■ For Students

MyAccountingLab provides students with a personalized interactive learning environment, where they can learn at their own pace and measure their progress.

Interactive Tutorial Exercises ▼

MyAccountingLab's homework and practice questions are correlated to the textbook, and they regenerate algorithmically to give students unlimited opportunity for practice and mastery. Questions include guided solutions, DemoDoc examples, and learning aids for extra help at point-of-use, and they offer helpful feedback when students enter incorrect answers.

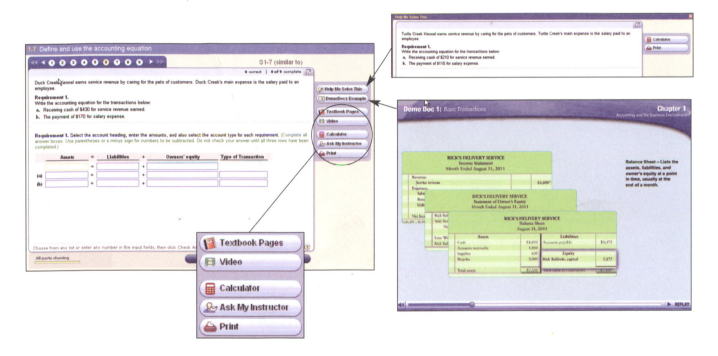

Study Plan for Self-Paced Learning ▶

MyAccountingLab's study plan helps students monitor their own progress, letting them see at a glance exactly which topics they need to practice. MyAccountingLab generates a personalized study plan for each student based on his or her test results, and the study plan links directly to interactive, tutorial exercises for topics the student hasn't yet mastered. Students can regenerate these exercises with new values for unlimited practice, and the exercises include guided solutions and multimedia learning aids to give students the extra help they need.

View a guided tour of MyAccountingLab at http://www.myaccountinglab.com/support/tours.

FINANCIAL ACCOUNTING

Jeffrey Waybright
Spokane Community College

Robert Kemp
University of Virginia

Prentice Hall

Boston   Columbus   Indianapolis   New York   San Francisco   Upper Saddle River
Amsterdam   Cape Town   Dubai   London   Madrid   Milan   Munich   Paris   Montréal   Toronto
Delhi   Mexico City   São Paulo   Sydney   Hong Kong   Seoul   Singapore   Taipei   Tokyo

VP/Editorial Director: Sally Yagan
AVP/Executive Editor: Jodi McPherson
AVP/Director of Marketing: Kate Valentine
AVP/Director of Digital Learning & Assessments:
   Richard Keaveny
AVP/Director of Product Development: Lisa Strite
Product Development Manager: Ashley Santora
Editorial Project Manager: Rebecca Knauer
Editorial Media Project Manager: Allison Longley
Development Editor: Mignon Tucker, J.D., Brava
   360° Publishing Solutions
Supplements Development Editor: Claire Hunter
Editorial Assistant: Jane Avery
Sr. Marketing Manager: Maggie Moylan
Marketing Assistant: Justin Jacob
Senior Managing Editor: Cynthia Zonneveld

Sr. Production Project Manager: Rhonda Aversa
Media Production Project Manager: John Cassar
Permissions Coordinator: Charles Morris
Associate Director of Manufacturing: Alexis Heydt
Senior Operations Supervision: Natacha Moore
Senior Art Director: Jonathan Boylan
Interior and Cover Designer: Jonathan Boylan
Manager, Rights and Permissions: Zina Arabia
Manager, Visual Research: Beth Brenzel
Manager, Cover Visual Research & Permissions:
   Karen Sanatar
Cover Art: Comstock Images \Getty Images Inc. RF
Image Permission Coordinator: Craig Jones
Photo Researcher: Kathy Ringrose
Composition: GEX Publishing Services
Full-Service Project Management: GEX Publishing
   Services

Credits and acknowledgments borrowed from other sources and reproduced, with permission, in this textbook appear on appropriate page within text (or on page 740).

Library of Congress Cataloging-in-Publication Data
Waybright, Jeffrey.
   Financial accounting / Jeffrey Waybright.
      p. cm.
   Includes index.
   ISBN 0-13-606048-X (978-0-13-606048-2)
   1. Accounting. 2. Accounting--Textbooks. I. Title.
HF5636.W39 2010
657--dc22   2009044137

Prentice Hall
is an imprint of

www.pearsonhighered.com

ISBN-13: 978-0-13-606048-2
ISBN-10: 0-13-606048-X

Dedication

My family—I couldn't have done this without their
support and encouragement
Jim Kahl—Jim has been a mentor, a colleague, and above all, a
tremendous friend for my entire teaching career
My students, past, present, and future—without them I would not be
doing that which I love to do, teaching accounting

Jeffrey Waybright

About the Authors

Jeffrey Waybright teaches accounting at Spokane Community College, which is part of a multi-college district in eastern Washington. He has been a full-time, tenured, community college instructor for over 16 years. In addition to teaching at the community college level, he has also taught upper division courses for Linfield College. Jeffrey is a recent co-recipient of the Washington Society of CPA's Outstanding Educator Award.

Jeffrey received his B.A. in business administration (emphasis in accounting) and MBA from Eastern Washington University. Before becoming a professor, Jeffrey spent eight years as a practicing CPA in Washington State and still holds his license. During his teaching career, he has taught in many disciplines of accounting including financial, managerial, computerized, and payroll accounting as well as in the disciplines of economics, business math, and general business. Jeffrey developed online courses in accounting, teaches online and traditional courses for financial and managerial accounting, and advises students. Jeffrey is passionate about teaching students the subject of accounting.

Robert S. Kemp, DBA, CPA Professor Kemp is the Ramon W. Breeden, Sr. Research Professor at the McIntire School of Commerce, University of Virginia. He is a Certified Public Accountant and possesses a baccalaureate, master and doctorate in business administration.

Professor Kemp is an accomplished scholar, conducting research and writing in the theory and practice of contemporary business. He currently is conducting research in the funding of pensions, the management of financial institutions, and corporate finance. His scholarly works include 70 completed projects, including monographs, articles, cases, research presentations, and working papers. His work is published in, among other places, The Financial Review; The Journal of Financial Research; Advances in Accounting, A Research Journal; Benefits Quarterly; The Journal of Mathematics Applied in Business and Industry; The Journal of Accountancy; The Journal of Commercial Bank Lending; The Journal of Bank Accounting and Auditing; and The Journal of Business Economics.

Professor Kemp is likewise an accomplished teacher, to both University students and executives throughout the world. During his 30 years at the University of Virginia, he has taught numerous undergraduate and graduate courses. He has taught classes using lectures, case studies, discussion groups, and distance learning. His consistently high evaluations by students reflect his devotion to the classroom. This high quality is likewise seen in his teaching of business executives. He has worked with and taught for organizations such as Bank of America, the FDIC, Navigant - Tucker Alan, the Siberian Banking Institute, the Barents Group, KPMG, Gerson Lehrman, Wellington Management, the Russian Bankers Association, the Central Asian American Enterprise Fund, the American Institute of Certified Public Accountants, and the Consumer Bankers Association.

Brief Contents

Contents

Chapter 10

Corporations: Paid-In Capital and Retained Earnings   486

Chapter 11

The Statement of Cash Flows   538

Chapter 12

Financial Statement Analysis   596

With
Financial Accounting
Student Text, Study Resources,
and MyAccountingLab,
students will have more
"I get it!"
moments!

Students will "get it" anytime, anywhere

Students understand (or "get it") right after the instructor does a problem in class. Once they leave the classroom, however, students often struggle to complete the homework on their own. This frustration can cause them to give up on the material altogether and fall behind in the course, resulting in an entire class falling behind as the instructor attempts to keep everyone on the same page.

MyAccountingLab

Study Resources

Text

With the *Financial Accounting* **Student Learning System**, all the features of the student textbook, study resources, and online homework system are designed to work together to provide students with the consistency, repetition, and high level of detail that will keep both the instructor and students on track, providing more "I get it!" moments inside and outside the classroom.

Replicating the Classroom Experience with Demo Doc Examples

The Demo Doc examples consist of entire problems, worked through step-by-step, from start to finish, narrated with the kind of comments that instructors would say in class. The Demo Docs are available in specific chapters of the text and for every chapter in the study guide. In addition to the printed Demo Docs, Flash-animated versions are available so that students can watch the problems as they are worked through while listening to the explanations and details. Demo Docs will aid students when they are trying to solve exercises and problems on their own, duplicating the classroom experience outside of class.

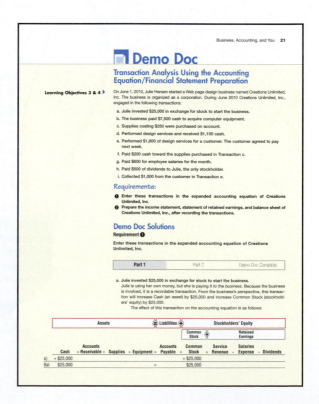

with the Student Learning System!

Consistency, Repetition, and a High Level of Detail Throughout the Learning Process

The concepts, materials, and practice problems are presented with clarity and consistency across all mediums—textbook, study resources, and online homework system. No matter which platform students use they will continually experience the same look, feel, and language, minimizing confusion and ensuring clarity.

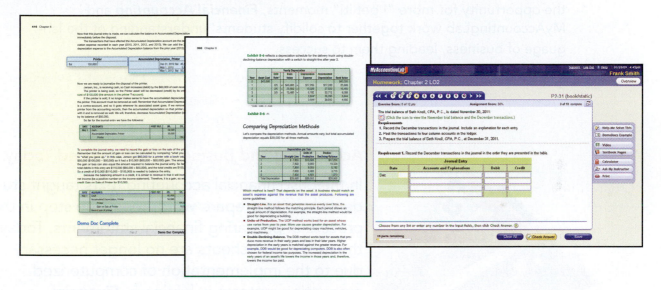

Experiencing the Power of Practice with MyAccountingLab: www.myaccountinglab.com

MyAccountingLab is an online homework system that gives students more "I get it!" moments through the power of practice. With **MyAccountingLab**, students can

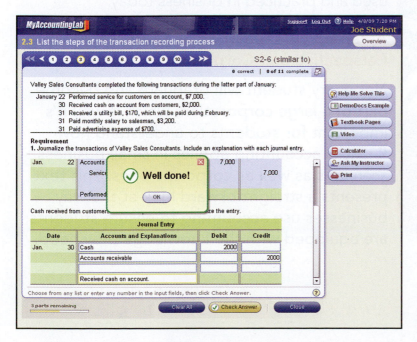

- work on the exact end-of-chapter material and/or similar problems assigned by the instructor.
- use the Study Plan for self-assessment and customized study outlines.
- use the Help Me Solve This tool for a step-by-step tutorial.
- view the Demo Docs example to see an animated demonstration of where the numbers came from.
- watch a video to see additional information pertaining to the lecture.
- open textbook pages to find the material they need to get help on specific problems.

Waybright & Kemp, *Financial Accounting*

Once students see that accounting is the language of business, they are on their way to academic and professional success. Authors Jeffrey Waybright and Robert Kemp's new text, *Financial Accounting*, in combination with MyAccountingLab translates the essentials of accounting to students so they understand "why" and "when" financially sound decisions are made in business today. Providing students the opportunity for more "I get it!" moments, *Financial Accounting* and MyAccountingLab work together to solidify students' understanding of the language of business, leading them to success.

Accounting and Business: As Practiced Today.

In the past, financial accounting texts taught students how to prepare worksheets as a step in the process of preparing financial statements. Today, the use of worksheets are no longer necessary due to the implementation of computerized accounting systems in business. *Financial Accounting* recognizes these changes in procedure and presents accounting to students as it is used and practiced in business today.

A Perfect Balance of Small Business Perspective and Corporate Coverage.

Not every student will graduate and become part of a large corporation, which is why it's important for students to understand how financial accounting applies in small business scenarios as well as corporate ones. This text presents a straightforward look at the way businesses use accounting to ensure students are equipped with the knowledge they need.

Helping students understand accounting as the language of business.

Presenting Concepts with Clarity and Purpose.
The first thing that will distract students is jargon and difficult language, especially when it comes to understanding accounting concepts. Waybright and Kemp have crafted a text that is written the way a great teacher would speak in class, with both clarity and purpose.

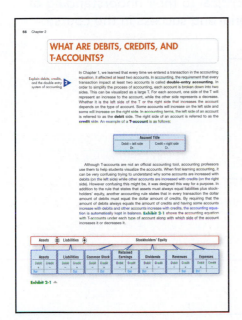

Question and Answer Format.
Some of the most teachable moments happen when a student asks a key question that gets straight to the heart of a topic. This text mirrors that approach by providing key questions in the headers, followed by clear, direct, and detailed explanations.

Accounting in Your World, found in every chapter, personalizes accounting challenges, issues, and ethical situations for students to evaluate from their own perspective.

Waybright & Kemp, *Financial Accounting*

Seeing it All Together.

Waybright and Kemp introduce a slight twist on the visuals found in this text to effectively illustrate the connection between accounting equations and big picture concepts. Instead of presenting the details of the journal entries, general ledger, and T-accounts in isolation, *Financial Accounting* shows these details within the context of the accounting equation and financial statements. This approach helps students appreciate the steps involved in preparing and interpreting financial statements, which is critical to their understanding of the material and success in the course.

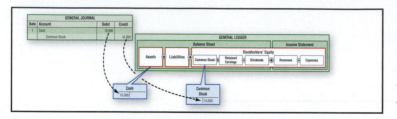

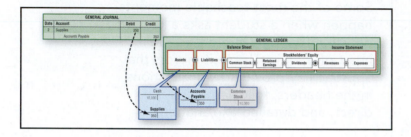

☑ Concept Check

Jill just completed a problem that was assigned in her accounting class. She told Alan, one of her classmates, that she was confident that she did the problem correctly because the debits equal the credits on the trial balance. According to Alan, just because the debits equal the credits on the trial balance does not mean that everything was done correctly. Who is right Jill or Alan?

Answer

Alan is correct. The following are some of the errors that can occur and yet the trial balance will still be in balance:

- A transaction can be recorded for the wrong amount in a journal entry.

- An entire journal entry can be recorded twice, or not recorded at all.

- The wrong accounts can be debited or credited in a journal entry. For example, when recording a payment on an account payable it is possible to debit accounts receivable instead of accounts payable.

Concept Checks appear throughout the chapter so that students can review their understanding and interpretation of the material. By showing "what it is" and "why and when it matters" together, these checks allow students a place to pause and interpret what they've just learned.

Focus on Decision Making.

Beginning with Chapter 1, an emphasis is placed on the importance of making financially sound business decisions. This emphasis helps students determine how much risk and impact is involved in the types of decisions they may encounter in their future careers. Ethics and ratio coverage are also woven throughout the text to continually support this decision-making focus.

Helping students understand accounting as the language of business.

Decision Guidelines.

Decision Guidelines summarize the chapter's key terms, concepts, and formulas in the context of business decisions. Found throughout and at the end of each chapter, Decision Guidelines show students each decision and how to evaluate it so they can readily see the value in, and for, a business. Overall, these guidelines continue to reinforce how accounting information is used to make decisions in business.

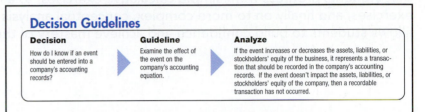

Decision Guidelines

Decision	Guideline	Analyze
How do I know if an event should be entered into a company's accounting records?	Examine the effect of the event on the company's accounting equation.	If the event increases or decreases the assets, liabilities, or stockholders' equity of the business, it represents a transaction that should be recorded in the company's accounting records. If the event doesn't impact the assets, liabilities, or stockholders' equity of the company, then a recordable transaction has not occurred.

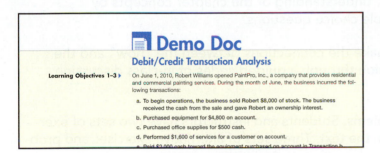

Demo Doc

Debit/Credit Transaction Analysis

Learning Objectives 1–3 ▶ On June 1, 2010, Robert Williams opened PaintPro, Inc., a company that provides residential and commercial painting services. During the month of June, the business incurred the following transactions:

a. To begin operations, the business sold Robert $8,000 of stock. The business received the cash from the sale and gave Robert an ownership interest.

b. Purchased equipment for $4,800 on account.

c. Purchased office supplies for $500 cash.

d. Performed $1,600 of services for a customer on account.

e. Paid $2,000 cash toward the equipment purchased on account in Transaction b.

Demo Docs in Every Chapter.

Worked-through problems, representative of the chapter material, help students navigate through the computations and concepts in a step-by-step format for overall comprehension. Additional Demo Docs are available in the study guide and MyAccountingLab.

An Emphasis on Ethics and Internal Control.

From the very beginning of Chapter 1, Waybright and Kemp emphasize ethics and continue in greater detail in Chapter 6: Ethics, Internal Control, and IFRS.

IFRS Coverage.

Arguably the most important shift in the future of financial accounting, IFRS is introduced in this text at a basic level, focusing on capturing student awareness. IFRS is first presented in Chapter 1 and then coverage is carried throughout each chapter as needed, with an icon or footnote indicating a potential shift in reporting requirements. The differences between U.S. GAAP and IFRS can be found in Chapter 6.

www.pearsonhighered.com/waybright

Waybright & Kemp, *Financial Accounting*

Progressive, Expansive, and Challenging End-of-Chapter Material.
Waybright and Kemp understand that the key to students' accounting success is in the practice and work completed in the end-of-chapter content. With this in mind, this text presents the material so that students progress from simple calculative exercises, to a mixture of calculative and conceptual exercises, and finally on to more complex, conceptual analysis problems and cases. This progression allows students to build confidence and achieve mastery of the material.

End-of-Chapter Material.

- **Self Check** quickly audits the students' understanding of the chapter concepts by presenting them with a series of multiple choice questions.

- **Discussion Questions** help students make the connections between the "how" and the "why" of financial accounting information through a guided series of in-class discussion questions.

- **"A" and "B" Set of Exercises and Problems.** Students and instructors have two sets of exercises and problems provided for them in the text. Three sets of alternative exercises and problems are also available in MyAccountingLab to give students more practice opportunities.

- **The Continuing Exercise** highlights the same small business from chapter to chapter, allowing students to apply their understanding of chapter concepts in a business context. As students move through the text, they complete additional steps in this comprehensive exercise. Students, again, see the big picture and learn how the topics build off one another. The Continuing Exercise can be assigned and completed within MyAccountingLab.

- **The Continuing Problem** is a more comprehensive version of the Continuing Exercise. Once again, students learn how accounting is a process and the Continuing Problem helps them put it all together.

Helping students understand accounting as the language of business.

The Importance of Cash.

- **The Know Your Business** section, found at the end of each chapter, compares and contrasts companies in the same industry and big and small businesses so that students can understand the significance of cash flows, financial statement analysis, and industry analysis as a means to evaluate the financial health of a company.

- **The Small Business Analysis** feature found in the end-of-chapter material takes the importance of cash one step further by allowing students the opportunity to work case problems and see the importance of cash flows for small business.

KNOW YOUR BUSINESS

FINANCIAL ANALYSIS

Purpose: To help familiarize you with the financial reporting of a real company in order to further your understanding of the chapter material you are learning.

Although we do not have access to the journals used by Columbia Sportswear, we can still understand various business transactions that Columbia Sportswear had as seen on the financial statements in its annual report. Refer to the Columbia Sportswear income statements, "Statements of Operations," and the Columbia Sportswear balance sheet's in Appendix A. Assume Columbia Sportswear completed the following transactions during January, 2008:

SMALL BUSINESS ANALYSIS

Purpose: To help you understand the importance of cash flows in the operation of a small business.

You're sitting in your CPA office late on a Friday afternoon when you get an e-mail from a friend. You know that she has been working on setting up a new accounting system in her office for a new business that she just started. You figured that this would eventually generate some communication between the two of you because you know that she has relatively limited accounting knowledge. Here's her e-mail to you.

"Jerry, I'm pretty frustrated right now! As you know, I've been installing this new accounting system here in the office and I've run into a problem. I don't understand this cash account. I have purchased some items on my debit card and I've purchased some items on my credit card. So logically, when I purchased the items on my debit card, I debited the cash account.

Critical Thinking Activities.

One of the best qualities a student can bring to their future career is the ability to think critically. This text cultivates this skill by including the following critical thinking activities:

- **Ethics in Action Cases**
- **Team Projects**
- **Know Your Business:** includes a series of interrelated case problems that show students the importance of financial statement analysis, industry analysis, and cash flows for a small business
- **Written Communication Activity**

 ® **NEW! End-of-Chapter Material is Integrated with MyAccountingLab.**

Students need practice and repetition in order to successfully learn the fundamentals of accounting. To provide unlimited practice, MyAccountingLab not only includes all of the questions from the book, but students also have access to algorithmically generated questions as well—all of which are automatically graded. For more information, visit **www.myaccountinglab.com**.

www.pearsonhighered.com/waybright

MyAccountingLab is Web-based tutorial and assessment software for accounting that gives students more "I get it!" moments. **MyAccountingLab** provides students with a personalized interactive learning environment where they can complete their course assignments with immediate tutorial assistance, learn at their own pace, and measure their progress.

In addition to completing assignments and reviewing tutorial help, students have access to the following resources in **MyAccountingLab**:

- Pearson eText
- Study Guide
- Animated Demo Docs
- Excel in Practice

- Videos
- Audio and Student PowerPoints
- Working Papers in both Excel and PDF
- MP3 Files with Chapter Objectives and Summaries
- Flashcards

Study Guide and Study Guide CD with Demo Docs
This chapter-by-chapter learning aid helps students learn financial accounting while getting the maximum benefit from study time. Animated Demo Docs are available on the accompanying study guide CD in Flash so students can easily refer to them when they need them.

Student Resource Website: www.pearsonhighered.com/waybright
- Excel in Practice
- Working Papers in both Excel and PDF

Student Reference Cards

International Financial Reporting Standards Student Reference Card

Accounting Tips Student Reference Card

Math for Accounting Student Reference Card

This four-page laminated reference card includes an overview of IFRS, why it matters and how it compares to U.S. standards, and highlights key differences between IFRS and U.S. GAAP.

This four-page laminated reference card illustrates the key steps in the accounting cycle.

This six-page laminated reference card provides students with a study tool for the basic math they will need to be successful in accounting, such as rounding, fractions, converting decimals, calculating interest, break-even analysis, and more!

Instructor Supplements

The primary goal of the Instructor Resources is to help instructors deliver their course with ease, using any delivery method—traditional, self-paced, or online.

www.myaccountinglab.com

MyAccountingLab not only gives students more "I get it" moments, but also can be used by instructors to make technology an integral part of their course or as a supplementary resource for students. MyAccountingLab offers the exact same end-of-chapter material found in the text along with algorithmic options that can be assigned for homework. **MyAccountingLab** also features the same look as the text so that students are familiar and comfortable working with the material.

Instructor's Manual

The Instructor's Manual, available electronically or in print, offers course-specific content including a guide to available resources, a road map for using **MyAccountingLab**, a first-day handout for students, sample syllabi, guidelines for teaching an online course, and content-specific material including chapter overviews, teaching outlines, student summary handouts, lecture outline tips, assignment grids, ten-minute quizzes, and more!

Instructor Resource Center: www.pearsonhighered.com/waybright

For your convenience, many of the instructor supplements are available for download from the textbook's catalog page or in your **MyAccountingLab**. Available resources include the following:

- **Solutions Manual** contains the fully worked-through and accuracy-checked solutions for every question, exercise, and problem in the text.
- **Test Item File with TestGen Software** offers over 1,600 multiple choice, true/false, and problem-solving questions that are correlated by learning objective and difficulty level as well as AACSB and AICPA standards.
- **Four Sets of PowerPoints** provide flexibility and choices for your courses. There are 508 Compliant Instructor PowerPoints with extensive notes for on-campus or online classes, Student PowerPoints, Clicker Response System (CRS) PowerPoints, and Audio Narrated PowerPoints.
- **Excel in Practice**
- **Image Library**
- **Working Papers and Solutions in Excel and PDF formats**
- **Instructor's Manual**

Course Cartridges

Course Cartridges for Blackboard, WebCT, CourseCompass, and other learning management systems are available upon request.

www.pearsonhighered.com/waybright

Acknowledgments

For the first edition of *Financial Accounting*, we had the help of instructors from across the country who participated in online surveys, chapter reviews, and focus groups. Their comments and suggestions for both the text and the supplements have been a great help in planning and carrying out the vision of this textbook, and we thank them for their contributions.

Online Table of Contents Reviewers

John Babich, Kankakee Community College
George Bernard, Seminole Community College
Joseph Berry, Campbell University
Swati Bhandarkar, University of Georgia
Donald Bond, Texas Southern University
Jerold K. Braun, Daytona State College
Dr. Linda Bressler, University of Houston-Downtown
Marci L. Butterfield, University of Utah
Ernest Carraway, North Carolina State University
Dr. Joan A. Cezair, Fayetteville State University
Leslie Cohen, University of Arizona
John Daugherty, Pitt Community College
Vaun Day, Central Arizona College
Jap Efendi, University of Texas at Arlington
Patricia Feller, Nashville State Community College
Calvin Fink, Bethune-Cookman University
Donna Free, Oakland University
Marina Grau, Houston Community College
Ann Gregory, South Plains College
Patrick A. Haggerty, Lansing Community College
Becky Hancock, El Paso Community College
Rob Hochschild, Ivy Tech Community College
Ron Lazer, University of Houston
Patsy Lee, University of Texas at Arlington
Donald Lucy, Indian River State College
Suzanne McCaffrey, University of Mississippi
Florence McGovern, Bergen Community College
Heidi H. Meier, Cleveland State University
Terri Meta, Seminole Community College
Melanie Middlemist, Colorado State University
Birendra Mishra, University of California Riverside
Carol A. Murphy, Quinsigamond Community College
Khursheed Omer, University of Houston, Downtown
Sandra Pelfrey, Oakland University
Stanley M. Quon, Sacramento City College
Allan M Rabinowitz, Pace University

Judy Ramage, Lawrence Christian Brothers University
Louis Rosamilia, Hudson Valley Community College
Christine Schalow, University of Wisconsin-Stevens Point
Randy Serrett, University of Houston-Downtown
Lily Sieux, California State University East Bay
Dennis Spector, Naugatuck Valley Community College
Joe Standridge, Sonoma State University
Dennis Stovall, Grand Valley State University
Ellen L. Sweatt, Georgia Perimeter College
Peter Theuri, Northern Kentucky University
Steven Thoede, Texas State University-San Marcos
Robin E. Thomas, North Carolina State University
Jack Topiol, Community College of Philadelphia
Jinhee Trone, Santa Ana College
Suzanne Ward, University of Louisiana at Lafayette
Marvin Williams, University of Houston-Downtown
Laura Young, University of Central Arkansas

Chapter Reviewers

Dawn Addington, Central New Mexico Community College
Sheila Ammons, Austin Community College
Beverly Beatty, Anne Arundel Community College
Anna Boulware, St. Charles Community College
Amy Bourne, Oregon State University
Jerold Braun, Daytona State College
Nina Brown, Tarrant County College, Northwest Campus
Kelley Butler, Ivy Tech Community College Lafayette
Marci Butterfield, University of Utah
Yunhao Chen, Florida International University
Leslie Cohen, University of Arizona
Barry N. Cooper, Borough of Manhattan Community College (BMCC)
Dori Danko, Grand Valley State University
Jimmy Dong, Sacramento City College
Patricia Doherty, Boston University School of Management
Patricia Feller, Nashville State Community College
Janice Fergusson, University of South Carolina
Philip Fink, University of Toledo
Linda Flowers, Houston Community College
Donald Foster, Tacoma Community College
Brenda Fowler, Alamance Community College
Andy Garcia, Bowling Green State University
Lisa Gillespie, Loyola University - Chicago
Marina Grau, Houston Community College
Anthony Greig, Purdue University
Bowe Hansen, University of New Hampshire
Carol Hutchinson, AB Tech
Janice Klimek, University of Central Missouri
Patti Lopez, Valencia Community College
Diane Marker, University of Toledo
Michele Martinez, Hillsborough Community College
Suzanne McCaffrey, University of Mississippi

Bruce McClain, Cleveland State University
Jeanine Metzler, Northampton Community College
Earl Mitchell, Santa Ana College
Rama Ramamurthy, College of William & Mary
Patrick Rogan, Cosumnes River College
Miles Romney, University of San Diego
Tracy Schmeltzer, Wayne Community College
Randy Serrett, University of Houston-Downtown
Sheila Shain, Santa Ana College
Carol Shaver, Louisiana Tech University
Margaret L. Shelton, University of Houston-Downtown
Nancy Snow, University of Toledo
Barbara Squires, Corning Community College
Rick Street, Spokane Community College
Gloria Stuart, Georgia Southern University
Pavani Tallapally, Slippery Rock University
Samantha Ternes, Kirkwood Community College
Christian Wurst Jr., Temple University
Judith Zander, Grossmont College

Supplements Authors and Reviewers

Courtney Baillie, Nebraska Wesleyan University
Cheryl Bartlett, Central New Mexico Community College
Michelle Berube, Corinthian Colleges
Nabanita Bhattacharya, Northwest Florida State College
Robert Braun, Southern Louisiana University
Dr. Anna Lusher, Slippery Rock University School of Business
Michelle Maggio, Westfield State College
Diane Marker, University of Toledo
Allan Sheets, International Business College
Rick Street, Spokane Community College
Samantha Ternes, Kirkwood Community College
Shannon Tincup
Judith Zander, Grossmont College

Jeffrey Waybright would especially like to thank the individuals below for their support and guidance throughout the project:
Jodi McPherson
Jodi Bolognese
Maggie Moylan
Rebecca Knauer
Rhonda Aversa
Carol O'Rourke
Cindy Zonneveld
Jonathan Boylan
Claire Hunter
Mignon Tucker, Brava 360° (You're the best!)
Everyone at GEX Publishing Services, who worked on the book
Rick Street, Spokane Community College
Dr. Clayton Hock, Miami University
Carrie Everman, U.S. Bank Merchant Services

Business, Accounting, and You

Do you want to open your own business someday or perhaps work for a large, multinational company? Whether your goal is to start your own business or to work for another company, the study of financial accounting can help you reach that goal. Accounting will help you answer questions such as "How much money is the business making?" or "Where does the business stand financially?" Knowing the answers to these and other important questions gives you a competitive advantage in the business world.

Chapter Outline:

Learning Objectives:

1 Describe the major types of business organizations

2 Know the key accounting principles and concepts

3 Analyze transactions using the basic accounting equation

4 Understand, and be able to prepare, basic financial statements

WHY STUDY ACCOUNTING?

Accounting Teaches the Language of Business

Many students who enroll in accounting classes often ask the question "Why do I have to take accounting anyway? I am not going to be an accountant." Perhaps the most compelling reason for taking an accounting course, especially if you do not plan on becoming an accountant, is that accounting teaches "the language of business." No matter what your intended area of study, if you want to be successful in business, you need to know how to speak the language of business.

Consider a patient in the hospital. Many health-care professionals, in addition to the doctor, are responsible for ensuring the overall health and welfare of the patient. There are nurses, nursing assistants, x-ray technicians, and others involved in the treatment and care of the patient. Additionally, many pieces of equipment monitor the patient's condition. If the doctor is the only person able to speak "the language of medicine" and read and interpret information provided about the patient's health, the ability of the other health-care professionals to provide quality care to the patient is severely limited. Therefore, all individuals in the health-care profession are required to speak "the language of medicine." They must understand how to speak, read, and interpret information relative to the health of the patients they serve in order to provide the highest level of care. Similarly, if only the accountants in a business organization are able to speak, read, and interpret financial information regarding the health of the business, the ability of others within the organization to manage the affairs of the business in a manner that ensures the health of the business will be limited. Whether your intended area of study is marketing or management, or even cosmetology or automotive, an understanding of accounting will allow you to monitor and manage the health of the organization for which you work.

Accounting Emphasizes the Importance of Ethical Business Behavior

Proper ethical behavior has taken on renewed importance in the wake of recent accounting scandals, such as Enron, that have occurred in the United States as well as in other countries. **Ethics** refers to the principles of right behavior that guide decision making. Individuals from top management to front line workers may be confronted with ethical dilemmas in their jobs. Ethical dilemmas often arise when the actions that most benefit an individual differ from the actions that most benefit the organization. Ethical dilemmas are also created when personal beliefs or organizational culture differ from ethical principles.

The study of accounting will help individuals better identify situations that create ethical dilemmas within an organization. More importantly, it helps them discern the proper course of action to take in these situations.

⊕ Accounting in Your World

How would you respond to the following situations?

❶ The company CEO asks you to falsify the company's accounting records. He or she says that the company cannot afford to report that it is performing poorly. If it does, some stores will likely have to be closed and people will lose their jobs. The CEO implies that if you are not a "team player" and falsify the records that it will be your fault these people are unemployed.

❷ At the end of the month, your supervisor asks you to create fictitious sales invoices. He or she tells you that your department is just a little bit shy of reaching the sales goal necessary for each member of the department to receive a quarterly bonus. Your supervisor says that you can just delete the fictitious sales at the beginning of the next month and that no one will ever know.

❸ A coworker of yours confides in you that he or she has stolen several MP3 players from the store at which you both work. Your coworker offers to give you one of the players. He or she says that you both deserve it for all of the long hours you have worked for the company lately.

You may find yourself faced with an ethical dilemma at any time during your career. You only have one chance to make the right decision. In Chapter 6 we take a closer look at ethics and reveal the consequences of other people's poor choices.

An Understanding of Accounting Helps Individuals Ensure That the Business Is Profitable

Many small business owners and managers within larger businesses are very knowledgeable with regards to many aspects of their position but often fail due to a lack of accounting knowledge. Individuals in these positions often know a lot about the products they sell but are unable to answer questions such as the following:

- What is the true cost of what I am selling?
- Am I being "ripped off" by my employees or my customers?
- How much will it cost my company (or department) to achieve the growth that has been projected for the upcoming quarter?

An understanding of accounting will allow an individual to answer these, and other questions, and monitor the operations that will help the company be profitable.

WHAT IS ACCOUNTING?

Have you noticed how many kids play little league sports these days, and wondered why so many kids compete in these sports? Some kids play to get into better shape and some kids play just for the fun, but most kids play because they want to win. If you think about it, we live in a very competitive world. This competitiveness makes the job of the scorekeeper very important because without the scorekeeper, nobody would know which team won the contest. In addition to keeping track of who wins, the scorekeeper in an athletic contest tracks many other statistics, which help the coach and the players judge individual performances.

The world of business is very much like little league sports. **Businesses** exist to win, which is usually defined as making money. The scorekeepers in the world of business are the accountants. Their job is to "keep score" to determine if the business has won or lost through a process known as **financial accounting**. An accountant also tracks other types of information in addition to whether the company made or lost money to help employees and managers judge individual performance. It is the job of the accountant to provide useful information to various users regarding the performance of the organization. The information is used mostly to determine whether or not to invest capital or lend money to a business. Financial accounting produces reports called **financial statements** that show financial information about a business. These reports are "historical" reports that communicate financial information about a business to people or organizations outside the company. Financial statements

- allow investors and creditors to make investment decisions.
- enable suppliers and customers to determine the financial condition of a business.
- report to regulatory agencies such as the Securities and Exchange Commission, the Internal Revenue Service, and the Federal Trade Commission.

This book teaches students the process of **accounting**, or "scorekeeping," for a business organization.

HOW ARE BUSINESSES ORGANIZED?

 Describe the major types of business organizations

Types of Businesses

The three types of business are a **service business**, a **merchandising business**, and a **manufacturing business**.

- A service business provides services to its customers. In other words, what it sells is time. Common types of service businesses are law firms, accounting firms, physical therapy offices, painting companies, automotive repair shops, etc.

- A merchandise business sells physical goods or products to its customers. Common types of merchandise businesses are grocery stores, automobile dealerships, sporting goods stores, etc. A merchandise business may be either a **wholesale business** or a **retail business**.

- Manufacturing businesses produce the physical goods that they sell to their customers. Common types of manufacturing businesses are automobile manufacturers, the makers of clothing, soft drink manufacturers, etc.

Choice of Business Organizations

A business can be organized as a sole proprietorship, partnership, corporation, or limited liability company. But how do you know what type of business organization is best for your business?

- A **sole proprietorship** is a business entity that has one owner. For legal purposes and for tax purposes the business and the owner are considered the same. The business owner is personally responsible for all of the debts and obligations of the business. If somebody wants to sue the business, he or she would have to sue the owner. In addition, all of the income or loss generated by the business is reported on the owner's personal tax return and taxed at individual tax rates.

- A **partnership** is very similar to a sole proprietorship except that it has two or more owners. For legal purposes, the owners (partners) and the business are considered the same. If somebody sues the business, he or she would need to sue one or more of the business owners. For tax purposes, the partners divide all of the income or loss of the partnership amongst themselves and report it on their personal tax returns. Therefore, it is taxed at individual tax rates just like a sole proprietorship. One advantage of a partnership is flexibility regarding the division of the business income between the partners.

- A **corporation** differs from a sole proprietorship or a partnership because it is a separate legal entity from the owners. This legal separation is very attractive to the business owners because it limits their personal liability to what they have invested in the corporation. The corporation may sue another person or business and it may be sued by another person or business. For tax purposes, the corporation is a separate entity from the owners. Therefore, federal income tax is imposed on the income of the corporation at corporate tax rates. Any remaining income that is distributed to the owners, or **shareholders**, in the form of dividends is then taxed at the shareholder's individual income tax rates, in effect, double taxing the business owners. Many business owners desire to have the legal protection that the corporate form of organization offers but they do not want to be subject to the "double taxation" that also occurs. Owners of small corporations are able to make an **S-corporation** election, which allows them to have the legal separation that the corporate form of organization provides but also requires that all of the income or loss from the corporation be reported on the owner's personal tax returns and be taxed at individual tax rates. One of the disadvantages to an S-corporation is that there is no flexibility in how earnings and losses are distributed. Earnings and losses must be distributed based on each owner's percentage of ownership in the business.

- A **limited liability company** is a relatively new form of business organization. The owners of a limited liability company enjoy the same legal separation that a corporation provides, but for tax purposes a limited liability company's income is treated similar to a sole proprietorship or a partnership by the IRS. All of the income of the limited liability company is divided amongst the owners and is taxed at their personal rates. In many ways, a limited liability company is similar to an S-corporation. However, unlike an S-corporation, a limited liability company can be very flexible in how it distributes earnings amongst the owners.

Exhibit 1-1 summarizes the different types of business organizations:

Type of Business	Legal Status	Tax Status	Benefits	Drawbacks
Sole Proprietorship	Business and owner are considered to be the same entity	Business income is allocated to the owner and taxed at owner's personal tax rate	• Ease of formation • No double taxation	• Unlimited liability of owner • Difficult to raise capital • Limited life
Partnership	Business and owners are considered to be the same entity	Business income is allocated to the owners and taxed at owners' personal tax rates	• Ease of formation • No double taxation • Shared investment/knowledge	• Unlimited liability of owners • Disagreements between partners • Limited life
Corporation	Business and owners are considered to be **separate** entities	Business income is taxed at corporate tax rates. Any income distributed to the owners is also taxed at owners' personal tax rates. Also referred to as a C Corporation.	• Limited liability of owners • Easier to raise capital • Unlimited life	• More difficult and costly to form • Double taxation • More paperwork • More regulations
S-Corporation	Business and owners are considered to be **separate** entities	Business income is allocated to the owners and taxed at owners' personal tax rates	• Limited liability of owners • No double taxation • Easier to raise capital • Unlimited life	• More difficult and costly to form • More paperwork • More regulations
Limited Liability Company	Business and owners are considered to be **separate** entities	Business income is allocated to the owners and taxed at owners' personal tax rates	• Limited liability of owners • No double taxation • More flexibility than with S-Corp	• More difficult and costly to form • Limited life

Exhibit 1-1 ▲

Although the process of accounting for the different types of business organizations is similar, there are slight variations depending on the type of organization. In this book, we will focus our attention on accounting for corporations.

Decision Guidelines

Decision	Guideline	Analyze
What form of business organization should be chosen? 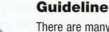	There are many ways to organize a business including the following: a sole proprietorship, partnership, corporation or S corporation, or limited liability company. Each type of business organization has different advantages and disadvantages.	Know the tax and legal treatments of each type of organization. Weigh the best treatment of taxes and legal liability of each type and pick the format that is most advantageous for the business owners.

WHAT ACCOUNTING PRINCIPLES AND CONCEPTS GOVERN THE FIELD OF ACCOUNTING?

 Know the key accounting principles and concepts **2**

Generally Accepted Accounting Principles

In sports there are established rules and principles that dictate how each game is to be played and how the score it to be kept.

In the United States, financial accounting must follow **Generally Accepted Accounting Principles (GAAP)**, which are the rules, principles, and concepts established by the accounting profession that govern financial accounting. Existing and potential investors and creditors can more easily compare different companies if both companies have prepared financial statements using these rules. While many sources provide the rules that make up GAAP, the majority are written by the **Financial Accounting Standards Board (FASB)**. The FASB is a seven-person group primarily responsible for the establishment of standards of financial accounting and reporting. The main objective of financial reporting is to provide information useful for making investment and lending decisions. To be useful, information must be relevant, reliable, and comparable. Therefore, many of the rules that make up GAAP center on some basic accounting principles and concepts.

The Business Entity Concept

The most basic concept in accounting is that of the business **entity**. The business entity concept dictates that the financial affairs of a business organization must be kept separate from the personal financial affairs of the business owners. This separation is necessary because if the owners of a business choose to place personal assets into the business, then those assets are now considered to belong to the business and no longer to the owners. For example, if a business owner invests a used car into his or her business, that car should no longer be used by the business owner for personal purposes.

The Reliability (Objectivity) Principle

The **reliability**, or **objectivity**, principle requires that the accounting information for a business be arrived at objectively so that it may be relied upon by outside users. The information should be independently verifiable. For example, a company's checking account at a bank is supported by a statement from the bank. This statement provides objective evidence that the account exists. Without the reliability principle, accounting information might be based on what people think or feel it should be rather than what it really is. This would make it easier to manipulate the information for fraudulent purposes.

The Cost Principle

The cost principle states that when a business acquires assets or services, they should be recorded at their actual cost, also called **historical cost**. In other words, the amount paid for the asset or service is the amount recorded as its value. Other values such as market value, appraised value, etc. are not important even if they are known at the time of the purchase. The cost principle also requires that the accounting records keep the historical cost of an asset throughout its useful life because this cost is a reliable measure.

International Financial Reporting Standards

International Financial Reporting Standards (IFRS) are accounting standards that are developed by the International Accounting Standards Board. IFRS were originally utilized by businesses located in countries that did not have their own accounting standards. However, many countries that have their own accounting standards have started to allow the use of IFRS in addition to, or instead of, their own standards. The United States is currently considering a switch from U.S. GAAP to IFRS. However, because the adoption of IFRS by the United States is not certain, and in any event would be years away, this book will focus on U.S. GAAP. Chapter 6 has a more in-depth discussion of IFRS and margin icons are utilized throughout the book to indicate items that will most likely be affected by the adoption of IFRS.

HOW IS THE ACCOUNTING EQUATION USED TO RECORD BUSINESS TRANSACTIONS?

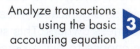

Analyze transactions using the basic accounting equation **3**

As we said earlier, the accountant's job is really the job of being the scorekeeper for the business. The accountant needs to keep track of information so he or she can tell people how the company is performing. The accountant must keep track of two main things at the same time. First, the accountant must track what the company has that has value. In accounting, the things of value the company has are called **assets**. In addition, the accountant must track the ownership rights to the assets. In other words, if the business were to close its doors at any given time, who would have a right to the company assets? Two possibilities for ownership rights to the company's assets are people other than the owners of the company (called a **third party**) and the owners of the company themselves (called the **stockholders**). If third parties have an ownership interest in the company's assets then the company owes them that amount of assets. In accounting terminology, the amount a business owes to third parties is called **liabilities**. Assets not owned by third parties must belong to the stockholders. In accounting terminology, the amount of assets owned by the stockholders of the company is called **stockholders' equity**. The amount of assets that a company has must always equal the ownership of those assets. This concept can be expressed as an equation, referred to as the **fundamental accounting equation**:

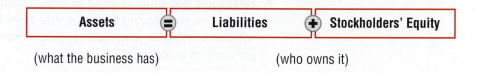

| **Assets** | = | **Liabilities** | + | **Stockholders' Equity** |

(what the business has)   (who owns it)

☑ Concept Check

At the end of its first month of operations, Robinson Consulting, Inc., has assets totaling $57,000 and stockholders' equity totaling $32,000. What is the amount of Robinson Consulting's total liabilities at the end of the month?

Answer:

We can use the fundamental accounting equation to figure out what Robinson Consulting's total liabilities are. First, it helps to restate the equation in a different format by subtracting stockholders' equity from both sides of the equation as follows:

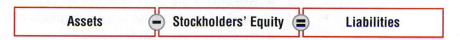

| **Assets** | − | **Stockholders' Equity** | = | **Liabilities** |

Next, insert the amount of Robinson Consulting's total assets and the total stockholders' equity into the restated formula.

$$\$57{,}000 - \$32{,}000 = \text{Liabilities}$$

Finally, solve the equation to get the total liabilities of $25,000.

$$\$57{,}000 - \$32{,}000 = \$25{,}000$$

Transaction Analysis

Accountants will record the effects of transactions in this equation. A **transaction** is any event that has a financial impact on the business. If something changes either what the company has or who owns it, it must be recorded in the accounting equation. When the accountant records a transaction that affects the business, he or she will record what effect the transaction has on the assets of the business and he or she will record what effect it has on the ownership of those assets. This process is called transaction analysis.

Stockholders' Equity

Before we start looking at how transactions affect the accounting equation, let's take a closer look at the stockholders' equity section of the equation. In order to provide more useful information to various people, the stockholders' equity section of the equation can be broken down into smaller subcategories:

- **Common stock** is used to reflect stockholders' equity which is the result of the owners of the business investing assets into the business. In other words, the assets of the company increased because the stockholders invested those assets into the company.

- **Retained earnings** is used to reflect stockholders' equity which is the result of the business having earnings that have been retained in the business. As we will see shortly, earnings are created when the business provides goods or services to customers.

An expanded version of the accounting equation would look like this:

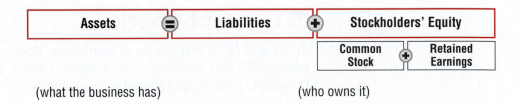

(what the business has)   (who owns it)

The retained earnings subcategory can now be further broken down into smaller subcategories to help the accountant provide even better information. These subcategories and what they reflect are as follows:

- **Revenues** are used to reflect an increase in retained earnings which is the result of the business providing goods and services.

- **Expenses** are used to reflect a decrease in retained earnings which is the result of the business incurring costs related to providing goods and services.

- **Dividends** are used to reflect a decrease in retained earnings which is the result of the owners receiving assets (usually cash) from the business.

An expanded version of the accounting equation would now look like this:

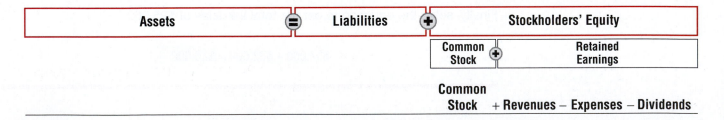

Retained Earnings and, therefore, Stockholders' Equity is increased by adding amounts to Revenues. Retained Earnings and, therefore, Stockholders' Equity is decreased by adding amounts to Expenses and Dividends. These subcategories will make more sense as we see how they are used to record the effects of business transactions. To illustrate, let us analyze the effects of several transactions on the accounting equation for the month of January 2010 for Osborne Consulting, Inc., a new computer consulting business started by Cindy Osborne.

1. **Sale of stock.** Cindy Osborne invests $10,000 to start the business. Osborne Consulting, Inc., sells Cindy $10,000 of common stock in exchange for her cash investment. The effect of this transaction on the accounting equation is to increase Assets and increase Stockholders' Equity as follows:

	Assets	=	Liabilities	+	Stockholders' Equity		
					Common Stock ⊕		Retained Earnings
	Cash	=	Accounts Payable	+	Common Stock	+ Revenues − Expenses − Dividends	
(1)	+ $10,000				+ $10,000		
Bal	$10,000	=			$10,000		

Remember for each transaction that the amount on the left side of the equation must equal the amount on the right side. The amount of assets will be increased by $10,000 because the business now has $10,000 of cash that it did not have before. In order to keep track of what type of assets the business has, the accountant will create a subcategory under assets for each different type of asset that the business has, so a subcategory for Cash was created. Since the assets have increased, there is now a need to increase the ownership side of the equation. The business does not owe the $10,000 to a third party so the $10,000 ownership interest must belong to Cindy and must be entered in the Stockholders' Equity section of the equation. If we look at the Stockholders' Equity side of the equation, we can see that there are two possible places the $10,000 can be entered in order to increase Stockholders' Equity: Common Stock and Retained Earnings. Based on the definitions of when each of these would be used, as discussed previously, we see that the $10,000 should be entered in the Common Stock section of Stockholders' Equity because this increase in Stockholders' Equity was the result of Cindy investing assets into the business.

2. **Purchase supplies on credit.** Osborne Consulting purchases office supplies agreeing to pay $350 within 30 days. The effect of this transaction on the accounting equation is to increase Assets and increase Liabilities as follows:

	Assets			=	Liabilities	+	Stockholders' Equity		
							Common Stock ⊕		Retained Earnings
	Cash	+	Supplies	=	Accounts Payable	+	Common Stock	+ Revenues − Expenses − Dividends	
Bal	$10,000			=			$10,000		
(2)			+ $350		+ $350				
Bal	$10,000	+	$350	=	$350	+	$10,000		

The Supplies account is an asset because the supplies that were purchased have not been used yet. Supplies are an example of what we call **prepaid expenses**. A prepaid expense is considered an asset until it has been used up in the business operations. The agreement to pay for them later creates an **accounts payable**, a liability, because the business owes $350 to a third party.

3. Purchase equipment for cash. The business purchases equipment, paying cash of $4,000. The effect of this transaction on the accounting equation is to increase one asset and decrease another asset as follows:

		Assets			=	Liabilities	+		Stockholders' Equity			
									Common Stock +		Retained Earnings	
	Cash	+	Supplies	+	Equipment =	Accounts Payable	+	Common Stock	+ Revenues	– Expenses	– Dividends
Bal	$10,000	+	$350		=	$350	+	$10,000			
(3)	– $ 4,000				+ $4,000						
Bal	$ 6,000	+	$350	+	$4,000 =	$350	+	$10,000			

The cash purchase of equipment increases one asset, Equipment, and decreases another asset, Cash, by the same amount. After the transaction is completed, Osborne Consulting has total assets of $10,350, liabilities of $350 and stockholders' equity of $10,000. This type of transaction is referred to as a **shift in assets**. Because there has been no change in the total amount of assets, there should be no change in ownership; therefore, there will be no change in the amount of Stockholders' Equity.

4. Borrow cash from the bank. Osborne Consulting borrows $12,000 cash from the bank and signs a two-year note payable to the bank. The effect of this transaction on the accounting equation is to increase Assets and increase Liabilities as follows:

		Assets			=	Liabilities	+		Stockholders' Equity			
									Common Stock +		Retained Earnings	
	Cash	+	Supplies	+	Equipment =	Accounts Payable +	Notes Payable +	Common Stock	+ Revenues	– Expenses	– Dividends
Bal	$ 6,000	+	$350	+	$4,000 =	$350		+ $10,000			
(4)	+ $12,000						+ $12,000				
Bal	$18,000	+	$350	+	$4,000 =	$350	+ $12,000 +	$10,000			

A **note payable** is a written promise to pay a specified amount in the future. Often businesses will borrow money from the bank in order to purchase assets or to make sure enough cash is available to operate the business. Borrowing cash from the bank increases the asset Cash because the business has $12,000 that it did not have before. It also increases the liability, Notes Payable, by $12,000 because the business owes $12,000 to the bank. In other words, the bank has an ownership interest in $12,000 of Osborne Consulting's assets. Note that total assets of $22,350 still equal the total liabilities of $12,350 plus the stockholders' equity of $10,000.

5. Provide services for cash. Osborne Consulting earns service revenue by providing consulting services for clients. Osborne collects $1,200 cash for services provided. The effect of this transaction on the accounting equation is to increase Assets and increase Stockholders' Equity as follows:

Assets	=	Liabilities	+	Stockholders' Equity		
				Common Stock ⊕		Retained Earnings

	Cash	+	Supplies	+	Equipment	=	Accounts Payable	+	Notes Payable	+	Common Stock	+ Revenues	− Expenses	− Dividends
Bal	$18,000	+	$350	+	$4,000	=	$350	+	$12,000	+	$10,000			
(5)	+ $ 1,200											+ $1,200		
Bal	$19,200	+	$350	+	$4,000	=	$350	+	$12,000	+	$10,000	+ $1,200		

Providing services increases both Cash and Revenues by $1,200. Cash is increased because the business has $1,200 that it did not have before and Revenues is increased because Stockholders' Equity must be increased to reflect the fact that Cindy, the sole stockholder, has an ownership interest in the increased assets. As was previously discussed, the specific subcategory that is used to increase Retained Earnings (and, therefore, Stockholders' Equity) because of providing goods and services is Revenues.

6. Provide services on credit. A business can also earn service revenue even if it has not yet received cash for these services. Osborne Consulting performs $1,900 of services and, in return, receives customers' promises to pay this $1,900 within one month. In accounting, we say that Osborne performed this service **on account**. A client's promise to pay is called an **account receivable**. It is an asset because the business has the right to collect the cash in the future. The effect on the accounting equation is to increase Assets and increase Stockholders' Equity as follows:

Assets	=	Liabilities	+	Stockholders' Equity		
				Common Stock ⊕		Retained Earnings

	Cash	+ Accounts Receivable	+ Supplies	+ Equipment	=	Accounts Payable	+	Notes Payable	+	Common Stock	+ Revenues	− Expenses	− Dividends
Bal	$19,200		+ $350	+ $4,000	=	$350	+	$12,000	+	$10,000	+ $1,200		
(6)		+ $1,900									+ $1,900		
Bal	$19,200	+ $1,900	+ $350	+ $4,000	=	$350	+	$12,000	+	$10,000	+ $3,100		

Notice the Revenue account was increased just as it was in the previous transaction when Osborne Consulting performed services and received cash. The Revenue account was increased to reflect the fact that there has been an increase in the stockholders' ownership interest in the assets of the business.

In Transaction 5 the assets increased because the business received cash and in Transaction 6 the assets increased because the business received an account receivable.

7. **Partial payment of accounts payable.** Osborne Consulting pays $150 to the store where it purchased $350 worth of supplies in Transaction 2. In accounting this is referred to as "paying on account." The effect on the accounting equation is to decrease Assets and decrease Liabilities as follows:

	Assets			=	Liabilities	+		Stockholders' Equity		
							Common Stock (+)		Retained Earnings	

	Cash	+ Accounts Receivable	+ Supplies	+ Equipment	= Accounts Payable	+ Notes Payable	+ Common Stock	+ Revenues	– Expenses	– Dividends
Bal	$19,200	+ $1,900	+ $350	+ $4,000	= $350	+ $12,000	+ $10,000	+ $3,100		
(7)	– $ 150				– $150					
Bal	$19,050	+ $1,900	+ $350	+ $4,000	= $200	+ $12,000	+ $10,000	+ $3,100		

The payment of cash on account has no effect on Supplies because the payment does not affect the amount of supplies that the business has. Likewise, the payment on account does not affect Expenses because the business is paying off an amount owed, not using those supplies. The Cash account decreases because the business has less cash and the Accounts Payable account decreases because the business owes less to a third party.

8. **Payment of expenses.** During the month, Osborne Consulting paid $1,700 cash for expenses incurred such as wages, building rent, and utilities. Later on we will see that each different type of expense will be shown separately in the accounting equation, but for now we will lump them all together under the heading "Expenses." The effect on the accounting equation is to decrease Assets and decrease Stockholders' Equity as follows:

	Assets			=	Liabilities	+		Stockholders' Equity		
							Common Stock (+)		Retained Earnings	

	Cash	+ Accounts Receivable	+ Supplies	+ Equipment	= Accounts Payable	+ Notes Payable	+ Common Stock	+ Revenues	– Expenses	– Dividends
Bal	$19,050	+ $1,900	+ $350	+ $4,000	= $200	+ $12,000	+ $10,000	+ $3,100		
(8)	– $ 1,700								+ $1,700	
Bal	$17,350	+ $1,900	+ $350	+ $4,000	= $200	+ $12,000	+ $10,000	+ $3,100	– $1,700	

For this transaction, Cash decreases and Expenses increase. Because Expenses are subtracted from Retained Earnings, Retained Earnings (and, therefore, Stockholders' Equity) will decrease. This decrease in Stockholders' Equity reflects that the assets for the business have decreased and, therefore, there has to be less ownership reported. Remember that Expenses are used to decrease Retained Earnings when needed as the result of the business incurring costs related to providing goods and services.

9. Cash dividends. Osborne Consulting pays $500 of cash dividends to Cindy Osborne, the stockholder. The effect on the accounting equation is to decrease Assets and decrease Stockholders' Equity as follows:

Assets	=	Liabilities	+	Stockholders' Equity	
				Common Stock +	Retained Earnings

	Cash	+ Accounts Receivable	+ Supplies	+ Equipment	=	Accounts Payable	+ Notes Payable	+ Common Stock	+ Revenues	− Expenses	− Dividends
Bal	$17,350	+ $1,900	+ $350	+ $4,000	=	$200	+ $12,000	+ $10,000	+ $3,100	− $1,700	
(9)	− $ 500										+ $500
Bal	$16,850	+ $1,900	+ $350	+ $4,000	=	$200	+ $12,000	+ $10,000	+ $3,100	− $1,700	− $500

The payment of dividends causes a decrease in Cash of $500 and an increase in Dividends of $500. Because Dividends are subtracted from Retained Earnings, Retained Earnings (and, therefore, Stockholders' Equity) will decrease. This decrease in Stockholders' Equity reflects that the assets for the business have decreased and, therefore, there has to be less ownership reported. Dividends are different from expenses because the cash is paid directly to the owners rather than being paid for costs that were related to providing goods or services. Once again we can see that the total assets of $23,100 still equal the total liabilities of $12,200, plus stockholders' equity of $10,900 so the accounting equation continues to balance. Remember that total Stockholders' Equity equals the Common Stock of $10,000 plus the Retained Earnings of $900 and that the Retained Earnings was arrived at by calculating earnings of $1,400 (subtracting the Expenses from the Revenues) and then subtracting the Dividends.

WHAT DO FINANCIAL STATEMENTS REPORT, AND HOW ARE THEY PREPARED?

Understand, and be able to prepare, basic financial statements **4** ▶

To present the results of a business's transactions for a period, financial statements need to be prepared. These reports show the entity's financial information to interested stakeholders both inside and outside the organization. Four basic financial statements are prepared by most organizations:

■ Income statement
■ Statement of retained earnings
■ Balance sheet
■ Statement of cash flows

The Income Statement

An **income statement** is prepared to answer the question, "Is the organization making any money or making a **profit**?" Just as a scoreboard shows how many points a team earned for a specific period of time, a business prepares an income statement to show, for a specific time period, the revenue earned and the expenses incurred to produce that revenue. Like the scoreboard that shows whether the team is winning or losing, the income statement shows whether the business had **net income** (total revenues were greater than total expenses) or a **net loss** (total revenues are less than total expenses). To prepare an income statement, we set up a format that includes a heading and the body of the statement. The heading of all financial statements should show "who," what," and "when." The "who" is the name of the business, the "what" is the name of the financial statement, and the "when" is the time period covered by the statement. The body of the income statement lists the revenues, then the expenses, and finally the net income or net loss. When revenues are greater than expenses, the business earns net income, or profit. When expenses are greater than revenues, the business has a net loss. We can prepare an income statement for Osborne Consulting for the month of January 2010 by referring to the ending balances in the accounting equation that we recently completed.

If we look at **Exhibit 1-2** we can see what the income statement for Osborne Consulting looks like. In the first month of operations, Osborne Consulting, Inc., earned $3,100 in revenue and had $1,700 in expenses which resulted in net income of $1,400. This amount can remain part of the stockholders' equity in the business and can be used to "grow" or expand the business or, the business can use all or part of these funds to pay dividends to the stockholders.

Osborne Consulting, Inc.
Income Statement
Month Ended January 31, 2010

Revenue		$3,100
Expenses		1,700
Net Income		$1,400

Osborne Consulting, Inc.
Statement of Retained Earnings
Month Ended January 31, 2010

Retained Earnings, January 1, 2010		$ 0
Add: Net Income for the month		1,400
Subtotal		1,400
Less: Dividends		500
Retained Earnings, January 31, 2010		$ 900

Osborne Consulting, Inc.
Balance Sheet
January 31, 2010

ASSETS		LIABILITIES	
Cash	$16,850	Accounts Payable	$ 200
Accounts Receivable	1,900	Note Payable	12,000
Supplies	350	Total Liabilities	12,200
Equipment	4,000		
		STOCKHOLDERS' EQUITY	
		Common Stock	10,000
		Retained Earnings	900
		Total Stockholders' Equity	10,900
		Total Liabilities &	
Total Assets	$23,100	Stockholders' Equity	$23,100

Exhibit 1-2 ▲

Notice the dollar signs on the first and last amounts and the double underline under the last amount, net income, presented on the statement. It is common practice to place a dollar sign on the first number and the last number in each column on a financial statement and to double underline the final amount.

Decision Guidelines

Decision	Guideline	Analyze
How do I determine if a business is profitable? 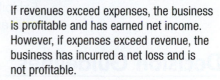	Use the income statement to determine the profitability of a business. The income statement reports the revenues and expenses of a business. Revenues represent what a business earns as a result of providing goods or services. Expenses represent the cost to the business of providing those goods or services.	If revenues exceed expenses, the business is profitable and has earned net income. However, if expenses exceed revenue, the business has incurred a net loss and is not profitable.

The Statement of Retained Earnings

"How much has the corporation made and kept during the current accounting period?" The **statement of retained earnings** answers this question by presenting the amount of the retained earnings and the changes to it during a specific time period, such as a month or a year. Increases in retained earnings come from net income and decreases result from either a net loss or the payment of dividends.

To prepare the statement of retained earnings, we set up a format that includes a heading and body similar to what we did for the income statement. The heading includes the name of the business, the name of the financial statement, and the time period covered by the statement. The body of the statement lists the beginning retained earnings balance, any net income earned or net loss incurred, any dividends paid, and the ending balance of Retained Earnings. Using the information from the income statement that we just prepared and the dividend information from our accounting equation, we can prepare a statement of retained earnings.

Exhibit 1-2 shows what Osborne Consulting's statement of retained earnings looks like. Because this is the first month that Osborne Consulting has been in business, there is a zero balance in beginning retained earnings. During the first month of operations, Osborne Consulting, Inc., paid dividends of $500, which when combined with the $1,400 of net income for January leaves an ending retained earnings balance at January 31 of $900. We can see that of the $1,400 that Osborne Consulting earned during January, $900 was retained in the business.

Decision Guidelines

Decision	Guideline	Analyze
If the company was profitable, what did it do with the profits?	Use the statement of retained earnings to find out. The statement of retained earnings shows whether the net income of a business was paid out as dividends or retained in the business.	If a business is planning on growth, it will often issue low or no dividends to shareholders. This way, it retains the income in the business.

The Balance Sheet

"What assets does the company have and who has ownership rights to those assets?" The **balance sheet** answers this question by listing all of an entity's assets, liabilities, and stockholders' equity as of a specific date, usually the end of a month or a year. Basically the balance sheet shows the accounting equation for a business and reflects the fact that assets equal liabilities plus stockholders' equity. The balance sheet is also known as the **statement of financial position**. Using the information from the statement of retained earnings that we just prepared and information from our accounting equation, we can prepare a balance sheet for Osborne Consulting. Exhibit 1-2 shows what Osborne Consulting's balance sheet will look like. Notice that total assets equal total liabilities and stockholders' equity.

Decision Guidelines

Decision	Guideline	Analyze
If a business were to close its doors, who would get its assets?	Use the balance sheet to determine who has claims to the company's assets.	The liabilities of a business reflect the claims of third parties to the assets of the business. Once those claims are settled, the remaining assets belong to the stockholders (the owners) of the business. This amount is reflected by the stockholders' equity on the balance sheet.

The Statement of Cash Flows

"Where did the business get the money it needed to operate and where did it spend its money?" The **statement of cash flows** answers this question by showing stakeholders all of the sources and all of the uses of cash by a business for a specified period of time. The statement of cash flows is a complex statement to prepare; therefore, we will postpone the coverage of the statement of cash flows until Chapter 11.

Decision Guidelines

Decision	Guideline	Analyze
Where does a business get its cash and where is it spent?	Use the statement of cash flows to see all of the sources and uses of cash for a business.	You can see whether a company's operations generated cash for the business and how much cash the business invested in the purchase of assets such as buildings and equipment. If a company's operations generated insufficient funds to finance its investments in assets, you can determine how the business financed these acquisitions.

Relationships Between the Financial Statements

The financial statements are prepared in the following order:

1. Income statement
2. Statement of retained earnings
3. Balance sheet
4. Statement of cash flows

The reason for this order is that the net income figure from the income statement is needed in order to prepare the statement of retained earnings. Likewise, the ending retained earnings balance from the statement of retained earnings is needed to prepare the balance sheet. Finally, information from both the income statement and the balance sheet is needed in order to prepare the statement of cash flows.

Demo Doc

Transaction Analysis Using the Accounting Equation/Financial Statement Preparation

Learning Objectives 3 & 4 ▶

On June 1, 2010, Julie Hansen started a Web page design business named Creations Unlimited, Inc. The business is organized as a corporation. During June 2010 Creations Unlimited, Inc., engaged in the following transactions:

a. Julie invested $25,000 in exchange for stock to start the business.

b. The business paid $7,500 cash to acquire computer equipment.

c. Supplies costing $350 were purchased on account.

d. Performed design services and received $1,100 cash.

e. Performed $1,800 of design services for a customer. The customer agreed to pay next week.

f. Paid $200 cash toward the supplies purchased in Transaction c.

g. Paid $600 for employee salaries for the month.

h. Paid $500 of dividends to Julie, the only stockholder.

i. Collected $1,000 from the customer in Transaction e.

Requirements:

❶ Enter these transactions in the expanded accounting equation of Creations Unlimited, Inc.

❷ Prepare the income statement, statement of retained earnings, and balance sheet of Creations Unlimited, Inc., after recording the transactions.

Demo Doc Solutions

Requirement ❶

Enter these transactions in the expanded accounting equation of Creations Unlimited, Inc.

Part 1	Part 2	Demo Doc Complete

a. Julie invested $25,000 in exchange for stock to start the business.

Julie is using her own money, but she is paying it *to the business*. Because the business is involved, it is a recordable transaction. From the business's perspective, this transaction will increase Cash (an asset) by $25,000 and increase Common Stock (stockholders' equity) by $25,000.

The effect of this transaction on the accounting equation is as follows:

	Assets				= Liabilities +	Stockholders' Equity			
							Common Stock		**Retained Earnings**
	Cash	+ Accounts Receivable +	Supplies	+ Equipment =	Accounts Payable +	Common Stock	+ Service Revenue	− Salaries Expense	− Dividends
a)	+ $25,000					+ $25,000			
Bal	$25,000				=	$25,000			

To record this transaction in the equation, we add $25,000 to Cash and add $25,000 to Common Stock. Before we move on, we bring down the account balances and check to see that the left side of the equation equals the right side. It is important to remember that the equation must balance after each transaction is recorded.

b. The business paid $7,500 cash to acquire computer equipment.

Equipment (an asset) is increased by $7,500, while Cash (an asset) is decreased by $7,500.

The effect of this transaction on the accounting equation is as follows:

	Assets				= Liabilities +		Stockholders' Equity			
						Common Stock +	Retained Earnings			
	Cash	+ Accounts Receivable +	Supplies +	Equipment =	Accounts Payable +	Common Stock +	Service Revenue −	Salaries Expense −	Dividends
Bal	$25,000			=		$25,000			
b)	− $ 7,500			+ $7,500					
Bal	$17,500	+		$7,500 =		$25,000			

Notice that transactions do not have to affect both sides of the equation. However, the accounting equation *must always balance*.

c. Supplies costing $350 were purchased on account.

Supplies is an asset that is increased by $350. However, the supplies were not paid for in cash, but instead *on account*. This transaction involves accounts *pay*able (because it will have to be *paid* later). Because we now have *more* money that has to be paid later, it is an increase in Accounts Payable (a liability) of $350.

The effect of this transaction on the accounting equation is as follows:

	Assets				= Liabilities +		Stockholders' Equity			
						Common Stock +	Retained Earnings			
	Cash	+ Accounts Receivable +	Supplies +	Equipment =	Accounts Payable +	Common Stock +	Service Revenue −	Salaries Expense −	Dividends
Bal	$17,500		+	$7,500 =		$25,000			
c)			+ $350		+ $350				
Bal	$17,500	+	$350 +	$7,500 =	$350 +	$25,000			

Remember that the supplies will be recorded as an asset until the time that they are used by the business (we will learn how to adjust for supplies used in a later chapter). The obligation to pay the $350 will remain in Accounts Payable until it is paid.

d. Performed design services and received $1,100 cash.

When the business designs Web pages, it is doing work for customers. Doing work for customers (or performing services) is the way that the business makes money. By performing these services, the business is earning service revenues. This means that Service Revenue increases (which increases Retained Earnings) by $1,100. Because the customer paid in cash, this transaction also results in an increase in Cash (an asset) of $1,100.

The effect of this transaction on the accounting equation is as follows:

	Assets				=	Liabilities	+	Stockholders' Equity			

								Common Stock	+	Retained Earnings	

	Cash	+ Accounts Receivable +	Supplies	+ Equipment =	Accounts Payable +	Common Stock	+ Service Revenue	− Salaries Expense	− Dividends
Bal	$17,500	+	$350	+ $7,500 =	$350 +	$25,000			
d)	+ $ 1,100						+ $1,100		
Bal	$18,600	+	$350	+ $7,500 =	$350 +	$25,000 +	$1,100		

e. Performed $1,800 of design services for a customer. The customer agreed to pay next week.

Again, the business is performing services for customers, which means that it is earning service revenues. This transaction results in an increase in Service Revenue (Retained Earnings) of $1,800.

This transaction is similar to Transaction d, except that the business is not receiving the cash immediately. Should we wait to record the revenue until the cash is received? No because Creations Unlimited, Inc., should recognize the revenue when the service is performed, regardless of whether or not it has received the cash.

However, this time the client did not pay in cash but instead agreed to pay later, which is the same as charging the services *on account*. The business will *receive* this money in the future (when the customer eventually pays), so it is called an account *receivable*. Accounts Receivable (an asset) is increased by $1,800. Accounts Receivable represents amounts owed to the business and decreases when a customer pays.

The effect of this transaction on the accounting equation is as follows:

	Assets				=	Liabilities	+	Stockholders' Equity			

								Common Stock	+	Retained Earnings	

	Cash	+ Accounts Receivable +	Supplies	+ Equipment =	Accounts Payable +	Common Stock	+ Service Revenue	− Salaries Expense	− Dividends
Bal	$18,600	+	$350	+ $7,500 =	$350 +	$25,000	$1,100		
e)		+ $1,800					+ $1,800		
Bal	$18,600	+ $1,800 +	$350	+ $7,500 =	$350 +	$25,000 +	$2,900		

f. Paid $200 cash toward the supplies purchased in Transaction c.

Think of Accounts Payable (a liability) as a list of companies to which the business owes money. In other words, it is a list of companies to which the business will *pay* money. In this particular problem, the business owes money to the company from which it purchased supplies on account in Transaction c. When the business *pays* the money in full, it can cross this company off of the list. Right now, the business is paying only *part* of the money owed.

This transaction results in a decrease to Accounts Payable (a liability) of $200 and a decrease to Cash (an asset) of $200. Because the business is only paying part of the money it owes to the supply store, the balance to Accounts Payable is still $150 ($350 − $200).

You should note that this transaction does not affect Supplies because we are not buying more supplies. We are simply paying off a liability, not acquiring more assets or incurring a new expense.

The effect of this transaction on the accounting equation is as follows:

					Assets			=	Liabilities	+			Stockholders' Equity		

											Common Stock	+			Retained Earnings		

	Cash	+	Accounts Receivable	+	Supplies	+	Equipment	=	Accounts Payable	+	Common Stock	+	Service Revenue	−	Salaries Expense	−	Dividends
Bal	$18,600	+	$1,800	+	$350	+	$7,500	=	$350	+	$25,000	+	$2,900				
f)	− $ 200								− $200								
Bal	$18,400	+	$1,800	+	$350	+	$7,500	=	$150	+	$25,000	+	$2,900				

g. Paid $600 for employee salaries for the month.

The work the employees have given to the business has *already been used*. By the end of June, Creations Unlimited's employees have worked for the entire month. Therefore, the *benefit* of the employees' work has *already been received*, which means that it is a salary *expense*. Salaries Expense increases by $600, which is a decrease to Retained Earnings. Remember, Expenses *decrease* Retained Earnings.

The salaries were paid in cash, so Cash (an asset) also decreases by $600.

The effect of this transaction on the accounting equation is as follows:

					Assets			=	Liabilities	+			Stockholders' Equity		

											Common Stock	+			Retained Earnings		

	Cash	+	Accounts Receivable	+	Supplies	+	Equipment	=	Accounts Payable	+	Common Stock	+	Service Revenue	−	Salaries Expense	−	Dividends
Bal	$18,400	+	$1,800	+	$350	+	$7,500	=	$150	+	$25,000	+	$2,900				
g)	− $ 600														+ $600		
Bal	$17,800	+	$1,800	+	$350	+	$7,500	=	$150	+	$25,000	+	$2,900	−	$600		

h. Paid $500 of dividends to Julie, the only stockholder.

A decrease to Cash (an asset) is recorded because the business paid Julie $500. This transaction also results in a $500 increase to the Dividend account, which results in a decrease of $500 to Retained Earnings. You should note that *the dividend is not an expense* because the cash is not used by the business. The cash withdrawn is for the owner's personal use.

The effect of this transaction on the accounting equation is as follows:

					Assets			=	Liabilities	+			Stockholders' Equity		

											Common Stock	+			Retained Earnings		

	Cash	+	Accounts Receivable	+	Supplies	+	Equipment	=	Accounts Payable	+	Common Stock	+	Service Revenue	−	Salaries Expense	−	Dividends
Bal	$17,800	+	$1,800	+	$350	+	$7,500	=	$150	+	$25,000	+	$2,900	−	$600		
h)	− $ 500																+ $500
Bal	$17,300	+	$1,800	+	$350	+	$7,500	=	$150	+	$25,000	+	$2,900	−	$600	−	$500

i. **Collected $1,000 from the customer in Transaction e.**

Think of Accounts Receivable (an asset) as a list of people/companies from which the business will *receive* money at some point in the future. Later, when the business collects (receives) the cash in full from any particular customer, it can cross that customer off the list.

In Transaction e, Creations Unlimited, Inc., performed services for a client who did not pay at that time. Now Creations Unlimited, Inc., is receiving *part* of the money owed ($1,000). Because cash is received, this is an increase to Cash (an asset) of $1,000. This collection also decreases Accounts Receivable (an asset) by $1,000 because the customer no longer owes this amount to Creations Unlimited, Inc.

The effect of this transaction on the accounting equation is as follows:

Assets					**= Liabilities +**		**Stockholders' Equity**							
							Common Stock **+**				Retained Earnings			
	Cash	+ Accounts Receivable +	Supplies	+ Equipment =	Accounts Payable +	Common Stock +	Service Revenue −	Salaries Expense −	Dividends
Bal	$17,300 +	$1,800 +	$350 +	$7,500 =	$150 +	$25,000 +	$2,900 −	$600 −	$500
i)	+ $ 1,000	− $1,000							
Bal	$18,300 +	$ 800 +	$350 +	$7,500 =	$150 +	$25,000 +	$2,900 −	$600 −	$500

Requirement ❷

Prepare the income statement, statement of retained earnings, and balance sheet of Creations Unlimited, Inc., after recording the transactions.

Part 1	**Part 2**	Demo Doc Complete

Income Statement

The income statement is the first statement that should be prepared because the other financial statements rely upon the net income number calculated on the income statement.

The income statement reports the profitability of the business. To prepare an income statement, begin with the proper heading. A proper heading includes the name of the company (Creations Unlimited, Inc.), the name of the statement (Income Statement), and the time period covered (Month Ended June 30, 2010). Notice that we are reporting income for a period of time, rather than a single date.

The income statement lists all revenues and expenses. It uses the following formula to calculate net income:

Revenues − Expenses = Net Income or Net Loss

First, you should list revenues. Secondly, list the expenses. After you have listed and totaled the revenues and expenses, you subtract the total expenses from total revenues to determine net income or net loss. If you have a positive number, then you report net income. A negative number indicates that expenses exceeded revenues, and you will report a net loss.

In the case of Creations Unlimited, Inc., Transactions d and e increased service revenue (by $1,100 and $1,800, respectively). These transactions mean that total service revenue for the month was $2,900 ($1,100 + 1,800).

The only expenses incurred were in Transaction g, which resulted in a salary expense of $600. The income statement for Creations Unlimited, Inc., is presented next:

Creations Unlimited, Inc. Income Statement Month Ended June 30, 2010		
Revenue:		
Service Revenue		$2,900
Expenses:		
Salaries Expense		600
Net Income		$2,300

You will use the $2,300 net income on the statement of retained earnings.

Statement of Retained Earnings

The statement of retained earnings shows the changes in retained earnings for a period of time. To prepare a statement of retained earnings, begin with the proper heading. A proper heading includes the name of the company (Creations Unlimited, Inc.), the name of the statement (Statement of Retained Earnings), and the time period covered (Month Ended June 30, 2010). As with the income statement, we are reporting changes for a period of time, rather than a single date.

Net income is used on the statement of retained earnings to calculate the new balance in the Retained Earnings account. This calculation uses the following formula:

Beginning Retained Earnings
+ Net Income or − Net Loss
− Dividends
= Ending Retained Earnings

You will begin the body of the statement by reporting the retained earnings at the beginning of the period (June 1). List Retained Earnings and the beginning date to the left, and enter the dollar amount to the right. Then, list the net income as an addition to retained earnings. If the business had a net loss it would be listed as a subtraction from retained earnings. You should notice that the amount of net income comes directly from the income statement. Next, arrive at a subtotal by adding net income to (or subtracting a net loss from) beginning retained earnings. Following this subtotal, you will report dividends as a deduction from retained earnings. The last step is to subtract the dividends from the subtotal to arrive at the ending retained earnings for the period (June 30).

In this case, because the company is new, the beginning retained earnings is zero. The net income of $2,300 is added to the zero balance in retained earnings for a subtotal of $2,300. The $500 of dividends is subtracted from the $2,300 subtotal to arrive at the ending balance in retained earnings of $1,800. Creations Unlimited's statement of retained earnings would appear as follows:

Creations Unlimited, Inc. Statement of Retained Earnings Month Ended June 30, 2010		
Retained Earnings, June 1, 2010		$ 0
Add: Net Income for the month		2,300
Subtotal		2,300
Less: Dividends		500
Retained Earnings, June 30, 2010		$1,800

You will use the $1,800 ending balance in retained earnings on the balance sheet.

Balance Sheet

The balance sheet reports the financial position of the business. To prepare a balance sheet, begin with the proper heading. A proper heading includes the name of the company (Creations Unlimited, Inc.), the name of the statement (Balance Sheet), and the date (June 30, 2010). Unlike the income statement and statement of retained earnings, we are reporting the financial position of the company for a *specific date*, rather than a period of time.

The balance sheet is just a listing of all assets, liabilities, and equity, with the equality of the accounting equation verified at the bottom.

To prepare the body of the statement, begin by listing assets. Next, list the liabilities and stockholders' equity. Notice that the balance sheet is organized in the same order as the accounting equation. You should also note that the amount of retained earnings comes from the ending retained earnings on your statement of retained earnings. You should then total both sides to make sure that they are equal. If they are not equal, you need to look for an error.

The figures for assets and liabilities come directly from the accounting equation. In this case, assets include the total cash balance of $18,300, accounts receivable of $800, supplies worth $350, and the equipment's value of $7,500, for a total of $26,950 in assets. Liabilities total $150: the balance in the Accounts Payable account. The $25,000 common stock balance is added to the ending retained earnings of $1,800 (from the statement of retained earnings) to give us total stockholders' equity of $26,800. The stockholders' equity is then added to the liabilities to get total liabilities and stockholders' equity of $26,950. The $26,950 of total assets equals the $26,950 of total liabilities plus stockholders' equity, which confirms the accounting equation: Assets = Liabilities + Stockholders' Equity.

Creations Unlimited, Inc.			
Balance Sheet			
June 30, 2010			
ASSETS		**LIABILITIES**	
Cash	$18,300	Accounts Payable	$ 150
Accounts Receivable	800		
Supplies	350		
Equipment	7,500		
		STOCKHOLDERS' EQUITY	
		Common Stock	25,000
		Retained Earnings	1,800
		Total Stockholders' Equity	26,800
		Total Liabilities &	
Total Assets	$26,950	Stockholders' Equity	$26,950

Demo Doc Complete

Part 1	Part 2	**Demo Doc Complete**

Decision Guidelines

Suppose you open a business. Here are some questions you should consider:

Decision	Guideline	Analyze
What form of business organization is the best?	There are many ways to organize a business including the following: a sole proprietorship, partnership, corporation or S corporation, or limited liability company. Each type of business organization has different advantages and disadvantages.	Know the tax and legal treatments of each type of organization. Weigh the best treatment of taxes and legal liability of each type and pick the format that is most advantageous for the business owners.
How do I determine if a business is profitable?	Use the income statement to determine the profitability of a business. The income statement reports the revenues and expenses of a business. Revenues represent what a business earns as a result of providing goods or services. Expenses represent the cost to the business of providing those goods or services.	If revenues exceed expenses, the business is profitable and has earned net income. However, if expenses exceed revenue, the business has incurred a net loss and isnot profitable.
If the company was profitable, what did it do with the profits?	Use the statement of retained earnings to find out. The statement of retained earnings shows whether the net income of a business was paid out as dividends or retained in the business.	If a business is planning on growth, it will often issue low or no dividends to shareholders. This way, it retains the income in the business.
If a business were to close its doors, who would get its assets?	Use the balance sheet to determine who has claims to the company's assets.	The liabilities of a business reflect the claims of third parties to the assets of the business. Once those claims are settled, the remaining assets belong to the stockholders (the owners) of the business. This amount is reflected by the stockholders' equity on the balance sheet.
Can I tell where a business got its cash and where it spent it?	Use the statement of cash flows to see all of the sources and all of the uses of cash for a business.	You can see whether a company's operations generated cash for the business and how much cash the business invested in the purchase of assets such as buildings and equipment. If a company's operations generated insufficient funds to finance its investments in assets, you can determine how the business financed these acquisitions.

ACCOUNTING VOCABULARY

THE LANGUAGE OF BUSINESS

Accounts payable (p. 13) A liability backed by the general reputation and credit standing of the debtor.

Accounts receivable (p. 15) An asset representing amounts due from customers to whom the business has sold goods or for whom the business has performed services.

Accounting (p. 6) The information system that measures business activity, processes the results of activities into reports, and communicates the results to decision makers.

Assets (p. 10) Items of value that a business possesses; also referred to as the resources of the business.

Balance sheet (p. 20) Summary of an entity's assets, liabilities, and stockholders' equity as of a specific date; also called the *statement of financial position*.

Businesses (p. 6) Organizations that sell products or services to customers.

Common stock (p. 12) Represents the investment of assets made by stockholders into a corporation.

Corporation (p. 7) A business owned by stockholders that is an entity legally separate from its owners. Also referred to as a C corporation.

Dividends (p. 12) Distribution of earnings by a corporation to its stockholders.

Entity (p. 9) An organization or a section of an organization that, for accounting purposes, stands apart as a separate economic unit.

Ethics (p. 4) Principles of socially responsible behavior.

Expenses (p. 12) Decreases to retained earnings caused by using resources to deliver goods or provide services to customers.

Financial accounting (p. 6) A process used to track business transactions and to provide financial information about a business.

Financial Accounting Standards Board (FASB) (p. 9) The primary organization that determines how accounting is practiced in the United States.

Financial statements (p. 6) Historical, objective reports, prepared according to GAAP, that communicate financial information about a business.

Fundamental accounting equation (p. 11) The basic tool of accounting that measures the resources of a business and the claims to those resources: Assets = Liabilities + Stockholders' Equity.

Generally Accepted Accounting Principles (GAAP) (p. 9) Accounting rules, created by the Financial Accounting Standards Board, that govern how accountants measure, process, and communicate financial information.

Historical cost (p. 10) Actual cost of assets and services acquired.

Income statement (p. 17) Summary of a business's revenues, expenses, and net income or net loss for a specific period.

Liabilities (p. 11) Third party claims to the assets of a business; the debts owed to third parties.

Limited liability company (p. 8) A hybrid business entity having characteristics of both a *corporation* and a *partnership*.

Manufacturing business (p. 7) Businesses that make their own products that are sold to the final customer or to other companies.

Merchandising business (p. 7) Businesses that sell products made by another company; also called *wholesale* and *retail companies*.

Net income (p. 17) The excess of total revenues over total expenses; also called *profit*.

Net loss (p. 18) The excess of total expenses over total revenues.

Note payable (p. 14) A written promise of future payment made by the business.

Objectivity (p. 10) Verifiable and confirmable by any independent observer; also called *reliability*.

On account (p. 15) Buying or selling on credit.

Partnership (p. 7) A business with two or more owners.

Prepaid expenses (p. 13) Amounts that are assets of a business because they represent items that have been paid for but will be used later.

Profit (p. 17) The difference between the revenues (the sales price of the goods or services sold by the business) and expenses (the cost of the resources used to provide these goods and services); also called *net income*.

Reliability (p. 10) Verifiable, confirmable by any independent observer; also called *objectivity*.

Retail business (p. 7) A business that sells products purchased from another company to the final consumer.

Retained earnings (p. 12) Earnings of a business that are kept, or retained, in the business.

Revenues (p. 12) Increases to retained earnings created by delivering goods or providing services to customers.

S-corporation (p. 8) A corporation that does not pay income tax. Instead, its earnings are passed through to its owners.

Service business (p. 7) Businesses that provide services to customers.

Shareholder (p. 7) A person who owns stock in a corporation; also called *stockholder*.

Shift in assets (p. 14) Exchanging one asset for another; this generally has no effect on liabilities or stockholders' equity.

Sole proprietorship (p. 7) A business with a single owner.

Statement of cash flows (p. 20) Summary of the changes in a business's cash balance for a specific period.

Statement of financial position (p. 20) Summary of business's assets, liabilities, and stockholders' equity as of a specific date; also called the *balance sheet*.

Statement of retained earnings (p. 19) Summary of the changes in a business's retained earnings during a period.

Stockholder (p. 11) A person who owns stock in a corporation. Also called a *shareholder*.

Stockholders' equity (p. 11) Represents the stockholders' ownership interest in the assets of a corporation.

Third party (p. 11) People or organizations unrelated to the organization.

Transaction (p. 11) An event that has a financial impact on a business entity.

Wholesale business (p. 7) A businesses that purchases products from a manufacturer and sells them to a retail business.

ACCOUNTING PRACTICE

DISCUSSION QUESTIONS

1. The text states that accounting is the "language of business." What does this mean? Why is it important to know the language?

2. Would you describe accounting as being primarily a technical discipline or primarily an ethical discipline? Why?

3. Financial statements are defined as "historical reports that communicate financial information about a business to people or organizations outside the company." Why is the word "historical" used?

4. What are some reasons why accounting has adopted "historical" financial statements as the model? What are some disadvantages associated with presenting "historical" financial statements?

5. What are some of the uses of financial statements?

6. What is the primary way in which corporations differ from proprietorships and partnerships? What are some of the factors that might affect a person's decision about the form of organization that would be best in a given situation?

7. What is the fundamental accounting equation? Define each of the components of this equation.

8. How is the accounting equation affected by each of the following transactions?
   a. Owners contribute cash to start the business.
   b. The company borrows money from the bank.
   c. The company provides services for a client who promises to pay later.
   d. The company collects from the customer in option c.

9. In what order would the financial statements be prepared? Why?

10. Which financial statement would be most useful to answer each of the following questions:
    a. Does the corporation have enough resources to pay its short-term debts?
    b. What is the corporation's policy toward "growing the company" versus distributing its wealth to owners?
    c. Did the corporation pay its operating costs with resources generated from operations, money borrowed from banks, or money generated from selling off its buildings and equipment?
    d. Did the corporation make a profit last year?

SELF CHECK

1. Which type of business organization is owned by its stockholders?
   a. Proprietorship
   b. Partnership
   c. Corporation
   d. All the above are owned by stockholders.

2. Generally Accepted Accounting Principles (GAAP) are created by the
   a. Securities and Exchange Commission (SEC).
   b. Financial Accounting Standards Board (FASB).
   c. Institute of Management Accountants (IMA).
   d. American Institute of Certified Public Accountants (AICPA).

3. Which accounting concept or principle specifically states that we should record trans-actions at amounts that can be verified?

   a. Entity concept
   b. Reliability principle
   c. Cost principle
   d. Going-concern concept

4. Boardmaster is famous for custom skateboards. At the end of a recent year, Boardmaster's total assets added up to $622 million, and stockholders' equity was $487 million. How much did Boardmaster owe creditors?

   a. $1,109 million
   b. $622 million
   c. $135 million
   d. $487 million

5. Assume that Boardmaster sold skateboards to a department store for $35,000 cash. How would this transaction affect Boardmaster's accounting equation?

   a. Increase both assets and stockholders' equity by $35,000
   b. Increase both assets and liabilities by $35,000
   c. Increase both liabilities and stockholders' equity by $35,000
   d. It will not effect the accounting equation because the effects cancel out.

6. Assume that Boardmaster sold skateboards to another department store for $22,000 on account. Which parts of the accounting equation does a sale on account affect?

   a. Accounts Receivable and Accounts Payable
   b. Accounts Payable and Cash
   c. Accounts Payable and Retained Earnings
   d. Accounts Receivable and Retained Earnings

7. Assume that Boardmaster paid expenses totaling $38,000. How does this transaction affect Boardmaster's accounting equation?

   a. Increases assets and decreases liabilities
   b. Increases both assets and stockholders' equity
   c. Decreases both assets and stockholders' equity
   d. Decreases assets and increases liabilities

8. Consider the overall effects of transactions in questions 5, 6, and 7 on Boardmaster. What is Boardmaster's net income or net loss?

   a. Net income of $57,000
   b. Net loss of $3,000
   c. Net income of $19,000
   d. It cannot be determined from the data given.

9. The balance sheet reports

   a. financial position on a specific date.
   b. results of operations on a specific date.
   c. financial position for a specific period.
   d. results of operations for a specific period.

10. The income statement reports

   a. financial position on a specific date.
   b. results of operations on a specific date.
   c. financial position for a specific period.
   d. results of operations for a specific period.

   Answers are given after Written Communication.

SHORT EXERCISES

S1-1. Accounting principles (*Learning Objective 2*) 5–10 min.

Place the corresponding letter of the definition next to the term.

a. An organization that stands as a separate economic unit must not have its financial affairs confused with that of other entities.

b. Data must be verifiable.

c. Standards developed by FASB.

d. Acquired assets and services should be recorded at their actual cost.

_____ 1. Cost principle

_____ 2. Entity concept

_____ 3. Generally accepted accounting principles

_____ 4. Reliability principle

S1-2. Accounting principles (*Learning Objective 2*) 5–10 min.

Jill Riggins owns and operates Jill's Java coffee shop. She proposes to account for the shop's assets at their current market value in order to have current amounts on the balance sheet. Which accounting concept or principle does Jill violate?

a. Cost principle

b. Entity concept

c. Going-concern concept

d. Reliability principle

S1-3. Accounting terminology (*Learning Objectives 1 & 3*) 10–15 min.

Place the corresponding letter of the definition next to the term.

_____ 1. Liabilities

_____ 2. Assets

_____ 3. Corporation

_____ 4. Dividends

_____ 5. Sole proprietorship

_____ 6. Partnership

_____ 7. Transaction

a. Any event that affects financial position.

b. Organization form with a single owner.

c. Organization form with two or more owners.

d. Organization form that can have an indefinite life.

e. Debt owed to outsiders.

f. Economic resource of the business.

g. Payment of cash to the owners of a corporation.

S1-4. Basic accounting equation (*Learning Objective 3*) 5–10 min

Determine the missing amounts in the following accounting equations.

	Assets	=	Liabilities	+	Stockholders' Equity
a.	$75,000	=	$32,000	+	?
b.	?	=	$43,000	+	$37,000
c.	$92,000	=	?	+	$60,000

S1-5. Basic accounting equation (*Learning Objective 3*) 5–10 min

Bill Allen owns Bill's Lawncare Service. The business has cash of $3,000 and equipment that costs $12,000. Debts of the business include accounts payable of $6,000 and a $5,000 note payable. Determine the amount of stockholders' equity Bill has in the business. Write the accounting equation for Bill's Lawncare Service.

S1-6. Basic accounting equation (*Learning Objective 3*) 5–10 min.

Apex Accounting, Inc., has cash of $2,000, supplies costing $800, and stockholders' equity of $1,300. Determine the liabilities of the business. Write the accounting equation for Apex Accounting, Inc.

S1-7. Basic accounting equation (*Learning Objective 3*) 5–10 min.

Bond Back Clinic, Inc., started a business when Dr. Bond purchased $8,000 of stock in the business. Before starting operations, Bond Back Clinic, Inc., borrowed $5,000 cash by signing a note payable to First State Bank. Account for these two transactions in the accounting equation.

S1-8. Entering transactions in the accounting equation (*Learning Objective 3*) 5–10 min.

T & T Towing Service, Inc., earns service revenue by towing vehicles for AAA. T & T Towing Service's main expenses are the salaries paid to its employees. Account for the following transactions in the expanded accounting equation:

a. T & T Towing Service, Inc., earned $14,000 of service revenue on account.

b. T & T Towing Service, Inc., paid $8,000 in salaries expense.

S1-9. Basic accounting equation (*Learning Objective 3*) 5–10 min.

Match each of the following items with its location in the accounting equation. Use the most detailed category appropriate:

a. Assets

b. Liabilities

c. Stockholders' Equity

d. Revenues

e. Expenses

_____ 1. Utilities Expense

_____ 2. Accounts Receivable

_____ 3. Common Stock

_____ 4. Office Supplies

_____ 5. Lease Expense, Computer

_____ 6. Salary Expense

_____ 7. Cash

_____ 8. Rent Expense, Office

_____ 9. Service Revenue

_____ 10. Accounts Payable

_____ 11. Land

S1-10. Basic financial statements (*Learning Objective 4*) 5–10 min.

Label each of the items listed with the abbreviation of the financial statement on which it appears. Items may appear on more than one statement.

Income Statement (IS)

Balance Sheet (BS)

Statement of Retained Earnings (RE)

_____ 1. Accounts Receivable

_____ 2. Notes Payable

_____ 3. Advertising Expense

_____ 4. Service Revenue

_____ 5. Retained Earnings

_____ 6. Office Supplies

S1-11. Entering transactions in the accounting equation (*Learning Objective 3*) 5–10 min.

As a manager of a department store, you must deal with a variety of business transactions. Place the letter of each of the following transactions next to the effect it has on the accounting equation.

a. Paid cash to the stockholders as a distribution of earnings.

b. Purchased land for building site.

c. Paid cash on an account payable.

d. Sold stock to stockholders.

e. Received cash from the bank in exchange for a note payable.

____ 1. Increase an asset and increase stockholders' equity.

____ 2. Increase an asset and increase a liability.

____ 3. Increase one asset and decrease another asset.

____ 4. Decrease an asset and decrease stockholders' equity.

____ 5. Decrease an asset and decrease a liability.

S1-12. Transaction analysis (*Learning Objective 3*) 5–10 min.

PWC Motorsports, Inc., a corporation, sells and services personal watercraft. The business experienced the following events. State whether each event (a) increased, (b) decreased, or (c) had no effect on the total assets of the business, and identify the asset(s) involved in each transaction.

1. PWC Motorsports, Inc., sold additional stock to stockholders.

2. Purchased land as a building site for cash.

3. Paid cash on accounts payable.

4. Purchased machinery and equipment; signed a promissory note in payment.

5. Performed service for a customer on account.

6. Paid cash to the stockholders as a distribution of earnings.

7. Received cash from a customer on accounts receivable.

8. Sold land for a price equal to the cost of the land; received cash.

9. Borrowed money from the bank.

S1-13. Transaction analysis (*Learning Objective 3*) 5–10 min.

Presented here are nine transactions and the analysis used to account for them. Evaluate each of the suggested accounting treatments and indicate whether it is true or false.

1. Received cash of $38,000 from the stockholders, who bought stock in the business.

Answer: Increase asset, increase stockholders' equity. ____ True ____ False

2. Paid $450 cash to purchase supplies.

Answer: Increase asset, increase stockholders' equity. ____ True ____ False

3. Earned service revenue on account, $500.

Answer: Increase asset, increase retained earnings. ____ True ____ False

4. Purchased office furniture on account at a cost of $850.

Answer: Increase asset, increase liability. ____ True ____ False

5. Received cash on account, $1,400.

Answer: Increase asset, decrease asset. ____ True ____ False

6. Paid cash on account, $675.

Answer: Increase asset, increase liability. ____ True ____ False

7. Sold land for $38,000, which was the cost of the land.

Answer: Increase asset, decrease asset. ____ True ____ False

8. Serviced automobiles and received cash of $680.

   Answer: Increase asset, increase revenue. ____ True ____ False

9. Paid monthly office rent of $1,200.

   Answer: Decrease asset, increase stockholders' equity. ____ True ____ False

---

S1-14. Transaction analysis and calulating net income (*Learning Objectives 3 & 4*)
5–10 min.

The analysis of Nelson's Painting Service's first seven transactions follows. The business only sold stock once and paid no dividends.

	Cash	+ Accounts Receivable	+ Equipment	=	Accounts Payable	+ Notes Payable	+	Common Stock	+ Retained Earnings
1.	+ $40,000			=				+ $40,000	
2.	− 1,200		+ $ 1,200	=					
3.			+ 25,000	=		+ $25,000			
4.		+ $400		=					+ 400
5.	− 750			=					− 750
6.	+ 1,800			=					+ 1,800
7.	+ 200	− 200		=					

Assets = Liabilities + Stockholders' Equity

1. Label each of the transactions in the preceding analysis with the corresponding letter of the description that best fits it:

   a. Earned revenue for painting services provided, but customer will pay later.

   b. Customers paid cash for painting services completed earlier in the month.

   c. Received cash for revenue earned by providing painting services.

   d. Paid cash for expenses incurred to operate the business.

   e. Paid cash to purchase painting equipment.

   f. Sold stock to start the painting service business.

   g. Borrowed money from the bank to purchase painting equipment.

2. If these transactions fully describe the operations of Nelson's Painting Service, Inc., during the month, what was the amount of its net income or net loss?

EXERCISES (GROUP A)

E1-15A. Basic accounting equation (*Learning Objective 3*) 10–15 min.

Determine the missing amounts in the following accounting equations.

	Assets	=	Liabilities	+	Stockholders' Equity
Inland Equipment, Corp.	?	=	$52,700	+	$18,000
Peter's Hardware, Inc.	$ 96,000	=	?	+	$42,000
Sparky's Electric, Inc.	$107,400	=	$88,200	+	?

E1-16A. Basic accounting equation (*Learning Objective 3*) 10–15 min.

Styles Salon had $87,000 of total assets and $52,000 of total stockholders' equity at December 31, 2010. At December 31, 2011, Styles Salon had assets totaling $153,000 and stockholders' equity totaling $81,000.

After analyzing the data, answer the following questions:

Quick solution: $37,000 increase.

1. What was the amount of the increase or decrease in liabilities?
2. Identify a possible reason for the change in liabilities during the year.

E1-17A. Basic accounting equation (*Learning Objective 3*) 10–15 min.

Anthony's Consulting, Inc., started business in 2010 with total assets of $32,000 and total liabilities of $14,000. At the end of 2010, Anthony's total assets were $42,000, and total liabilities were $18,500.

After analyzing the data, answer the following questions:

1. What was the amount of the increase or decrease in stockholders' equity?
2. Identify two possible reasons for the change in stockholders' equity during the year.

E1-18A. Using the accounting equation to determine net income (*Learning Objectives 3 & 4*) 15–20 min.

The balance sheet data for Quick Care, Inc. at August 31, 2010, and September 30, 2010, follow:

	Aug 31, 2010	Sep 30, 2010
Total Assets	$130,000	$165,000
Total Liabilities	87,000	131,000
Common Stock	15,000	15,000
Total Stockholders' Equity	?	?

Requirement

1. The following are three *independent* assumptions about the business during September. For each assumption, compute the amount of net income or net loss during September 2010. Find the solution by preparing the statement of retained earnings. First, use the amounts of total assets, total liabilities, and common stock given previously and the accounting equation to determine the beginning and ending retained earnings amounts. Then plug those and the other amounts given in each assumption into the statement of retained earnings to determine the net income or net loss.

   a. The business paid no dividends.
   b. The business paid $8,000 of dividends.
   c. The business paid $14,000 of dividends.

E1-19A. Transaction analysis (*Learning Objective 3*) 15–20 min.

Suzanne Luken opened a medical practice titled Suzanne Luken M.D., Inc. During March, the first month of operations, the business experienced the following events:

Mar	2	Luken bought $65,000 of stock in the business by opening a bank account in the name of Suzanne Luken M.D., Inc.
	6	The business paid $55,000 cash for land with the intention of building an office building on the land.
	11	The business purchased medical supplies for $1,000 on account.
	15	The business officially opened for business.
	17	The business treated patients and earned service revenue of $7,000, receiving cash.
	19	The business paid office rent, $1,800.
	22	The business sold supplies to another doctor for the cost of those supplies, $250.
	30	The business paid $500 on account related to the March 11 purchase.

Requirement

1. Analyze the effects of these events on the accounting equation of the medical practice of Suzanne Luken M.D., Inc. Use headings for Cash, Medical Supplies, Land, Accounts Payable, Common Stock, Service Revenue, and Rent Expense.

E1-20A. Types of business organizations and balance sheet preparation (*Learning Objectives 1 & 4*) 10–15 min.

The following are the balances of the assets, liabilities, and equity of Hair Today Salon at July 31, 2010:

Cash	$3,500	Office Equipment	$6,300
Retained Earnings	2,200	Common Stock	3,000
Accounts Payable	2,500	Note Payable	4,000
Accounts Receivable	1,200	Supplies	700

Requirements

1. What type of business organization is Hair Today Salon?
2. Prepare the balance sheet of the business at July 31, 2010.
3. What does the balance sheet report?

E1-21A. Types of accounts and income statement preparation (*Learning Objectives 3 & 4*) 15–20 min.

Selected accounts of Armstrong Consulting, Inc., a financial services business, have the following balances at December 31, 2010, the end of its first year of operations. During the year, Lori Armstrong, the only stockholder, bought $20,000 of stock in the business.

Office Furniture	$ 28,000	Rent Expense	$36,000
Utilities Expense	12,600	Cash	5,400
Accounts Payable	3,800	Office Supplies	800
Note Payable	21,500	Salary Expense	43,000
Service Revenue	141,500	Salaries Payable	2,000
Accounts Receivable	9,500	Property Tax Expense	2,300
Supplies Expense	4,200	Equipment	22,000

Requirements

1. Identify each as an asset, liability, revenue, or expense.
2. Prepare the income statement of Armstrong Consulting, Inc., for the year ended December 31, 2010. What is the result of operations for 2010?
3. Assuming the balance in Retained earnings on December 31, 2010, was $18,400, what was the amount of the dividends during the year? Answer by preparing a statement of retained earnings to solve for the dividends. Recall that the business has just completed its first year and has no beginning balance for retained earnings.

E1-22A. Using the accounting equation to determine net income (*Learning Objectives 3 & 4*) 15–20 min.

Presented here is information for Telco, Inc., for the year ended December 31, 2010.

	Telco, Inc.	
Beginning:		
Assets		$66,000
Liabilities		15,000
Ending:		
Assets		$94,000
Liabilities		28,000
Stockholders' Equity:		
Sale of Stock		$ 7,000
Payment of Dividends		20,000

Requirements

1. What is the beginning stockholders' equity of Telco, Inc.?
2. What is the ending stockholders' equity of Telco, Inc.?
3. What is the net income or net loss for the year?

EXERCISES (GROUP B)

E1-23B. Basic accounting equation (*Learning Objective 3*) 10–15 min.

Determine the missing amounts in the following accounting equations.

	Assets	=	Liabilities	+	Stockholders' Equity
Style Cuts Corp.	?	=	$52,700	+	$ 2,500
Your Basket, Inc.	$102,000	=	?	+	$48,000
Perfect Cleaners, Inc.	$108,800	=	$87,100	+	?

E1-24B. Basic accounting equation (*Learning Objective 3*) 10–15 min.

Great Wall Chinese Cuisine had $93,000 of total assets and $31,000 of total stockholders' equity at May 31, 2010. At May 31, 2011, Great Wall Chinese Cuisine had assets totaling $147,000 and stockholders' equity totaling $87,000.

After analyzing the data, answer the following questions:

1. What was the amount of the increase or decrease in liabilities?
2. Identify a possible reason for the change in liabilities during the year.

E1-25B. Basic accounting equation (*Learning Objective 3*) 10–15 min.

Kablossom started a business in 2010 with total assets of $35,000 and total liabilities of $32,000. At the end of 2010, Kablossom's total assets were $65,000, and total liabilities were $20,000.

After analyzing the data, answer the following questions:

1. What was the amount of the increase or decrease in stockholders' equity?
2. Identify two possible reasons for the change in stockholders' equity during the year.

E1-26B. Using the accounting equation to determine net income (*Learning Objectives 3 & 4*) 15–20 min.

The balance sheet data for Bob's Electronics, Co., at October 31, 2010, and November 30, 2010, follow:

	Oct 31, 2010	Nov 30, 2010
Total Assets	$140,000	$175,000
Total Liabilities..	75,000	117,000
Common Stock	45,000	45,000
Total Stockholders' Equity	?	?

Requirement

1. The following are three *independent* assumptions about the business during November. For each assumption, compute the amount of net income or net loss during November 2010. Find the solution by preparing the statement of retained earnings. First, use the amounts of total assets, total liabilities, and common stock given previously and the accounting equation to determine the beginning and ending retained earnings amounts. Then plug those and the other amounts given in each assumption into the statement of retained earnings to determine the net income or net loss.

   a. The business paid no dividends.

   b. The business paid $17,000 of dividends.

   c. The business paid $25,000 of dividends.

E1-27B. Transaction analysis (*Learning Objective 3*) 15–20 min.

Sherene Lynch opened a medical practice titled Sherene Lynch M.D., Inc. During January, the first month of operations, the business experienced the following events:

Jan 2	Lynch bought $80,000 of stock in the business by opening a bank account in the name of Sherene Lynch M.D., Inc.
6	The business paid $30,000 cash for land with the intention of building an office building on the land.
11	The business purchased medical supplies for $600 on account.
15	The business officially opened for business.
17	The business treated patients and earned service revenue of $13,000, receiving cash.
19	The business paid office rent, $1,100.
22	The business sold supplies to another doctor for the cost of those supplies, $400.
30	The business paid $150 on account related to the January 11 purchase.

Requirement

1. Analyze the effects of these events on the accounting equation of the medical practice of Sherene Lynch M.D., Inc. Use headings for Cash, Medical Supplies, Land, Accounts Payable, Common Stock, Service Revenue, and Rent Expense.

E1-28B. Types of business organizations and balance sheet preparation (*Learning Objectives 1 & 4*) 10–15 min.

The following are the balances of the assets, liabilities, and equity of Kite Runner, Inc., at August 31, 2010:

Cash	$24,000	Office Equipment	$4,100
Retained Earnings	18,400	Common Stock	5,000
Accounts Payable	5,000	Note Payable	1,000
Accounts Receivable	600	Supplies	700

Requirements

1. What type of business organization is Kite Runner, Inc.?
2. Prepare the balance sheet of the business at August 31, 2010.
3. What does the balance sheet report?

E1-29B. Types of accounts and income statement preparation (*Learning Objectives 3 & 4*) 15–20 min.

Selected accounts of Albright Consulting, Inc., a financial services business, have the following balances at January 31, 2010, the end of its first year of operations. During the year, Lilly Albright, the only stockholder, bought $49,700 of stock in the business.

Office Furniture	$ 20,000	Rent Expense	$36,000
Utilities Expense	13,500	Cash	15,600
Accounts Payable	9,500	Office Supplies	1,400
Notes Payable	21,500	Salary Expense	43,000
Service Revenue	155,000	Salaries Payable	1,000
Accounts Receivable	10,500	Property Tax Expense	3,000
Supplies Expense	3,700	Equipment	40,000

Requirements

1. Identify each as an asset, liability, revenue, or expense.
2. Prepare the income statement of Albright Consulting, Inc., for the year ended January 31, 2010. What is the result of operations for 2010?
3. Assuming the balance in Retained Earnings on January 31, 2010, was $5,800, what was the amount of the dividends during the year? Answer by preparing a statement of retained earnings to solve for the dividends. Recall that the business has just completed its first year and has no beginning balance for retained earnings.

E1-30B. Using the accounting equation to determine net income (*Learning Objectives 3 & 4*) 15–20 min.

Presented here is information for Eliason, Inc., for the year ended August 31, 2010.

Eliason, Inc.	
Beginning:	
Assets	$ 99,000
Liabilities	15,000
Ending:	
Assets	$164,000
Liabilities	70,000
Stockholders' Equity:	
Sale of Stock	$ 17,000
Payment of Dividends	55,000

Requirements

1. What is the beginning stockholders' equity of Eliason, Inc.?
2. What is the ending stockholders' equity of Eliason, Inc.?
3. What is the net income or net loss for the year?

EXERCISES (ALTERNATES 1, 2, AND 3)

These alternative exercise sets are available for your practice benefit at
www.myaccountinglab.com

PROBLEMS (GROUP A)

P1-31A Transaction analysis and the calculation of net income (*Learning Objectives 3 & 4*) 20–25 min.

Dan Oliver worked as an accountant at a local accounting firm for five years after graduating from college. Recently, he opened his own accounting practice, which he operates as a corporation. The name of the new entity is Oliver and Associates, Inc. Dan experienced the following events during the first month of operations. Some of the events were personal and did not affect the accounting practice. Others were business transactions and should be accounted for by the business.

Jun	3	Received $30,000 cash proceeds from refinancing his house.
	5	$60,000 of stock in the business was sold to Dan Oliver. The cash proceeds were deposited in a new business bank account titled Oliver and Associates, Inc.
	7	Paid $450 cash for office supplies for the new accounting practice.
	9	Purchased $3,800 of office furniture for the accounting practice and agreed to pay the vendor within three months.
	10	Dan sold 500 shares of General Motors stock, which he had owned for several years, receiving $48,000 cash. The cash from the sale of stock was deposited in his personal bank account.
	14	A representative of a large company telephoned Dan and told him of the company's intention to hire Oliver and Associates, Inc., as its accountants.
	20	Finished accounting work for a client and sent the client a bill for $3,800. The client is expected to pay within two weeks.
	27	Paid office rent, $1,600.
	30	Paid $1,000 of dividends to Oliver and Associates, Inc., shareholders.

Requirements

1. Enter each transaction in the expanded accounting equation of Oliver and Associates, Inc., as needed, calculating new balances after each transaction.
2. Determine the following items:
   a. Total assets
   b. Total liabilities
   c. Total stockholders' equity
   d. Net income or net loss for June

P1-32A Income statement and balance sheet transactions; prepare the income statement and balance sheet (*Learning Objectives 3 & 4*) 25–30 min.

Donna Adams started an interior design company called Interiors by Donna, Inc., on September 1, 2010. The following amounts summarize the financial position of her business on September 14, 2010, after the first two weeks of operations:

Assets					= Liabilities +		Stockholders' Equity			
							Common Stock +		Retained Earnings	

Cash	+	Accounts Receivable	+	Supplies	+	Equipment	=	Accounts Payable	+	Common Stock	+	Service Revenue	–	Salaries Expense	–	Dividends
$1,540	+	$3,680	+		+	$24,000	=	$5,100	+	$21,000	+	$5,100	–	$1,980		

During the remainder of September, the following events occurred:

a. Adams received $10,000 as a gift and used it to buy stock in the business.

b. Paid off the beginning balance of Accounts Payable.

c. Performed services for a client and received cash of $2,500.

d. Collected cash from a customer on account, $850.

e. Purchased supplies on account, $600.

f. Consulted on the interior design of a major office building and billed the client for services performed, $5,000.

g. Sold an additional $2,500 of stock in the business.

h. Paid salaries of $2,400.

i. Sold supplies at cost to another interior designer for $110 cash.

j. Paid dividends of $1,500 to Adams.

Requirements

1. Enter the remaining transactions for the month of September into the expanded accounting equation, calculating new balances after each transaction.

2. Prepare the income statement of Interiors by Donna, Inc., for the month ended September 30, 2010.

3. Prepare the statement of retained earnings of Interiors by Donna, Inc., for the month ended September 30, 2010.

4. Prepare the balance sheet of Interiors by Donna, Inc., at September 30, 2010.

P1-33A Prepare the income statement, statement of retained earnings, and balance sheet (*Learning Objective 4*) 20–25 min.

Gear Heads, Inc., restores antique automobiles. The retained earnings balance of the corporation was $32,000 at December 31, 2009. During 2010, the corporation paid $40,000 in dividends to its stockholders. At December 31, 2010, the business's accounting records show these balances:

Accounts Receivable	$ 5,000	Cash	$ 7,000
Note Payable	25,000	Accounts Payable	2,000
Retained Earnings	?	Advertising Expense	3,000
Salary Expense	14,000	Service Revenue	72,000
Equipment	78,000	Common Stock	20,000
Insurance Expense	4,000		

Requirement

1. Prepare the following financial statements for Gear Heads, Inc.:

   a. Income statement for the year ended December 31, 2010

   b. Statement of retained earnings for the year ended December 31, 2010

   c. Balance sheet at December 31, 2010

Quick solution:

a. Net income = $51,000
b. Ending Retained earnings = $43,000
c. Total assets = $90,000

P1-34A Prepare the income statement and balance sheet; identify certain financial information (*Learning Objective 4*) 25–30 min.

Presented here are the amounts of Assets, Liabilities, Stockholders' Equity, Revenues, and Expenses of The Better Body, Inc., at December 31, 2010. The items are listed in alphabetical order.

Accounts Payable	$ 15,000	Interest Expense	$ 9,000
Accounts Receivable	14,000	Land	40,000
Advertising Expense	13,000	Note Payable	65,000
Building	130,000	Property Tax Expense	3,000
Cash	16,000	Rent Expense	24,000
Common Stock	40,000	Salary Expense	71,000
Dividends	36,000	Salary Payable	2,000
Equipment	45,000	Service Revenue	185,000
Insurance Expense	1,000	Supplies	2,000

The retained earnings balance of the business was $97,000 at December 31, 2009.

Requirements

1. Identify each amount shown as an asset, liability, or stockholders' equity.
2. Prepare the company's income statement and statement of retained earnings for the year ended December 31, 2010.
3. Prepare the company's balance sheet at December 31, 2010.
4. Answer these questions about the company:
   a. What was the profit or loss for the year?
   b. What was the increase or decrease of retained earnings for the year?
   c. What is the amount of economic resources on December 31, 2010?
   d. What is the amount owed on December 31, 2010?

P1-35A Error analysis and preparation of balance sheet (*Learning Objective 4*) 20–25 min.

The IT manager of Aztec Realty, Inc., prepared the balance sheet of the company while the accountant was ill. The balance sheet contains numerous errors. In particular, the IT manager knew that the balance sheet should balance, so she plugged in the retained earnings amount to achieve this balance. The retained earnings amount, however, is not correct. All other amounts are accurate, but some are out of place.

Aztec Realty, Inc.
Balance Sheet
Month Ended June 30, 2010

ASSETS		LIABILITIES	
Cash	$ 9,000	Accounts Payable	$ 200
Rent Expense	1,000	Utilities Expense	900
Supplies Expense	350	Accounts Receivable	1,400
Salaries Payable	1,750	Notes Payable	5,700
Equipment	7,500		
		STOCKHOLDERS' EQUITY	
		Common Stock	8,000
		Supplies	800
		Retained Earnings	2,600
		Total Stockholders' Equity	11,400
		Total Liabilities &	
Total Assets	$19,600	Stockholders' Equity	$19,600

Requirement

1. Prepare a new, corrected balance sheet for Aztec Realty, Inc.

PROBLEMS (GROUP B)

P1-36B Transaction analysis and the calculation of net income (*Learning Objectives 3 & 4*) 20–25 min.

Don Griffin worked as an accountant at a local accounting firm for five years after graduating from college. Recently, he opened his own accounting practice, which he operates as a corporation. The name of the new entity is Griffin and Associates, Inc. Don experienced the following events during the first month of operations. Some of the events were personal and did not affect the accounting practice. Others were business transactions and should be accounted for by the business.

Apr	3	Received $20,000 cash proceeds from refinancing his house.
	5	$90,000 of stock in the business was sold to Don Griffin. The cash proceeds were deposited in a new business bank account titled Griffin and Associates, Inc.
	7	Paid $600 cash for office supplies for the new accounting practice.
	9	Purchased $4,000 of office furniture for the accounting practice and agreed to pay the vendor within three months.
	10	Don sold 1,200 shares of Mercedes stock, which he had owned for several years, receiving $22,000 cash. The cash from the sale of stock was deposited in his personal bank account.
	14	A representative of a large company telephoned Don and told him of the company's intention to hire Griffin and Associates, Inc., as its accountants.
	20	Finished accounting work for a client and sent the client a bill for $3,900. The client is expected to pay within two weeks.
	27	Paid office rent, $1,200.
	30	Paid $500 of dividends to Griffin and Associates, Inc., shareholders.

Requirements

1. Enter each transaction in the expanded accounting equation of Griffin and Associates, Inc., as needed, calculating new balances after each transaction.

2. Determine the following items:

   a. Total assets

   b. Total liabilities

   c. Total stockholders' equity

   d. Net income or net loss for April

P1-37B Income statement and balance sheet transactions; prepare the income statement and balance sheet (*Learning Objectives 3 & 4*) 25–30 min.

Deanna Golds started an interior design company called Interiors by Deanna, Inc., on November 1, 2010. The following amounts summarize the financial position of her business on November 14, 2010, after the first two weeks of operations:

Assets	=	Liabilities	+	Stockholders' Equity

				Common Stock	+	Retained Earnings

Cash	+	Accounts Receivable	+	Supplies	+	Equipment	=	Accounts Payable	+	Common Stock	+	Service Revenue	–	Salaries Expense	–	Dividends
$1,750	+	$3,210	+		+	$24,000	=	$5,400	+	$18,020	+	$6,900	–	$1,360		

During the remainder of November, the following events occurred:

a. Golds received $6,900 as a gift and used it to buy stock in the business.

b. Paid off the beginning balance of Accounts Payable.

c. Performed services for a client and received cash of $1,500.

d. Collected cash from a customer on account, $850.

e. Purchased supplies on account, $400.

f. Consulted on the interior design of a major office building and billed the client for services performed, $9,000.

g. Sold an additional $5,500 of stock in the business.

h. Paid salaries of $2,550.

i. Sold supplies at cost to another interior designer for $250 cash.

j. Paid dividends of $1,200 to Golds.

Requirements

1. Enter the remaining transactions for the month of November into the expanded accounting equation, calculating new balances after each transaction.

2. Prepare the income statement of Interiors by Deanna, Inc., for the month ended November 30, 2010.

3. Prepare the statement of retained earnings of Interiors by Deanna, Inc., for the month ended November 30, 2010.

4. Prepare the balance sheet of Interiors by Deanna, Inc., at November 30, 2010.

P1-38B Prepare the income statement, statement of retained earnings, and balance sheet (*Learning Objective 4*) 20–25 min.

Barrett, Inc., restores antique automobiles. The retained earnings balance of the corporation was $28,500 at December 31, 2009. During 2010, the corporation paid $35,000 in dividends to its stockholders. At December 31, 2010, the business's accounting records show these balances:

Accounts Receivable	$ 5,000	Cash	$10,000
Note Payable	16,000	Accounts Payable	2,000
Retained Earnings	?	Advertising Expense	3,500
Salary Expense	16,000	Service Revenue	70,000
Equipment	70,000	Common Stock	32,000
Insurance Expense	9,000		

Requirement

1. Prepare the following financial statements for Barrett, Inc.:

   a. Income statement for the year ended December 31, 2010

   b. Statement of retained earnings for the year ended December 31, 2010

   c. Balance sheet at December 31, 2010

P1-39B Prepare the income statement and balance sheet; identify certain financial information (*Learning Objective 4*) 25–30 min.

Presented here are the amounts of Assets, Liabilities, Stockholders' Equity, Revenues, and Expenses of Camp Out, Inc., at October 31, 2011. The items are listed in alphabetical order.

Accounts Payable	$ 13,000	Interest Expense	$ 7,000
Accounts Receivable	21,000	Land	36,000
Advertising Expense	17,000	Note Payable	64,000
Building	150,000	Property Tax Expense	2,500
Cash	17,000	Rent Expense	22,000
Common Stock	75,000	Salary Expense	71,000
Dividends	33,000	Salary Payable	1,900
Equipment	50,000	Service Revenue	195,000
Insurance Expense	1,000	Supplies	1,100

The retained earnings balance of the business was $79,700 at October 31, 2010.

Requirements

1. Identify each amount shown as an asset, liability, or stockholders' equity.
2. Prepare the company's income statement and statement of retained earnings for the year ended October 31, 2011.
3. Prepare the company's balance sheet at October 31, 2011.
4. Answer these questions about the company:
   a. What was the profit or loss for the year?
   b. What was the increase or decrease of retained earnings for the year?
   c. What is the amount of economic resources on October 31, 2011?
   d. What is the amount owed on October 31, 2011?

P1-40B Error analysis and preparation of balance sheet (*Learning Objective 4*) 20–25 min.

The IT manager of Right Away Realty, Inc., prepared the balance sheet of the company while the accountant was ill. The balance sheet contains numerous errors. In particular, the IT manager knew that the balance sheet should balance, so she plugged in the retained earnings amount to achieve this balance. The retained earnings amount, however, is not correct. All other amounts are accurate, but some are out of place.

Right Away Realty, Inc.
Balance Sheet
Month Ended September 30, 2010

ASSETS		LIABILITIES	
Cash	$14,000	Accounts Payable	$ 300
Rent Expense	1,600	Utilities Expense	700
Supplies Expense	100	Accounts Receivable	2,200
Salaries Payable	1,950	Notes Payable	7,000
Equipment	8,300		
		STOCKHOLDERS' EQUITY	
		Common Stock	12,000
		Supplies	600
		Retained Earnings	3,150
		Total Stockholders' Equity	15,750
		Total Liabilities &	
Total Assets	$25,950	Stockholders' Equity	$25,950

Requirement

1. Prepare a new, corrected balance sheet for Right Away Realty, Inc.

PROBLEMS (ALTERNATES 1, 2, AND 3)

These alternative problem sets are available for your practice benefit at
www.myaccountinglab.com

CONTINUING EXERCISE

This exercise is the first exercise in a sequence that begins an accounting cycle. The cycle is continued in Chapter 2 and completed in Chapter 3.

Graham's Yard Care, Inc., began operations and completed the following transactions during June:

Jun 1   Received $1,000 and issued 100 shares of common stock. Deposited this amount in bank account titled Graham's Yard Care, Inc.

3   Purchased on account a mower, $1,000, and weed whacker, $400. The equipment is expected to remain in service for four years.

5   Purchased $20 of gas. Wrote check #1 from the new bank account.

6   Performed lawn services for client on account, $200.

8   Purchased $50 of fertilizer from the lawn store. Wrote check #2 from the new bank account.

17   Completed landscaping job for client, received cash $500.

30   Received $50 on account from June 6 sale.

Requirement

1. Analyze the effects of Graham's Yard Care, Inc.'s transactions on the accounting equation. Include these headings: Cash, Accounts Receivable, Lawn Supplies, Equipment, Accounts Payable, Common Stock, Retained Earnings, Dividends, Service Revenue, and Fuel Expense.

In Chapter 2, we will account for these same transactions a different way—as the accounting is actually performed in practice.

CONTINUING PROBLEM

This problem is the first problem in a sequence that begins an accounting cycle. The cycle is continued in Chapter 2 and completed in Chapter 3.

Mike Hanson recently left his job at a local pool company to open his own pool and spa maintenance business. Mike Hanson took all of the money he and his wife had in their personal savings account and used it to open Aqua Elite, Inc., on May 1, 2010. Presented next are the transactions for the first month of operations for Aqua Elite, Inc.:

May

1   Mike invested $15,000 cash and a used truck worth $13,500 in the business in exchange for company stock.

3   Paid $4,700 cash to purchase office equipment.

7   Purchased $860 of supplies on account.

12   Performed services for cash customers and received $850.

15   Paid salaries of $675 to the office receptionist.

16   Sold the company truck for $13,500.

18   Signed a note payable for $31,000 to purchase a new truck.

21   Performed $3,200 of services on account for a local hotel chain.

27   Paid $500 of the amount owed from the purchase of supplies on May 7.

30   Received $2,000 on account from credit customers.

31   Received the utility bill for the month of May, $480. The bill is not due until the 15th of June.

31   Paid $1,000 dividends to the shareholder, Mike Hanson.

Requirements

1. Enter the transactions for Aqua Elite, Inc., for the month of May into the expanded accounting equation. Calculate the ending balances at the end of May.

2. Prepare the income statement for Aqua Elite, Inc., for the first month of operations.

3. Prepare the statement of retained earnings for Aqua Elite, Inc., for the first month of operations.

4. Prepare the balance sheet for Aqua Elite, Inc., for the first month of operations.

5. Did Mike make a wise decision leaving his job to start Aqua Elite, Inc.?

APPLY YOUR KNOWLEDGE

ETHICS IN ACTION

Case 1. Wendy Brown and her husband Jeff were the owners of WJ Enterprises, Inc. They applied for a small business loan, and the bank requested the most recent business financial statements. When Wendy compiled the balance sheet, she noticed that the business assets and related owner's equity were small. Accordingly, she told Jeff that they should contribute some of their personal assets to the business so that the assets and equity would appear much larger and thus the bank would more likely agree to the business loan. Jeff agreed that the balance sheet would appear stronger with more assets and equity but his concern was with the income statement. The sales for the latest period were low, which resulted in a slight net loss because expenses were slightly higher than revenues. Jeff reasoned that contributing assets would show a stronger balance sheet but felt something had to be done to also improve the income statement. He then told Wendy that their business could "sell" back some of the assets they had contributed and report higher sales on the income statement, which would result in net income rather than the actual net loss. Wendy did not feel comfortable buying back assets from their business just to increase reported sales.

Discuss any ethical concerns you may have with Wendy's proposal. Discuss any ethical concerns you may have with Jeff's proposal. Do you think it is ethical for a business to "dress up" its financial statements when applying for a loan?

Case 2. Eagle Ridge, Inc., was in the final phase of completing a land development project it started earlier in the year. Eagle Ridge, Inc., had acquired 100 acres of raw land for $250,000 and then spent an additional $1,650,000 in land development costs to create a new subdivision with 200 residential lots. With a total cost of $1,900,000 and 200 lots, each lot had a cost of $9,500; however, the lots were listed for sale at $32,000 per lot. Eagle Ridge, Inc., was applying for a business loan and needed to provide current financial statements to the bank. Jill Hamilton, the company president, wanted to include the total current value of the lots, $6,400,000 (20 lots x $32,000 per lot), rather than the total cost currently listed on the balance sheet, $1,900,000. Dave Jamison, the company accountant, told Jill that the lots were inventory and the cost principle required that they be included on the balance sheet at the $1,900,000 rather than the fair market value. Furthermore, even though the lots were listed for sale at $32,000 each, there was no guarantee that they would actually all sell at this value, and according to the objectivity principle, the more reliable cost figure should be used for this reason, too.

Should the balance sheet for Eagle Ridge, Inc., list the lots at the total cost of $1,900,000 or the total selling price of $6,400,000? Could Eagle Ridge, Inc., provide one balance sheet using historical cost and another balance sheet using market value?

KNOW YOUR BUSINESS

FINANCIAL ANALYSIS

Purpose: To help familiarize you with the financial reporting of a real company in order to further your understanding of the chapter material you are learning.

Each chapter will have a financial statement case that will focus on material contained in that chapter. You will be asked questions and you will then refer to Appendix A at the end of the book where you will find the annual report for Columbia Sportswear Company. Use the annual report to answer these questions. As you progress through each chapter, you will gain a real understanding of actual corporate financial reporting in addition to the basic accounting concepts you are learning within each textbook chapter. This added learning experience will further reinforce your understanding of accounting.

Requirements

1. Look at all the financial statements starting on page 681 of Appendix A and see whether you can identify the balance sheet, income statement, and statement of cash flows. (Note that the term *Consolidated* simply means combined.)

2. What was the total amount of assets Columbia Sportswear reported as of December 31, 2008? (Keep in mind that the numbers are in thousands.) Did the total assets increase or decrease from December 2007?

3. Did you see that Columbia Sportswear titled its income statement "Statements of Operations"? Were you able to identify it? (Note that some companies use this title.)

4. What was the total amount of revenues (net sales) Columbia Sportswear reported for the year ended December 31, 2008? (Keep in mind that the numbers are in thousands.) Did the revenues increase or decrease from the previous years presented?

INDUSTRY ANALYSIS

Purpose: To help you understand and compare the performance of two companies in the same industry.

Go to the Columbia Sportswear Company Annual Report located in Appendix A and find the Consolidated Balance Sheets on page 681. Now access the 2008 Annual Report for Under Armour, Inc. To do this from the Internet, go to their Web page for the Investor Relations at http://investor.underarmour.com/investors.cfm and under Downloads on the right-hand side, go to 2008 Annual Report. Their Consolidated Balance Sheet is located on page 49.

Columbia Sportswear Company and Under Armour, Inc., are in the same industry, which is manufacturing and selling sportswear. It is helpful to compare a company's financial data against other companies in their industry.

Requirement

1. Look at the data from the Consolidated Balance Sheets for each of the companies. Which company's stockholders have a higher claim to their company's assets? To find out, divide the total stockholders' equity for each company by its total liabilities and stockholders' equity.

SMALL BUSINESS ANALYSIS

Purpose: To help you understand the importance of cash flows in the operation of a small business.

You have just received your year-end financial statements from your CPA and you notice one very disturbing item. The net income from your income statement shows $40,000! Your very first thought is "where is it?" Then you look at your cash balance and see that it decreased $10,000 from last year to this year. You're thinking there has to be something wrong here. So you call up your CPA and ask for a meeting to discuss this obvious error. After all, how can you possibly have a positive net income and have your cash balance **decrease**?

At the meeting, the CPA lays out the financial statements in front of you and begins to explain how this would have happened. The following is a condensed income statement, statement of retained earnings, and balance sheet.

BCS Consultants, Inc.
Income Statement
For the Year Ended December 31, 2010

	Total Revenue		$150,000
	Total Expenses		110,000
	Net Income		$ 40,000

BCS Consultants, Inc.
Statement of Retained Earnings
For the Year Ended December 31, 2010

	Beginning Retained Earnings		$ 91,000
	Net Income	$ 40,000	
	Dividends Paid	(13,000)	27,000
	Ending Retained Earnings		$118,000

BCS Consultants, Inc.
Balance Sheet
December 31, 2010 & 2009

		2010	2009
	Assets:		
	Cash	$ 30,000	$ 40,000
	Equipment	158,000	146,000
	Total Assets	$188,000	$186,000
	Liabilities:		
	Notes Payable—Bank	$ 50,000	$ 75,000
	Stockholder's Equity:		
	Common Stock	20,000	20,000
	Retained Earnings	118,000	91,000
	Total Stockholders' Equity	138,000	111,000
	Total Liabilities and Stockholders' Equity	$188,000	$186,000

Requirement

1. By looking at the three financial statements, can you anticipate what the CPA is going to tell you about why the cash decreased even though you had net income for the year? What changed from 2009 to 2010? And are transactions that affect the income statement the only transactions that affect your cash balance?

WRITTEN COMMUNICATION

You just got an e-mail from a potential new client who contacted you from your Web site. This client has indicated to you that he or she is planning to start a new business. The client would like to find out from you what different types of business organizations are available. And also, he or she is wondering exactly what role an accountant would have in the running of the client's business.

Requirement

1. Prepare an e-mail back to this potential client addressing his or her questions about the different types of business organizations and why he or she needs to have an accountant involved in the business.

Self Check Answers
1. c 2. b 3. b 4. c 5. a 6. d 7. c 8. c 9. a 10. d

Analyzing and Recording Business Transactions

Now that you know why an understanding of accounting is important to everyone, you might ask yourself "How is accounting done in the *real world*?" You may wonder how to determine if a transaction has occurred, and if it has, how is it recorded? Maybe you have heard that accountants use things called debits and credits and wondered what they are. In this chapter, we will explore these questions as we learn about the process of accounting.

Chapter Outline:

Learning Objectives:

1. Define accounts and understand how they are used in accounting

2. Explain debits, credits, and the double entry system of accounting

3. Demonstrate the use of the general journal and the general ledger to record business transactions

4. Use a trial balance to prepare financial statements

HOW ARE ACCOUNTS USED TO KEEP BUSINESS TRANSACTIONS ORGANIZED?

Define accounts and understand how they are used in accounting **1**

As we discussed in Chapter 1, accounting provides useful information to various users. In order for the information to be useful, it has to be detailed information. Therefore, to facilitate the detail required, accountants will create many categories to track information in. These categories are referred to as **accounts**. We have already seen accounts in use. When recording transactions in the accounting equation in Chapter 1, we created accounts such as Cash, Equipment, and Accounts Payable.

Organizing Accounts

Numbering helps keep the accounts organized. Account numbers usually have two or more digits. The first digit indicates the type of account. Generally, if an account starts with:

- 1, it is an asset account.
- 2, it is a liability account.
- 3, it is a stockholders' equity account other than a revenue or expense account.
- 4, it is a revenue account.
- 5, it is an expense account.

Accounts that start with 6, 7, 8, or 9 are used by some businesses to record special types of accounts such as other revenues and expenses.

The remaining digits in an account number are used to specify the exact account. For example, cash may be numbered 101 and accounts receivable may be numbered 131. A gap in numbers is usually left between the different accounts to allow for additional accounts to be added later. A listing of all of the accounts is referred to as a **chart of accounts**. The accounts are typically listed in the chart of accounts in the order that they appear in the accounting equation. Therefore, assets would be listed first, followed by the liabilities, and then the stockholders' equity accounts. Typical types of accounts for many businesses are as follows:

Assets

As described in Chapter 1, assets represent things of value that a business has. Most businesses use the following asset accounts:

- **Cash.** Cash typically includes the business's bank account balance, paper currency, coins, and checks.
- **Accounts Receivable.** A business may sell goods or services in exchange for a promise of a future cash receipt. Such sales are said to be made on credit or on account. The Accounts Receivable account reflects the amounts that customers owe the business for goods or services that have already been provided. In other words, it shows how much money the company can expect to *receive* from customers in the future.
- **Notes Receivable.** A business may sell goods or services or loan money and receive a promissory note. A note receivable is a written promise that the customer or borrower will pay a fixed amount of money by a certain date. Notes Receivable reflects the amount of the **promissory notes** that the business expects to collect in cash at a later date.

- **Prepaid Expenses.** A business often pays certain expenses, such as rent and insurance, in advance. A prepaid expense is an asset because the prepayment provides a future benefit for the business. A separate asset account is used for each prepaid expense. Prepaid Rent and Prepaid Insurance are examples of prepaid expense accounts.
- **Land.** The Land account is used to track of the cost of land a business owns and uses in its operations.
- **Buildings.** The cost of a business's buildings, offices, warehouses, etc. is recorded in the Buildings account.
- **Equipment, Furniture, and Fixtures.** A business typically has a separate asset account for each type of equipment. Examples include Computer Equipment, Office Equipment, Store Equipment, and Furniture and Fixtures.

Liabilities

As defined in Chapter 1, liabilities are amounts owed to third parties. A business generally has fewer liability accounts than asset accounts because a business's liabilities can be summarized in a few categories such as the following:

- **Accounts Payable.** A business may purchase goods or services in exchange for a promise of future payment. Such purchases are said to be made on credit or on account. The Accounts Payable account reflects how much cash the business must pay to suppliers for goods or services that have already been received.
- **Notes Payable.** Notes Payable represents amounts the business must pay because it signed promissory notes to borrow money or to purchase goods or services.
- **Accrued Liabilities.** An accrued liability is a liability for an expense that has been incurred but has not yet been paid. Taxes Payable, Interest Payable, and Wages Payable are examples of accrued liability accounts.

Stockholders' Equity

As we saw in Chapter 1, the owners' claim to the assets of the business is called Stockholders' Equity. We have already discussed the different types of stockholders' equity accounts and what they're used for but they are listed here again for review.

- **Common Stock.** The Common Stock account represents the investment of assets, usually cash, the stockholders have invested into a business in exchange for the company's stock.
- **Retained Earnings.** The Retained Earnings account tracks the cumulative earnings of the business since it began, less any dividends given to stockholders.
- **Revenues.** Increases in Retained Earnings (and, therefore, Stockholders' Equity) created by selling goods or services to customers are called revenues. This account represents amounts *earned* by the company even if the company has not yet been paid for the goods and services provided. A business may have several revenue accounts depending on how many ways it earns its revenue.
- **Expenses.** Expenses are decreases in Retained Earnings (and, therefore, Stockholders' Equity) from using resources to deliver goods and services to customers. A business needs a separate account for each type of expense, such as Insurance Expense, Rent Expense, Wages Expense, and Utilities Expense. Businesses often have numerous expense accounts because many different types of costs are associated with providing goods and services to customers.
- **Dividends.** This account reflects the amount of earnings that have been distributed to the stockholders. Dividends decrease Retained Earnings (and, therefore, Stockholders' Equity).

WHAT ARE DEBITS, CREDITS, AND T-ACCOUNTS?

Explain debits, credits, and the double entry system of accounting ▶ **2**

In Chapter 1, we learned that every time we entered a transaction in the accounting equation, it affected at least two accounts. In accounting, the requirement that every transaction impact at least two accounts is called **double-entry accounting**. In order to simplify the process of accounting, each account is broken down into two sides. This can be visualized as a large T. For each account, one side of the T will represent an increase to the account, while the other side represents a decrease. Whether it is the left side of the T or the right side that increases the account depends on the type of account. Some accounts will increase on the left side and some will increase on the right side. In accounting terms, the left side of an account is referred to as the **debit** side. The right side of an account is referred to as the **credit** side. An example of a **T-account** is as follows:

Account Title	
Debit = left side Dr.	Credit = right side Cr.

Although T-accounts are not an official accounting tool, accounting professors use them to help students visualize the accounts. When first learning accounting, it can be very confusing trying to understand why some accounts are increased with debits (on the left side) while other accounts are increased with credits (on the right side). However confusing this might be, it was designed this way for a purpose. In addition to the rule that states that assets must always equal liabilities plus stockholders' equity, another accounting rule states that in every transaction the dollar amount of debits must equal the dollar amount of credits. By requiring that the amount of debits always equals the amount of credits and having some accounts increase with debits and other accounts increase with credits, the accounting equation is automatically kept in balance. **Exhibit 2-1** shows the accounting equation with T-accounts under each type of account along with which side of the account increases it or decreases it.

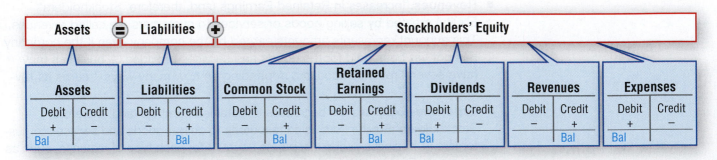

Exhibit 2-1 ▲

When trying to learn which accounts are increased with debits and which accounts are increased with credits, it is helpful to think of the acronym ADE and the acronym LCR. In the acronym ADE, the A stands for Assets, the D for Dividends, and the E for Expenses. These accounts are increased on the debit side (think of the DE in ADE). In the acronym LCR, the L stands for Liabilities, the C stands for Common Stock, and the R stands for both Revenues and Retained Earnings. These accounts are increased on the credit side (think of the CR in LCR).

Accounting in Your World

Jill recently purchased something over the phone and used her debit card to pay for it. When she checked her bank account activity online, the bank "debited" her account when it took money out of her account to pay for the purchase. Jill read in the textbook that a debit would increase her cash account. Now Jill is really confused.

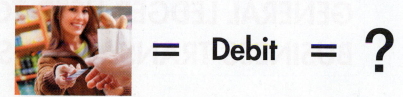

Many students feel this way when first introduced to debits and credits. It is really just a matter of perspective. You see, your bank account is an asset to you because it represents cash that is yours. However, your account is a liability to the bank because it represents money that the bank owes you. So, when the bank removes money from your account, it will debit the account to lower the liability because it no longer owes you the money. This is why it is called a *debit* card. You would actually need to credit your cash account, an asset, to show a decrease to your cash. Because you view your account as an asset and the bank views it as a liability, what you do (debit or credit) to the account to increase or decrease it will be exactly opposite of what the bank does.

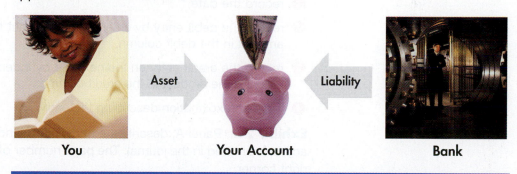

You   Your Account   Bank

Normal Balance

You would expect an account to have a positive balance; therefore, the **normal balance** of an account is on the increase side of an account:

- Assets increase on the debit side, so the normal balance of an asset is on the debit side.
- Liabilities increase on the credit side, so the normal balance of a liability is on the credit side.

- Common Stock increases on the credit side, so the normal balance of this account is on the credit side.
- Retained Earnings increases on the credit side, so the normal balance of this account is on the credit side.
- Dividends increase on the debit side, so the normal balance of the Dividends account is on the debit side.
- Revenues increase on the credit side, so the normal balance of a revenue is on the credit side.
- Expenses increase on the debit side, so the normal balance of an expense is on the debit side.

HOW ARE THE GENERAL JOURNAL AND GENERAL LEDGER USED TO KEEP TRACK OF BUSINESS TRANSACTIONS?

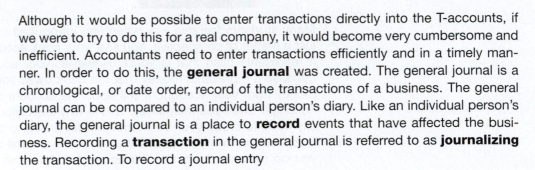
Demonstrate the use of the general journal and the general ledger to record business transactions

Although it would be possible to enter transactions directly into the T-accounts, if we were to try to do this for a real company, it would become very cumbersome and inefficient. Accountants need to enter transactions efficiently and in a timely manner. In order to do this, the **general journal** was created. The general journal is a chronological, or date order, record of the transactions of a business. The general journal can be compared to an individual person's diary. Like an individual person's diary, the general journal is a place to **record** events that have affected the business. Recording a **transaction** in the general journal is referred to as **journalizing** the transaction. To record a journal entry

1 record the date.

2 record the debit entry by entering the account title and then entering the amount in the debit column.

3 record the credit entry on the next line by indenting the account title and then entering the amount in the credit column.

4 write an explanation describing the entry.

Exhibit 2-2, Panel A, describes a transaction, and Panel B shows how this transaction is entered in the journal. The page number of the journal appears in its upper right corner.

Because the information in the general journal is organized by date and not by account, the information that it provides is not very useful. In order to be more useful, information must be organized by account. Therefore, the **general ledger** was created. The general ledger is a grouping of all the accounts of a business with their balances in balance sheet order. It shows the amount of Assets, Liabilities, and the Stockholders' Equity accounts on a given date. Once transactions have been entered in the general journal, the information is then transferred to the general ledger. The process of transferring information from the general journal to the general ledger is called **posting**. Posting simply means copying the amounts from the journal to the ledger. Debits in the journal are posted as debits in the ledger, and credits in the journal are posted as credits in the ledger. Exhibit 2-2, Panel C, demonstrates how an entry is posted from the journal to the ledger.

PANEL A—Illustrative Transaction:

DATE	TRANSACTION
Jan 1, 2010	Osborne Consulting, Inc., sold $10,000 of stock to Cindy Osborne, who was investing in the business.

PANEL B—Journal:

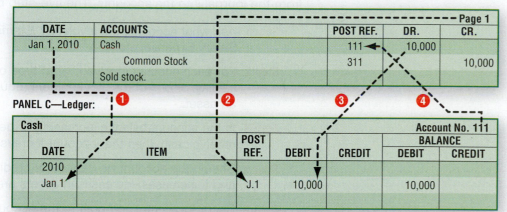

Page 1

DATE	ACCOUNTS	POST REF.	DR.	CR.
Jan 1, 2010	Cash	111	10,000	
	Common Stock	311		10,000
	Sold stock.			

PANEL C—Ledger:

Cash — Account No. 111

DATE	ITEM	POST REF.	DEBIT	CREDIT	BALANCE DEBIT	BALANCE CREDIT
2010 Jan 1		J.1	10,000		10,000	

Common Stock — Account No. 311

DATE	ITEM	POST REF.	DEBIT	CREDIT	BALANCE DEBIT	BALANCE CREDIT
2010 Jan 1		J.1		10,000		10,000

Exhibit 2-2 ▲

The posting process demonstrated in Exhibit 2-2 includes four steps. The four steps required to post the first part of the journal entry are as follows:

Arrow ① Copy the transaction date from the journal to the Cash account in the ledger.

Arrow ② Copy the journal page number from the journal to the **Posting Reference** column in the Cash account in the ledger. "J.1" refers to Journal page 1. This provides a reference that links the entry in the ledger back to the journal.

Arrow ③ Copy the dollar amount of the debit, $10,000, from the journal as a debit into the Cash account in the ledger.

Arrow ④ Copy the account number, 111, from the Cash account in the ledger back to the Posting Reference column in the journal. This step indicates that the $10,000 debit to Cash was posted to the Cash account in the ledger.

The journal entry is posted to Cash first because this is the first account listed in the entry. Once posting to Cash is complete, repeat the process to post the entry to Common Stock. The account format that is utilized in Exhibit 2-2 is called a four-column account. The first pair of debit and credit columns contains the individual transaction amounts that have been posted from journal entries, such as the $10,000 debit. The second pair of debit and credit columns is used to show the account's balance after each entry. Posting used to be performed on a periodic basis, such as daily or weekly. However, most modern computerized accounting systems post transactions immediately after they have been entered.

Transaction Analysis

To properly record, or journalize, transactions in the general journal it is helpful to complete a five-step process. Steps 1 through 4 analyze the transaction for the journal entry and Step 5 reflects the journalizing of the transaction and the posting from the journal into the accounts. The five-step process is as follows:

Step 1 Ask what accounts are involved? *Example*: Cash, Accounts Payable, Salary Expense, etc.

Step 2 For each account involved, what type of account is it? Is it an asset, liability, or one of the stockholders' equity accounts? *Example*: Cash is an asset.

Step 3 Is the account balance increasing or decreasing? *Example*: If you receive cash, then that account increases.

Step 4 Should the account be debited or credited? *Example*: Cash is an asset and it increases; increases in assets are recorded as debits.

Step 5 Record the entry and post to the accounts in the general ledger.

The five-step analysis looks like the following in chart form:

Step 1	Step 2	Step 3	Step 4	Step 5
Accounts Affected	Type	↑↓	Dr. or Cr.	Journalize entry and post to ledger

Applying Transaction Analysis

Check out how the transactions for the first month of operations for Osborne Consulting, Inc., are analyzed and recorded. *For illustration purposes, journal entries are shown being posted to T-accounts within the accounting equation. In actual practice, the journal entries would be posted to four-column accounts in the general ledger.*

1. Sale of stock. The business sold Cindy Osborne $10,000 of stock.

Analysis of Transaction (1)

Step 1 What accounts are involved? The business received cash in exchange for stock so the accounts involved are Cash and Common Stock.

Step 2 What type of account is it? Cash is an asset. Common Stock is an account within stockholders' equity.

Step 3 Does the account balance increase or decrease? Because cash was received, Cash is increased. Common Stock also increased because there has been more stock issued.

Step 4 Do you debit or credit the account in the journal entry? According to the rules of debits and credits, an increase in an asset is recorded with a debit. An increase in Common Stock is recorded with a credit.

The first four steps can be summarized as follows:

1 Accounts Affected	2 Type	3 ↑↓	4 Dr. or Cr.
Cash	Asset	↑	Dr.
Common Stock	Stockholders' Equity	↑	Cr.

Step 5 Journalize and post the transaction as follows:

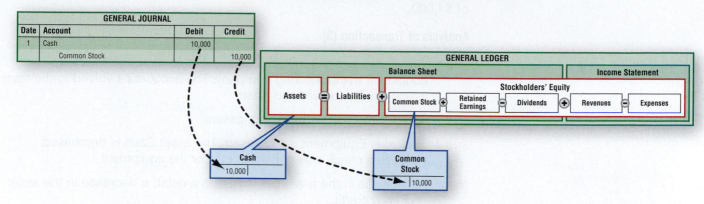

Notice that the name of the account being credited is indented in the journal. This format is a standard way to differentiate the accounts which are credited from the accounts which are debited. Also, note again, that every transaction affects at least two accounts and that the total amount added to the debit side equals the total amount added to the credit side. This demonstrates double-entry accounting, which keeps the accounting equation in balance.

2. **Purchase supplies on credit.** Osborne Consulting purchases office supplies agreeing to pay $350 within 30 days.

Analysis of Transaction (2)

Step 1 The business received supplies in exchange for a promise to pay cash to the supplier next month. The accounts involved in the transaction are Supplies and Accounts Payable.

Step 2 Supplies is an asset; Accounts Payable is a liability.

Step 3 The asset Supplies is increased. The liability Accounts Payable is increased because the business owes more than it did before this transaction.

Step 4 An increase in the asset Supplies is a debit; an increase in the liability Accounts Payable is a credit.

1 Accounts Affected	2 Type	3 ↑↓	4 Dr. or Cr.
Supplies	Asset	↑	Dr.
Accounts Payable	Liability	↑	Cr.

Step 5 Journalize and post the transaction as follows:

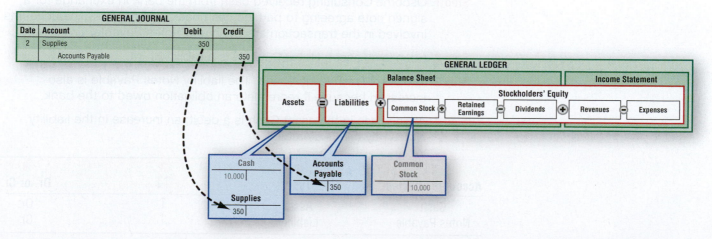

3. **Purchase equipment for cash.** The business purchases equipment, paying cash of $4,000.

Analysis of Transaction (3)

Step 1 The business received equipment in exchange for cash paid to the equipment manufacturing company. The accounts involved in the transaction are Equipment and Cash.

Step 2 Equipment and Cash are both assets.

Step 3 The asset Equipment is increased. The asset Cash is decreased because a check was written to pay for the equipment.

Step 4 An increase in the asset Equipment is a debit; a decrease in the asset Cash is a credit.

1 Accounts Affected	2 Type	3 ↑↓	4 Dr. or Cr.
Equipment	Asset	↑	Dr.
Cash	Asset	↓	Cr.

Step 5 Journalize and post the transaction as follows:

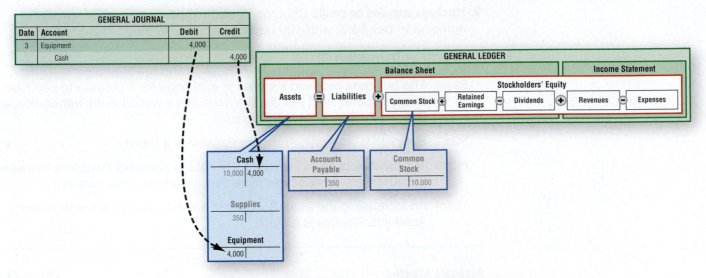

4. **Borrow cash from the bank.** Osborne Consulting borrows $12,000 cash from the bank and signs a two-year note payable to the bank.

Analysis of Transaction (4)

Step 1 Osborne Consulting received cash from the bank in exchange for a signed note agreeing to pay the cash back in two years. The accounts involved in the transaction are Cash and Notes Payable.

Step 2 Cash is an asset; Notes Payable is a liability.

Step 3 The asset Cash is increased. The liability Notes Payable is also increased because it represents an obligation owed to the bank.

Step 4 An increase in the asset Cash is a debit; an increase in the liability Notes Payable is a credit.

1 Accounts Affected	2 Type	3 ↑↓	4 Dr. or Cr.
Cash	Asset	↑	Dr.
Notes Payable	Liability	↑	Cr.

Step 5 Journalize and post the transaction as follows:

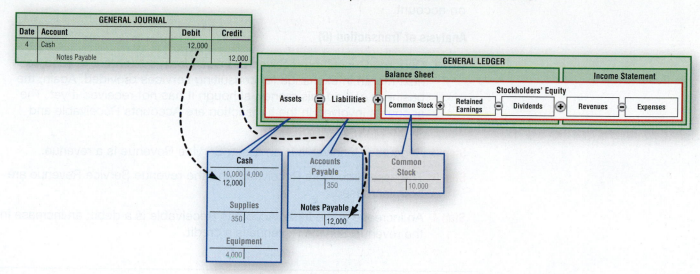

5. **Provide services for cash.** Osborne collects $1,200 of cash for services provided.

Analysis of Transaction (5)

Step 1 The business received cash in exchange for computer consulting services. The accounts involved in the transaction are Cash and Service Revenue.

Step 2 Cash is an asset; Service Revenue is a revenue.

Step 3 The asset Cash is increased. The revenue Service Revenue is increased also because the business has earned revenue by providing services.

Step 4 An increase in the asset Cash is a debit; an increase in the revenue, Service Revenue, is a credit.

1 Accounts Affected	2 Type	3 ↑↓	4 Dr. or Cr.
Cash	Asset	↑	Dr.
Service Revenue	Revenue	↑	Cr.

Step 5 Journalize and post the transaction as follows:

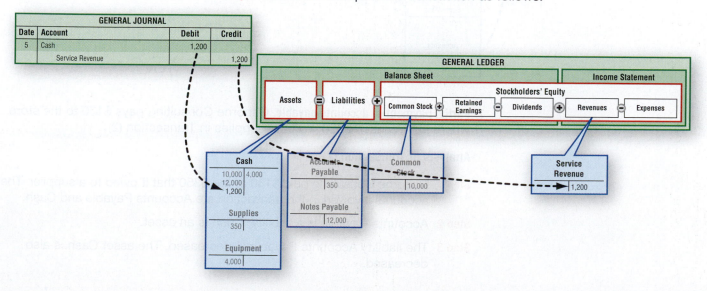

6. Provide services on credit. Osborne Consulting performs $1,900 of services on account.

Analysis of Transaction (6)

Step 1   Osborne Consulting received promises from customers to send cash next month in exchange for consulting services provided. Again, the business *earned* this money, although it has not received it yet. The accounts involved in the transaction are Accounts Receivable and Service Revenue.

Step 2   Accounts Receivable is an asset; Service Revenue is a revenue.

Step 3   The asset Accounts Receivable and the revenue Service Revenue are both increased.

Step 4   An increase in the asset Accounts Receivable is a debit; an increase in the revenue Service Revenue is a credit.

1 Accounts Affected	2 Type	3 ↑↓	4 Dr. or Cr.
Accounts Receivable	Asset	↑	Dr.
Service Revenue	Revenue	↑	Cr.

Step 5   Journalize and post the transaction as follows:

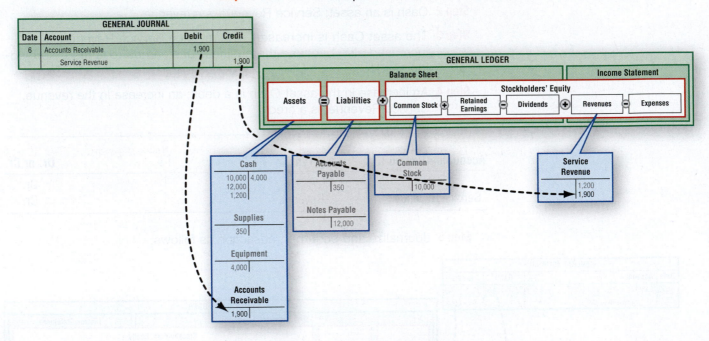

7. Partial payment of accounts payable. Osborne Consulting pays $150 to the store where it purchased $350 worth of supplies in Transaction (2).

Analysis of Transaction (7)

Step 1   Osborne Consulting paid $150 of the $350 that it owed to a supplier. The accounts involved in the transaction are Accounts Payable and Cash.

Step 2   Accounts Payable is a liability; Cash is an asset.

Step 3   The liability Accounts Payable is decreased. The asset Cash is also decreased.

Step 4 A decrease in the liability Accounts Payable is a debit; a decrease in the asset Cash is a credit.

1 Accounts Affected	2 Type	3 ↑↓	4 Dr. or Cr.
Accounts Payable	Liability	↓	Dr.
Cash	Asset	↓	Cr.

Step 5 Journalize and post the transaction as follows:

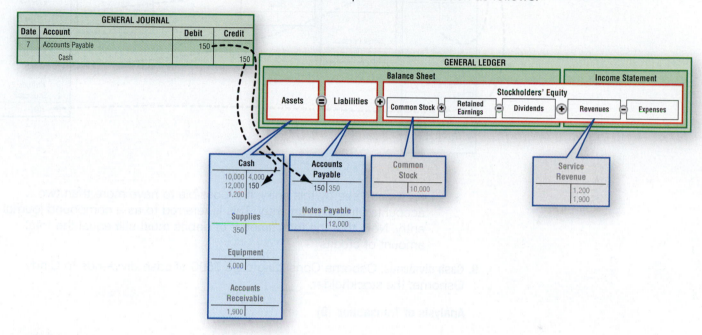

8. Payment of expenses. During the month, Osborne Consulting paid cash of $1,700 for expenses incurred such as wages ($600), building rent ($900), and utilities ($200).

Analysis of Transaction (8)

Step 1 The business paid $1,700 in exchange for employee services, the use of the building, and for utilities consumed as part of operating the business. The accounts involved in the transaction are Wages Expense, Rent Expense, Utilities Expense, and Cash.

Step 2 Wages Expense, Rent Expense, and Utilities Expense are expenses; Cash is an asset.

Step 3 The expense accounts are increased. The asset Cash is decreased.

Step 4 An increase in an expense is a debit; a decrease in the asset Cash is a credit.

1 Accounts Affected	2 Type	3 ↑↓	4 Dr. or Cr.
Wages Expense	Expense	↑	Dr.
Rent Expense	Expense	↑	Dr.
Utilities Expense	Expense	↑	Dr.
Cash	Asset	↓	Cr.

Step 5 Journalize and post the transaction as follows:

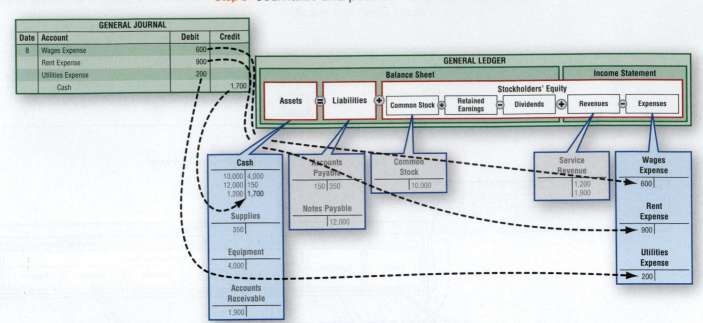

As we can see by this entry, it is possible to have more than two accounts utilized in an entry. This is referred to as a compound journal entry. Note that the total amount of debits must still equal the total amount of credits.

9. **Cash dividends.** Osborne Consulting pays $500 of cash dividends to Cindy Osborne, the stockholder.

Analysis of Transaction (9)

Step 1 The stockholder received cash dividends. The business reduced the stockholders' equity interest because of dividends paid to the stockholder. The accounts involved in the transaction are Dividends and Cash.

Step 2 Dividends is an account within stockholders' equity and Cash is an asset.

Step 3 The Dividends account is increased because the amount of money distributed to the stockholder increased. The asset Cash is decreased.

Step 4 An increase in Dividends is a debit; a decrease in the asset Cash is a credit.

1 Accounts Affected	2 Type	3 ↑↓	4 Dr. or Cr.
Dividends	Stockholders' Equity	↑	Dr.
Cash	Asset	↓	Cr.

Step 5 Journalize and post the transaction as follows:

GENERAL JOURNAL

Date	Account	Debit	Credit
9	Dividends	500	
	Cash		500

GENERAL LEDGER

Balance Sheet: Assets = Liabilities + Stockholders' Equity (Common Stock + Retained Earnings − Dividends) + Income Statement (Revenues − Expenses)

Cash
10,000 | 4,000
12,000 | 150
1,200 | 1,700
| 500

Supplies 350

Equipment 4,000

Accounts Receivable 1,900

Accounts Payable 150 | 350

Notes Payable | 12,000

Common Stock | 10,000

Dividends 500

Service Revenue | 1,200 | 1,900

Wages Expense 600

Rent Expense 900

Utilities Expense 200

Decision Guidelines

Decision	Guideline	Analyze
How do I know if an event should be entered into a company's accounting records?	Examine the effect of the event on the company's accounting equation.	If the event increases or decreases the assets, liabilities, or stockholders' equity of the business, it represents a transaction that should be recorded in the company's accounting records. If the event doesn't impact the assets, liabilities, or stockholders' equity of the company, then a recordable transaction has not occurred.

Balancing the T-Accounts

After the transactions are recorded and posted to the T-accounts, you will calculate each account's **balance**. The balance is the difference between the account's total debits and its total credits. Every account has a balance as shown as "Bal" in the following T-account:

Cash 101

(1) Bal	0	(3)	300
(2)	1,000		
(4) Bal	700		

❶ The beginning balance for the current accounting period is the ending balance brought forward from the previous period. In this example, the business is new, so its beginning balance is $0.

② If, for example, the business receives $1,000 from the sale of stock during the first accounting period, this transaction will show up as a debit to the Cash account.

③ If the company then pays $300 cash for supplies purchased, the amount will be entered on the credit side of the account.

④ Because the company just started, this account had a beginning debit balance of $0. Add increases of $1,000 that appear on the debit side, and subtract decreases of $300 that appear on the credit side. The resulting ending balance of Cash is $700. The Cash account normally has a debit balance because debits increase this account.

A horizontal line separates the transaction amounts from the account balance at the end of an accounting period. The "Bal 700" under the horizontal line shows that the balance in Cash at the end of the accounting period was $700. In the next accounting period, this balance will be the new beginning balance and will change as the business receives more cash and pays out more cash.

If an account's total debits are more than its total credits, then that account has a debit balance. If an account's total credits are more than its total debits, then that account has a credit balance. The ending balance of any T-account can be found in the same way that we just did for the Cash account.

The ending balances for Osborne Consulting would be as follows:

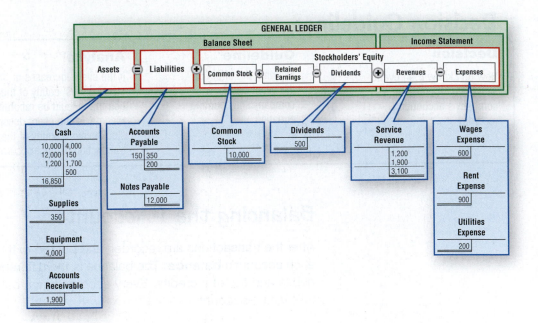

HOW IS A TRIAL BALANCE PREPARED AND WHAT IS IT USED FOR?

Use a trial balance to prepare financial statements **4** ▶

Once transactions have been recorded in the journal and posted to accounts in the ledger, a **trial balance** is prepared. The first step in preparing a trial balance is to complete the heading. Similar to the financial statements that were prepared in Chapter 1, the heading should show the company name, the statement name, and the period covered by the statement. Next, the name of each account is entered into the first column of the trial balance in the order that the account appears in the general ledger. Now, two columns are created labeled "debit" and "credit" and the balance of each account is entered into the correct column. Finally, the debit and credit columns are totaled. As was done when preparing the financial statements in Chapter 1, the first and last amount in each column has a dollar sign placed before it and the last amounts in both columns are double underlined. It should be noted that the trial balance is not an "official" financial statement. Its purpose is to summarize all account balances to be certain that total debits equal total credits after the entries have been journalized and posted. A trial balance can be prepared at any time, but is most commonly done at the end of the **accounting period**. An accounting period is usually defined as a month, a quarter, or a year. **Exhibit 2-3** shows the trial balance for Osborne Consulting, Inc., after all transactions have been journalized and posted for January 2010.

Osborne Consulting, Inc.
Trial Balance
January 31, 2010

ACCOUNT	DEBIT	CREDIT
Cash	$16,850	
Accounts Receivable	1,900	
Supplies	350	
Equipment	4,000	
Accounts Payable		$ 200
Notes Payable		12,000
Common Stock		10,000
Retained Earnings		0
Dividends	500	
Service Revenues		3,100
Rent Expense	900	
Wages Expense	600	
Utilities	200	
Total	$25,300	$25,300

Exhibit 2-3 ▲

☑ Concept Check

Jill just completed a problem that was assigned in her accounting class. She told Alan, one of her classmates, that she was confident that she did the problem correctly because the debits equal the credits on the trial balance. According to Alan, just because the debits equal the credits on the trial balance does not mean that everything was done correctly. Who is right Jill or Alan?

Answer

Alan is correct. The following are some of the errors that can occur and yet the trial balance will still be in balance:

■ A transaction can be recorded for the wrong amount in a journal entry.

■ An entire journal entry can be recorded twice, or not recorded at all.

■ The wrong accounts can be debited or credited in a journal entry. For example, when recording a payment on an account payable it is possible to debit accounts receivable instead of accounts payable.

Correcting Errors

If an error has occurred, the steps required to correct it depends on the type of error that was made. If a journal entry has been made to the wrong accounts or for the wrong amount, it is easiest to reverse, or undo, the incorrect entry. A new entry should then be prepared that contains the correct accounts or amount. To correct an entry that has been made twice, one of the entries should be reversed. If an entry was erroneously omitted, it simply needs to be entered.

Decision Guidelines

Decision		Guideline		Analyze
How do I know the amount of assets, liabilities, or stockholders' equity in the business at any point in time?		Review the trial balance or the general ledger.		The trial balance is a summary of all of a company's accounts with their respective balances on a given day. The general ledger provides the detail of all of the transactions that have impacted an account along with a running balance of the account. Having quick access to the account balances often allows managers and owners to make better decisions.

Preparation of Financial Statements

After completing the trial balance, you can use it to prepare the financial statements because it shows all of the accounts with their balances. First, set up the financial statements as we did in Chapter 1. Now, using the account balances from the trial balance, insert the account names and their balances into the financial statements, starting with the income statement, then the statement of retained earnings, and finishing with the balance sheet. Make sure the balance sheet is in balance! That is, total Assets equal total Liabilities plus Stockholders' Equity.

Exhibit 2-4 on the following page shows the income statement, statement of retained earnings, and balance sheet for Osborne Consulting, Inc., at January 31, 2010. You can see once again how the information flows from one statement to another.

These statements look the same as they did in Chapter 1, except now on the income statement we see detailed information for revenues and expenses. Also, notice that the income statement now has two columns. Many students assume, erroneously, that these columns represent debits and credits as they did on the trial balance. On financial statements, columns are used in order to make the statement more organized and easier to read; they are not used to signify debits and credits.

Osborne Consulting, Inc.
Income Statement
Month Ended January 31, 2010

Revenue:			
Service Revenues			$3,100
Expenses:			
Rent Expense		$900	
Wages Expense		600	
Utilities Expense		200	
Total Expenses			1,700
Net Income			$1,400

Osborne Consulting, Inc.
Statement of Retained Earnings
Month Ended January 31, 2010

Retained Earnings, January 1, 2010		$ 0
Add: Net Income for the month		1,400
Subtotal		1,400
Less: Dividends		500
Retained Earnings, January 31, 2010		$ 900

Osborne Consulting, Inc.
Balance Sheet
January 31, 2010

ASSETS		LIABILITIES	
Cash	$16,850	Accounts Payable	$ 200
Accounts Receivable	1,900	Note Payable	12,000
Supplies	350	Total Liabilities	12,200
Equipment	4,000		
		STOCKHOLDERS' EQUITY	
		Common Stock	10,000
		Retained Earnings	900
		Total Stockholders' Equity	10,900
		Total Liabilities &	
Total Assets	$23,100	Stockholders' Equity	$23,100

Exhibit 2-4 ▲

Decision Guidelines

Decision	Guideline	Analyze
How can I tell how well a business is performing?	A company's financial statements will provide feedback regarding the performance of the company.	The income statement reflects how profitable a business has been for a specified period of time. The statement of retained earnings shows how much of a company's earnings have been distributed to the stockholders during the period. And, the balance sheet reflects the business's financial position on a given date. In other words, it shows what assets the business has and who has rights to those assets.

The process of analyzing transactions, entering them into the journal, posting them to the ledger, preparing a trial balance, and preparing financial statements is only a part of what is called the **accounting cycle**. This accounting cycle is completed by a business for every accounting period and then it is repeated for the next accounting period, and the next, and the next, and so on. Shown next is a visual representation of the accounting cycle:

In the next chapter, you will learn the remaining steps in the accounting cycle, which includes preparing adjusting and closing entries.

 # Demo Doc

Debit/Credit Transaction Analysis

Learning Objectives 1–3 ▶

On June 1, 2010, Robert Williams opened PaintPro, Inc., a company that provides residential and commercial painting services. During the month of June, the business incurred the following transactions:

a. To begin operations, the business sold Robert $8,000 of stock. The business received the cash from the sale and gave Robert an ownership interest.

b. Purchased equipment for $4,800 on account.

c. Purchased office supplies for $500 cash.

d. Performed $1,600 of services for a customer on account.

e. Paid $2,000 cash toward the equipment purchased on account in Transaction b.

f. Received $2,300 in cash for services provided to a new customer.

g. Paid $350 cash to repair equipment.

h. Paid $1,150 cash in salary expense.

i. Received $700 cash from customers on account.

j. Paid $1,000 of dividends to its only stockholder, Robert Williams.

Requirements:

1 **Create blank T-accounts for the following accounts:** Cash, 111; Accounts Receivable, 121; Supplies, 131; Equipment, 141; Accounts Payable, 211; Common Stock, 311; Dividends, 322; Service Revenue, 411; Salary Expense, 511; and Repairs Expense, 521.

2 **Journalize the transactions and show how they are posted in T-accounts.**

3 **Total all the T-accounts to determine their balances at the end of the month.**

Demo Doc Solutions

Requirement **1**

Create blank T-accounts for the following accounts:

Cash, 111; Accounts Receivable, 121; Supplies, 131; Equipment, 141; Accounts Payable, 211; Common Stock, 311; Dividends, 322; Service Revenue, 411; Salary Expense, 511; and Repairs Expense, 521.

| Part 1 | Part 2 | Part 3 | Demo Doc Complete |

Opening a T-account simply means drawing a blank account (the T) and putting the account title (and the account number, if used) on top. To help find the accounts later, they are usually organized into assets, liabilities, stockholders' equity, revenue, and expenses (in that order). Note that the account numbers also follow this order.

Draw empty T-accounts for every account listed in the question.

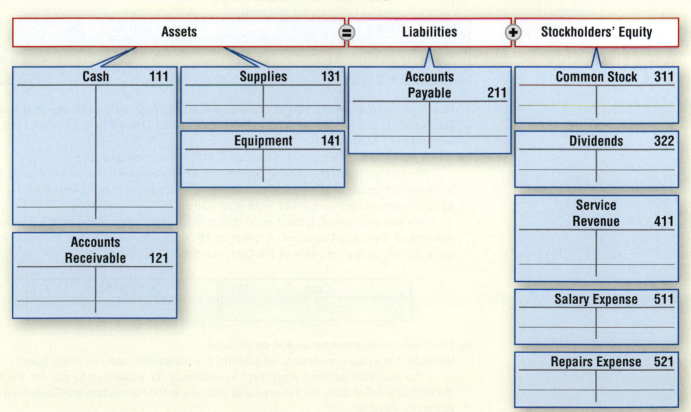

Requirement ❷

Journalize the transactions and show how they are posted in T-accounts.

Part 1	**Part 2**	Part 3	Demo Doc Complete

a. To begin operations, the business sold Robert $8,000 of stock. The business received the cash from the sale and gave Robert an ownership interest.

Remember the transaction analysis steps listed earlier in the chapter. First, we must determine which accounts are affected.

The business received $8,000 cash when it sold Robert stock. In exchange, Robert received an equity interest in the business. So, the accounts involved are Cash and Common Stock.

The next step is to determine what type of accounts they are. Cash is an asset, while common stock is part of stockholders' equity.

The next step is to determine whether these accounts increased or decreased. From *the business's* point of view, Cash (an asset) increased. Common Stock (equity) also increased.

Now we must determine whether these accounts should be debited or credited. According to the rules of debits and credits, an increase in assets is a debit, while an increase in common stock (equity) is a credit.

So, Cash (an asset) increases, which is a debit. Common Stock (equity) also increases, which is a credit.

1 Accounts Affected	2 Type	3 ↑↓	4 Dr. or Cr.
Cash	Asset	↑	Dr.
Common Stock	Stockholders' Equity	↑	Cr.

The journal entry would be as follows:

DATE	ACCOUNTS	POST REF.	DR.	CR.
a.	Cash		8,000	
	Common Stock			8,000
	Sold Stock.			

Note that the total dollar amounts of debits will equal the total dollar amounts of credits. Remember to use the transaction letters for references. This will help when we post this entry to the T-accounts.

Posting to the T-accounts is the last step in transaction analysis.

To post the transaction to the T-accounts, simply transfer the amount of each debit to its correct account as a debit (left side) entry, and transfer the amount of each credit to its correct account as a credit (right side) entry.

For this transaction, a debit of $8,000 to Cash means that we enter $8,000 on the left side of the Cash T-account. A credit of $8,000 to Common Stock means that we enter $8,000 on the right side of the Common Stock T-account:

Cash	111		Common Stock	311
(a) 8,000				(a) 8,000

b. Purchased equipment for $4,800 on account.

Because it is a new transaction, we perform the transaction analysis steps again.

The business received equipment in exchange for a promise to pay for the cost ($4,800) at a future date. So the accounts involved in the transaction are Equipment and Accounts Payable.

Equipment is an asset, and Accounts Payable is a liability. Equipment (an asset) increased. Accounts Payable (a liability) also increased.

According to the debit and credit rules, an increase in assets is a debit, while an increase in liabilities is a credit.

So, Equipment (an asset) increases, which is a debit. Accounts Payable (a liability) also increases, which is a credit.

1 Accounts Affected	2 Type	3 ↑↓	4 Dr. or Cr.
Equipment	Asset	↑	Dr.
Accounts Payable	Liability	↑	Cr.

The journal entry would be as follows:

DATE	ACCOUNTS	POST REF.	DR.	CR.
b.	Equipment		4,800	
	Accounts payable			4,800
	Purchased equipment on account.			

We enter $4,800 on the debit (left) side of the Equipment T-account and $4,800 on the credit (right) side of the Accounts Payable T-account.

Equipment	141
(b) 4,800	

Accounts Payable	211
	(b) 4,800

c. **Purchased office supplies for $500 cash.**

The business purchased supplies in exchange for cash ($500). The accounts involved in the transaction are Supplies and Cash.

Supplies and Cash are both assets. Supplies (an asset) increased. Cash (an asset) decreased.

An increase in assets is a debit, while a decrease in assets is a credit.

So, Supplies (an asset) increases, which is a debit. Cash (an asset) decreases, which is a credit.

1 Accounts Affected	2 Type	3 ↑↓	4 Dr. or Cr.
Supplies	Asset	↑	Dr.
Cash	Asset	↓	Cr.

The journal entry would be as follows:

DATE	ACCOUNTS	POST REF.	DR.	CR.
c.	Supplies		500	
	Cash			500
	Purchased supplies for cash.			

We enter $500 on the debit (left) side of the Supplies T-account and $500 on the credit (right) side of the Cash T-account.

Cash	111
(a) 8,000	(c) 500

Supplies	131
(c) 500	

Notice the $8,000 already on the debit side of the Cash account from Transaction a.

d. Performed $1,600 of services for a customer on account.

The business received promises from customers to send cash ($1,600) next month in exchange for painting services rendered. So the accounts involved in the transaction are Accounts Receivable and Service Revenue.

Accounts Receivable is an asset and Service Revenue is a revenue. Accounts Receivable (an asset) increased. Service Revenue (revenue) also increased.

An increase in assets is a debit, while an increase in a revenue is a credit.

So, Accounts Receivable (an asset) increases, which is a debit. Service Revenue (revenue) increases, which is a credit.

1 Accounts Affected	2 Type	3 ↑↓	4 Dr. or Cr.
Accounts Receivable	Asset	↑	Dr.
Service Revenue	Revenue	↑	Cr.

The journal entry is as follows:

DATE	ACCOUNTS	POST REF.	DR.	CR.
d.	Accounts Receivable		1,600	
	Service Revenue			1,600
	Performed services on account.			

We enter $1,600 on the debit (left) side of the Accounts Receivable T-account and $1,600 on the credit (right) side of the Service Revenue T-account.

Accounts Receivable 121		Service Revenue 411	
(d) 1,600			(d) 1,600

e. Paid $2,000 cash toward the equipment purchased on account in Transaction b.

The business paid *some* of the money that was owed on the purchase of equipment in Transaction b. The accounts involved in the transaction are Accounts Payable and Cash.

Accounts Payable is a liability, and Cash is an asset. Accounts Payable (a liability) decreased. Cash (an asset) also decreased.

Remember, the Accounts Payable account is the total amount owed to creditors to which the business will have to make payments in the future (a liability). When the business makes these payments to the creditors, the amount of this account decreases, because the business now owes less (in this case, it reduces from $4,800—in Transaction b—to $2,800).

A decrease in liabilities is a debit, while a decrease in assets is a credit.

So, Accounts Payable (a liability) decreases, which is a debit. Cash (an asset) decreases, which is a credit.

1 Accounts Affected	2 Type	3 ↑↓	4 Dr. or Cr.
Accounts Payable	Liability	↓	Dr.
Cash	Asset	↓	Cr.

The journal entry is as follows:

DATE	ACCOUNTS	POST REF.	DR.	CR.
e.	Accounts Payable		2,000	
	Cash			2,000
	Made a partial payment on account.			

We enter $2,000 on the debit (left) side of the Accounts Payable T-account and $2,000 on the credit (right) side of the Cash T-account.

Cash			111
(a)	8,000	(c)	500
		(e)	2,000

Accounts Payable			211
(e)	2,000	(b)	4,800

f. Received $2,300 in cash for services provided to a new customer.

The business received cash ($2,300) in exchange for painting services rendered to a client. The accounts involved in the transaction are Cash and Service Revenue.

Cash is an asset, and Service Revenue is a revenue. Cash (an asset) increased. Service Revenue (revenue) also increased.

An increase in assets is a debit, while an increase in a revenue is a credit.

So, Cash (an asset) increases, which is a debit. Service Revenue (revenue) increases, which is a credit.

1 Accounts Affected	2 Type	3 ↑↓	4 Dr. or Cr.
Cash	Asset	↑	Dr.
Service Revenue	Revenue	↑	Cr.

The journal entry is as follows:

DATE	ACCOUNTS	POST REF.	DR.	CR.
f.	Cash		2,300	
	Service Revenue			2,300
	Received cash for services performed.			

We enter $2,300 on the debit (left) side of the Cash T-account and $2,300 on the credit (right) side of the Service Revenue T-account.

Cash			111
(a)	8,000	(c)	500
(f)	2,300	(e)	2,000

Service Revenue			411
		(d)	1,600
		(f)	2,300

Notice how we keep adding onto the T-accounts. The values from previous transactions are already in place.

g. Paid $350 cash to repair equipment.

The business paid $350 cash to repair equipment. Because the benefit of the repairs has already been used, the repairs are recorded as Repairs Expense. Because the repairs were paid in cash, the Cash account is also involved.

Repairs Expense is an expense and Cash is an asset. Repairs Expense (an expense) increased. Cash (an asset) decreased.

An increase in expenses is a debit, while a decrease in an asset is a credit.

So, Repairs Expense (an expense) increases, which is a debit. Cash (an asset) decreases, which is a credit.

1 Accounts Affected	2 Type	3 ↑↓	4 Dr. or Cr.
Repairs Expense	Expense	↑	Dr.
Cash	Asset	↓	Cr.

The journal entry is as follows:

DATE	ACCOUNTS	POST REF.	DR.	CR.
g.	Repairs Expense		350	
	Cash			350
	Paid cash for repairs.			

We enter $350 on the debit (left) side of the Repairs Expense T-account and $350 on the credit (right) side of the Cash T-account.

Cash		111		Repairs Expense	521
(a)	8,000	(c)	500	(g)	350
(f)	2,300	(e)	2,000		
		(g)	350		

h. **Paid $1,150 cash in salary expense.**

The business paid employees $1,150 in cash. Because the benefit of the employee's work has already been used, the salary is recorded as Salary Expense. Because the salary was paid in cash, the Cash account is also involved.

Salary Expense is an expense, and Cash is an asset. Salary Expense (an expense) increased. Cash (an asset) decreased.

An increase in expenses is a debit, while a decrease in an asset is a credit.

So, Salary Expense (an expense) increases, which is a debit. Cash (an asset) decreases, which is a credit.

1	2	3	4
Accounts Affected	**Type**	↑↓	**Dr. or Cr.**
Salary Expense	Expense	↑	Dr.
Cash	Asset	↓	Cr.

The journal entry is as follows:

DATE	ACCOUNTS	POST REF.	DR.	CR.
h.	Salary Expense		1,150	
	Cash			1,150
	Paid salary with cash.			

We enter $1,150 on the debit (left) side of the Salary Expense T-account and $1,150 on the credit (right) side of the Cash T-account.

Cash		111		Salary Expense	511
(a)	8,000	(c)	500	(h)	1,150
(f)	2,300	(e)	2,000		
		(g)	350		
		(h)	1,150		

i. **Received $700 cash from customers on account.**

The business received payments ($700) from customers for services previously provided in Transaction d. The accounts involved in this transaction are Cash and Accounts Receivable.

Cash and Accounts Receivable are both assets. Cash (an asset) increased. Accounts Receivable (an asset) decreased.

Remember, accounts receivable is the total amount due from customers from which the business will receive money. When the business receives these payments from its customers, the amount of this account decreases, because the business now has less to receive in the future (in this case, it reduces from $1,600—in Transaction d—to $900).

An increase in assets is a debit, while a decrease in assets is a credit.

So Cash (an asset) increases, which is a debit. Accounts Receivable (an asset) decreases, which is a credit.

1 Accounts Affected	2 Type	3 ↑↓	4 Dr. or Cr.
Cash	Asset	↑	Dr.
Accounts Receivable	Asset	↓	Cr.

The journal entry is as follows:

DATE	ACCOUNTS	POST REF.	DR.	CR.
i.	Cash		700	
	Accounts Receivable			700
	Collected cash from customers on account.			

We enter $700 on the debit (left) side of the Cash T-account and $700 on the credit (right) side of the Accounts Receivable account.

Cash		111		Accounts Receivable		121
(a)	8,000	(c) 500	(d)	1,600	(i)	700
(f)	2,300	(e) 2,000				
(i)	700	(g) 350				
		(h) 1,150				

j. Paid $1,000 of dividends to its only stockholder, Robert Williams.

The business distributed $1,000 of earnings to Robert by paying him dividends. The business paid cash to Robert, whose ownership interest (equity) decreased. The accounts involved in the transaction are Dividends and Cash.

Dividends is a stockholders' equity account, and Cash is an asset. Dividends increased and Cash (an asset) decreased.

An increase in dividends is a debit, while a decrease in an asset is a credit.

1 Accounts Affected	2 Type	3 ↑↓	4 Dr. or Cr.
Dividends	Stockholders' Equity	↑	Dr.
Cash	Asset	↓	Cr.

The journal entry is as follows:

DATE	ACCOUNTS	POST REF.	DR.	CR.
j.	Dividends		1,000	
	Cash			1,000
	Paid dividends.			

We enter $1,000 on the debit (left) side of the Dividends T-account and $1,000 on the credit (right) side of the Cash account.

Cash			111
(a)	8,000	(c)	500
(f)	2,300	(e)	2,000
(i)	700	(g)	350
		(h)	1,150
		(j)	1,000

Dividends		322
(j)	1,000	

Now we will summarize the journal entries for the month:

DATE	ACCOUNTS	POST REF.	DR.	CR.
a.	Cash	111	8,000	
	Common Stock	311		8,000
	Sold Stock.			
b.	Equipment	141	4,800	
	Accounts Payable	211		4,800
	Purchased equipment on account.			
c.	Supplies	131	500	
	Cash	111		500
	Purchased supplies for cash.			
d.	Accounts Receivable	121	1,600	
	Service Revenue	411		1,600
	Performed services on account.			
e.	Accounts Payable	211	2,000	
	Cash	111		2,000
	Made a partial payment on account.			
f.	Cash	111	2,300	
	Service Revenue	411		2,300
	Received cash for services performed.			
g.	Repairs Expense	521	350	
	Cash	111		350
	Paid cash for repairs.			
h.	Salary Expense	511	1,150	
	Cash	111		1,150
	Paid salary with cash.			
i.	Cash	111	700	
	Accounts Receivable	121		700
	Collected cash from customers on account.			
j.	Dividends	322	1,000	
	Cash	111		1,000
	Paid dividends.			

Notice how the posting reference field now contains the account number that indicates that the entries have been posted to the general ledger (or in this case, the T-accounts).

Requirement ❸

Total all the T-accounts to determine their balances at the end of the month.

Part 1	Part 2	**Part 3**	Demo Doc Complete

To compute the balance in a T-account (total the T-account), add up the numbers on the debit/left side of the account and (separately) the credit/right side of the account. Subtract the smaller number from the bigger number and put the difference on the side of the bigger number. This procedure gives the balance in the T-account (the net total of both sides combined).

For example, for the Cash account, the numbers on the left side total $8,000 + $2,300 + $700 = $11,000. The credit/right side = $500 + $2,000 + $350 + $1,150 + $1,000 = $5,000. The difference is $11,000 – $5,000 = $6,000. We put the $6,000 on the debit side because it is the side of the bigger number of $11,000.

Another way to think of adding up (totaling) T-accounts is the following:

> Beginning Balance in T-account
> + Increases to T-account
> – Decreases to T-account
> = Ending Balance in T-account

The T-accounts should look like the following after posting all transactions and totaling each account:

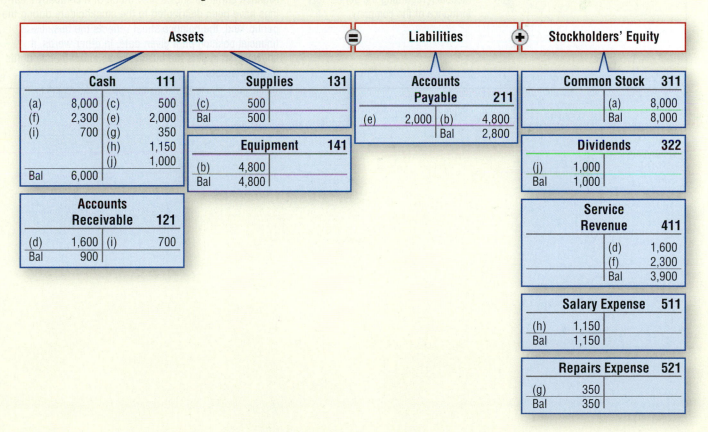

Demo Doc Complete

Decision Guidelines

Recording Business Transactions

Here are some decisions that you would make as you record and summarize transactions in your business:

Decision		Guideline		Analyze
How do I know if an event should be entered into a company's accounting records?		Examine the effect of the event on the company's accounting equation.		If the event increases or decreases the assets, liabilities, or stockholders' equity of the business, it represents a transaction that should be recorded in the company's accounting records. If the event doesn't impact the assets, liabilities, or stockholders' equity of the company, then a recordable transaction has not occurred.
How do I know the amount of assets, liabilities, or stockholders' equity in the business at any point in time?		Review the trial balance or the general ledger.		The trial balance is a summary of all of a company's accounts with their respective balances on a given day. The general ledger provides the detail of all of the transactions that have impacted an account along with a running balance of the account. Having quick access to the account balances often allows managers and owners to make better decisions.
How can I tell how well a business is performing?		A company's financial statements will provide feedback regarding the performance of the company.		The income statement reflects how profitable a business has been for a specified period of time. The statement of retained earnings shows how much of a company's earnings have been distributed to the stockholders during the period. And, the balance sheet reflects the business's financial position on a given date. In other words, it shows what assets the business has and who has rights to those assets.

ACCOUNTING VOCABULARY

THE LANGUAGE OF BUSINESS

Account (p. 54) The basic summary device of accounting; the detailed record of all the changes in a specific asset, liability, or stockholders' equity item as a result of transactions.

Accounting cycle (p.72) The sequence of steps used to record and report business transactions.

Accounting period (p. 69) Generally, the time period reflected by a set of financial statements.

Balance (p. 67) The difference between an account's total debit and total credit amounts; the ending value of an account.

Chart of accounts (p. 54) A list of all the accounts of a business and the numbers assigned to those accounts.

Credit (p. 56) The right side of any account; an entry made to the right side of an account.

Debit (p. 56) The left side of any account; an entry made to the left side of an account.

Double-entry accounting (p. 56) The rule of accounting that specifies every transaction involves at least two accounts and is recorded with equal amounts of debits and credits.

General journal (p. 58) The chronological accounting record of the transactions of a business.

General ledger (p. 58) The accounting record summarizing, in accounts, the transactions of a business and showing the resulting account balances.

Journalize (p. 58) Entering a transaction in a journal; also called *record*.

Normal balance (p. 57) The balance that appears on the side of an account where increases are recorded; the expected balance of an account.

Posting (p. 58) Copying information from the general journal to accounts in the general ledger.

Posting reference (p. 59) A notation in the journal and ledger that links these two accounting records together.

Promissory note (p. 54) A written pledge to pay a fixed amount of money at a later date.

Record (p. 58) Entering a transaction in a journal; also called *journalize*.

T-account (p. 56) An informal account form used to summarize transactions, where the top of the T holds the account title and the base divides the debit and credit sides of the account.

Transaction (p. 58) An event that has a financial impact on a business entity.

Trial balance (p. 68) A list of all the accounts of a business and their balances in balance sheet order; its purpose is to verify that total debits equal total credits.

ACCOUNTING PRACTICE

DISCUSSION QUESTIONS

1. The order in which assets were listed and described in the text is the order in which you will see them listed on the balance sheet. What is the organizing principle behind the order in which assets are listed?

2. What type of transaction would result in the recording of a prepaid asset? What do you think will happen to that prepaid asset eventually?

3. How is revenue related to retained earnings?

4. Distinguish between an event and a transaction. Are all transactions events? Are all events transactions? Why or why not? What are the implications of your answers with respect to journal entries?

5. What is a "normal balance"? What are normal balances for the following accounts?
   a. Accounts Receivable
   b. Prepaid Expenses
   c. Notes Payable
   d. Retained Earnings
   e. Salaries Expense

6. You learned in this chapter that cash is increased with a debit. When you deposit your paycheck in your account, however, the teller might say that he or she is going to credit your account. Why?

7. What would be the implications of a credit balance in the cash account?

8. Distinguish between journalizing and posting.

9. True or false: If the trial balance is in balance, the financial statements will be accurate. Why or why not?

10. When it comes time to prepare the financial statements, from where do the financial statement numbers come?

SELF CHECK

1. Which sequence of actions correctly summarizes the accounting process?
   a. Prepare a trial balance, journalize transactions, post to the accounts
   b. Post to the accounts, journalize transactions, prepare a trial balance
   c. Journalize transactions, post to the accounts, prepare a trial balance
   d. Journalize transactions, prepare a trial balance, post to the accounts

2. The left side of an account is used to record
   a. debits.
   b. credits.
   c. debits or credits, depending on the type of account.
   d. increases.

3. Suppose Sunshine Florists, Inc., has cash of $40,000, receivables of $30,000, and furniture and fixtures totaling $170,000. Sunshine Florists, Inc., owes $60,000 on account and has a $120,000 note payable. How much is the stockholders' equity?
   a. $240,000
   b. $120,000
   c. $180,000
   d. $60,000

4. Lori's Catering, Inc., purchased $400 of supplies on account. The journal entry to record this transaction is denoted by which of the following?

DATE	ACCOUNTS	POST REF.	DR.	CR.
a.	Inventory		400	
	Accounts Payable			400
b.	Accounts Payable		400	
	Supplies			400
c.	Supplies		400	
	Accounts Payable			400
d.	Supplies		400	
	Accounts Receivable			400

5. Posting a $800 purchase of supplies on account appears as which of the following?

a.
Supplies		Accounts Receivable
800		800

b.
Supplies		Accounts Payable
800		800

c.
Supplies		Accounts Payable
800		800

d.
Cash		Supplies
800		800

6. Which journal entry records obtaining a bank loan of $15,000?

DATE	ACCOUNTS	POST REF.	DR.	CR.
a.	Notes Payable		15,000	
	Accounts Receivable			15,000
b.	Notes Payable		15,000	
	Cash			15,000
c.	Cash		15,000	
	Notes Payable			15,000
d.	Cash		15,000	
	Accounts Payable			15,000

7. S & S Janitorial, Inc., paid $600 for supplies and purchased additional supplies on account for $800. S & S Janitorial, Inc., also paid $300 of the accounts payable. What is the balance in the Supplies account?

a. $800
b. $1,100
c. $1,400
d. $1,700

8. The Blue Ox Restaurant recorded a cash collection on account by debiting Cash and crediting Accounts Payable. What will the trial balance show for this error?

a. Too much for liabilities
b. Too much for assets
c. The trial balance will not balance
d. Both a and b

9. Tim Walters, an attorney, had a law corporation, Tim Walters, Attorney, Inc., that began the year with total assets of $110,000, total liabilities of $80,000, and stockholders' equity of $30,000. During the year, Tim Walters, Attorney, Inc., earned revenue of $90,000 and paid expenses of $40,000. Tim Walters, Attorney, Inc., also sold an additional $10,000 of stock and paid $20,000 in dividends. How much is the stockholders' equity in Tim Walters, Attorney, Inc., at year-end?

a. $70,000
b. $110,000
c. $130,000
d. $160,000

10. The entry to record the payment of $1,200 rent expense would be which of the following?

DATE	ACCOUNTS	POST REF.	DR.	CR.
a.	Rent Expense		1,200	
	Accounts Payable			1,200
b.	Cash		1,200	
	Rent Expense			1,200
c.	Rent Expense		1,200	
	Cash			1,200
d.	Accounts Payable		1,200	
	Rent Expense			1,200

Answers are given after Written Communication.

SHORT EXERCISES

S2-1. Accounting terms (*Learning Objective 1*) 5–10 min.

Match the accounting terms at the left with the corresponding definitions at the right.

_____ 1. Account   a. Any economic event that has a financial impact on the business

_____ 2. Assets   b. The detailed record of the changes in a particular asset, liability, or stockholders' equity

_____ 3. Stockholders' Equity   c. Economic resources that provide a future benefit for a business

_____ 4. Expenses   d. Debts or obligations of a business

_____ 5. Liabilities   e. Stockholders' claim to the assets of a corporation

_____ 6. Revenues   f. Increases in stockholders' equity from selling goods or services to customers

_____ 7. Transactions   g. Decreases in stockholders' equity from using resources to sell goods or services

---

S2-2. Account types (*Learning Objective 1*) 5–10 min.

For each of the following accounts, place the corresponding letter(s) of its account type in the space provided. Use the most detailed account type appropriate.

(A) Asset (L) Liability (SE) Stockholders' Equity (R) Revenue (E) Expense

_SE_   Dividends

_____ 1. Accounts Payable

_____ 2. Cash

_____ 3. Service Revenue

_____ 4. Prepaid Rent

_____ 5. Rent Expense

_____ 6. Common Stock

S2-3. Accounting cycle steps (*Learning Objectives 2, 3, & 4*) 5–10 min.

The following list names the activities involved in the accounting process of recording and summarizing business transactions. Place the number corresponding with the order the activity occurs next to the activity, starting with 1.

_1_   Transaction occurs.

_____ Prepare the financial statements.

_____ Prepare the trial balance.

_____ Post the transactions from the journal to the ledger.

_____ Record the transactions in the journal.

S2-4. Account types (*Learning Objective 1*) 5–10 min.

For each of the following accounts, indicate the account type by labeling it as an asset (A), liability (L), stockholders' equity (SE), revenue (R), or expense (E). Also give the digit each account number would begin with in the chart of accounts. Use the most detailed account type appropriate.

_A,1_   Land

_____ 1. Service Revenue

_____ 2. Dividends

_____ 3. Accounts Receivable

_____ 4. Salary Expense

_____ 5. Notes Payable

_____ 6. Common Stock

_____ 7. Rent Expense

S2-5. Accounting terminology (*Learning Objective 2, 3, & 4*) 5–10 min.

Demonstrate your knowledge of accounting terminology by filling in the blanks to review some key definitions.

Dillon Baker is describing the accounting process for a friend who is a psychology major. Dillon states, "The basic summary device in accounting is the _____. The left side of an account is called the _____ side, and the right side is called the _____ side. We record transactions first in a _____. Then we post, or copy, the data to the _____. It is helpful to list all the accounts with their balances on a _____ _____."

S2-6. Effects of debits and credits on accounts (*Learning Objective 2*) 5–10 min.

For each of the following accounts, indicate if the account's normal balance is a debit balance (DR) or a credit balance (CR).

_DR_ Cash

_____ 1. Rent Expense

_____ 2. Accounts Payable

_____ 3. Service Revenue

_____ 4. Office Furniture

_____ 5. Common Stock

_____ 6. Land

_____ 7. Dividends

S2-7. Balancing accounts and normal balances (*Learning Objective 2*) 5–10 min.

Calculate each account balance.

	Supplies	132		Note Payable	221
3/8	400	3/27 600	3/20	2,000	3/5 10,000
3/17	500		3/31	4,000	

S2-8. Types of accounts and effects of debits and credits (*Learning Objective 2*) 5–10 min.

Complete the following table. For each account listed, identify the type of account, how the account is increased (debit or credit), and how the account is decreased (debit or credit). Use the most detailed account type appropriate.

Account	Type	↑	↓
Office Equipment	Asset	Dr.	Cr.
Dividends			
Service Revenue			
Accounts Payable			
Rent Expense			
Cash			

S2-9. Recreating journal entries from T-account postings (*Learning Objective 2*) 15–20 min.

IPW, Inc., began operations on January 1, 2010. The seven transactions recorded during January by the company accountant, are shown in the following T-accounts:

Cash			111
(1)	15,000	(2)	3,000
		(5)	250
		(6)	2,300
		(7)	1,000
Bal	8,450		

Accounts Receivable			112
(4)	4,500		
Bal	4,500		

Supplies			113
(3)	600		
Bal	600		

Equipment			114
(2)	3,000		
Bal	3,000		

Accounts Payable			211
(5)	250	(3)	600
		Bal	350

Common Stock			311
		(1)	15,000
		Bal	15,000

Dividends			322
(7)	1,000		
Bal	1,000		

Service Revenue			411
		(4)	4,500
		Bal	4,500

Operating Expenses			511–524
(6)	2,300		
Bal	2,300		

Complete the following table. For each transaction shown, determine the accounts affected, the type of account, whether the account increases or decreases, and whether it would be recorded in the journal on the debit or credit side.

Transaction	Accounts Affected	Type	↑↓	Dr. or Cr.
(1)	Cash	Asset	Increase	Dr.
	Common Stock	Stockholders' Equity	Increase	Cr.

S2-10. Journalizing transactions (*Learning Objective 3*) 10–15 min.

Shawn Andrews opened a dental practice in Spokane, Washington as a corporation. The following transactions took place in June:

Jun	1	Sold $20,000 of stock to Andrews to start the business.
	5	Purchased dental supplies on account, $4,600.
	7	Paid monthly office rent of $2,400.
	10	Provided $4,000 of dental services to patients. Received cash of $1,700 for these services and sent bills to patients for the remainder.

Using the steps outlined in the five-step transaction analysis, record the transactions in the journal.

S2-11. Journalizing transactions (*Learning Objective 3*) 10–15 min.

After operating for a month, Shawn Andrews' dental practice completed the following transactions during July:

Jul	3	The business borrowed $25,000 from the bank, signing a note payable.
	9	Performed service for patients on account, $2,900.
	16	Received cash on account from patients, $1,200.
	22	Received a utility bill, $550, which will be paid during August.
	31	Paid the monthly salary to its dental assistance, $1,900.
	31	Paid interest expense of $125 on the bank loan.

Using the steps outlined in the five-step transaction analysis, record the transactions in the journal.

S2-12. Prepare trial balance (*Learning Objective 4*) 10–15 min.

The accounting records for Airborne Services, Corp., contain the following amounts on December 31, 2010. The accounts appear in no particular order.

Service Revenues	$79,000	Utilities Expense	$24,000
Prepaid Rent	4,000	Note Payable	15,000
Accounts Payable	1,000	Cash	14,000
Equipment	18,000	Rent Expense	36,000
Dividends	6,000	Common Stock	7,000

Prepare the trial balance for Airborne Services at December 31, 2010. List the accounts in proper order.

S2-13. Preparation of financial statements from a trial balance (*Learning Objective 4*) 5–10 min.

To the left of each account listed on the trial balance, indicate the financial statement that will include the account: income statement (IS), statement of retained earnings (RE), or balance sheet (BS).

Wirt's Dirt, Inc.
Trial Balance
December 31, 2010

		ACCOUNT	DEBIT	CREDIT
		Cash	$13,900	
		Accounts Receivable	2,100	
		Supplies	400	
		Equipment	5,200	
		Accounts Payable		$ 1,900
		Notes Payable		11,000
		Common Stock		8,000
		Dividends	500	
		Service Revenues		3,300
		Wages Expense	1,300	
		Rent Expense	600	
		Utilities Expense	200	
		Total	$24,200	$24,200

S2-14. Accounting terminology (*Learning Objectives 1, 2, & 3*) 5–10 min.

Accounting has its own vocabulary and basic relationships. Match the accounting terms at the left with the corresponding phrase at the right.

____ 1. Posting	a. Chronological record of transactions
____ 2. Normal balance	b. An asset
____ 3. Payable	c. Left side of an account
____ 4. Journal	d. Side of an account where increases are recorded
____ 5. Receivable	e. Copying data from the journal to the ledger
____ 6. Chart of accounts	f. List of all accounts with their balances
____ 7. Debit	g. A liability
____ 8. Trial balance	h. List of all of the accounts of a business
____ 9. Credit	i. Right side of an account

EXERCISES (GROUP A)

E2-15A. Journalizing transactions (*Learning Objective 2 & 3*) 10–15 min.

The following are six transactions for Gonzalez Engineering, Inc., during the month of July.

Jul 1	Paid advertising expense, $275.
3	Performed service for customers and received cash, $3,000.
5	Purchased supplies on account, $450.
9	Received cash of $1,200 from credit customers on account.
12	Paid $900 on accounts payable.
17	Performed service for customers on account, $2,800.

Requirement

1. Complete the following table. For each transaction shown, determine the accounts affected, the type of account, whether the account increases or decreases, and whether it would be recorded in the journal on the debit or credit side.

Transaction #	Accounts Affected	Account Type	↑↓	Dr. or Cr.
(1)	Advertising Expense	Stockholders' Equity	↑	Dr.
	Cash	Asset	↓	Cr.

E2-16A. Journalizing transactions (*Learning Objective 3*) 15–20 min.

Using the steps outlined in the five-step transaction analysis, record the following transactions in the general journal for Alread Plumbing, Inc. Explanations are not required.

Feb 1	Paid interest expense, $300.
5	Purchased office furniture on account, $2,200.
10	Performed service on account for a customer, $1,700.
12	Borrowed $4,500 cash, signing a note payable.
19	Sold for $85,000 land that had cost the company $85,000.
21	Purchased building for $290,000; signed a note payable.
27	Paid $1,500 on account.

E2-17A. Journalizing transactions (*Learning Objective 3*) 15–20 min.

Williams & Associates, Inc., completed the following transactions during October 2010, its first month of operations:

Oct 1	Sold $50,000 of stock to Kirsten Williams to start the business.
3	Purchased supplies on account, $300.
5	Paid cash for a building to use for storage, $42,000.
6	Performed service for customers and received cash, $1,600.
11	Paid on accounts payable, $200.
18	Performed service for customers on account, $2,400.
24	Received cash from a customer on account, $800.
31	Paid the following expenses: salary, $500; and rent, $1,200.

Requirement

1. Using the steps outlined in the five-step transaction analysis, journalize the transactions of Williams & Associates, Inc. List transactions by date. Use the following accounts: Cash, Accounts Receivable, Supplies, Building, Accounts Payable, Common Stock, Service Revenue, Salary Expense, and Rent Expense.

E2-18A. Balance accounts and prepare trial balance (*Learning Objectives 3 & 4*)
10–15 min.

The transactions for Little Tykes Daycare, Inc., for the month of January 2010 are posted in the following T-accounts.

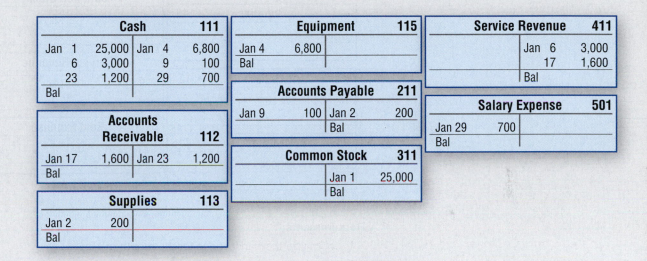

	Cash		111
Jan 1	25,000	Jan 4	6,800
6	3,000	9	100
23	1,200	29	700
Bal			

	Accounts Receivable		112
Jan 17	1,600	Jan 23	1,200
Bal			

	Supplies		113
Jan 2	200		
Bal			

	Equipment		115
Jan 4	6,800		
Bal			

	Accounts Payable		211
Jan 9	100	Jan 2	200
		Bal	

	Common Stock		311
		Jan 1	25,000
		Bal	

	Service Revenue		411
		Jan 6	3,000
		17	1,600
		Bal	

	Salary Expense		501
Jan 29	700		
Bal			

Quick solution:

1. Cash balance = $21,600;
2. Trial balance totals = $29,700

Requirements

1. Calculate account balances.

2. Prepare the trial balance for Little Tykes Daycare, Inc., at January 31, 2010.

E2-19A. Record transactions and prepare a trial balance (*Learning Objectives 1 & 2*)
15–20 min.

Baldwin Realty, Inc., had the following transactions for the month of May, 2010.

May	2	Paid Rent Expense, $600.
	4	Performed service for a customer and received cash, $1,000.
	8	Purchased supplies on account, $400.
	11	Received cash from credit customers on account, $1,200.
	15	Sold an additional $5,000 of Common Stock.
	19	Paid $500 on account.
	27	Performed service for customers on account, $1,600.
	31	Made a payment on the Notes Payable, $3,000.

The following T-accounts have been set up, for Baldwin Realty, Inc., with their beginning balances as of May 1, 2010.

Cash		111
May 1	3,000	

Accounts Payable		211
	May 1	800

Accounts Receivable		112
May 1	1,800	

Notes Payable		212
	May 1	10,000

Supplies		113
May 1	300	

Common Stock		311
	May 1	30,000

Service Revenue		411
	May 1	2,100

Office Furniture		114
May 1	1,200	

Rent Expense		511
May 1	600	

Building		116
May 1	36,000	

Requirements

1. Journalize the transactions for the month of May.
2. Post the journal entries to the appropriate T-accounts. Identify all items by date.
3. Calculate the balance of each account at May 31, 2010.
4. Prove that the total of all the debit balances equals the total of all of the credit balances by preparing a trial balance.

E2-20A. Journalize transactions, prepare a trial balance and balance sheet (*Learning Objectives 3 & 4*) 20–25 min.

The transactions for Crazy Curlz, Inc., for the month of June 2010 have been posted to the accounts as follows:

Cash			
(1)	16,000	(4)	8,000
		(5)	5,000
		(6)	300

Supplies	
(2)	800

Equipment	
(4)	8,000

Building	
(3)	60,000

Accounts Payable			
(6)	300	(2)	800

Notes Payable			
(5)	5,000	(3)	60,000

Common Stock	
	(1) 16,000

Requirements

1. Prepare the journal entries that served as the sources for the six transactions.
2. Calculate the balance in each account.
3. Prepare the trial balance for Crazy Curlz, Inc., at June 30, 2010.
4. Prepare a balance sheet for Crazy Curlz, Inc., as of June 30, 2010.

E2-21A. Journalizing, posting, trial balance, income statement, and balance sheet (*Learning Objectives 3 & 4*) 25–30 min.

McDonald Consulting, Inc., completed the following transactions during December 2010, its first month of operations:

Dec	2	Sold $10,000 of stock to Dan McDonald to start the consulting practice.
	3	Paid monthly office rent, $800.
	6	Paid cash for a new computer, $1,600.
	8	Purchased office furniture on account, $2,100.
	11	Purchased supplies on account, $200.
	19	Performed consulting service for a client on account, $900.
	20	Paid utility expenses, $300.
	28	Performed service for a client and received cash for the full amount of $1,100.

Requirements

1. Open, or set up, T-accounts in the ledger: Cash, Accounts Receivable; Supplies; Equipment; Furniture; Accounts Payable; Common Stock; Service Revenue; Rent Expense; Utilities Expense.

2. Record transactions in the journal. Explanations are not required.

3. Post the transactions to the T-accounts, identify all items by date. Calculate the balance in each account.

4. Prepare a trial balance at December 31, 2010.

5. Prepare the income statement, statement of retained earnings, and balance sheet.

E2-22A. Error correction (*Learning Objective 4*) 20–25 min.

Julie Palmer has trouble keeping her debits and credits equal. During a recent month, Julie made the following errors:

a. Julie recorded a $750 payment of rent by debiting rent expense for $75 and crediting Cash for $75.

b. In recording a $250 payment on account, Julie debited Accounts Receivable and credited Cash.

c. Julie recorded the receipt of cash for service revenue by debiting Cash for $130 instead of the correct amount of $310. Julie also credited Service Revenue for $130, the incorrect amount.

d. Julie recorded a $120 purchase of supplies on account by debiting Accounts Payable and crediting Supplies.

e. In preparing the trial balance, Julie omitted a $15,000 note payable.

Requirements

1. For each of these errors, state whether Julie's mistake would cause the total debits and total credits on the trial balance to be unequal.

2. Identify each account with an incorrect balance, and indicate the amount and direction of the error.

Use the following format:

Effect on Trial Balance	Account(s) Misstated
Total debits = Total credits	Cash
	$675 too high
	Rent Expense
	$675 too low

EXERCISES (GROUP B)

E2-23B. Journalizing transactions (*Learning Objective 2 & 3*) 10–15 min.

The following are six journal entries Keene Engineering, Inc., made during the month of April.

Apr 1	Paid advertising expense, $275.
3	Paid $4,000 cash to purchase a new piece of equipment.
5	Issued stock in exchange for $7,000 cash.
9	Borrowed $5,000 on a note payable from the bank.
12	Paid monthly telephone bill, $325.
17	Purchased supplies for $175, paid cash.

Requirement

1. For each transaction shown, determine the accounts affected, the type of account, whether the account increases or decreases, and whether it would be recorded in the journal on the debit or credit side. The first transaction has been analyzed for you.

Transaction	Accounts Affected	Type	Increase/Decrease	Dr. or Cr.
(1)	Advertising Expense	Stockholders' Equity	Increase	Dr.
	Cash	Asset	Decrease	Cr.

E2-24B. Journalizing transactions (*Learning Objective 3*) 15–20 min.

Using the steps outlined in the five-step transaction analysis, record the following transactions in the general journal for Laverden Plumbing, Inc. Explanations are not required.

May 1	Paid interest expense, $500.
5	Purchased office furniture on account, $2,500.
10	Performed service on account for a customer, $2,700.
12	Borrowed $4,500 cash, signing a note payable.
19	Sold for $50,000 land that had cost the company $50,000.
21	Purchased building for $800,000; signed a note payable.
27	Paid $700 on account.

E2-25B. Journalizing transactions (*Learning Objective 3*) 15–20 min.

Welch & Associates, Inc., completed the following transactions during September 2010, its first month of operations:

Sep 1	Sold $40,000 of stock to Katie Welch to start the business.
3	Purchased supplies on account, $200.
5	Paid cash for a building to use for storage, $32,000.
6	Performed service for customers and received cash, $3,000.
11	Paid on accounts payable, $100.
18	Performed service for customers on account, $2,900.
24	Received cash from a customer on account, $1,500.
30	Paid the following expenses: salary, $650; and rent, $1,100.

Requirement

1. Using the steps outlined in the five-step transaction analysis, journalize the transactions of Welch & Associates, Inc. List transactions by date.

E2-26B. Balancing accounts and prepare trial balance (*Learning Objectives 2 & 3*) 10–15 min.

The transactions for Learning Fun Daycare, Inc., for the month of May 2010 are posted in the following T-accounts.

Cash			111
May 1	45,000	May 4	12,700
6	7,500	9	200
23	900	29	1,100
Bal			

Equipment		115
May 4	12,700	
Bal		

Service Revenue			411
		May 6	7,500
		17	3,600
		Bal	

Accounts Receivable			112
May 17	3,600	May 23	900
Bal			

Accounts Payable			211
May 9	200	May 2	700
		Bal	

Salary Expense		501
May 29	1,100	
Bal		

Common Stock			311
		May 1	45,000
		Bal	

Supplies		113
May 2	700	
Bal		

Requirements

1. Calculate account balances.
2. Prepare the trial balance for Learning Fun Daycare, Inc., at May 31, 2010.

E2-27B. **Record transactions and prepare a trial balance (*Learning Objectives 1 & 2*)**
15–20 min.

Baltimore Realty, Inc., had the following transactions for the month of June 2010.

Jun	2	Paid Rent Expense, $900.
	4	Performed service for a customer and received cash, $1,500.
	8	Purchased supplies on account, $900.
	11	Received cash from credit customers on account, $1,100.
	15	Sold an additional $15,000 of Common Stock.
	19	Paid $600 on account.
	27	Performed service for customers on account, $3,000.
	30	Made a payment on the Notes Payable, $3,500.

The following T-accounts have been set up, for Baltimore Realty, Inc., with their beginning balances as of June 1, 2010.

Cash		111
Jun 1	9,000	

Accounts Payable			211
		Jun 1	2,600

Accounts Receivable		112
Jun 1	1,800	

Notes Payable			212
		Jun 1	10,000

Supplies		113
Jun 1	600	

Common Stock			311
		Jun 1	34,500

Office Furniture		114
Jun 1	1,900	

Service Revenue			411
		Jun 1	3,700

Building		116
Jun 1	36,000	

Rent Expense		511
Jun 1	1,500	

Requirements

1. Journalize the transactions for the month of June.
2. Post the journal entries to the appropriate T-accounts. Identify all items by date.
3. Calculate the balance of each account at June 30, 2010.
4. Prove that the total of all the debit balances equals the total of all of the credit balances by preparing a trial balance.

E2-28B. Journalize transactions, prepare a trial balance and balance sheet (*Learning Objectives 3 & 4*) 20–25 min.

The transactions for Dancing Antz, Inc., for the month of September 2010 have been posted to the accounts as follows:

Cash				Supplies		Equipment		Building	
(1)	28,000	(4)	2,000	(2)	600	(4)	2,000	(3)	80,000
		(5)	6,000						
		(6)	150						

Accounts Payable				Notes Payable				Common Stock	
(6)	150	(2)	600	(5)	6,000	(3)	80,000	(1)	28,000

Requirements

1. Prepare the journal entries that served as the sources for the six transactions.
2. Calculate the balance in each account.
3. Prepare the trial balance for Dancing Antz, Inc., at September 30, 2010.
4. Prepare a balance sheet for Dancing Antz, Inc., as of September 30, 2010.

E2-29B. Journalizing, posting, trial balance, income statement, and balance sheet (*Learning Objectives 3 & 4*) 25–30 min.

Meo Consulting, Inc., completed the following transactions during February 2010, its first month of operations:

Feb	2	Sold $65,000 of stock to Drake Meo to start the consulting practice.
	3	Paid monthly office rent, $800.
	6	Paid cash for a new computer, $1,900.
	8	Purchased office furniture on account, $2,500.
	11	Purchased supplies on account, $500.
	19	Performed consulting service for a client on account, $2,700.
	20	Paid utility expenses, $450.
	28	Performed service for a client and received cash for the full amount of $2,000.

Requirements

1. Record transactions in the journal. Explanations are not required.
2. Post them to the T-accounts that have been set up for you. Identify all items by date. Calculate the balance in each account.
3. Prepare a trial balance at February 28, 2010.
4. Prepare the income statement, statement of retained earnings, and balance sheet.

E2-30B. Error correction (*Learning Objective 4*) 20–25 min.

Sheri Neylon has trouble keeping her debits and credits equal. During a recent month, Sheri made the following errors:

a. Sheri recorded a $850 payment of rent by debiting Rent Expense for $85 and crediting Cash for $85.
b. In recording a $600 payment on account, Sheri debited Accounts Receivable and credited Cash.

c. Sheri recorded the receipt of cash for service revenue by debiting Cash for $280 instead of the correct amount of $820. Sheri also credited Service Revenue for the $280, the incorrect amount.

d. Sheri posted a $350 purchase of supplies on account by debiting Accounts Payable and crediting Supplies.

e. In preparing the trial balance, Sheri omitted a $50,000 note payable.

Requirements

1. For each of these errors, state whether Sheri's mistake would cause the total debits and total credits on the trial balance to be unequal.

2. Identify each account with an incorrect balance, and indicate the amount and direction of the error.

EXERCISES (ALTERNATES 1, 2, AND 3)

These alternative exercise sets are available for your practice benefit at
www.myaccountinglab.com

PROBLEMS (GROUP A)

P2-31A. Journalizing transactions (*Learning Objective 3*) 15–20 min.

Angela Rodriguez practices law under the business title Angela Rodriguez Attorney at Law, Inc. During June, her law practice engaged in the following transactions:

Jun	1	Sold $60,000 of stock to Rodriguez to start the business.
	3	Paid $500 for the purchase of office supplies.
	8	Paid $34,000 cash to purchase land for an office site.
	12	Purchased office equipment on account, $3,800.
	17	Borrowed $15,000 from the bank. Rodriguez signed a note payable to the bank in the name of the business.
	26	Paid $2,500 on account.
	30	Revenues earned during the month included $7,000 cash and $9,000 on account.
	30	Paid employees' salaries, $2,800; office rent, $3,600; and utilities, $600.
	30	Paid $6,000 of dividends to stockholder, Rodriguez.

Rodriguez's business uses the following accounts: Cash, Accounts Receivable, Supplies, Land, Office Equipment, Accounts Payable, Notes Payable, Common Stock, Dividends, Service Revenue, Salary Expense, Rent Expense, and Utilities Expense.

Requirement

1. Journalize each transaction. Omit explanations.

P2-32A. Journalizing transactions (*Learning Objective 3*) 15–20 min.

Advantage Advertising, Inc., engaged in the following business transactions during November of 2010:

Nov	1	Borrowed $200,000 from First State Bank. The company president signed a note payable to the bank in the name of Advantage Advertising, Inc.
	3	Paid $145,000 cash to purchase an office building.
	6	Provided services to customers on account, $14,700.
	9	Purchased $1,600 of office supplies on account.
	13	Provided services to cash customers, $8,100.
	15	Paid $6,000 of dividends to company stockholders.
	17	Received payment on account from credit customers, $6,600.
	18	Paid property tax expense on office building, $1,600.
	22	Paid employee salaries, $2,800.
	26	Paid cash to purchase supplies, $700.
	30	Paid $2,000 on account.

Advantage Advertising, Inc., uses the following accounts: Cash, Accounts Receivable, Supplies, Building, Accounts Payable, Notes Payable, Common Stock, Dividends, Sales Revenue, Salary Expense, and Property Tax Expense.

Requirement

1. Journalize each transaction. Omit explanations.

P2-33A. Journalizing, posting, and trial balance preparation (*Learning Objectives 3 & 4*) 20–25 min.

Tom Slater opened an accounting firm on March 1, 2010. During the month of March, the business completed the following transactions:

Mar	1	The business sold $40,000 of stock to open the firm, Slater & Associates, Inc.
	3	Purchased supplies, $400, and furniture, $2,100, on account.
	5	Performed accounting service for a client and received cash, $1,700.
	8	Paid cash to acquire land for a future office site, $18,000.
	11	Prepared tax returns for a client on account, $500.
	14	Paid assistant's salary, $1,100.
	16	Paid for the furniture purchased March 3 on account.
	19	Received $800 cash for accounting services performed.
	23	Billed a client for $1,300 of accounting services.
	28	Received $300 from client on account.
	31	Paid secretary's salary, $900.
	31	Paid rent expense, $1,200.
	31	Paid $1,800 of dividends.

Requirements

1. Open, or set up, the following T-accounts: Cash, Accounts Receivable, Supplies, Furniture, Land, Accounts Payable, Common Stock, Dividends, Service Revenue, Salary Expense, and Rent Expense.

2. Journalize transactions. Explanations are not required.

3. Post the transactions to the T-accounts, using transaction dates as posting references.

4. Calculate the balance in each account.

5. Prepare the trial balance for Slater & Associates, Inc., at the end of March.

P2-34A. Journalizing, posting, and trial balance preparation (*Learning Objectives 3 & 4*) 25–30 min.

The trial balance for TDR Systems, Inc., at July 15, 2010, follows:

	TDR Systems, Inc. Trial Balance July 15, 2010		
ACCT #	**ACCOUNT**	**DEBIT**	**CREDIT**
110	Cash	$ 3,500	
112	Accounts Receivable	7,700	
115	Supplies	700	
140	Equipment	13,200	
210	Accounts Payable		$ 4,500
311	Common Stock		20,000
315	Dividends	2,600	
411	Service Revenues		6,700
511	Salary Expense	2,200	
515	Rent Expense	1,300	
	Total	$31,200	$31,200

During the remainder of July, TDR Systems, Inc., completed the following transactions:

Jul 16	Collected $2,500 cash from a client on account.
18	Performed services on account, $1,900.
21	Received $1,700 cash for services performed.
23	Purchased supplies on account, $600.
25	Paid $1,400 in dividends.
27	Paid $3,200 on account.
29	Received $2,900 cash for services performed.
30	Paid rent, $1,200.
30	Paid employees' salaries, $2,500.

Quick solution:

2. Cash balance = $2,300;
3. Trial balance totals = $35,100

Requirements

1. Journalize the transactions that occurred July 16 to July 30 on page 6 of the journal.

2. Open the ledger accounts listed in the trial balance together with their beginning balances at July 15. Use the four-column account format illustrated in the chapter. Enter "Bal" for the previous balance in the Item column. Post the transactions to the ledger using dates, account numbers, and posting references. Calculate the new account balances.

3. Prepare the trial balance for TDR Systems, Inc., at the end of July.

P2-35A. **Prepare a trial balance, income statement, statement of retained earnings, and balance sheet (*Learning Objective 4*) 20–25 min.**

The accounts of Cascade Consulting, Inc., follow with their normal balances at December 31, 2010. The accounts are listed in no particular order.

Account	Balance
Common Stock	$ 65,000
Insurance Expense	1,700
Accounts Payable	3,700
Service Revenue	83,000
Land	24,000
Supplies Expense	2,800
Cash	8,300
Salary Expense	51,000
Building	110,000
Rent Expense	12,800
Dividends	13,500
Utilities Expense	6,400
Retained Earnings	9,700
Accounts Receivable	6,500
Notes Payable	76,000
Supplies	400

Requirements

1. Prepare the company's trial balance at December 31, 2010, listing accounts in the proper order. List the largest expense first, the second-largest expense next, and so on.

2. Prepare the financial statements: income statement, statement of retained earnings, and balance sheet. The retained earnings balance of $9,700 is the beginning balance for the year; it has not been updated for the current year's income or loss.

3. Was it a profitable year for Cascade Consulting, Inc.? Why or why not?

P2-36A. Error correction (*Learning Objective 4*) 15–20 min.

The following errors occurred in the accounting records of Pacific Outfitters, Inc.:

a. The company accountant recorded the receipt of cash for service revenue by debiting Cash for $890 instead of the correct amount of $980. Service Revenue was also credited for $890, the incorrect amount.

b. A $270 purchase of supplies on account was recorded by debiting Accounts Payable and crediting Supplies.

c. The company accountant recorded a $1,200 payment of rent by debiting rent expense for $12,000 and crediting Cash for $12,000.

d. In recording a $850 payment on account, Accounts Receivable was debited and cash was credited.

Requirements

1. Prepare the necessary journal entries to correct each of these errors.

2. For each of the errors, determine if the error would cause net income to be overstated, understated, or unchanged.

PROBLEMS (GROUP B)

P2-37B. Journalizing transactions (*Learning Objective 3*) 15–20 min.

Arleen O'Neil practices law under the business title Arleen O'Neil Attorney at Law, Inc. During November, her law practice engaged in the following transactions:

Nov	1	Sold $55,000 of stock to O'Neil to start the business.
	3	Paid $200 for the purchase of office supplies.
	8	Paid $28,000 cash to purchase land for an office site.
	12	Purchased office equipment on account, $2,800.
	17	Borrowed $50,000 from the bank. O'Neil signed a note payable to the bank in the name of the business.
	26	Paid $2,700 on account.
	30	Revenues earned during the month included $12,000 cash and $23,000 on account.
	30	Paid employees' salaries, $2,100; office rent, $2,500; and utilities, $300.
	30	Paid $2,000 of dividends to stockholder, O'Neil.

O'Neil's business uses the following accounts: Cash, Accounts Receivable, Supplies, Land, Office Equipment, Accounts Payable, Notes Payable, Common Stock, Dividends, Service Revenue, Salary Expense, Rent Expense, and Utilities Expense.

Requirement

1. Journalize each transaction. Omit explanations.

P2-38B. Journalizing transactions (*Learning Objective 3*) 15–20 min.

Tip Top Advertising, Inc., engaged in the following business transactions during July of 2010:

Jul	1	Borrowed $190,000 from Oakville Bank. The company president signed a note payable to the bank in the name of Tip Top Advertising, Inc.
	3	Paid $110,000 cash to purchase an office building.
	6	Provided services to customers on account, $18,400.
	9	Purchased $1,200 of office supplies on account.
	13	Provided services to cash customers, $8,500.
	15	Paid $3,000 of dividends to company stockholders.
	17	Received payment on account from credit customers, $2,900.
	18	Paid property tax expense on office building, $1,400.
	22	Paid employee salaries, $3,150.
	26	Paid cash to purchase supplies, $500.
	31	Paid $2,200 on account.

Tip Top Advertising, Inc., uses the following accounts: Cash, Accounts Receivable, Supplies, Building, Accounts Payable, Notes Payable, Common Stock, Dividends, Sales Revenue, Salary Expense, and Property Tax Expense.

Requirement

1. Journalize each transaction. Omit explanations.

P2-39B. Journalizing, posting, and trial balance preparation (*Learning Objectives 3 & 4*) 20–25 min.

Teddy Sargent opened an accounting firm on May 1, 2010. During the month of May, the business completed the following transactions:

May	1	The business sold $80,000 of stock to open the firm, Sargent & Associates, Inc.
	3	Purchased supplies, $500, and furniture, $1,200, on account.
	5	Performed accounting service for a client and received cash, $2,700.
	8	Paid cash to acquire land for a future office site, $22,000.
	11	Prepared tax returns for a client on account, $2,500.
	14	Paid assistant's salary, $1,200.
	16	Paid for the furniture purchased May 3 on account.
	19	Received $700 cash for accounting services performed.
	23	Billed a client for $1,300 of accounting services.
	28	Received $400 from client on account.
	31	Paid secretary's salary, $1,200.
	31	Paid rent expense, $1,700.
	31	Paid $1,200 of dividends.

Requirements

1. Open, or set up, the following T-accounts: Cash, Accounts Receivable, Supplies, Furniture, Land, Accounts Payable, Common Stock, Dividends, Service Revenue, Salary Expense, and Rent Expense.
2. Journalize transactions. Explanations are not required.
3. Post the transactions to the T-accounts that have been set up for you, using transaction dates as posting references.
4. Calculate the balance in each account.
5. Prepare the trial balance for Sargent & Associates, Inc., at the end of May.

P2-40B. Journalizing, posting, and trial balance preparation (*Learning Objectives 3 & 4*) 25–30 min.

The trial balance for BFF Systems, Inc., at March 15, 2010, follows:

BFF Systems, Inc.
Trial Balance
March 15, 2010

ACCT #	ACCOUNT	DEBIT	CREDIT
110	Cash	$ 4,400	
112	Accounts Receivable	8,900	
115	Supplies	100	
140	Equipment	16,000	
210	Accounts Payable		$ 4,100
311	Common Stock		23,900
315	Dividends	2,800	
411	Service Revenue		7,700
511	Salary Expense	2,200	
515	Rent Expense	1,300	
	Total	$35,700	$35,700

During the remainder of March, BFF Systems, Inc., completed the following transactions:

Mar 16	Collected $1,700 cash from a client on account.
18	Performed services on account, $1,900.
21	Received $1,500 cash for services performed.
23	Purchased supplies on account, $700.
25	Paid $1,300 in dividends.
27	Paid $3,300 on account.
29	Received $2,500 cash for services performed.
30	Paid rent, $1,600.
30	Paid employees' salaries, $2,600.

Requirements

1. Journalize the transactions that occurred March 16 to March 30 on page 6 of the journal.

2. The four-column ledger accounts, together with their beginning balances, have been opened for you. Post the transactions to the ledger, using dates, account numbers, and posting references. Calculate the new account balances.

3. Prepare the trial balance for BFF Systems, Inc., at the end of March.

P2-41B. Prepare a trial balance, income statement, statement of retained earnings, and balance sheet (*Learning Objective 4*) 20–25 min.

The accounts of Highland Consulting, Inc., follow with their normal balances at August 31, 2010. The accounts are listed in no particular order.

Account	Balance
Common Stock	$107,700
Insurance Expense	1,300
Accounts Payable	4,000
Service Revenue	86,500
Land	89,000
Supplies Expense	3,100
Cash	9,200
Salary Expense	56,000
Building	91,000
Rent Expense	8,700
Dividends	10,000
Utilities Expense	5,400
Retained Earnings	13,600
Accounts Receivable	5,500
Notes Payable	68,000
Supplies	600

Requirements

1. Prepare the company's trial balance at August 31, 2010, listing accounts in the proper order. List the largest expense first, the second-largest expense next, and so on.

2. Prepare the financial statements: income statement, statement of retained earnings, and balance sheet. The retained earnings balance of $13,600 is the beginning balance for the year; it has not been updated for the current year's net income or loss.

3. Was it a profitable year for Highland Consulting, Inc.? Why or why not?

P2-42B. Error correction (*Learning Objective 4*) 15–20 min.

The following errors occurred in the accounting records of Over Side, Inc.:

a. The company accountant recorded the receipt of cash for service revenue by debiting Cash for $1,140 instead of the correct amount of $1,410. Service revenue was also credited for $1,140, the incorrect amount.

b. A $150 purchase of supplies on account was recorded by debiting Accounts Payable and crediting Supplies.

c. The company accountant recorded a $800 payment of rent by debiting Rent Expense for $8,000 and crediting Cash for $8,000.

d. In recording an $815 payment on account, Accounts Receivable was debited and Cash was credited.

Requirements

1. Prepare the necessary journal entries to correct each of these errors.

2. For each of the errors, determine if the error would cause net income to be overstated, understated, or unchanged.

PROBLEMS (ALTERNATES 1, 2, AND 3)

These alternative problem sets are available for your practice benefit at
www.myaccountinglab.com

CONTINUING EXERCISE

This exercise continues with the business of Graham's Yard Care, Inc., begun in the continuing exercise in Chapter 1. Here you will account for Graham's Yard Care, Inc.'s transactions in the general journal. Graham's Yard Care, Inc., completed the following transactions during June:

Jun 1	Received $1,000 and issued 100 shares of common stock. Deposited this amount in bank account titled Graham's Yard Care, Inc.
3	Purchased on account a mower, $1,000, and weed whacker, $400. The equipment is expected to remain in service for four years.
5	Purchased $20 of gas. Wrote check #1 from the new bank account.
6	Performed lawn services for client on account, $200.
8	Purchased $50 of fertilizer from the lawn store. Wrote check #2 from the new bank account.
17	Completed landscaping job for client, received cash $500.
30	Received $50 on account from June 6 sale.

Requirements

1. Open T-accounts in the ledger: Cash, Accounts Receivable, Lawn Supplies, Equipment, Accounts Payable, Common Stock, Retained Earnings, Service Revenue, and Fuel Expense.

2. Journalize the transactions. Explanations are not required.

3. Post to the T-accounts. Key all items by date and denote an account balance as *Bal*. Formal posting references are not required.

4. Prepare a trial balance at June 30, 2010.

CONTINUING PROBLEM

This problem continues with the business of Aqua Elite, Inc., begun in the continuing problem in Chapter 1. Here you will account for Aqua Elite, Inc.'s transactions using formal accounting practices. The trial balance for Aqua Elite, Inc., as of May 31, 2010, is presented below.

Aqua Elite, Inc. Trial Balance May 31, 2010		
ACCOUNT	**DEBIT**	**CREDIT**
Cash	$24,475	
Accounts Receivable	1,200	
Supplies	860	
Equipment	4,700	
Vehicles	31,000	
Accounts Payable		$ 840
Notes Payable		31,000
Common Stock		28,500
Dividends	1,000	
Service Revenues		4,050
Salary Expense	675	
Utilities Expense	480	
Total	$64,390	$64,390

During June the following transactions occurred:

Jun	1	Paid receptionist's salary, $675.
	2	Paid cash to acquire land for a future office site, $15,000.
	3	Moved into a new location for the business and paid the first month's rent, $1,800.
	4	Performed service for a customer and received cash, $1,700.
	5	Received $500 on account.
	8	Purchased $750 of supplies on account.
	11	Billed customers for services performed, $3,800.
	13	Sold an additional $10,000 of stock to Mike Hanson.
	16	Paid receptionist's salary, $675.
	17	Received $1,350 cash for services performed.
	18	Received $1,500 from customers on account.
	19	Paid $325 to be listed in the yellow pages telephone directory.
	21	Paid $1,000 on account.
	22	Purchased office furniture on account, $3,300.
	24	Paid miscellaneous expenses, $275.
	26	Billed customers for services provided, $1,100.
	28	Received $300 from customers on account.
	30	Paid utility bill, $745.
	30	Paid receptionist's salary, $675.
	30	Paid $1,800 of dividends.

Requirements

1. Journalize the transactions that occurred in June, omit explanations.

2. Open the ledger accounts listed in the trial balance together with their beginning balances at May 31. Use the four-column account format illustrated in the chapter. Enter "Bal" for the previous balance in the Item column. Post the transactions to the ledger creating new ledger accounts as necessary, omit posting references. Calculate the new account balances.

3. Prepare the trial balance for Aqua Elite, Inc., at the end of June.

APPLY YOUR KNOWLEDGE

ETHICS IN ACTION

Case 1. Jamie Hanson was recording the daily transactions of Alpine Physical Therapy, Inc., into the accounting records so she could prepare financial statements and apply for a bank loan. Some of the business expenses were higher than she had expected, and Jamie was worried about the effect of these expenses on net income. Jamie was recording a $5,000 payment for legal fees incurred by the business by debiting Legal Expense and crediting Cash to properly record the journal entry. She then thought that, rather than debiting the expense account for the $5,000 payment, she could debit the Dividends account, which also had a normal debit balance. Jamie knew that debits had to equal credits so debiting the Dividends account instead of the Legal Expense account would not affect the trial balance. Further, the net income would be $5,000 higher because now no legal expense would be recorded. She thought that either way the retained earnings would be lower, and besides, it really didn't matter how the $5,000 payment was shown as long as she showed it somewhere.

Should Jamie debit the Dividends account rather than the Legal Expense account? Do you agree with her thought that it really doesn't matter how the $5,000 payment is shown as long as it is shown somewhere? Considering that Jamie owns all of the Alpine Physical Therapy, Inc., common stock, does she have any ethical responsibilities to properly record each business transaction?

Case 2. Jim Peterson is the accountant for ProCare Lawnservice, Inc. During the month, numerous payments were made for wages, and therefore, he was properly debiting the Wage Expense account and crediting Cash. Jim became concerned that if he kept debiting the Wage Expense account it would end up with a balance much higher than any of the other expense accounts. Accordingly, he began debiting other expense accounts for some of the wage payments and thus, "spread the expenses around" to other expense accounts. When he was done posting all the journal entries to the ledger accounts, he printed a trial balance. He saw that the Wage Expense debit balance was $38,000 and the total of all the other expense accounts was $24,000. Had he properly posted all the wage expense transactions, Wage Expense would have totaled $52,000 and the other expense accounts would have totaled $10,000. Jim reasoned that his actions provided for "more balanced" expense account totals and, regardless of his postings, the total expenses were still $62,000, so the overall net income would be the same.

Were Jim's actions justified? Do they cause any ethical concerns? If you were the owner of ProCare Lawnservice, Inc., would you have a problem with what Jim did?

KNOW YOUR BUSINESS

FINANCIAL ANALYSIS

Purpose: To help familiarize you with the financial reporting of a real company in order to further your understanding of the chapter material you are learning.

Although we do not have access to the journals used by Columbia Sportswear, we can still understand various business transactions that Columbia Sportswear had as seen on the financial statements in its annual report. Refer to the Columbia Sportswear income statements, "Statements of Operations," and the Columbia Sportswear balance sheet's in Appendix A. Assume Columbia Sportswear completed the following transactions during January, 2008:

Jan	3	Purchased $485,000 of equipment for cash.
	7	Had cash sales of $26,360,000.
	10	Purchased $32,845,000 of inventory on account.
	15	Made $642,000 of sales on account.
	29	Paid $16,750,000 on account from the January 10 purchase.

Requirements

1. Prepare journal entries to record the transactions listed. Use the account titles found in the Columbia Sportswear financial statements: Cash; Accounts Receivable; Property, Plant, and Equipment; Accounts Payable; and Net Sales.

2. Look at the financial statements and locate the accounts that you included in your journal entries. Note that the balances Columbia Sportswear reported include millions of dollars in transactions for the year. Imagine how much activity and how many transactions Columbia Sportswear has every day!

INDUSTRY ANALYSIS

Purpose: To help you understand and compare the performance of two companies in the same industry.

Go to the Columbia Sportswear Company Annual Report located in Appendix A. Now access the 2008 Annual Report for Under Armour, Inc. To do this from the Internet, go to their Web page for Investor Relations at *http://investor.underarmour.com/investors.cfm* and under Downloads on the right-hand side, go to 2008 Annual Report.

Requirements

Answer these questions about the two companies:

1. In terms of total revenue, which is the larger company? Which financial statement did you look at to find that information?

2. In terms of total assets, which is the larger company? Which financial statement did you look at to find that information?

3. Which company has more total debt? Which financial statement did you look at to find that information?

4. Which company has the higher gross profit percentage? Don't know that one? On the Consolidated Statements of Operations, divide Gross Profit by Net Sales (or Net Revenues). What exactly does this mean?

5. Who paid more cash dividends to its stockholders in 2008? Which financial statement did you look at to find that information?

6. Which company's stock would you rather own? Why?

SMALL BUSINESS ANALYSIS

Purpose: To help you understand the importance of cash flows in the operation of a small business.

You're sitting in your CPA office late on a Friday afternoon when you get an e-mail from a friend. You know that she has been working on setting up a new accounting system in her office for a new business that she just started. You figured that this would eventually generate some communication between the two of you because you know that she has relatively limited accounting knowledge. Here's her e-mail to you.

"Jerry, I'm pretty frustrated right now! As you know, I've been installing this new accounting system here in the office and I've run into a problem. I don't understand this cash account. I have purchased some items on my debit card and I've purchased some items on my credit card. So logically, when I purchased the items on my debit card, I debited the cash account. But when I used my credit card, it made sense to credit my cash account. And to make things even worse, my cash account ends up with a credit balance, and I'm pretty sure that's not right. This is too confusing and it's Friday afternoon; I'm going home!"

The following journal entries were attached to your client's e-mail.

DATE	ACCOUNTS	POST REF.	DR.	CR.
May 5	Cash		400	
	Supplies			400
	Purchased supplies using debit card.			

DATE	ACCOUNTS	POST REF.	DR.	CR.
May 6	Utilities Expense		250	
	Cash			250
	Paid utilities bill using credit card.			

Requirement

1. Since Cash is the lifeblood of any business, having a correct balance in the cash account is of utmost importance. Correctly entering cash transactions is equally as important. Suggest to your client the corrections that need to be made to the journal entries she made.

WRITTEN COMMUNICATION

Consider the situation that was presented in the Small Business Analysis. Your client had two concerns that she asked you about. The first one is that she was concerned that her cash balance was showing as a credit balance instead of a debit balance. And even after the corrections were made, the cash balance was still a credit. The second concern she had was how to record transactions when she uses her debit card as opposed to transactions when she uses her credit card.

Write a short memo or letter to your client addressing these two situations and what you would consider to be the proper accounting treatment for each of the two. More specifically, if the cash account was showing as a credit balance, how would that have happened? Is it possible for that to happen? And regarding the use of the debit card versus the credit card, from the information contained in the chapter, explain the difference between the two types of cards and how each transaction should be recorded from an accounting point of view.

Self Check Answers
1. c 2. a 3. d 4. c 5. b 6. c 7. c 8. d 9. a 10. c

3

Adjusting and Closing Entries

Now that you have an understanding of how to analyze and record transactions, it is time to explore a couple more important questions. The first question is "How does a company make sure that it is reporting its income accurately?" And, the second question is "How does a company prepare for a new accounting period?" In this chapter, we will see the answers to these questions when discussing adjusting and closing entries.

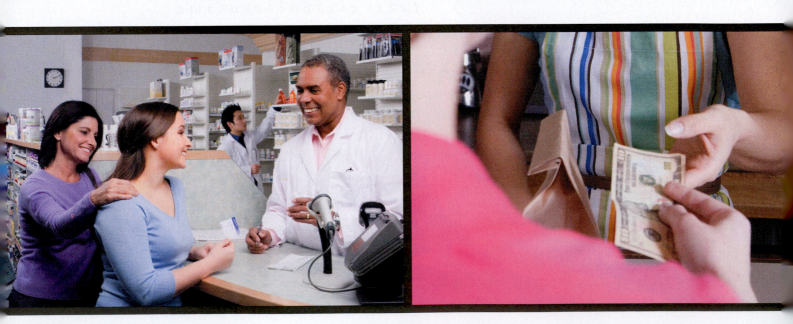

Chapter Outline:

HOW DOES A COMPANY ACCURATELY REPORT ITS INCOME? (p. 110)

WHAT IS THE ROLE OF ADJUSTING ENTRIES, AND WHEN ARE THEY PREPARED? (p. 111)

HOW ARE FINANCIAL STATEMENTS PREPARED FROM AN ADJUSTED TRIAL BALANCE? (p. 120)

HOW DOES A COMPANY PREPARE FOR A NEW ACCOUNTING PERIOD? (p. 123)

Learning Objectives

1. Understand the revenue recognition and matching principles
2. Understand the four types of adjustments and prepare adjusting entries
3. Prepare financial statements from an adjusted trial balance
4. Prepare closing entries and a post-closing trial balance

In Chapter 2, we learned about journalizing and posting transactions for a business as well as how to prepare a trial balance and financial statements. These were steps one, two, three, and six of the accounting cycle. Once again the **accounting cycle** looks like this:

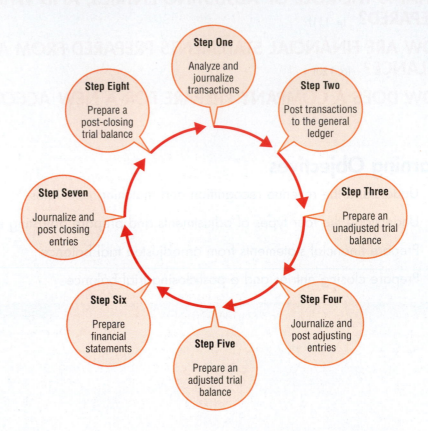

Here in Chapter 3, we will learn how to prepare steps four, five, seven, and eight. The accounting cycle is repeated for every **accounting period**. The accounting period can be defined as a month, a quarter, or a year. The annual accounting period for most large companies runs the calendar year from January 1 through December 31, although some companies use a fiscal year that does not coincide with the calendar year. A **fiscal year** is any consecutive 12-month period that a business chooses. It may begin on any day of the year and end 12 months later. Usually, the fiscal year-end date is the low point in business activity for the year. Although we will focus primarily on an annual time period, financial statements are usually also prepared monthly, quarterly, or semiannually so that businesses have an idea of how they are doing before the year ends.

HOW DOES A COMPANY ACCURATELY REPORT ITS INCOME?

Revenue Recognition and Matching Principles

Understand the revenue recognition and matching principles ▶ **1**

In Chapter 1, we learned that financial statements are prepared in order to provide useful information to various users. However, in order for financial statements to be useful, they must be accurate and up to date. To ensure that financial statements are up to date, GAAP requires the use of **accrual accounting**. To practice accrual accounting, a business must follow the next two accounting principles:

- The **revenue recognition principle** states that revenues should be recognized, or recorded, when they are earned regardless of when cash is received.
- The **matching principle** states that expenses should be matched with the revenues they helped generate. In other words, expenses should be recorded when they are incurred regardless of when they are paid for.

Accruals and Deferrals

It is possible for a business to record revenues only when cash is received and record expenses only when cash is paid. This is referred to as **cash-basis accounting**. In many instances, when a company uses cash-basis accounting, its financial statements do not present an accurate picture of how the company is performing. This is because a business may provide goods and services to customers "on account." In this case, the business has earned revenue prior to receiving cash from the customer. A business may also purchase goods and services from suppliers on account. In this case, expenses are incurred before cash is paid. When revenues are earned before cash is received, or expenses are incurred before cash is paid, it is called an **accrual**. We have already seen accruals in Chapters 1 and 2 when we recorded transactions in Accounts Receivable and Accounts Payable.

Businesses may also receive cash from customers prior to the delivery of goods or services to the customer. In this case, cash is received before revenue is earned. In addition, businesses may pay for goods or services prior to receiving those goods or services from the supplier. In this case, cash is paid before an expense is incurred. When cash is received for goods or services prior to the recognition of a revenue, or cash is paid for goods or services prior to the recognition of the expense, it is called a **deferral**. We have also seen deferrals in Chapters 1 and 2 when we purchased supplies and equipment. Accruals and deferrals can be summarized as follows:

	Now	**Later**
Accrued Revenue	Revenue is recognized	Cash is received
Accrued Expense	Expense is recognized	Cash is paid
Deferred Revenue	Cash is received	Revenue is recognized
Deferred Expense	Cash is paid	Expense is recognized

As we saw in Chapter 2, a business records transactions throughout the accounting period as the transactions occur. At the end of the period, the accountant prepares a trial balance and uses it to prepare financial statements. However, before most businesses can prepare accurate, up-to-date, financial statements, the accountant will have to prepare **adjusting entries**.

WHAT IS THE ROLE OF ADJUSTING ENTRIES, AND WHEN ARE THEY PREPARED?

Understand the four types of adjustments and prepare adjusting entries **2**

Adjusting entries are journal entries used to ensure the revenue recognition principle and the matching principle are followed. Adjustments may be needed for accruals when revenues have been earned, or expenses have been incurred, before cash is exchanged. Since cash has not been exchanged, it is possible that the revenue or expense has not been recorded, so an adjusting entry is needed to record the revenue or expense.

- Two types of adjustments are made for accruals:

1. Accrue, or record, unrecorded revenues. Revenues are recorded in the current period by debiting a receivable and crediting revenue.

2. Accrue, or record, unrecorded expenses. Record the expenses in the current period by debiting an expense and crediting a liability.

A deferral is created when cash is exchanged before the related revenue or expense is recognized. Examples include receiving cash from customers prior to providing services or purchasing supplies that are not used immediately.

- Two types of adjustments are made for deferrals:

1. Divide **unearned revenues** between periods. When payment is received in advance from a customer for goods or services, cash is debited. The liability account, Unearned Revenues, is credited because the customer is owed the goods or services. Once the customer receives the goods or services, an adjusting entry is prepared in which the unearned revenue account is debited to reduce it and a revenue is credited.

2. Divide **prepaid expenses**, supplies, buildings, equipment, and other assets between periods. These items are recorded as assets when they are purchased because the item that was paid for has not yet been used up. Therefore, an asset account is debited and cash is credited to record the purchase. Once part, or all, of the item is used up, an adjusting entry is prepared in which an expense account is debited and the related asset is credited to reduce it.

At the end of the accounting period, the accountant prepares a trial balance from the account information contained in the general ledger. This trial balance lists most of the revenues and expenses of the business, but these amounts are incomplete because the adjusting entries have not yet been prepared. Therefore, this trial balance is called an **unadjusted trial balance** (step three in the accounting cycle). Remember Osborne Consulting, Inc., from Chapter 2? **Exhibit 3-1** shows the unadjusted trial balance for Osborne Consulting, Inc. at the end of its first quarter of operations, at March 31, 2010.

	Osborne Consulting, Inc. (Unadjusted) Trial Balance March 31, 2010		
		BALANCE	
ACCOUNT TITLE		**DEBIT**	**CREDIT**
Cash		$26,300	
Accounts Receivable		3,100	
Supplies		900	
Prepaid Rent		3,000	
Equipment		12,600	
Accounts Payable			$13,100
Unearned Service Revenue			450
Common Stock			20,000
Retained Earnings			9,500
Dividends		3,200	
Service Revenue			7,000
Salary Expense		550	
Utilities Expense		400	
Total		$50,050	$50,050

Exhibit 3-1 ▲

Remember from Chapter 2 that transactions are recorded in the journal and posted to accounts in the general ledger. This process is still used when adjusting the accounts. In this chapter, we will show how to record adjusting entries and how to post them to accounts. However, instead of using the real ledger account form, we will post adjustments to T-accounts. We use this method because it is easier to see how these entries affect the specific accounts as well as the accounting equation.

Accruing Revenues

Accounts Receivable Businesses sometimes earn revenue by providing goods or services before they receive cash. Assume that a local car dealership hires Osborne Consulting, Inc., on March 15 as a computer consultant. Osborne Consulting agrees to a monthly fee of $500, which the car dealership pays on the 15 of each month beginning on April 15. During March, Osborne earns half a month's fee, $250 ($500 × 1/2 month), for consulting work performed March 15 through March 31. On March 31, Osborne makes the following adjusting entry to reflect the accrual of the revenue earned during March (the beginning balance of each account is found on the unadjusted trial balance presented in Exhibit 3-1):

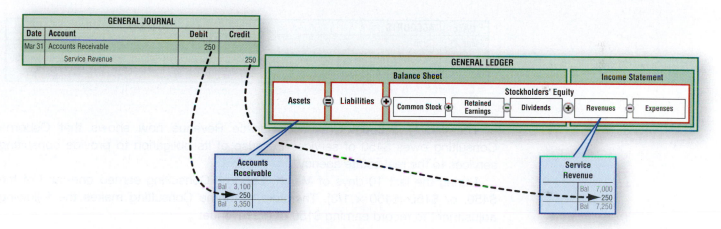

Without the adjustment, Osborne Consulting's financial statements are inaccurate because they would understate both Accounts Receivable and Service Revenue.

Accruing Expenses

Salary Payable Suppose Osborne Consulting pays its employee a monthly salary of $550. Osborne pays the employee on the 15 of each month for the past month's work. On March 31, the following adjustment must be made to record the salary expense for the month of March:

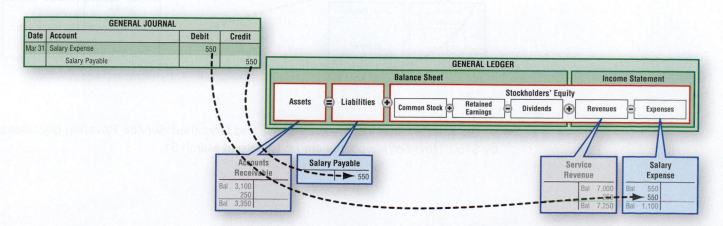

This is referred to as accruing the expense. **Accrued expenses**, such as the accrual for salary expense, are expenses that the business has incurred but not paid. The adjusting entry to accrue the expense always creates a liability, such as Salary Payable, Taxes Payable, or Interest Payable.

Adjusting Deferred Revenues

Unearned Revenues It is possible for a business to collect cash from customers prior to providing goods or services. Receiving cash from a customer before earning it creates a liability called unearned revenue, or **deferred revenue**. It is classified as a liability because the company owes a product or service to the customer. Even though the account has the word "revenue" in its title, it is not a revenue account because the amounts in the account represents what has *not* yet been earned.

Suppose a local real estate agency hires Osborne Consulting to provide consulting services, agreeing to pay $450 monthly, beginning immediately. Osborne Consulting collects the first amount from the real estate agency on March 21. Osborne Consulting records the cash receipt and a liability as follows:

DATE	ACCOUNTS	POST REF.	DR.	CR.
Mar 21	Cash		450	
	Unearned Service Revenue			450
	Collected revenue in advance.			

The liability account Unearned Service Revenue now shows that Osborne Consulting owes $450 of services because of its obligation to provide consulting services to the real estate agency.

During the last 10 days of March, Osborne Consulting earned one-third of the $450, or $150 ($450 × 1/3). Therefore, Osborne Consulting makes the following adjustment to record earning $150 of the revenue:

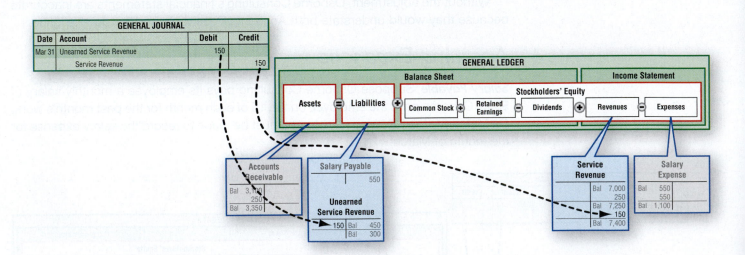

Service Revenue increases by $150, and Unearned Service Revenue decreases by $150. Now both accounts are up to date at March 31.

Adjusting Deferred Expenses

Prepaid Rent Prepaid rent and prepaid insurance are examples of prepaid expenses, also called **deferred expenses**. Prepaid expenses represent items that are paid for before they are used. Often, renters are required to pay rent in advance. This prepayment creates an asset for the renter. Suppose Osborne Consulting, Inc., moves to a new office and prepays three months' office rent on March 1, 2010. If the lease specifies a monthly rental of $1,000, the amount of cash paid is $3,000 ($1,000 × 3 months). The entry to record the payment is as follows:

DATE	ACCOUNTS	POST REF.	DR.	CR.
Mar 1	Prepaid Rent		3,000	
	Cash			3,000
	Paid three months' rent in advance.			

After posting, Prepaid Rent has a $3,000 debit balance. During March, Osborne Consulting uses the rented space for one month; therefore, the balance in Prepaid Rent is reduced by $1,000 (one month's rent). The required adjusting entry is as follows:

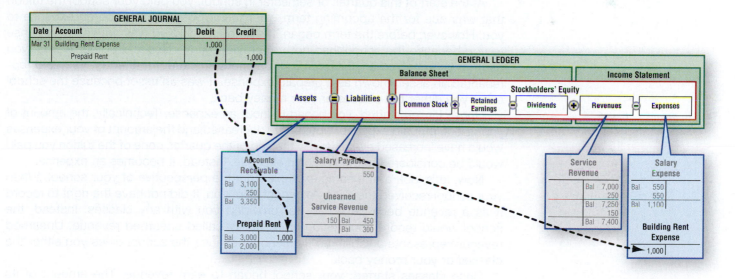

The Building Rent Expense account is increased with a debit, which reduces Retained Earnings and, therefore, Stockholders' Equity. The asset account Prepaid Rent is decreased with a credit for the same amount. After posting, Prepaid Rent and Building Rent Expense show the correct ending balances. If Osborne Consulting, Inc., had prepaid insurance, the same analysis would also apply to this asset account. The difference in the adjusting entry would be in the account titles, which would be Prepaid Insurance instead of Prepaid Rent, and Insurance Expense instead of Building Rent Expense. The amount of the entry would also be different.

🌐 Accounting in Your World

In order to better understand the difference between a prepaid expense and an unearned revenue, consider this example:

At the start of this quarter, or semester in school, you paid your school the tuition that was due for the upcoming term. Your tuition will ultimately be an expense to you. However, before the term began, the amount you paid was not yet an expense to you because the school had not yet provided any classes. In other words, you had not yet received anything for your payment. Instead, the amount you paid represented an asset known as a prepaid expense. It was an asset because the school owes you either the classes or your money back.

Once classes started, you began to incur an expense. Technically, the amount of your asset, prepaid expense, would have decreased and the amount of your expenses would have increased every day. By the end of the quarter, none of the tuition you paid would be considered to be a prepaid expense. Instead, it becomes an expense.

Now, let's look at the same example from the perspective of your school. When your school received the tuition payment from you, it did not have the right to record it as a revenue because it had not provided you with any classes. Instead, the school would record your tuition as a liability called unearned revenue. Unearned revenue represents a liability to the school because the school owes you either the classes or your money back.

Once classes started, your school began to earn revenue. The amount of its unearned revenue would have decreased and the amount of its revenue would have increased every day. By the end of the quarter, the entire amount of tuition you paid would be considered to be revenue to your school. As you can see, one entity's prepaid expense is another entity's unearned revenue and vice versa.

Supplies Supplies receive the same treatment as prepaid expenses. On March 5, Osborne Consulting pays $900 for office supplies. The asset accounts, Supplies and Cash, are both affected. Supplies increased by $900, while Cash decreased by $900, as shown here:

DATE	ACCOUNTS	POST REF.	DR.	CR.
Mar 5	Supplies		900	
	Cash			900
	Purchased office supplies.			

The March 31 trial balance, as shown in Exhibit 3-1 on page 112, shows Supplies with a $900 debit balance. During March, Osborne Consulting uses some of these supplies to conduct business. Therefore, Osborne Consulting's March 31 Balance Sheet should *not* report supplies of $900. To figure out the amount of supplies used, Osborne Consulting counts the supplies on hand at the end of March. The supplies on hand are still an asset to the business. Assume that Osborne Consulting has supplies costing $600 at March 31st. The supplies purchased ($900) minus the supplies on hand at the end of March ($600) equals the value of the supplies used during the month ($300). The amount of supplies used during the month will become supplies expense. The March 31 adjusting entry updates the Supplies account and records Supplies Expense for the month:

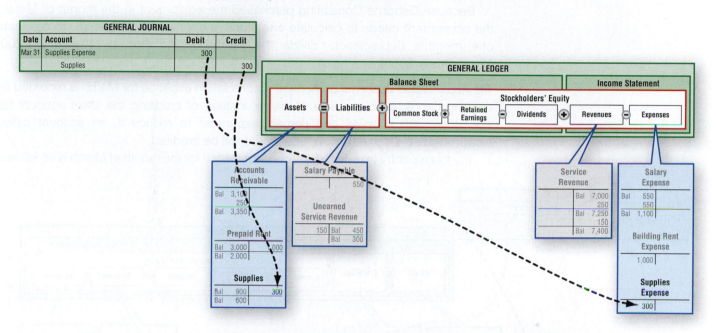

After the entry is posted to the general ledger, the correct account balances for Supplies and Supplies Expense will be reflected.

Depreciation of long-term assets **Long-term assets**, or fixed assets, are assets that last for more than one year. Examples include land, buildings, equipment, and furniture. All of these assets, except land, are used up over time. As a long-term asset is used up, part of the asset's cost becomes an expense, just as supplies become supplies expense when they are used up. The expensing of a long-term asset's cost over its useful life is called **depreciation**. No depreciation is recorded for land because it is never really used up.

We account for long-term assets in the same way as prepaid expenses and supplies because they are all assets. The major difference is the length of time it takes for the asset to be used up. Prepaid expenses and supplies are typically used within a year, while most long-term assets remain functional for several years. Suppose that on March 8, Osborne Consulting purchases equipment on account for $12,600 and makes this journal entry:

DATE	ACCOUNTS	POST REF.	DR.	CR.
Mar 8	Equipment		12,600	
	Accounts Payable			12,600
	Purchased equipment on account.			

After posting the entry, the Equipment account has a $12,600 balance. It is difficult to measure the amount of a long-term asset that has been used up over time so the amount must be estimated. Several methods can be used to estimate the amount of depreciation. The most common method, which Osborne Consulting utilizes, is called the **straight-line depreciation** method. Osborne Consulting believes the equipment will be useful for three years and will be worthless and have no **salvage value** at the end of its life. Depreciation of this equipment is calculated using the straight-line method as follows:

$$\text{Depreciation Expense per Year} = \frac{\text{Cost of Asset} - \text{Salvage Value of Asset}}{\text{Useful Life of Asset}} = \frac{\$12,600}{3} = \$4,200$$

Because Osborne Consulting purchased the equipment in the month of March, the accountant needs to calculate one month's depreciation expense. To calculate one month's depreciation, divide the yearly depreciation by twelve ($4,200/ 12 months = $350).

The Accumulated Depreciation Account Depreciation expense for March is recorded by debiting depreciation expense. However, instead of crediting the asset account (as was done with supplies and prepaid expenses) to reduce it, an account called **Accumulated Depreciation**, Equipment will be credited.

The journal entry to record depreciation expense for the month of March is as follows:

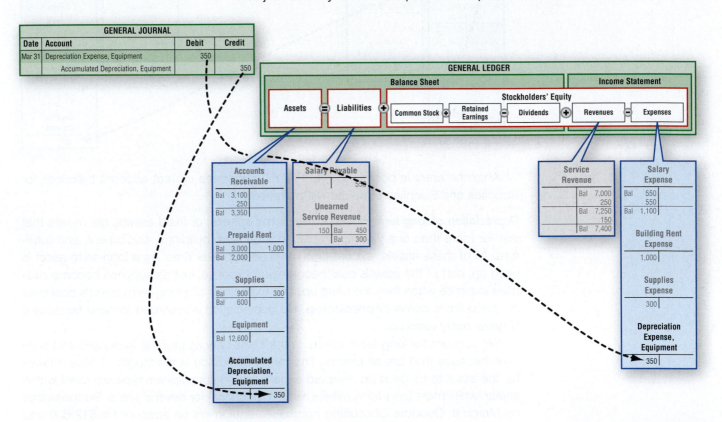

Accumulated Depreciation, Equipment, is a contra-asset. A **contra-account** has three main characteristics:

- A contra-account is linked to another account and will always appear with this account in the financial statements.
- A contra-account's normal balance is always opposite of the account it is linked to.
- The balance in a contra-account is subtracted from the balance of the account it is linked to in order to find the **net value** of the two accounts.

Because it is linked to Equipment, an asset account, Accumulated Depreciation, Equipment will appear on the balance sheet. Being an asset, the Equipment account has a debit balance, so the Accumulated Depreciation, Equipment account will have a credit balance because it is a contra-asset. Since it's a contra-account, the balance of Accumulated Depreciation, Equipment is subtracted from Equipment. The net amount of a long-term asset is called its **book value**, or **carrying value**, and is calculated as follows:

	Book Value of a Long-Term Asset	
Cost	Equipment..	$12,600
− Accumulated Depreciation	Less: Accumulated Depreciation, Equipment.............	350
= Book (or Carrying) Value	Book Value...	$12,250

Accumulated Depreciation, Equipment increases over the life of the asset as the asset is used up, which reduces the book value of the equipment. By keeping the cost of the equipment separate from its accumulated depreciation, financial statement users can look at the Equipment account to see how much the asset originally cost and also look at the Accumulated Depreciation, Equipment account to see how much of the original cost has been used up. A business usually keeps an accumulated depreciation account for each type of depreciable long-term asset. If Osborne Consulting, Inc., had both buildings and equipment, it would use two accumulated depreciation accounts, Accumulated Depreciation, Buildings, and Accumulated Depreciation, Equipment. Depreciation will be covered more in depth in Chapter 8.

☑ Concept Check

Jim Oliver is the accountant for Crazy Critters, Inc., a local veterinary clinic. After Jim finished preparing the financial statements for the year he realized that he failed to make an adjusting entry to record $1,800 of depreciation expense for the year. What effect did this error have on Crazy Critter's financial statements?

Answer

In order to determine the effects of omitting an adjusting entry we must examine what the adjusting entry should have been. The adjusting entry Jim should have made is as follows:

DATE	ACCOUNTS	POST REF.	DR.	CR.
	Depreciation Expense		1,800	
	Accumulated Depreciation			1,800

As we can see from the journal entry, Depreciation Expense should have been debited (increased), which would have increased total expenses for the year. An increase in total expenses causes a decrease in Net Income. So, the omission of the adjusting entry for depreciation expense causes Net Income, and therefore, Retained Earnings, to be overstated. We also see that the Accumulated Depreciation account should have been credited (increased), which would cause total assets to decrease because Accumulated Depreciation is a contra-asset account. So, the omission of the adjusting entry for depreciation expense also causes the total assets to be overstated.

Decision Guidelines

Decision	Guideline	Analyze
How do I know if my financial statements are accurate?	To produce accurate financial information the revenue recognition principle and the matching principle should be followed.	The revenue recognition principle requires that revenues be recorded only when they are earned regardless of when cash is received.
		The matching principle requires that expenses be recorded when they are incurred regardless of when cash is paid. This ensures that expenses are matched with the revenues they helped generate.
		When the revenue recognition principle and the matching principle are followed it is referred to as *accrual accounting*.

HOW ARE FINANCIAL STATEMENTS PREPARED FROM AN ADJUSTED TRIAL BALANCE?

Prepare financial statements from an adjusted trial balance

The Adjusted Trial Balance

Earlier in the chapter, the unadjusted trial balance in Exhibit 3-1 on page 112 showed the account balances for Osborne Consulting, Inc., before the adjustments had been made. After adjustment, Osborne Consulting's accounts would appear as presented in **Exhibit 3-2**.

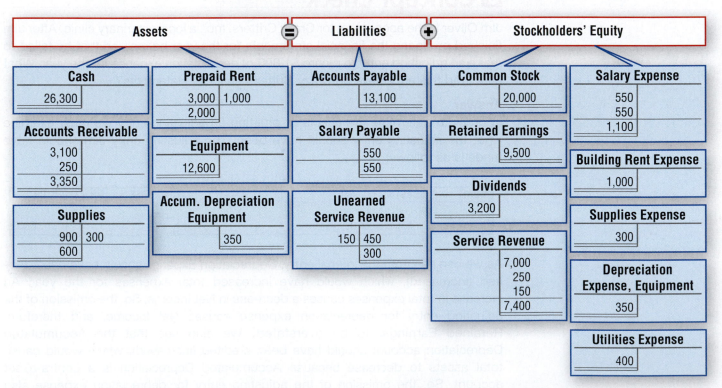

Exhibit 3-2 ▲

Prior to preparing the financial statements, an **adjusted trial balance** is prepared to make sure total debits still equal total credits after adjusting entries have been recorded and posted. The adjusted trial balance for Osborne Consulting is presented in **Exhibit 3-3**.

		ACCOUNT	DEBIT	CREDIT
		Cash	$26,300	
		Accounts Receivable	3,350	
		Supplies	600	
		Prepaid Rent	2,000	
		Equipment	12,600	
		Accumulated Depreciation, Equipment		$ 350
		Accounts Payable		13,100
		Salary Payable		550
		Unearned Service Revenue		300
		Common Stock		20,000
		Retained Earnings		9,500
		Dividends	3,200	
		Service Revenue		7,400
		Salary Expense	1,100	
		Building Rent Expense	1,000	
		Utilities Expense	400	
		Depreciation Expense, Equipment	350	
		Supplies Expense	300	
		Total	$51,200	$51,200

Osborne Consulting, Inc.
Adjusted Trial Balance
March 31, 2010

Exhibit 3-3 ▲

Preparing the Financial Statements

The March financial statements of Osborne Consulting, Inc., are prepared from the adjusted trial balance in Exhibit 3-3. The financial statements should be prepared in the same order that we used in previous chapters:

❶ The income statement (**Exhibit 3-4**) reports the revenues and the expenses to determine net income or net loss for a period of time.

❷ The statement of retained earnings (**Exhibit 3-5**) shows the changes in retained earnings during the period and computes the ending balance of retained earnings. Notice that the Retained Earnings balance of $9,500 on the adjusted trial balance does *not* represent the ending Retained Earnings balance because the account has not yet been updated for the current period's earnings or dividends.

❸ The balance sheet (**Exhibit 3-6**) reports the assets, liabilities, and stockholders' equity to see the financial position of the business at a specific point in time.

As we first discussed in Chapter 1, all financial statements include these elements:

■ Heading
1. Name of the entity, such as Osborne Consulting, Inc.
2. Title of the statement: income statement, statement of retained earnings, or balance sheet
3. Date, or period, covered by the statement: Month ended March 31, 2010, or March 31, 2010
■ Body of the statement

Osborne Consulting, Inc.
Income Statement
Month Ended March 31, 2010

Revenue:			
Service Revenue			$7,400
Expenses:			
Salary Expense		$1,100	
Building Rent Expense		1,000	
Utilities Expense		400	
Depreciation Expense, Equipment		350	
Supplies Expense		300	
Total Expenses			3,150
Net Income			$4,250

Exhibit 3-4 ▲

Osborne Consulting, Inc.
Statement of Retained Earnings
Month Ended March 31, 2010

Retained Earnings, March 1, 2010	$ 9,500
Add: Net Income	4,250
Subtotal	13,750
Less: Dividends	3,200
Retained Earnings, March 31, 2010	$10,550

Exhibit 3-5 ▲

Osborne Consulting, Inc.
Balance Sheet
March 31, 2010

ASSETS			LIABILITIES	
Cash		$26,300	Accounts Payable	$13,100
Accounts Receivable		3,350	Salary Payable	550
Supplies		600	Unearned Service Revenue	300
Prepaid Rent		2,000	Total Liabilities	13,950
Equipment	$12,600			
Less: Accumulated			**STOCKHOLDERS' EQUITY**	
Depreciation,	350		Common Stock	20,000
Equipment		12,250	Retained Earnings	10,550
			Total Stockholders' Equity	30,550
			Total Liabilities &	
Total Assets		$44,500	Stockholders' Equity	$44,500

Exhibit 3-6 ▲

On the income statement, expenses may be listed in descending order from the largest amount to the smallest amount, as Osborne Consulting did, or they may be listed in some other order, such as alphabetical order.

HOW DOES A COMPANY PREPARE FOR A NEW ACCOUNTING PERIOD?

Completing the Accounting Cycle

Prepare closing entries and a post-closing trial balance **4**

We have now seen steps one through six in the accounting cycle completed for Osborne Consulting. The entire accounting cycle can be completed by finishing steps seven and eight. Step seven of the accounting cycle is the journalizing and posting of the closing entries, and step eight is the preparation of a post-closing trial balance.

In order to complete the accounting cycle, **closing entries** must be journalized and posted. Earlier in the chapter, we processed the transactions for Osborne Consulting and prepared the financial statements for the month of March. If we continue recording information in the revenue, expense, and dividend accounts, we will lose track of what activity happened in March compared to what happens in April, making it impossible to prepare accurate financial statements for the month of April.

In order to not confuse the transactions from the two different months, the revenue, expense, and dividend accounts must be reset back to zero before we start recording transactions for April. It is similar to resetting the scoreboard at the end of a game before you start a new game. Since we must keep the accounting equation in balance, we cannot just erase the balances in the revenue, expense, and dividend accounts because it would cause the equation to become unbalanced. To keep the accounting equation in balance and still be able to zero out these accounts, we will use closing entries. Closing entries are utilized to accomplish two things:

- The revenue, expense, and dividend account balances from the current accounting period are set back to zero so that accounting for the next period can begin.
- The revenue, expense, and dividend account balances from the current accounting period are transferred into Retained Earnings so that the accounting equation stays in balance. Transferring the revenue and expense account balances into retained earnings actually transfers the net income, or net loss, for the current period into Retained Earnings. Transferring the dividend account balance into Retained Earnings decreases Retained Earnings by the amount of dividends for the period.

The revenue, expense, and dividend accounts are known as **temporary accounts**. They are called temporary because they are used temporarily to record activity for a specific period, the accounting period, and then they are closed into Retained Earnings. It is easy to remember the temporary accounts if you think of the color RED. The R in RED stands for revenues, the E stands for expenses, and the D stands for dividends. The RED accounts are closed at the end of each accounting period.

Before closing the accounts, the accounting equation for a corporation would be as follows:

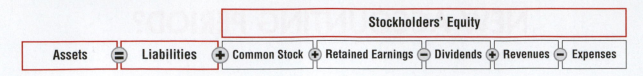

After closing the accounts, the accounting equation would be as follows:

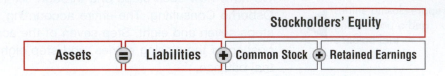

The accounts that remain in the accounting equation after closing are called **permanent accounts**. Assets, liabilities, common stock, and retained earnings are *not* closed at the end of the period because they are not used to measure activity for a specific period. Consider Cash, Accounts Receivable, Accounts Payable, and Common Stock. These accounts do not represent business activity for a single period, so they are not closed at the end of the period. Their balances carry over to the next period. For example, the Cash balance at March 31, 2010, becomes the beginning balance on April 1, 2010.

The Three Closing Entries: Revenues, Expenses, and Dividends

To journalize closing entries, complete the following steps:

Step 1 Close the revenue accounts and move their balances into the Retained Earnings account. To close revenues, debit each revenue account for the amount of its credit balance. Transfer the revenue balances to Retained Earnings by crediting the Retained Earnings account for the total amount of the revenues. This closing entry transfers total revenues to the credit side of Retained Earnings.

Step 2 Close the expense accounts and move their balances into the Retained Earnings account. To close expenses, credit each expense account for the amount of its debit balance. Transfer the expense balances to Retained Earnings by debiting the Retained Earnings account for the total amount of the expenses. This closing entry transfers total expenses to the debit side of Retained Earnings.

Step 3 Close the Dividends account and move its balance into the Retained Earnings account. To close the Dividends account, credit it for the amount of its debit balance and debit the Retained Earnings account. This entry transfers the dividends to the debit side of Retained Earnings.

Remember that Net Income is equal to Revenues minus Expenses. So, closing the Revenues and Expenses into Retained Earnings, Steps 1 and 2, has the effect of adding Net Income for the period to, or deducting a Net Loss for the period from, Retained Earnings. Once the Dividends account has been subtracted from Retained Earnings, Step 3, the balance in the Retained Earnings account should match ending retained earnings on the statement of retained earnings.

The process for making closing entries is the same as it is for making any entry; record the entries in the journal and post them to the proper accounts in the ledger.

Now, let's apply this process to Osborne Consulting, Inc., for the month of March:

Step 1

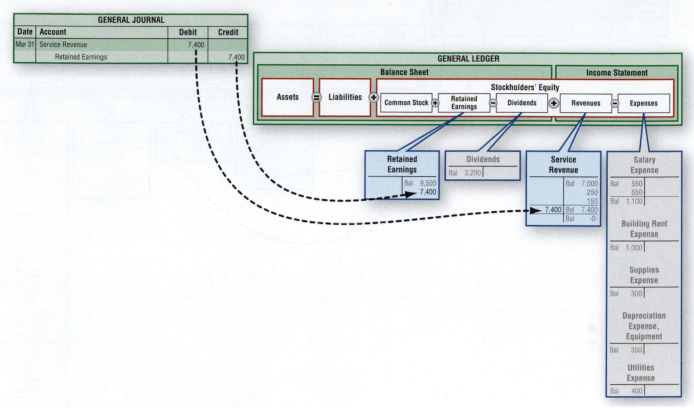

Step 2

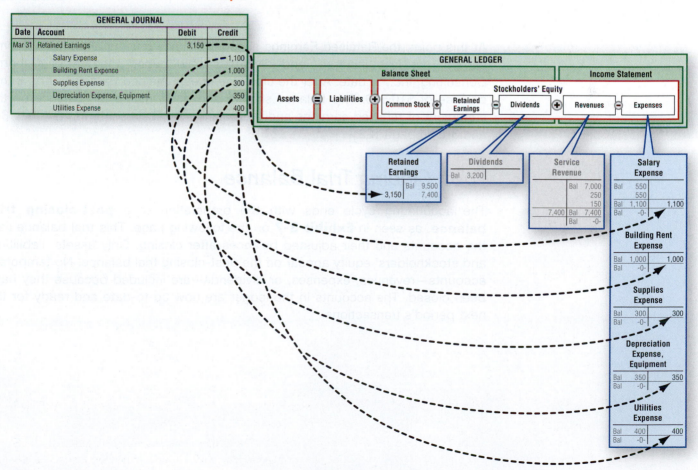

Step 3

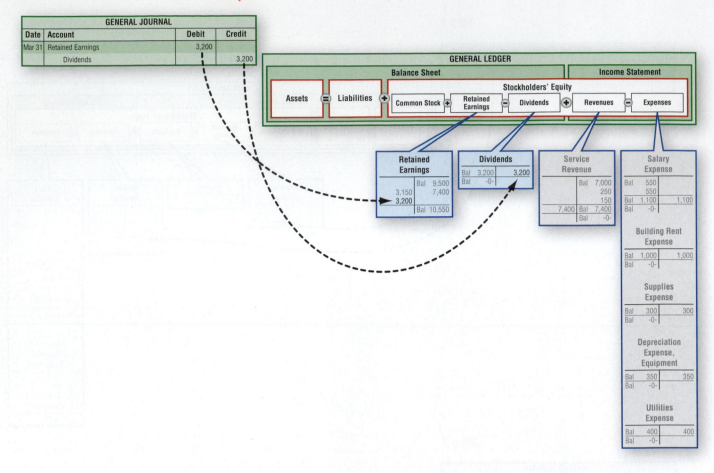

At this point, the Retained Earnings account balance reflects all the net income earned, net loss incurred, and dividends paid during the life of Osborne Consulting, Inc., to date. After the closing entries, Retained Earnings ends with a balance of $10,550. This balance should, and does, match the balance on the statement of retained earnings and the balance sheet presented in Exhibits 3-5 and 3-6 on page 122.

Post-Closing Trial Balance

The accounting cycle ends with the preparation of a **post-closing trial balance**, as seen in **Exhibit 3-7** on the following page. This trial balance lists the accounts and their adjusted balances after closing. Only assets, liabilities, and stockholders' equity appear on the post-closing trial balance. No temporary accounts—revenues, expenses, or dividends—are included because they have been closed. The accounts in the ledger are now up-to-date and ready for the next period's transactions.

		BALANCE	
Osborne Consulting, Inc. **Post-Closing Trial Balance** March 31, 2010			
ACCOUNT TITLE		**DEBIT**	**CREDIT**
Cash		$26,300	
Accounts Receivable		3,350	
Supplies		600	
Prepaid Rent		2,000	
Equipment		12,600	
Accumulated Depreciation, Equipment			$ 350
Accounts Payable			13,100
Salary Payable			550
Unearned Service Revenue			300
Common Stock			20,000
Retained Earnings			10,550
Total		$44,850	$44,850

Exhibit 3-7 ▲

Decision Guidelines

Decision		**Guideline**		**Analyze**
How do I ensure that my accounting records are ready to start a new period?		Prepare *closing entries* for the *temporary accounts*: • Revenues • Expenses • Dividends	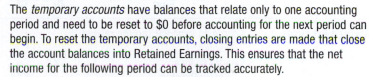	The *temporary accounts* have balances that relate only to one accounting period and need to be reset to $0 before accounting for the next period can begin. To reset the temporary accounts, closing entries are made that close the account balances into Retained Earnings. This ensures that the net income for the following period can be tracked accurately. Assets, Liabilities, Common Stock, and Retained Earnings do not get closed. These accounts are referred to as *permanent accounts*. Their balances are carried forward into the next period. After temporary accounts have been closed, a post-closing trial balance is prepared to ensure that all of the temporary accounts were properly closed.

Summary of the Adjusting and Closing Process

Businesses record adjusting entries at the *end* of the accounting period to accomplish two purposes:

❶ Report net income or net loss accurately on the income statement.

❷ Reflect the correct account balances on the balance sheet.

Each adjusting entry will always affect one income statement account, a revenue or an expense, and one balance sheet account, an asset or a liability. *Cash is never included in an adjusting entry because cash is always recorded accurately at the time it is received or paid*.

Deferrals and accruals can be summarized as follows:

❶ A *deferred revenue or expense* is paid first, and recorded as a revenue or expense later as the revenue is earned or the expense is incurred.

❷ An *accrued revenue or expense* is recorded as a revenue or expense first as the revenue is earned or the expense is incurred, and paid later.

Exhibit 3-8 summarizes the accrual and deferral adjustments.

				Adjusting Entries		
Deferrals: Cash transaction comes first.						
	First	Dr.	Cr.	Later	Dr.	Cr.
Prepaid Expenses,	*Pay cash and record an asset:*			*Record an expense and decrease the asset:*		
Depreciable Assets	Prepaid Rent	XXX		Rent Expense	XXX	
	Cash		XXX	Prepaid Rent		XXX
Unearned Revenues	*Receive cash and record a liability:*			*Record a revenue and decrease the liability:*		
	Cash	XXX		Unearned Service Revenue	XXX	
	Unearned Service Revenue		XXX	Service Revenue		XXX
Accruals: Cash transaction comes later.						
	First	Dr.	Cr.	Later	Dr.	Cr.
Accrued Expenses	*Accrue an expense and the related liability:*			*Pay cash and decrease the liability:*		
	Salary Expense	XXX		Salary Payable	XXX	
	Salary Payable		XXX	Cash		XXX
Accrued Revenues	*Accrue a revenue and the related asset:*			*Receive cash and decrease the asset:*		
	Accounts Receivable	XXX		Cash	XXX	
	Service Revenue		XXX	Accounts Receivable		XXX

Exhibit 3-8 ▲

Businesses record closing entries at the *end* of the accounting period to accomplish two purposes:

■ Zero out the revenue, expense, and dividend accounts.

■ Transfer the balance of the revenue, expense, and dividend accounts into Retained Earnings.

Closing entries are the end-of-period journal entries that get the temporary accounts-revenues, expenses, and dividends ready for the next accounting period by zeroing them out. Closing entries also transfer the balances from the temporary accounts into the Retained Earnings account. The post-closing trial balance is the final step in the accounting cycle. The post-closing trial balance is prepared to ensure that debits still equal credits before a new accounting period is started.

Demo Doc

Preparation of Adjusting Entries, Adjusted Trial Balance, Financial Statements, Closing Entries, and Post-Closing Trial Balance

Learning Objectives 2–4 ▶ Apex Architects, Inc., has the following unadjusted trial balance at December 31, 2010:

Apex Architects, Inc. Unadjusted Trial Balance December 31, 2010		
ACCOUNT	**DEBIT**	**CREDIT**
Cash	$124,000	
Accounts Receivable	96,000	
Supplies	3,500	
Prepaid Rent	24,000	
Land	48,000	
Building	270,000	
Accumulated Depreciation, Building		$135,000
Accounts Payable		118,000
Unearned Service Revenue		36,000
Common Stock		50,000
Retained Earnings		64,700
Dividends	46,000	
Service Revenue		486,000
Salary Expense	245,000	
Rent Expense	32,000	
Miscellaneous Expense	1,200	
Total	$889,700	$889,700

Apex Architects, Inc., must make adjusting entries related to the following items:

a. Supplies on hand at year-end, $800.

b. Six months of rent ($24,000) was paid in advance on September 1, 2010. No rent expense has been recorded since that date.

c. Depreciation expense has not been recorded on the building for 2010. The building has a useful life of 30 years.

d. Employees work Monday through Friday. The weekly payroll is $3,500 and is paid every Friday. December 31, 2010, is a Wednesday.

e. Service revenue of $18,000 must be accrued.

f. A client paid $36,000 in advance on August 1, 2010, for services to be provided evenly from August 1, 2010, through January 31, 2011. None of the revenue from this client has been recorded.

Requirements:

❶ Open the ledger T-accounts with their unadjusted balances.

❷ Journalize Apex Architects' adjusting entries at December 31, 2010, and post the entries to the T-accounts.

❸ Total all the T-accounts in the ledger.

❹ Prepare an adjusted trial balance.

⑤ Prepare the income statement, the statement of retained earnings, and the balance sheet. Draw arrows linking the three financial statements.

⑥ Journalize and post Apex Architects' closing entries.

⑦ Prepare a post-closing trial balance.

Demo Doc Solution

Requirement ❶

Open the ledger T-accounts with their unadjusted balances.

Part 1	Part 2	Part 3	Part 4	Part 5	Part 6	Part 7	Demo Doc Complete

Remember from Chapter 2 that opening a T-account means drawing a blank account that looks like a capital T and putting the account title across the top. To help find the accounts later, they are usually organized into assets, liabilities, stockholders' equity, revenue, and expenses (in that order). If the account has a beginning balance, it *must* be put in on the correct side.

Remember that debits are always on the left side of the T-account and credits are always on the right side. This rule is true for *every* account.

The correct side to enter each account's beginning balance is the side of *increase* in the account. We expect all accounts to have a *positive* balance, or more increases than decreases.

For assets, an increase is a debit, so we would expect all assets to have a debit balance. For liabilities and stockholders' equity, an increase is a credit, so we would expect all of these accounts to have a credit balance. By the same reasoning, we expect revenues to have a credit balance and expenses and dividends to have a debit balance.

The unadjusted balances to be posted into the T-accounts are simply the amounts from the unadjusted trial balance.

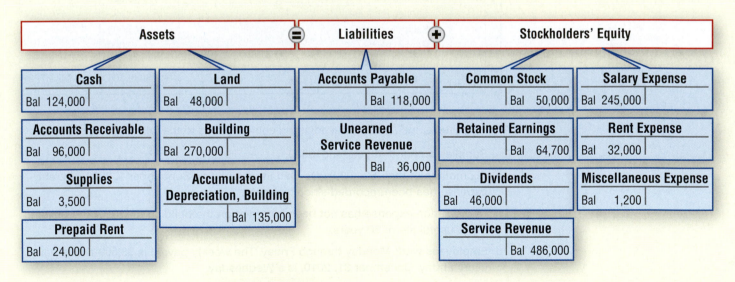

Requirement ❷

Journalize Apex Architects' adjusting entries at December 31, 2010, and post the entries to the T-accounts.

Part 1	**Part 2**	Part 3	Part 4	Part 5	Part 6	Part 7	Demo Doc Complete

a. Supplies on hand at year-end, $800.

On December 31, 2010, the unadjusted balance in supplies was $3,500. However, a count shows that only $800 of supplies actually remains on hand. The supplies that are no longer there have been used. When assets/benefits are used, an expense is created.

Apex Architects, Inc., will need to make an adjusting journal entry to reflect the correct amount of supplies on the balance sheet. The amount to be shown on the balance sheet is the actual amount of supplies on hand of $800. However, right now the Supplies account shows $3,500 (as we can see from the trial balance). This $3,500 is the "cost of asset available."

$$\text{Cost of asset available} - \frac{\text{Cost of asset on hand at}}{\text{the end of the period}} = \frac{\text{Cost of asset used (expense)}}{\text{during the period}}$$

$$\$3,500 \quad - \quad \$800 \quad = \quad \$2,700$$

The supplies have decreased because they have been used up. The $2,700 of supplies expense must be recorded to show the value of supplies that were used.

DATE	ACCOUNTS	POST REF.	DR.	CR.
Dec 31	Supplies Expense		2,700	
	Supplies			2,700
	Record supply expense.			

After posting, Supplies and Supplies Expense reflect correct ending balances:

ASSETS

Supplies

Bal	3,500	(a)	2,700
Bal	800		

EXPENSES

Supplies Expense

(a)	2,700	
Bal	2,700	

b. **Six months of rent ($24,000) was paid in advance on September 1, 2010. No rent expense has been recorded since that date.**

When something is prepaid, it is a *future* benefit (an asset) because the business is now entitled to receive goods or services. Once those goods or services are received (in this case, once Apex Architects, Inc., has occupied the building being rented), they become a *past* benefit, and therefore, an expense.

Apex Architects, Inc., prepaid $24,000 for six months of rent on September 1, which means that Apex Architects, Inc., pays $24,000/6 = $4,000 a month for rent. At December 31, prepaid rent is adjusted for the amount of the asset that has been used up. Because Apex Architects, Inc., occupied the building being rented for four months, we know that four months of the prepayment has been used. The amount of rent used is as follows:

$$4 \times \$4,000 = \$16,000$$

The amount of prepaid rent that will appear on the balance sheet is the amount of prepaid rent that has not been used. In this case, two months' worth of prepaid rent has not been used. 2 × $4,000 = $8,000. However, right now the Prepaid Rent account shows $24,000 (as we can see from the trial balance). This $24,000 is the "total asset to account for."

$$\text{Total asset to account for} - \frac{\text{Asset remaining}}{\text{at end of period}} = \frac{\text{Cost of asset used (expense)}}{\text{during the period}}$$

$$\$24,000 \quad - \quad \$8,000 \quad = \quad \$16,000$$

Because the $16,000 of prepaid rent is a *past* benefit, an expense is recorded. Rent Expense must be increased (a debit) and Prepaid Rent (an asset) must be decreased (a credit).

DATE	ACCOUNTS	POST REF.	DR.	CR.
Dec 31	Rent Expense		16,000	
	Prepaid Rent			16,000
	Record rent expense.			

ASSETS

EXPENSES

Prepaid Rent			
Bal	24,000	(b)	16,000
Bal	8,000		

Rent Expense		
Bal	32,000	
(b)	16,000	
Bal	48,000	

c. Depreciation expense has not been recorded on the building for 2010. The building has a useful life of 30 years.

Depreciation expense per year is calculated as follows:

$$\text{Depreciation Expense per Year} = \frac{(\text{Cost of Asset} - \text{Salvage Value of Asset})}{\text{Useful Life of Asset}}$$

The cost principle compels us to keep the original cost of a plant asset in that asset account. Because the Building account has a balance of $270,000, we know that this is the original cost of the building. No salvage value is mentioned in the question, so we assume it is $0. We are told in the question that the building's useful life is 30 years.

$$\text{Depreciation Expense per Year} = \frac{(\$270,000 - \$0)}{30 \text{ Years}}$$

$$= \$9,000 \text{ per Year}$$

We will record depreciation of $9,000 in the adjusting journal entry.

The journal entry to record depreciation expense is *always* the same. It is only the *number* (dollar amount) in the entry that changes. It always involves an increase to Depreciation Expense (a debit) and an increase to the contra-asset account of Accumulated Depreciation (a credit).

DATE	ACCOUNTS	POST REF.	DR.	CR.
Dec 31	Depreciation Expense		9,000	
	Accumulated Depreciation, Building			9,000
	Record depreciation expense.			

ASSETS

EXPENSES

ASSET

CONTRA-ASSET

Building		
Bal	270,000	
Bal	270,000	

Accumulated Depreciation, Building		
	Bal	135,000
	(c)	9,000
	Bal	144,000

Depreciation Expense, Building		
(c)	9,000	
Bal	9,000	

The book value of the building is its original cost (the amount in the Building T-account) minus the accumulated depreciation on the building:

Book Value of Plant Assets	
Building..	$ 270,000
Less: Accumulated Depreciation, Building............	(144,000)
Book Value of the Building................................	$ 126,000

d. **Employees work Monday through Friday. The weekly payroll is $3,500 and is paid every Friday. December 31, 2010, is a Wednesday.**

Salary is an accrued expense. That is, it is a liability that incurs from an *expense* that hasn't been paid yet. Most employers pay their employees *after* the work has been done, which means that the work is a *past* benefit. This is salary expense, and it grows each pay period until payday.

Apex Architects' employees are paid $3,500 for five days of work (Monday through Friday), which means they earn $3,500/5 = $700 per day. By the end of the day on Wednesday, December 31, the employees have worked for three days and have not been paid. Therefore, Apex Architects, Inc., owes employees $700 × 3 = $2,100 of salary at December 31.

If the salaries have not been paid, then they are pay*able* (or in other words, they are *owed*). They must be recorded in a payable account. We might be tempted to use Accounts Payable, but this account is usually reserved for *bills* received. Employees do not typically send their employers a bill. They simply expect to be paid and Apex Architects, Inc., knows that the salaries are owed. For this reason, we put this amount into another payable account. In this case, Salary Payable is most appropriate.

Because salary is not owed until work is performed, we know that Apex Architects' employees have already worked. We need to record an expense (in this case, Salary Expense) for the past benefit Apex Architects, Inc., received from its employees.

We record an increase to Salary Expense (a debit) and an increase to the liability Salary Payable (a credit) of $2,100.

DATE	ACCOUNTS	POST REF.	DR.	CR.
Dec 31	Salary Expense		2,100	
	Salary Payable			2,100
	Accrue salary expense.			

EXPENSES   **LIABILITIES**

Salary Expense			Salary Payable	
Bal	245,000		(d)	2,100
(d)	2,100		Bal	2,100
Bal	247,100			

e. **Service revenue of $18,000 must be accrued.**

Accrued revenue is another way of saying "receivable" (or receipt in the future). If *accrued* revenue is recorded, it means that a receivable is also recorded. Customers have received goods or services from the business, but the business has not yet received the cash. The business is entitled to these receivables because the revenue has been earned.

Service Revenue must be increased by $18,000 (a credit) and the Accounts Receivable asset must be increased by $18,000 (a debit).

DATE	ACCOUNTS	POST REF.	DR.	CR.
Dec 31	Accounts Receivable		18,000	
	Service Revenue			18,000
	Accrue service revenue.			

ASSETS

Accounts Receivable

Bal	96,000		
(e)	18,000		
Bal	114,000		

REVENUES

Service Revenue

		Bal	486,000
		(e)	18,000
		Bal	504,000

f. A client paid $36,000 in advance on August 1, 2010, for services to be provided evenly from August 1, 2010, through January 31, 2011. None of the revenue from this client has been recorded.

Apex Architects, Inc., received cash in advance for work not yet performed for the client. By accepting the cash, Apex Architects, Inc., also accepted the obligation to perform that work (or provide a refund if it did not). In accounting, an obligation is a liability. We call this liability "unearned revenue" because it *will* be revenue (after the work is performed) but it is not revenue *yet*.

The $36,000 paid in advance is still in the Unearned Service Revenue account. However, some of the revenue has been earned as of December 31. Five months of the earnings period have passed (August 1 through December 31), so five months' worth of the revenue have been earned.

The entire revenue earnings period is six months (August 1 through January 31), so the revenue earned per month is $36,000/6 = $6,000. The five months of revenue earned total:

$$5 \times \$6,000 = \$30,000$$

The amount of unearned revenue that will appear on the balance sheet is the amount of unearned revenue that remains at the end of the period. In this case, one month of unearned revenue remains: $1 \times \$6,000 = \$6,000$. However, right now the Unearned Service Revenue account shows a balance of $36,000 (as we can see from the trial balance). This $36,000 is the "total to account for."

Total unearned revenue to account for	−	Unearned revenue remaining at the end of period	=	Revenue earned during the period
$36,000	−	$6,000	=	$30,000

So Unearned Service Revenue, a liability, must be decreased by $30,000 (a debit). Because the revenue is now earned, it can be recorded as normal service revenue. Therefore, Service Revenue also increases by $30,000 (a credit).

DATE	ACCOUNTS	POST REF.	DR.	CR.
Dec 31	Unearned Service Revenue		30,000	
	Service Revenue			30,000
	Record unearned service revenue that has been earned.			

Essentially, the $30,000 has been shifted from "unearned" to "earned" revenue.

LIABILITIES

Unearned Service Revenue

(f)	30,000	Bal	36,000
		Bal	6,000

REVENUES

Service Revenue

		Bal	486,000
		(e)	18,000
		(f)	30,000
		Bal	534,000

Now we will summarize all of the adjusting journal entries:

DATE	ACCOUNTS	POST REF.	DR.	CR.
Dec 31	Supplies Expense		2,700	
	Supplies			2,700
	Record supply expense.			
Dec 31	Rent Expense		16,000	
	Prepaid Rent			16,000
	Record rent expense.			
Dec 31	Depreciation Expense, Building		9,000	
	Accumulated Depreciation, Building			9,000
	Record depreciation expense.			
Dec 31	Salary Expense		2,100	
	Salary Payable			2,100
	Accrue salary expense.			
Dec 31	Accounts Receivable		18,000	
	Service Revenue			18,000
	Accrue service revenue.			
Dec 31	Unearned Service Revenue		30,000	
	Service Revenue			30,000
	Record unearned service revenue that has been earned.			

Requirement ❸

Total all the T-accounts in the ledger.

Part 1	Part 2	**Part 3**	Part 4	Part 5	Part 6	Part 7	Demo Doc Complete

After posting all of these entries and totaling all of the T-accounts, we have the following:

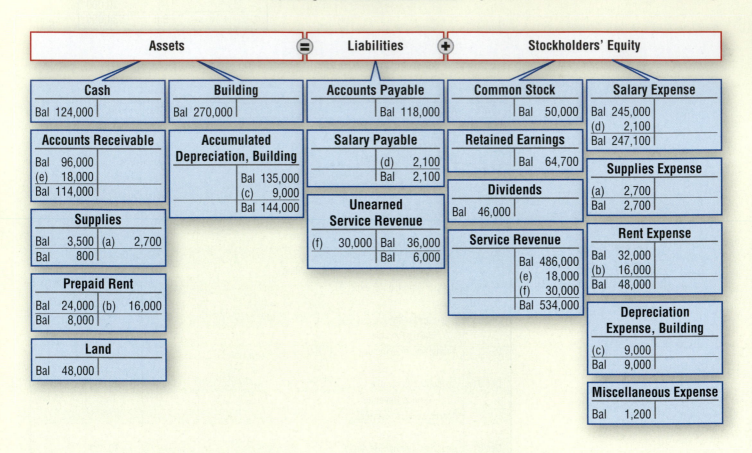

Assets = **Liabilities** + **Stockholders' Equity**

Cash
Bal 124,000

Building
Bal 270,000

Accounts Payable
| | Bal 118,000 |

Common Stock
| | Bal 50,000 |

Salary Expense
Bal 245,000
(d) 2,100
Bal 247,100

Accounts Receivable
Bal 96,000
(e) 18,000
Bal 114,000

Accumulated Depreciation, Building
	Bal 135,000
	(c) 9,000
	Bal 144,000

Salary Payable
| (d) 2,100 |
| Bal 2,100 |

Retained Earnings
| | Bal 64,700 |

Supplies Expense
(a) 2,700
Bal 2,700

Supplies
| Bal 3,500 | (a) 2,700 |
| Bal 800 | |

Unearned Service Revenue
| (f) 30,000 | Bal 36,000 |
| | Bal 6,000 |

Dividends
Bal 46,000

Rent Expense
Bal 32,000
(b) 16,000
Bal 48,000

Prepaid Rent
| Bal 24,000 | (b) 16,000 |
| Bal 8,000 | |

Service Revenue
	Bal 486,000
	(e) 18,000
	(f) 30,000
	Bal 534,000

Depreciation Expense, Building
(c) 9,000
Bal 9,000

Land
Bal 48,000

Miscellaneous Expense
Bal 1,200

Requirement ❹

Prepare an adjusted trial balance.

| Part 1 | Part 2 | Part 3 | **Part 4** | Part 5 | Part 6 | Part 7 | Demo Doc Complete |

<table>
<tr><td colspan="3" align="center">Apex Architects, Inc.
Adjusted Trial Balance
December 31, 2010</td></tr>
<tr><td>ACCOUNT</td><td>DEBIT</td><td>CREDIT</td></tr>
<tr><td>Cash</td><td>$124,000</td><td></td></tr>
<tr><td>Accounts Receivable</td><td>114,000</td><td></td></tr>
<tr><td>Supplies</td><td>800</td><td></td></tr>
<tr><td>Prepaid Rent</td><td>8,000</td><td></td></tr>
<tr><td>Land</td><td>48,000</td><td></td></tr>
<tr><td>Building</td><td>270,000</td><td></td></tr>
<tr><td>Accumulated Depreciation, Building</td><td></td><td>$144,000</td></tr>
<tr><td>Accounts Payable</td><td></td><td>118,000</td></tr>
<tr><td>Salary Payable</td><td></td><td>2,100</td></tr>
<tr><td>Unearned Service Revenue</td><td></td><td>6,000</td></tr>
<tr><td>Common Stock</td><td></td><td>50,000</td></tr>
<tr><td>Retained Earnings</td><td></td><td>64,700</td></tr>
<tr><td>Dividends</td><td>46,000</td><td></td></tr>
<tr><td>Service Revenue</td><td></td><td>534,000</td></tr>
<tr><td>Salary Expense</td><td>247,100</td><td></td></tr>
<tr><td>Rent Expense</td><td>48,000</td><td></td></tr>
<tr><td>Depreciation Expense, Building</td><td>9,000</td><td></td></tr>
<tr><td>Supplies Expense</td><td>2,700</td><td></td></tr>
<tr><td>Miscellaneous Expense</td><td>1,200</td><td></td></tr>
<tr><td>Total</td><td>$918,800</td><td>$918,800</td></tr>
</table>

Requirement ❺

Prepare the income statement, the statement of retained earnings, and the balance sheet. Draw arrows linking the three financial statements.

Part 1	Part 2	Part 3	Part 4	**Part 5**	Part 6	Part 7	Demo Doc Complete

Apex Architects, Inc.
Income Statement
Year Ended December 31, 2010

Revenue:			
Service Revenue			$534,000
Expenses:			
Salary Expense		$247,100	
Rent Expense		48,000	
Depreciation Expense, Building		9,000	
Supplies Expense		2,700	
Miscellaneous Expense		1,200	
Total Expenses			308,000
Net Income			$226,000

Apex Architects, Inc.
Statement of Retained Earnings
Year Ended December 31, 2010

Retained Earnings, January 1, 2010		$ 64,700
Add: Net Income for the Year		226,000
Subtotal		290,700
Less: Dividends		46,000
Retained Earnings, December 31, 2010		$244,700

Apex Architects, Inc.
Balance Sheet
December 31, 2010

ASSETS			LIABILITIES		
Cash		$124,000	Accounts Payable	$118,000	
Accounts Receivable		114,000	Salary Payable	2,100	
Supplies		800	Unearned Service		
Prepaid Rent		8,000	Revenue	6,000	
Land		48,000	Total Liabilities		$126,100
Building	$270,000				
Less: Accumulated			**STOCKHOLDERS'**		
Depreciation	144,000	126,000	**EQUITY**		
			Common Stock	50,000	
			Retained Earnings	244,700	
			Total Stockholders'		
			Equity		294,700
			Total Liabilities &		
			Stockholders'		
Total Assets		$420,800	Equity		$420,800

Requirement ⑥

Journalize and post Apex Architects' closing entries.

Part 1	Part 2	Part 3	Part 4	Part 5	**Part 6**	Part 7	Demo Doc Complete

We prepare closing entries for two reasons. First, we need to clear out the temporary accounts (the revenue, expense, and dividends accounts) to a zero balance. They need to begin the next period empty so that the next period's income statement can begin fresh. Second, we need to update the Retained Earnings account.

The first step in the closing process is to close the revenue accounts. Apex Architects, Inc., only has one revenue account, Service Revenue. Because the Service Revenue account has a credit balance we will need to debit it to bring its balance to zero. The credit side of the entry is to Retained Earnings. The effect of this entry is to move the revenues into the Retained Earnings account.

DATE	ACCOUNTS	POST REF.	DR.	CR.
Dec 31	Service Revenue		534,000	
	Retained Earnings			534,000
	Close revenue accounts.			

Service Revenue					Retained Earnings			
		Bal	486,000				Bal	64,700
		(e)	18,000				Clo	534,000
		(f)	30,000					
Clo	534,000	Bal	534,000					
		Bal	-0-					

The next step in the closing process is to close the expenses into the Retained Earnings account.

Each of the expenses has a *debit* balance. In order to bring the accounts to zero, we must *credit* them. The debit side of the entry will go to the Retained Earnings account:

DATE	ACCOUNTS	POST REF.	DR.	CR.
Dec 31	Retained Earnings		308,000	
	Salary Expense			247,100
	Rent Expense			48,000
	Depreciation Expense, Building			9,000
	Supplies Expense			2,700
	Miscellaneous Expense			1,200
	Close expense accounts.			

Salary Expense			
Bal	245,000		
(d)	2,100		
Bal	247,100	Clo	247,100
Bal	0		

Supplies Expense			
(a)	2,700		
Bal	2,700	Clo	2,700
Bal	0		

Rent Expense			
Bal	32,000		
(b)	16,000		
Bal	48,000	Clo	48,000
Bal	0		

Miscellaneous Expense			
Bal	1,200	Clo	1,200
Bal	0		

Retained Earnings			
Clo	308,000	Bal	64,700
		Clo	534,000

Depreciation Expense, Building			
(c)	9,000		
Bal	9,000	Clo	9,000
Bal	0		

The final step in the closing process is to close the Dividends account to the Retained Earnings account, which moves the amount from Dividends to Retained Earnings. The Dividends account has a debit balance of $46,000, so to bring that to zero, we *credit* the Dividends account for $46,000. The balancing debit goes to the Retained Earnings account:

DATE	ACCOUNTS	POST REF.	DR.	CR.
Dec 31	Retained Earnings		46,000	
	Dividends			46,000
	Close Dividends account.			

Dividends			
Bal	46,000	Clo	46,000
Bal	0		

Retained Earnings			
Clo	308,000	Bal	64,700
Clo	46,000	Clo	534,000
		Bal	244,700

Notice that all temporary accounts (that is the revenue, the expense, and the dividends accounts) now return to a zero balance and are ready to begin the next year.

Requirement ❼

Prepare a post-closing trial balance.

Part 1	Part 2	Part 3	Part 4	Part 5	Part 6	**Part 7**	Demo Doc Complete

Apex Architects, Inc.
Post-Closing Trial Balance
December 31, 2010

ACCOUNT	DEBIT	CREDIT
Cash	$124,000	
Accounts Receivable	114,000	
Supplies	800	
Prepaid Rent	8,000	
Land	48,000	
Building	270,000	
Accumulated Depreciation, Building		$144,000
Accounts Payable		118,000
Salary Payable		2,100
Unearned Service Revenue		6,000
Common Stock		50,000
Retained Earnings		244,700
Total	$564,800	$564,800

Notice that the post-closing trial balance only contains permanent accounts. This is because all of the temporary accounts have been closed and have zero balances.

DemoDoc Complete

Part 1	Part 2	Part 3	Part 4	Part 5	Part 6	Part 7	**Demo Doc Complete**

Decision Guidelines

Completing the Accounting Cycle

In completing the accounting cycle for your business, you might encounter the following decisions:

Decision	Guideline	Analyze
How do I know if my financial statements are accurate?	To produce accurate financial information, the revenue recognition principle and the matching principle should be followed.	The revenue recognition principle requires that revenues be recorded only when they are earned regardless of when cash is received.
		The matching principle requires that expenses be recorded when they are incurred regardless of when cash is paid. This ensures that expenses are matched with the revenues they helped generate.
		When the revenue recognition principle and the matching principle are followed it is referred to as *accrual accounting*.
How do I ensure that my accounting records are ready to start a new period?	Prepare *closing entries* for the *temporary accounts*: • Revenues • Expenses • Dividends	The *temporary accounts* have balances that relate only to one accounting period and need to be reset to $0 before accounting for the next period can begin. To reset the temporary accounts, closing entries are made that close the account balances into Retained Earnings. This ensures that the net income for the following period can be tracked accurately.
		Assets, Liabilities, Common Stock, and Retained Earnings do not get closed. These accounts are referred to as *permanent accounts*. Their balances are carried forward into the next period.
		After temporary accounts have been closed, a post-closing trial balance is prepared to ensure that all of the temporary accounts were properly closed.

ACCOUNTING VOCABULARY
THE LANGUAGE OF BUSINESS

Accounting cycle (p. 110) The sequence of steps used to record and report business transactions for a period of time.

Accounting period (p. 110) A period of time for which a business reports financial information; typically a month, a quarter, or a year.

Accrual accounting (p. 111) Accounting method that records revenues when earned and expenses when incurred without regard to when cash is exchanged.

Accruals (p. 111) Revenues earned or expenses incurred before cash has been exchanged.

Accrued expenses (p. 114) Expenses that have been incurred prior to being paid for.

Accumulated depreciation (p. 118) A contra-asset account that reflects all of the depreciation recorded for an asset to date.

Adjusted trial balance (p. 120) A list of all the accounts of a business with their adjusted balances.

Adjusting entries (p. 111) Journal entries made at the end of the accounting period to measure the period's income accurately and bring the related asset and liability accounts to correct balances before the financial statements are prepared.

Book value (p. 119) The asset's cost minus its accumulated depreciation; also called *carrying value*.

Carrying value (p. 119) The asset's cost minus its accumulated depreciation; also called *book value*.

Cash-basis accounting (p. 111) Accounting method that records revenues when cash is received and expenses when cash is paid.

Closing entries (p. 123) Journal entries that are prepared at the end of the accounting period. Closing entries zero out the revenue, expense, and dividends accounts so that accounting can begin for the next period.

Contra-account (p. 118) An account that is linked to another account. A contra-account will have a normal balance opposite of the account it is linked to.

Deferrals (p. 111) Cash received or paid before revenues have been earned or expenses have been incurred.

Deferred expenses (p. 115) Amounts that are assets of a business because they represent items which have been paid for but will be used later. Also called *prepaid expenses*.

Deferred revenue (p. 114) A liability created when a business collects cash from customers in advance of providing goods or services; also called *unearned revenue*.

Depreciation (p. 117) Allocation of the cost of a long-term asset to expense over its useful life.

Fiscal year (p. 110) Any consecutive, 12-month period that a business adopts as its accounting year.

Long-term assets (p. 117) Long-lived, tangible assets such as land, buildings, equipment, and furniture used in the operation of a business lasting for more than a year.

Matching principle (p. 111) Recording expenses in the time period they were incurred to produce revenues, thus matching them against the revenues earned during that same period.

Net value (p. 118) The amount found by subtracting the balance of a contra-account from the balance of the account it is linked to.

Permanent accounts (p. 124) The asset, liability, and stockholders' equity accounts; these accounts are not closed at the end of the period.

Prepaid expenses (p. 112) Amounts that are assets of a business because they represent items that have been paid for but will be used later; also called *deferred expenses*.

Post-closing trial balance (p. 126) A list of the accounts and their balances at the end of the accounting period after closing entries have been journalized and posted.

Revenue recognition principle (p. 111) Recording revenues when they are earned by providing goods or services to customers.

Salvage value (p. 118) The estimated value at the end of a long-term asset's useful life.

Straight-line depreciation (p. 118) A method of estimating depreciation: (Cost of the Asset – Salvage Value)/Useful Life of the Asset.

Temporary accounts (p. 123) The revenue, expense, and dividend accounts; these accounts are closed at the end of the period.

Unadjusted trial balance (p. 112) A trial balance that is prepared prior to the adjusting entries being made.

Unearned revenue (p. 112) A liability created when a business collects cash from customers in advance of providing goods or services; also called *deferred revenue*.

ACCOUNTING PRACTICE

DISCUSSION QUESTIONS

1. If XYZ Consulting performs a consulting service and bills the customer on June 28 and receives payment from the customer on July 19, on what date would revenue be recorded if

    a. XYZ uses the cash basis of accounting?

    b. XYZ uses the accrual basis of accounting?

2. What does the matching principle require companies to match?

3. Why does the time period in which revenue is recognized matter?

4. What is a deferral? Under which basis of accounting, cash or accrual, would deferrals come into play? Under what circumstances would a company record a deferral?

5. Why do companies prepare adjusting entries?

6. What are some similarities and differences between assets and expenses?

7. What type of account (asset, liability, revenue, or expense) would Joe's towing debit when it pays (credits) cash for each of the following transactions?

    a. Pays $100 to fill tow truck with gas

    b. Pays $1,000 to have a gas company deliver gas for its on-site refueling station

    Did you choose the same type of account or different ones? Why?

8. Describe the type of transaction that gives rise to a deferred revenue journal entry during the year. Why might deferred revenues require adjustment?

9. What kind of account is accumulated depreciation? How is it reported on the financial statements?

10. What are the objectives of the closing process? Which kind of accounts get closed? What is the only account that is affected by the closing process but not closed?

SELF CHECK

1. The revenue recognition principle says

    a. record revenue only after you have earned it.

    b. record revenue only when you receive cash.

    c. match revenues and expenses in order to compute net income.

    d. divide time into equal periods to measure net income or net loss properly.

2. Adjusting the accounts is the process of

    a. recording transactions as they occur during the period.

    b. updating the accounts at the end of the period.

    c. zeroing out account balances to prepare for the next period.

    d. subtracting expenses from revenues to measure net income.

3. Which of the following terms describe the types of adjusting entries?

    a. Deferrals and depreciation

    b. Expenses and revenues

    c. Deferrals and accruals

    d. Prepaid expenses and prepaid revenues

4. Assume that the weekly payroll of IDT, Inc., is $3,500. December 31, the end of the year, falls on Tuesday, but the company won't pay employees for the full week until its usual payday, Friday. What adjusting entry will IDT, Inc., make on Tuesday, December 31?

DATE	ACCOUNTS	POST REF.	DR.	CR.
a.	Salary Expense		1,400	
	Accumulated Salary			1,400
b.	Salary Expense		1,400	
	Cash			1,400
c.	Salary Payable		1,400	
	Salary Expense			1,400
d.	Salary Expense		1,400	
	Salary Payable			1,400

5. Unearned Revenue is always

   a. a liability.
   b. revenue.
   c. an asset.
   d. stockholders' equity.

6. The adjusted trial balance shows

   a. amounts that may be out of balance.
   b. revenues and expenses only.
   c. assets, liabilities, and common stock only.
   d. amounts that are ready for the financial statements.

7. Which of the following accounts is not closed?

   a. Salary Expense
   b. Service Revenue
   c. Accumulated Depreciation, Equipment
   d. Dividends

8. What do closing entries accomplish?

   a. Transfer revenues, expenses, and dividends to retained earnings
   b. Zero out the revenues, expenses, and dividends to prepare them for the next period
   c. Bring the Retained earnings account to its correct ending balance
   d. All of the above

9. Which of the following is not a closing entry?

DATE	ACCOUNTS	POST REF.	DR.	CR.
a.	Retained Earnings		300	
	Building Rent Expense			300
b.	Salary Payable		700	
	Retained Earnings			700
c.	Service Revenue		1,100	
	Retained Earnings			1,100
d.	Retained Earnings		600	
	Dividends			600

10. Which correctly represents the flow of information from one financial statement to another?

a. Income statement to the statement of retained earnings

b. Statement of retained earnings to the balance sheet

c. Both a and b are correct

d. None of the above is correct

Answers are given after Written Communication.

SHORT EXERCISES

S3-1. Accounting principles (*Learning Objective 1*) 5–10 min.

Match the accounting term with the corresponding definition.

_____ 1. Accrual basis accounting

_____ 2. Matching principle

_____ 3. Revenue recognition principle

_____ 4. Fiscal period

a. Any consecutive 12-month period.

b. Records the impact of a business event as it occurs regardless of whether the transaction affected cash.

c. Records expenses when incurred to sell goods or provide services.

d. Records revenue when it is earned.

S3-2. Accounting terminology (*Learning Objectives 2 & 3*) 5–10 min.

Match the accounting term with the corresponding definition.

_____ 1. Accumulated depreciation

_____ 2. Adjusted trial balance

_____ 3. Adjusting entry

_____ 4. Book value

_____ 5. Contra-account

_____ 6. Depreciation

_____ 7. Long-term asset

a. An account whose normal balance is opposite that of its companion account.

b. Entry made to assign revenues to the period in which they are earned and expenses to the period incurred.

c. A list of accounts with their adjusted balances.

d. The cumulative sum of all depreciation recorded for an asset.

e. The allocation of a long-term asset's cost to expense over its useful life.

f. The asset's cost less its accumulated depreciation.

g. Long-lived asset used to operate the business.

S3-3. Types of adjusting entries (*Learning Objective 2*) 5–10 min.

The trial balance of Sampson & Associates includes the following balance sheet accounts. For each account, identify the type of adjusting entry that is typically made for the account (deferred expense, deferred revenue, accrued expense, or accrued revenue), and give the related income statement account used in that adjustment. Example: Prepaid Insurance: deferred expense; Insurance Expense

a. Interest Payable

b. Unearned Service Revenue

c. Accounts Receivable

d. Supplies

e. Accumulated Depreciation

S3-4. Adjusting journal entry—prepaid rent (*Learning Objective 2*) 5–10 min.

Alpine Ski Shop's Prepaid Rent balance is $4,500 on June 1. This prepaid rent represents six months' rent. Journalize and post the adjusting entry on June 30 to record one month's rent. Compute the balances of the two accounts involved.

S3-5. Adjusting journal entry—supplies (*Learning Objective 2*) 5–10 min.

Alpine Ski Shop's Office Supplies balance on September 1 is $1,200 and the balance in Office Supplies Expense is $0. On September 30, there is $500 of supplies on hand. Journalize and post the adjusting entry on September 30 for the supplies used. Compute the balances of the two accounts involved.

S3-6. Adjusting journal entry—interest expense (*Learning Objective 2*) 5–10 min.

In order to purchase equipment and supplies, ProPaint, Inc., borrowed $30,000 on August 1 by signing a note payable to First State Bank. Interest expense for ProPaint, Inc., is $200 per month. Journalize an adjusting entry to accrue interest expense at December 31, assuming no other adjusting entries have been made for the year. Post to the two accounts affected by the adjustment.

S3-7. Adjusting journal entry—magazine subscriptions (*Learning Objective 2*) 5–10 min.

Wild Wonders, an outdoor magazine, collected $2,400 on April 1 for one-year subscriptions from subscribers in advance. Journalize and post the adjusting entry on December 31 to record the revenue that Wild Wonders has earned, assuming no other adjusting entries have been made for the year. Compute the balances of the two accounts involved.

S3-8. Adjusting journal entry—salaries, accured revenue, interest expense (*Learning Objective 2*) 5–10 min.

Journalize the following adjusting entries at December 31:

1. Services provided but not recorded, $1,500.
2. Salaries earned by employees but not recorded, $2,300.
3. Accrued interest on a note payable, $375.

S3-9. Adjusting journal entry—accrued service revenue (*Learning Objective 2*) 5–10 min.

Suppose you work summers mowing yards. Most of your customers pay you immediately after their lawn is mowed, but a few customers ask you to bill them at the end of the month. It is now September 30 and you have collected $1,200 from cash-paying customers. Your remaining customers owe you $150. How much service revenue would you record according to accrual basis accounting?

S3-10. Closing entires (*Learning Objective 4*) 5–10 min.

From the following list of accounts from the adjusted trial balance, identify each as an asset, liability, stockholders' equity, revenue, or expense. Use the most detailed account type appropriate. Also state whether each account is a permanent or temporary account, and if it is an account that gets closed at the end of the accounting period. Following the accounts is a sample of the format to use.

1. Depreciation Expense
2. Sales Revenue
3. Building
4. Cash
5. Unearned Service Revenue
6. Prepaid Rent
7. Dividends

Account	Type of Account	Permanent/Temporary	Closed
Supplies	Asset	Permanent	No

S3-11. Financial statements and closing entries (*Learning Objectives 3 & 4*) 10–15 min.

The following selected accounts and balances appear on the adjusted trial balance for Ray Service, Inc., on December 31, 2010:

Service Revenue	$1,200
Building Rent Expense	200
Salary Expense	300
Dividends	500
Common Stock	4,000
Retained Earnings	3,500

1. What is the net income or net loss?
2. What is the change in Retained Earnings?
3. Journalize the closing entries required.

S3-12. Adjusting and closing entries (*Learning Objectives 2 & 4*) 5–10 min.

For the following series of journal entries, indicate whether each is an adjusting entry (ADJ) or a closing entry (CL).

TYPE OF ENTRY (ADJ OR CL)	ACCOUNTS	POST REF.	DR.	CR.
	Salary Expense		400	
	Salary Payable			400
	Service Revenue		900	
	Retained Earnings			900
	Retained Earnings		1,500	
	Dividends			1,500
	Unearned Revenue		800	
	Service Revenue			800

S3-13. Preparing a post-closing trial balance (*Learning Objective 4*) 5–10 min.

After closing its accounts at October 31, 2010, Simmons Realty, Inc., had the following account balances:

Notes Payable	$2,000	Cash	1,850
Prepaid Rent	975	Service Revenue	0
Accounts Receivable	2,450	Retained Earnings	1,075
Prepaid Insurance	1,300	Common Stock	5,000
Accounts Payable	300	Salary Expense	0
Building	$1,800		

Prepare Simmons Realty's post-closing trial balance at October 31, 2010. List accounts in proper order.

EXERCISES (GROUP A)

E3-14A. Adjusting journal entries—unearned revenue and accrued revenue (*Learning Objective 2*) 10–15 min.

Suppose you started up your own landscaping business. A customer paid you $175 in advance to mow his or her lawn while he or she was on vacation. You performed landscaping services for a local business but the business hasn't paid you the $340 fee yet. A customer pays you $150 cash for landscaping services. Answer the following questions about the correct way to account for your revenue under accrual basis accounting:

1. Name the accounts used to record these events.
2. Prepare the journal entries to record the three transactions.

E3-15A. Adjusting journal entry—prepaid advertising (*Learning Objective 2*) 5–10 min.

Calculate the missing amounts for each of the following Prepaid Insurance situations. For situation A, journalize the adjusting entry. Consider each situation separately.

	Situation			
	A	B	C	D
Beginning Prepaid Insurance	$ 300	$ 600	?	$ 400
Payments for Prepaid Insurance during the year	1,200	?	1,300	?
Total amount to account for	?	?	2,000	1,900
Ending Prepaid Insurance	400	500	?	?
Insurance Expense	$?	$1,000	$1,200	$ 800

E3-16A. Common adjusting journal entries (*Learning Objective 2*) 10–15 min.

Journalize the adjusting entries for the following adjustments at December 31, the end of the accounting period, omitting explanations.

a. Employee salaries owed for Monday through Thursday of a five-day workweek equals $6,000.
b. Unearned service revenue now earned, $750.
c. Depreciation, $1,800.
d. Prepaid rent expired, $450.
e. Interest revenue accrued, $875.

E3-17A. Error analysis (*Learning Objective 2*) 10–15 min.

The adjusting entries for the following adjustments were omitted at year-end:

a. Prepaid insurance expired, $2,400.
b. Depreciation, $1,800.
c. Employee salaries owed for Monday through Wednesday of a five-day work-week, $2,700.
d. Supplies used during the year, $700.
e. Unearned service revenue now earned, $3,500.

Requirement

1. Compute the amount that net income for the year is overstated or understated by for each omitted entry. Use the following format to help analyze the transactions.

Transaction	Overstated/Understated	Amount
Sample a., b., etc.	Overstated	$5,000

E3-18A. Common adjusting journal entries (*Learning Objective 2*) 15–20 min.

Journalize the adjusting entry needed at October 31, the fiscal year-end, for each of the following independent situations. No other adjusting entries have been made for the year.

a. On September 1, we collected $4,800 rent in advance. We debited Cash and credited Unearned Rent Revenue. The tenant was paying six months' rent in advance.

b. The business holds a $30,000 note receivable. Interest revenue of $650 has been earned on the note but not yet received.

c. Salary expense is $1,700 per day, Monday through Friday, and the business pays employees each Friday. This year, October 31 falls on a Thursday.

d. The unadjusted balance of the Supplies account is $2,200. Supplies on hand total $700.

e. Equipment was purchased last year at a cost of $18,000. The equipment's useful life is four years.

f. On June 1, when we prepaid $1,500 for a one-year insurance policy, we debited Prepaid Insurance and credited Cash.

E3-19A. Common adjusting journal entries (*Learning Objective 2*) 15–20 min.

The accounting records of Vacations Unlimited include the following unadjusted balances at June 30: Accounts Receivable, $1,500; Supplies, $800; Salary Payable, $0; Unearned Service Revenue, $900; Service Revenue, $3,900; Salary Expense, $1,700; and Supplies Expense, $0. The following data pertain to the June 30 adjusting entries:

a. Service revenue accrued, $1,200.

b. Unearned service revenue that has been earned, $500.

c. Supplies on hand, $150.

d. Salary owed to employees, $1,100.

Requirement

1. Record the adjustments, then post them to T-accounts, labeling each adjustment by letter. Calculate each account's adjusted balance.

E3-20A. Income statement preparation (*Learning Objective 3*) 15–20 min.

The accountant for Henderson Roofing, Inc., posted adjusting entries (a) through (e) to the accounts at December 31, 2010. Selected balance sheet accounts and all the revenues and expenses of the entity follow in T-account form.

Accounts Receivable		Supplies			Accumulated Depreciation, Equipment		Accumulated Depreciation, Building	
21,000		2,800	(a)	1,200		5,600		28,000
(e) 1,500					(b)	1,400	(c)	2,000

Salary Payable				Service Revenue	
	(d) 2,900				97,000
				(e)	1,500

Salary Expense		Supplies Expense		Depreciation Expense, Equipment		Depreciation Expense, Building	
14,000		(a) 1,200		(b) 1,400		(c) 2,000	
(d) 2,900							

Requirements

1. Calculate balances in the accounts and use the appropriate accounts to prepare the income statement of Henderson Roofing, Inc., for the year-ended December 31, 2010. List expenses in order from largest to smallest.

2. Were the 2010 operations successful? Give the reason for your answer.

E3-21A. Statement of retained earnings preparation (*Learning Objective 3*) 10–15 min.

Sigma Security, Inc., began the year with $15,000 of common stock and $32,000 of retained earnings. On May 5, investors bought $12,000 of additional stock in the business. On August 22, the business purchased land valued at $65,000. The income statement for the year ended December 31, 2010, reported a net loss of $11,000. During this fiscal year, the business paid $800 each month for dividends.

Requirements

1. Prepare Sigma Security's statement of retained earnings for the year ended December 31, 2010.

2. Did the retained earnings of the business increase or decrease during the year? What caused this change?

E3-22A. Recreating adjusting journal entries (*Learning Objective 2*) 10–15 min.

The adjusted trial balances of PDQ, Inc., at December 31, 2010, and December 31, 2011, include these amounts:

	2010	2011
Supplies	$ 2,800	$ 1,700
Salary Payable	2,800	3,700
Unearned Service Revenue	18,000	16,300

Analysis of the accounts at December 31, 2011, reveals these transactions for 2011:

Purchase of supplies	$ 8,700
Cash payments for salaries	52,300
Cash receipts in advance for services revenue	106,400

Requirement

1. Compute the amount of supplies expense, salary expense, and service revenue PDQ, Inc., will report for the year ended December 31, 2011. Solve by making T-accounts and posting the information to solve for the unknown amounts.

E3-23A. Financial statement preparation (*Learning Objective 3*) 15–20 min.

The adjusted trial balance for Country Cookin Catering, Inc., is presented next. Prepare the income statement, statement of retained earnings, and balance sheet for Country Cookin Catering, Inc., for the month ended March 31, 2010.

Country Cookin Catering, Inc. Adjusted Trial Balance March 31, 2010		
ACCOUNT	**DEBIT**	**CREDIT**
Cash	$ 4,000	
Accounts Receivable	8,000	
Supplies	1,300	
Equipment	22,500	
Accumulated Depreciation, Equipment		$ 8,800
Accounts Payable		2,100
Salary Payable		600
Unearned Service Revenue		1,400
Common Stock		5,000
Retained Earnings		5,800
Dividends	800	
Service Revenues		18,600
Salary Expense	3,600	
Rent Expense	1,200	
Depreciation Expense, Equipment	600	
Supplies Expense	300	
Total	$42,300	$42,300

E3-24A. Prepare closing entries (*Learning Objective 4*) 10–15 min.

Requirements

1. Using the following selected accounts of A to Z Electrical, Inc., at April 30, 2010, prepare the entity's closing entries:

Common Stock	$ 18,000	Accounts Receivable	9,000
Service Revenue	127,000	Retained Earnings	6,500
Unearned Revenues	1,800	Salary Payable	800
Salary Expense	18,500	Depreciation Expense	8,200
Accumulated Depreciation	32,600	Building Rent Expense	5,100
Supplies Expense	1,700	Dividends	18,000
Interest Revenue	800	Supplies	1,800
Interest Expense	$ 2,300		

2. What is A to Z Electrical's ending Retained Earnings balance at April 30, 2010?

E3-25A. Statement of retained earnings preparation (*Learning Objective 3*) 10–15 min.

From the following accounts of Kurlz Salon, Inc., prepare the business's statement of retained earnings for the year ended December 31, 2010:

Retained Earnings					Dividends			
Clo	95,000	Jan 1	188,000	Mar 31	18,000			
Clo	76,000	Clo	234,000	Jun 30	14,000			
		Bal	251,000	Sep 30	23,000			
				Dec 31	21,000			
				Bal	76,000	Clo	76,000	

E3-26A. Prepare a post-closing trial balance (*Learning Objective 4*) 10–15 min.

The following post-closing trial balance was prepared for Cunningham Photography, Inc. Prepare a corrected post-closing trial balance. Assume all accounts have normal balances and the amounts are correct.

Cunningham Photography, Inc.
Post-Closing Trial Balance
December 31, 2010

ACCOUNT	DEBIT	CREDIT
Cash	$ 9,450	
Accounts Receivable	33,100	
Supplies		$ 1,900
Equipment		68,000
Accumulated Depreciation, Equipment	19,700	
Accounts Payable	11,450	
Salary Payable		2,500
Unearned Service Revenue	5,600	
Common Stock		30,000
Retained Earnings	43,200	
Total	$122,500	$102,400

E3-27A. Prepare closing entries (*Learning Objective 4*) 10–15 min.

The following is the adjusted trial balance of Qwik Care Clinic, Inc., for December 31, 2010.

Requirement

1. Journalize the closing entries at December 31.

Qwik Care Clinic, Inc.
Adjusted Trial Balance
December 31, 2010

ACCOUNT	DEBIT	CREDIT
Cash	$ 7,400	
Accounts Receivable	8,700	
Supplies	200	
Furniture	4,800	
Accumulated Depreciation, Furniture		$ 1,200
Equipment	32,000	
Accumulated Depreciation, Equipment		8,800
Accounts Payable		1,300
Salary Payable		3,500
Unearned Service Revenue		3,100
Common Stock		10,000
Retained Earnings		18,500
Dividends	14,000	
Service Revenues		73,000
Salary Expense	31,000	
Rent Expense	18,600	
Depreciation Expense, Equipment	1,600	
Depreciation Expense, Furniture	400	
Supplies Expense	700	
Total	$119,400	$119,400

EXERCISES (GROUP B)

E3-28B. Adjusting journal entries—unearned revenue and accrued revenue (*Learning Objective 2*) 10–15 min.

Suppose you started up your own landscaping business. A customer paid you $120 in advance to mow his or her lawn while he or she was on vacation. You performed landscaping services for a local business but the business hasn't paid you the $425 fee yet. A customer pays you $110 cash for landscaping services. Answer the following questions about the correct way to account for your revenue under accrual basis accounting:

1. Name the accounts used to record these events.
2. Prepare the journal entries to record the three transactions.

E3-29B. Adjusting journal entry—prepaid advertising (*Learning Objective 2*) 5–10 min.

Calculate the missing amounts for each of the Prepaid Insurance situations.

For situation A, journalize the adjusting entry. Consider each situation separately.

	Situation			
	A	**B**	**C**	**D**
Beginning Prepaid Insurance	$ 800	$1,100	?	$ 300
Payments for Prepaid Insurance during the year	1,500	?	1,600	?
Total amount to account for	?	?	3,200	2,700
Ending Prepaid Insurance	700	1,200	?	?
Insurance Expense	?	$ 500	$2,600	$1,400

E3-30B. Common adjusting journal entries (*Learning Objective 2*) 10–15 min.

Journalize the adjusting entries at May 31, the end of the accounting period. Omit explanations.

a. Employee salaries owed for Monday through Thursday of a five-day work week equals $7,500.

b. Unearned service revenue now earned, $1,250.

c. Depreciation, $1,900.

d. Prepaid rent expired, $550.

e. Interest revenue accrued, $980.

E3-31B. Error analysis (*Learning Objective 2*) 10–15 min.

The adjusting entries for the following adjustments were omitted at year-end:

a. Prepaid rent expired, $2,500.

b. Depreciation, $1,000.

c. Employee salaries owed for Monday through Wednesday of a five-day work-week, $3,100.

d. Supplies used during the year, $800.

e. Unearned service revenue now earned, $4,500.

Requirement

1. Compute the amount that net income for the year is overstated or understated by for each omitted entry. Use the following format to help analyze the transactions.

Transaction	Overstated/Understated	Amount
Sample a., b., etc.	Overstated	$5,000

E3-32B. Common adjusting journal entries (*Learning Objective 2*) 15–20 min.

Journalize the adjusting entry needed at August 31, the fiscal year-end, for each of the following independent situations. No other adjusting entries have been made for the year.

a. On July 1, we collected $3,000 rent in advance. We debited Cash and credited Unearned Rent Revenue. The tenant was paying six months' rent in advance.

b. The business holds a $35,000 note receivable. Interest revenue of $520 has been earned on the note but not yet received.

c. Salary expense is $2,900 per day, Monday through Friday, and the business pays employees each Friday. This year, August 31 falls on a Tuesday.

d. The unadjusted balance of the Supplies account is $1,400. Supplies on hand total $200.

e. Equipment was purchased last year at a cost of $8,000. The equipment's useful life is 10 years.

f. On April 1, when we prepaid $1,560 for a one-year insurance policy, we debited Prepaid Insurance and credited Cash.

E3-33B. Common adjusting journal entries (*Learning Objective 2*) 15–20 min.

The accounting records of Weddings Unlimited include the following unadjusted balances at April 30: Accounts Receivable, $1,900; Supplies, $1,100; Salary Payable, $0; Unearned Service Revenue, $1,300; Service Revenue, $5,300; Salary Expense, $3,100; and Supplies Expense, $0. The following data pertains to April 30 adjusting entries:

a. Service revenue accrued, $2,200.

b. Unearned service revenue that has been earned, $300.

c. Supplies on hand, $150.

d. Salary owed to employees, $700.

Requirement

1. Record the adjustments, then post them to T-accounts, labeling each adjustment by letter. Calculate each account's adjusted balance.

E3-34B. Income statement preparation (*Learning Objective 3*) 15–20 min.

The accountant for Metal Main, Inc., posted adjusting entries (a) through (e) to the accounts at August 31, 2010. Selected balance sheet accounts and all the revenues and expenses of the entity follow in T-account form.

Accounts Receivable			Supplies			Accumulated Depreciation, Equipment			Accumulated Depreciation, Building		
	19,200			2,200	(a) 1,600			4,200			46,000
(e)	2,250						(b)	1,400		(c)	1,000

Salary Payable				Service Revenue		
	(d) 2,500					6,400
					(e)	2,250

Salary Expense			Supplies Expense			Depreciation Expense, Equipment			Depreciation Expense, Building		
	13,500		(a)	1,600		(b)	1,400		(c)	1,000	
(d)	2,500										

Requirements

1. Calculate balances in the accounts and use the appropriate accounts to prepare the income statement of Metal Main, Inc., for the year-ended August 31, 2010. List expenses in order from largest to smallest.

2. Were the 2010 operations successful? Give the reason for your answer.

E3-35B. Statement of retained earnings preparation (*Learning Objective 3*) 10–15 min.

Zeta Safety, Inc., began the year with $15,000 of common stock and $34,000 of retained earnings. On August 5, investors bought $19,000 of additional stock in the business. On October 22, the business purchased land valued at $45,000. The income statement for the year ended December 31, 2010, reported a net loss of $5,000. During this fiscal year, the business paid $550 each month for dividends.

Requirements

1. Prepare Zeta Safety's statement of retained earnings for the year ended December 31, 2010.

2. Did the retained earnings of the business increase or decrease during the year? What caused this change?

E3-36B. Recreating adjusting journal entries (*Learning Objective 2*) 10–15 min.

The adjusted trial balances of CAS, Inc., at March 31, 2010, and March 31, 2011, include these amounts:

	2010	2011
Supplies	$ 1,700	$ 1,200
Salary Payable	4,000	4,500
Unearned Service Revenue	17,000	15,100

Analysis of the accounts at March 31, 2011, reveals these transactions for 2011:

Purchases of supplies	$ 9,000
Cash payments for salaries	55,500
Cash receipts in advance for service revenue	58,000

Requirement

1. Compute the amount of supplies expense, salary expense, and service revenue CAS, Inc., will report for the year ended March 31, 2011. Solve by making T-accounts and posting the information to solve for the unknown amounts.

E3-37B. Financial statement preparation (*Learning Objective 3*) 15–20 min.

The adjusted trial balance for Spruce Up Catering, Inc., is presented next. Prepare the income statement, statement of retained earnings, and balance sheet for Spruce Up Catering, Inc., for the month ended January 31, 2010.

Spruce Up Catering, Inc. Adjusted Trial Balance January 31, 2010		
ACCOUNT	**DEBIT**	**CREDIT**
Cash	$ 6,500	
Accounts Receivable	6,000	
Supplies	400	
Equipment	26,600	
Accumulated Depreciation, Equipment		$ 6,800
Accounts Payable		2,300
Salary Payable		1,100
Unearned Service Revenue		1,900
Common Stock		5,200
Retained Earnings		11,100
Dividends	1,100	
Service Revenue		20,100
Salary Expense	3,800	
Rent Expense	1,700	
Depreciation Expense, Equipment	1,500	
Supplies Expense	900	
Total	$48,500	$48,500

E3-38B. Prepare closing entries (*Learning Objective 4*) 10–15 min.

Requirements

1. Using the following selected accounts of Juba Electrical, Inc., at September 30, 2010, prepare the entity's closing entries:

Common Stock	$17,000	Accounts Receivable	$14,000
Service Revenue	49,000	Retained Earnings	7,900
Unearned Revenues	2,500	Salary Payable	700
Salary Expense	21,900	Depreciation Expense	5,000
Accumulated Depreciation	32,600	Building Rent Expense	5,600
Supplies Expense	2,300	Dividends	14,000
Interest Revenue	300	Supplies	2,300
Interest Expense	2,400		

2. What is Juba Electrical's ending Retained Earnings balance at September 30, 2010?

E3-39B. Statement of retained earnings preparation (*Learning Objective 3*) 10–15 min.

From the following accounts of Resch Restore, Inc., prepare the business's statement of retained earnings for the year ended January 31, 2010:

Retained Earnings					Dividends			
Clo	110,000	Feb 1	77,000	Apr 30	17,000			
Clo	82,000	Clo	299,000	Jul 31	14,000			
		Bal	184,000	Oct 31	24,000			
				Jan 31	27,000			
				Bal	82,000	Clo	82,000	

E3-40B. Prepare a post-closing trial balance (*Learning Objective 4*) 10–15 min.

The following post-closing trial balance was prepared for Fonzarelli Photo, Inc. Prepare a corrected post-closing trial balance. Assume all accounts have normal balances and the amounts are correct.

Fonzarelli Photo, Inc.
Post-Closing Trial Balance
March 31, 2010

ACCOUNT	DEBIT	CREDIT
Cash	$10,250	
Accounts Receivable	25,000	
Supplies		$ 600
Equipment		17,000
Accumulated Depreciation, Equip.	5,000	
Accounts Payable	8,800	
Salary Payable		5,200
Unearned Service Revenue	2,200	
Common Stock		20,000
Retained Earnings	11,650	
Total	$62,900	$42,800

E3-41B. Prepare closing entries (*Learning Objective 4*) 10–15 min.

The following is the adjusted trial balance of Happy Health, Inc., for August 31, 2010.

Requirement

1. Journalize the closing entries at August 31.

Happy Health, Inc. Adjusted Trial Balance August 31, 2010		
ACCOUNT	**DEBIT**	**CREDIT**
Cash	$ 9,000	
Accounts Receivable	11,000	
Supplies	170	
Furniture	5,200	
Accumulated Depreciation, Furniture		$ 1,800
Equipment	39,000	
Accumulated Depreciation, Equipment		4,500
Accounts Payable		1,200
Salary Payable		3,500
Unearned Service Revenue		2,200
Common Stock		18,000
Retained Earnings		7,970
Dividends	14,000	
Service Revenue		77,000
Salary Expense	27,000	
Rent Expense	6,000	
Depreciation Expense, Equipment	1,500	
Depreciation Expense, Furniture	1,300	
Supplies Expense	2,000	
Total	$116,170	$116,170

EXERCISES (ALTERNATES 1, 2, AND 3)

These alternative exercise sets are available for your practice benefit at
www.myaccountinglab.com

PROBLEMS (GROUP A)

P3-42A. Common adjusting journal entries (*Learning Objective 2*) 15–20 min.

Journalize the adjusting entry needed on December 31, the end of the current accounting year, for each of the following independent cases affecting Outdoor Adventures, Inc. No other adjusting entries have been made for the year.

a. Prior to making the adjusting entry on December 31, the balance in Prepaid Insurance is $2,400. Outdoor Adventures, Inc., pays liability insurance each year on April 30.

b. Outdoor Adventures, Inc., pays employees each Friday. The amount of the weekly payroll is $6,500 for a five-day workweek. December 31, the fiscal year-end, is a Tuesday.

c. Outdoor Adventures, Inc., received notes receivable from some customers for services provided. For the current year, accrued interest amounts to $350 and will be collected next year.

d. The beginning balance of Supplies was $1,800. During the year, $3,700 of supplies were purchased. At December 31, the supplies on hand total $2,200.

e. During the year, Outdoor Adventures, Inc., received $8,800 in advance for services to be provided at a later date. As of December 31, Outdoor Adventures, Inc., earned $5,100 of the total fees received during the current year.

f. Depreciation for the current year includes Vehicles, $2,850, and Equipment, $1,200.

P3-43A. Recreating adjusting journal entries from trial balance (*Learning Objective 2*)
15–20 min.

Assume the unadjusted and adjusted trial balances for Kristy's Consulting, Inc., at June 30, 2010, show the following data:

Kristy's Consulting, Inc.
Trial Balance
June 30, 2010

ACCOUNT	UNADJUSTED TRIAL BALANCE DR.	UNADJUSTED TRIAL BALANCE CR.	ADJUSTED TRIAL BALANCE DR.	ADJUSTED TRIAL BALANCE CR.
Cash	$ 6,200		$ 6,200	
Accounts Receivable	5,800		5,800	
Supplies	1,400		300	
Prepaid Rent	2,800		2,100	
Equipment	18,000		18,000	
Accumulated Depreciation, Equipment		$ 7,500		$ 7,750
Accounts Payable		1,800		1,800
Salary Payable				1,250
Interest Payable				150
Unearned Service Revenue		2,600		900
Notes Payable		7,000		7,000
Common Stock		5,000		5,000
Retained Earnings		4,900		4,900
Dividends	13,600		13,600	
Service Revenues		47,400		49,100
Salary Expense	23,400		24,650	
Rent Expense	3,500		4,200	
Depreciation Expense, Equipment	1,250		1,500	
Interest Expense	250		400	
Supplies Expense			1,100	
Total	$76,200	$76,200	$77,850	$77,850

Requirement

1. Journalize the adjusting entries that account for the differences between the two trial balances.

P3-44A. Prepare adjusting journal entries and an adjusted trial balance (*Learning Objectives 2 & 3*) 25–30 min.

The trial balance of Alpha Advertising, Inc., at November 30, 2010, and the data needed for the month-end adjustments follow:

	Alpha Advertising, Inc. Trial Balance November 30, 2010		
ACCOUNT		**DEBIT**	**CREDIT**
	Cash	$ 22,800	
	Accounts Receivable	39,400	
	Prepaid Insurance	2,700	
	Supplies	900	
	Equipment	83,800	
	Accumulated Depreciation, Equipment		$ 64,300
	Accounts Payable		1,900
	Salary Payable		
	Unearned Service Revenue		2,200
	Common Stock		50,000
	Retained Earnings		29,300
	Dividends	3,600	
	Service Revenues		8,400
	Salary Expense	2,900	
	Insurance Expense		
	Depreciation Expense, Equipment		
	Utilities Expense		
	Supplies Expense		
	Total	$156,100	$156,100

a. Insurance coverage still remaining at November 30, $300.

b. Supplies used during the month, $250.

c. Depreciation for the month, $1,200.

d. Accrued utilities expense at November 30, $300. (Use Accounts Payable as the liability account needed.)

e. Accrued salaries at November 30, $450.

f. Service revenue still unearned at November 30, $800.

Requirements

1. Open T-accounts for the accounts listed in the trial balance and insert their November 30 unadjusted balances.

2. Journalize the adjusting entries and post them to the T-accounts. Reference the posted amounts by letters, (a) through (f). Calculate the adjusted balance in each account.

3. Prepare the adjusted trial balance.

4. How will the company use the adjusted trial balance?

P3-45A. Effects of adjusting journal entries on income statement accounts (*Learning Objectives 2 & 3*) 20–25 min.

Helgeson Enterprises, Corp., completed the following selected transactions and prepared these adjusting entries during January:

Jan	1	Prepaid insurance for January through March, $750.
	3	Performed service on account, $1,800.
	6	Purchased office furniture on account, $350.
	8	Paid property tax expense, $600.
	12	Purchased office equipment for cash, $1,400.
	18	Performed services and received cash, $4,700.
	23	Collected $900 on account.
	26	Paid the account payable from the January 6 transaction.
	30	Paid salary expense, $2,400.
	31	Recorded an adjusting entry for January insurance expense related to the January 1 transaction.
	31	Recorded an adjusting entry for unearned revenue now earned, $400.

Requirements

1. State whether the transaction would increase revenues, decrease revenues, increase expenses, decrease expenses, or have no effect on revenues or expenses. If revenues or expenses are affected, give the amount of the impact on revenues or expenses for January. Use the following format for your answer.

	Revenues and Expenses for January	
Date	**Impact on Revenues or Expenses**	**$ Effect on Revenues or Expenses**
Jan XX	Increase Revenues	$500

2. Compute January net income or net loss under the accrual basis of accounting.

3. State why the accrual basis of accounting results in an accurate measurement of income.

P3-46A. Prepare financial statements (*Learning Objective 3*) 20–25 min.

The adjusted trial balance of Lighthouse Realty, Inc., at December 31, 2010, follows:

Lighthouse Realty, Inc.
Adjusted Trial Balance
December 31, 2010

ACCOUNT	DEBIT	CREDIT
Cash	$ 6,300	
Accounts Receivable	11,600	
Prepaid Rent	1,200	
Supplies	900	
Equipment	48,000	
Accumulated Depreciation, Equipment		$ 12,000
Accounts Payable		5,400
Unearned Service Revenue		2,100
Interest Payable		750
Salary Payable		1,800
Notes Payable		12,000
Common Stock		20,000
Retained Earnings		8,200
Dividends	14,000	
Service Revenue		97,000
Interest Revenue		650
Salary Expense	51,000	
Rent Expense	18,000	
Depreciation Expense, Equipment	4,200	
Utilities Expense	2,700	
Interest Expense	1,300	
Supplies Expense	700	
Total	$159,900	$159,900

Requirements

1. Prepare Lighthouse Realty's 2010 income statement, statement of retained earnings, and year-end balance sheet. List expenses in decreasing order on the income statement.

2. **a.** Which financial statement reports Lighthouse Realty's results of operations? Were operations successful during 2010? Cite specifics from the financial statements to support your evaluation.

   b. Which statement reports the company's financial position?

P3-47A. Prepare closing entries and a post-closing trial balance (*Learning Objective 4*) 20–25 min.

The June 30, 2010, adjusted trial balance of Energized Espresso, Inc., is shown next.

Energized Espresso, Inc. Adjusted Trial Balance June 30, 2010		
ACCOUNT	**DEBIT**	**CREDIT**
Cash	$ 4,900	
Accounts Receivable	9,600	
Prepaid Rent	1,800	
Supplies	600	
Equipment	26,000	
Accumulated Depreciation, Equipment		$ 4,200
Accounts Payable		2,400
Unearned Service Revenue		1,100
Salary Payable		1,800
Notes Payable		3,000
Common Stock		10,000
Retained Earnings		11,950
Dividends	2,000	
Service Revenue		43,000
Interest Revenue		400
Salary Expense	24,500	
Rent Expense	6,000	
Depreciation Expense, Equipment	1,200	
Utilities Expense	700	
Supplies Expense	550	
Total	$77,850	$77,850

Quick solution:

2. Retained Earnings = $20,400
3. Trial balance totals = $42,900

Requirements

1. Prepare the June closing entries for Energized Espresso, Inc.
2. Calculate the ending balance in Retained Earnings.
3. Prepare a post-closing trial balance.

PROBLEMS (GROUP B)

P3-48B. Common adjusting journal entries (*Learning Objective 2*) 15–20 min.

Journalize the adjusting entries needed at December 31, the end of the current accounting year, for each of the following independent cases affecting Waterfall Heights, Inc. No other adjusting entries have been made for the year.

a. Prior to making the adjusting entry on December 31, the balance in Prepaid Insurance is $3,000. Waterfall Heights, Inc., pays liability insurance each year on September 30.

b. Waterfall Heights, Inc., pays employees each Friday. The amount of the weekly payroll is $19,000 for a five-day workweek. December 31, the fiscal year-end, is a Thursday.

c. Waterfall Heights, Inc., received notes receivable from some customers for services provided. For the current year, accrued interest amounts to $875 and will be collected next year.

d. The beginning balance of Supplies was $1,600. During the year, $4,400 of supplies were purchased. At December 31, the supplies on hand total $2,500.

e. During the year, Waterfall Heights, Inc., received $14,500 in advance for services to be provided at a later date. As of December 31, Waterfall Heights, Inc., earned $5,100 of the total fees received during the current year.

f. Depreciation for the current year includes Vehicles, $2,170, and Equipment, $1,300.

P3-49B. Recreating adjusting journal entries from trial balance (*Learning Obejctive 2*) 15–20 min.

Assume the unadjusted and adjusted trial balances for Milky Way Theater, Inc., at November 30, 2010, show the following data:

Milky Way Theater, Inc.
Trial Balance
November 30, 2010

ACCOUNT	UNADJUSTED TRIAL BALANCE DR.	UNADJUSTED TRIAL BALANCE CR.	ADJUSTED TRIAL BALANCE DR.	ADJUSTED TRIAL BALANCE CR.
Cash	$ 9,200		$ 9,200	
Accounts Receivable	6,200		6,200	
Supplies	2,200		800	
Prepaid Rent	3,600		2,700	
Equipment	26,000		26,000	
Accumulated Depreciation, Equipment		$ 4,700		$ 6,200
Accounts Payable		2,600		2,600
Salary Payable				1,250
Interest Payable				290
Unearned Service Revenue		3,000		2,100
Notes Payable		7,000		7,000
Common Stock		15,000		15,000
Retained Earnings		2,900		2,900
Dividends	12,000		12,000	
Service Revenue		53,400		54,300
Salary Expense	23,600		24,850	
Rent Expense	4,800		5,700	
Depreciation Expense, Equipment	750		2,250	
Interest Expense	250		540	
Supplies Expense			1,400	
Total	$88,600	$88,600	$91,640	$91,640

Requirement

1. Journalize the adjusting entries that account for the differences between the two trial balances.

P3-50B. Prepare adjusting journal entries and an adjusted trial balance (*Learning Objectives 2 & 3*) 25–30 min.

The trial balance of Nina's Novelty, Inc., at September 30, 2010, and the data needed for the month-end adjustments follow:

		ACCOUNT	DEBIT	CREDIT
		Nina's Novelty, Inc.		
		Trial Balance		
		September 30, 2010		
		Cash	$ 25,000	
		Accounts Receivable	17,400	
		Prepaid Insurance	2,400	
		Supplies	1,200	
		Equipment	59,000	
		Accumulated Depreciation, Equipment		$ 50,000
		Accounts Payable		2,000
		Salary Payable		
		Unearned Service Revenue		2,400
		Common Stock		25,000
		Retained Earnings		22,800
		Dividends	9,700	
		Service Revenue		16,200
		Salary Expense	3,700	
		Insurance Expense		
		Depreciation Expense		
		Utilities Expense		
		Supplies Expense		
		Total	$118,400	$118,400

a. Insurance coverage still remaining at September 30, $800.

b. Supplies used during the month, $900.

c. Depreciation for the month, $2,200.

d. Accrued utilities expense at September 30, $1,000. (Use Accounts Payable as the liability account needed.)

e. Accrued salaries at September 30, $800.

f. Service revenue still unearned at September 30, $1,600.

Requirements

1. Journalize the adjusting entries.

2. The unadjusted balances have been entered in the T-accounts for you. Post the adjusting entries to the T-accounts. Reference the posted amounts by letters, (a) through (f). Calculate the adjusted balance in each account.

3. Prepare the adjusted trial balance.

4. How will the company use the adjusted trial balance?

P3-51B. Effects of adjusting journal entries on income statement accounts (*Learning Objectives 2 & 3*) 20–25 min.

Moore, Corp., completed the following selected transactions and prepared these adjusting entries during May:

May	1	Prepaid insurance for May through July, $2,700.
	3	Performed service on account, $2,500.
	6	Purchased office furniture on account, $900.
	8	Paid property tax expense, $500.
	12	Purchased office equipment for cash, $1,500.
	18	Performed services and received cash, $3,500.
	23	Collected $800 on account.
	26	Paid the account payable from the May 6 transaction.
	30	Paid salary expense, $1,300.
	31	Recorded an adjusting entry for May insurance expense related to the May 1 transaction.
	31	Recorded an adjusting entry for unearned revenue now earned, $1,100.

Requirements

1. State whether the transaction would increase revenues, decrease revenues, increase expenses, decrease expenses, or have no effect on revenues or expenses. If revenues or expenses are affected, give the amount of the impact on revenues or expenses for May. Use the following format for your answer.

Revenues and Expenses for May		
Date	**Impact on Revenues or Expenses**	**$ Effect on Revenues or Expenses**
May XX	Increase Revenues	$XXX

2. Compute May net income or net loss under the accrual basis of accounting.

3. State why the accrual basis of accounting results in an accurate measurement of income.

P3-52B. Prepare financial statements (*Learning Objective 3*) 20–25 min.

The adjusted trial balance for Destination Realty, Inc., at October 31, 2010, follows:

ACCOUNT	DEBIT	CREDIT
Destination Realty, Inc.		
Adjusted Trial Balance		
October 31, 2010		
Cash	$ 6,500	
Accounts Receivable	12,100	
Prepaid Rent	2,500	
Supplies	500	
Equipment	42,500	
Accumulated Depreciation, Equipment		$ 11,300
Accounts Payable		4,300
Unearned Service Revenue		2,800
Interest Payable		720
Salary Payable		9,000
Notes Payable		8,000
Common Stock		3,960
Retained Earnings		9,700
Dividends	5,000	
Service Revenue		85,000
Interest Revenue		420
Salary Expense	40,000	
Rent Expense	20,000	
Depreciation Expense, Equipment	2,500	
Utilities Expense	1,800	
Interest Expense	1,100	
Supplies Expense	700	
Total	$135,200	$135,200

Requirements

1. Prepare Destination Realty's income statement, statement of retained earnings, and year-end balance sheet. List expenses in decreasing order on the income statement.

2. a. Which financial statement reports Destination Realty's results of operations? Were operations successful during 2010? Cite specifics from the financial statements to support your evaluation.

   b. Which statement reports the company's financial position?

P3-53B. Prepare closing entries and a post-closing trial balance (*Learning Objective 4*)
20–25 min.

The September 30, 2010, adjusted trial balance of Java Jolt, Inc., is shown next.

		ACCOUNT	DEBIT	CREDIT
		Java Jolt, Inc.		
		Adjusted Trial Balance		
		June 30, 2010		
		Cash	$ 5,800	
		Accounts Receivable	7,000	
		Prepaid Rent	2,300	
		Supplies	300	
		Equipment	30,000	
		Accumulated Depreciation, Equipment		$ 3,800
		Accounts Payable		3,000
		Unearned Service Revenue		1,900
		Salary Payable		1,400
		Notes Payable		10,000
		Common Stock		3,100
		Retained Earnings		11,200
		Dividends	4,000	
		Service Revenue		41,000
		Interest Revenue		1,000
		Salary Expense	18,500	
		Rent Expense	5,400	
		Depreciation Expense, Equipment	1,700	
		Utilities Expense	800	
		Supplies Expense	600	
		Total	$76,400	$76,400

Requirements

1. Prepare the September closing entries for Java Jolt, Inc.
2. Calculate the ending balance in Retained Earnings.
3. Prepare a post-closing trial balance.

PROBLEMS (ALTERNATES 1, 2, AND 3)

These alternative problem sets are available for your practice benefit at
www.myaccountinglab.com

CONTINUING EXERCISE

This exercise continues the accounting process for Graham's Yard Care, Inc., from the continuing exercise in Chapter 2. Refer to the T-accounts and the trial balance that you prepared for Graham's Yard Care, Inc., at June 30, 2010.

Requirements

1. Open these additional T-accounts: Accumulated Depreciation, Equipment, Depreciation Expense, Equipment, Supplies Expense.
2. A physical count shows $20 of lawn supplies on hand at June 30, 2010. Depreciation on equipment for the month totals $30. Journalize any required adjusting journal entries and post to the T-accounts, identifying all items by date.

3. Prepare the adjusted trial balance.

4. Journalize and post the closing entries at June 30. Denote each closing amount as *Clo* and an account balance as *Bal.*

5. Prepare a post-closing trial balance.

CONTINUING PROBLEM

This problem continues the accounting process for Aqua Elite, Inc., from the continuing problem in Chapter 2. The trial balance for Aqua Elite, Inc., at June 30, 2010, should look like this:

		Aqua Elite, Inc. Trial Balance June 30, 2010		
		ACCOUNT	DEBIT	CREDIT
		Cash	$16,855	
		Accounts Receivable	3,800	
		Supplies	1,610	
		Land	15,000	
		Furniture	3,300	
		Equipment	4,700	
		Vehicles	31,000	
		Accounts Payable		$ 3,890
		Notes Payable		31,000
		Common Stock		38,500
		Dividends	2,800	
		Service Revenue		12,000
		Salary Expense	2,700	
		Rent Expense	1,800	
		Utilities Expense	1,225	
		Advertising Expense	325	
		Miscellaneous Expense	275	
		Total	$85,390	$85,390

During July, the following transactions occurred:

Jul	1	Paid three months' rent, $5,400.
	4	Performed service for a customer and received cash, $2,100.
	9	Received $3,600 from customers for services to be performed later.
	12	Purchased $750 of supplies on account.
	15	Billed customers for services performed, $2,800.
	16	Paid receptionist's salary, $675.
	22	Received $3,100 on account.
	25	Paid $2,800 on account.
	28	Received $1,200 cash for services performed.
	30	Paid $600 of dividends.

Requirements

1. Journalize the transactions that occurred in July. Omit explanations.

2. Using the four-column accounts from the continuing problem in Chapter 2, post the transactions to the ledger creating new ledger accounts as necessary, omit posting references. Calculate the new account balances.

3. Prepare the unadjusted trial balance for Aqua Elite, Inc., at the end of July.

4. Journalize and post the adjusting entries for July based on the following adjustment information.

   a. Record the expired rent.

   b. Supplies on hand, $350.

   c. Depreciation; $400 equipment, $210 furniture, $650 vehicles.

   d. Services performed but unbilled, $1,900.

   e. Accrued salaries, $675.

   f. Unearned service revenue earned as of July 31, $800.

5. Prepare an adjusted trial balance for Aqua Elite, Inc., at the end of July.

6. Prepare the income statement, statement of retained earnings, and balance sheet for the three-month period May through July, 2010.

7. Prepare and post closing entries.

8. Prepare a post-closing trial balance for the end of the period.

APPLY YOUR KNOWLEDGE

ETHICS IN ACTION

Case 1. Jennifer Baxter was preparing the adjusting journal entries for Jennifer's Java, a business that uses the accrual basis of accounting, in order to prepare the adjusted trial balance and financial statements. She knew that $750 of salaries related to the current accounting period had accrued but wouldn't be paid until the next period. Jennifer thought that simply not including the adjustment for these salaries would mean that salary expense would be lower, and reported net income would be higher than it would have been if she had made the adjustment. Further, she knew that the Salary Payable account would be zero, so the liabilities reported on the balance sheet would be less, and her business would look even better. Besides, she reasoned that these salaries would be reported eventually, so it was merely a matter of showing them in one period instead of another. Dismissing the reporting as just a timing issue, she ignored the adjustment for the additional salary expense.

Is Jennifer acting unethically by failing to record the adjustment for accrued salaries? Does it matter that, shortly into the new accounting period, the wages will ultimately be paid? Is it really simply a matter of timing? What are the potential problems of failing to include all the adjusting journal entries?

Case 2. Jim Anderson and his banker were reviewing the quarterly income statements for his consulting business, Anderson and Associates, Inc. The banker was impressed with the growth of sales revenue and net income for the second quarter this year as compared to the second quarter of last year. Jim knew it had been a good quarter, but didn't think it had been spectacular. Suddenly, Jim realized that he failed to close out the revenue and expense accounts for the prior quarter, which ended in March. Because those temporary accounts were not closed out, their balances were included in the second quarter amounts for the current year. Jim then realized that the banker had the financial statements but not the general ledger or any trial balances. Thus, the banker would not be able to see that the accounting cycle was not properly closed and that this failure was creating a misstated income statement for the second quarter of the current year. The banker then commented that the business appeared to be performing so well that he would approve a line of credit for the business. Jim decided to not say anything because he did not want to lose the line of credit. Besides, he thought, it really did not matter that the income statement was misstated because his business would be sure to repay any amounts borrowed.

Should Jim have informed the banker of the mistake made and should he have redone the second quarter's income statement? Was Jim's failure to close the prior quarter's revenue and expense accounts unethical? Does the fact that the business will repay the loan matter?

KNOW YOUR BUSINESS

FINANCIAL ANALYSIS

Purpose: To help familiarize you with the financial reporting of a real company in order to further your understanding of the chapter material you are learning.

This case will help you to better understand the effect of adjusting journal entries on the financial statements. You know that adjusting journal entries are entered in the journal and then posted to the ledger accounts. We do not have access to the journals and ledgers used by Columbia Sportswear, but we can see some of the adjusted accounts on the company's financial statements. Refer to the Columbia Sportswear income statements, "Statements of Operations," and the Columbia Sportswear balance sheets, in Appendix A. Also find footnote 4 titled "Property, plant, and equipment, net" and footnote 6 titled "Accrued Liabilities," which are two of the many footnotes included after the financial statements.

Requirements

1. Open T-accounts for the following accounts and their balances as of December 31, 2007. (Note that amounts from the Columbia Sportswear financial statements are in thousands.)

Accumulated Depreciation	$168,067
Accrued Salaries, Bonus, Vacation, and Other Benefits	$ 34,952
Accrued Product Warranty	$ 10,862
Accrued Cooperative Advertising	$ 6,877
Other Accrued Liabilities	$ 9,858

2. Using the following information for Columbia Sportswear's 2008 operations, make the appropriate journal entries.
   a. Full payment of the December 31, 2007, balances in the accrued liability accounts.
   b. Depreciation expense, $22,839.
   c. Accrued salaries and benefits expense, $29,437.
   d. Accrued product warranty expense, $9,746.
   e. Accrued cooperative advertising expense, $6,457.
   f. Accrued other (miscellaneous) expenses, $12,445.

3. Post the journal entries to the T-accounts you set up. Check the updated ending balances in each account against the balances reported by Columbia Sportswear as of December 31, 2008.

INDUSTRY ANALYSIS

Purpose: To help you understand and compare the performance of two companies in the same industry.

Go to the Columbia Sportswear Company Annual Report located in Appendix A. Now access the 2008 Annual Report for Under Armour, Inc. To do this from the Internet, go to the company's Web page for Investor Relations at *http://investor.underarmour.com/investors.cfm* and under Downloads on the right-hand side, go to 2008 Annual Report.

Requirement

1. By reviewing the financial statements of both companies, can you determine which method of accounting, cash or accrual basis, each of the companies used? How did you determine this? If one of the companies used the cash-basis and the other used the accrual basis, would it affect your ability to compare the two companies? Explain your answer.

SMALL BUSINESS ANALYSIS

Purpose: To help you understand the importance of cash flows in the operation of a small business.

It's the end of the month and cash flow has been a little slow, as it usually is during this time of the accounting period. It just seems to be a little slower this month. You know that Wednesday the 31st is payday, which always requires a large cash outlay. However, you also know that your bank is looking for a set of financial statements as of the end of the month because the loan on your building is coming up for renewal soon. In some of the previous meetings with your bankers, you know that they were always concerned with the cash balance, so you want to have your cash balance as high as possible.

You come up with a tentative plan to not only preserve some of your cash balance at the end of the month, but you believe it will also help your bottom line, your net income. That's the other thing that the bankers are always concerned about. You don't want to make any mistakes with your financial statements at this crucial point, so you decide to contact your CPA to run the idea by her. The conversation goes something like this:

"Good morning, Linda. This is Jerry from BCS Consultants, Inc. Our financial statements have to look really good this month because the bank is going to be scrutinizing them pretty closely for our pending loan renewal. I know that the two things they concentrate on are the cash balance and the net income. So, I've got a plan to help in both of those areas. I'm going to hold off paying my employees until after the first of the month. Plus, last month, I made a big insurance payment to cover me for the next six months, so I won't need to show any insurance expense this month. Both of those will help my net income because I won't be showing those expenses on my income statement. Plus, by not writing the paychecks until the first of the month, I'll be helping to show a higher cash balance. It's really only one day, but the bank won't know that my cash balance should be lower. These certainly sound like some good ideas that would help with my situation, but just in case, I wanted to check with you to see what you thought. Any comments?"

The first words out of the CPA's mouth are "Jerry, you know that your financial statements are prepared using the accrual basis of accounting."

Requirement

1. Complete the thought process of the CPA concerning Jerry's plan. What does she mean by the accrual basis of accounting? What affect will that have on the net income? Is Jerry correct in his assessment of the big insurance payment he made last month covering the next six months? What affect will that have on the net income? And in regard to the last item, what about Jerry's plan to keep the cash balance as high as possible and his statement "the bank won't know that my cash balance should be lower"?

WRITTEN COMMUNICATION

You received a letter from a disgruntled client concerning this year's tax return that you just completed for his or her company. The client's business is in the second year of operations, and you remembered that it seemed to be much more profitable this year than during the first year of operations. You also recall that this particular client's year-end work was assigned to a relatively new staff accountant, which might be part of the problem. The gist of the letter is that last year's taxable net income was about $25,000, and according to the company's calculations, the net income from this year should have been about $50,000. And so the client is wondering why the company is showing taxable net income of $75,000 on this year's return and paying income tax on that amount. You retrieve the file to review it and immediately see the problem. The staff accountant failed to make the closing entries at the end of the first year of operations!

Requirement

1. Prepare a letter to this client explaining the situation and most importantly, explaining the importance of doing closing entries at the end of each and every year. Also, suggest a solution to this problem for the client, knowing that just explaining the accounting issue might not be enough to retain this client in the future.

COMPREHENSIVE PROBLEM

JOURNALIZING, POSTING, ADJUSTING, PREPARING FINANCIAL STATEMENTS, AND CLOSING

Waters Landscaping, Inc., completed the following transactions during its first month of operations for January 2010:

a. Gary Waters invested $7,500 cash and a truck valued at $15,000 to start Waters Landscaping, Inc. The business issued common stock in exchange for these assets.

b. Purchased $300 of supplies on account.

c. Paid $1,200 for a six-month insurance policy.

d. Performed landscape services for a customer and received $800 cash.

e. Completed a $4,500 landscaping job on account.

f. Paid employee salary, $600.

g. Received $1,100 cash for performing landscaping services.

h. Collected $1,500 in advance for landscaping service to be performed later.

i. Collected $2,500 cash from a customer on account.

j. Purchased fuel for the truck, paying $80 with a company credit card. Credit Accounts Payable.

k. Performed landscaping services on account, $1,600.

l. Paid the current month's office rent, $750.

m. Paid $50 on account.

n. Paid cash dividends of $500.

Requirements

1. Record each transaction in the general journal. Use the letter corresponding to each transaction as the transaction date. Explanations are not required.

2. Post the transactions that you recorded in Requirement 1 in the following T-accounts.

Cash	Salary Payable	Service Revenue
Accounts Receivable	Unearned Service Revenue	Salary Expense
Supplies	Common Stock	Depreciation Expense
Prepaid Insurance	Retained Earnings	Insurance Expense
Truck	Dividends	Fuel Expense
Accumulated Depreciation		Rent Expense
Accounts Payable		Supplies Expense

3. Prepare an unadjusted trial balance as of January 31, 2010.

4. Journalize and post the adjusting journal entries based on the following information:

    a. Accrued salary expense, $600.

    b. Depreciation expense, $375.

    c. Record the expiration of one month's insurance.

    d. Supplies on hand, $75.

    e. Earned 1/3 of the Unearned Service Revenue during January.

5. Prepare an adjusted trial balance as of January 31, 2010. Use the adjusted trial balance to prepare Waters Landscaping's income statement, statement of retained earnings, and balance sheet for January. On the income statement list expenses in decreasing order by amount—that is, the largest expense first, the smallest expense last.

6. Journalize and post the closing entries.

7. Prepare a post-closing trial balance at January 31, 2010.

CHAPTER 4

Accounting for a Merchandising Business

Although service businesses are the predominant type of business in the U.S., they are not the only type. The U.S. also has a significant number of merchandising businesses. Now that you have learned how to account for a service business, maybe you wonder how much different the accounting is for a merchandiser. Do the financial statements that a merchandiser prepares differ from those of a service organization? In Chapter 4, you will discover the answers to these questions as we explore accounting for merchandise organizations.

Chapter Outline:

Learning Objectives

1. Describe the relationship between wholesalers, retailers, and customers

2. Define periodic and perpetual inventory systems

3. Journalize transactions for the purchase of inventory

4. Journalize transactions for the sale of inventory

5. Understand shipping terms and journalize transactions for freight charges and other selling expenses

6. Prepare a multi-step income statement and a classified balance sheet

7. Compute the gross profit percentage and the current ratio

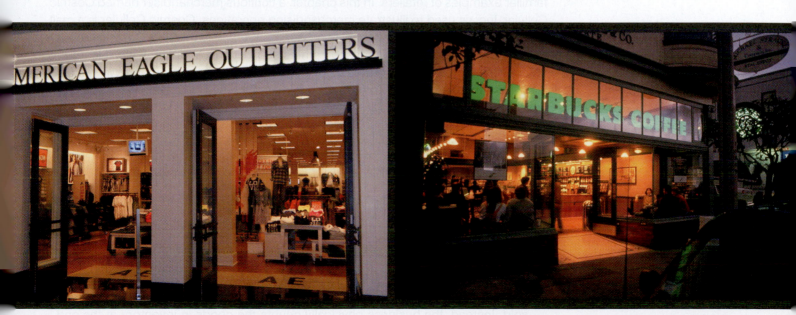

WHAT IS THE RELATIONSHIP BETWEEN WHOLESALERS, RETAILERS, AND CUSTOMERS?

Describe the relationship between wholesalers, retailers, and customers **1**

In Chapters 1–3, you learned how to account for a service business. In this chapter, you will learn how to account for a merchandising business. A merchandising business buys and sells products, called **merchandise inventory**, instead of services. Inventory is a very important asset to a merchandising business because it reflects the amount of goods the business has available to sell to its customers. Throughout the remainder of the book, we will refer to merchandise inventory simply as **inventory**.

A merchandising business can be either a **wholesaler** or a **retailer**. Wholesalers generally purchase large lots of products from manufacturers and resell them to retailers. Retailers buy goods from wholesalers and resell them to the final consumers, the general public. It is also possible for a retailer to purchase products directly from a manufacturer. **Exhibit 4-1** shows the relationship between manufacturers, wholesalers, retailers, and customers.

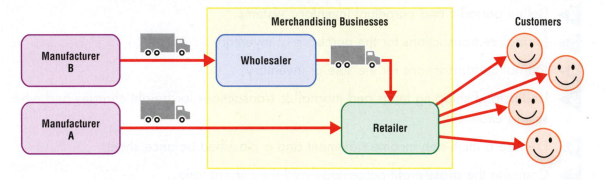

Exhibit 4-1 ▲

The discount chain Wal-Mart and the Internet merchandiser, Amazon.com are familiar examples of retailers. In this chapter, a fictitious merchandiser named Cosmic Cellular, Inc., is used to illustrate merchandising operations. Cosmic Cellular is a mall retailer that sells cell phones and accessories. We will learn how Cosmic Cellular records entries related to purchases from its suppliers. In addition, we will learn the entries Cosmic uses to record sales of merchandise to its customers. We will also learn how the type of inventory tracking system chosen by Cosmic will impact the journal entries that it must make.

HOW DO PERIODIC AND PERPETUAL INVENTORY SYSTEMS DIFFER?

Define periodic and perpetual inventory systems **2**

Merchandisers use one of two inventory tracking systems:

- The **periodic inventory system** is a system of accounting for inventory that does *not* keep a continuous, running record of inventory as it is bought and sold. Instead, the business physically counts the goods in inventory at the end of the accounting period. It then multiplies the quantity of each item by its cost to get the total value of the ending inventory. Once the ending inventory has been determined, a business will calculate the cost of the inventory it has sold during the period using the following formula:

$$
\begin{array}{l}
\text{Beginning Inventory} \\
\text{+ Purchases} \\
\hline
\text{= Cost of Goods Available for Sale} \\
\text{− Ending Inventory} \\
\hline
\text{= Cost of Goods Sold}
\end{array}
$$

Historically, businesses that sold large quantities of relatively inexpensive goods used the periodic inventory system because it was too costly and time consuming to track the inventory items that were sold. Currently, thanks to innovations in inventory tracking technology, most businesses utilize a perpetual inventory system.

- The **perpetual inventory system** is a system of accounting for inventory that keeps a running record of inventory as it is bought and sold. Every time the business engages in a transaction involving inventory, the balance in the inventory account is immediately updated. By doing this, the inventory balance is *perpetually* up-to-date. However, the business must still physically count inventory at least once a year to see whether any goods have been lost, damaged, or stolen. Just because the accounting records indicate that a certain amount of inventory exists, it doesn't mean that this amount is actually on hand. If the actual inventory count is different than the perpetual records indicate, the perpetual records are adjusted to reflect the physical count. The general ledger is also updated by debiting or crediting the inventory account as needed. The offsetting debit or credit is to the Cost of Goods Sold account. Technology makes it easier for almost any business to use the perpetual system. Usually, a cash register used in a perpetual system is connected to a bar code scanner. When an inventory item is scanned, not only is the sale recorded, but the inventory records are simultaneously updated. Because the perpetual inventory system is more commonly used, we will use it to illustrate the transactions for Cosmic Cellular.

Decision Guidelines

Decision		Guideline		Analyze
Which inventory system should my business use?		This decision depends on whether or not you plan on utilizing a computer system to help with inventory management.		The *perpetual system* shows the current, correct amounts of inventory on hand and the cost of goods sold at all times.
				The *periodic system* requires that a physical count of the inventory be taken in order to know the correct balances of inventory and cost of goods sold.
				Before computers, only businesses that sold smaller quantities of higher cost items could use the perpetual method. Today, thanks to computers and other technology, most companies utilize the perpetual method even if they sell a high quantity of low cost items.

HOW DO YOU ACCOUNT FOR THE PURCHASE OF INVENTORY?

Journalize transactions for the purchase of inventory **3**

Throughout the year, merchandisers engage in a number of inventory transactions with suppliers including cash purchases, credit purchases, **purchase returns and allowances**, and **purchase discounts**. Let's examine how Cosmic Cellular accounts for these types of transactions.

Cash and Credit Purchases

Cosmic Cellular purchases 300 cell phone cases from Accessories Unlimited on account at a cost of $25 each. Therefore, the total value of Cosmic's purchase is $7,500 (300 cases × $25). Cosmic Cellular receives the goods on February 1 and records this purchase as follows:

DATE	ACCOUNTS	POST REF.	DR.	CR.
Feb 1	Inventory		7,500	
	Accounts Payable—Accessories Unlimited			7,500
	Record purchase of inventory on account.			

The purchase of inventory on account increases both Cosmic Cellular's assets and liabilities. The Inventory account reflects the cost of goods purchased for resale. The balance increases every time inventory is purchased. Inventory is an asset until it is sold because, as discussed in Chapter 1, assets represent things of value that the business has.

Notice that the name of the supplier is listed in the journal entry following Accounts Payable. The supplier's name is used because the amount owed to each individual supplier will be posted to a **subsidiary ledger** in addition to the Accounts Payable account in the general ledger. The subsidiary ledger contains a record for each separate supplier. If everything has been posted correctly, the total of the account balances in the accounts payable subsidiary ledger will equal the accounts payable account balance in the general ledger. This way, a merchandiser can keep track of the amount of accounts payable owed to each individual supplier.

Some suppliers may require cash to be paid at the time of shipment. If Accessories Unlimited required cash payment for the 300 cell phone cases at the time of sale, Cosmic Cellular would record the cash purchase as follows:

DATE	ACCOUNTS	POST REF.	DR.	CR.
Feb 1	Inventory		7,500	
	Cash			7,500
	Record purchase of inventory for cash.			

Purchase Returns and Allowances

Occasionally, merchandisers buy goods that are not satisfactory. In these cases, most suppliers allow the goods to be returned. Or, they may allow the merchandiser to keep the unsuitable goods and receive a deduction, or allowance, from the amount they owe for the merchandise. Both purchase returns and allowances decrease the merchandiser's cost of the inventory.

Suppose Cosmic Cellular buys 20 hands free headsets for $20 each from Mega Mobile, and these headsets become damaged in shipment. If Cosmic returns the merchandise to Mega Mobile, it will issue a **debit memorandum**. A debit memorandum is a document that supports the return of goods to the supplier, as illustrated in **Exhibit 4-2**.

COSMIC CELLULAR
1471 E. Union St.
Seattle, WA

DEBIT MEMORANDUM #47

To: Mega Mobile   Date: April 5, 2010
9 Rio Rancho Drive
San Antonio, TX

We debit your account balance for the following:

20 T180 Headsets @ $20 each   **$400**

Exhibit 4-2 ▲

A debit memorandum gets its name from the fact that the issuer's Accounts Payable account will be debited as a result of the return of the goods. Upon issuing the debit memorandum, Cosmic will *debit*, or reduce, its Accounts Payable balance for the value of the merchandise returned. Cosmic will also reduce the inventory account by the amount of the return because it no longer has this inventory. Cosmic records the purchase return as follows:

DATE	ACCOUNTS	POST REF.	DR.	CR.
Apr 5	Accounts Payable—Mega Mobile		400	
	Inventory			400
	Record inventory returned to manufacturer.			

Purchase Discounts

Exhibit 4-3 on the following page illustrates Accessories Unlimited's invoice for Cosmic's $7,500 purchase of inventory. A **sales invoice** is a bill that documents the sale of goods to a business customer. The invoice includes **credit terms**, or the payment terms, for customers who buy on account. A customer may pay cash when it receives the goods or it may pay within a period of time following the receipt of those goods. Merchandisers use credit terms on sales to communicate to the customer when payment is due. Often, merchandisers will use the term **n/30**, which means that the sales price for the goods must be paid within 30 days after the date of the invoice. If the amount is due at the end of the month, the invoice will include the phrase **n/eom** or just **eom**.

All businesses want to have enough cash to pay their bills on time. Therefore, suppliers often offer merchandisers purchase discounts for early payment in order to improve their cash inflow. By rewarding the merchandiser for paying amounts before the due date, these companies get cash sooner. The time period in which the

Accessories UNLIMITED					Invoice	
Accessories Unlimited P.O. Box 873 Redding, CA					Date	Number
					2/1/10	644
Shipped to:	Cosmic Cellular 1471 E. Union St. Seattle, WA				Terms: 3/15, n/30	
Quantity	Item			Unit Price		Total
300 each	Cell phone cases			$ 25		$ 7,500
			Subtotal			$ 7,500
			Shipping Charge			–
			Tax			–
			Total			$ 7,500

Exhibit 4-3 ▲

merchandiser may pay and receive the discount is called the **discount period**. If the merchandiser takes advantage of this offer and pays early, then these discounts represent a reduction in the cost of the merchandise purchased.

Review Accessories Unlimited's invoice in Exhibit 4-3. Accessories Unlimited's credit terms of "3/15, n/30" mean that Cosmic Cellular may deduct 3% of the total amount due to Accessories Unlimited if it pays within 15 days of the invoice date. Otherwise, the full amount is due in 30 days. In this case, the discount period covers 15 days. However, if Accessories Unlimited listed terms of "n/30" instead of "3/15, n/30," it would mean that it was not offering a discount at all, and payment is due 30 days after the invoice date.

If Cosmic Cellular pays within the discount period, it will pay $7,275, or 97% of the purchase invoice amount of $7,500:

Invoice Total	$7,500	(100% of invoice amount)
– Purchase Discount	(225)	(3% of invoice amount, or .03 × $7,500)
= Cash Paid	$7,275	(97% of invoice amount, or .97 × $7,500)

Cosmic records its payment on February 13, which is within the discount period, as shown:

DATE	ACCOUNTS	POST REF.	DR.	CR.
Feb 13	Accounts Payable—Accessories Unlimited		7,500	
	Cash			7,275
	Inventory			225
	Record payment of inventory purchases within the discount period.			

Note that the discount is credited to the Inventory account. This is because the discount decreases the cost of the cell phone cases that Cosmic Cellular bought from Accessories Unlimited. However, if Cosmic Cellular pays this invoice after the discount period, it pays the full amount of $7,500. In this case, it records the payment as follows:

DATE	ACCOUNTS	POST REF.	DR.	CR.
Feb 24	Accounts Payable—Accessories Unlimited		7,500	
	Cash			7,500
	Record payment of inventory purchases after the discount period.			

It is important to note that discounts are not granted on any portion of a purchase that is returned to the supplier.

HOW DO YOU ACCOUNT FOR THE SALE OF INVENTORY?

Journalize transactions for the sale of inventory **4**

Merchandisers engage in several different types of business transactions with customers:

- Cash sales: Goods are sold for cash.
- Credit sales: Goods are sold on account.
- Sales returns and allowances: Damaged goods are returned by a customer for a refund. However, sometimes the customer keeps the damaged goods and accepts an allowance (price reduction) on the goods.
- Sales discounts: Suppliers grant customers a reduction in the amount owed as an incentive for paying within a discount period.

Let's examine how Cosmic Cellular accounts for these types of transactions.

Cash Sales

Merchandisers, such as Cosmic Cellular, often receive cash at the time they sell merchandise. The journal entry to record a cash sale increases the asset, Cash, and, also, increases the revenue account, **Sales Revenue**. Sales Revenue is the account used by merchandisers to track the value of merchandise sold to customers at the price that the merchandiser charges those customers.

Remember that Cosmic Cellular uses the perpetual inventory system to account for its inventory. At the time of a sale, in addition to recording the sales revenue, Cosmic also reduces the Inventory balance for the value of the merchandise sold. By doing this, the Inventory account is updated so that it always, or perpetually, reflects the current balance. The value of the merchandise sold is accounted for in the **Cost of Goods Sold** account. This income statement account reflects the cost of merchandise sold during the period. The Cost of Goods Sold is deducted from Sales Revenue as a step in determining the amount of net income or loss for the period.

Assume that on June 9, Cosmic Cellular sells $3,000 of merchandise to customers for cash. The goods that Cosmic sold its customers cost Cosmic $1,900. The journal entry to record the sale is as follows:

DATE	ACCOUNTS	POST REF.	DR.	CR.
Jun 9	Cash		3,000	
	Sales Revenue			3,000
	Cost of Goods Sold		1,900	
	Inventory			1,900
	Record sale of inventory for cash.			

Remember that when a product is sold, a merchandiser recognizes the following:

1 Sales revenue for the selling price of the product to the customer

2 Cost of goods sold for the merchandiser's cost of the product

A journal entry that involves more than two accounts is called a **compound journal entry**. A compound entry may include more than one debit amount or more than one credit amount.

Some merchandisers allow customers to use credit cards and debit cards rather than currency. These transactions are treated as cash sales because the merchandiser receives cash from the credit/debit card company. The credit/debit card company then collects the amount due from the customer. The merchandiser, however, usually must pay a service charge to the credit/debit card company in exchange for its processing of the transactions. Accounting for debit and credit card sales is discussed in Chapter 7 in more detail.

Credit Sales

Many merchandisers establish charge accounts for their customers. Assume that Cosmic Cellular sold on account a cell phone and accessories to Jim Kahl on June 11 for $500. The goods cost Cosmic $290. The entry to record this transaction is similar to accounting for a cash sale except Accounts Receivable is debited instead of Cash. Cosmic records this sale on account and the cost of goods sold as follows:

DATE	ACCOUNTS	POST REF.	DR.	CR.
Jun 11	Accounts Receivable—Jim Kahl		500	
	Sales Revenue			500
	Cost of Goods Sold		290	
	Inventory			290
	Record sale of inventory on account, invoice no. 322.			

When Jim sends Cosmic his payment for this merchandise, Cosmic records the cash receipt on account as follows:

DATE	ACCOUNTS	POST REF.	DR.	CR.
Jun 19	Cash		500	
	Accounts Receivable—Jim Kahl			500
	Record payment received on invoice no. 322.			

Notice that the name of the customer is listed in the journal entry following Accounts Receivable. This is similar to what is done for Accounts Payable. A separate account is kept in an accounts receivable subsidiary ledger for each charge customer. Each entry affecting accounts receivable is posted to the customer's account in the subsidiary ledger as well as to the Accounts Receivable account in the general ledger. After all entries are posted, the total of the account balances in the accounts receivable subsidiary ledger will equal the Accounts Receivable account balance in the general ledger. This way, the merchandiser can keep track of the amount of accounts receivable owed by each individual customer.

Sales Returns and Allowances

Merchandisers may allow customers to return unwanted merchandise or they may let customers keep the goods and request an allowance. A business tracks these returns so that it can analyze and manage the causes behind the returns and measure the related costs to the business. In order to track returns accurately, the amount of returns is recorded in a contra-account called **Sales Returns and Allowances**. Remember from Chapter 3 that a contra-account is an account with a balance opposite of the account to which it is linked. Sales Returns and Allowances is linked to Sales Revenue, which has a credit balance. Therefore, Sales Returns and Allowances will have a debit balance. As we will see later, Sales Returns and Allowances appears on the income statement and is deducted from Sales Revenue to arrive at Net Sales.

Exhibit 4-4 illustrates a **credit memorandum**, a document that acknowledges the return of goods from a customer. The credit memo gets its name from the effect that it has on the balance of the customer's account. Because the credit memo decreases the amount due from the customer, the merchandiser *credits* the accounts receivable balance for that customer. The merchandiser sends a credit memorandum to the customer as notification that an adjustment has been made to the amount the customer owes the merchandiser.

COSMIC CELLULAR

1471 E. Union St.
Seattle, WA

CREDIT MEMORANDUM #14

To: Jill Harris   Date: August 15, 2010
2194 S.E. 31st Ave.
Olympia, WA

We credit your account balance for the following:

3 Car chargers @ $25 each	**$75**

Exhibit 4-4 ▲

Sales Returns

When a customer returns goods, the merchandiser will

- decrease net sales revenue by increasing Sales Returns and Allowances, and decrease the customer's Accounts Receivable account balance for the sales price of those goods.
- decrease Cost of Goods Sold and increase Inventory for the cost of the returned goods.

Let's see how Cosmic records the return illustrated in the credit memo in Exhibit 4-4. The credit memo reflects the return of three car chargers, originally purchased for $75, by Jill Harris, a customer. The returned car chargers cost Cosmic $30. Cosmic Cellular records the sales return as follows:

DATE	ACCOUNTS	POST REF.	DR.	CR.
Aug 15	Sales Returns and Allowances		75	
	Accounts Receivable—Jill Harris			75
	Inventory		30	
	Cost of Goods Sold			30
	Record receipt of returned goods, credit memo no. 14.			

Accounts Receivable decreases because the customer no longer owes Cosmic for the returned goods. Cosmic also updates its inventory because its perpetual inventory system needs to reflect the increase to Inventory because of the return of the goods. Cosmic also decreases the Cost of Goods Sold because the goods are no longer sold.

Sales Allowances

Rather than return goods to the merchandiser, some customers may be willing to keep unwanted goods and accept an allowance. Assume Cosmic Cellular grants credit customer Bill Logan a $100 sales allowance for damaged goods. Cosmic records the sales allowance as follows:

DATE	ACCOUNTS	POST REF.	DR.	CR.
Aug 29	Sales Returns and Allowances		100	
	Accounts Receivable—Bill Logan			100
	Record sales allowance for damaged goods, credit memo no. 15.			

Notice that the journal entry for a sales allowance does not affect Inventory or Cost of Goods Sold because the customer did not return any goods to the merchandiser.

☑ Concept Check

If a customer returned $2,500 of merchandise and the transaction was recorded by debiting Sales and crediting Accounts Receivable, instead of debiting Sales Returns and Allowances and crediting Accounts Receivable, would the net income on the income statement be incorrect?

Answer:
No. Let's assume that the company has $20,000 of total sales at the time the return is made and that this is the first time merchandise is returned during the period. If the transaction is recorded by debiting Sales, the Sales balance will be reduced to $17,500. Because there have been no other sales returns, the balance in the Sales Returns and Allowances will be zero. Therefore, the amount of Net Sales will be $17,500. If instead of debiting Sales, the Sales Returns and Allowances account is debited, the Sales account will have a balance of $20,000 and the Sales Returns and Allowances account will have a balance of $2,500. Therefore, the amount of Net Sales will still be $17,500 ($20,000 – $2,500). If the amount of Net Sales is $17,500 regardless of which way the transaction is recorded, the net income will be the same. The reason for using the Sales Returns and Allowances account is simply to keep track of the amount of merchandise returned during the period. Managers often use this information to determine if there are quality issues with their products.

Sales Discounts

Do you recall the discount that Cosmic Cellular received from Accessories Unlimited for early payment? It is possible for Cosmic to offer discounts to its credit customers for early payment. Let's assume that Cosmic sells merchandise to Kelly Harding for $450. The sale is made on account with credit terms of 2/15, n/30. If Kelly chooses to pay the invoice within the 15-day discount period, she will get a 2%, or $9, discount on her $450 purchase ($450 × .02). Kelly will pay $441, or 98% of the invoice amount of $450. This discount represents a reduction in the value of sales to Cosmic.

Businesses track the amount of these sales discounts so they can measure the impact on their sales revenue. To do so, businesses record these discounts in a contra-account called **Sales Discounts**. Because Sales Discounts is linked to Sales Revenue, it will normally have a debit balance. The Sales Discounts account tracks decreases in sales revenue, which results from a discount to customers. Similar to the treatment of Sales Returns and Allowances, Sales Discounts appears on the income statement and is deducted from Sales Revenue to arrive at Net Sales. Because the Sales Returns and Allowances and the Sales Discount accounts have debit balances, they will be closed along with the expense accounts at the end of the period.

Assume that Cosmic receives payment of $441 from Kelly on February 13 within the discount period. The journal entry to record the receipt of cash and the sales discount is as follows:

DATE	ACCOUNTS	POST REF.	DR.	CR.
Feb 13	Cash		441	
	Sales Discounts		9	
	A/R—Kelly Harding			450

If Kelly fails to pay within the 15-day discount period, she will have to pay the full invoice price of $450. If Cosmic receives payment from Kelly on February 24, it records the payment as follows:

DATE	ACCOUNTS	POST REF.	DR.	CR.
Feb 24	Cash		450	
	A/R—Kelly Harding			450

HOW DO YOU ACCOUNT FOR FREIGHT CHARGES AND OTHER SELLING EXPENSES?

Understand shipping terms and journalize transactions for freight charges and other selling expenses **5**

In addition to purchases and sales transactions, a merchandiser also accounts for shipping costs and other selling expenses. Merchandisers often pay costs related to

- receiving goods from suppliers.
- delivering goods to customers.
- advertising and other selling costs.

When merchandisers order items, they often pay the cost of shipping the items to their place of business. These shipping costs are often referred to as **freight charges**.

⬛ Accounting in Your World

Have you ever purchased something online, or from a catalog, and thought you received a really great deal until you received the bill and realized that the company charged you a significant amount for "shipping and handling"? The reason that you were required to pay these shipping charges is because the merchandise was sold with shipping terms of "FOB Shipping Point." Next time, you should purchase items from a company that offers "FOB Destination" shipping terms.

Buyers and sellers specify who pays shipping costs by agreeing to shipping terms. In addition to dictating who is responsible for paying shipping costs, shipping terms also specify the point at which ownership of the goods, or **title**, transfers from seller to buyer. Shipping terms may be **free on board (FOB) shipping point** or **free on board (FOB) destination**.

- Under free on board (FOB) shipping point, ownership transfers from the seller to the buyer at the point where the goods are *shipped*. Also, this term means that the buyer pays the shipping charges to have the merchandise delivered to their place of business. The buyer adds the shipping costs to inventory by debiting Inventory because these amounts increase the cost of the goods purchased.
- Free on board (FOB) destination denotes the opposite arrangement. Ownership transfers from the seller to the buyer when the goods reach their *destination*. This term means that the seller must pay to ship goods to that point. The seller records the shipping costs with a debit to Delivery Expense.

Exhibit 4-5 on the following page summarizes FOB terms.

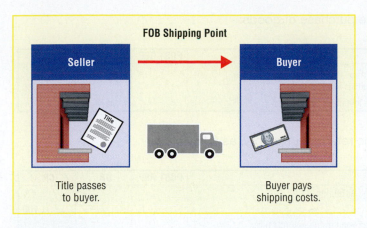

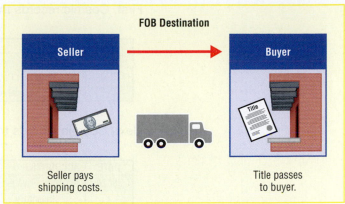

Exhibit 4-5 ▲

Costs Related to the Receipt of Goods from Suppliers

Let us see how Cosmic Cellular records shipping costs when it purchases goods. When it buys products under FOB shipping point, Cosmic either pays the shipping company directly or reimburses the seller for the freight charges if they have been prepaid by the seller. When Cosmic buys products under FOB destination, the supplier pays the freight charges.

FOB Shipping Point, Pay the Shipping Company

Suppose Cosmic Cellular incurs shipping costs related to the purchase of merchandise (FOB shipping point) from Accessories Unlimited. Cosmic pays $60 to the carrier for the February 1 shipment. Cosmic Cellular's entry to record payment of the shipping charge is as follows:

DATE	ACCOUNTS	POST REF.	DR.	CR.
Feb 1	Inventory		60	
	Cash			60
	Record payment of shipping bill for the February 1 purchase.			

Cosmic debits Inventory to increase the cost of the merchandise bought and credits Cash for the shipping costs.

FOB Shipping Point, Repay the Seller for Prepaid Shipping Costs

Under FOB shipping point, the seller sometimes prepays the shipping costs as a convenience to the buyer. These costs are added to the invoice for the merchandise.

Let's see how Cosmic records the following purchase transactions. On July 15, Cosmic buys $1,000 of goods on account from Celltel, Inc. The terms of the purchase are 2/10, n/30, FOB shipping point. Celltel prepaid $80 of shipping costs and added the charges to the invoice for an invoice total of $1,080. Cosmic then returns $100 of these goods for credit on July 20. On July 25, Cosmic makes payment in full for the purchase.

First, Cosmic records the purchase of goods:

DATE	ACCOUNTS	POST REF.	DR.	CR.
Jul 15	Inventory		1,080	
	Accounts Payable—CellTel, Inc.			1,080
	Record purchase of inventory on account.			

Next, Cosmic records the return of inventory, as follows:

DATE	ACCOUNTS	POST REF.	DR.	CR.
Jul 20	Accounts Payable—CellTel, Inc.		100	
	Inventory			100
	Record inventory returned to the manufacturer.			

Finally, it records the payment for the purchase by calculating the purchase discount and the balance due. Cosmic pays on July 25, which is within the 10-day discount period, so it receives a discount of $18: 2% of the $1,000 original cost of the goods minus $100 of returned goods, or .02 × $900. Although shipping costs increase the invoice amount of the merchandise purchased, they are not included in the calculation of any purchase discount. The purchase discount is computed only on the amount due to the supplier for the goods purchased. The calculation of the payment amount is as follows:

Purchase Amount	$1,000
+ Shipping Costs	80
− Purchase Return	(100)
− Purchase Discount	(18) ($1,000 − $100 = $900; $900 × .02 = $18)
= Cash Paid	$ 962

The journal entry to record the cash payment is as follows:

DATE	ACCOUNTS	POST REF.	DR.	CR.
Jul 25	Accounts Payable—CellTel, Inc.			
	($1,000 + $80 − $100)		980	
	Inventory [($1,000 − $100) × 0.02]			18
	Cash ($1,000 + $80 − $100 − $18)			962
	Record payment of inventory puchases within the			
	discount period.			

FOB Destination

Under FOB destination, the seller pays to ship the goods to the destination requested by the customer. If Cosmic Cellular purchased goods under these terms, it has no shipping costs to record because the supplier pays the freight.

Costs Related to Delivering Goods to Customers

The cost of shipping goods to customers is recorded in an expense account titled Delivery Expense. This cost occurs when the seller agrees to shipping terms of FOB destination. Delivery Expense is an expense on the income statement and, as an expense account, normally has a debit balance.

Let's see how the sale of goods and payment of shipping costs affect Cosmic Cellular in different situations. Rob Macklin, a frequent customer at Cosmic Cellular, has an account with the store. Rob buys a blue tooth headset as a Christmas gift for his sister who lives in Las Vegas. Cosmic purchases the head set for $45 and sells it to Rob for $100. Shipping costs to Las Vegas total $15.

FOB Destination

Let's assume that Cosmic advertises that shipping costs are free with any purchase of $100 or more. Assume Rob buys the headset on November 30 and charges it to his account. He asks Cosmic to ship it to Las Vegas. Cosmic records the sale and payment of shipping costs as follows:

In this case, income from the sale is $40 ($100 – $45 – $15).

DATE	ACCOUNTS	POST REF.	DR.	CR.
Nov 30	Accounts Receivable—Rob Macklin		100	
	Sales Revenue			100
	Cost of Goods Sold		45	
	Inventory			45
	Record sale of inventory on account.			

DATE	ACCOUNTS	POST REF.	DR.	CR.
Nov 30	Delivery Expense		15	
	Cash			15
	Record shipping on sale.			

FOB Shipping Point

Now, let's assume that Cosmic does not offer free shipping. Because Cosmic sold the goods FOB shipping point, Rob pays for the shipping costs. Rob purchases the headset on November 30 and takes it home to wrap and send with another gift. Cosmic would record the sale as follows:

DATE	ACCOUNTS	POST REF.	DR.	CR.
Nov 30	Accounts Receivable—Rob Macklin		100	
	Sales Revenue			100
	Cost of Goods Sold		45	
	Inventory			45
	Record sale of inventory on account.			

In this situation, income from sale would be $55 ($100 – $45).

FOB Shipping Point, Seller Agrees to Prepay the Shipping Costs

Now assume that Rob buys the headset on November 30 and asks Cosmic to ship it to Las Vegas for him. Again, because the goods are sold FOB shipping point, Rob is responsible for the shipping charges. In this case, Cosmic pays for shipping the goods and adds the cost to Rob's invoice. Cosmic records the sale, including the payment of shipping costs as follows:

DATE	ACCOUNTS	POST REF.	DR.	CR.
Nov 30	Accounts Receivable—Rob Macklin		100	
	Sales Revenue			100
	Cost of Goods Sold		45	
	Inventory			45
	Record sale of inventory on account.			

DATE	ACCOUNTS	POST REF.	DR.	CR.
Nov 30	Accounts Receivable—Rob Macklin		15	
	Cash			15
	Record prepayment of shipping costs.			

Income from the sale is again $55 ($100 – $45). The $15 Cosmic paid to ship the headset to Las Vegas is not an expense as it will be reimbursed by Rob. A comparison reveals that the income from the sale under FOB shipping point remains the same whether or not Cosmic prepays the shipping charges:

	FOB destination	FOB Shipping Point	FOB Shipping Point, Seller Prepays
Sales Revenue	$100	$100	$100
– Cost of Goods Sold	(45)	(45)	(45)
– Delivery Expense	(15)	—	—
= Income from Sale	$ 40	$ 55	$ 55

Other Selling Costs

Selling expenses represent the costs associated with advertising and selling inventory. Examples of selling expenses usually found on a merchandiser's income statement include the following:

- Sales salaries, wages, and commissions
- Advertising and promotion
- Depreciation for the use of stores, parking lots, counters, displays, shelves, vehicles of salespeople, and storage space (such as warehouses and refrigerators)
- Delivery of merchandise to customers

As we will see in the next section, selling expenses are a deduction when arriving at the net income of a merchandiser.

HOW DO YOU PREPARE A MERCHANDISER'S FINANCIAL STATEMENTS?

The Income Statement

Prepare a multi-step income statement and a classified balance sheet **6**

In earlier chapters, you learned how to complete the financial statements for a service business. Most service businesses use a **single-step income statement**. The single-step income statement groups all revenues together and all expenses together. Then, the total expenses are subtracted from total revenues in a single step without calculating any subtotals. The advantage of the single-step format is that it clearly distinguishes revenues from expenses. Although Cosmic Cellular is a merchandiser,

Exhibit 4-6 illustrates its income statement for the year ended December 31, 2010, prepared using the single-step format.

Cosmic Cellular, Inc. Income Statement Year Ended December 31, 2010		
Revenues:		
Net Sales Revenue		$167,900
Expenses:		
Cost of Goods Sold	$90,300	
Selling Expenses	1,200	
General and Administrative Expenses	19,650	
Interest Expense	1,100	
Total Expenses		112,250
Net Income		$ 55,650

Exhibit 4-6 ▲

Most merchandisers use a **multi-step income statement**. The multi-step income statement is prepared in steps. Important subtotals are computed as part of the calculation of net income or net loss. Investors prefer this format because it provides step-by-step information about the profitability of the business. This format makes it more useful for managers within the business as well as investors outside of the business. The multi-step income statement for most merchandisers will contain most, but not necessarily all, of the following items:

- **Net Sales Revenue** is presented first, and is calculated by subtracting both Sales Returns and Allowances and Sales Discounts from Sales Revenue. Keep in mind that a company may not offer its customers any sales discounts. Also, even if sales discounts are offered, customers may not take advantage of them. Therefore, it is possible that no sales discounts will appear on a company's income statement.
- The cost of the merchandise that is sold appears next as Cost of Goods Sold.
- **Gross Profit**, also called **Gross Margin**, is a subtotal computed next. The gross profit equals Net Sales Revenue minus Cost of Goods Sold.
- **Operating Expenses** are the expenses, other than cost of goods sold, of operating the business. Operating Expenses are listed after Gross Profit. Many companies report operating expenses in two categories:
  1. Selling Expenses include sales salaries, commissions, advertising, promotion, depreciation for items used in sales, and delivery costs to customers.
  2. **General and Administrative Expenses** include office expenses, such as the salaries of the company president and office employees, depreciation of items used in administration, rent, utilities, and property taxes on the office building.
- On the multi-step income statement, Gross Profit minus Operating Expenses equals **Operating Income**, or **Income from Operations**. Operating income measures the results of the entity's primary, ongoing business activities.
- The last section of a multi-step income statement is **Other Revenues and Expenses**. This category reports revenues and expenses that fall outside of a business's main operations. Examples include interest revenue, interest expense, dividend revenue, and gains and losses on the sale of long-term

assets. Because not every business has revenues and expenses outside its business operations, not all income statements will include this section.

- The last line of the multi-step income statement is Net Income or Net Loss. To calculate, add Other Revenues and subtract Other Expenses from Operating Income. The final results of operations, net income or net loss, is a company's *bottom line, a commonly used business term*.

Cosmic Cellular's multi-step income statement for the year ended December 31, 2010, appears in **Exhibit 4-7** on page 194 along with the Statement of Retained Earnings and the Balance Sheet.

After you review Cosmic Cellular's multi-step income statement in Exhibit 4-7, look again at its single-step version in Exhibit 4-6. Notice that in both formats net income is exactly the same. The format of the income statement does not change the net income or net loss of a business. It simply changes how the calculation of net income or net loss is presented.

Decision Guidelines

Decision	Guideline	Analyze
Which income statement format is the best to use?	This depends on who the intended users of the financial statements are.	The *single-step format* shows the calculation of net income or net loss by subtracting all expenses from all revenues in a single step. The single-step format typically shows summary information and is intended for users who do not need much detail. This format would not be a good format for creditors or investors to use but it would be great to use in a press release or newspaper article. The *multi-step format* shows the calculation of net income or net loss in a series of steps with subtotals for *gross profit* and *operating income*. This format shows detailed information and is best suited for creditors and investors.

The Statement of Retained Earnings

A merchandiser's statement of retained earnings looks exactly like that of a service business. Cosmic's statement of retained earnings is presented in Exhibit 4-7.

The Balance Sheet

In order to provide more useful information, merchandisers, as well as most service businesses, usually prepare a **classified balance sheet**. A classified balance sheet lists assets in classes in the order of their **liquidity**. Liquidity refers to how close an asset is to becoming cash or being used up. Similar to the assets, the liabilities are listed in classes based on how soon the obligation will be paid or fulfilled. By listing the assets and liabilities in these classes, financial statement users can better analyze the business's ability to pay its bills on time.

Assets

The most liquid assets are presented on a classified balance sheet in a class called **Current Assets**. Current Assets are assets that will be converted to cash, sold, or used up during the next 12 months or within a business's normal **operating cycle** if longer than one year.

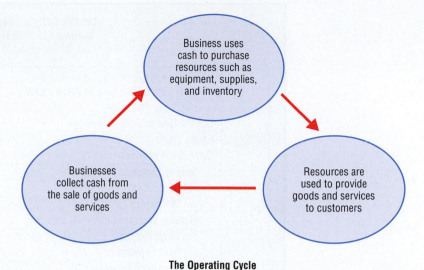

The Operating Cycle

For most businesses, the operating cycle is a few months. Cash, Accounts Receivable, Notes Receivable due within one year, and Prepaid Expenses are all current assets. If the business is a merchandiser, then the major difference between its balance sheet and that of a service business is that it also shows Inventory as a current asset.

All assets other than current assets are reported in a class called **long-term assets**. One category of long-term assets is called **plant assets** or **fixed assets**. This category is labeled on the balance sheet as **property, plant, and equipment**. Land, buildings, furniture, fixtures, and equipment are examples of these assets.

Liabilities

The debts or obligations of a business that must be paid for or fulfilled within one year (or within the entity's operating cycle if the cycle is longer than a year) are reported in a class called **current liabilities**. Accounts Payable, Notes Payable due within one year, Salary Payable, Interest Payable, and Unearned Revenue are current liabilities.

Obligations that extend beyond one year are reported as **long-term liabilities**. Often, a business owner signs a contract to repay a note or mortgage over several years. The portion of the note or mortgage that must be paid within one year is classified as a current liability. However, the remaining balance is a long-term liability.

The balance sheet for Cosmic Cellular is presented in Exhibit 4-7. Cosmic's balance sheet is presented in **account form**. The account form lists the assets on the left and the liabilities and stockholders' equity on the right, just as these accounts appear in the accounting equation. It is also acceptable to present the balance sheet in **report form**, which lists the assets at the top and the liabilities and stockholders' equity on the bottom.

Cosmic Cellular, Inc.
Income Statement
Year Ended December 31, 2010

Sales Revenue			$171,300	
Less: Sales Returns and Allowances			3,400	
Net Sales Revenue				$167,900
Cost of Goods Sold				90,300
Gross Profit				77,600
Operating Expenses:				
Selling Expenses:				
Advertising		$ 1,000		
Delivery Expense		200	1,200	
General and Administrative Expenses:				
Wage Expense		10,200		
Rent Expense		7,300		
Insurance Expense		1,000		
Depreciation Expense, Office Equipment		600		
Supplies Expense		550	19,650	20,850
Operating Income				56,750
Other Revenues and (Expenses):				
Interest Expense				(1,100)
Net Income				$ 55,650

Cosmic Cellular, Inc.
Statement of Retained Earnings
Year Ended December 31, 2010

Retained Earnings, December 31, 2009		$ 20,900
Add: Net Income		55,650
Subtotal		76,550
Less: Dividends		55,900
Retained Earnings, December 31, 2010		$ 20,650

Cosmic Cellular, Inc.
Classified Balance Sheet
December 31, 2010

ASSETS			LIABILITIES		
Current Assets:			Current Liabilities:		
Cash	$ 3,150		Accounts Payable	$30,000	
Accounts Receivable	4,600		Wages Payable	400	
Supplies	100		Unearned Sales Revenue	700	
Inventory	39,700		Total Current Liabilities		$31,100
Prepaid Insurance	200		Long-Term Liabilities		
Total Current Assets		$47,750	Mortgage Payable		10,000
Long-term Assets:			Total Liabilities		41,100
Office Equipment	32,000				
Less: Accumulated			**STOCKHOLDERS'**		
Depreciation, Office			**EQUITY**		
Equipment	3,000	29,000	Common Stock	15,000	
			Retained Earnings	20,650	
			Total Stockholders' Equity		35,650
			Total Liabilities &		
Total Assets		$76,750	Stockholders' Equity		$76,750

Exhibit 4-7 ▲

FOCUS ON DECISION MAKING: RATIOS

The Gross Profit Percentage

Compute the gross profit percentage and the current ratio **7**

Gross profit, also called gross margin, is a key tool in evaluating merchandising operations. Remember that gross profit is net sales revenue minus the cost of goods sold. Thus, gross profit is the amount left over from sales after deducting the cost of the merchandise sold. Merchandisers strive to maximize gross profit in order to help maximize net income. The **gross profit percentage**, also called the **gross margin percentage**, shows how well a merchandising business meets this goal. The gross profit percentage measures the relationship between gross profit and sales.

The gross profit percentage is one of the most carefully watched measures of profitability by investors and business managers. This information is used to compare changes in gross profit from year to year for the business. Also, it is used to compare the company to other businesses in the same industry. For most businesses, the gross profit percentage changes little from year to year. To investors, a significant change in the gross profit percentage signals a significant change in the business's operations meriting further investigation.

To compute the gross profit percentage, divide gross profit by net sales revenue. Based on information provided from the income statement in Exhibit 4-7, the gross profit percentage for Cosmic Cellular is 46.2%, calculated as follows:

$$\text{Gross Profit Percentage} = \frac{\text{Gross Profit}}{\text{Net Sales Revenue}} = \frac{\$77,600}{\$167,900} = 0.462 = 46.2\%$$

A 46.2% gross margin percentage means that each dollar of net sales generates 46.2 cents of gross profit. Every time Cosmic Cellular sells $1 of merchandise, it produces 46.2 cents of gross profit that hopefully covers operating expenses and generates net income.

The Current Ratio

The **current ratio** is one of the most widely used tools investors, creditors, and suppliers use to evaluate a company's ability to pay its obligations as they come due. The granting of credit is often based upon a company having a strong current ratio. The current ratio measures a company's ability to pay its current liabilities by comparing those liabilities to its current assets. The formula for calculating the current ratio is as follows:

$$\text{Current Ratio} = \text{Current Assets/Current Liabilities}$$

A high current ratio is desired because that means a company has plenty of current assets to pay its current liabilities. An increasing current ratio over time indicates improvement in a company's ability to pay current debts. A rule of thumb is that a strong current ratio is 1.50. This indicates that the company has $1.50 in current assets for every $1.00 in current liabilities. A company with a current ratio of 1.50 would probably have little trouble paying its current liabilities. A current ratio below 1.00 is considered low.

Based on information provided from the balance sheet in Exhibit 4-7, the current ratio for Cosmic Cellular is 1.54, calculated as follows:

$$\text{Current Ratio} = \frac{\text{Current Assets}}{\text{Current Liabilities}} = \frac{\$47{,}750}{\$31{,}100} = 1.54$$

It appears that Cosmic Cellular should have no trouble paying its obligations as they come due.

Decision Guidelines

Decision	Guideline	Evaluate
Is there a quick way to analyze a business's performance?	Key ratios are often used as a quick way to measure a business's performance.	The *gross profit percentage* helps analyze the profitability of a merchandiser. The gross profit percentage provides a measurement of how much of each sales dollar remains after covering the cost of the inventory. The *current ratio* can be used to determine a business's ability to pay its obligations as they come due. A current ratio that is above 1.5 is generally considered to be good. However, if a current ratio gets too high it can be an indicator that the business has too much tied up in current assets and, therefore, is not utilizing its assets as effectively as it could be.

Demo Doc

Transaction Analysis for a Merchandiser Using the Perpetual Inventory System

Learning Objectives 3–5 ▶

Spokane Paper Products, Inc., had the following transactions in March 2010:

Mar	1	Purchased $1,500 of inventory on account. Terms were 2/10, n/30, FOB destination.
	2	Sold inventory for cash, $800 (cost, $550).
	7	Returned $400 of the inventory purchased on March 1 because it was defective.
	9	Paid supplier for goods purchased on March 1.
	11	Purchased inventory for $1,800 on account. Terms were 3/15, n/30, FOB shipping point.
	14	Paid freight bill on merchandise purchased on March 11, $125.
	18	Sold inventory for $2,200 (cost, $1,500) on account. Terms were 2/10, n/30, FOB shipping point.
	24	Paid supplier for goods purchased on March 11.
	26	The customer from the March 18 sale returned $750 ($500 cost) of goods.
	28	Received cash in full settlement of its account from the customer who purchased inventory on March 18.

Requirement:

1 Journalize these transactions, omit explanations.

Demo Doc Solution
Requirement ❶

Journalize these transactions, omit explanations.

Part 1	Demo Doc Complete

Mar 1   Purchased $1,500 of inventory on account. Terms were 2/10, n/30, FOB destination.

The purchase of inventory causes the Inventory account to increase by $1,500. The Inventory account is an asset and is, therefore, increased with a debit. Because the purchase was made on account, Accounts Payable is increased (credited) by $1,500. The credit terms are not relevant until the *payment* is made to the supplier. The freight terms indicate that the supplier is responsible for paying the freight charges.

DATE	ACCOUNTS	POST REF.	DR.	CR.
Mar 1	Inventory		1,500	
	Accounts Payable			1,500

Mar 2   Sold inventory for cash, $800 (cost, $550).

Under the perpetual inventory method, the entry required to account for a sale requires two parts. The first part of the entry is required to record the recognition of revenue. Because the sale was a cash sale, the Cash account is increased (debited) by $800. When merchandise is sold (and delivered) to a customer, the company earns sales revenue. By selling merchandise, Spokane Paper Products, Inc., has earned sales revenue of $800. Therefore, Sales Revenue is increased (credited) by $800.

The second part of the entry is required to record the cost of the goods sold. The Cost of Goods Sold account is increased (debited) for $550 (Spokane Paper Products' cost of the merchandise). Remember, Cost of Goods Sold is an *expense*. Because goods from inventory were given to the customer, the Inventory account is decreased (credited) by $550.

DATE	ACCOUNTS	POST REF.	DR.	CR.
Mar 2	Cash		800	
	Sales Revenue			800
	Cost of Goods Sold		550	
	Inventory			550

Mar 7   Returned $400 of the inventory purchased on March 1 because it was defective.

Because Spokane Paper Products, Inc., has not yet paid for the purchase, the return of the merchandise will result in a $400 decrease (debit) to Accounts Payable. Also, because the goods were returned to the supplier, the Inventory account will be decreased (credited) by $400.

DATE	ACCOUNTS	POST REF.	DR.	CR.
Mar 7	Accounts Payable		400	
	Inventory			400

Mar 9   Paid supplier for goods purchased on March 1.

Because the original purchase was made on account, we need to consider the credit terms, which were 2/10, n/30. Because Spokane Paper Products, Inc., is paying within the 10-day discount period, it is entitled to take a 2% discount. However, the discount does not apply to the $400 of goods that Spokane Paper Products, Inc., has returned. It only applies to the net account payable that Spokane Paper Products, Inc., owes after the return.

Original purchase price of goods	$1,500
Less amount of goods returned	$ 400
Net account payable.................................	$1,100

The discount, and the amount of cash paid, is calculated as follows:

Net account payable..............	$ 1,100	
Less 2% discount	$ (22)	(2% × $1,100)
Total cash paid	$ 1,078	

Accounts Payable is decreased (debited) by the remaining amount due of $1,100. The cash account will be decreased (credited) by the $1,078 of cash paid. The $22 difference is the discount and is treated as a reduction to the Inventory account because it represents a reduction in the cost of the inventory. So, Inventory is decreased (credited) by the $22 amount of the discount.

DATE	ACCOUNTS	POST REF.	DR.	CR.
Mar 9	Accounts Payable		1,100	
	Cash			1,078
	Inventory			22

Mar 11 Purchased inventory for $1,800 on account. Terms were 3/15, n/30, FOB shipping point.

The purchase of inventory causes the Inventory account to increase (debit) by $1,800. Because the purchase was made on account, Accounts Payable is increased by $1,800 with a credit. The credit terms are not relevant until the *payment* is made to the supplier. The freight terms indicate that the Spokane Paper Products, Inc., is responsible for paying the freight charges.

DATE	ACCOUNTS	POST REF.	DR.	CR.
Mar 11	Inventory		1,800	
	Accounts Payable			1,800

Mar 14 Paid freight bill on merchandise purchased on March 11, $125.

The shipping terms of FOB shipping point means that Spokane Paper Products, Inc., is responsible for paying the freight charges. Because the freight charges represent an increase in the cost of the inventory to Spokane Paper Products, the Inventory account will be increased (debited) by $125. Cash will be decreased (credited) by $125.

DATE	ACCOUNTS	POST REF.	DR.	CR.
Mar 14	Inventory		125	
	Cash			125

Mar 18 Sold inventory for $2,200 (cost, $1,500) on account. Terms were 2/10, n/30, FOB shipping point.

Remember, under the perpetual inventory method, the entry required to account for a sale requires two parts. The first part of the entry is required to record the recognition of revenue. Because the sale was on account, the Accounts Receivable account is increased (debited) by $2,200. Sales revenue is increased (credited) by $2,200. The second part of the entry is required to record the cost of the goods sold. The Cost of Goods Sold account is increased (debited) for $1,500 and Inventory is decreased (credited) by $1,500.

DATE	ACCOUNTS	POST REF.	DR.	CR.
Mar 18	Accounts Receivable		2,200	
	Sales Revenue			2,200
	Cost of Goods Sold		1,500	
	Inventory			1,500

Mar 24   Paid supplier for goods purchased on March 11.

Because the original purchase was made on account, we need to consider the credit terms, which were 3/15, n/30. Because Spokane Paper Products, Inc., is paying within the 15-day discount period, it is entitled to take a 3% discount. There were no returns related to this purchase so the discount, and the amount of cash paid, is calculated as follows:

Net account payable.................................	$ 1,800
Less 3% discount (3% × $1,800)	$ (54)
Total cash paid	$ 1,746

Accounts Payable is decreased (debited) by the amount due of $1,800. The cash account will be decreased (credited) by the $1,746 of cash paid. The $54 difference is the discount and is treated as a reduction to the Inventory account because it represents a reduction in the cost of the inventory. So, Inventory is decreased (credited) by the $54 amount of the discount.

DATE	ACCOUNTS	POST REF.	DR.	CR.
Mar 24	Accounts Payable		1,800	
	Cash			1,746
	Inventory			54

Mar 26   The customer from the March 18 sale returned $750 ($500 cost) of goods.

Just as the sale of goods under the perpetual inventory method requires a two-part entry, so does the return of goods from a customer. The first part of the entry "undoes" the sale and is recorded by increasing (debiting) the contra-account Sales Returns and Allowances by $750. The customer has not yet paid the account, so the return of the goods will result in a decrease (credit) to Accounts Receivable for $750. The second part of the entry will record the physical return of the goods. The Inventory account is increased (debited) by $500, the value of the goods returned. Because the goods were returned, they are no longer "sold," so the Cost of Goods Sold account is decreased (credited) by $500.

DATE	ACCOUNTS	POST REF.	DR.	CR.
Mar 26	Sales Returns and Allowances		750	
	Accounts Receivable			750
	Inventory		500	
	Cost of Goods Sold			500

Mar 28   Received cash in full settlement of its account from the customer who purchased inventory on March 18.

Because the original purchase was made on account, we need to consider the credit terms, which were 2/10, n/30. Because the customer is paying within the 10-day discount period, he or she is entitled to take a 2% discount. However, the discount does not apply to the $750 of goods that the customer returned. It only applies to the net account receivable that the customer still owes to Spokane Paper Products, Inc., after the return.

Original sales price of goods.....................	$2,200
Less amount of goods returned...............	$ 750
Net account receivable.............................	$1,450

The discount, and the amount of cash Spokane Paper Products, Inc., receives, is calculated as follows:

Net account receivable.............................	$ 1,450
Less 2% discount (2% × $1,450).............	$ (29)
Total cash received..................................	$ 1,421

The cash account will be increased (debited) by the $1,421 of cash received. The amount of the discount, $29, is recorded as an increase (debit) to the contra-account, Sales Discounts. Accounts Receivable is decreased (credited) by the net account receivable of $1,450.

DATE	ACCOUNTS	POST REF.	DR.	CR.
Mar 28	Cash		1,421	
	Sales Discounts		29	
	Accounts Receivable			1,450

DemoDoc Complete

Part 1	**Demo Doc Complete**

Decision Guidelines

Accounting for a Merchandising Business

As a merchandiser, you might be faced with decisions such as the following:

Decision	Guideline	Analyze
Which inventory system should my business use?	This decision depends on whether or not you plan on utilizing a computer system to help with inventory management.	The *perpetual system* shows the current, correct amounts of inventory on hand and the cost of goods sold at all times. The *periodic system* requires that a physical count of the inventory be taken in order to know the correct balances of inventory and cost of goods sold. Before computers, only businesses that sold smaller quantities of higher cost items could use the perpetual method. Today, thanks to computers and other technology, most companies utilize the perpetual method even if they sell a high quantity of low cost items.
Which income statement format is the best to use?	This determination depends on the intended users of the financial statements.	The *single-step format* shows the calculation of net income or net loss by subtracting all expenses from all revenues in a single step. The single-step format typically shows summary information and is intended for users who do not need much detail. This format would not be a good format for creditors or investors to use but it would be great to use in a press release or newspaper article. The *multi-step format* shows the calculation of net income or net loss in a series of steps with subtotals for *gross profit* and *operating income*. This format shows detailed information and is best suited for creditors and investors.
Is there a quick way to analyze a business's performance?	Key ratios are often used as a quick way to measure a business's performance.	The *gross profit percentage* helps analyze the profitability of a merchandiser. The gross profit percentage provides a measurement of how much of each sales dollar remains after covering the cost of the inventory. The *current ratio* can be used to determine a business's ability to pay its obligations as they come due. A current ratio that is above 1.5 is generally considered to be good. However, if a current ratio gets too high it can be an indicator that the business has too much tied up in current assets and, therefore, is not utilizing its assets as effectively as it could be.

ACCOUNTING VOCABULARY

THE LANGUAGE OF BUSINESS

Account form (p. 193) A balance sheet format that lists assets on the left of the report and liabilities and stockholders' equity on the right, just as those accounts appear in the accounting equation.

Classified balance sheet (p. 192) A balance sheet that separates assets and liabilities into current and long-term classes.

Compound journal entry (p. 182) A journal entry affecting more than two accounts; an entry that has more than one debit and/or more than one credit.

Cost of Goods Sold (p. 181) The cost of the inventory that the business has sold to customers.

Credit memorandum (p. 183) A document that supports the return of goods from the customer and the adjustment to the customer's account balance.

Credit terms (p. 179) The payment terms for customers who buy on account.

Current Assets (p. 192) Assets that are expected to be converted to cash, sold, or consumed within one year or the business's operating cycle if the cycle is longer than a year.

Current liabilities (p. 193) Debts due to be paid with cash or fulfilled with goods and services within one year or the entity's operating cycle if the cycle is longer than a year.

Current ratio (p. 195) The ratio of current assets to current liabilities; a key measure of liquidity.

Debit memorandum (p. 179) A document that supports the return of goods to the supplier and the adjustment to the balance owed to the supplier.

Discount period (p. 180) Period in which the buyer can make early payment for a purchase and receive a discount on that purchase.

eom (p. 179) Credit term specifying that payment for a purchase is due by the end of the month; also referred to as *n/eom*.

Fixed assets (p. 193) The long-lived assets of a business including land, buildings, furniture, fixtures, and equipment; also called plant assets and commonly shown on the balance sheet as property, plant, and equipment.

Free on board (FOB) destination (p. 186) A shipping term specifying that title to goods passes to the buyer when the goods are received at buyer's destination; thus, the seller pays the cost of shipping the goods to this destination.

Free on board (FOB) shipping point (p. 186) A shipping term specifying that title to goods passes to the buyer when the goods are shipped at the seller's place of business; thus, the buyer pays the cost of shipping the goods to its location.

Freight charges (p. 186) The cost of shipping merchandise from the seller to the buyer.

General and Administrative Expenses (p. 191) Office expenses, such as the salaries of the company president and office employees, depreciation of items used in administration, rent, utilities, and property taxes on the office building.

Gross Margin (p. 191) Net sales revenue minus cost of goods sold; also called gross profit.

Gross margin percentage (p. 195) A measure of profitability equal to gross margin divided by net sales revenue; also called *gross profit percentage*.

Gross Profit (p. 191) Net sales revenue minus cost of goods sold; also called *gross margin*.

Gross profit percentage (p. 195) A measure of profitability equal to gross profit divided by net sales revenue; also called *gross margin percentage*.

Income from Operations (p. 191) Gross profit minus operating expenses; also called *operating income*.

Inventory (p. 176) Goods purchased for resale to customers in the normal course of merchandising operations; also called merchandise inventory.

Liquidity (p. 192) The ability to convert an asset to cash quickly.

Long-term assets (p. 193) Assets other than those that are current.

Long-term liabilities (p. 193) Liabilities other than those that are current.

Merchandise inventory (p. 176) Goods purchased for resale to customers in the normal course of merchandising operations; also called *inventory*.

Multi-step income statement (p. 191) Income statement format that calculates net income or net loss by listing important subtotals, such as gross profit and operating income.

n/30 (p. 179) Credit term specifying that payment for a purchase is due within 30 days after the date of the invoice.

n/eom (p. 179) Credit term specifying that payment for a purchase is due by the end of the month; also referred to as *eom*.

Net Sales Revenue (p. 191) Sales revenue less sales discounts and sales returns and allowances.

Operating cycle (p. 192) The time span during which the business obtains resources, uses them to sell goods and services to customers, and collects cash from these customers.

Operating expenses (p. 191) Expenses of operating a business other than cost of goods sold. Examples include depreciation, rent, salaries, utilities, advertising, delivery expense, property taxes, and supplies expense.

Operating Income (p. 191) Gross profit minus operating expenses. Also called income from operations.

Other Revenues and Expenses (p. 191) Revenues and expenses that fall outside the main operations of a business, such as interest expense and a loss on the sale of long-term assets.

Periodic inventory system (p. 176) An inventory system in which the business does not keep a continuous record of inventory on hand. At the end of the period, a physical count of inventory is taken and determines the inventory owned as well as the cost of the goods sold.

Perpetual inventory system (p. 177) An inventory system in which the business keeps a continuous record of inventory on hand and the cost of the goods sold.

Plant assets (p. 193) The long-lived assets of a business including land, buildings, furniture, fixtures, and equipment; also called *fixed assets* and commonly shown on the balance sheet as property, plant, and equipment.

Property, plant, and equipment (p. 193) A heading often seen on the balance sheet used to describe fixed, or plant, assets.

Purchase discount (p. 178) Discount received on purchases by paying early within a discount period.

Purchase returns and allowances (p. 178) A reduction in the amount owed for a purchase due to returning merchandise or accepting damaged goods.

Report form (p. 193) A balance sheet format that reports assets at the top of the report, followed by liabilities, and ending with stockholders' equity at the end of the report.

Retailers (p. 176) Businesses that buy goods from manufacturers or wholesalers and resell them to the general public.

Sales Discount (p. 185) Discount granted on sales for the customer's early payment within a discount period; a contra-account to Sales Revenue.

Sales invoice (p. 179) A bill that documents the sale of goods to a business customer.

Sales Returns and Allowances (p. 183) A reduction in the amount of sales due to customers returning merchandise or accepting damaged goods; a contra-account to Sales Revenue.

Sales revenue (p. 181) The amount that a retailer earns from selling its inventory.

Selling expenses (p. 190) Expenses related to advertising and selling products including sales salaries, sales commissions, advertising, depreciation on items used in sales, and delivery expense.

Single-step income statement (p. 190) Income statement format that groups all revenues together and lists all expenses together, subtracting total expenses from total revenues and calculating net income or net loss without computing any subtotals.

Subsidiary ledger (p. 178) An accounting record that contains details, such as a list of customers and the accounts receivable due from each, or a list of suppliers and the accounts payable due to each.

Title (p. 186) Ownership.

Wholesalers (p. 176) Businesses that buy goods from manufacturers and resell them to retailers.

ACCOUNTING PRACTICE

DISCUSSION QUESTIONS

1. What accounts will appear on the financial statements of a merchandiser that will not appear on those of a service-oriented company?

2. What are some reasons why a merchandiser might prefer to use a perpetual inventory system over a periodic inventory system?

3. Why do businesses use subsidiary ledgers?

4. What do the terms 2/10, n/30 mean? If you were advising a company who bought goods under these terms, what would you advise it to do with respect to payment? Why?

5. How many accounts are involved in recording the sale of merchandise on credit?

6. What kind of account is Sales Returns and Allowances? Where would it appear on the financial statements?

7. What is a debit memorandum? What is a credit memorandum? Give an example of the types of transactions in which each would be used.

8. What does the term "free on board" mean? Why is this an important term to understand if you are involved in making decisions about the purchasing of inventory or the setting of prices for your products?

9. What is the difference between a single-step and multi-step income statement? To what type of business is a multi-step income statement most appropriate?

10. What situation might explain why a company's gross profit percentage went down from 60% to 40% from one year to the next?

SELF CHECK

1. Which account does a merchandiser use that a service company does not use?
   a. Cost of goods sold
   b. Inventory
   c. Sales revenue
   d. All of the above

2. The two main inventory accounting systems are the
   a. perpetual and periodic.
   b. purchase and sale.
   c. returns and allowances.
   d. cash and accrual.

3. The journal entry for the purchase of $900 of inventory on account is as follows:

DATE	ACCOUNTS	POST REF.	DR.	CR.
a.	Cost of Goods Sold		900	
	Accounts Payable			900
b.	Inventory		900	
	Accounts Payable			900
c.	Accounts Payable		900	
	Inventory			900
d.	Inventory		900	
	Cash			900

4. Apex Electrical Supply, Inc., purchased inventory for $2,000 and also paid $125 freight to have the inventory delivered. Apex Electrical Supply, Inc., returned $500 of the goods to the seller and later took a 2% purchase discount. What is the final cost of the inventory that Apex Electrical Supply, Inc., kept?
   a. $2,083
   b. $2,085
   c. $1,595
   d. $1,593

5. Suppose Bonzai Boards, Inc., had sales of $180,000 and sales returns of $22,000. Cost of goods sold was $110,000. How much gross profit did Bonzai Boards, Inc., report?
   a. $48,000
   b. $70,000
   c. $92,000
   d. $158,000

6. Suppose Apex Electrical Supply's Inventory account showed a balance of $43,000. A physical count showed $41,800 of goods on hand. To adjust the inventory account, Apex Electrical Supply, Inc., would make the following entry:

DATE	ACCOUNTS	POST REF.	DR.	CR.
a.	Cost of Goods Sold		1,200	
	Inventory			1,200
b.	Accounts Payable		1,200	
	Inventory			1,200
c.	Inventory		1,200	
	Cost of Goods Sold			1,200
d.	Inventory		1,200	
	Accounts Payable			1,200

7. If Bonzai Boards, Inc., returned $3,600 of snowboards to a supplier it would record the transaction as follows:

DATE	ACCOUNTS	POST REF.	DR.	CR.
a.	Cost of Goods Sold		3,600	
	Inventory			3,600
b.	Accounts Payable		3,600	
	Sales Returns and Allowances			3,600
c.	Inventory		3,600	
	Accounts Payable			3,600
d.	Accounts Payable		3,600	
	Inventory			3,600

8. An asset is classified as current if it
   a. was purchased within the last six months.
   b. will become cash, be sold, or be used up within 12 months.
   c. was purchased with cash.
   d. will last longer than one year.

9. The income statement format that shows important subtotals is referred to as
   a. a classified income statement.
   b. a single-step income statement.
   c. a multi-step income statement.
   d. a subtotaled income statement.

10. Suppose Bonzai Boards, Inc., had sales of $210,000 and sales returns of $18,000. Cost of goods sold was $125,000. What was Bonzai Boards' gross profit percentage (rounded) for this period?
    a. 35%
    b. 54%
    c. 40%
    d. 32%

Answers are given after Written Communication.

SHORT EXERCISES

S4-1. Inventory methods (*Learning Objective 2*) 5–10 min.

The following characteristics are related to either periodic inventory or perpetual inventory systems.

   a. A physical count of goods on hand at year end is required.

   b. Inventory records are continuously updated.

   c. Purchases of inventory are recorded in an asset account at the time of purchase.

   d. Bar code scanners are often utilized when using this inventory system.

   e. It is necessary to calculate the cost of goods sold at the end of the year with this inventory system.

Identify each characteristic as one of the following:

   a. Periodic inventory

   b. Perpetual inventory

   c. Both periodic and perpetual inventory

   d. Neither periodic nor perpetual inventory.

S4-2. Adjusting inventory based on a physical count (*Learning Objective 2*) 5–10 min.

Charleston's Furniture uses the perpetual inventory method. At the end of the year, Charleston's Furniture's Inventory account had a ledger balance of $87,000. A physical inventory count revealed that the actual inventory on hand totaled $85,300.

Journalize the transaction necessary to adjust the Inventory account at the end of the year.

S4-3. Journalizing inventory purchases (*Learning Objective 3*) 5–10 min.

Suppose Sports-R-Us purchases $40,000 of sportswear on account from Pacific Trail on March 1, 2010. Credit terms are 2/10, net 30. Sports-R-Us pays Pacific Trail on March 8, 2010.

   1. Journalize the transactions for Sports-R-Us on March 1, 2010, and March 8, 2010.

   2. What was the final cost of this inventory for Sports-R-Us?

S4-4. Inventory purchases and returns (*Learning Objective 3*) 5–10 min.

Sonny's Spas, Inc., purchased $8,000 worth of inventory from the Pool Warehouse on account, terms of 2/10, n/30. Some of the goods are damaged in shipment, so Sonny's Spas, Inc., returns $1,100 of the merchandise to the Pool Warehouse.

How much must Sonny's Spas, Inc., pay the Pool Warehouse

   a. after the discount period?

   b. within the discount period?

S4-5. Journalizing inventory purchases and returns (*Learning Objective 3*) 5–10 min.

Sonny's Spas, Inc., purchased $8,000 worth of inventory from the Pool Warehouse on account, terms of 2/10, n/30. Some of the goods are damaged in shipment, so Sonny's Spas, Inc., returns $1,100 of the merchandise to the Pool Warehouse.

Journalize the following transactions for Sonny's Spas, Inc. Explanations are not required.

   a. Purchase of the goods

   b. Return of the damaged goods

   c. Payment for the goods within the discount period

S4-6. Journalizing inventory purchases and freight charges (*Learning Objectives 3 & 5*) 5–10 min.

Journalize the following transactions for the Jazz Man music store.

    a. Purchased $8,700 of merchandise on account, terms 2/10, n/30, FOB shipping point.

    b. Paid $175 to the freight company for the delivery of the merchandise purchased.

    c. Paid for the inventory purchased in part a within the discount period.

S4-7. Journalizing sales transactions (*Learning Objective 4*) 5–10 min.

Journalize the following transactions for the Pool Warehouse. Explanations are not required.

    a. The Pool Warehouse sold $55,000 of merchandise to Sonny's Spas, Inc., on account, terms 2/15, n/30. The merchandise cost the Pool Warehouse $30,250.

    b. Received payment for the goods from Sonny's Spas, Inc., within the discount period.

S4-8. Journalizing sales and return transactions (*Learning Objective 4*) 5–10 min.

Suppose Peter's Hardware sells merchandise on account, terms 2/10, n/45, for $750 (cost of the inventory is $460) on May 17, 2010. Peter's Hardware later received $225 of goods (cost, $140) as sales returns on May 21, 2010. The customer paid the balance due on May 26, 2010.

Journalize the May, 2010 transactions for Peter's Hardware.

S4-9. Calculate income statement items (*Learning Objective 6*) 5–10 min.

Suppose Peter's Hardware sells merchandise on account, terms 2/10, n/45, for $750 (cost of the inventory is $460) on May 17, 2010. Peter's Hardware later received $225 of goods (cost, $140) as sales returns on May 21, 2010. The customer paid the balance due on May 26, 2010.

    1. Calculate net sales revenue for May 2010.

    2. Calculate gross profit for May 2010.

S4-10. Calculate classified balance sheet amounts (*Learning Objective 6*) 5–10 min.

Selected account balances for Jill's Java at the end of the month are listed below in random order:

Accounts Payable	19,500
Unearned Revenue	2,000
Equipment	33,000
Inventory	37,000
Accounts Receivable	6,000
Wages Payable	1,500
Note Payable, Long-Term	28,000
Accumulated Depreciation, Equipment	4,500
Common Stock	25,000
Supplies	3,400
Building	87,000
Cash	5,200
Accumulated Depreciation, Building	24,000
Prepaid Rent	6,200
Retained Earnings	15,000

Identify or compute the following amounts for Jill's Java:

    a. Total current assets

    b. Total current liabilities

    c. Book value of plant assets

    d. Total long-term liabilities

S4-11. Prepare a multi-step income statement (*Learning Objective 6*) 10–15 min.

The accounting records for ADR, Inc., reflected the following amounts at the end of August 2010:

Cash	$3,500	Cost of Goods Sold	$19,500
Total Operating Expense	3,700	Equipment, Net	6,100
Accounts Payable	4,500	Accrued Liabilities	1,900
Total Stockholders' Equity	5,200	Net Sales Revenue	28,000
Long-Term Notes Payable	2,300	Accounts Receivable	2,900
Inventory	1,700	Prepaid Rent	800
Wages Payable	1,100		

Prepare ADR's multi-step income statement for the fiscal year ended August 31, 2010.

S4-12. Prepare a classified balance sheet (*Learning Objective 6*) 10–15 min.

The accounting records for ADR, Inc., reflected the following amounts at the end of August 2010:

Cash	$3,500	Cost of Goods Sold	$19,500
Total Operating Expense	3,700	Equipment, Net	6,100
Accounts Payable	4,500	Accrued Liabilities	1,900
Total Stockholders' Equity	5,200	Net Sales Revenue	28,000
Long-Term Notes Payable	2,300	Accounts Receivable	2,900
Inventory	1,700	Prepaid Rent	800

Prepare the ADR, Inc., classified balance sheet at August 31, 2010. Use the report format.

S4-13. Calculate gross profit and current ratio (*Learning Objective 7*) 10–15 min.

The accounting records for ADR, Inc., reflected the following amounts at the end of August, 2010:

Cash	$3,500	Cost of Goods Sold	$19,500
Total Operating Expense	3,700	Equipment, Net	6,100
Accounts Payable	4,500	Accrued Liabilities	1,900
Total Stockholders' Equity	5,200	Net Sales Revenue	28,000
Long-Term Notes Payable	2,300	Accounts Receivable	2,900
Inventory	1,700	Prepaid Rent	800
Wages Payable	1,100		

Calculate the gross profit percentage and current ratio for 2010.

EXERCISES (GROUP A)

E4-14A. Adjusting inventory based on a physical count (*Learning Objective 2*) 5–10 min.

The Inventory account for McCormack Tire Company had a balance of $112,600 at the end of its fiscal year. A physical count taken at year end revealed that the value of inventory on hand amounted to $110,800.

Requirements

1. Journalize the adjustment for inventory shrinkage.

2. What could cause the inventory balance according to the physical count to be different from the ledger balance?

E4-15A. Journalizing inventory purchases, returns, and freight transactions (*Learning Objectives 3 & 5*) 10–15 min.

On June 15, 2010, Bailey's Department Store purchased $4,300 of inventory on account from one of its suppliers. The terms were 3/15, n/45, FOB shipping point. On June 18 Bailey's Department Store paid freight charges of $350 related to the delivery of the goods purchased on June 15. Upon receiving the goods, Bailey's Department Store checked the order and found $900 of unsuitable merchandise, which was returned to the supplier on June 20. Then, on June 28, Bailey's Department Store paid the invoice.

Requirement

1. Journalize all necessary transactions for Bailey's Department Store. Omit explanations.

E4-16A. Journalizing inventory purchases, returns, and freight transactions (*Learning Objective 3 & 5*) 10–15 min.

Journalize the following transactions for Amazing Audio, Inc., that occurred during the month of March.

Mar	3	Purchased $4,600 of merchandise on account, terms 2/10, n/30, FOB shipping point. The supplier prepaid freight charges of $250 and added the amount to the invoice.
	6	Returned damaged goods to the supplier and received a credit memorandum in the amount of $600.
	12	Paid for the goods purchased on March 3.

E4-17A. Journalizing inventory sales, returns, and freight transactions (*Learning Objectives 4 & 5*) 10–15 min.

On September 14, 2010, C & T Machinery, Inc., sold $2,300 of inventory (cost is $1,350) on account to one of its customers. The terms were 1/10, n/30, FOB destination. On September 16, C & T Machinery, Inc., paid freight charges of $75 related to the delivery of the goods sold on September 14. On September 20, $900 of damaged goods (cost is $540) were returned by the customer. On September 23, C & T Machinery, Inc., received payment in full from the customer.

Requirement

1. Journalize all necessary transactions for C & T Machinery, Inc. Omit explanations.

E4-18A. Journalizing inventory sales, returns, and freight transactions (Learning Objectives 4 & 5) 10–15 min.

Journalize the following transactions for Amazing Audio, Inc., that occurred during the month of November. Amazing Audio's cost of inventory is 65% of the sales price.

Nov 3	Sold $1,600 of merchandise on account, terms 2/15, n/45, FOB shipping point. Amazing Audio, Inc., prepaid $85 of shipping costs and added the amount to the customer's invoice.
7	Issued a credit memo to the customer acknowledging the return of $250 of damaged goods.
16	Received payment in full from the customer for the November 3 invoice.

E4-19A. Journalizing inventory purchases, sales, returns, and freight transactions (Learning Objectives 3, 4, & 5) 15–20 min.

The following transactions occurred during April 2010, for Angelo's Garden Center, Inc.:

Apr 3	Purchased $3,500 of goods on account. Terms, 2/10, n/30, FOB shipping point.
6	Returned $400 of defective merchandise purchased on April 3.
8	Paid freight charges of $110 for delivery of goods purchased on April 3.
11	Sold $4,300 of inventory to a customer on account. Terms, 3/15, n/45, FOB shipping point. The cost of the goods was $2,100.
12	Paid amount owed on the April 3 purchase.
18	Granted a $300 sales allowance on the April 11 sale because the goods were the wrong color.
25	Received payment in full from customer for the April 11 sale.

Requirement

1. Journalize the April transactions for Angelo's Garden Center, Inc. Omit explanations.

E4-20A. Calculate multi-step income statement items (Learning Objective 6) 10–15 min.

Consider the following incomplete table of a merchandiser's profit data:

Sales	Sales Discounts	Net Sales	Cost of Goods Sold	Gross Profit
(a)	2,500	(b)	68,300	32,100
64,000	1,700	(c)	44,600	(d)
102,000	(e)	93,500	(f)	28,600
(g)	2,100	86,300	57,700	(h)

Requirement

1. Complete the table by computing the missing amounts.

E4-21A. Prepare a single-step income statement (*Learning Objective 6*) 10–15 min.

The account balances for Atlantis Aquatics, Inc., for the year ended December 31, 2010, are presented next in random order:

Cash	$ 3,700	Cost of Goods Sold	$136,400
Equipment	13,700	Accumulated Depreciation,	
Accounts Payable	4,500	Equipment	6,100
Common Stock	35,000	Unearned Revenues	1,900
Long-Term Notes Payable	10,000	Sales Revenue	243,500
General Expenses	18,200	Accounts Receivable	3,200
Wages Payable	1,100	Accumulated Depreciation,	
Supplies	900	Building	18,500
Building	125,000	Mortgage Payable	
Sales Returns and		(Long-Term)	37,000
Allowances	4,800	Dividends	34,000
Prepaid Rent	800	Sales Discounts	2,200
Retained Earnings	13,800	Selling Expenses	26,800
		Inventory	1,700

Requirements

1. Prepare Atlantis Aquatics' *single-step* income statement.

2. Would you recommend the use of the single-step income statement format by a merchandiser? Why?

Quick solution:

1. Net Income = $55,100.

E4-22A. Prepare a multi-step income statement; calculate gross profit percentage (*Learning Objectives 6 & 7*) 15–20 min.

Use the data for Atlantis Aquatics, Inc., from E4-21A.

Requirements

1. Prepare Atlantis Aquatics' *multi-step* income statement.

2. Calculate the gross profit percentage.

3. The gross profit percentage for 2009 was 38.7%. Did the gross profit percentage improve or deteriorate during 2010?

E4-23A. Prepare a classified balance sheet; calculate current ratio (*Learning Objectives 6 & 7*) 15–20 min.

Use the data for Atlantis Aquatics, Inc., from E4-21A.

Requirements

1. Prepare Atlantis Aquatics' classified balance sheet. Use the account format. The balance shown for retained earnings represents the balance prior to closing the temporary accounts for the year.

2. Calculate the current ratio.

3. The current ratio for 2009 was 1.25. Did the current ratio improve or deteriorate during 2010?

E4-24A. Calculate gross profit percentage and current ratio (*Learning Objective 7*) 10–15 min.

Apex, Inc., had Sales Revenue of $47 million, Sales Returns and Allowances of $2 million and Sales Discounts of $0.5 million in 2010. Cost of goods sold was $24 million, and net income was $7 million for the year. At December 31, the company had total assets of $36 million of which total current assets amounted to

$15 million. Apex's current liabilities were $9 million and its long-term liabilities were $4 million.

Requirement

1. Compute Apex's gross profit percentage and current ratio for 2010.

EXERCISES (GROUP B)

E4-25B. Adjusting inventory based on a physical count (*Learning Objective 2*) 5–10 min.

The Inventory account for Brady Company had a balance of $137,900 at the end of its fiscal year. A physical count taken at year end revealed that the value of inventory on hand amounted to $136,400.

Requirements

1. Journalize the adjustment for inventory shrinkage.
2. What could cause the inventory balance according to the physical count to be different from the ledger balance?

E4-26B. Journalizing inventory purchases, returns, and freight transactions (*Learning Objectives 3 & 5*) 10–15 min.

On November 15, 2010, Chandler's Department Store purchased $5,100 of inventory on account from one of its suppliers. The terms were 3/15, n/45, FOB shipping point. On November 18 Chandler's Department Store paid freight charges of $175 related to the delivery of the goods purchased on November 15. Upon receiving the goods, Chandler's Department Store checked the order and found $600 of unsuitable merchandise, which was returned to the supplier on November 20. Then, on November 28, Chandler's Department Store paid the invoice.

Requirement

1. Journalize all necessary transactions for Chandler's Department Store. Omit explanations.

E4-27B. Journalizing inventory purchases, returns, and freight transactions (*Learning Objectives 3 & 5*) 10–15 min.

Journalize the following transactions for Antique Furniture, Inc., that occurred during the month of January.

Jan	3	Purchased $5,700 of merchandise on account, terms 1/10, n/30, FOB shipping point. The supplier prepaid freight charges of $225 and added the amount to the invoice.
	6	Returned damaged goods to the supplier and received a credit memorandum in the amount of $500.
	12	Paid for the goods purchased on January 3.

E4-28B. Journalizing inventory sales, returns, and freight transactions (*Learning Objectives 4 & 5*) 10–15 min.

On November 14, 2010, Amazing Sound, Inc., sold $3,100 of inventory (cost is $1,330) on account to one of its customers. The terms were 3/10, n/30, FOB destination. On November 16, Amazing Sound, Inc., paid freight charges of $65 related to the delivery of the goods sold on November 14. On November 20, $800 of damaged goods (cost is $420) were returned by the customer. On November 23, Amazing Sound, Inc., received payment in full from the customer.

Requirement

1. Journalize all necessary transactions for Amazing Sound, Inc. Omit explanations.

E4-29B. Journalizing inventory sales, returns, and freight transactions (Learning Objectives 4 & 5) 10–15 min.

Journalize the following transactions for Antique Furniture, Inc., that occurred during the month of April. Antique Furniture's cost of inventory is 70% of the sales price.

Apr	3	Sold $2,100 of merchandise on account, terms 1/15, n/45, FOB shipping point. Antique Furniture, Inc., prepaid $50 of shipping costs and added the amount to the customer's invoice.
	7	Issued a credit memo to the customer acknowledging the return of $225 of damaged goods.
	16	Received payment in full from the customer for the April 3 invoice.

E4-30B. Journalizing inventory purchases, sales, returns, and freight transactions (Learning Objectives 3, 4, & 5) 15–20 min.

The following transactions occurred during April 2010, for Sandy Salon Products, Inc.:

Apr	3	Purchased $3,400 of goods on account. Terms, 1/15, n/30. FOB shipping point.
	6	Returned $500 of defective merchandise purchased on April 3.
	8	Paid freight charges of $130 for delivery of goods purchased on April 3.
	11	Sold $2,800 of inventory to a customer on account. Terms, 3/15, n/45, FOB shipping point. The cost of the goods was $1,600.
	12	Paid amount owed on the April 3 purchase.
	18	Granted a $225 sales allowance on the April 11 sale because the goods were the wrong color.
	25	Received payment in full from customer for the April 11 sale.

Requirement

1. Journalize the April transactions for Sandy Salon Products, Inc. Omit explanations.

E4-31B. Calculate multi-step income statement items (Learning Objective 6) 10–15 min.

Consider the following incomplete table of a merchandiser's profit data:

Sales	Sales Discounts	Net Sales	Cost of Goods Sold	Gross Profit
(a)	1,700	(b)	67,500	37,700
89,600	2,900	(c)	55,700	(d)
103,000	(e)	94,300	(f)	31,500
(g)	1,400	88,000	51,900	(h)

Requirement

1. Complete the table by computing the missing amounts.

E4-32B. Prepare a single-step income statement (*Learning Objective 6*) 10–15 min.

The account balances for Great Gadget, Inc., for the year ended December 31, 2010, are presented next in random order:

Cash	$ 9,300	Cost of Goods Sold	$135,000
Equipment	39,800	Accumulated Depreciation,	
Accounts Payable	6,300	Equipment	13,700
Common Stock	25,000	Unearned Revenues	1,900
Long-Term Notes Payable	35,000	Sales Revenue	257,000
General Expenses	18,200	Accounts Receivable	4,500
Wages Payable	1,300	Accumulated Depreciation,	
Supplies	3,300	Building	25,900
Building	130,000	Mortgage Payable	
Sales Returns and		(Long-Term)	43,500
Allowances	2,900	Dividends	41,000
Prepaid Rent	2,600	Sales Discounts	1,500
Retained Earnings	25,700	Selling Expenses	43,500
		Inventory	3,700

Requirements

1. Prepare Great Gadget's *single-step* income statement.
2. Would you recommend the use of the single-step income statement format by a merchandiser? Why?

E4-33B. Prepare a multi-step income statement; calculate gross profit percentage (*Learning Objectives 6 & 7*) 15–20 min.

Use the data for Great Gadget, Inc., from E4-32B.

Requirements

1. Prepare Great Gadget's *multi-step* income statement.
2. Calculate the gross profit percentage.
3. The gross profit percentage for 2009 was 52.3%. Did the gross profit percentage improve or deteriorate during 2010?

E4-34B. Prepare a classified balance sheet; calculate current ratio (*Learning Objectives 6 & 7*) 15–20 min.

Use the data for Great Gadget, Inc., from E4-32B.

Requirements

1. Prepare Great Gadget's classified balance sheet. Use the account format. The balance shown for retained earnings represents the balance prior to closing the temporary accounts for the year.
2. Calculate the current ratio.
3. The current ratio for 2009 was 3.62. Did the current ratio improve or deteriorate during 2010?

E4-35B. Calculate gross profit percentage and current ratio (*Learning Objective 7*) 10–15 min.

Sunny Day Sunlamps, Inc., had Sales Revenue of $53 million, Sales Returns and Allowances of $2 million, and Sales Discounts of $0.3 million in 2010. Cost of goods sold was $23 million, and net income was $12 million for the year. At December 31, the company had total assets of $33 million of which total current assets amounted to $13 million. Sunny Day Sunlamps' current liabilities were $7 million and its long-term liabilities were $4 million.

Requirement

1. Compute Sunny Day Sunlamps' gross profit percentage and current ratio for 2010.

EXERCISES (ALTERNATES 1, 2, AND 3)

These alternative exercise sets are available for your practice benefit at
www.myaccountinglab.com

PROBLEMS (GROUP A)

P4-36A. Journalizing inventory purchases, returns, and freight transactions (*Learning Objective 3 & 5*) 15–20 min.

The following purchase related transactions for Axiom, Inc., occurred during the month of February.

Feb	3	Purchased $5,400 of merchandise, paid cash.
	9	Purchased $650 of supplies on account from Supplies Unlimited. Terms, n/30, FOB destination.
	16	Purchased $6,800 of merchandise on account from A to Z, Inc. Terms, 2/15, n/30, FOB shipping point.
	22	Received a credit memo in the amount of $1,200 from A to Z, Inc., for damaged goods from the February 16 purchase that were returned.
	28	Paid for the supplies purchased on February 9.
	28	Paid A to Z, Inc., in full for the February 16 purchase.

Requirement

1. Journalize the transactions for Axiom, Inc. Omit explanations.

P4-37A. Journalizing inventory sales, returns, and freight transactions (*Learning Objective 3 & 5*) 15–20 min.

The following sale related transactions for PDR, Inc., occurred during the month of June.

Jun	3	Sold $3,200 (cost $2,100) of merchandise on account to J. Henderson. Terms, 2/15, n/45, FOB destination.
	4	Paid $250 to ship the goods sold on June 3 to J. Henderson.
	10	Sold $1,800 (cost $1,200) of merchandise to cash customers.
	17	Received payment in full from J. Henderson for the June 3 sale.
	22	Sold $4,700 (cost $3,100) of merchandise to M. Perez. Terms, 3/10, n/30, FOB shipping point.
	26	Granted M. Perez a $600 allowance on the June 22 sale due to minor defects in the goods shipped.
	30	Received payment in full from M. Perez for the June 22 sale.

Requirement

1. Journalize the transactions for PDR, Inc. Omit explanations.

P4-38A. Journalizing inventory purchases, sales, returns, and freight transactions (*Learning Objectives 3, 4, & 5*) 20–25 min.

The following transactions occurred between Kinzer Furniture and M & L Furniture Warehouse during May of the current year:

May	4	Kinzer Furniture purchased $5,800 of merchandise from M & L Furniture Warehouse on account. Terms, 2/15, n/30. FOB shipping point. The goods cost M & L Furniture Warehouse $3,300.
	7	Kinzer Furniture paid a $125 freight bill for delivery of the goods purchased on May 4.
	10	Kinzer Furniture returned $1,400 of the merchandise purchased on May 4. The goods cost M & L Furniture Warehouse $800.
	18	Kinzer Furniture paid $2,000 of the May 4 invoice less the discount.
	31	Kinzer Furniture paid the remaining amount owed on the May 4 invoice.

Requirements

1. Journalize these transactions on the books of Kinzer Furniture.
2. Journalize these transactions on the books of M & L Furniture Warehouse.

P4-39A. Journalizing inventory purchases, sales, returns, and freight transactions; calculate gross profit (*Learning Objectives 3, 4, 5, & 6*) 25–30 min.

The following transactions for Liberty Tire, Co., occurred during October:

Oct	4	Purchased $5,900 of merchandise on account from Firerock Tire. Terms, 2/15, n/45, FOB shipping point. Firerock Tire prepaid the $300 shipping cost and added the amount to the invoice.
	7	Purchased $350 of supplies on account from OfficeMaxx. Terms, 2/10, n/30, FOB destination.
	9	Sold $950 (cost, $500) of merchandise on account to L. Simpson. Terms, 3/15, n/45, FOB destination.
	11	Paid $75 freight charges to deliver goods to L. Simpson.
	13	Returned $1,400 of the merchandise purchased on October 4 and received a credit.
	15	Sold $650 (cost, $350) of merchandise to cash customers.
	16	Paid for the supplies purchased on October 7.
	18	Paid Firerock Tire the amount due from the October 4 purchase in full.
	20	L. Simpson returned $175 (cost, $100) of merchandise from the October 9 sale.
	22	Purchased $2,100 of inventory. Paid cash.
	23	Received payment in full from L. Simpson for the October 9 sale.

Quick solution:

2. Gross Profit for the month of October = $651.75.

Requirements

1. Journalize the transactions on the books of Liberty Tire, Co.
2. What was Liberty Tire's gross profit for the month of October?

P4-40A. Prepare a multi-step income statement; calculate gross profit percentage (*Learning Objectives 6 & 7*) 20–25 min.

The adjusted trial balance for Sparky's Electrical Supply, Inc., as of November 30, 2010, is presented next:

	ACCOUNT	DEBIT	CREDIT
	Sparky's Electrical Supply, Inc.		
	Trial Balance		
	November 30, 2010		
	Cash	$ 15,000	
	Accounts Receivable	37,300	
	Inventory	18,500	
	Supplies	900	
	Equipment	68,000	
	Accumulated Depreciation, Equipment		$ 8,000
	Accounts Payable		12,900
	Unearned Sales Revenue		5,300
	Note Payable, Long-Term		15,000
	Common Stock		10,000
	Retained Earnings		73,300
	Dividends	22,000	
	Sales Revenue		193,200
	Sales Returns and Allowances	8,700	
	Sales Discounts	2,600	
	Cost of Goods Sold	103,400	
	Selling Expense	25,200	
	General Expense	16,100	
	Total	$317,700	$317,700

Requirements

1. Prepare the multi-step income statement for November for Sparky's Electrical Supply, Inc.

2. Calculate the gross profit percentage for November for Sparky's Electrical Supply, Inc.

3. What does Sparky's Electrical Supply Inc.'s gross profit percentage mean?

P4-41A. Prepare a multi-step income statement, a statement of retained earnings, and a classified balance sheet (*Learning Objective* 6) 25–30 min.

The account balances for the year ended December 31, 2010, for Williams Industries are listed next:

Sales Revenue	$322,800	Cost of Goods Sold	$158,400
Equipment	104,000	Accumulated Depreciation,	
Accounts Payable	16,500	Equipment	26,400
Sales Discounts	2,200	Unearned Sales Revenue	2,500
Advertising Expense	12,600	Prepaid Rent	1,200
Interest Expense	1,700	Office Salaries Expense	52,000
Wages Payable	1,600	Accumulated Depreciation,	
Accounts Receivable	6,900	Building	40,500
Building	140,000	Rent Expense	5,800
Sales Returns and		Dividends	14,000
Allowances	6,700	Cash	7,800
Common Stock	35,000	Retained Earnings	87,600
Utilities Expense	10,300	Delivery Expense	1,300
Inventory	16,400	Insurance Expense	5,700
Commission Expense	22,300	Mortgage Payable	
		(Long-Term)	37,000
		Supplies	600

Requirements

1. Prepare Williams' Industries' *multi-step* income statement.
2. Prepare Williams' Industries' statement of retained earnings.
3. Prepare Williams' Industries' classified balance sheet in *report form*.

P4-42A. Calculate gross profit percentage and current ratio (*Learning Objective* 7) 20–25 min.

The account balances for the year ended December 31, 2010, for Williams Industries are listed next:

Sales Revenue	$322,800	Cost of Goods Sold	$158,400
Equipment	104,000	Accumulated Depreciation,	
Accounts Payable	16,500	Equipment	26,400
Sales Discounts	2,200	Unearned Sales Revenue	2,500
Advertising Expense	12,600	Prepaid Rent	1,200
Interest Expense	1,700	Office Salaries Expense	52,000
Wages Payable	1,600	Accumulated Depreciation,	
Accounts Receivable	6,900	Building	40,500
Building	140,000	Rent Expense	5,800
Sales Returns and		Dividends	14,000
Allowances	6,700	Cash	7,800
Common Stock	35,000	Retained Earnings	87,600
Utilities Expense	10,300	Delivery Expense	1,300
Inventory	16,400	Insurance Expense	5,700
Commission Expense	22,300	Mortgage Payable	37,000
		Supplies	600

Requirements

1. Calculate the gross profit percentage for Williams Industries for the year.
2. The gross profit percentage for 2009 was 51.3%. Did the gross profit percentage improve or deteriorate during 2010?
3. Calculate the current ratio for Williams Industries.
4. The current ratio for 2009 was 1.47. Did the current ratio improve or deteriorate during 2010?

PROBLEMS (GROUP B)

P4-43B. Journalizing inventory purchases, returns, and freight transactions (*Learning Objectives 3 & 5*) 15–20 min.

The following purchase related transactions for Lavery, Inc., occurred during the month of September.

Sep	3	Purchased $5,100 of merchandise, paid cash.
	9	Purchased $800 of supplies on account from Chandler Unlimited. Terms, n/30, FOB destination.
	16	Purchased $4,300 of merchandise on account from Garden Supplies, Inc. Terms, 3/15, n/30, FOB shipping point.
	22	Received a credit memo in the amount of $1,100 from Garden Supplies, Inc., for damaged goods from the Sep 16 purchase that were returned.
	30	Paid for the supplies purchased on Sep 9.
	30	Paid Garden Supplies, Inc., in full for the Sep 16 purchase.

Requirement

1. Journalize the transactions for Lavery, Inc. Omit explanations.

P4-44B. Journalizing inventory sales, returns, and freight transactions (*Learning Objectives 3 & 5*) 15–20 min.

The following sale related transactions for Beautiful Decor, Inc., occurred during the month of April.

Apr	3	Sold $3,600 (cost $1,700) of merchandise on account to A. Klecans. Terms, 3/15, n/45, FOB destination.
	4	Paid $75 to ship the goods sold on April 3 to A. Klecans.
	10	Sold $2,700 (cost $1,200) of merchandise to cash customers.
	17	Received payment in full from A. Klecans for the April 3 sale.
	22	Sold $5,100 (cost $2,500) of merchandise to M. Perez. Terms, 2/10, n/30, FOB shipping point.
	26	Granted M. Perez a $200 allowance on the April 22 sale due to minor defects in the goods shipped.
	30	Received payment in full from M. Perez for the April 22 sale.

Requirement

1. Journalize the transactions for Beautiful Decor, Inc. Omit explanations.

P4-45B. Journalizing inventory purchases, sales, returns, and freight transactions (*Learning Objectives 3, 4, & 5*) 20–25 min.

The following transactions occurred between Retro Furniture and E & S Furniture Warehouse during October of the current year:

Oct	4	Retro Furniture purchased $8,000 of merchandise from E & S Furniture Warehouse on account. Terms, 1/15, n/30. FOB shipping point. The goods cost E & S Furniture Warehouse $2,900.
	7	Retro Furniture paid a $200 freight bill for delivery of the goods purchased on October 4.
	10	Retro Furniture returned $1,000 of the merchandise purchased on October 4. The goods cost E & S Furniture Warehouse $450.
	18	Retro Furniture paid $2,000 of the October 4 invoice less the discount.
	31	Retro Furniture paid the remaining amount owed on the October 4 invoice.

Requirements

1. Journalize these transactions on the books of Retro Furniture.
2. Journalize these transactions on the books of E & S Furniture Warehouse.

P4-46B. Journalizing inventory purchases, sales, returns, and freight transactions; calculate gross profit (*Learning Objectives 3, 4, 5, & 6*) 25–30 min.

The following transactions for Best Deal Tire, Co., occurred during May:

May	4	Purchased $5,400 of merchandise on account from Bargain Tire. Terms, 3/15, n/45, FOB shipping point. Bargain Tire prepaid the $125 shipping cost and added the amount to the invoice.
	7	Purchased $375 of supplies on account from Office Maxx. Terms, 3/10, n/30, FOB destination.
	9	Sold $950 (cost, $250) of merchandise on account to W. Furmick. Terms, 3/15, n/45, FOB destination.
	11	Paid $25 freight charges to deliver goods to W. Furmick.
	13	Returned $600 of the merchandise purchased on May 4 and received a credit.
	15	Sold $900 (cost, $350) of merchandise to cash customers.
	16	Paid for the supplies purchased on May 7.
	18	Paid Bargain Tire the amount due from the May 4 purchase in full.
	20	W. Furmick returned $175 (cost, $100) of merchandise from the May 9 sale.
	22	Purchased $3,900 of inventory. Paid cash.
	23	Received payment in full from W. Furmick for the May 9 sale.

Requirements

1. Journalize the transactions on the books of Best Deal Tire, Co.
2. What was Best Deal Tire's gross profit for the month of May?

P4-47B. Prepare a multi-step income statement; calculate gross profit percentage (*Learning Objectives 6 & 7*) 20–25 min.

The adjusted trial balance for CED Electric, Inc., as of June 30, 2010, is presented next:

		ACCOUNT	DEBIT	CREDIT
		CED Electric, Inc.		
		Trial Balance		
		June 30, 2010		
		Cash	$ 13,600	
		Accounts Receivable	32,600	
		Inventory	19,600	
		Supplies	2,600	
		Equipment	69,000	
		Accumulated Depreciation, Equipment		$ 13,700
		Accounts Payable		5,100
		Unearned Sales Revenue		2,800
		Note Payable, Long-term		40,000
		Common Stock		25,000
		Retained Earnings		68,200
		Dividends	48,000	
		Sales Revenues		197,500
		Sales Returns and Allowances	4,800	
		Sales Discount	3,100	
		Cost of Goods Sold	101,400	
		Selling Expense	37,000	
		General Expense	20,600	
		Total	$352,300	$352,300

Requirements

1. Prepare the multi-step income statement for June for CED Electric, Inc.
2. Calculate the gross profit percentage for June for CED Electric, Inc.
3. What does CED Electric Inc.'s gross profit percentage mean?

P4-48B. Prepare a multi-step income statement, a statement of retained earnings and a classified balance sheet (*Learning Objective 6*) 25–30 min.

The accounts of for the year ended March 31, 2010, for Clark Industries, Inc. are listed next:

Sales Revenue...............	$275,100	Cost of Goods Sold...............	$119,000
Equipment......................	27,000	Accumulated Depreciation,	
Accounts Payable...........	16,500	Equipment........................	13,000
Sales Discounts	2,500	Unearned Sales Revenue	2,500
Advertising Expense........	11,500	Prepaid Rent	5,000
Interest Expense	700	Office Salaries Expense..........	54,000
Wages Payable...............	1,000	Accumulated Depreciation,	
Accounts Receivable........	8,800	Building............................	52,500
Building..........................	190,000	Rent Expense	5,200
Sales Returns and		Dividends............................	12,000
Allowances..................	4,900	Cash....................................	22,500
Common Stock................	35,000	Retained Earnings.................	112,800
Utilities Expense.............	14,000	Delivery Expense...................	1,200
Inventory........................	29,000	Insurance Expense................	10,200
Commission Expense........	31,700	Mortgage Payable	
		(Long-Term)	42,000
		Supplies	1,200

Requirements

1. Prepare Clark Industries' *multi-step* income statement.
2. Prepare Clark Industries' statement of retained earnings.
3. Prepare Clark Industries' classified balance sheet in *report form*.

P4-49B Calculate gross profit percentage and current ratio (*Learning Objective 7*) 20–25 min.

The income statement and balance sheet for Clark Industries at March 31, 2010, are presented next:

Sales Revenue	$275,100	Cost of Goods Sold	$119,000
Equipment	27,000	Accumulated Depreciation,	
Accounts Payable	16,500	Equipment	13,000
Sales Discounts	2,500	Unearned Sales Revenue	2,500
Advertising Expense	11,500	Prepaid Rent	5,000
Interest Expense	700	Office Salaries Expense	54,000
Wages Payable	1,000	Accumulated Depreciation,	
Accounts Receivable	8,800	Building	52,500
Building	190,000	Rent Expense	5,200
Sales Returns and		Dividends	12,000
Allowances	4,900	Cash	22,500
Common Stock	35,000	Retained Earnings	112,800
Utilities Expense	14,000	Delivery Expense	1,200
Inventory	29,000	Insurance Expense	10,200
Commission Expense	31,700	Mortgage Payable	
		(Long-Term)	42,000
		Supplies	1,200

Requirements

1. Calculate the gross profit percentage for Clark Industries for the year.
2. The gross profit percentage for 2009 was 39.1%. Did the gross profit percentage improve or deteriorate during 2010?
3. Calculate the current ratio for Clark Industries.
4. The current ratio for 2009 was 2.33. Did the current ratio improve or deteriorate during 2010?

PROBLEMS (ALTERNATES 1, 2, AND 3)

These alternative problem sets are available for your practice benefit at
www.myaccountinglab.com

CONTINUING EXERCISE

Let's continue our accounting for Graham's Yard Care, Inc., from Chapter 3. Starting in July, Graham's Yard Care, Inc., has begun selling plants that it purchases from a wholesaler. During July, Graham's Yard Care, Inc., completed the following transactions:

Jul 2	Completed lawn service and received cash of $500.
5	Purchased 100 plants on account for inventory, $250, plus freight in of $10.
15	Sold 40 plants on account, $400 (cost $104).
17	Consulted with a client on landscaping design for a fee of $150 on account.
20	Purchased 100 plants on account for inventory, $300.
21	Paid on account, $100.
25	Sold 100 plants for cash, $700 (cost $276).
31	Recorded the following adjusting entries: Accrued salaries for the month of July equal $225 Depreciation on equipment $30 Physical count of plant inventory, 50 plants (cost $150)

Refer to the T-accounts for Graham's Yard Care, Inc., from the continuing exercise in Chapter 3.

Requirements

1. Journalize and post the July transactions. Omit explanations. Compute each account balance, and denote the balance as *Bal*. Open additional accounts as necessary.

2. Prepare the July income statement of Graham's Yard Care, Inc., using the single-step format.

CONTINUING PROBLEM

In this problem, we continue the accounting for Aqua Elite, Inc. from Chapter 3. On August 1, Aqua Elite, Inc., expanded its business and began selling and installing swimming pools and spas. The post closing trial balance for Aqua Elite, Inc., as of July 31, 2010, is presented next.

Aqua Elite, Inc. Trial Balance July 31, 2010		
ACCOUNT	**DEBIT**	**CREDIT**
Cash	$17,380	
Accounts Receivable	5,400	
Supplies	350	
Prepaid Rent	3,600	
Land	15,000	
Furniture	3,300	
Accumulated Depreciation, Furniture		$ 210
Equipment	4,700	
Accumulated Depreciation, Equipment		400
Vehicles	31,000	
Accumulated Depreciation, Vehicles		650
Accounts Payable		1,840
Salary Payable		675
Unearned Service Revenue		2,800
Notes Payable		31,000
Common Stock		38,500
Retained Earnings		4,655
Total	$80,730	$80,730

The following transactions occurred during the month of August:

Aug	2	Paid the receptionist's salary, which was accrued on July 31.
	3	Purchased $20,600 of merchandise on account from the Spa Superstore. Terms, 3/15, n/45, FOB shipping point.
	5	Purchased $750 of supplies. Paid cash.
	6	Paid freight charges of $475 related to the August 3 purchase.
	8	Sold a spa for $5,800 (cost, $3,600) on account to R. Tanaka. Terms, 2/15, n/30, FOB shipping point.
	10	Purchased office furniture for $1,200. Paid cash.
	11	Paid advertising expense, $625.
	12	Returned a defective spa, which was purchased on August 3. Received a $3,400 credit from the Spa Superstore.
	13	Sold a spa for $6,750 (cost, $3,360) to a cash customer.
	15	Granted R. Tanaka a $300 allowance because of imperfections she detected upon receiving her spa.
	16	Paid receptionist's salary, $675.
	17	Paid the Spa Superstore the amount due from the August 3 purchase in full.
	19	Purchased $12,100 of inventory on account from Pool Universe. Terms, 2/10, n/30, FOB destination.
	21	Sold an above ground pool for $13,700 (cost, $8,500) on account to B. Wagoner. Terms, 2/10, n/30, FOB destination.
	22	Received payment in full from R. Tanaka for the August 8 sale.
	24	Paid freight charges of $560 to have the pool sold to B. Wagoner on August 21 delivered.
	25	Purchased equipment on account from Betterbuy, Inc., for $2,600. Terms, n/30, FOB destination.
	27	Received payment in full from B. Wagoner for the August 21 sale.
	28	Paid in full the invoice from the August 19 purchase from Pool Universe.
	30	Paid monthly utilities, $850.
	31	Paid sales commissions of $1,300 to the sales staff.

Requirements

1. Journalize the transactions that occurred in August.

2. Using the four-column accounts from the continuing problem in Chapter 3, post the transactions to the ledger creating new ledger accounts as necessary; omit posting references. Calculate the new account balances.

3. Prepare the unadjusted trial balance for Aqua Elite, Inc., at the end of August.

4. Journalize and post the adjusting entries for August based on the following adjustment information.

   a. Record the expired rent.

   b. Supplies on hand, $445.

   c. Depreciation; $575 equipment, $380 furniture, $650 vehicles.

   d. A physical count of inventory revealed $13,387 of inventory on hand.

5. Prepare an adjusted trial balance for Aqua Elite, Inc., at the end of August.

6. Prepare the multi-step income statement, statement of retained earnings, and classified balance sheet for the month of August.

7. Prepare and post closing entries.

8. Prepare a post closing trial balance for the end of the period.

APPLY YOUR KNOWLEDGE
ETHICS IN ACTION

Case 1. Tim Jackson works as a salesperson at Conway, Inc. In addition to a base monthly salary, Tim receives a commission that is based on the amount of sales that he makes during the month. Tim was hoping to have enough money for a down payment on a new car but sales have been low due to a downturn in the economy. Tim was aware that Conway, Inc., granted credit terms of 2/10, n/30 to its credit customers. In addition, Tim knew that Conway, Inc., had a "no questions asked" return policy. Based on this knowledge, Tim had an idea. Tim contacted a regular customer and convinced the customer to make a substantial purchase of merchandise so that he could earn the commission on the sale. Tim explained to the customer that they would not have to pay for the goods for thirty days and that they could return part, or all, of the goods prior to paying for them. However, Tim asked the customer not to return any of the goods until the following month to ensure that he would earn the full commission.

Requirements
1. Do you feel Tim acted unethically? Why or why not?
2. How can Conway, Inc., deter actions like Tim's?

Case 2. Tina Adams owns and operates the Cottage Café. Tina has requested a credit application from UMT, Inc., a major food supplier, that she hopes to begin purchasing inventory from. UMT, Inc., has requested that Tina submit a full set of financial statements for the Cottage Café with the credit application. Tina is concerned because the most recent balance sheet for the Cottage Café reflects a current ratio of 1.24. Tina has heard that most creditors like to see a current ratio that is 1.5 or higher. In order to increase the Cottage Café's current ratio, Tina has convinced her parents to loan the business $25,000 on an 18-month long-term note payable. Tina's parents are apprehensive about having their money "tied up" for over a year. Tina reassured them that even though the note is an 18-month note, the Cottage Café can, and probably will, repay the $25,000 sooner.

Requirements
1. Discuss the ethical issues related to the loan from Tina's parents?
2. Why do you think creditors like to see current ratios of 1.5 or higher?

KNOW YOUR BUSINESS
FINANCIAL ANALYSIS

Purpose: To help familiarize you with the financial reporting of a real company in order to further your understanding of the chapter material you are learning.

This case uses both the income statement (statement of operations) and the balance sheet of Columbia Sportswear in Appendix A at the end of the book.

Requirements
1. What income statement format does Columbia Sportswear use? How can you tell?
2. Calculate the gross profit ratio for Columbia Sportswear for 2006, 2007, and 2008. Has the gross profit rate been improving or deteriorating?
3. Does Columbia Sportswear report a classified balance sheet? How can you tell?
4. Calculate the current ratio for Columbia Sportswear for 2007 and 2008. Has the current ratio improved or deteriorated?

INDUSTRY ANALYSIS

Purpose: To help you understand and compare the performance of two companies in the same industry.

Find the Columbia Sportswear Company Annual Report located in Appendix A and go to the financial statements starting on page 681. Now access the 2008 Annual Report for Under Armour, Inc., from the Internet. Go to the company's Web page for Investor Relations at http://investor.underarmour.com/investors.cfm and under Downloads on the right-hand side, go to 2008 Annual Report. The company's financial statements start on page 49.

Which of these companies would be considered to be merchandising businesses? If your answer was "both companies are merchandising businesses," you would be correct. But how did you know that? If you didn't know anything about either of these two companies (maybe you're already familiar with them through their advertising campaigns), how would you know that they are merchandising businesses? Can you tell that by looking at the consolidated balance sheets for both companies? What about the consolidated statements of income (or operations)? Which accounts on these two financial statements tell you that these companies are merchandising businesses?

SMALL BUSINESS ANALYSIS

Purpose: To help you understand the importance of cash flows in the operation of a small business.

The end of the year is approaching. You're going to meet with your CPA next week to do some end of the year tax planning, so in preparation for that meeting you look at your last month's income statement. You know that you've had a pretty good year, which means that you're going to have to pay some income taxes. But you know if you can get your taxable income down, you won't have to pay as much in income taxes.

You remember that one of your suppliers was offering a pretty good discount if you purchased from the company in bulk. The only problem is you have to pay for the purchases at the time of purchase. Knowing that you want to decrease your taxable income, you call up the supplier and place a large order and write the supplier a check.

At your meeting with the CPA, you tell of the large inventory purchase for cash that you just made and how much income tax that will save you on this year's income tax return. The CPA has a rather troubled look on his face; that look usually means you've made some kind of an error. So you pose this question to him:

"Steve, you got that look on your face right after I told you about the big inventory purchase that I made. Even though I used up a lot of my available cash, the reason I did it was to save money on my tax return. A big purchase like that has to knock down my taxable income pretty good, huh? And besides, I got these products for a really good price, which means I'll make more profit when I sell them. So why do you have that look? Did I mess up?"

Requirement

1. If you were the CPA, how would you respond to this client? Is the large inventory purchase going to have any effect on his income statement? What about the fact that he paid for this large purchase in cash? Was that a good idea to use a large portion of available cash for a purchase like this? Keeping in mind that inventory can have a significant amount of carrying cost (storage, personnel, opportunity cost of the money, etc.) would you tell your client that this was a good thing that he did, or not?

WRITTEN COMMUNICATION

You just got a letter from one of your good customers complaining about the shipment of your product that he or she just received. Football season is approaching and the customer had ordered a large shipment of regulation size footballs. Instead, he or she received youth size footballs for half of the order. The customer is asking you what can be done about this mistake. Knowing that this client is located halfway across the country, it's not feasible to just have him or her drop by your facility and trade out the footballs.

The customer also had a question about a line item on his or her invoice under shipping terms. It said FOB Destination and the customer noticed that he or she was charged freight, which the customer normally doesn't have to pay. The customer wants to know if that is correct.

Requirement

1. Write a letter to your customer explaining how you intend to handle this purchase return or this purchase allowance (you choose which one you're going to do). Explain the accounting forms that will need to be prepared to document this transaction. Also address the customer's concern about the shipping terms.

Self Check Answers

1. d 2. a 3. b 4. c 5. a 6. a 7. d 8. b 9. c 10. a

Inventory

If you have ever worked in a retail establishment, it is very likely that you have witnessed, or maybe even participated in, the counting of inventory. If so, did you wonder why the inventory had to be counted or what would happen if the count was done incorrectly? Did you ever hear the terms FIFO or LIFO and wonder what they had to do with inventory? Let's explore the answers to these questions in Chapter 5 as we learn how to account for inventory.

Chapter Outline:

Learning Objectives:

1. Describe the four different inventory costing methods

2. Compute inventory costs using first-in, first-out (FIFO); last-in, first-out (LIFO); and average cost methods and journalize inventory transactions

3. Compare the effects of the different costing methods on the financial statements

4. Value inventory using the lower-of-cost-or-market (LCM) rule

5. Illustrate the reporting of inventory in the financial statements

6. Determine the effect of inventory errors on the financial statements

7. Use the gross profit method to estimate ending inventory

8. Compute the inventory turnover rate

WHAT INVENTORY COSTING METHODS ARE ALLOWED?

Describe the four different inventory costing methods ▶**1**

As discussed in Chapter 4, merchandise inventory represents the goods that a merchandiser has available to sell to its customers. A manufacturer also has goods it holds for sale to its customers. These goods are called **finished goods** inventory. In addition, a manufacturer maintains two other types of inventory: **raw materials** inventory, which it uses to produce the goods it sells, and **work in process** inventory, which represents partially completed goods. In other words, work in process inventory represents goods that are in the process of becoming finished goods. A more detailed discussion of the inventory accounts of a manufacturer will be left to a managerial or cost accounting course. In this chapter, we focus on managing and accounting for inventory in merchandise businesses. Inventory represents a key asset for a merchandiser and is probably the business's largest current asset.

Recall from Chapter 4 that most companies utilize a perpetual inventory system. Under a perpetual system, the cost of goods purchased is added to the Inventory account in the general ledger when goods are purchased. When the goods are sold, the cost of the goods is removed from the Inventory account and added to the Cost of Goods Sold account. Most merchandisers purchase large quantities of identical items. Due to inflation and other market forces, the cost the merchandiser pays for the items often differs from one purchase to the next. This raises an important accounting dilemma. If the goods are identical, but have different costs, how does the business know which costs to remove from the Inventory account and transfer to Cost of Goods Sold at the time merchandise is sold?

According to Generally Accepted Accounting Principles (GAAP), a business can assign costs using one of four different inventory costing methods. The four costing methods allowed by GAAP are as follows:

❶ **Specific-identification** method—Assumes that the cost assigned to an inventory item when it is sold is the actual cost paid for that item. Therefore, the Cost of Goods Sold represents the actual cost of the items that were sold. Also, the Ending Inventory represents the actual cost of the goods remaining in inventory. Under specific-identification, the cost flow of the goods through the accounting records will *exactly* match the physical flow of the goods through the business.

❷ **First-in, first-out (FIFO)** method—Assumes that the earliest inventory costs are assigned to items as they are sold. The Cost of Goods Sold represents the oldest costs incurred to purchase inventory items. The Ending Inventory represents the most recent costs incurred to purchase inventory items. Under FIFO, the cost flow of the goods through the accounting records will closely match the physical flow of the goods through the business.

 ▶ ❸ **Last-in, first-out (LIFO)** method—Assumes that the most recent inventory costs are assigned to items as they are sold. The Cost of Goods Sold represents the latest costs incurred to purchase inventory items. The Ending Inventory represents the earliest costs incurred to purchase inventory. Under LIFO, the cost flow of the goods through the accounting records will be nearly opposite of the physical flow of the goods through the business.

❹ **Average cost** method—Assumes that a weighted-average cost per item of the entire inventory purchased is assigned to items as they are sold. Both the Cost of Goods Sold and the Ending Inventory represent an average of the cost incurred to purchase inventory items. Under the average cost method, the Cost of Goods Sold and the Ending Inventory will fall between the amounts arrived at using FIFO and LIFO assuming that costs are steadily rising or falling.

🌐 Accounting in Your World

Does this taste funny to you?

Jill was at the grocery store the other day picking up a gallon of milk when she started thinking about LIFO, which she had been learning about in her accounting class. It did not make sense to her that any company would want to use LIFO. After all she reasoned, if the grocery store used LIFO, it would be selling milk that it just purchased first which would leave older milk on the shelves. Jill wonders how she can be sure that the gallon of milk she took off the shelf is fresh and not one that has been on the shelf for weeks, or even months.

Jill is confusing the flow of costs through the accounting records with the physical flow of inventory through a store. LIFO refers to the flow of costs through the accounting records and not to the physical flow of goods. The flow of costs through the accounting records can match, or be exactly opposite of, the physical flow of goods through a store. Jill can rest assured that even if the store uses LIFO, her milk is fresh.

Cost Flow Versus Physical Flow of Inventory

The inventory costing method (FIFO, LIFO, etc.) refers to the flow of costs through a merchandiser's accounting records rather than to the physical flow of the goods through the business. The physical flow of the goods through the business will depend on how the goods are stocked and in what order customers, or employees, remove the goods from the shelves when they are sold. The flow of the *costs* through the accounting records will depend upon which inventory costing method the business chooses.

Imagine that every inventory item that is purchased has a "yellow sticky note" attached to it with the price that was paid for the item written on the "sticky note." Next, assume that when the business receives a shipment of inventory items, the "sticky notes" reflecting the cost of the items are removed from each item and given to the Accounting Department. The Accounting Department will keep track of the "sticky notes" for each separate purchase in what is referred to as an **inventory layer**. The quantity purchased of each item along with the purchase price is tracked as an inventory layer for every separate purchase.

The physical inventory will most likely be managed in a manner that causes the oldest inventory to be sold first followed by more recent purchases and so on. The physical flow of the inventory is maintained in this manner to prevent inventory items from spoiling if they are perishable, or to prevent having items that look outdated should the manufacturer choose to change the packaging of the items. The Accounting Department calculates the cost flow of the inventory without any consideration of the actual physical flow of the merchandise (unless the specific-identification inventory method is used). The Accounting Department only needs to know *how many* units were sold, not *which* units were sold. The Accounting Department then applies the cost flow method (FIFO, LIFO, etc.) to the inventory layers that it has recorded. In other words, the inventory costs are assigned based on the layers of "sticky notes." **Exhibit 5-1** demonstrates the difference between cost flow and physical flow.

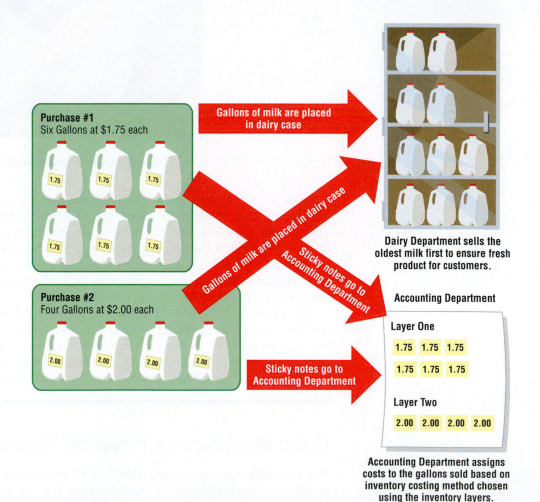

Purchase #1
Six Gallons at $1.75 each

Purchase #2
Four Gallons at $2.00 each

Gallons of milk are placed in dairy case

Gallons of milk are placed in dairy case

Sticky notes go to Accounting Department

Sticky notes go to Accounting Department

Dairy Department sells the oldest milk first to ensure fresh product for customers.

Accounting Department

Layer One

| 1.75 | 1.75 | 1.75 |
| 1.75 | 1.75 | 1.75 |

Layer Two

| 2.00 | 2.00 | 2.00 | 2.00 |

Accounting Department assigns costs to the gallons sold based on inventory costing method chosen using the inventory layers.

Exhibit 5-1 ▲

Decision Guidelines

Decision	Guideline	Analyze
How do I determine the cost of the inventory I sell?	The physical flow of the inventory and the cost flow of the inventory can be different. The cost assigned to the units sold may be based on one of the following four methods: • Specific-identification • First-in, first-out (FIFO) • Last-in, first-out (LIFO) • Average cost	*Specific-identification*: Inventory items are specifically labeled or identified and the actual cost of each item sold is assigned to cost of goods sold. *First-in, first-out (FIFO)*: The first inventory costs incurred are the first costs to be assigned to cost of goods sold. *Last-in, first-out (LIFO)*: The last inventory costs incurred are the first costs to be assigned to cost of goods sold. *Average cost*: After each purchase of inventory, a new weighted-average cost per unit is computed and assigned to cost of goods sold.

HOW ARE THE FOUR INVENTORY COSTING METHODS APPLIED?

Compute inventory costs using first-in, first-out (FIFO); last-in, first-out (LIFO); and average cost methods and journalize inventory transactions

Inventory Cost Flows

Recollect from Chapter 4 that in a perpetual inventory system purchases of goods for resale increase the balance of the Inventory account, while sales of goods to customers decrease the account. The Inventory account also reflects purchase discounts, purchase returns and allowances, and shipping costs related to the purchase of goods:

Inventory			
Bal	XX		
Purchases	XX	Purchase Discounts	XX
Shipping	XX	Purchase Returns and Allowances	XX
		Sales	XX
Bal	XX		

The cost of the inventory flows through the Inventory account as items are purchased and sold. The cost of the units on hand in inventory at the beginning of the period is added to the net cost of units purchased for the period to determine the **cost of goods available for sale**. The objective of tracking the inventory cost is to allocate the cost of the goods available for sale between the following:

■ Units sold, which is recorded as Cost of Goods Sold and is subtracted from net sales revenue on the income statement to arrive at gross profit
■ Units on hand, or unsold, which is reflected as ending inventory, a current asset on the balance sheet

Let's follow the September inventory activity for ski parkas sold by Northwest Outfitters, Inc., assuming the following:

Sep 1	One parka costing $40 is on hand, unsold from the previous month.
5	Purchased six parkas for $45 each.
15	Sold four parkas for $80 each.
26	Purchased seven parkas for $50 each.
30	Sold eight parkas for $80 each.
30	Two parkas are on hand, unsold.

During September, Northwest Outfitters had 14 parkas available for sale: 1 unit on hand in beginning inventory plus 13 units purchased during the month. Northwest Outfitters goods available for sale would be calculated as follows:

Beginning Inventory	(1 @ $40)	= $ 40
+ Purchases	(6 @ $45) = $270	
	(7 @ $50) = 350	620
= Goods Available for Sale		$660

Of the 14 parkas available for sale, Northwest sold 12 parkas and still had 2 parkas on hand in ending inventory at the end of the month. What would be the cost of the goods sold for the month and the ending inventory balance for that month? The answer depends on which inventory costing method Northwest Outfitters elects to use. **Exhibit 5-2** illustrates the objective of calculating inventory costs for Northwest Outfitters.

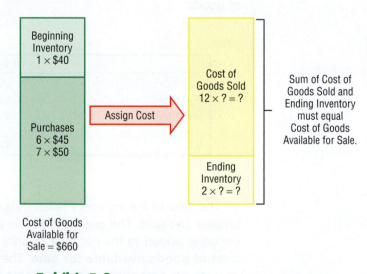

Exhibit 5-2

As we shall see, the various inventory costing methods produce different values for ending inventory and cost of goods sold.

Specific-Identification Method

The specific-identification method is also called the **specific-unit cost** method. This method values inventory according to the specific cost of each item of inventory. This method is used predominately by businesses that sell unique items with very different costs. Some examples are businesses that sell automobiles, houses, and artwork. For instance, an automobile dealer may have two vehicles on its car lot, a "basic" model that costs $22,000 and a "fully-equipped" model that costs $29,000. Accordingly, the sales price of the basic model would be less than the sales price for the fully equipped model. It would not make sense for the dealer to assign the cost of the fully-equipped model to the basic model when the basic model is sold. This would cause gross profit to be inaccurately stated because the higher cost of the fully-equipped model would be subtracted from the lower selling price of the basic model. The dealer would want to specifically identify which model it sold and assign the actual cost of that model to the cost of goods sold. In order to utilize the specific-identification method, each inventory item must be able to be distinguished from other items with some identifying mark such as a serial number. Because the specific-identification method of inventory valuation is not widely used, we will focus on the more popular inventory costing methods. Let's see how to compute inventory amounts using the FIFO, LIFO, and average cost methods for Northwest Outfitters.

First-In, First-Out (FIFO) Method

Assume that Northwest Outfitters uses the FIFO method to account for its inventory. Under FIFO, the first inventory costs incurred by Northwest each period are the first costs to be assigned to cost of goods sold. *Simply put, FIFO assumes that the first inventory items Northwest purchased are the first inventory items it sold.* In order to efficiently track inventory costs, a **perpetual inventory record** is often utilized. The perpetual inventory record maintains the detail supporting the quantity of, and costs assigned to, the inventory items as they are purchased and sold. It also maintains a running balance of the inventory on hand. When preparing the perpetual inventory record, it is critical that the inventory "layers" are kept in the proper order. An inventory layer consists of the quantity of inventory and its purchase cost. **Exhibit 5-3** (on the next page) illustrates the FIFO perpetual inventory record for Northwest Outfitters, while **Exhibit 5-4** (on the next page) illustrates the flow of costs using FIFO.

Northwest began September with one parka that cost $40. After the September 5 purchase, the inventory on hand consists of seven units: one at $40 plus six at $45. On September 15, Northwest sold four units. Under FIFO, the cost of the first unit sold is the oldest cost, $40 per unit. The next three units sold come from the layer that cost $45 per unit. That leaves three units in inventory on hand, and those units cost $45 each. The remainder of the perpetual inventory record is completed in the same manner.

The FIFO monthly summary on September 30 is as follows:

- Cost of Goods Sold: 12 units that cost a total of $560
- Ending Inventory: 2 units that cost a total of $100

Look for these amounts in the last row of the perpetual inventory record in Exhibit 5-3 as well as in Exhibit 5-4. If Northwest uses the FIFO method, it will use these amounts for the cost of goods sold and inventory in its financial statements. Notice that the sum of the cost of goods sold plus ending inventory equals the cost of goods available for sale, $660 ($560 + $100).

Parkas									
	Purchases			Cost of Goods Sold			Inventory on Hand		
Date	Quantity	Unit Cost	Total Cost	Quantity	Unit Cost	Total Cost	Quantity	Unit Cost	Total Cost
Sep 1							1	$40	$ 40
5	6	$45	$270				1	$40	$ 40
							6	$45	$270
15				1	$40	$ 40			
				3	$45	$135	3	$45	$135
26	7	$50	$350				3	$45	$135
							7	$50	$350
30				3	$45	$135			
				5	$50	$250	2	$50	$100
30	**13**		**$620**	**12**		**$560**	**2**		**$100**

Exhibit 5-3 ▲

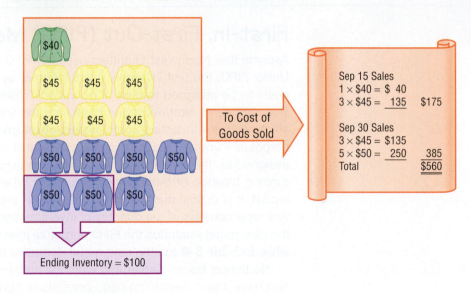

Exhibit 5-4 ▲

IFRS ▸

Last-In, First-Out (LIFO) Method

Now imagine that Northwest uses the LIFO method instead of FIFO. Under the LIFO method, the last, most recent costs incurred are the first costs assigned to the cost of goods sold. *Accordingly, LIFO assumes that the last inventory items purchased are the first inventory items sold.* The ending inventory's cost comes from the oldest, earliest purchases of the inventory. Remember, LIFO costing does not follow the actual physical flow of goods for most companies. LIFO is simply a method of *assigning* costs to the physical units that were sold. The LIFO method perpetual inventory record for Northwest Outfitters is presented in **Exhibit 5-5**. **Exhibit 5-6** illustrates the assignment of costs using LIFO.

Again, Northwest had one parka at the beginning of September. After the purchase on September 5, Northwest holds seven units of inventory: one at $40 plus six

Parkas									
	Purchases			**Cost of Goods Sold**			**Inventory on Hand**		
Date	**Quantity**	**Unit Cost**	**Total Cost**	**Quantity**	**Unit Cost**	**Total Cost**	**Quantity**	**Unit Cost**	**Total Cost**
Sep 1							1	$40	$ 40
5	6	$45	$270				1	$40	$ 40
							6	$45	$270
15				4	$45	$180	1	$40	$ 40
							2	$45	$ 90
26	7	$50	$350				1	$40	$ 40
							2	$45	$ 90
							7	$50	$350
30				7	$50	$350			
				1	$45	$ 45	1	$40	$ 40
							1	$45	$ 45
30	**13**		**$620**	**12**		**$575**	**2**		**$ 85**

Exhibit 5-5 ▲

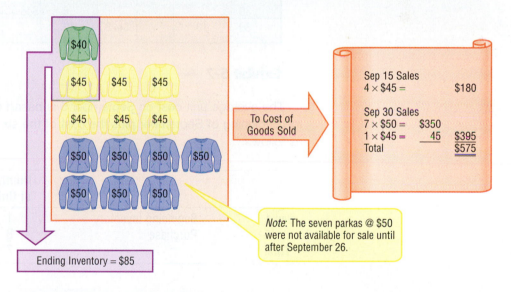

To Cost of Goods Sold

Sep 15 Sales
4 × $45 = $180

Sep 30 Sales
7 × $50 = $350
1 × $45 =   45 $395
Total $575

Note: The seven parkas @ $50 were not available for sale until after September 26.

Ending Inventory = $85

Exhibit 5-6 ▲

at $45. Northwest then sells four units on September 15. Under LIFO, the cost of goods sold always comes from the latest purchase. That leaves three parkas in inventory on September 15: one at $40 plus two at $45. The purchase of seven units on September 26 adds a new $50 layer to inventory. Then the sale of eight units on September 30 removes units from inventory in LIFO order.

The LIFO monthly summary on September 30 is as follows:

- Cost of Goods Sold: 12 units that cost a total of $575
- Ending Inventory: 2 units that cost a total of $85

These amounts can be seen in the last row of the perpetual inventory record in Exhibit 5-5 as well as in Exhibit 5-6. If Northwest uses the LIFO method, it will use these amounts for the cost of goods sold and inventory in its financial statements. Notice that the sum of cost of goods sold and ending inventory still equals the cost of goods available for sale, $660 ($575 + $85).

Average Cost Method

Suppose Northwest Outfitters uses the average cost method to account for its inventory of parkas. *With this method, the business computes a new, weighted-average cost per unit after each purchase* based on the number of items purchased at each price. Ending inventory and cost of goods sold are then based on the average cost per unit. **Exhibit 5-7** shows a perpetual inventory record for the average cost method. We round average unit cost to the nearest cent and total cost to the nearest dollar.

Parkas

Date	Purchases Quantity	Unit Cost	Total Cost	Cost of Goods Sold Quantity	Unit Cost	Total Cost	Inventory on Hand Quantity	Unit Cost	Total Cost
Sep 1							1	$40.00	$ 40
5	6	$45	$270				7	$44.29	$310
15				4	$44.29	$177	3	$44.29	$133
26	7	$50	$350				10	$48.30	$483
30				8	$48.30	$386	2	$48.30	$ 97
30	13		$620	12		$563	2		$ 97

Exhibit 5-7 ▲

The average unit cost on September 5 is based on the cost of the unit on hand at the beginning of September plus the cost of the six units purchased on September 5 as follows:

		Number of Units	Unit Cost	Total Cost
Sep 1	Beginning Inventory	1	$40	$ 40
5	Purchase	6	$45	$270
Total		7		$310

Total Cost of Inventory on Hand ÷ Number of Units on Hand = Average Cost per Unit		
$310	7 Units	$44.29

The four items sold on September 15 are assigned a cost of $44.29 per unit and the remaining three units are carried forward at a cost of $44.29 each. Northwest then computes a new average cost after the September 26 purchase in the same manner. The average cost monthly summary on September 30 is as follows:

- Cost of Goods Sold: 12 units that cost a total of $563
- Ending Inventory: 2 units that cost a total of $97

Once again, these amounts can be seen in the last row of the perpetual inventory record presented in Exhibit 5-7. If Northwest uses the average cost method, it will use these amounts to prepare its financial statements. Yet again the sum of the cost of goods sold and ending inventory equals the cost of goods available for sale, $660 ($563 + $97).

Journalizing Inventory Transactions

The journal entries to record the inventory transactions for Northwest Outfitters for the month of September are presented in **Exhibit 5-8** using the following information:

- All purchases and sales in September were made on account.
- The sales price of a parka charged to a customer was $80.

	DATE	ACCOUNTS	FIFO DR.	FIFO CR.	LIFO DR.	LIFO CR.	AVERAGE COST DR.	AVERAGE COST CR.
Purchase inventory on account (six parkas @ $45 each)	Sep 5	Inventory	270		270		270	
		Accounts Payable		270		270		270
Sold four parkas for $80 each	15	Accounts Receivable	320		320		320	
		Sales Revenue		320		320		320
		Cost of Goods Sold	175		180		177	
		Inventory		175		180		177
Purchased inventory on account (seven parkas @ $50 each)	26	Inventory	350		350		350	
		Accounts Payable		350		350		350
Sold eight parkas for $80 each	30	Accounts Receivable	640		640		640	
		Sales Revenue		640		640		640
		Cost of Goods Sold	385		395		386	
		Inventory		385		395		386

Exhibit 5-8 ▲

Notice that the journal entries to record the purchases of inventory on account are the same, regardless of the costing method chosen. *The differences occur in the second part of the sales entries that removes the cost of the parkas sold from the inventory account and transfers it to cost of goods.*

WHAT EFFECT DO THE DIFFERENT COSTING METHODS HAVE ON NET INCOME?

Compare the effects of the different costing methods on the financial statements 3

The choice of inventory costing method often has an effect on the amount of net income a company reports on its income statement.

☑ Concept Check...

Anderson's Outdoor Equipment, Inc., has recently opened for business. The owners of the business are trying to determine which inventory costing method to choose. The owners would like to pay the least amount of income tax possible. Which inventory method will allow Anderson's Outdoor Equipment, Inc., to pay the least amount of taxes?

Answer

It depends on whether the cost of inventory is expected to increase or decrease during the period. If inventory costs are expected to increase, Anderson's Outdoor Equipment, Inc., should choose LIFO. However, if inventory costs are expected to decrease, Anderson's Outdoor Equipment, Inc., should choose FIFO. If inventory costs are expected to remain constant, the choice of inventory costing method will have no effect on the net income for the period.

Exhibit 5-9 compares the FIFO, LIFO, and average cost methods of costing inventory assuming that, over time, inventory costs are *increasing*. As you can see, different methods have different benefits. FIFO is the most popular inventory costing method, followed by LIFO and then by average cost.

Inventory Costing Method	Description	Benefit
First-In, First-Out (FIFO)	Cost of goods sold has older, lower costs. Ending inventory has the newer, higher costs.	Most closely matches actual flow of goods in most cases. Maximizes net income. Use method to attract investors or borrow money.
Last-In, First-Out (LIFO)	Cost of goods sold has newer, higher costs. Ending inventory has the older, lower costs.	Minimizes net income and income tax and minimizes ending inventory. Use method to reduce income tax and cash needed to pay tax.
Average Cost	Averages costs in ending inventory and cost of goods sold.	A "middle-ground solution" for reporting net income and inventory and paying income tax.

Exhibit 5-9 ▲

Exhibit 5-10 summarizes the results of the three inventory methods as used for Northwest Outfitters. It shows Sales Revenue, Cost of Goods Sold, and Gross Profit for FIFO, LIFO, and average cost. All data come from Exhibits 5-3, 5-5, and 5-7.

Exhibit 5-10 shows that FIFO produces the lowest cost of goods sold and the highest gross profit. Net income is also the highest under FIFO when inventory costs are rising. Many companies choose this method when they want to report high income in order to attract investors and borrow on attractive terms.

LIFO results in the highest cost of goods sold and, therefore, the lowest gross profit when inventory costs are increasing. Lower gross profit results in lower net income and lower income taxes. A drawback to using LIFO when inventory costs are rising is that the company reports lower net income.

	FIFO	LIFO	Average Cost
Sales Revenue	$960	$960	$960
Cost of Goods Sold	560	575	563
Gross Profit	$400	$385	$397

Exhibit 5-10 ▲

The average cost method generates gross profit, net income, and income tax amounts that fall between the extremes of FIFO and LIFO. Therefore, companies that seek a "middle-ground" solution choose the average cost method for valuing inventory.

Based upon the previous information given, it appears that a business could "manage its income" by switching back and forth between costing methods depending upon the circumstances. This is not the case due to the **consistency** principle mandated by GAAP. The consistency principle states that businesses should use the same accounting methods and procedures from period to period. The consistency principle does not mean that a company can never change its accounting methods, for instance changing from the LIFO to FIFO inventory valuation method, but that it can only do so if it can justify the change. Also, any changes in accounting methods must be disclosed to the financial statement users.

Suppose you are analyzing a company's net income pattern over a two-year period and costs are rising. If the company switched from LIFO to FIFO during that time, its net income likely increased significantly. The problem is that much, if not all, of the increase in income could be the result of the change in inventory method. If you were unaware of the change, you might believe that the company's income increased because of improved operations. Therefore, companies must report any changes in the accounting methods they use and they generally must retrospectively apply the impact of the change as an adjustment to beginning retained earnings, unless it is impractical to do so. Consistency helps investors compare a company's financial statements from one period to the next and make better decisions.

Decision Guidelines

Decision	Guideline	Analyze
Which inventory costing method is the best for my company?	It depends on whether costs are rising or declining and whether you want to report higher or lower net income.	When costs are rising • FIFO reports the highest ending inventory value and lowest cost of goods sold and, therefore, the highest net income. • LIFO reports the lowest ending inventory value and highest cost of goods sold and, therefore, the lowest net income. • average cost reports an average cost for the value of ending inventory and cost of goods sold. Average cost can be used to stabilize fluctuations in net income if inventory costs are continually fluctuating.

WHAT ELSE DETERMINES HOW INVENTORY IS VALUED?

Value inventory using the lower-of-cost-or-market (LCM) rule

Another important accounting principle is the principle of **conservatism**. Conservatism in accounting means reporting items in the financial statements at amounts that lead to the most cautious immediate results. A conservative approach will mean that when there are two reasonable options present the option should be chosen that causes assets and income to be understated, rather than overstated. A conservative approach will also mean that liabilities and expenses are overstated, rather than understated. The goal is for financial statements to report figures that minimize the risk of overstating the company's financial position.

Merchandisers are often faced with a situation where the cost of replacing an inventory item is lower than what was originally paid for the item. In order to take a conservative approach when these situations arise, businesses will often apply the

lower-of-cost-or-market (LCM) rule. The LCM rule requires businesses to report inventory in the financial statements at whichever is lower, the amount originally paid (the historical cost) or the replacement cost (the current market value) of each inventory item. If the replacement cost of inventory is less than its historical cost, a company writes down the inventory value by decreasing inventory and increasing cost of goods sold. In this way, net income is decreased in the period in which the decrease in the market value of the inventory occurred.

Let's look at the process of valuing inventory according to lower-of-cost-or-market rule for the inventory in **Exhibit 5-11**.

■ Prepare a table listing each inventory item, its quantity, unit cost, and market value.

■ Calculate the total cost and total market value for each item. Inventory Item 122A, for example, has a total cost of $2,000 (40 units × $50 cost per unit) and a total market value of $2,080 (40 units × $52 market value per unit).

■ Place the lower of the cost or market value for each item in the "Lower of C or M" column. Item 122A would have a value of $2,000.

■ Add the amounts in each column to obtain the total cost, total market value, and total lower-of-cost-or-market amounts.

■ Adjust the inventory balance to reflect the lower-of-cost-or-market amount. The total cost is $14,800 and the total LCM amount is $14,425, so a journal entry is made to reduce the inventory amount by the difference of $375 ($14,800 − $14,425).

Inventory Item	Inventory Quantity	Unit Cost	Unit Market Value	Total		
				Cost	Market	Lower of C or M
122A	40	$ 50	$ 52	$ 2,000	$ 2,080	$ 2,000
1587L	75	$ 80	$ 75	6,000	5,625	5,625
394CZ	68	$100	$101	6,800	6,868	6,800
				$14,800	$14,573	$14,425

Exhibit 5-11 ▲

The application of LCM is actually more complex than what is demonstrated in Exhibit 5-11; however, more in depth coverage will be left to a more advanced accounting course. The LCM rule may be applied to inventory on an item-by-item basis as in Exhibit 5-11, to broad categories of items, or to the entire inventory taken as a whole. Application of the LCM rule is a continuation of the process of valuing inventory. Businesses using LCM will record inventory transactions, assigning a cost to each inventory item sold using the specific-identification, FIFO, LIFO, or average cost method. Then, at the end of the accounting period, they will apply the LCM rule to the ending inventory. In this way, businesses report conservative values for inventory and net income.

Most businesses will report inventory on the balance sheet at the lower-of-cost-or-market value; however, others will use the concept of **materiality** to decide whether inventory needs to be written down to its current replacement cost. The materiality concept states that a company must perform strictly proper accounting *only* for items that have a material effect on the company's financial statements. An item is considered to have a material *effect* when it would cause someone to change a decision; stated differently, a material amount is one large enough to make a difference to a user of the financial statements. For example, if the lower-of-cost-or-market comparison in Exhibit 5-11 resulted in a difference between total cost and total LCM of $3, the company would have been appropriate in ignoring any adjustment to inventory for the $3. Hence, the materiality concept frees accountants from having to report every account in strict accordance with GAAP, yet still report items properly.

HOW IS INVENTORY REPORTED ON THE BALANCE SHEET?

Illustrate the reporting of inventory in the financial statements **5**

Inventory is reported as a current asset and is often listed after receivables on the balance sheet. In addition to showing the inventory amount, a business must disclose the costing method used to value inventory (specific-identification, FIFO, LIFO, or average cost) and whether the inventory is valued using LCM. This discloser helps a business adhere to the **full-disclosure** principle. The full-disclosure principle requires that a company's financial statements report enough information for outsiders to make knowledgeable decisions about the company. To provide this information, accountants typically include a set of **footnotes** that accompany the financial statements. Footnote disclosures help ensure that companies report relevant, reliable, and comparable financial information. A common footnote related to inventory would look like this:

NOTE 2: Statement of Significant Accounting Policies:
Inventory. Inventory is carried at the *lower of cost or market*. Cost is determined using the first-in, first-out method.

Suppose a banker is comparing two companies, one using LIFO and the other FIFO. When prices are rising, the company using the FIFO inventory costing method reports higher net income, but only because it uses FIFO. Without knowledge of the accounting methods the companies are using, the banker could lend money to the wrong business, or lend the wrong amount of money to each.

Inventory Shrinkage

The perpetual inventory method keeps a continuous record of the inventory on hand at all times. However, the actual amount of inventory on hand may differ from the amount on hand according to the accounting records due to errors in recording inventory related transactions or due to **inventory shrinkage**. Inventory shrinkage represents a loss of inventory. Inventory shrinkage is most often the result of employee theft, customer theft, and the damage, spillage, or spoilage of inventory items.

A physical inventory count is used to determine the amount of inventory actually on hand at the end of the accounting period. A number of commonly used procedures help ensure the accuracy of the count. It usually occurs when the store is closed. Individuals assigned to the count can use maps of inventory locations, prenumbered count sheets, ink pens, and may count in pairs. The count may also involve prewritten inventory instructions and tags to identify merchandise to be counted, and is typically supervised. To save time and increase objectivity for the count, an outside inventory-taking firm may be used to take counts instead of, or in addition to, employees. If the entity has its financial statements audited, a representative of the audit firm will usually be present at the count to take test counts and determine whether inventory instructions are being adequately followed. This allows the auditor to evaluate whether inventory and cost of goods sold are fairly presented in the statements.

The inventory value derived from the physical inventory count is used as the inventory account balance on the balance sheet. The accounting records are adjusted for any difference between the inventory value determined by the count and the value according to the perpetual records. The Inventory account is debited or credited as necessary with a corresponding credit or debit to the Cost of Goods Sold account.

HOW DO INVENTORY ERRORS AFFECT THE FINANCIAL STATEMENTS?

Determine the effect of inventory errors on the financial statements **6**

A correct count of the inventory items on hand is necessary to ensure the accurate reporting of the inventory's value. However, errors in the inventory count can and do occur such as the following:

- Improperly counting inventory
- Double counting inventory; for example, counting it in one location and then moving it to another location where it is counted again
- Not counting one section of the storeroom or excluding incoming goods shipped FOB shipping point
- Failure to recognize obsolete or damaged goods, resulting in failure to write down their value accordingly

What is the impact of a counting error? Remember that in a perpetual inventory system, the inventory account balance is adjusted to reflect the value arrived at by the physical count. A wrong count, a count that disagrees with the accounting records of inventory, will result in making a journal entry that causes both the Inventory balance and the Cost of Goods Sold to be incorrect.

To demonstrate, let's look at the income statements for a company for two consecutive years. In order to keep the example simple, we will assume that the company has a $20,000 balance in both beginning inventory and ending inventory for the first year. We will also assume that it has a $20,000 balance in ending inventory in the second year (remember that the beginning balance in the inventory account in year 2 is the ending inventory balance from year 1). We will also assume that the company made purchases of $75,000 and that it had sales of $160,000 and operating expenses of $40,000 in both years. In other words, the activity for both years is exactly the same. **Exhibit 5-12**, Panel A, illustrates the income statements for both years assuming that inventory was properly counted.

Now, let's assume that the ending inventory was incorrectly valued at $25,000 (instead of the correct amount of $20,000) due to an error in the physical count. Exhibit 5-12, Panel B, illustrates the income statements for both years assuming that ending inventory was overstated by $5,000.

Panel A—Ending Inventory correctly stated		Year 1		Year 2	
Sales Revenue			$160,000		$160,000
Cost of Goods Sold:					
Beginning Inventory	$20,000	▶$ 20,000			
Purchases	75,000	75,000			
Cost of Goods Available for Sale	95,000	95,000			
Ending Inventory	20,000	20,000			
Cost of Goods Sold			75,000		75,000
Gross Profit			85,000		85,000
Operating Expenses			40,000		40,000
Net Income			$45,000		$45,000

Panel B—Ending Inventory overstated by $5,000		Year 1		Year 2	
Sales Revenue			$160,000		$160,000
Cost of Goods Sold:					
Beginning Inventory	$20,000	▶$ 25,000			
Purchases	75,000	75,000			
Cost of Goods Available for Sale	95,000	100,000			
Ending Inventory	25,000	20,000			
Cost of Goods Sold			70,000		80,000
Gross Profit			90,000		80,000
Operating Expenses			40,000		40,000
Net Income			$ 50,000		$ 40,000

Exhibit 5-12 ▲

A comparison of the statements in Panel A and Panel B of Exhibit 5-12 reveals the following for year one:

- Cost of Goods Sold is understated by $5,000.
- Gross Profit is overstated by $5,000.
- Net Income is overstated by $5,000.
- Retained Earnings will be overstated because Net Income is closed into Retained Earnings.

Recall from Chapter 3 that Inventory, as an asset, is a permanent account that carries its balance over to the next period. So, one period's ending inventory becomes the next period's beginning inventory. Thus, the error in ending inventory in year 1 carries over as an error in the beginning inventory in year 2. A comparison of the statements in Panel A and Panel B of Exhibit 5-12 reveals the following for year 2:

- Cost of Goods Available for Sale is overstated by $5,000.
- Cost of Goods Sold is overstated by $5,000.
- Gross Profit is understated by $5,000.
- Net Income is understated by $5,000.
- Retained Earnings will now be correctly stated because the understatement in Net Income in year 2 will offset the overstatement from year 1 when the Net Income from year 2 is closed into Retained Earnings.

As you can see, the error cancels out after two periods. The total net income, $90,000, from Panel B for the two periods combined when there is an error is the same as it is in Panel A for the two periods when there are no errors. The effects of inventory errors are summarized in **Exhibit 5-13** on the following page.

Inventory Error	Period 1		Period 2	
	Cost of Goods Sold	Gross Profit and Net Income	Cost of Goods Sold	Gross Profit and Net Income
Period 1 Ending Inventory *Overstated*	Understated	Overstated	Overstated	Understated
Period 1 Ending Inventory *Understated*	Overstated	Understated	Understated	Overstated

Exhibit 5-13 ▲

Decision Guidelines

Decision	Guideline	Analyze

What is the effect of a misstatement of ending inventory?	In addition to causing an overstatement or understatement of Inventory on the balance sheet, a misstatement of ending inventory will cause an error on the income statement.	If ending inventory is overstated, then
		• Cost of Goods Sold is understated.
		• Gross Profit is overstated.
		• Net Income is overstated.
		
		If ending inventory is understated, then
		• Cost of Goods Sold is overstated.
		• Gross Profit is understated.
		• Net Income is understated.
		
		Because ending inventory for one period becomes beginning inventory for the next period, the Cost of Goods Sold, Gross Profit, and Net Income of the next period are also misstated.

IS IT POSSIBLE TO ESTIMATE THE VALUE OF INVENTORY IF THE INVENTORY IS ACCIDENTALLY DESTROYED?

Use the gross profit method to estimate ending inventory **7**

Often a business must estimate the value of its inventory. Suppose the company suffers a fire loss. To collect insurance, it must estimate the cost of the inventory destroyed, that is, it must estimate the ending inventory.

The **gross profit method** estimates inventory by using the format for the Cost of Goods Sold:

> Beginning Inventory
> + Purchases (Net of Discounts and Returns and Allowances,
>   Plus Shipping Costs)
> = Cost of Goods Available for Sale
> − Ending Inventory
> = Cost of Goods Sold

Rearranging ending inventory and cost of goods sold helps to estimate ending inventory. Let's look at an example. We can estimate ending inventory through the following steps and amounts, as shown in **Exhibits 5-14** and **5-15**:

Step 1 Calculate the cost of goods available for sale. Add the beginning balance of inventory and the net cost of purchases for the accounting period ($14,000 + $66,000 = $80,000).

Step 2 Estimate the cost of goods sold. Do you remember calculating the gross profit percentage in Chapter 4? The historical gross profit percentage of a business can be used to estimate the current period's gross profit. Calculate the estimated gross profit by multiplying the net sales revenue by the historical gross profit percentage ($100,000 × 40% = $40,000). Subtract the estimated gross profit from the net sales revenue to get the estimated cost of goods sold ($100,000 − $40,000 = $60,000).

Step 3 Estimate the ending inventory. Subtract estimated cost of goods sold from the cost of goods available for sale ($80,000 − $60,000 = $20,000).

Step 1	Beginning Inventory		$ 14,000
	+ Purchases (net)		66,000
	= Cost of Goods Available for Sale		80,000
Step 2	Estimated Cost of Goods Sold:		
	Net Sales Revenue	$100,000	
	− Estimated Gross Profit of 40% ($100,000 × 40%)	(40,000)	
	= Estimated Cost of Goods Sold		(60,000)
Step 3	Estimated Ending Inventory		$ 20,000

Exhibit 5-14 ▲

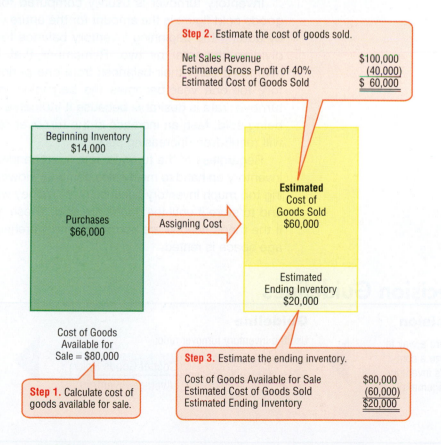

Step 2. Estimate the cost of goods sold.

Net Sales Revenue	$100,000
Estimated Gross Profit of 40%	(40,000)
Estimated Cost of Goods Sold	$ 60,000

Beginning Inventory
$14,000

Purchases
$66,000

Assigning Cost

Estimated
Cost of
Goods Sold
$60,000

Estimated
Ending Inventory
$20,000

Cost of Goods
Available for
Sale = $80,000

Step 1. Calculate cost of goods available for sale.

Step 3. Estimate the ending inventory.

Cost of Goods Available for Sale	$80,000
Estimated Cost of Goods Sold	(60,000)
Estimated Ending Inventory	$20,000

Exhibit 5-15 ▲

FOCUS ON DECISION MAKING: RATIOS

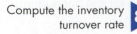 Compute the inventory turnover rate **8**

The Rate of Inventory Turnover

Inventory is the most important asset for a merchandising business because it is often the largest current asset and the focus of a company's operations. Owners and managers strive to sell inventory quickly because inventory generates no profit until it is sold. The faster a business produces sales, the higher the sales revenue available to create income will be. **Inventory turnover**, the ratio of cost of goods sold to average inventory, measures the number of times a company sells, or *turns over*, its average level of inventory during a period. To demonstrate the inventory turnover we will use the financial statements for Cosmic Cellular from Exhibit 4-7 in Chapter 4. Cosmic Cellular's Rate of Inventory Turnover is calculated as follows:

$$\text{Inventory Turnover} = \frac{\text{Cost of Goods Sold}}{\text{Average Inventory}} = \frac{\text{Cost of Goods Sold}}{(\text{Beginning Inventory} + \text{Ending Inventory})/2}$$

$$= \frac{\$90,300}{(\$40,000^* + \$39,700)/2} = \quad 2.27 \text{ Times Per Year}$$

*The $40,000 beginning inventory balance is the ending inventory balance for the prior period and is not shown in Exhibit 4-7.

Cosmic's inventory turnover rate shows that it is selling its merchandise inventory a little more than two times a year.

Inventory turnover is usually computed for an annual period, so the cost of goods sold figure is the amount for the entire year. Average inventory is computed by adding the beginning inventory balance to the ending inventory balance, and dividing the total by two. Remember that balance sheet accounts, such as Inventory, carry their balances from one period to the next, so the ending inventory for one year becomes the beginning inventory for the next year. A high turnover rate is desirable because it indicates that the inventory is turning over, or being sold, fast; an increase in the turnover rate usually means increasing profits will result from increasing sales.

Regardless of the turnover rate, merchandisers need to keep sufficient levels of inventory on hand to meet sales demand. However, they also need to avoid purchasing too much inventory because more money will be needed to pay for the inventory and to store it until the goods are sold. These actions will increase interest expense if the funds needed are borrowed, and warehouse rent expense, if warehouse storage space is rented.

Decision Guidelines

Decision	**Guideline**	**Analyze**
Is there a way to analyze a company's inventory management?	Use the inventory turnover ratio: $\text{Inventory Turnover} = \dfrac{\text{Cost of Goods Sold}}{\text{Average Inventory}}$	The inventory turnover ratio can be an indicator that a business is poorly managing its inventory. For example, a ratio that is low compared to the industry average or a ratio that has declined from the prior year may indicate that the business has damaged or obsolete inventory.

Demo Doc

Inventory Costing

Learning Objective 2 ▶

Mackay Specialty Products, Inc., which uses the perpetual inventory method, had the following inventory information for the month of June, 2010:

Jun	1	Beginning inventory was 200 units costing $9.00 per unit.
	3	Purchased 125 units at $9.25 per unit.
	7	Sold 180 units.
	13	Purchased 100 units at $9.40 per unit.
	18	Sold 115 units.
	25	Sold 65 units.

Requirements:

❶ Without resorting to calculations, determine which costing method, FIFO or LIFO, will result in the highest reported income for Mackay Specialty Products, Inc.

❷ Calculate the cost of goods sold and the value of ending inventory for Mackay Specialty Products, Inc., for the month of June 2010 under the following costing methods:

a. FIFO

b. LIFO

c. Average cost

Demo Doc Solutions

Requirement ❶

Without resorting to calculations, determine which costing method, FIFO or LIFO, will result in the highest reported income for Mackay Specialty Products, Inc.

Part 1	Part 2	Demo Doc Complete

In order to determine whether the FIFO or LIFO costing method would result in the highest income, we must first look to see if the cost of inventory is increasing or decreasing. A review of the data indicates that the cost of inventory has steadily increased from $9.00 to $9.40 per unit during the month. In order to have the highest income possible, we must choose the inventory costing method that results in the lowest cost of goods sold. The FIFO costing method assumes that the earliest inventory costs become part of cost of goods sold, which leaves the most recent costs in ending inventory. The LIFO method is exactly opposite. It assumes that the most recent costs become part of cost of goods sold, which leaves the earliest costs in ending inventory. Because the inventory costs for Mackay Specialty Products, Inc., have steadily increased, the earliest inventory costs are lower than the most recent purchases. Therefore, choosing the FIFO costing method will result in the highest income for Mackay Specialty Products, Inc., as it will result in the lowest cost of goods sold.

Requirement ❷

Calculate the cost of goods sold and the value of ending inventory for Mackay Specialty Products, Inc., for the month of June 2010 under the following costing methods:

Part 1	Part 2	Demo Doc Complete

a. FIFO

An easy way to determine the cost of goods sold and the value of ending inventory is to prepare a perpetual inventory record. The first entry necessary in the record records the beginning inventory of 200 units at $9.00 each for a total of $1,800.00. This information is entered in the inventory on hand columns of the record as follows:

Date	Purchases Quantity	Purchases Unit Cost	Purchases Total Cost	Cost of Goods Sold Quantity	Cost of Goods Sold Unit Cost	Cost of Goods Sold Total Cost	Inventory on Hand Quantity	Inventory on Hand Unit Cost	Inventory on Hand Total Cost
Jun 1							200	$9.00	$1,800.00

Next, we enter the June 3 purchase of 125 units costing $9.25 each for a total of $1,156.25 in the purchases columns of the record.

Date	Purchases Quantity	Purchases Unit Cost	Purchases Total Cost	Cost of Goods Sold Quantity	Cost of Goods Sold Unit Cost	Cost of Goods Sold Total Cost	Inventory on Hand Quantity	Inventory on Hand Unit Cost	Inventory on Hand Total Cost
Jun 1							200	$9.00	$1,800.00
Jun 3	125	$9.25	$1,156.25						

The inventory on hand columns are completed by carrying down the original layer of inventory (200 units at $9.00) and then adding the new layer (125 units at $9.25).

Date	Purchases Quantity	Purchases Unit Cost	Purchases Total Cost	Cost of Goods Sold Quantity	Cost of Goods Sold Unit Cost	Cost of Goods Sold Total Cost	Inventory on Hand Quantity	Inventory on Hand Unit Cost	Inventory on Hand Total Cost
Jun 1							200	$9.00	$1,800.00
Jun 3	125	$9.25	$1,156.25				200	$9.00	$1,800.00
							125	$9.25	$1,156.25

Next, we will enter the June 7 sale transaction. Under FIFO, costs are assigned to cost of goods sold based on the *oldest* units on hand (the *first* units in). The oldest units we have are the units in beginning inventory (200 units at $9.00 each). The 180 units sold are, therefore, assigned a cost of $9.00 each for a total of $1,620.00. This information is entered into the cost of goods sold columns of the record.

Date	Purchases Quantity	Purchases Unit Cost	Purchases Total Cost	Cost of Goods Sold Quantity	Cost of Goods Sold Unit Cost	Cost of Goods Sold Total Cost	Inventory on Hand Quantity	Inventory on Hand Unit Cost	Inventory on Hand Total Cost
Jun 1							200	$9.00	$1,800.00
Jun 3	125	$9.25	$1,156.25				200	$9.00	$1,800.00
							125	$9.25	$1,156.25
Jun 7				180	$9.00	$1,620.00			

The inventory on hand columns are now completed. Of the original 200 units in beginning inventory, only 20 (200 – 180) are left. We also still have the 125 units purchased on June 3 for $9.25 each.

Date	Purchases Quantity	Unit Cost	Total Cost	Cost of Goods Sold Quantity	Unit Cost	Total Cost	Inventory on Hand Quantity	Unit Cost	Total Cost
Jun 1							200	$9.00	$1,800.00
Jun 3	125	$9.25	$1,156.25				200	$9.00	$1,800.00
							125	$9.25	$1,156.25
Jun 7				180	$9.00	$1,620.00	20	$9.00	$ 180.00
							125	$9.25	$1,156.25

The June 13 purchase of 100 units at $9.40 each is entered into the purchases columns of the record.

Date	Purchases Quantity	Unit Cost	Total Cost	Cost of Goods Sold Quantity	Unit Cost	Total Cost	Inventory on Hand Quantity	Unit Cost	Total Cost
Jun 1							200	$9.00	$1,800.00
Jun 3	125	$9.25	$1,156.25				200	$9.00	$1,800.00
							125	$9.25	$1,156.25
Jun 7				180	$9.00	$1,620.00	20	$9.00	$ 180.00
							125	$9.25	$1,156.25
Jun 13	100	$9.40	$ 940.00						

The inventory on hand columns are now completed by carrying down the layers of inventory from June 7 and adding a layer consisting of the 100 units purchased on June 13.

Date	Purchases Quantity	Unit Cost	Total Cost	Cost of Goods Sold Quantity	Unit Cost	Total Cost	Inventory on Hand Quantity	Unit Cost	Total Cost
Jun 1							200	$9.00	$1,800.00
Jun 3	125	$9.25	$1,156.25				200	$9.00	$1,800.00
							125	$9.25	$1,156.25
Jun 7				180	$9.00	$1,620.00	20	$9.00	$ 180.00
							125	$9.25	$1,156.25
Jun 13	100	$9.40	$ 940.00				20	$9.00	$ 180.00
							125	$9.25	$1,156.25
							100	$9.40	$ 940.00

On June 18, 115 units are sold. Remember that under FIFO we must assign the oldest cost to cost of goods sold first. The oldest cost of inventory on hand is the 20 units at $9.00 each. Because we sold more than 20 units, we must look to the next inventory layer for the cost to assign to the remaining 95 units (115 − 20). These 95 units are assigned a cost of $9.25 each. The sale is entered into the cost of goods sold columns of the record as follows:

Date	Purchases Quantity	Unit Cost	Total Cost	Cost of Goods Sold Quantity	Unit Cost	Total Cost	Inventory on Hand Quantity	Unit Cost	Total Cost
Jun 1							200	$9.00	$1,800.00
Jun 3	125	$9.25	$1,156.25				200	$9.00	$1,800.00
							125	$9.25	$1,156.25
Jun 7				180	$9.00	$1,620.00	20	$9.00	$ 180.00
							125	$9.25	$1,156.25
Jun 13	100	$9.40	$ 940.00				20	$9.00	$ 180.00
							125	$9.25	$1,156.25
							100	$9.40	$ 940.00
Jun 18				20	$9.00	$ 180.00			
				95	$9.25	$ 878.75			

After this sale, all of the beginning inventory items are assumed to be sold as well as 95 of the units costing $9.25. Therefore, the remaining inventory is made up of 30 units (125 – 95) at $9.25 and 100 units at $9.40. These amounts are entered into the inventory on hand columns of the record.

Date	Purchases Quantity	Unit Cost	Total Cost	Cost of Goods Sold Quantity	Unit Cost	Total Cost	Inventory on Hand Quantity	Unit Cost	Total Cost
Jun 1							200	$9.00	$1,800.00
Jun 3	125	$9.25	$1,156.25				200	$9.00	$1,800.00
							125	$9.25	$1,156.25
Jun 7				180	$9.00	$1,620.00	20	$9.00	$ 180.00
							125	$9.25	$1,156.25
Jun 13	100	$9.40	$ 940.00				20	$9.00	$ 180.00
							125	$9.25	$1,156.25
							100	$9.40	$ 940.00
Jun 18				20	$9.00	$ 180.00	30	$9.25	$ 277.50
				95	$9.25	$ 878.75	100	$9.40	$ 940.00

In the last transaction on June 25, 65 units were sold. Of these 65 units, 30 are assumed to cost $9.25 and the remaining 35 (65 – 30) are assumed to cost $9.40.

Date	Purchases			Cost of Goods Sold			Inventory on Hand		
	Quantity	Unit Cost	Total Cost	Quantity	Unit Cost	Total Cost	Quantity	Unit Cost	Total Cost
Jun 1							200	$9.00	$1,800.00
Jun 3	125	$9.25	$1,156.25				200	$9.00	$1,800.00
							125	$9.25	$1,156.25
Jun 7				180	$9.00	$1,620.00	20	$9.00	$ 180.00
							125	$9.25	$1,156.25
Jun 13	100	$9.40	$ 940.00				20	$9.00	$ 180.00
							125	$9.25	$1,156.25
							100	$9.40	$ 940.00
Jun 18				20	$9.00	$ 180.00	30	$9.25	$ 277.50
				95	$9.25	$ 878.75	100	$9.40	$ 940.00
Jun 25				30	$9.25	$ 277.50			
				35	$9.40	$ 329.00			

After this sale, all units costing $9.25 are assumed to be sold as well as 35 of the units costing $9.40. Therefore, the remaining inventory is made up of 65 units (100 – 35) at $9.40. These amounts are entered into the inventory on hand columns of the record.

Date	Purchases			Cost of Goods Sold			Inventory on Hand		
	Quantity	Unit Cost	Total Cost	Quantity	Unit Cost	Total Cost	Quantity	Unit Cost	Total Cost
Jun 1							200	$9.00	$1,800.00
Jun 3	125	$9.25	$1,156.25				200	$9.00	$1,800.00
							125	$9.25	$1,156.25
Jun 7				180	$9.00	$1,620.00	20	$9.00	$ 180.00
							125	$9.25	$1,156.25
Jun 13	100	$9.40	$ 940.00				20	$9.00	$ 180.00
							125	$9.25	$1,156.25
							100	$9.40	$ 940.00
Jun 18				20	$9.00	$ 180.00	30	$9.25	$ 277.50
				95	$9.25	$ 878.75	100	$9.40	$ 940.00
Jun 25				30	$9.25	$ 277.50			
				35	$9.40	$ 329.00	65	$9.40	$ 611.00

The perpetual inventory record is completed by calculating the total quantity and total cost for the purchases, cost of goods sold, and inventory on hand columns and entering the results in the last row. Notice that the amounts in the inventory on hand columns only reflect the amounts that existed after the last transaction.

Date	Purchases Quantity	Purchases Unit Cost	Purchases Total Cost	Cost of Goods Sold Quantity	Cost of Goods Sold Unit Cost	Cost of Goods Sold Total Cost	Inventory on Hand Quantity	Inventory on Hand Unit Cost	Inventory on Hand Total Cost
Jun 1							200	$9.00	$1,800.00
Jun 3	125	$9.25	$1,156.25				200	$9.00	$1,800.00
							125	$9.25	$1,156.25
Jun 7				180	$9.00	$1,620.00	20	$9.00	$ 180.00
							125	$9.25	$1,156.25
Jun 13	100	$9.40	$ 940.00				20	$9.00	$ 180.00
							125	$9.25	$1,156.25
							100	$9.40	$ 940.00
Jun 18				20	$9.00	$ 180.00	30	$9.25	$ 277.50
				95	$9.25	$ 878.75	100	$9.40	$ 940.00
Jun 25				30	$9.25	$ 277.50			
				35	$9.40	$ 329.00	65	$9.40	$ 611.00
Jun 30	225		$2,096.25	360		$3,285.25	65		$ 611.00

We can double-check our calculations using the following formula:

$$\text{Cost of Goods Sold} = (\text{Beginning Inventory} + \text{Purchases} - \text{Ending Inventory})$$

Using this formula, the cost of goods sold is $3,285.25 ($1,800.00 + $2,096.25 – $611.00). This agrees with the cost of goods sold total on the perpetual inventory record so our calculations are correct.

b. LIFO

In order to calculate the cost of goods sold and the value of ending inventory using LIFO we need to prepare another perpetual inventory record. The first entry necessary in the record is for the amount of the beginning inventory of 200 units at $9.00 each for a total of $1,800.00. This information is entered in the inventory on hand columns of the record as follows:

Date	Purchases Quantity	Purchases Unit Cost	Purchases Total Cost	Cost of Goods Sold Quantity	Cost of Goods Sold Unit Cost	Cost of Goods Sold Total Cost	Inventory on Hand Quantity	Inventory on Hand Unit Cost	Inventory on Hand Total Cost
Jun 1							200	$9.00	$1,800.00

Next, we enter the June 3 purchase of 125 units costing $9.25 each for a total of $1,156.25 in the purchases columns of the record.

Date	Purchases Quantity	Purchases Unit Cost	Purchases Total Cost	Cost of Goods Sold Quantity	Cost of Goods Sold Unit Cost	Cost of Goods Sold Total Cost	Inventory on Hand Quantity	Inventory on Hand Unit Cost	Inventory on Hand Total Cost
Jun 1							200	$9.00	$1,800.00
Jun 3	125	$9.25	$1,156.25						

The inventory on hand columns are completed by carrying down the original layer of inventory (200 units at $9.00) and then adding the new layer (125 units at $9.25).

	Purchases			Cost of Goods Sold			Inventory on Hand		
Date	Quantity	Unit Cost	Total Cost	Quantity	Unit Cost	Total Cost	Quantity	Unit Cost	Total Cost
Jun 1							200	$9.00	$1,800.00
Jun 3	125	$9.25	$1,156.25				200	$9.00	$1,800.00
							125	$9.25	$1,156.25

Next, we will enter the June 7 sale transaction. Under LIFO, costs are assigned to cost of goods sold based on the most recently purchased units on hand (the last units in). The most recently purchased units are the 125 units at $9.25 each. Because we sold more than 125 units, we must look to the next inventory layer for the cost to assign to the remaining 55 units (180 − 125). These 55 units are assigned a cost of $9.00 each. The sale is entered into the cost of goods sold columns of the record as follows:

	Purchases			Cost of Goods Sold			Inventory on Hand		
Date	Quantity	Unit Cost	Total Cost	Quantity	Unit Cost	Total Cost	Quantity	Unit Cost	Total Cost
Jun 1							200	$9.00	$1,800.00
Jun 3	125	$9.25	$1,156.25				200	$9.00	$1,800.00
							125	$9.25	$1,156.25
Jun 7				125	$9.25	$1,156.25			
				55	$9.00	$ 495.00			

The inventory on hand columns are now completed. The 125 units at $9.25 are assumed to be sold as well as 55 of the beginning inventory units costing $9.00. Therefore, the remaining inventory is made up of 145 units (200 − 55) at $9.00. These amounts are entered into the inventory on hand columns of the record.

	Purchases			Cost of Goods Sold			Inventory on Hand		
Date	Quantity	Unit Cost	Total Cost	Quantity	Unit Cost	Total Cost	Quantity	Unit Cost	Total Cost
Jun 1							200	$9.00	$1,800.00
Jun 3	125	$9.25	$1,156.25				200	$9.00	$1,800.00
							125	$9.25	$1,156.25
Jun 7				125	$9.25	$1,156.25			
				55	$9.00	$ 495.00	145	$9.00	$1,305.00

The June 13 purchase of 100 units at $9.40 each is entered into the purchases columns of the record.

Date	Purchases Quantity	Unit Cost	Total Cost	Cost of Goods Sold Quantity	Unit Cost	Total Cost	Inventory on Hand Quantity	Unit Cost	Total Cost
Jun 1							200	$9.00	$1,800.00
Jun 3	125	$9.25	$1,156.25				200	$9.00	$1,800.00
							125	$9.25	$1,156.25
Jun 7				125	$9.25	$1,156.25			
				55	$9.00	$ 495.00	145	$9.00	$1,305.00
Jun 13	100	$9.40	$ 940.00						

The inventory on hand columns are now completed by carrying down the layer of inventory from June 7 and adding a layer consisting of the 100 units purchased on June 13.

Date	Purchases Quantity	Unit Cost	Total Cost	Cost of Goods Sold Quantity	Unit Cost	Total Cost	Inventory on Hand Quantity	Unit Cost	Total Cost
Jun 1							200	$9.00	$1,800.00
Jun 3	125	$9.25	$1,156.25				200	$9.00	$1,800.00
							125	$9.25	$1,156.25
Jun 7				125	$9.25	$1,156.25			
				55	$9.00	$ 495.00	145	$9.00	$1,305.00
Jun 13	100	$9.40	$ 940.00				145	$9.00	$1,305.00
							100	$9.40	$ 940.00

On June 18, 115 units are sold. Remember that under LIFO we must assign the most recent cost to cost of goods sold first. The most recent cost of inventory on hand is the 100 units at $9.40 each so, 100 units will be assigned a cost of $9.40. Because we sold more than 100 units, we must look to the next inventory layer for the cost to assign to the remaining 15 units (115 − 100). These 15 units are assigned a cost of $9.00 each. The sale is entered into the cost of goods sold columns of the record as follows:

Date	Purchases Quantity	Unit Cost	Total Cost	Cost of Goods Sold Quantity	Unit Cost	Total Cost	Inventory on Hand Quantity	Unit Cost	Total Cost
Jun 1							200	$9.00	$1,800.00
Jun 3	125	$9.25	$1,156.25				200	$9.00	$1,800.00
							125	$9.25	$1,156.25
Jun 7				125	$9.25	$1,156.25			
				55	$9.00	$ 495.00	145	$9.00	$1,305.00
Jun 13	100	$9.40	$ 940.00				145	$9.00	$1,305.00
							100	$9.40	$ 940.00
Jun 18				100	$9.40	$940.00			
				15	$9.00	$135.00			

After this sale, all of the inventory items costing $9.40 are assumed to be sold as well as 15 of the units costing $9.00. Therefore, the remaining inventory is made up of 130 units (145 − 15) at $9.00. These amounts are entered into the inventory on hand columns of the record.

	Purchases			Cost of Goods Sold			Inventory on Hand		
Date	Quantity	Unit Cost	Total Cost	Quantity	Unit Cost	Total Cost	Quantity	Unit Cost	Total Cost
Jun 1							200	$9.00	$1,800.00
Jun 3	125	$9.25	$1,156.25				200	$9.00	$1,800.00
							125	$9.25	$1,156.25
Jun 7				125	$9.25	$1,156.25			
				55	$9.00	$ 495.00	145	$9.00	$1,305.00
Jun 13	100	$9.40	$ 940.00				145	$9.00	$1,305.00
							100	$9.40	$ 940.00
Jun 18				100	$9.40	$ 940.00			
				15	$9.00	$ 135.00	130	$9.00	$1,170.00

In the last transaction on June 25, 65 units were sold. These 65 units are assigned a cost of $9.00 because the only layer of inventory left is the 130 units at $9.00.

	Purchases			Cost of Goods Sold			Inventory on Hand		
Date	Quantity	Unit Cost	Total Cost	Quantity	Unit Cost	Total Cost	Quantity	Unit Cost	Total Cost
Jun 1							200	$9.00	$1,800.00
Jun 3	125	$9.25	$1,156.25				200	$9.00	$1,800.00
							125	$9.25	$1,156.25
Jun 7				125	$9.25	$1,156.25			
				55	$9.00	$ 495.00	145	$9.00	$1,305.00
Jun 13	100	$9.40	$ 940.00				145	$9.00	$1,305.00
							100	$9.40	$ 940.00
Jun 18				100	$9.40	$ 940.00			
				15	$9.00	$ 135.00	130	$9.00	$1,170.00
Jun 25				65	$9.00	$ 585.00			

After this sale, the remaining inventory is made up of 65 units (130 – 65) at $9.00. These amounts are entered into the inventory on hand columns of the record.

	Purchases			Cost of Goods Sold			Inventory on Hand		
Date	Quantity	Unit Cost	Total Cost	Quantity	Unit Cost	Total Cost	Quantity	Unit Cost	Total Cost
Jun 1							200	$9.00	$1,800.00
Jun 3	125	$9.25	$1,156.25				200	$9.00	$1,800.00
							125	$9.25	$1,156.25
Jun 7				125	$9.25	$1,156.25			
				55	$9.00	$ 495.00	145	$9.00	$1,305.00
Jun 13	100	$9.40	$ 940.00				145	$9.00	$1,305.00
							100	$9.40	$ 940.00
Jun 18				100	$9.40	$ 940.00			
				15	$9.00	$ 135.00	130	$9.00	$1,170.00
Jun 25				65	$9.00	$ 585.00	65	$9.00	$ 585.00

The perpetual inventory record is completed by calculating the total quantity and total cost for the purchases, cost of goods sold, and inventory on hand columns and entering the results in the last row. Notice that the amounts in the inventory on hand columns only reflect the amounts that existed after the last transaction.

Date	Purchases Quantity	Purchases Unit Cost	Purchases Total Cost	Cost of Goods Sold Quantity	Cost of Goods Sold Unit Cost	Cost of Goods Sold Total Cost	Inventory on Hand Quantity	Inventory on Hand Unit Cost	Inventory on Hand Total Cost
Jun 1							200	$9.00	$1,800.00
Jun 3	125	$9.25	$1,156.25				200	$9.00	$1,800.00
							125	$9.25	$1,156.25
Jun 7				125	$9.25	$1,156.25			
				55	$9.00	$ 495.00	145	$9.00	$1,305.00
Jun 13	100	$9.40	$ 940.00				145	$9.00	$1,305.00
							100	$9.40	$ 940.00
Jun 18				100	$9.40	$ 940.00			
				15	$9.00	$ 135.00	130	$9.00	$1,170.00
Jun 25				65	$9.00	$ 585.00	65	$9.00	$ 585.00
Jun 30	225		$2,096.25	360		$3,311.25	65		$ 585.00

We can double-check our calculations by calculating the cost of goods sold using the same formula that we used in step a. Using this formula, the cost of goods sold is $3,311.25 ($1,800.00 + $2,096.25 – $585.00). This agrees with the cost of goods sold total on the perpetual inventory record so our calculations are correct.

c. Average cost

We will now complete a perpetual inventory record using average cost. As we did for the FIFO and LIFO inventory records, the first entry is to record the beginning inventory of 200 units costing $9.00 each.

Date	Purchases Quantity	Purchases Unit Cost	Purchases Total Cost	Cost of Goods Sold Quantity	Cost of Goods Sold Unit Cost	Cost of Goods Sold Total Cost	Inventory on Hand Quantity	Inventory on Hand Unit Cost	Inventory on Hand Total Cost
Jun 1							200	$9.00	$1,800.00

The entry for the first purchase of 125 units on June 3 is the same as for the FIFO and LIFO inventory records.

Date	Purchases Quantity	Purchases Unit Cost	Purchases Total Cost	Cost of Goods Sold Quantity	Cost of Goods Sold Unit Cost	Cost of Goods Sold Total Cost	Inventory on Hand Quantity	Inventory on Hand Unit Cost	Inventory on Hand Total Cost
Jun 1							200	$9.00	$1,800.00
Jun 3	125	$9.25	$1,156.25						

Once a purchase is made, the average cost per unit must be calculated. The average cost per unit is calculated by dividing the total cost of inventory on hand by the total quantity of inventory on hand. The total cost of inventory equals $2,956.25 ($1,800.00 beginning inventory + $1,156.25 purchased on June 3). The total quantity of inventory on hand equals the 200 units in beginning inventory plus the 125 units purchased for a total of 325 units. The average cost per unit is calculated as follows:

$$\frac{\$2,956.25}{325} = \$9.10^* \text{ per unit}$$

*Rounded

The inventory on hand consists of 325 units at $9.10 each. This information is entered into the inventory on hand columns of the inventory record.

Date	Purchases Quantity	Unit Cost	Total Cost	Cost of Goods Sold Quantity	Unit Cost	Total Cost	Inventory on Hand Quantity	Unit Cost	Total Cost
Jun 1							200	$9.00	$1,800.00
Jun 3	125	$9.25	$1,156.25				325	$9.10	$2,957.50

On June 7, 180 units are sold. The units in inventory have an average cost of $9.10 each, so the units sold are assigned a cost of $9.10 for a total of $1,638.00. This information is entered into the cost of goods sold columns of the record.

Date	Purchases Quantity	Unit Cost	Total Cost	Cost of Goods Sold Quantity	Unit Cost	Total Cost	Inventory on Hand Quantity	Unit Cost	Total Cost
Jun 1							200	$9.00	$1,800.00
Jun 3	125	$9.25	$1,156.25				325	$9.10	2,957.50
Jun 7				180	$9.10	$1,638.00			

This transaction leaves 145 units (325 − 180) in inventory at $9.10 each. This information is now entered in the inventory on hand columns of the record.

Date	Purchases Quantity	Unit Cost	Total Cost	Cost of Goods Sold Quantity	Unit Cost	Total Cost	Inventory on Hand Quantity	Unit Cost	Total Cost
Jun 1							200	$9.00	$1,800.00
Jun 3	125	$9.25	$1,156.25				325	$9.10	$2,957.50
Jun 7				180	$9.10	$1,638.00	145	$9.10	$1,319.50

The June 13 purchase of 100 units at $9.40 each is now entered into the purchases columns of the inventory record.

Date	Purchases Quantity	Unit Cost	Total Cost	Cost of Goods Sold Quantity	Unit Cost	Total Cost	Inventory on Hand Quantity	Unit Cost	Total Cost
Jun 1							200	$9.00	$1,800.00
Jun 3	125	$9.25	$1,156.25				325	$9.10	$2,957.50
Jun 7				180	$9.10	$1,638.00	145	$9.10	$1,319.50
Jun 13	100	$9.40	$ 940.00						

Because another purchase has been made, the average cost per unit must be recalculated. The total cost of inventory equals $2,259.50 ($1,319.50 June 7 remaining inventory + $940.00 purchased on June 13). The total quantity of inventory on hand equals the 145 units remaining in inventory on June 7 plus the 100 units purchased for a total of 245 units. The average cost per unit is calculated as follows:

$$\frac{\$2,259.50}{245} = \$9.22^* \text{ per unit}$$

*Rounded

The inventory on hand consists of 245 units at $9.22 each. This information is entered into the inventory on hand columns of the inventory record.

Date	Purchases Quantity	Unit Cost	Total Cost	Cost of Goods Sold Quantity	Unit Cost	Total Cost	Inventory on Hand Quantity	Unit Cost	Total Cost
Jun 1							200	$9.00	$1,800.00
Jun 3	125	$9.25	$1,156.25				325	$9.10	$2,957.50
Jun 7				180	$9.10	$1,638.00	145	$9.10	$1,319.50
Jun 13	100	$9.40	$940.00				245	$9.22	$2,258.90

On June 18, 115 units are sold. The units in inventory have an average cost of $9.22 each, so the units sold are assigned a cost of $9.22 for a total of $1,060.30. This information is entered into the cost of goods sold columns of the record.

Date	Purchases Quantity	Unit Cost	Total Cost	Cost of Goods Sold Quantity	Unit Cost	Total Cost	Inventory on Hand Quantity	Unit Cost	Total Cost
Jun 1							200	$9.00	$1,800.00
Jun 3	125	$9.25	$1,156.25				325	$9.10	$2,957.50
Jun 7				180	$9.10	$1,638.00	145	$9.10	$1,319.50
Jun 13	100	$9.40	$940.00				245	$9.22	$2,258.90
Jun 18				115	$9.22	$1,060.30			

This transaction leaves 130 units (245 − 115) in inventory at $9.22 each. This information is now entered in the inventory on hand columns of the record.

Date	Purchases Quantity	Unit Cost	Total Cost	Cost of Goods Sold Quantity	Unit Cost	Total Cost	Inventory on Hand Quantity	Unit Cost	Total Cost
Jun 1							200	$9.00	$1,800.00
Jun 3	125	$9.25	$1,156.25				325	$9.10	$2,957.50
Jun 7				180	$9.10	$1,638.00	145	$9.10	$1,319.50
Jun 13	100	$9.40	$940.00				245	$9.22	$2,258.90
Jun 18				115	$9.22	$1,060.30	130	$9.22	$1,198.60

The last transaction on June 25 was for the sale of 65 units. Because there have been no purchases since the last transaction, there is no need to recalculate the average cost per unit. So the cost assigned to the 65 units will be $9.22 each. This information is entered into the cost of goods sold columns of the record.

Date	Purchases Quantity	Unit Cost	Total Cost	Cost of Goods Sold Quantity	Unit Cost	Total Cost	Inventory on Hand Quantity	Unit Cost	Total Cost
Jun 1							200	$9.00	$1,800.00
Jun 3	125	$9.25	$1,156.25				325	$9.10	$2,957.50
Jun 7				180	$9.10	$1,638.00	145	$9.10	$1,319.50
Jun 13	100	$9.40	$ 940.00				245	$9.22	$2,258.90
Jun 18				115	$9.22	$1,060.30	130	$9.22	$1,198.60
Jun 25				65	$9.22	$ 599.30			

This transaction leaves 65 units (130 – 65) in inventory at $9.22 each. This information is now entered in the inventory on hand columns of the record.

Date	Purchases Quantity	Unit Cost	Total Cost	Cost of Goods Sold Quantity	Unit Cost	Total Cost	Inventory on Hand Quantity	Unit Cost	Total Cost
Jun 1							200	$9.00	$1,800.00
Jun 3	125	$9.25	$1,156.25				325	$9.10	$2,957.50
Jun 7				180	$9.10	$1,638.00	145	$9.10	$1,319.50
Jun 13	100	$9.40	$ 940.00				245	$9.22	$2,258.90
Jun 18				115	$9.22	$1,060.30	130	$9.22	$1,198.60
Jun 25				65	$9.22	$ 599.30	65	$9.22	$ 599.30

As we did with FIFO and LIFO, the perpetual inventory record is completed by calculating the total quantity and total cost for the purchases, cost of goods sold, and inventory on hand columns and entering the results in the last row. Notice that the amounts in the inventory on hand columns only reflect the amounts that existed after the last transaction.

Date	Purchases Quantity	Unit Cost	Total Cost	Cost of Goods Sold Quantity	Unit Cost	Total Cost	Inventory on Hand Quantity	Unit Cost	Total Cost
Jun 1							200	$9.00	$1,800.00
Jun 3	125	$9.25	$1,156.25				325	$9.10	$2,957.50
Jun 7				180	$9.10	$1,638.00	145	$9.10	$1,319.50
Jun 13	100	$9.40	$ 940.00				245	$9.22	$2,258.90
Jun 18				115	$9.22	$1,060.30	130	$9.22	$1,198.60
Jun 25				65	$9.22	$ 599.30	65	$9.22	$ 599.30
Jun 30	225		$2,096.25	360		$3,297.60	65		$ 599.30

Once again, we can double-check our calculations by calculating the cost of goods sold using the same formula that we used in steps a and b. Using this formula, the cost of goods sold is $3,296.95 ($1,800.00 + $2,096.25 - $599.30). The difference ($0.65) between this amount and the cost of goods sold found on our perpetual inventory record ($3,297.60) is due to rounding when calculating the average unit costs and is immaterial.

DemoDoc Complete

Part 1	Part 2	**Demo Doc Complete**

Decision Guidelines

Inventory

If you own or work for a merchandiser, here are some decisions related to inventory that you may encounter.

Decision	Guideline	Analyze
Decision	**Guideline**	**Analyze**
How do I determine the cost of the inventory I sell?	The physical flow of the inventory and the cost flow of the inventory can be different. The cost assigned to the units sold may be based on one of the following four methods: • Specific-identification • First-in, first-out (FIFO) • Last-in, first-out (LIFO) • Average cost	*Specific-identification*: Inventory items are specifically labeled or identified and the actual cost of each item sold is assigned to cost of goods sold. *First-in, first-out (FIFO)*: The first inventory costs incurred are the first costs to be assigned to cost of goods sold. *Last-in, first-out (LIFO)*: The last inventory costs incurred are the first costs to be assigned to cost of goods sold. *Average cost*: After each purchase of inventory, a new weighted-average cost per unit is computed and assigned to cost of goods sold
Which inventory costing method is the best for my company?	It depends on whether costs are rising or declining and whether you want to report higher or lower net income.	When costs are rising • FIFO reports the highest ending inventory value and lowest cost of goods sold and, therefore, the highest net income. • LIFO reports the lowest ending inventory value and highest cost of goods sold and, therefore, the lowest net income. • average cost reports an average cost for the value of ending inventory and cost of goods sold. Average cost can be used to stabilize fluctuations in net income if inventory costs are continually fluctuating.

What is the effect of a misstatement of ending inventory?	In addition to causing an overstatement or understatement of Inventory on the balance sheet, a misstatement of ending inventory will cause an error on the income statement.	If ending inventory is overstated, then
		• Cost of Goods Sold is understated.
		• Gross Profit is overstated.
		• Net Income is overstated.
		
		If ending inventory is understated, then
		• Cost of Goods Sold is overstated.
		• Gross Profit is understated.
		• Net Income is understated.
		
		Because ending inventory for one period becomes beginning inventory for the next period, the Cost of Goods Sold, Gross Profit, and Net Income of the next period are also misstated.

Is there a way to analyze a company's inventory management?	Use the inventory turnover ratio: 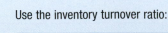 $$\text{Inventory Turnover} = \frac{\text{Cost of Goods Sold}}{\text{Average Inventory}}$$	The inventory turnover ratio can be an indicator that a business is poorly managing its inventory. For example, a ratio that is low compared to the industry average or a ratio that has declined from the prior year may indicate that the business has damaged or obsolete inventory.

ACCOUNTING VOCABULARY

THE LANGUAGE OF BUSINESS

Average cost (p. 230) Inventory costing method where, after each purchase of inventory, a new weighted average cost per unit is computed and is used to value ending inventory and cost of goods sold.

Conservatism (p. 241) Accounting principle that states that a business must report all items in the financial statements at amounts that lead to the most cautious immediate results.

Consistency (p. 241) Accounting principle that states that a business should use the same accounting methods and procedures from period to period.

Cost of goods available for sale (p. 233) The cost of inventory on hand at the beginning of the period plus the net cost of inventory purchased during the period.

Finished goods (p. 230) Inventory of goods ready to sell.

First-in, first-out (FIFO) (p. 230) Inventory costing method in which the first inventory costs incurred are the first costs to be assigned to cost of goods sold; FIFO leaves in ending inventory the last, the most recent, costs incurred.

Footnotes (p. 243) Disclosures that accompany the financial statements.

Full disclosure (p. 243) Accounting principle that states that a company's financial statements should report enough information for users to make knowledgeable decisions about the company.

Gross profit method (p. 246) A way of estimating inventory by estimating gross profit, using estimated gross profit to estimate cost of goods sold, and using estimated cost of goods sold to estimate ending inventory.

Inventory layer (p. 232) A record of the quantity of and the cost of inventory items made in a single purchase.

Inventory shrinkage (p. 243) The loss of inventory.

Inventory turnover (p. 248) The ratio of cost of goods sold to average inventory.

Last-in, first-out (LIFO) (p. 230) Inventory costing method in which the last inventory costs incurred are the first costs to be assigned to cost of goods sold; LIFO leaves in ending inventory the first, the oldest, costs incurred.

Lower-of-cost-or-market (LCM) rule (p. 242) The rule that a business must report inventory in the financial statements at whichever is lower, the historical cost or the market value, of each inventory item.

Materiality (p. 242) Accounting principle that states that a company must perform strictly proper accounting *only* for items that are significant for the business's financial statements. Information is significant, or material, when its presentation in the financial statements would cause someone to change a decision.

Perpetual inventory record (p. 235) A record that tracks the quantity of, and cost assigned to, inventory items as they are purchased and sold.

Raw materials (p. 230) Inventory items used in the production of goods.

Specific-identification (p. 230) Inventory costing method in which a business uses the specific cost of each unit of inventory; also called the *specific-unit cost* method.

Specific-unit cost (p. 235) Inventory costing method in which a business uses the specific cost of each unit of inventory; also called the *specific-identification* method.

Work in process (p. 230) Inventory of partially completed goods.

ACCOUNTING PRACTICE

DISCUSSION QUESTIONS

1. The introduction to this chapter suggests that the chapter will explore the answers to some questions about inventory. Did you get the answers to those questions? Specifically,
   a. why does inventory need to be counted?
   b. what would happen if the count was done incorrectly?
   c. what do the terms FIFO and LIFO have to do with inventory?

2. How are the financial statements of a manufacturer different from those of a merchandiser with respect to inventory?

3. What is a cost-flow assumption? Why is a cost-flow assumption necessary in accounting for inventory?

4. If a company had two units that cost $1 each in its beginning inventory and purchased two more units for $2 each, what would be the cost of goods sold associated with a sale of three units under each of the following assumptions?

   a. FIFO
   b. LIFO
   c. Average cost

5. If a company had two units that cost $1 each in its beginning inventory and purchased two more units for $2 each, what would be the gross profit reported on the income statement under each of the following assumptions if three units were sold for $3 each?

   a. FIFO
   b. LIFO
   c. Average cost

6. In a period of rising prices, which cost-flow assumption would produce the highest net income? Why?

7. Let's say that two companies, identical in every way except that one used FIFO and one used LIFO, went into a bank on the same day to get a loan to deal with the rising cost of acquiring inventory. Despite the fact that they both engaged in the same transactions at the same dollar values, one company reported higher net income and higher total assets on the financial statements. Which one was it? If the banker made the decision based on the company that would have better cash flow associated with the inventory costing method choice, which company would have received the loan?

8. Describe some business and economic conditions that might make the lower-of-cost-or-market rule more likely to be used.

9. Under which of the inventory methods, periodic or perpetual, would a company be better equipped to detect inventory shrinkage? Why?

10. If a company is having a harder time selling its products, even at discounted prices compared to last year, would this year's inventory turnover rate be higher or lower than last year's rate? What about the gross profit rate?

SELF CHECK

1. During February, Peter's Hardware made sales of $38,600 and ended the month with inventories totaling $5,400. Cost of Goods Sold was $23,200. Total operating expenses were $8,700. How much net income did Peter's Hardware earn for the month?

   a. $1,300
   b. $15,400
   c. $6,700
   d. $10,000

2. Which inventory costing method assigns the newest, most recent, costs incurred during the period to ending inventory?

   a. Specific-unit cost
   b. First-in, first-out (FIFO)
   c. Last-in, first-out (LIFO)
   d. Average cost

3. Which inventory costing method results in the lowest net income during a period of declining inventory costs?

   a. Average cost
   b. Specific-unit cost
   c. First-in, first-out (FIFO)
   d. Last-in, first-out (LIFO)

4. Assume HPC, Inc., began December with 60 units of inventory that cost a total of $720. During December, HPC, Inc., purchased and sold goods as follows:

Dec 6	Purchased 120 units @ $13 each
15	Sold 145 units @ $28 each
22	Purchased 100 units @ $15
30	Sold 85 units @ $29 each

HPC, Inc., uses perpetual inventory. Under the FIFO inventory method, how much is HPC's cost of goods sold for the sale on December 15?

a. $455   b. $1,740
c. $1,860   d. $1,825

5. Assume HPC, Inc., began December with 60 units of inventory that cost a total of $720. During December, HPC, Inc., purchased and sold goods as follows:

Dec	6	Purchased 120 units @ $13 each
	15	Sold 145 units @ $28 each
	22	Purchased 100 units @ $15 each
	30	Sold 85 units @ $29 each

HPC, Inc., uses perpetual inventory. Under the LIFO inventory method, how much is HPC's cost of inventory on hand after the sale on December 30?

a. $645   b. $750
c. $600   d. $650

6. Assume HPC, Inc., began December with 60 units of inventory that cost a total of $720. During December, HPC, Inc., purchased and sold goods as follows:

Dec	6	Purchased 120 units @ $13 each
	15	Sold 145 units @ $28 each
	22	Purchased 100 units @ $15 each
	30	Sold 85 units @ $29 each

HPC, Inc., uses perpetual inventory. Under the average cost inventory method, how much is HPC's cost of goods sold for the sale on December 15? Round unit cost to the nearest cent.

a. $1,812.50   b. $1,837.15
c. $1,825.75   d. $1,934.30

7. Which of the following prevents a company from switching its inventory costing method to a different method each year?

a. Disclosure principle   b. Consistency principle
c. Matching principle   d. Materiality concept

8. Which of the following is most closely linked to accounting conservatism?

a. Materiality concept   b. Consistency principle
c. Disclosure principle   d. Lower-of-cost-or-market rule

9. At December 31, 2010, Inland Equipment understated ending inventory by $2,800. How does this error affect cost of goods sold and net income for 2010?

a. Overstates cost of goods sold and understates net income
b. Understates costs of goods sold and overstates net income
c. Overstates both cost of goods sold and net income
d. Leaves both cost of goods sold and net income correct because the errors cancel each other

10. Suppose Ironman, Inc., lost all of its inventory in a flood. Beginning inventory was $43,000, net purchases totaled $524,000, and sales came to $875,000. Ironman's normal gross profit percentage is 44%. Use the gross profit method to estimate the cost of the inventory lost in the flood.

a. $308,000   b. $182,000
c. $77,000   d. $34,000

Answers are given after Written Communication.

SHORT EXERCISES

S5-1. Inventory methods (*Learning Objective 1*) 5 min.

Motion Auto would like to assign the oldest costs of inventory items to its ending inventory.

Which inventory costing method should Motion Auto choose?

S5-2. Inventory methods (*Learning Objective 1*) 5–10 min.

Hamilton Furniture doesn't expect prices to change dramatically and wants to use a method that averages price changes.

Which inventory method would best meet Hamilton Furniture's goal? What if Hamilton Furniture wanted to expense out the newer purchases of goods instead? Which inventory would best meet that need?

S5-3. FIFO (*Learning Objective 2*) 5–10 min.

Mike's Powersports uses the FIFO inventory method. Mike's Powersports started August with 10 helmets that cost $54 each. On August 19, Mike's Powersports bought 15 helmets at $56 each. On August 28, Mike's Powersports sold 12 helmets.

Prepare a perpetual inventory record for Mike's Powersports.

S5-4. LIFO (*Learning Objective 2*) 5–10 min.

Mike's Powersports uses the LIFO inventory method. Mike's Powersports started August with 10 helmets that cost $54 each. On August 19, Mike's Powersports bought 15 helmets at $56 each. On August 28, Mike's Powersports sold 12 helmets.

Prepare a perpetual inventory record for Mike's Powersports.

S5-5. Average cost (*Learning Objective 2*) 5–10 min.

Mike's Powersports uses the average cost inventory method. Mike's Powersports started August with 10 helmets that cost $54 each. On August 19, Mike's Powersports bought 15 helmets at $56 each. On August 28, Mike's Powersports sold 12 helmets.

Prepare a perpetual inventory record for the average cost method. Round average cost per unit to the nearest cent and all other amounts to the nearest dollar.

S5-6. Recording inventory transactions (*Learning Objective 2*) 5–10 min.

Mike's Powersports uses the (perpetual) LIFO inventory method. Mike's Powersports started August with 10 helmets that cost $54 each. On August 19, Mike's Powersports bought 15 helmets at $56 each. On August 28, Mike's Powersports sold 12 helmets.

1. The August 19 purchase of inventory was on account.
2. The August 28 sale of inventory was on account. Mike's Powersports sold each helmet for $95.

Prepare the required journal entries for the purchase and sale of inventory.

S5-7. FIFO versus LIFO (*Learning Objective 2*) 5–10 min.

Consider the FIFO, LIFO, and average cost inventory costing methods. Answer the following questions assuming that inventory costs are increasing:

1. Which method of inventory costing will produce the lowest cost of goods sold?
2. Which method of inventory costing will produce the highest cost of goods sold?
3. If prices had been declining instead of rising, which inventory method will produce the highest cost of goods sold?

S5-8. Inventory terms (*Learning Objectives 4 & 5*) 5–10 min.

Match the terms with the definitions.

a. Full disclosure

b. Materiality

c. Consistency

d. Conservatism

_____ 1. A company must perform strictly proper accounting only for items that are significant to the business's financial statements

_____ 2. Reporting the least favorable figures in the financial statements

_____ 3. A business's financial statements must report enough information for users to make knowledgeable decisions about the company

_____ 4. A business should use the same accounting methods and procedures from period to period

S5-9. Lower-of-cost-or-market (*Learning Objective 4*) 5–10 min.

Assume that Bonsai Boards has the following LIFO perpetual inventory record for snowboards for the month of November:

Snowboards			
Date	Purchases	Cost of Goods Sold	Inventory on Hand
Nov 1			$1,320
8	$ 840		$2,160
19		$1,640	$ 520
30	$1,130		$1,650

At November 30, the accountant for Bonsai Boards determines that the current replacement cost of the ending inventory is $1,615. Make any adjusting entry needed to apply the lower-of-cost-or-market rule. Inventory would be reported on the balance sheet at what value on November 30?

S5-10. Reporting inventory on the balance sheet (*Learning Objective 5*) 5–10 min.

At the end of the current year, Cuppa Joes' inventory account balance was $12,600. A physical count of the inventory revealed that inventory on hand totaled $12,200.

What amount should Cuppa Joes report on its balance sheet?

S5-11. Inventory principles and terminology (*Learning Objectives 1, 4, & 5*) 5–10 min.

Match the accounting terms on the left with the corresponding definitions on the right.

_____ 1. Conservatism

_____ 2. Full disclosure

_____ 3. LIFO

_____ 4. Average cost

_____ 5. FIFO

_____ 6. Consistency

_____ 7. Materiality

_____ 8. Specific-Identification

a. Assigns the most recent inventory costs to ending inventory.

b. Results in cost of goods sold that falls between what FIFO and LIFO produce assuming rising prices.

c. This principle is the basis for using lower-of-cost-or-market rule.

d. Principle that prevents a company from using a different inventory costing method each year.

e. Identifies exactly which inventory item was sold. Usually used for unique inventory items.

f. Requires that a company report enough information for outsiders to make decisions.

g. Treats the most recent/newest purchases as the first units sold.

h. Principle that states significant items must conform to GAAP.

S5-12. Inventory errors (*Learning Objective 6*) 5–10 min.

Bonsai Board's income statement data for the year ended December 31, 2010, follow.

Sales Revenue	$237,500
Cost of Goods Sold	142,800
Gross Profit	$ 94,700

Assume that the ending inventory was accidentally overstated by $3,300.

What are the correct amounts for cost of goods sold and gross profit?

S5-13. Inventory errors (*Learning Objective 6*) 10–15 min.

Bonsai Board's income statement data for the year ended December 31, 2010, follow.

Sales Revenue	$237,500
Cost of Goods Sold	142,800
Gross Profit	$ 94,700

Assume that the ending inventory was accidentally overstated by $3,300. How would the inventory error affect Bonsai Boards' cost of goods sold and gross profit for the year ended December 31, 2011, if the error is not corrected in 2010?

S5-14. Estimating ending inventory (*Learning Objective 7*) 10–15 min.

Inland Lumber began the year with inventory of $52,200 and made purchases of $316,700 during the year. Sales for the year are $503,800, and Inland Lumber's gross profit percentage is 42% of sales.

Compute Inland Lumber's estimated cost of ending inventory using the gross profit method.

S5-15. Inventory turnover (*Learning Objective 8*) 5–10 min.

Mackay Industries' sales for the year ended December 31, 2010, were $1,287,000 and cost of goods sold amounted to $707,000. Beginning inventory was $58,000 and ending inventory was $77,000.

Compute Mackay Industries' rate of inventory turnover for the year ended December 31, 2010. Round answer to the nearest tenth.

EXERCISES (GROUP A)

E5-16A. FIFO (*Learning Objective 2*) 10–15 min.

Austin's Jewelers carries a line of waterproof watches. Austin's Jewelers uses the FIFO method and a perpetual inventory system. The sales price of each watch is $175. Company records indicate the following activity for waterproof watches for the month of March:

Date	Item	Quantity	Unit Cost
Mar 1	Balance	3	$ 96
7	Purchase	10	$ 98
11	Sale	12	
19	Purchase	15	$104
28	Sale	10	

Requirements

1. Prepare a perpetual inventory record for the waterproof watches to determine the amount Austin's Jewelers should report for ending inventory and cost of goods sold using the FIFO method.

2. Journalize Austin's Jewelers' inventory transactions using the FIFO method. Assume that all purchases and sales are on account.

E5-17A. LIFO (*Learning Objective 2*) 10–15 min.

Refer to the data for E5-16A. However, instead of the FIFO method, assume Austin's Jewelers uses the LIFO method.

Requirements

1. Prepare a perpetual inventory record for the watches on the LIFO basis to determine the cost of ending inventory and cost of goods sold for the month.

2. Journalize Austin's Jewelers' inventory transactions using the perpetual LIFO method. Assume that all purchases and sales are on account.

E5-18A. Average cost (*Learning Objective 2*) 10–15 min.

Refer to the data for E5-16A. However, instead of the FIFO method, assume Austin's Jewelers uses the average cost method.

Requirements

1. Prepare a perpetual inventory record for the watches on the average cost basis to determine the cost of ending inventory and cost of goods sold for the month. Round average cost per unit to the nearest cent and all other amounts to the nearest dollar.

2. Journalize Austin's Jewelers' inventory transactions using the perpetual average cost method. Assume that all purchases and sales are on account.

E5-19A. FIFO versus LIFO (*Learning Objective 2*) 10–15 min.

Assume that Midway Cycles bought and sold a line of mountain bikes during May as follows:

Date	Item	Quantity	Unit Cost
May 1	Balance	10	$243
5	Sale	5	
12	Purchase	12	$252
21	Sale	7	
30	Sale	6	

Midway Cycles uses the perpetual inventory system.

Requirements

1. Compute the cost of ending inventory under FIFO.

2. Compute the cost of ending inventory under LIFO.

3. Which method results in higher cost of ending inventory?

E5-20A. FIFO versus LIFO (*Learning Objective 2*) 10–15 min.

Refer to the data for Midway Cycles in E5-19A.

Requirements

1. Compute the cost of goods sold under FIFO.

2. Compute the cost of goods sold under LIFO.

3. Which method results in the higher cost of goods sold?

Quick solution: 1. FIFO cost of goods sold = $4,446; 2. LIFO cost of goods sold = $4,482

E5-21A. FIFO versus LIFO versus average-cost (*Learning Objectives 2 & 3*) 15–20 min.

Assume that a Firestone Tire Store completed the following perpetual inventory transactions for a line of tires.

Beginning Inventory	34 tires @ $ 82
Purchase	25 tires @ $ 88
Sale	40 tires @ $134

Requirements

1. Compute cost of goods sold and gross profit under FIFO.
2. Compute cost of goods sold and gross profit using LIFO.
3. Compute cost of goods sold and gross profit using average cost. Round average cost per unit to the nearest cent and all other amounts to the nearest dollar.
4. Which method results in the largest gross profit and why?

E5-22A. Lower of cost or market (*Learning Objective 4*) 10–15 min.

GDL Enterprises has the following account balances at December 31, 2010. The inventory balance was determined using FIFO.

Inventory		Cost of Goods Sold		Sales Revenue	
Beg Bal	26,500	Bal	106,000		
End Bal	31,800			Bal	176,000

GDL Enterprises has determined that the replacement cost (current market value) of the December 31, 2010, ending inventory is $32,400.

Requirements

1. What value would GDL Enterprises report on the balance sheet at December 31, 2010, for inventory assuming the company uses the lower-of-cost–or-market rule?
2. Prepare any adjusting journal entry required from the information given.

E5-23A. Reporting inventory on the balance sheet (*Learning Objective 5*) 5–10 min.

Eagle Eye Sunglasses had the following FIFO perpetual inventory record at June 30, the end of the fiscal year.

	Purchases			Cost of Goods Sold			Inventory on Hand		
Date	Quantity	Unit Cost	Total Cost	Quantity	Unit Cost	Total Cost	Quantity	Unit Cost	Total Cost
Jun 1							200	$9.00	$1,800.00
Jun 3	125	$9.25	$1,156.25				200	$9.00	$1,800.00
							125	$9.25	$1,156.25
Jun 7				180	$9.00	$ 1,620.00	20	$9.00	$ 180.00
							125	$9.25	$1,156.25
Jun 13	100	$9.40	$ 940.00				20	$9.00	$ 180.00
							125	$9.25	$1,156.25
							100	$9.40	$ 940.00
Jun 18				20	$9.00	$ 180.00	30	$9.25	$ 277.50
				95	$9.25	$ 878.75	100	$9.40	$ 940.00
Jun 25				30	$9.25	$ 277.50			
				35	$9.40	$ 329.00	65	$9.40	$ 611.00
Jun 30	225		$2,096.25	360		$3,285.25	65		$ 611.00

A physical count of the inventory performed at year end revealed $587.00 of inventory on hand.

Requirements

1. Journalize the adjusting entry for inventory, if any is required.
2. What could have caused the value of the ending inventory based on the physical count to be lower than the amount based on the perpetual inventory record?

E5-24A. Inventory errors (*Learning Objective 6*) 10–15 min.

Motion Auto reported sales revenue of $138,000 and cost of goods sold of $76,000.

Requirements

1. Compute Motion Auto's correct gross profit assuming the company's ending inventory is overstated by $1,300. Show your work.
2. Compute Motion Auto's correct gross profit assuming the company's ending inventory is understated by $2,700. Show your work.

E5-25A. Inventory errors (*Learning Objective 6*) 10–15 min.

Hanson's Furniture Outlet reported the following comparative income statement for the years ended June 30, 2010 and 2009.

Hanson's Furniture Outlet
Comparative Income Statement
For the years ended December 31, 2010 and 2009

	2010		2009	
Sales Revenue		$187,600		$164,000
Cost of Goods Sold:				
Beginning Inventory	$ 12,300		$ 9,100	
Net Purchases	114,500		101,600	
Cost of Goods Available	126,800		110,700	
Ending Inventory	14,600		12,300	
Cost of Goods Sold		112,200		98,400
Gross Profit		75,400		65,600
Operating Expenses		32,900		26,700
Net Income		$ 42,500		$ 38,900

During 2010, Hanson's Furniture Outlet discovered that the 2009 ending inventory, as previously reported, was understated by $2,100.

Requirements

1. Prepare the corrected comparative income statement for the two-year period, complete with a heading for the statement.
2. What was the effect of the error on net income for the two years combined? Explain your answer.

E5-26A. Estimating ending inventory (*Learning Objective 7*) 5–10 min.

Totally Tunes sells and installs audio equipment. During a recent fire that occurred at its warehouse, Totally Tunes' entire inventory was destroyed. Totally Tunes' accounting records reflect the following information.

Beginning Inventory	$ 46,400
Net Purchases	243,900
Net Sales	404,000
Gross Profit Rate	35%

Requirement

1. Use the gross profit method to estimate the amount of Totally Tunes' inventory loss.

E5-27A. Inventory turnover (*Learning Objective 8*) 10–15 min.

Gibson's Nursery has the following information as of December 31, 2010:

Sales Revenue		$1,287,500
Cost of Goods Sold:		
Beginning Inventory	$ 44,300	
Net Purchases	750,600	
Cost of Goods Available	794,900	
Ending Inventory	48,700	
Cost of Goods Sold		746,200
Gross Profit		541,300
Operating Expenses		388,700
Net Income		$ 152,600

Requirements

1. Compute the rate of inventory turnover for Gibson's Nursery for the year ended December 31, 2010. Round the result to two decimal places.

2. The rate of inventory turnover for Gibson's Nursery was 17.36 in 2009. Has the rate improved or deteriorated?

EXERCISES (GROUP B)

E5-28B. FIFO (*Learning Objective 2*) 10–15 min.

Underwater Way carries a line of waterproof watches. Underwater Way uses the FIFO method and a perpetual inventory system. The sales price of each watch is $188. Company records indicate the following activity for waterproof watches for the month of August:

Date	Item	Quantity	Unit Cost
Aug 1	Balance	4	$106
7	Purchase	13	$110
11	Sale	16	
19	Purchase	18	$112
28	Sale	11	

Requirements

1. Prepare a perpetual inventory record for the waterproof watches to determine the amount Underwater Way should report for ending inventory and cost of goods sold using the FIFO method.

2. Journalize Underwater Way's inventory transactions using the FIFO method. Assume that all purchases and sales are on account.

E5-29B. LIFO (*Learning Objective 2*) 10–15 min.

Refer to the data for E5-28B. However, instead of the FIFO method, assume Underwater Way uses the LIFO method.

Requirements

1. Prepare a perpetual inventory record for the watches on the LIFO basis to determine the cost of ending inventory and cost of goods sold for the month.

2. Journalize Underwater Way's inventory transactions using the perpetual LIFO method. Assume that all purchases and sales are on account.

E5-30B. Average cost (*Learning Objective 2*) 10–15 min.

Refer to the data for E5-28B. However, instead of the FIFO method, assume that Underwater Way uses the average cost method.

Requirements

1. Prepare a perpetual inventory record for the watches on the average cost basis to determine the cost of ending inventory and cost of goods sold for the month. Round average cost per unit to the nearest cent and all other amounts to the nearest dollar.

2. Journalize Underwater Way's inventory transactions using the perpetual average cost method. Assume that all purchases and sales are on account.

E5-31B. FIFO vs. LIFO (*Learning Objective 2*) 10–15 min.

Assume that Cycle Guys bought and sold a line of mountain bikes during December as follows:

Date	Item	Quantity	Unit Cost
Dec 1	Balance	12	$225
5	Sale	6	
12	Purchase	10	$220
21	Sale	8	
30	Sale	6	

Cycle Guys uses the perpetual inventory system.

Requirements

1. Compute the cost of ending inventory under FIFO.

2. Compute the cost of ending inventory under LIFO.

3. Which method results in a higher cost of ending inventory?

E5-32B. FIFO versus LIFO (*Learning Objective 2*) 10–15 min.

Refer to the data for Cycle Guys in E5-31B.

Requirements

1. Compute the cost of goods sold under FIFO.

2. Compute the cost of goods sold under LIFO.

3. Which method results in a higher cost of goods sold?

E5-33B. FIFO versus LIFO versus average cost (*Learning Objectives 2 & 3*) 15–20 min.

Assume that a RB Tire Store completed the following perpetual inventory transactions for a line of tires.

Beginning Inventory..	32 tires @ $ 73
Purchase..	37 tires @ $ 67
Sale...	38 tires @ $154

Requirements

1. Compute cost of goods sold and gross profit under FIFO.
2. Compute cost of goods sold and gross profit using LIFO.
3. Compute cost of goods sold and gross profit using average cost. Round average cost per unit to the nearest cent and all other amounts to the nearest dollar.
4. Which method results in the largest gross profit and why?

E5-34B. Lower of cost or market (*Learning Objective 4*) 10–15 min.

Clarmont Resources has the following account balances at October 31, 2010. The inventory balance was determined using FIFO.

Inventory		Cost of Goods Sold		Sales Revenue	
Beg Bal 22,400					
End Bal 35,500		Bal 114,000			Bal 188,000

Clarmont Resources has determined that the replacement cost (current market value) of the October 31, 2010, ending inventory is $38,000.

Requirements

1. What value would Clarmont Resources report on the balance sheet at October 31, 2010, for inventory assuming the company uses the lower-of-cost-or-market rule?
2. Prepare any adjusting journal entry required from the information given.

E5-35B. Reporting inventory on the balance sheet (*Learning Objective 5*) 5–10 min.

Ray Blocker Sunglasses had the following FIFO perpetual inventory record at April 30, the end of the fiscal year.

Date	Purchases Quantity	Unit Cost	Total Cost	Cost of Goods Sold Quantity	Unit Cost	Total Cost	Inventory on Hand Quantity	Unit Cost	Total Cost
Apr 1							150	$9.00	$1,350.00
Apr 3	150	$9.50	$1,425.00				150	$9.00	$1,350.00
							150	$9.50	$1,425.00
Apr 7				110	$9.00	$ 990.00	40	$9.00	$ 360.00
							150	$9.50	$1,425.00
Apr 13	110	$9.70	$1,067.00				40	$9.00	$ 360.00
							150	$9.50	$1,425.00
							110	$9.70	$1,067.00
Apr 18				40	$9.00	$ 360.00	90	$9.50	$ 855.00
				60	$9.50	$ 570.00	110	$9.70	$1,067.00
Apr 25				90	$9.50	$ 855.00			
				35	$9.70	$ 339.50	75	$9.70	$ 727.50
Apr 30	260		$2,492.00	335		$3,114.50	75		$ 727.50

A physical count of the inventory performed at year end revealed $672.50 of inventory on hand.

Requirements

1. Journalize the adjusting entry for inventory, if any is required.
2. What could have caused the value of the ending inventory based on the physical count to be lower than the amount based on the perpetual inventory record?

E5-36B. Inventory errors (*Learning Objective 6*) 10–15 min.

Boston Auto reported sales revenue of $160,000 and cost of goods sold of $90,000.

Requirements

1. Compute Boston Auto's correct gross profit assuming the company's ending inventory is overstated by $1,400. Show your work.
2. Compute Boston Auto's correct gross profit assuming the company's ending inventory is understated by $2,400. Show your work.

E5-37B. Inventory errors (*Learning Objective 6*) 10–15 min.

Healthy Bite Mart reported the following comparative income statement for the years ended November 30, 2010 and 2009.

Healthy Bite Mart Comparative Income Statements For the years ended November 30, 2010 and 2009		2010		2009	
Sales Revenue			$137,000		$120,000
Cost of Goods Sold:					
Beginning Inventory		$15,500		$11,000	
Net Purchases		70,000		69,000	
Cost of Goods Available		85,500		80,000	
Ending Inventory		18,500		15,500	
Cost of Goods Sold			67,000		64,500
Gross Profit			70,000		55,500
Operating Expenses			24,000		20,000
Net Income			$ 46,000		$ 35,500

During 2010, Healthy Bite Mart discovered that the 2009 ending inventory, as previously reported, was understated by $2,500.

Requirements

1. Prepare the corrected comparative income statement for the two-year period, complete with a heading for the statement.

2. What was the effect of the error on net income for the two years combined? Explain your answer.

E5-38B. Estimating ending inventory (*Learning Objective 7*) 5–10 min.

Speaker Shop sells and installs audio equipment. During a recent fire that occurred at its warehouse, Speaker Shop's entire inventory was destroyed. Speaker Shop's accounting records reflect the following information.

Beginning Inventory	$ 47,500
Net Purchases	288,500
Net Sales	440,000
Gross Profit Rate	30%

Requirement

1. Use the gross profit method to estimate the amount of Speaker Shop's inventory loss.

E5-39B. Inventory turnover (*Learning Objective 8*) 10–15 min.

Pete's Plants has the following information as of October 31, 2010:

Sales Revenue		$1,345,000
Cost of Goods Sold:		
Beginning Inventory	$ 30,000	
Net Purchases	840,600	
Cost of Goods Available	870,600	
Ending Inventory	41,000	
Cost of Goods Sold		829,600
Gross Profit		515,400
Operating Expenses		109,000
Net Income		$ 406,400

Requirements

1. Compute the rate of inventory turnover for Pete's Plants for the year ended October 31, 2010. Round the result to two decimal places.

2. The rate of inventory turnover for Pete's Plants was 21.96 in 2009. Has the rate improved or deteriorated?

EXERCISES (ALTERNATES 1, 2, AND 3)

These alternative exercise sets are available for your practice benefit at
www.myaccountinglab.com

PROBLEMS (GROUP A)

P5-40A. Computing LIFO and journalizing inventory transactions (*Learning Objectives 1 & 2*) 15–20 min.

Inland Equipment sells hand held engine analyzers to automotive service shops. Inland Equipment started April with an inventory of 85 units that cost a total of $12,750. During the month, Inland Equipment purchased and sold merchandise on account as follows:

Apr 6	Purchased 125 units @ $160
13	Sold 110 units @ $310
19	Purchased 130 units @ $168
25	Sold 80 units @ $310
29	Sold 75 units @ $310

Inland Equipment uses the LIFO method. Cash payments on account totaled $21,700. Operating expenses for the month were $12,000, with two-thirds paid in cash and the rest accrued as Accounts Payable.

Requirements

1. Which inventory method (excluding specific-unit) most likely mimics the physical flow of Inland Equipment's inventory?
2. Prepare a perpetual inventory record, using LIFO cost, for this merchandise.
3. Journalize all transactions using LIFO. Record the payments on account and the operating expenses on the 30th.

P5-41A. Computing LIFO and journalizing inventory transactions (*Learning Objectives 2 & 5*) 15–20 min.

Refer to the data for Inland Equipment in P5-40A. However, assume Inland Equipment uses the average cost method.

Requirements

1. Prepare a perpetual inventory record using average cost. Round the average unit cost to the nearest cent and all other amounts to the nearest dollar.
2. Prepare a multi-step income statement for Inland Equipment for the month of April.

P5-42A. FIFO, LIFO, and average cost (*Learning Objectives 2 & 3*) 15–20 min.

MAC Industries completed the following inventory transactions during the month of August:

Date	Item	Quantity	Unit Cost
Aug 1	Balance	25	$80
4	Purchase	40	$78
12	Sale	52	
22	Purchase	30	$77
31	Sale	22	

Requirements

1. Without resorting to calculations, determine which inventory method will result in MAC Industries paying the lowest income taxes.
2. Prepare a perpetual inventory record using FIFO.
3. Prepare a perpetual inventory record using LIFO.
4. Prepare a perpetual inventory record using average cost.

P5-43A. Lower of cost or market (*Learning Objective 4*) 10–15 min.

Titan Offroad Equipment uses the LIFO inventory method and values its inventory using the lower-of-cost-or-market (LCM) rule. Titan Offroad Equipment has the following account balances at December 31, 2010, prior to releasing the financial statements for the year:

Inventory			Cost of Goods Sold			Sales Revenue	
Beg Bal 54,300							
End Bal 61,100			Bal 258,600				Bal 419,500

The accountant for Titan Offroad Equipment has determined that the replacement cost (current market value) of the ending inventory as of December 31, 2010, is $58,300.

Requirements

1. Which accounting principle or concept is most relevant to Titan Offroad Equipment's decision to utilize LCM?
2. What value would Titan Offroad Equipment report on the balance sheet at December 31, 2010, for inventory?
3. Prepare any adjusting journal entry required from the information given.

P5-44A. Lower of cost or market (*Learning Objective 4*) 10–15 min.

Due to a nationwide recession, PC World's merchandise inventory is gathering dust. It is now December 31, 2010, and the $162,000 that PC World paid for its ending inventory is $14,000 higher than current replacement cost. Before any adjustments at the end of the period, PC World's Cost of Goods Sold account has a balance of $628,000. PC World uses lower of cost or market to value its ending inventory.

Requirements

1. What amount should PC World report for inventory on the balance sheet?
2. What amount should PC World report for cost of goods sold?
3. Journalize any required entries.

P5-45A. Inventory errors (*Learning Objective 6*) 20–25 min.

A & R Industrial Supply shows the following financial statement data for 2008, 2009, and 2010. Prior to issuing the 2010 statements, auditors found that the ending inventory for 2008 was understated by $8,000 and that the ending inventory for 2010 was overstated by $9,000. The ending inventory at December 31, 2009, was correct.

(In thousands)	2010		2009		2008	
Sales Revenue		$210		$191		$186
Cost of Goods Sold:						
Beginning Inventory	$ 12		$ 18		$ 15	
Net Purchases	143		121		128	
Cost of Goods Available	155		139		143	
Ending Inventory	16		12		18	
Cost of Goods Sold		139		127		125
Gross Profit		71		64		61
Operating Expenses		46		43		42
Net Income		$ 25		$ 21		$ 19

Requirements

1. State whether each year's net income before corrections is understated or overstated and indicate the amount of the understatement or overstatement.
2. Prepare corrected income statements for the three years.
3. What is the impact on the 2010 income statement if the 2008 inventory error is left uncorrected?

P5-46A. Estimating ending inventory (*Learning Objective 7*) 15–20 min.

Amtran Enterprises lost its entire inventory in a hurricane that occurred on May 31, 2010. Over the past five years, gross profit has averaged 32% of net sales. The company's records reveal the following data for the month of May:

Beginning Inventory	$ 38,600
Net Purchases	341,900
Sales	530,400
Sales Returns and Allowances	12,300
Sales Discounts	6,500

Requirements

1. Estimate the May 31 inventory, using the gross profit method.
2. Prepare the May income statement through gross profit for Amtran Enterprises.

Quick solution: *1. May 31 estimated inventory = $32,612; 2. Gross Profit = $163,712*

P5-47A. Inventory turnover (*Learning Objective 8*) 10–15 min.

Motion Auto has the following information for the years ending December 31, 2010 and 2009:

(In thousands)	2010		2009	
Sales Revenue		$242		$239
Cost of Goods Sold:				
Beginning Inventory	$ 22		$ 38	
Net Purchases	152		144	
Cost of Goods Available	174		182	
Ending Inventory	13		22	
Cost of Goods Sold		161		160
Gross Profit		81		79
Operating Expenses		55		54
Net Income		$ 26		$ 25

Requirements

1. Compute the rate of inventory turnover for Motion Auto for the years ended December 31, 2010 and 2009. Round the result to two decimal places.
2. What is a likely cause for the change in the rate of inventory turnover from 2009 to 2010?

PROBLEMS (GROUP B)

P5-48B. Computing LIFO and journalizing inventory transactions (*Learning Objectives 1 & 2*) 15–20 min.

Builder Bee Equipment sells hand held engine analyzers to automotive service shops. Builder Bee Equipment started April with an inventory of 45 units that cost a total of $5,760. During the month, Builder Bee Equipment purchased and sold merchandise on account as follows:

Apr	6	Purchased 115 units @ $142
	13	Sold 100 units @ $300
	19	Purchased 80 units @ $152
	25	Sold 40 units @ $300
	29	Sold 75 units @ $300

Builder Bee Equipment uses the LIFO method. Cash payments on account totaled $20,000. Operating expenses for the month were $15,000, with two-thirds paid in cash and the rest accrued as Accounts Payable.

Requirements

1. Which inventory method (excluding specific-unit) most likely mimics the physical flow of Builder Bee Equipment's inventory?
2. Prepare a perpetual inventory record, using LIFO cost, for this merchandise.
3. Journalize all transactions using LIFO. Record the payments on account and the operating expenses on the 30th.

P5-49B. Computing LIFO and journalizing inventory transactions (*Learning Objectives 2 & 5*) 15–20 min.

Refer to the data for Builder Bee Equipment in P5-48B. However, assume Builder Bee Equipment uses the average cost method.

Requirements

1. Prepare a perpetual inventory record using average cost. Round the average unit cost to the nearest cent and all other amounts to the nearest dollar.
2. Prepare a multi-step income statement for Builder Bee Equipment for the month of April.

P5-50B. FIFO, LIFO, and average cost (*Learning Objectives 2 & 3*) 15–20 min.

Widget, Corp., completed the following inventory transactions during the month of January:

Date	Item	Quantity	Unit Cost
Jan 1	Balance	15	$50
4	Purchase	55	$55
12	Sale	66	
22	Purchase	35	$58
31	Sale	24	

Requirements

1. Without resorting to calculations, determine which inventory method will result in Widget, Corp., paying the lowest income taxes.
2. Prepare a perpetual inventory record using FIFO.
3. Prepare a perpetual inventory record using LIFO.
4. Prepare a perpetual inventory record using average cost.

P5-51B. Lower of cost or market (*Learning Objective* 4) 10–15 min.

Richmond Sporting Goods uses the LIFO inventory method and values its inventory using the lower-of-cost-or-market (LCM) rule. Richmond Sporting Goods has the following account balances at May 31, 2010, prior to releasing the financial statements for the year:

Inventory		Cost of Goods Sold		Sales Revenue	
Beg Bal 41,800					
End Bal 68,900		Bal 206,000		Bal 303,000	

The accountant for Richmond Sporting Goods has determined that the replacement cost (current market value) of the ending inventory as of May 31, 2010, is $54,000.

Requirements

1. Which accounting principle or concept is most relevant to Richmond Sporting Goods' decision to utilize LCM?
2. What value would Richmond Sporting Goods report on the balance sheet at May 31, 2010, for inventory?
3. Prepare any adjusting journal entry required from the information given.

P5-52B. Lower of cost or market (*Learning Objective 4*) 10–15 min.

Due to a nationwide recession, Amesbury Systems' merchandise inventory is gathering dust. It is now October 31, 2010, and the $163,300 that Amesbury Systems paid for its ending inventory is $18,500 higher than current replacement cost. Before any adjustments at the end of the period, Amesbury Systems' Cost of Goods Sold account has a balance of $695,000. Amesbury Systems uses lower of cost or market to value its ending inventory.

Requirements

1. What amount should Amesbury Systems report for inventory on the balance sheet?
2. What amount should Amesbury Systems report for cost of goods sold?
3. Journalize any required entries.

P5-53B. Inventory errors (*Learning Objective 6*) 20–25 min.

Lally Industries shows the following financial statement data for 2008, 2009, and 2010.

(In thousands)	2010		2009		2008	
Net Sales Revenue		$205		$170		$175
Cost of Goods Sold:						
Beginning Inventory	$ 12		$ 27		$ 24	
Net Purchases	138		103		126	
Cost of Goods Available	150		130		150	
Ending Inventory	21		12		27	
Cost of Goods Sold		129		118		123
Gross Profit		76		52		52
Operating Expenses		47		31		36
Net Income		$ 29		$ 21		$ 16

Prior to issuing the 2010 statements, auditors found that the ending inventory for 2008 was understated by $5,000 and that the ending inventory for 2010 was overstated by $12,000. The ending inventory at December 31, 2009, was correct.

Requirements

1. State whether each year's net income before corrections is understated or overstated and indicate the amount of the understatement or overstatement.
2. Prepare corrected income statements for the three years.
3. What is the impact on the 2010 income statement if the 2008 inventory error is left uncorrected?

P5-54B. Estimating ending inventory (*Learning Objective 7*) 15–20 min.

Olympic Village Enterprises lost its entire inventory in a hurricane that occurred on July 31, 2010. Over the past five years, gross profit has averaged 30% of net sales. The company's records reveal the following data for the month of July:

Beginning Inventory	$ 37,100
Net Purchases	294,600
Sales	540,100
Sales Returns and Allowances	72,200
Sales Discounts	8,300

Requirements

1. Estimate the July 31 inventory, using the gross profit method.
2. Prepare the July income statement through gross profit for Olympic Village Enterprises.

P5-55B. Inventory turnover (*Learning Objective* 8) 10–15 min

Hulu's Hybrids has the following information for the years ending January 31, 2010 and 2009:

(In thousands)	2010		2009	
Sales Revenue		$235		$213
Cost of Goods Sold:				
Beginning Inventory	$ 23		$ 33	
Net Purchases	141		147	
Cost of Goods Available	164		180	
Ending Inventory	6		23	
Cost of Goods Sold		158		157
Gross Profit		77		56
Operating Expenses		59		42
Net Income		$ 18		$ 14

Requirements

1. Compute the rate of inventory turnover for Hulu's Hybrids for the years ended January 31, 2010 and 2009. Round the result to two decimal places.

2. What is a likely cause for the change in the rate of inventory turnover from 2009 to 2010?

PROBLEMS (ALTERNATES 1, 2, AND 3)

These alternative problem sets are available for your practice benefit at
www.myaccountinglab.com

CONTINUING EXERCISE

This exercise continues the Graham's Yard Care, Inc., exercise begun in Chapter 1. Consider the July transactions for Graham's Yard Care that were presented in Chapter 4. (Cost data has been removed from the sale transactions.)

Jul	2	Completed lawn service and received cash of $500.
	5	Purchased 100 plants on account for inventory, $250, plus freight in of $10.
	15	Sold 40 plants on account, $400.
	17	Consulted with a client on landscaping design for a fee of $150 on account.
	20	Purchased 100 plants on account for inventory, $300.
	21	Paid on account, $100.
	25	Sold 100 plants for cash, $700.
	31	Recorded the following adjusting entries:
		Accrued salaries for the month of July equal $225
		Depreciation on equipment $30
		Physical count of plant inventory, 50 plants

Refer to the T-accounts for Graham's Yard Care, Inc., from the continuing exercise in Chapter 3.

Requirements

1. Prepare perpetual inventory records for July for Graham's Yard Care, Inc., using the FIFO method.

2. Journalize and post the July transactions using the perpetual inventory record created in Requirement 1, omit explanations. Key all items by date. Compute each account balance, and denote the balance as *Bal*.

3. Journalize and post the adjusting entries. Denote each closing amount as *Adj*.

4. Journalize and post closing entries. After posting all closing entries, prove the equality of debits and credits in the ledger.

CONTINUING PROBLEM

This continues our accounting for Aqua Elite, Inc. As stated in the continuing problem in Chapter 4, Aqua Elite, Inc., began selling pools and spas in August. For this problem, we will focus on the purchase and sales of spas during the month of September. The purchases and sales of spa inventory for the month of September are as follows:

Spa Inventory		
	Unit @ Cost	**Total Cost**
August 31 balance	3 units @ $1,800/each	$ 5,400
September 5 purchase	5 units @ $2,000/each	$10,000
September 11 sale	4 units	
September 17 purchase	6 units @ $2,100/each	$12,600
September 21 sale	5 units	
September 25 purchase	5 units @ $2,200/each	$11,000
September 29 sale	4 units	

Requirements

1. Assuming that Aqua Elite, Inc., uses the FIFO inventory cost flow assumption, what is the September 30 ending spa inventory balance and September cost of goods sold for spas?

2. Assuming that Aqua Elite, Inc., uses the LIFO inventory cost flow assumption, what is the September 30 ending spa inventory balance and September cost of goods sold for spas?

3. Assuming that Aqua Elite, Inc., uses the average cost inventory cost flow assumption, what is the September 30 ending spa inventory balance and September cost of goods sold for spas?

APPLY YOUR KNOWLEDGE

ETHICS IN ACTION

Case 1. Julie Robertson recently went to work for K & K Enterprises as the accounting manager. At the end of the year, Jeffrey Baker, the CEO, called Julie into his office for a meeting. Mr. Baker explained to Julie that K & K Enterprises was in the midst of obtaining a substantial investment of cash by a major investor. Mr. Baker explained that he was concerned that the investor would decide not to invest in K & K Enterprises when it saw the current year's results of operations. Mr. Baker then asked Julie to revise the current year's financial statements by increasing the value of the ending inventory in order to decrease cost of goods sold and increase net income. Mr. Baker tried to reassure Julie by explaining that the company is undertaking a new advertising campaign that will result in a significant improvement in the company's income in the following year. Julie is concerned about the future of her job, as well as others within the company, if the company does not receive the investment of cash.

Requirements

1. What would you do if you were in Julie's position?

2. If Julie increases the value of the current year's ending inventory, what will be the effect on the following year's net income?

Case 2. Inland Standard Equipment, which sells industrial handling equipment, values its inventory using LIFO. During the recent year, Inland Standard Equipment has experienced a significant increase in the cost of its inventory items. Although the net income for the current year has been fairly good, Roberta Hill, the company president, wishes it was higher because the company has been considering borrowing money to purchase a new building. Mrs. Hill has heard that a company's choice of inventory valuation method can impact the net income of the company. Mrs. Hill has asked the controller, Vicki Simpson, to explore the possibility of changing the company's inventory valuation method.

Requirement

1. If you were in Vicki's position how would you respond to Mrs. Hill? Address potential ethical implications and applicable accounting principles in your answer.

KNOW YOUR BUSINESS

FINANCIAL ANALYSIS

Purpose: To help familiarize you with the financial reporting of a real company in order to further your understanding of the chapter material you are learning.

This case continues our examination of the financial statements of Columbia Sportswear. In addition to the income statement (statement of operations) and the balance sheet of Columbia Sportswear in Appendix A, you will also be investigating the notes to the financial statements.

Requirements

1. Which footnote discusses the inventory costing method used by Columbia Sportswear?

2. What inventory method does Columbia Sportswear use to value its inventory?

3. Calculate the rate of inventory turnover for Columbia Sportswear for 2008 and 2007 (the 2006 ending balance in inventory was $212,323,000). Has the rate of inventory turnover improved or deteriorated?

INDUSTRY ANALYSIS

Purpose: To help you understand and compare the performance of two companies in the same industry.

Find the Columbia Sportswear company annual report located in Appendix A and go to the financial statements starting on page 681. Now access the 2008 annual report for Under Armour, Inc., from the Internet. Go to the company's Web page for Investor Relations at *http://investor.underarmour.com/investors.cfm* and under downloads on the right-hand side, go to 2008 annual report. The company's financial statements start on page 49.

Requirement

1. Calculate the inventory turnover for both companies for 2008. Who has the highest inventory turnover? Is that good or bad? Is it better to have a high inventory turnover or a low inventory turnover?

SMALL BUSINESS ANALYSIS

Purpose: To help you understand the importance of cash flows in the operation of a small business.

It's the end of the year and your warehouse manager just finished taking a physical count of the inventory on hand. Because you are utilizing the perpetual inventory method with a relatively sophisticated inventory software program, you expect that the ending inventory balance will be pretty close to the balance on your general ledger. In the past, you've had to make some pretty large adjustments for inventory shrinkage, but with the new security measures you've installed to safeguard your inventory, you're hoping that any shrinkage adjustment this year will be minimal. At least you hope that's the case, because your net income can't take many more adjustments. This year's financial statements are very important to your banker because of the loan renewal coming up early next year.

You look at the amount from the final inventory count and it reads $467,450. You go to the general ledger Merchandise Inventory account and it reads $498,500. You look at the preliminary income statement, which doesn't reflect any of these adjustments yet, and the net income is $128,400. You remember that the banker said that he really wanted to see a net income of at least $100,000 this year.

Requirements

1. Calculate the effect that the required inventory adjustments will have on the net income for the year. Would your banker be happy or not so happy when you presented the financial statements to him after these adjustments?

2. If the adjustment you made for inventory shrinkage last year was only about $10,000, should that cause you any concern for the amount of adjustment you have to make this year?

3. In addition to the impact that the inventory adjustment might have on your loan renewal, what effect did it have on your cash flow during the year?

WRITTEN COMMUNICATION

You just got off the telephone with one of your clients who has decided to expand her business by beginning to offer some merchandise for sale. Previously the company had only been a consulting business, but now it has an opportunity to sell some product from a new line offered by one of its clients.

The client's question to you seems rather simple, at least in her eyes. Which inventory costing method should the client use that will give the highest amount of net income? Because the consulting part of the business has not been doing very well lately, the company wants to have a lot of net income from this new side of the business so that the income statement will look good at the end of the year. The company has heard that either LIFO or FIFO will result in higher net income, but it is not certain which it is. Plus, the company definitely plans to always sell the oldest merchandise first, so will this have any impact on which method it chooses? The question does seem simple, but is the answer simple?

Requirement

1. Respond to your client either with a memo, a letter, or an e-mail.

Self Check Answers
1. c 2. b 3. c 4. d 5. a 6. b 7. b 8. d 9. a 10. c

COMPREHENSIVE PROBLEM

THE ACCOUNTING CYCLE FOR A MERCHANDISER INCLUDING INVENTORY VALUATION

Wild Wheels, Inc., wholesales a line of custom mountain bikes. Wild Wheels' inventory as of November 30, 2010, consisted of 20 bikes costing $550 each. Wild Wheels' trial balance as of November 30 appears as follows:

<table>
<tr><td colspan="3" align="center">**Wild Wheels, Inc.**
Trial Balance
November 30, 2010</td></tr>
<tr><th>ACCOUNT</th><th>DEBIT</th><th>CREDIT</th></tr>
<tr><td>Cash</td><td>$ 9,150</td><td></td></tr>
<tr><td>Accounts Receivable</td><td>12,300</td><td></td></tr>
<tr><td>Inventory</td><td>11,000</td><td></td></tr>
<tr><td>Supplies</td><td>900</td><td></td></tr>
<tr><td>Office Equipment</td><td>18,000</td><td></td></tr>
<tr><td>Accumulated Depreciation, Office Equipment</td><td></td><td>3,000</td></tr>
<tr><td>Accounts Payable</td><td></td><td>1,325</td></tr>
<tr><td>Note Payable, Long-Term</td><td></td><td>5,000</td></tr>
<tr><td>Common Stock</td><td></td><td>8,500</td></tr>
<tr><td>Retained Earnings</td><td></td><td>21,425</td></tr>
<tr><td>Dividends</td><td>4,250</td><td></td></tr>
<tr><td>Sales Revenues</td><td></td><td>93,500</td></tr>
<tr><td>Sales Returns and Allowances</td><td>1,700</td><td></td></tr>
<tr><td>Sales Discounts</td><td>1,275</td><td></td></tr>
<tr><td>Cost of Goods Sold</td><td>46,750</td><td></td></tr>
<tr><td>Sales Commissions</td><td>11,300</td><td></td></tr>
<tr><td>Office Salaries Expense</td><td>7,425</td><td></td></tr>
<tr><td>Office Rent Expense</td><td>5,500</td><td></td></tr>
<tr><td>Shipping Expense</td><td>3,200</td><td></td></tr>
<tr><td>Total</td><td>$132,750</td><td>$132,750</td></tr>
</table>

Dec	4	Purchased 10 mountain bikes for $575 each from Slickrock Bicycle, Co., on account. Terms, 2/15, n/45, FOB destination.
	6	Sold 14 mountain bikes for $1,100 each on account to Allsport, Inc. Terms, 3/10, n/30, FOB destination.
	8	Paid $175 freight charges to deliver goods to Allsport, Inc.
	10	Received $6,200 from Cyclemart as payment on a November 17 purchase. Terms were n/30.
	12	Purchased $350 of supplies on account from OfficeMaxx. Terms, 2/10, n/30, FOB destination.
	14	Received payment in full from Allsport, Inc., for the Dec 6 sale.
	16	Purchased 15 mountain bikes for $600 each from Slickrock Bicycle, Co., on account. Terms, 2/15, n/45, FOB destination.
	18	Paid Slickrock Bicycle, Co., the amount due from the December 4 purchase in full.
	19	Sold 18 mountain bikes for $1,125 each on account to Bikeworld, Inc. Terms, 2/15, n/45, FOB shipping point.
	20	Paid for the supplies purchased on December 12.
	22	Paid sales commissions, $875.
	30	Paid current month's rent, $500.

During the month of December 2010 Wild Wheels, Inc., had the following transactions:

Requirements

1. Using the transactions previously listed, prepare a perpetual inventory record for Wild Wheels, Inc., for the month of December. Wild Wheels, Inc., uses the FIFO inventory costing method.

2. Open four-column general ledger accounts and enter the balances from the November 30 trial balance.

3. Record each transaction in the general journal. Explanations are not required. Post the journal entries to the general ledger, creating new ledger accounts as necessary. Omit posting references. Calculate the new account balances.

4. Prepare an unadjusted trial balance as of December 31, 2010.

5. Journalize and post the adjusting journal entries based on the following information, creating new ledger accounts as necessary:

    a. Depreciation expense on office equipment, $1,650.

    b. Supplies on hand, $125.

    c. Accrued salary expense for the office receptionist, $675.

6. Prepare an adjusted trial balance as of December 31, 2010. Use the adjusted trial balance to prepare Wild Wheels, Inc.'s multi-step income statement, statement of retained earnings, and classified balance sheet for the year ending December 31, 2010.

7. Journalize and post the closing entries.

8. Prepare a post-closing trial balance at December 31, 2010.

Ethics, Internal Control, and IFRS

Most likely you have heard of Enron and the accounting firm of Arthur Andersen because of the major accounting fraud that both companies played a part in back in 2002. In light of this, and other financial scandals that took place around the same time, perhaps you wonder what measures companies use to prevent and detect fraud. Or you may wonder, how did Congress respond to protect shareholders? Perhaps you have heard of something called the IFRS and wondered what they are all about. In Chapter 6, we will explore what fraud is and how businesses try to prevent it by implementing internal controls. We will examine the Sarbanes-Oxley Act, which was Congress's response to all of the scandals of the early 2000s. We will also learn what IFRS are and see how they differ from US GAAP.

Chapter Outline:

Learning Objectives:

1. Understand the role of ethics in business and accounting

2. Define fraud and describe the different types of fraud in business

3. Identify the three elements of the fraud triangle

4. Define Internal Control and describe the objectives of an internal control system

5. Identify the elements of a good internal control system

6. Describe the major requirements of the Sarbanes-Oxley Act

7. Understand the major provisions of International Financial Reporting Standards (IFRS)

In the early part of the 1990s, the management of a company called Phar-Mor committed an accounting **fraud** that amounted to somewhere between 350 and 500 million dollars. Unfortunately, this pales in comparison to some of the more recent scandals that have affected American businesses. Currently, it is impossible to talk about fraud without mentioning companies like Enron, WorldCom, Adelphia Communications, and Tyco International, whose recent fraudulent activities amounted to tens of billions of dollars. **Exhibit 6-1** outlines these recent scandals.

Company and Year Detected	Who Perpetrated Fraud	Nature of Fraud	Why They Did It	Fallout
Phar-Mor 1992	The Chief Financial Officer, Pat Finn, and the accounting department under the direction of the Chief Executive Officer, Mickey Monus	Inventory was overstated with a corresponding understatement of expenses.	To hide losses the company was incurring while it tried to grow rapidly and expand its market share. Mickey Monus also diverted over $10 million from the company for personal uses.	Phar-Mor filed for bankruptcy. Pat Finn and Mickey Monus were sentenced to federal prison.
Enron 2001	The Chairman of the Board, Ken Lay, the Chief Executive Officer, Jeffrey Skilling, the Chief Financial Officer, Andrew Fastow, as well as others under their direction	Complex relationships with offshore partnerships along with questionable accounting practices were used to overstate revenues, understate expenses, and hide the true amount of Enron's liabilities.	To hide losses in order to bolster the company's stock price on the stock market. The perpetrators of the fraud stood to gain from the high price of the stock due to their ownership of a significant number of Enron shares.	Enron filed for bankruptcy. Lay, Skilling, Fastow, and other top executives were convicted of fraud and/or other related charges. Numerous individuals were also convicted of insider trading. Enron's auditor, Arthur Anderson was convicted of obstruction of justice for shredding documents related to the audit. Arthur Anderson dissolved its U.S. operations despite the conviction being overturned by the U.S. Supreme Court.
Worldcom 2002	The Chief Executive Officer, Bernard Ebbers, the Chief Financial Officer, Scott Sullivan, the Controller, David Myers, and the Director of General Accounting, Buford "Buddy" Yates	Overstated revenues and understated expenses.	To hide losses in order to bolster the company's stock price on the stock market. Ebbers had significant ownership of WorldCom stock.	WorldCom filed for bankruptcy. Ebbers, Sullivan, Myers, and Yates were all convicted of fraud and/or other related charges.
Adelphia Communications 2002	Company founder, John Rigas and his son, Timothy Rigas	Revenues were overstated and liabilities were grossly understated. The Rigas men also funneled approximately $100 million from the company for personal use.	To fund extravagant lifestyles lived by the Rigas family and to bolster the company's stock price on the stock market.	Adelphia filed for bankruptcy. John and Timothy Rigas were convicted of fraud and related charges.
Tyco International 2002	Company CEO, Dennis Kozlowski and Finance Chief Mark Swartz	Kozlowski and Swartz pilfered hundreds of millions of dollars from Tyco.	To fund extravagant lifestyles. Kozlowski purchased a $6,000 shower curtain for his apartment with Tyco money.	Kozlowski and Swartz were convicted of fraud.

Exhibit 6-1 ▲

These, and other scandals, rocked the business community and eroded investor confidence. Innocent people lost their jobs, and the stock market suffered when stock prices dropped. Therefore, it is no surprise that these scandals ushered in a new era in the field of accounting and business in general—the need for higher ethical standards and improved internal controls.

WHY IS ETHICS IMPORTANT IN BUSINESS AND ACCOUNTING?

Understand the role of ethics in business and accounting **1**

Some accounting professionals contend that the accounting rules (GAAP) may have contributed to the recent accounting scandals. How could that be you might wonder? Well, GAAP did not always have as many specific rules as it now has. GAAP used to consist of a small number of overriding principles. Accountants were expected to exercise their professional judgment to ensure that proper accounting treatment was being applied in order to adhere to these overriding principles. Over time, GAAP has evolved into a system with numerous rules that have been adopted to address very specific accounting situations. With this evolution of the rules, some feel, has come an attitude that "if the rules don't prohibit a specific accounting treatment, then it must be acceptable and, therefore, I am not acting unethically if I utilize this accounting treatment." They contend that this attitude has encouraged some individuals to search for unique ways of accounting for certain transactions, that, although not specifically prohibited, most likely would have been considered to violate the original overriding accounting principles. They argue that it is impossible to write enough rules to cover every situation. In order to promote ethical behavior, they maintain, the accounting profession needs to return to a system with a small number of overriding principles and the expectation that sound judgment be applied to ensure that the principles are followed.

Whether or not the current system of accounting rules contributed to the recent accounting scandals is a topic for debate. What is certain is that most, if not all, of these scandals were the result of poor ethical behavior of one or more individuals. In Chapter 1, **ethics** was defined as principles of right behavior that guide decision making. Scandals, such as those that have occurred in the last decade do not result from decision making based on proper ethical behavior. Proper ethical behavior is more than just following the rules or doing what is legal; it is characterized by honesty, fairness, and integrity. Proper ethical behavior can be summarized by the "golden rule," which says "treat others the same way that you would want to be treated in the same situation." In order for organizations to earn and keep the public's trust, they must practice good ethical behavior at every level within the organization. Some of the steps that many organizations utilize to accomplish this include, but are not limited to, the following:

■ Develop a written **code of ethics**. A code of ethics defines standards of behavior all members of an organization are expected to follow.

■ Communicate the code of ethics to all members of the organization. A good idea is to distribute the code of ethics in written format to all employees at least annually. Then, have employees acknowledge in writing that they have received, read, and understand what is expected of them.

■ Ensure top management within the organization models good ethical behavior at all times because ethics is better "caught than taught." As any parent can tell you, expecting your children to "do as I say, not as I do" does not work very well.

- Establish a method that allows for ethics violations to be reported anonymously. A person who reports unethical behavior, a **whistleblower**, must be able to make a report without fear of punishment or retaliation.
- Enforce the ethics code. Ethics violations should always be addressed in a timely fashion. This helps ensure that the ethics code is taken seriously.

WHAT IS FRAUD AND WHO COMMITS IT?

Define fraud and describe the different types of fraud in business **2**

The scandalous activities referred to previously involve the commission of fraud by company management. So what exactly is fraud? Although there are many definitions of fraud, in its broadest sense, fraud can be defined as the use of deception or trickery for personal gain. In the United States, fraud is one of the fastest growing crimes. It accounts for more losses than robbery. In the business world, fraud is either committed by a business organization or against a business organization.

Management Fraud

An organization's top management is usually responsible for fraud that is committed by a business organization. This **management fraud** typically involves fraudulent financial reporting. Fraudulent financial reporting most often makes a company's earnings look better than they are. The goal of overstating earnings is to help increase a company's stock price or to ensure larger year-end bonuses for upper management. Fraudulent financial reporting is achieved when management does the following:

- Overstates revenues by
  1. overstating receivables related to revenue that has not yet been earned
  2. understating unearned revenue (recording revenue when cash is received even though goods or services have not yet been provided)
- Understates expenses by
  1. overstating the value of assets such as inventory, equipment, and buildings, or recording assets that do not exist
  2. understating amounts owed to suppliers, employees, or creditors

Employee Embezzlement

The primary form of fraud committed against a business organization is **employee embezzlement**. Employee embezzlement usually involves the misappropriation of business assets by an employee. Employees can

- steal cash, inventory, tools, supplies, or other assets from the employer.
- establish fake companies and have the employer pay these phony companies for goods or services that are never delivered then intercept and fraudulently cash the checks.
- engage in **disbursement schemes**. Employee embezzlement involving disbursement schemes takes place when an employee tricks a company into giving up cash for an invalid reason. Examples of disbursement schemes include the following:
  1. **Check tampering**: The employee writes a fraudulent check and makes the check payable to him- or herself. Alternatively, the employee obtains a check intended for an outside party, endorses the check, and then cashes it.

2. **Cash register schemes**: The employee gives a false refund for returned merchandise by filling out a refund form and putting it in the cash register. The employee then pockets the cash. Another related scheme happens when the employee accepts cash from a customer for a purchase but does not record the transaction in the cash register. The employee then keeps the cash for personal use.

3. **Expense schemes**: The employee over bills the company for travel, or other business-related expenses, such as lunches, hotels, air travel, parking fees, and cab fares.

Another form of employee embezzlement occurs when an employee takes **bribes** or **kickbacks** from

- suppliers in exchange for the employee turning a blind eye to a supplier charging the employer higher purchase prices.
- suppliers in exchange for the employee turning a blind eye to delivery of inferior goods.
- suppliers in exchange for the employee authorizing payments to the supplier for goods not delivered to the employer.
- customers in exchange for granting the customer a lower sales price.
- customers in exchange for giving the customer goods or services for which the employer is never paid.

Decision Guidelines

Decision		Guideline		Analyze
Should I be concerned about fraud?		Fraud is *deceit or trickery causing financial* harm. It may be perpetrated by management or by employees.		Management fraud typically involves fraudulent financial reporting. Fraudulent financial reporting occurs when financial information is manipulated so that the business looks more profitable than it really is. Managers may record revenues prematurely or fictitiously, or understate expenses.

Employee embezzlement usually involves the misappropriation of assets. Employee embezzlement can include stealing cash or other assets; taking kickbacks from suppliers or customers; or using check tampering, cash register schemes, and expense schemes that result in improper payment from the employer.

Both management fraud and employee embezzlement can cause financial ruin for a company as well as result in criminal prosecution for the perpetrators.

WHAT FACTORS ARE USUALLY PRESENT WHEN FRAUD IS COMMITTED?

Identify the three elements of the fraud triangle ▶ **3**

Anyone who has done much camping knows that it takes three things to build a fire: fuel, oxygen, and ignition. For fraud to occur, three factors must also exist: perceived pressure, rationalization, and perceived opportunity. **Exhibit 6-2** on the following page presents the **fraud triangle**, which shows the connection of the three factors necessary to commit fraud.

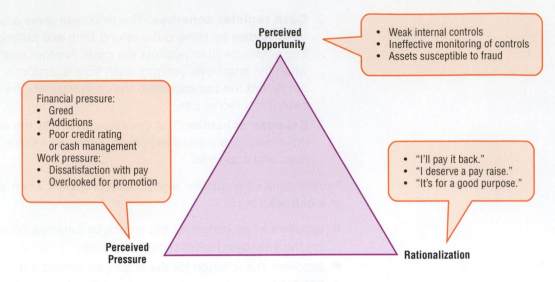

Perceived Opportunity
- Weak internal controls
- Ineffective monitoring of controls
- Assets susceptible to fraud

Financial pressure:
- Greed
- Addictions
- Poor credit rating or cash management

Work pressure:
- Dissatisfaction with pay
- Overlooked for promotion

- "I'll pay it back."
- "I deserve a pay raise."
- "It's for a good purpose."

Perceived Pressure

Rationalization

Exhibit 6-2 ▲

Let us take a closer look at the three elements of the fraud triangle.

Perceived Pressure

Numerous reasons exist that could cause an individual to feel pressured to commit fraud. However, the most likely source of **perceived pressure** is usually financial pressure or work-related pressure. Financial pressure can be caused by, but is not limited to, the following:

- Unexpected financial needs, such as medical bills
- A drug or alcohol habit
- Living beyond one's means
- A gambling addiction
- Unanticipated financial losses
- Excessive bills or personal debt

Work-related pressure also has several possible causes. An employee might feel dissatisfied with his or her job because of a sense of being underpaid or underappreciated. Or, an employee might have recently been overlooked for a promotion. Either of these things can motivate an employee to "get even" with the company by committing fraud. Also, if a company is performing poorly, it is possible for people within management to feel they are personally responsible. The perceived pressure caused by this feeling of personal responsibility can lead them to commit management fraud by falsifying the financial statements.

Rationalization

The next element of the fraud triangle that must be present in order for fraud to occur is **rationalization**. Rationalization is simply finding good reasons for doing things that we really know are wrong. Rationalization is human nature and very few people, if any, do not rationalize their behavior at some time or another. For example, you may have rationalized going out to a movie with your friends last night when you knew that you really needed to study for an important quiz. Employees who commit fraud attempt to justify their actions and convince themselves that fraud is not wrong by rationalizing their behavior. Common rationalizations used by individuals involved in fraud include the following:

- "I didn't steal the money; I only borrowed it and I will pay it back."
- "I deserve a pay raise. The company owes this to me."
- "It won't hurt anyone."
- "Once the company gets over its financial difficulties, I will correct the books."

Perceived Opportunity

The third, and final, element of the fraud triangle is **perceived opportunity**. An individual who commits fraud must perceive that an opportunity exists to commit the fraud, conceal it, and avoid punishment. An opportunity to commit fraud is often perceived when there is easy access to assets or when assets are poorly accounted for by an organization.

Removing any one of the three elements of the fraud triangle makes it much less likely that fraud will occur. Consider the following examples:

- No perceived pressure: An employee may see an opportunity to steal a company computer. He or she may even be able to justify taking the computer by telling him- or herself that the computer is an older one the company no longer uses. However, if he or she can afford to purchase a new computer, the employee will have a low incentive to commit fraud.
- No rationalization: An employee may desperately need cash to pay overdue bills and may see a way to steal money without detection. However, the employee's moral beliefs may make it impossible for him or her to justify taking the money.
- No perceived opportunity: An employee may feel pressured to steal money to cover a gambling debt. He or she may rationalize the theft by convincing him- or herself that he or she will repay the company next month. However, if it is not possible for the employee to steal money without detection, it is unlikely that he or she will commit fraud. This situation arises because the employee sees no opportunity to engage in fraudulent activity without discovery.

Out of the three elements of the fraud triangle, a business can have the most influence over the element of perceived opportunity. A business generally has limited control over perceived pressure felt by an employee or an employee's ability to rationalize unethical behavior. So, the most effective way for a business to prevent fraud is to reduce, or eliminate, the perceived opportunity for an employee to misappropriate company assets or for a manager to falsify financial information. Perceived opportunity can be reduced through a good system of **internal control**.

Decision Guidelines

Decision	Guideline	Analyze
Can I reduce the likelihood of fraud occurring?	When all three "legs," or elements, of the fraud triangle are present, fraud is more likely to occur. These elements are as follows: • Perceived pressure • Rationalization • Perceived opportunity	If you remove one of the legs from a three legged stool the stool will fall down. In a similar manner, if you can remove one of the elements of the fraud triangle, it is much less likely that fraud will occur. Perceived pressure and rationalization are influenced more by a perpetrator of fraud and are, therefore, very hard to remove. However, it is possible to control the element of perceived opportunity and, therefore, reduce the risk of fraud occurring.

WHAT IS AN INTERNAL CONTROL SYSTEM?

 4 Define Internal Control and describe the objectives of an internal control system

5 Identify the elements of a good internal control system

Internal control is a comprehensive system that helps an organization do the following:

- Safeguard assets
- Operate efficiently and effectively
- Ensure proper reporting of financial information
- Ensure compliance with applicable laws and regulations

An organization's management is responsible for the design and implementation of the internal control system. Internal control systems vary from one company to another. Usually, large companies have better developed, more complex internal control systems than small companies. Despite being less formal and less structured, the internal control systems of small companies can still be effective.

Elements of an Internal Control System

There are five key elements that affect an organization's internal control system. The complexity of, and the effectiveness of, the internal control system depends upon these elements. These elements are as follows:

- The control environment
- Risk assessment
- Control activities
- Information and communication
- Monitoring

Control Environment

The **control environment** is the foundation for all other components of internal control. The control environment reflects management and staff attitudes regarding internal control and sets the tone for the entire organization. Control environment factors include the following:

- Leadership philosophy and operating style (an effective control environment cannot exist if management has a "do as I say, not as I do" attitude)
- The competency of the employees within an organization
- The integrity and ethical values of the company personnel
- The organizational structure of the company, namely the delegation of authority and responsibility

Risk Assessment

Risk is a fact of life. Every day, a company will face a variety of risks from both internal and external sources. **Risk assessment** is an ongoing process that identifies and analyzes risks and takes steps to reduce them. For example, a fast food restaurant that hires predominately younger workers would be at a higher risk of violating "child labor laws." Also, a company that has a large amount of cash on hand will have a higher risk of having cash stolen from it.

Control Activities

There are two elements related to **control activities**: policies establishing what should be done and the procedures that should be followed to implement the policies. The types of control activities used by an organization vary from company to company. Control activities occur at all levels and in all functions throughout the entire organization. Generally, the controls chosen for an organization are based on its control environment, its assessment of risk, the size and structure of the organization, and the nature of its operations. Examples of common control activities include the following:

- Employment of competent personnel: Employees must be competent and trustworthy. They should have written job descriptions and be properly trained and adequately supervised.

- Separation of duties: Responsibility for more than one of the following functions should not be given to any one employee:

  1. Authorizing transactions
  2. Maintaining custody of assets
  3. Keeping accounting records

  Assigning an individual responsibility for more than one of these duties creates an opportunity for fraud. For example, if an employee has access to cash or other assets and he or she can record transactions, then they can steal from the company and falsify financial information to hide the theft.

- Mandatory vacations: Employees should be required to take annual vacations. If an employee knows that another person will be performing his or her duties while they are on vacation, there is less perceived opportunity to commit fraud. The vacationing employee will be concerned that any improper activities will be detected.

- Restricted access: Limit the number of employees who have access to company assets, such as cash, inventory, and supplies. For instance, use cash registers, vaults, and locked storage units to control access to assets. Also, access to computerized accounting records should be restricted to authorized personnel through the use of passwords. Allowing too many people access to assets and records creates opportunity for fraud to occur. It also makes it more difficult to find the perpetrator should fraud occur.

- Security measures: Proper security measures should be implemented to deter theft. These measures can include the use of security cameras and alarm systems. Cash registers that print a receipt should also be utilized with a requirement that all customers receive a receipt.

- Proper authorization: Requiring proper authorization for certain activities. For example, requiring proper authorization for all sales returns can help prevent improper refunds from being issued.

- Maintain adequate documents and records: A trail of business documents and records, called an **audit trail**, should be maintained. The audit trail provides evidence of, and the details supporting, business transactions. Documents should be pre-numbered so gaps in the numbered sequence draw attention. Creating an effective audit trail lowers the chance that inappropriate activity will go unnoticed.

🌐 Accounting in Your World

Who says there's no free lunch?

Have you ever eaten at a food court in a mall and seen a sign that says "If you do not get a receipt your meal is free"? Why would the business care if you get a receipt? This is actually part of the business's internal control activities. You see, the company doesn't really care if you get a receipt, they just care that a receipt is printed. This practice prevents an employee from taking your money and pocketing it because once the receipt is printed, the sale is recorded. If the employee pockets your payment, the daily cash count will not match the daily record of sales and the theft will be detected. This example is just one of many control activities that businesses utilize as part of their internal control systems.

Information and Communication

To maximize the effectiveness of an internal control system, information about the control environment, the risk assessment and the control activities must be communicated at all levels of the organization. This information should be communicated up, down, and across the organizational structure of the company. It is also critical that management communicates to all personnel that internal control must be taken seriously.

Monitoring

The internal control system must be continually monitored to locate weaknesses in the system. Monitoring can be accomplished through ongoing activities or through separate evaluations. Ongoing monitoring activities include regular management and supervisory activities. It also includes the assessment of the performance of the internal control system by employees as they perform their required duties. The need for separate evaluations depends on the effectiveness of the ongoing monitoring procedures.

Internal Control Limitations

A good internal control system reduces the risk of undetected errors and irregularities. However, an internal control system cannot provide absolute assurance that no errors will occur. It also does not guarantee that fraud will be prevented or detected. The effectiveness of an internal control system is limited because of the following:

- Employees can become tired, careless, or distracted and make mistakes. They may also use poor judgment or misunderstand policies and procedures.
- Controls can be poorly designed.
- Staff size limitations may hinder efforts to properly segregate duties.
- Two or more people can work together to circumvent controls. This is known as **collusion**.
- Management can override controls.
- The cost of implementing some internal controls may exceed the benefits of these controls.

Some examples of these limitations are as follows:

- An employee may forget to check authorization for the extension of credit to a customer when the phone rings in the middle of the transaction.
- A disgruntled employee may convince another employee to help them steal from the company.
- Management may override controls and direct the accounting staff to record revenue for services that have not yet been performed.
- In small businesses, the cost of employing enough people for a separation of duties may exceed the benefits of the segregation.

☑ Concept Check

Goodguys Tire Company is a small retail tire outlet located in Portland, Oregon. Bill Hanson, the president of Goodguys Tire Company, has assigned the bookkeeper the responsibility of processing all cash receipts as well as all cash disbursements. The bookkeeper also prepares the daily cash deposits and takes them to the bank. Bill knows that he has not achieved a very good separation of duties, but the limited number of employees (due to the size of the company) did not allow it. Is there anything Bill can do in light of the fact that there is not a good separation of duties to help prevent fraud from occurring?

Answer

Yes, although there is no substitute for proper separation of duties, some of the steps Bill could take to help detect/deter fraud include, but are not limited to, the following:

- Ensure that someone other than the bookkeeper receives the unopened bank statement and prepares a bank reconciliation on a monthly basis.
- Require that all adjustments to customer accounts be authorized by someone other than the bookkeeper. A periodic review of the customer account detail should also be performed by someone other than the bookkeeper. Any unauthorized adjustments to the accounts should be noted and investigated.
- Require that someone other than the bookkeeper authorize all cash disbursements. The cash disbursement detail should also be reviewed for unusual disbursements periodically by someone other than the bookkeeper.

Decision Guidelines

Decision	Guideline	Analyze
Is my system of internal control adequate?	A good system of internal control must achieve the following objectives: • Safeguard assets • Operate efficiently and effectively • Ensure proper reporting of financial information • Ensure compliance with applicable laws and regulations	The internal control system consists of all of the policies and procedures that a business has in place to achieve these objectives. One of the most important things that can be done to help prevent fraud is to ensure that there is adequate separation of duties within the organization. However, no matter how good a system of internal controls is, there are still limitations. For example, two or more employees can work together (collude) to commit fraud even though there is adequate separation of duties.

WHO IS RESPONSIBLE FOR INTERNAL CONTROL?

 Describe the major requirements of the Sarbanes-Oxley Act **6**

Audits confirm, or validate, the accounting records and reports of a business. Auditors examine the company's financial statements and the accounting system that produces them. Audits may be internal or external. Employees conduct **internal audits** of a business. These employees, or internal auditors, verify that company personnel are following policies and procedures, and that operations are running efficiently. Internal auditors also determine whether the company is following applicable legal requirements.

Certified Public Accountants (CPAs) are the auditors who perform **external audits** of an organization's financial statements. CPAs are independent of the organization. The Securities and Exchange Commission requires that all companies who sell stocks and bonds to the general public be audited by independent CPAs.

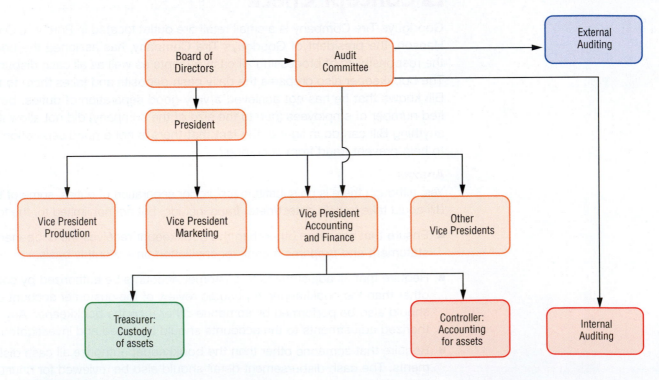

Exhibit 6-3 ▲

This audit includes an assessment of the company's financial statements to determine whether they are fairly presented in accordance with Generally Accepted Accounting Principles as well as an examination of the company's internal control system. **Exhibit 6-3** on the previous page illustrates a typical organizational chart.

Audit Opinions

The outcome of an external audit is the issuance of an opinion by the independent CPA. **Exhibit 6-4** describes the four different types of audit opinions:

Type of Opinion	Reason Supporting the Opinion	Impact as a Result of the Opinion
Unqualified (also called a "clean" opinion)	An unqualified opinion means that, in the auditors' opinion, the financial statements are fairly presented. In addition, they are free of material misstatements, and have been prepared in accordance with Generally Accepted Accounting Principles, unless otherwise noted.	This is the best type of opinion. It gives the financial statement users assurance that the financial statements can be relied upon.
Qualified (also called an "except for" opinion)	A qualified opinion is issued when one of the following occurs: • The auditors have taken exception to an accounting application or treatment the company being audited used. • The auditors were unable to gather the information they felt was necessary in order to issue an unqualified opinion. • The auditors were unable to determine the outcome of an uncertainty, which could have an effect on the financial statements.	A qualified opinion includes a separate paragraph outlining the reason for the qualification. A qualified opinion is used to help financial statement users make more informed decisions about the company. It allows the auditor to bring to the attention of the users circumstances or situations that may affect the user's reliance on the financial statements.
Adverse	By issuing an adverse opinion, the auditors are stating that in their opinion one of the following situations exists: • The financial statements are not fairly presented in accordance with GAAP • There are material misstatements in the financial statements	An adverse opinion will be accompanied by a paragraph explaining the reason for the negative opinion. An adverse opinion is very detrimental to a company as it basically informs users that the financial statements should not be relied upon.
Disclaimer	A disclaimer indicates that the auditors are unable to express an opinion based on their audit. A disclaimer of opinion may be issued because of the following: • A lack of independence on the auditors' part • The inability to obtain the evidence needed to support a different type of opinion • The existence of substantial doubts regarding the business's ability to continue as a "going concern" • Material uncertainties for which the auditors are unable to determine the outcome.	Since the auditors are unable, or unwilling, to express an opinion on the financial statements, investors will give considerable thought before investing in a company that has been issued a disclaimer of opinion.

Exhibit 6-4 ▲

The Sarbanes-Oxley Act

As discussed earlier in the chapter, an unprecedented number of accounting frauds perpetrated by upper management have occurred in the United States in recent years. This is despite the fact that the financial statements of the companies involved were all audited by independent auditors. As a response to these frauds, Congress passed the **Sarbanes-Oxley Act** in 2002. The Sarbanes-Oxley Act, commonly referred to as

SOX, is named after its co-sponsors, Senator Paul Sarbanes and Congressman Michael Oxley. The Sarbanes Oxley Act

- applies to publicly traded companies.
- established the Public Company Accounting Oversight Board (PCAOB). The PCAOB is a private sector, nonprofit corporation that oversees the auditors of public companies. The PCAOB protects the interests of investors by helping ensure fair, independent audit reports.
- requires that external auditors report to an audit committee, rather than to an organization's management. Prior to Sarbanes-Oxley, the external auditors often reported to a company's upper management.
- requires that a company's Chief Executive Officer (CEO) and Chief Financial Officer (CFO) certify all annual, or quarterly, reports filed by an organization. By signing the reports, the executives certify the following:
  1. They have reviewed the report.
  2. The report does not contain any materially untrue statements.
  3. The financial statements and related information contained in the report fairly present the financial condition and the results of operations in all material respects of the organization.
  4. The signing officers are responsible for internal controls and have evaluated these internal controls within the previous 90 days and have reported on their findings.
  5. They have disclosed
     a. a list of all deficiencies in the internal controls and information on any fraud that involves employees who are involved with internal activities.
     b. any significant changes in internal controls or related factors that could have a negative impact on the internal controls.

While SOX has been costly to implement for many companies, it has had a definite impact on improving internal controls in corporate America. As is true in any relationship, once trust has been broken, it takes time to rebuild. The implementation of SOX along with the business community's heightened awareness of the need for proper ethical behavior has started to restore the public's trust in corporate America.

WHAT ARE INTERNATIONAL FINANCIAL REPORTING STANDARDS?

Understand the major provisions of International Financial Reporting Standards (IFRS) **7**

In the 1970s a set of accounting standards was developed for use primarily by companies located in countries that did not have their own accounting standards. These standards, originally called International Accounting Standards, evolved into what is currently known as **International Financial Reporting Standards, or IFRS**. IFRS has become widespread throughout the world. As a matter of fact, many countries have abandoned their own accounting standards in favor of IFRS.

Currently, IFRS is used by over one-half of all of the countries in the world. The number of countries that have adopted IFRS is expected to increase to over three-fourths of the countries in the world by the year 2012. As of the writing of this book, the United States was considering a switch from U.S. GAAP to IFRS as early as the year 2014.

International Financial Reporting Standards are created by the International Accounting Standards Board. The members of the International Accounting Standards Board are appointed by the International Accounting Standards Committee. Both the International Accounting Standards Board and the International Accounting Standards Committee have members from many different regions throughout the world. This ensures that IFRS are the result of input from many different countries throughout the entire world. The goal of the International Accounting Standards Board is to create a set of global, high-quality, enforceable, accounting standards.

IFRS is referred to as a principles based system. As of 2009, IFRS was comprised of less than 40 standards that provide guidance on accounting issues. Instead of creating countless rules that need to be followed, IFRS relies on a small number of overriding principles coupled with sound decision making and good ethical behavior. In contrast, U.S. GAAP is referred to as a rules based system. U.S. GAAP is made up of a hierarchy of rules that number into the several hundreds. Many opponents of a switch from U.S. GAAP to IFRS make the point that U.S. GAAP started out as a principles based system. However, through the years it has evolved into the rules based system that it is today. They question how practical and effective it will be for the U.S. to return to a principles based system.

A significant difference between IFRS and U.S. GAAP is in the area of valuation. As discussed in Chapter 1, U.S. GAAP utilizes the cost principle. The cost principle states that historical cost should be used to value assets or services when they are acquired. The cost principle also requires that the accounting records keep the historical cost of an asset throughout its useful life because this cost is a reliable measure. In contrast, IFRS favors the use of current market value over historical cost. This causes the specific accounting treatment of many items under U.S. GAAP to be different than it would be if IFRS were followed. **Exhibit 6-5** on the following page summarizes some of the more significant items that will differ between U.S. GAAP and IFRS.

Topic	US GAAP Treatment	IFRS Treatment	Related Chapter
Inventory costing	The use of LIFO is allowed.	The use of LIFO is prohibited.	5
Inventory valuation using lower-of-cost-or-market	Market is typically defined as the current replacement cost.	Market is defined as the net realizable value (selling price) of the inventory.	5
Goodwill and other intangible assets	Generally valued at cost and only recognized if purchased.	Generally recognized if the future benefit of the intangible is probable and can be reliably measured. Intangible assets may be purchased or internally generated.	8
Research and development costs	Both research and development costs are expensed as incurred.	Research costs are expensed as incurred. Development costs are capitalized and amortized over time.	8
Contingent liabilities	Contingent liabilities are recorded only if they are probable and can be reasonably estimated. If they are possible, they are only disclosed in the footnotes.	Contingent liabilities are recorded if they are either probable or possible.	9
Cash flow statement	Interest and dividend income and interest expense are reported in the operating section of an indirect method cash flow statement as part of net income.	Interest and dividend income and interest expense can be removed from net income in the operating section of an indirect method cash flow statement (using adjustments similar to those used for depreciation or gains and losses). Interest and dividend income can be reported in the investing section of the cash flow statement. Interest expense can be reported in the financing section of the cash flow statement.	11
Extraordinary items	Extraordinary items are excluded from income from continuing operations and reported separately as a component of net income.	Extraordinary items are reported as part of income from continuing operations.	12

Exhibit 6-5 ▲

As pointed out in Chapter 1, margin icons are utilized throughout the book to indicate items that will most likely be affected by the adoption of IFRS.

Although the exact date that the United States will switch from U.S. GAAP to IFRS is uncertain, what does appear to be certain is that it is not a matter of if the switch will be made, but when it will be made. This is sure to elevate the importance of good ethical behavior as it relates to the accounting profession and to business in general in the United States.

Decision Guidelines

ACCOUNTING VOCABULARY

Internal Control

Successful businesses need good internal controls to help prevent the loss of assets and to help ensure accurate financial reporting. Here are some decisions you might encounter while establishing a system of internal control:

Decision	Guideline	Analyze
Should I be concerned about fraud?	Fraud is *deceit or trickery causing financial* harm. It may be perpetrated by management or by employees.	Management fraud typically involves fraudulent financial reporting. Fraudulent financial reporting occurs when financial information is manipulated so that the business looks more profitable than it really is. Managers may record revenues prematurely or fictitiously, or understate expenses. Employee embezzlement usually involves the misappropriation of assets. Employee embezzlement can include stealing cash or other assets; taking kickbacks from suppliers or customers; or using check tampering, cash register schemes, and expense schemes that result in improper payment from the employer. Both management fraud and employee embezzlement can cause financial ruin for a company as well as result in criminal prosecution for the perpetrators.
Can I reduce the likelihood of fraud occurring? 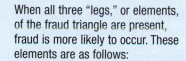	When all three "legs," or elements, of the fraud triangle are present, fraud is more likely to occur. These elements are as follows: • Perceived pressure • Rationalization • Perceived opportunity	If you remove one of the legs from a three legged stool the stool will fall down. In a similar manner, if you can remove one of the elements of the fraud triangle, it is much less likely that fraud will occur. Perceived pressure and rationalization are influenced more by a perpetrator of fraud and are, therefore, very hard to remove. However, it is possible to control the element of perceived opportunity and, therefore, reduce the risk of fraud occurring.
Is my system of internal control adequate? 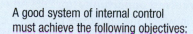	A good system of internal control must achieve the following objectives: • Safeguard assets • Operate efficiently and effectively • Ensure proper reporting of financial information • Ensure compliance with applicable laws and regulations	The internal control system consists of all of the policies and procedures that a business has in place to achieve these objectives. One of the most important things that can be done to help prevent fraud is to ensure that there is adequate separation of duties within the organization. However, no matter how good a system of internal controls is, there are still limitations. For example, two or more employees can work together (collude) to commit fraud even though there is adequate separation of duties.

ACCOUNTING VOCABULARY

THE LANGUAGE OF BUSINESS

Audit (p.300) An examination of a company's financial statements performed to determine their fairness.

Audit trail (p. 297) A trail of business documents and records that provides evidence of transactions.

Bribe (p. 293) The payment of money in order to influence the conduct of a person.

Cash register scheme (p. 293) A fraud scheme in which an employee steals cash by processing false refunds.

Certified Public Accountant (CPA) (p. 300) A licensed accountant who serves the general public rather than one particular company.

Check tampering (p. 292) A fraud scheme in which an employee writes a fraudulent check and makes the check payable to him- or herself, or obtains a check intended for an outside party, endorses the check, and then cashes it.

Code of ethics (p. 291) A formal written document that contains broad statements intended to guide proper ethical decision making.

Collusion (p. 299) Two or more individuals working together to commit fraud.

Control activities (p. 297) The policies and procedures implemented in an internal control system.

Control environment (p. 296) The overall attitude, awareness and actions of management and staff regarding the internal control system and its importance to the business.

Disbursement schemes (p. 292) A form of employee embezzlement in which an employee tricks a company into giving up cash for an invalid reason. Examples include check tampering, cash register schemes, and expense schemes.

Employee embezzlement (p. 292) Fraud where employees steal from employers by taking assets, bribes, or kickbacks, or engaging in disbursement schemes to steal cash.

Ethics (p. 291) Principles of right behavior.

Expense schemes (p. 293) A fraud scheme in which an employee overcharges the company for travel and other business-related expenses, such as lunches, hotels, air travel, parking fees, and cab fares.

External audit (p. 300) An audit of financial statements performed by Certified Public Accountants (CPAs).

Fraud (p. 290) Deceit or trickery involving intentional actions that cause harm to a business, its stakeholders, or both.

Fraud triangle (p. 293) The combination of perceived pressure, rationalization, and perceived opportunity necessary to commit fraud.

Internal audit (p. 300) Assessment of a company's compliance with laws and regulations, operations, and policies and procedures performed by employees of the company.

Internal control (p. 295) A system implemented within an organization to safeguard assets, operate efficiently and effectively, report financial information properly, and comply with applicable laws and regulations.

International Financial Reporting Standards (IFRS) (p. 302) Accounting standards developed by the International Accounting Standards Board for use throughout the world.

Kickback (p. 293) The return of part of a sum received because of a confidential agreement.

Management fraud (p. 292) Management's intentional misstatement of the financial statements, driven by greed or the pressure to show that a business is more profitable than it really is.

Perceived opportunity (p. 295) An element of the fraud triangle in which the employee believes a chance exists to commit fraud, conceal it, and avoid punishment.

Perceived pressure (p. 294) An element of the fraud triangle in which the employee feels a need to obtain cash or other assets.

Rationalization (p. 294) An element of the fraud triangle in which the employee justifies his or her actions and convinces him- or herself that fraud is not wrong.

Risk assessment (p. 296) The process of identifying risks and gauging the probability that they will occur.

Sarbanes-Oxley Act (p. 301) A law passed in 2002 by the U.S. Congress in response to recent, large-scale fraud in publicly owned companies.

SOX (p. 302) Acronym for the Sarbanes-Oxley Act.

Whistleblower (p. 292) A person who reports unethical behavior.

ACCOUNTING PRACTICE

DISCUSSION QUESTIONS

1. Can ethics be taught in the college classroom? Why or why not?

2. Is there a distinction between personal and professional ethics? What are the implications for the study of ethics in the college classroom?

3. What is management fraud? What is employee fraud? Give some examples of each.

4. What are the three components of the fraud triangle? How can they be helpful in fighting fraud in an organization?

5. Do you think the risk factors for management fraud are the same as the risk factors for employee fraud? Why or why not?

6. What is the control environment? Discuss how the control environment had a strong influence over a situation with which you are personally familiar (e.g., a place where you work, your family, your living group in college, a classroom, etc.).

7. What part of the fraud triangle is most closely associated with the control activities component of internal control? That is, if control activities are improved, which corner of the fraud triangle is most affected? Why?

8. What are the implications of the fact that every internal control structure has inherent limitations? That is, how does the knowledge that no internal control structure is perfect help management run the organization more effectively?

9. What effect does the Sarbanes-Oxley Act of 2002 have on the role and influence of the CEO in the corporation?

10. What is the difference between a rules-based system and a principles-based system of accounting rules? Under what circumstances would each be preferable? How does the distinction apply to the comparison of United States GAAP to IFRS?

SELF CHECK

1. Which of the following is necessary for fraud to occur?
   a. Perceived pressure
   b. Perceived opportunity
   c. Rationalization
   d. All three are necessary.

2. On what element of the fraud triangle do most organizations usually focus their fraud prevention efforts?
   a. Perceived pressure
   b. Perceived opportunity
   c. Rationalization
   d. All three are targeted.

3. Internal control is
   a. the act of stealing a business's assets.
   b. the preparation of fraudulent financial statements.
   c. the process that helps a business achieve its objectives, such as operating efficiently and effectively.
   d. the reconciliation of the bank's cash balance to the book's cash balance.

4. Which of the following is *not* an element of an internal control system?

   a. Auditing
   b. The control environment
   c. Monitoring
   d. Information and communication

5. Separation of duties refers to separating all of these functions *except* which of the following?

   a. Authorizing transactions
   b. Keeping accounting records
   c. Hiring personnel
   d. Maintaining custody of assets

6. Which of the following is *not* a control activity?

   a. Mandatory vacations
   b. Risk assessment
   c. Security measures
   d. Proper authorization

7. Darice Goodrich receives cash from customers as part of her job duties. Her other duty is to post the receipts to customer accounts receivable. Based on these duties, her company has weak

   a. ethics.
   b. fraud triangle.
   c. separation of duties.
   d. disbursement schemes.

8. Which of the following is *not* a limitation of internal control?

   a. Poorly designed controls
   b. Tired employees
   c. Collusion
   d. Rationalization

9. Internal auditors focus on ─────; external auditors are more concerned with ─────. (Fill in the blanks.)

   a. financial statements; risk assesment
   b. company policies and procedures; financial statements
   c. financial statements; laws and regulations
   d. e-commerce; fraud

10. Which of the following is *false* regarding the Sarbanes-Oxley act?

   a. It requires that external auditors report to the company president.
   b. It applies to publicly traded companies.
   c. It requires that the company CEO certify annual reports.
   d. It established the PCAOB.

   Answers are given after Written Communication.

SHORT EXERCISES

S6-1. Internal controls (*Learning Objective 2*) 5–10 min.

Indicate by letters the type of fraud committed:

Check tampering (CT)

Cash register scheme (CR)

Expense scheme (E)

Bribe (B)

Fraudulent financial reporting (F)

Here is an example:

<u>CT</u> Employee writes a fraudulent check making it payable to herself.

_____ 1. At the end of the year, the chief financial officer for Electra International recorded $100,000 in sales that had not been made.

_____ 2. Carrie is a cashier at a local restaurant. Once a day, she leaves the cash register open and does not record the sale in the cash register when she takes the customer's cash.

_____ 3. Harry's major customer in Iowa asked Harry to take 20% off of the sales price on the next shipment of jeans to his stores. In return, the customer will give him part of the money saved from the reduced sales price. Harry agrees to lower the price.

_____ 4. Frank Farmer, owner of Farmer Real Estate, asked the accountant to ignore any depreciation that should be recorded on assets owned.

_____ 5. Judson submits a cash reimbursement for a cab ride he never took.

S6-2. Fraud triangle (*Learning Objective 3*) 5–10 min.

Identify each of the following as an example of a perceived pressure (P), perceived opportunity (O), or rationalization (R) in the fraud triangle:

_____ 1. Job dissatisfaction

_____ 2. Greed

_____ 3. "It's for a good purpose."

_____ 4. Weak internal control

_____ 5. Gambling addiction

S6-3. Internal controls (*Learning Objective 4*) 5–10 min.

Internal controls are designed to safeguard assets, encourage employees to follow company policies, promote operational efficiency, and ensure accurate records.

Which objective is most important? Which must the internal controls accomplish for the business to survive? Give your reason.

S6-4. Internal controls (*Learning Objective 5*) 5–10 min.

Indicate by letters which of the following control activities match with the following descriptions:

Separation of duties (SD)

Restricted access (RA)

Proper authorization (PA)

Adequate documents and records (ADR)

_____ 1. Prenumbered invoices

_____ 2. Locking inventory in a warehouse

_____ 3. Manager approval of sales returns

_____ 4. Password protection of accounting software

_____ 5. Not allowing the accounts payable clerk to sign checks

S6-5. Internal controls (*Learning Objective 5*) 10–15 min.

Explain in your own words why separation of duties is often described as the cornerstone of internal control for safeguarding assets. Describe what can happen if the same person has custody of an asset and also accounts for the asset.

S6-6. Fraud triangle (*Learning Objective 3*) 5–10 min.

Look at each of the following employees of Agetro's Restaurant. Which of the elements of the fraud triangle apply?

Perceived pressure (P)

Perceived opportunity (O)

Rationalization (R)

____ 1. As the bartender puts $100 in tips in his pocket, he thinks, "Nobody will get hurt."

____ 2. Tina uses the stolen money to pay for her mother's high medical bills.

____ 3. Hector knows he will be fired if he doesn't record some fictitious sales.

____ 4. Roxanne, the night shift manager, knows that upper management does not monitor internal control.

____ 5. Leo, a waiter, drove to work in a BMW and bragged about his recent vacation to the French Riviera.

____ 6. Victoria, a cashier for the past five years, was caught stealing cash. When questioned about the theft, she said that she had not received a promotion and deserved more pay.

S6-7. Internal controls (*Learning Objectives 4 & 5*) 5–10 min.

Identify each of the following as an internal control objective (O), an internal control activity (A), or a limitation of internal control (L).

____ 1. Separation of duties

____ 2. Collusion

____ 3. Proper authorization

____ 4. Report financial information properly

____ 5. Mandatory vacations

____ 6. Management override

____ 7. Complies with laws and regulations

____ 8. Adequate documents and records

____ 9. Poor design

____10. Operates efficiently and effectively

S6-8. Internal controls (*Learning Objective 5*) 5–10 min.

Hazel's Video Store maintains the following policies/procedures with regard to internal control. Indicate by letter which of the following control activities applies to each of the following policies/procedures:

____ 1. Every day, all checks written are recorded in the accounting records, using the information on the check stubs.

____ 2. All stores utilize electronic theft detection systems.

____ 3. Purchases of new DVDs must be approved by the store manager.

____ 4. Daily sales are recorded in the accounting records by someone other than the sales associates.

____ 5. The company maintains passwords that limit access to its computerized accounting records.

a. Proper authorization

b. Adequate documents and records

c. Restricted access

d. Security measures

e. Separation of duties

S6-9. Internal controls (*Learning Objective 5*) 5–10 min.

The following situations suggest a strength or a weakness in internal control. Identify each as strength or weakness, and give the reason for your answer.

a. All employees must take at least five consecutive days off each year.

b. The accounting department orders merchandise and approves invoices for payment.

c. Cash received over the counter is controlled by the sales clerk, who rings up the sale and places the cash in the register. The daily sales are recorded in the accounting records by the accounting department.

d. The officer who signs the checks need not examine the payment packet because he is confident the amounts are correct.

S6-10. Internal controls (*Learning Objective 5*) 5–10 min.

Identify the missing internal control in the following situations. Select from these activities:

- Proper authorization
- Separation of duties
- Adequate documents and records

a. While reviewing the records of Discount Pharmacy, you find that the same employee orders merchandise and approves invoices for payment.

b. Business is slow at Fun City Amusement Park on Tuesday, Wednesday, and Thursday nights. To reduce expenses, the owner decides not to use a ticket taker on those nights. The ticket seller is told to keep the tickets as a record of the number sold.

c. When business is brisk, Stop-n-Go does not give customers a written receipt unless they ask for it.

d. Jim has worked for Peter's hardware for over 10 years. Due to his length of employment, he has been allowed to grant sales returns at his discretion.

e. At a grocery store, the manager decides to reduce paperwork. She eliminates the requirement that the receiving department prepare a receiving report.

S6-11. Fraud and internal controls (*Learning Objectives 2, 4, & 5*) 15-20 min.

Each of the following situations has an internal control weakness.

a. Betty Grable has been your trusted employee for 30 years. She performs all cash-handling and accounting duties. Betty Grable just purchased a new Lexus and a new home in an expensive suburb. As owner of the company you wonder how she can afford these luxuries because you pay her only $35,000 a year and she has no sources of outside income.

b. Sanchez Hardwoods, a private company, falsified sales and inventory figures in order to get an important loan. The loan went through, but Sanchez Hardwoods later went bankrupt and couldn't repay the bank.

c. The office supply company where Champ's Sporting Goods purchases its business forms recently notified Champ's Sporting Goods that its documents were no longer going to be prenumbered. Alex Champ, the owner, replied that he never uses the receipt numbers anyway.

d. Discount stores such as Target make most of their sales in cash, with the remainder in credit card sales. To reduce expenses, one store manager allows the cashiers to record sales in the accounting records.

Identify the missing internal control in each situation. Answers should include audit, documentation, and separation of duties. Identify the possible problem caused by each control weakness. Answers should include theft and unreliable financial statements. Propose a solution to each internal control problem.

S6-12. Sarbanes-Oxley act (*Learning Objective 6*) 20–25 min.

What are the main provisions of the Sarbanes-Oxley Act? Be specific.

S6-13. IFRS (*Learning Objective 7*) 20–25 min.

Describe the major differences between U.S. GAAP and International Financial Reporting Standards.

APPLY YOUR KNOWLEDGE

ETHICS IN ACTION

Case 1. Jake needed a summer job and was lucky enough to land a job as a ticket collector at a local amusement park. On his first day, he was assigned to work alongside Tim who had worked at the park for the past two summers. Tim explained to Jake that tickets are purchased from the box office outside the gate, and that park-goers present their tickets at the gate when they are ready to enter. Each ticket has a stub that is torn off and given back to the park-goer so they can leave and return the same day.

Jake decided this was not going to be a bad summer job considering that one of the "perks" of working at the park was that on his days off he could enter the park free. However, he had remembered from reading the employee handbook that only employees were admitted free. Any friends or family accompanying the employee must pay full price. Tim showed Jake the gate that employees used on their days off. He said, "just swipe your employee ID card through the card reader on the outside of the gate and you are in the park."

Soon after Jake started working at the park, he began to notice that many of the employees would hold the employee gate open while their friends and family entered without purchasing a ticket. One day Jake asked Tim about what he had saw. Tim replied, "Oh, nobody around here follows that policy. Last week I even saw the park superintendent come in with his entire family without paying."

A few weeks later on one of his days off, Jake was hanging out with his friends when one of them said, "Hey Jake, since you are working at the amusement park, can't you get us all in free today?" Jake thought about how much more fun it would be to go to the park with his friends and he began to reason "Why should I follow the rules if no one else does, not even the park superintendent? Anyway, it's not like I would really be stealing anything."

Requirement

1. What are the ethical considerations in this case?

Case 2. Marybeth Jones is the controller at Patterson Supply Company, a publicly-traded distributor of floral supplies. It is the end of the third quarter and Marybeth is working under a deadline to get the quarterly financial statements prepared before the board of directors meeting at 2 P.M. The board of directors approves the quarterly financial statements before they are sent to the Securities and Exchange Commission.

Unfortunately, Marybeth has a bit of a problem. The debit and credit columns of the general ledger trial balance do not balance. She is certain that this is a simple mistake that someone made in recording a journal entry, but she just doesn't have time to look for the mistake. In order to make the deadline, Marybeth decides to force the trial balance into balance by adding the $200,000 that she is out-of-balance to the Inventory account. Since inventory is the company's largest asset, Marybeth justified her actions by thinking that this wouldn't make a difference to anyone looking at the financial statements. She wished she had more time to look for the mistake, but the clock is ticking away.

Requirement

1. Is there any evidence of unethical behavior in this case? Explain your answer.

Case 3. Rex Banner is the manager of a Stop Mart convenience store. He has been employed by the company for 12 years, the last 9 years of which was as a store manager. Rex applied for a promotion to regional manager, which oversees all 30 locations, but was once again denied promotion. Had he been promoted, the regional manager salary would have given Rex $14,000 more per year.

Rex was upset and decided that if the company would not give him the additional compensation he deserved then he would give himself a raise at the expense of the company. He knew that whenever he hired a new employee, the required paperwork sent to the corporate headquarters was simply filed without being reviewed. Thus, Rex completed all the company employment forms for a fictitious new employee he named "Sam Jones." He figured that, when the company was notified by the Social Security Administration that the Social Security number for "Sam Jones" was fraudulent, Rex would simply report that the employee had just quit and that Rex had no way to contact him. Rex's scheme involved the following actions:

- He put "Sam" on the schedule.
- Every week, he submitted a signed time card for "Sam" along with all the other legitimate employee time cards.
- Every two weeks when Rex received the employee paychecks, he pulled "Sam's" paycheck and hid it in his briefcase.
- He then cashed the paycheck for "Sam" and enjoyed the extra money.

Requirement

1. While Rex's actions are clearly unethical, were they justified, given that he was again denied a promotion and therefore undercompensated? Will Rex be caught? Does the company bear some responsibility too? If the company required direct deposit of its employee paychecks, could this type of fraud be prevented? Can you recommend any other procedures the company could adopt that would help to prevent Rex's fraud?

Case 4. RAS, Inc., is a supplier of residence alarm systems to building contractors. Sam Jennings, the company's new CEO, is out to make a name for himself and makes it known to his management team that he plans for the company to meet, if not exceed, its sales target each quarter.

Sam begins to realize that the company is falling short of its goal and he quickly calls a management meeting to announce his new plan. He says he has arranged sweet deals with several of the company's largest customers. RAS will pay the contractors a 1% fee to buy a large quantity of alarm systems just before the end of each quarter, with the understanding that RAS will buy the alarm systems back shortly after the beginning of the next quarter. Sam uses the term "buy" loosely since there is no plan for an exchange of cash. RAS will record the sales transaction by debiting Accounts Receivable and crediting Sales Revenue. When the alarm systems are bought back, RAS will debit Inventory and credit Accounts Receivable, which, of course, will have no impact on the income statement.

Lisa Barlow, the company's accountant, tells Sam that there is a problem with his plan. She explains that under Generally Accepted Accounting Principles (GAAP), RAS has not earned revenue until inventory is delivered to customers. Sam quickly responds that he has everything under control. He explains to Lisa that the contractors have agreed to accept automatic shipments of the alarm systems and carry them in the company's inventory as of quarter-end. Sam says this is a "win-win" situation for everyone.

The plan did exactly what Sam hoped it would do. The company reported sales that consistently exceeded expectations. These inflated sales figures helped to boost the company's stock price to an all time high. Sam considered himself a true winner. His compensation package included a lucrative stock bonus plan tied to the company's sales growth. As a result of the company's reported sales revenue, Sam received stock in the company that he was able to sell for thousands of dollars at the inflated stock price.

Requirements

1. Is there any evidence of unethical behavior in this case? Explain your answer.
2. Other than Sam and the contractors, who could be harmed by Sam's plan?

Case 5. Mary Rel was hired as the new store manager for the Bargain Bin. The store used four cash registers, and 10 cashiers worked various shifts in the store. Store operations include the following procedures:

- At the start of each shift, a cashier counts the beginning cash balance in the drawer, which is supposed to be $550.
- At the end of each shift, the cashier then does the following:
  1. Counts the ending cash balance in the drawer and adds to it any amounts dropped in the safe
  2. Completes the shift cash form that reconciles the cash received to the total register sales tape
  3. Reports any difference between the cash on hand and the cash that should be on hand based on receipts

As a manager, Mary was responsible for preparing the cash drawers for each shift. She decided to test the honesty of the cashiers so she added an additional $50 to the beginning balance of one cash drawer. Mary planned to look at the shift cash form to see whether the cashier reported the extra $50 that was part of the beginning balance or just reported the $550 expected balance, taking the $50 for personal use.

Mary also tested her assistant manager. She gave him the bank deposit bag containing $5,246.24, but included a deposit ticket that was exactly $100 less, listing $5,146.24 as the deposit amount. Mary wanted to see whether the assistant manager would report the extra $100 in the deposit bag.

Mary planned to never let her employees or even her assistant manager know that she had tested them; instead she would just say that she made a simple mistake in counting the cash if they questioned her.

Requirement

1. Should Mary distrust her employees? Is it ethical for a manager to test employees without their knowledge? Should Mary ever inform the employees that they had been tested? Was it unethical for Mary to test an assistant manager?

Case 6. Assume that you were recently hired as a staff accountant for Environmental Solutions, Inc. You report to Karen, the director of financial reporting, who in turn reports to the CFO. One of your first assignments is to prepare the adjusting entries for the end of the second quarter and to draft the income statement. Karen instructs you to let her know as soon as you have the estimated earnings for the quarter. She says she will need to review the adjusting entries and earnings calculation with the CFO.

After reviewing your work with the CFO, Karen tells you to change the entry that you recorded for depreciation expense on the company's fleet of trucks from $229,000 to $184,000. At first you thought that you must have made some mistake in calculating the amount of depreciation, so you re-check your calculations. Surprisingly, you come up with the same amount again. So tactfully you ask Karen for an explanation for the change. She tells you that depreciation is only an estimate and that the CFO will change his mind about estimates based on earnings.

Requirements

1. What is the effect of the change in the amount of the depreciation expense on the company's second-quarter earnings?
2. What is the ethical dilemma that you face?
3. What are the alternatives that you might consider and what are the potential consequences of each alternative?
4. What are some of the common pitfalls used to rationalize unethical behavior?

Case 7. Marvin Silverstein, a trusted employee of Progressive Supply Company, found himself in a difficult financial situation. His son's college tuition had to be paid in full by the end of the month. The family had experienced some unexpected expenses and the money was just not there to pay the tuition. Marvin knew his son could not register for classes until the tuition was paid, and classes filled quickly, so this could cause his son not to get the classes that he needed to graduate on time.

Marvin considered himself a "true company man" who never missed work and was always willing to work until the job was finished. Although he had been with the company for 10 years and was entitled to two weeks vacation per year, Marvin never found time to take vacation. Because of his loyalty to the company over the years, he knew that his boss would probably loan him the money that he needed for his son's tuition, but he just couldn't bring himself to ask his boss for a loan. As Marvin thought about the situation, he realized how simple it would be for him to "borrow" some money from the company to help him through these rough times and pay it back before anyone noticed.

Marvin was responsible for all of the bookkeeping functions, plus opening the mail, counting the cash in the registers at the end of the day, and making the daily bank deposit. With these combined duties, Marvin found it fairly simple to give himself a "loan." He removed $2,500 in cash from the cash register and replaced it with a $2,500 check from the incoming mail that day. The check was from a customer who was paying his or her account in full. Marvin made a journal entry crediting *Accounts Receivable* to clear the customer's account, but rather than debiting Cash, he debited Inventory. Marvin knew that inventory was not counted and reconciled until year-end. This would give Marvin plenty of time to get the "loan" repaid before anyone noticed.

Requirements

1. What are the ethical considerations in this case?
2. Discuss the primary internal control weakness in this case that could have contributed to Marvin's actions.

Case 8. You are the controller for CrystalClean Services, a company that provides janitorial services to large commercial customers. The company has been very successful during its first two years of operations, but in order to expand its customer base, the company is in need of additional capital to be used for equipment purchases. The two brothers who started the business, Chuck and Josh Wisher, invested their life savings in the business, so they have contacted a local bank about securing a loan for $150,000.

The bank has asked for a set of financial statements, and Chuck, being the businessperson that he is, knows that the bank is going to be looking for a growth in earnings each year. Although the company's earnings have increased, Chuck would like the past year to look better than it does now.

Chuck stops by your office late in the afternoon on December 31 to find out when the financial statements will be ready. You explain that you still have to close out the end of the year, but should have them ready by the end of the week. Chuck tells you that he is aware of a major contract that Josh is working on that will be signed on January 2, and asks you to delay the closing process a couple of days so the new contract can be included in this year's operating results. You attempt to explain to Chuck that you cannot do that, but you can tell that he is not listening to you. Chuck interrupts by saying, "I don't know why you accountants get so worked up over a couple of days. Let me just say that *it would be in your best interest* to include this contract in the current year's operating results." Chuck left your office in a hurry and you heard him mutter under his breath as he turned the corner, "That accountant—who does he think he is trying to tell me how to run my business."

Requirements

1. What are the accounting issues related to Chuck's request?
2. What is the ethical issue involved in this case?
3. What would be the appropriate course of action for you to take?

KNOW YOUR BUSINESS

FINANCIAL ANALYSIS

Purpose: To help familiarize you with the financial reporting of a real company in order to further your understanding of the chapter material you are learning.

The annual report of Columbia Sportswear in Appendix A contains much more information than what is reported in the financial statements and related footnotes. In this case, you will explore other information presented in the annual report in order to determine the responsibilities of both management and the independent auditors for the annual report content. In addition, you will investigate the respective roles of both management and the auditors in the company's internal control system.

Refer to the Columbia Sportswear Annual Report in Appendix A. You will need to find and then read the following reports:

- Management's Report on the Consolidated Financial Statements (Item 8)
- Report of Independent Registered Public Accounting Firm on Consolidated Financial Statements (Item 8)
- Management's Report on Internal Control Over Financial Reporting (Item 9a)
- Report of Independent Registered Public Accounting Firm on Internal Control over Financial Reporting (Item 9a)

Requirements

1. Who is responsible for the information in the annual report? Who is responsible for recommending the independent accountants to the Board of Directors?

2. Who were the independent auditors? Under what standards did they conduct their audit? What was their opinion of the audited financial statements?

3. Who is responsible for establishing and maintaining adequate internal control over financial reporting? Is the effectiveness of the internal controls ever reviewed? Do you think that internal control procedures are necessary? Why?

4. Do the auditors have any responsibility with respect to the internal controls? What was the auditor's opinion regarding the management assessment of internal control effectiveness?

INDUSTRY ANALYSIS

Purpose: To help you understand and compare the performance of two companies in the same industry.

Find the Columbia Sportswear Company Annual Report located in Appendix A and go to the section entitled Design and Evaluation of Internal Control over Financial Reporting starting on page 708. Now access the 2008 Annual Report for Under Armour, Inc., from the Internet. Go to the company Web page for Investor Relations at *http://investor.underarmour.com/investors.cfm* and under Downloads on the right-hand side, go to 2008 Annual Report. On page 75 of the Annual Report, you'll find a section (Item 9A) where they discuss the company's Controls and Procedures.

Requirement

1. Compare the two Annual reports as they relate to their disclosure of internal control procedures and the system of internal control.

SMALL BUSINESS ANALYSIS

Purpose: To help you understand the importance of cash flows in the operation of a small business.

You're having a tough time figuring out why your actual cash is always coming up less than the amount that the general ledger says should be there. You would hate to think that any of your employees would be stealing from you, because they have all been with you since you opened the business five years ago. But maybe it's time to do a little investigative work. After all, cash is the lifeblood of the business, and if it's being misappropriated, you need to find out fast!

You start to think back over some of the observations you've made recently and some of the conversations you've overheard, and one startling conclusion is staring you in the face. Joe's been a good employee, but lately he's been bragging about his wild weekends and some of the gambling casinos he's been going to. Joe never used to be like that. You overheard one of his fellow employees ask him where he's getting all this money, and he said that his wife just got a really good raise at her job and they're celebrating. Then just last week, Joe drove to work in a new sports car and again you overheard him tell someone about the great deal his brother-in-law got for him on this car.

Joe is in charge of billing and collecting. Since your office is so small, you always felt like these two jobs could be done more efficiently by the same person. You also remember that Joe's uncle is one of your vendors and there was that situation last year where you discovered a double billing to his uncle's company. When you brought it to Joe's attention, he immediately admitted his error and took care of it.

Requirement

1. Respond to the following: You are wondering whether or not you should call Joe into your office and have a talk with him, or just observe a little bit more to see if you can discover any irregularities in Joe's area.

WRITTEN COMMUNICATION

You've been asked by your boss to write a brief description of what the control activities should be as part of the development of a strong internal control system in your office. You know that the office is small in terms of personnel, which does create some control problems. So your boss has also asked you to make some recommendations on ways to strengthen any weaknesses that you discover in the internal control system.

Self Check Answers
1. d 2. b 3. c 4. a 5. c 6. b 7. c 8. d 9. b 10. a

Cash and Receivables

If you ever have the opportunity of owning your own business or working in upper management, you will quickly learn how important cash is to a business. The need for cash can make the decision of whether or not to grant credit to customers a critical decision. If you do grant credit, how do you account for customers that fail to pay the amount they owe? Should your company accept debit and credit cards as a form of payment? In Chapter 7, we will explore the issues surrounding these important decisions as we study cash and receivables.

Chapter Outline:

Learning Objectives:

1. Discuss internal controls for cash and prepare a bank reconciliation

2. Report cash on the balance sheet

3. Identify the different types of receivables and discuss related internal controls for accounts receivable

4. Use the direct write-off and allowance methods to account for uncollectible accounts

5. Report Accounts Receivable on the balance sheet

6. Account for notes receivable

7. Calculate the quick ratio and accounts receivable turnover

8. (Appendix 7A) Account for the petty cash fund

In earlier chapters we have seen that net income is the result of deducting all of a business's expenses from its revenues. Therefore, it makes sense that in order to increase net income a business must either reduce its expenses or increase its revenues. The choice of what methods of payment a business is willing to accept from its customers can have a significant effect on the amount of revenues it is able to generate. The method of payment a business accepts is determined by the type of sales it makes.

WHAT ARE THE DIFFERENT TYPES OF SALES?

Cash Sales

Cash sales are the most desirable form of sales because the business receives cash immediately upon delivering goods or services. Cash sales are also the easiest type to track because customers give currency or a check at the time of sale. The business does not need to keep records of the individual customers. As demonstrated in earlier chapters, a cash sale is recorded as follows (assume the sale amount is $500):

DATE	ACCOUNTS	POST REF.	DR.	CR.
	Cash		500	
	Sales			500

Although cash sales are easy to account for, businesses may limit their sales potential by not providing options for customers to buy now and pay later.

Credit Card Sales

An alternative that helps businesses attract more customers is the acceptance of credit cards. There are two main types of credit cards:

- Credit cards issued by a financial institution such as a bank or a credit union. The most common types of these cards are Visa and MasterCard.
- Credit cards issued by a credit card company. Discover and American Express are the most common credit card companies.

One of the primary benefits of credit cards is that they allow customers to buy now and pay later. Retailers who accept credit card payments do not have to worry about collecting from the customer or keeping accounts receivable records because the entity that issued the card bears the responsibility of collecting the amounts due from the customers. Instead of collecting cash from the customer, the retailer will receive payment from the issuer of the card. Another benefit of credit card sales is that they facilitate purchases made via telephone or online due to the fact that no cash has to change hands at the time of sale. One drawback to accepting credit card payments is that retailers typically pay a service fee to cover the cost of processing the transaction.

Debit Card Sales

Businesses can also attract customers by accepting debit card payments in addition to cash and credit card payments. From the retailer's perspective, debit cards are nearly identical to credit cards and have the same benefits and drawbacks. The primary difference between a debit card and a credit card is how and when the cardholder must pay the card issuer.

Credit/Debit Card Processing

Most businesses hire a third party processor to process credit and debit card transactions. Transactions are typically entered into an electronic terminal that is often rented from the processor. Businesses may also purchase a terminal if they would rather own the terminal than rent it. As previously discussed, there is a fee associated with credit and debit card transactions. The fees vary depending on the type of card processed and depending upon the specific agreement the business has with the card processor. The agreement also specifies when and how fees are paid. The most common methods of fee payment follow:

- The fees are deducted from the proceeds of each sale at the time the sale proceeds are deposited into the business's bank account.
- The fees for all transactions processed are deducted from the business's bank account on a monthly basis.

Proceeds from credit and debit card transactions are typically deposited into a business's bank account within a one to three day period. Therefore, credit and debit card sales are journalized in a manner similar to cash sales. Assume a business has credit/debit card transactions which total $500 for the day and that $8 of processing fees are deducted from the proceeds. The journal entry to record the day's card sales is as follows:

DATE	ACCOUNTS	POST REF.	DR.	CR.
	Cash		492	
	Service Fee Expense		8	
	Sales			500

The expense associated with processing the transactions is recorded at the same time the sale proceeds are recorded. Now, assume that instead of having the processing fees deducted from the sales proceeds, the business has the fees deducted from its bank account at the end of each month. The journal entry to record the day's card sales would now look like this:

DATE	ACCOUNTS	POST REF.	DR.	CR.
	Cash		500	
	Sales			500

Notice that this entry is exactly the same as the entry required for cash sales. The expense associated with processing the transactions will be recorded at the time a statement is received from the processor or at the time the monthly bank reconciliation is prepared.

Sales on Account

In Chapter 4, we discussed sales of merchandise on account. When businesses agree to sell on credit, sales increase, but so does the risk of not being able to collect what is owed as a result of these sales. Accordingly, companies bear the risk of **bad debts**, or **uncollectible accounts**, which occur when a customer does not pay for the goods or services they received. Regardless of its size, a business must manage its customer relationships to avoid bad debts. We will account for bad debts later in the chapter.

Decision Guidelines

Decision		Guideline		Analyze
How can my business maximize sales?		Consider granting credit to your customers or accepting alternate forms of payment other than cash.		Granting credit to your customers is an excellent way to increase a business's sales. On the other hand, if the credit accounts are not properly managed, the costs associated with bad debts can exceed the profits generated by the extra sales.
				Accepting debit and credit cards can also positively affect the amount of sales a business generates. However, because of the fees associated with accepting debit and credit cards, the profitability of those sales will be less than it is for cash sales.

WHAT INTERNAL CONTROL PROCEDURES SHOULD BE USED FOR CASH?

Discuss internal controls for cash and prepare a bank reconciliation

Regardless of whether sales are cash sales, credit/debit card sales or sales on account, ultimately a business will collect cash from the transaction. Cash is one of the most vulnerable assets a business has. Cash is easy to conceal and has no identifying marks that link it to its owner, making it relatively easy to steal. Transactions that affect the cash account also impact other accounts, so misstatement of cash can result in misstatement of other items. As a result, it is important to have good internal controls over cash.

Internal Controls over Cash Receipts

Companies typically receive cash over the counter and through the mail. Good internal control dictates that all cash receipts be deposited in the bank quickly. Each source of cash needs its own security measures.

Over the Counter Cash Receipts

The cash register provides control over the cash receipts for a retail business. Consider a Target store. Target issues a receipt for each transaction to ensure that every sale is recorded; a customer cannot receive a receipt unless the register records the transaction. When the sales associate enters a transaction in the register, the machine records it and the cash drawer opens to receive cash. At the end of the day, the cash in the drawer is reconciled against the machine's record of cash sales to ensure the proper amount of cash is on hand. The machine's record of sales is then used as the source for the journal entry to record sales.

At the end of the day, or several times daily if the company is making a lot of sales, cash should be deposited in the bank. Any cash not in a cash register should be kept in a locked location within the business, such as a safe, until it can be deposited in the bank. These measures, coupled with oversight by management, help discourage theft.

Cash Receipts by Mail

Many companies receive cash by mail, especially if they sell products or services on credit. **Exhibit 7-1** shows how companies can control cash received by mail. Generally, an employee who has no other involvement in the sales or collection process, often a mailroom employee, opens all incoming mail and prepares a control listing of amounts received. At this time a remittance advice is prepared if one did not accompany the payment. The mailroom then sends all customer checks to the treasurer, who oversees having the money deposited in the bank. The remittance advices, often check stubs, go to the Accounting Department and serve as a basis for making journal entries to Cash and the customer accounts receivable. As a final step, the controller compares the bank deposit amount from the treasurer with the debit to Cash from the Accounting Department.

The amount of cash received according to the mailroom should match the debit to Cash and should equal the amount deposited in the bank. This procedure ensures that cash receipts are safe in the bank, and the company accounting records are up-to-date.

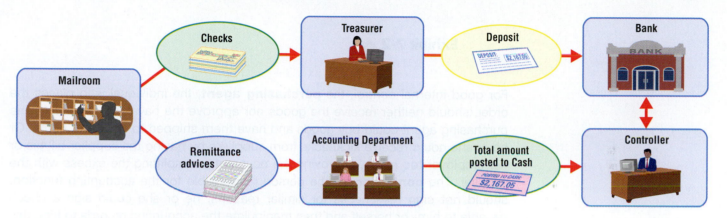

Exhibit 7-1 ▲

Internal Control over Cash Payments

A good separation of duties between operations and cash payments provides internal control over those payments. Also, making payments by check is another important control for several reasons:

- The check provides a written record of the payment.
- An authorized official studies the evidence supporting the payment.
- The official approves the payment by signing the check.

Purchase and Payment Process

To illustrate the internal control over cash payments by check in a company large enough to separate duties, suppose Joe's Sporting Goods buys snowboard inventory from Burton Snowboards. This purchase and payment process will generally follow steps similar to those shown in **Exhibit 7-2** on the following page:

1 Joe's Sporting Goods sends a **purchase order** to Burton Snowboards, its supplier. By preparing this document, Joe's is placing an order to buy snowboards.

2 Burton Snowboards ships the goods and sends an invoice back to Joe's.

3 Joe's receives the snowboards and prepares a **receiving report** as evidence that it received the goods.

4 After matching the information on these documents, Joe's sends a check to Burton Snowboards to pay for the goods.

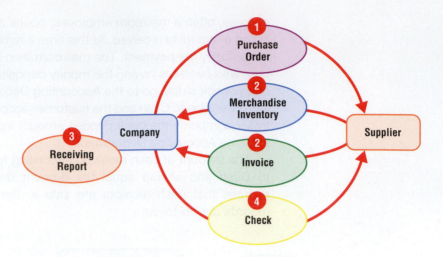

Exhibit 7-2 ▲

For good internal control, the **purchasing agent**, the individual who places the order, should neither receive the goods nor approve the payment. Otherwise, the purchasing agent could buy goods and have them shipped to his or her home. Or he or she could receive kickbacks from suppliers by having the supplier bill his or her employer too much, approving the payment and splitting the excess with the supplier. The **controller**, as the person responsible for the accounting function, should not sign the checks for similar reasons; he or she could sign a check payable to him- or herself and then manipulate the accounting records to hide this improper payment.

Before signing the check, the **treasurer**, who usually assumes responsibility for the custody of cash, should examine each set of documents including the purchase order, receiving report, purchase invoice, and check to prove that they agree. This helps the company ensure that

❶ the goods it received were the goods it ordered, as proved by the purchase order and receiving report.

❷ it is paying only for the goods ordered and received, as proved by the purchase order, receiving report, invoice, and check.

After payment, the check signer should deface the set of documents. This can be accomplished by punching a hole through the payment packet or stamping the documents "PAID." This hole or stamp confirms the bill has been paid and prevents the documents from being used to generate a second payment.

Streamlined Payment Procedures

For many companies, the purchase and payment process is made more efficient through the use of **electronic data interchange (EDI)**. EDI is a streamlined process that bypasses people and documents altogether. For example, in electronic data interchange Wal-Mart's computers communicate directly with the computers of suppliers such as Procter & Gamble and Hershey Foods. When Wal-Mart's inventory of Hershey chocolate candy reaches a low level, the computer sends a purchase order to Hershey. Hershey ships the candy and invoices Wal-Mart electronically. Then an **electronic funds transfer (EFT)** sends Wal-Mart's payment to Hershey via electronic communication.

The Bank Reconciliation

Preparing a **bank reconciliation** is an important internal control that should be performed regularly. On a monthly basis a company will receive a **bank statement** from its bank that shows the **bank balance**, the cash balance in the company's account according to the bank. This balance usually does not agree to the **book balance**, the cash balance according to the company's records. Differences between the bank balance and the book balance arise because of

- differences, called timing differences, between the time when the bank records a transaction and when the business records it.
- errors made by either the bank or the business.

The bank reconciliation identifies and explains the differences between the bank balance and the book balance and is used to arrive at the actual "true" balance of cash. The bank reconciliation serves as an internal control because it allows the correct amount of cash to be arrived at according to both bank and book records.

Preparing the Bank Reconciliation

The basic format, showing items that typically appear on a bank reconciliation, is illustrated in **Exhibit 7-3**. The bank reconciliation is divided into two sides, the bank side and the book side. When establishing the procedures for a bank reconciliation, keep in mind our discussion of separation of duties; the person who prepares the bank reconciliation should have no other responsibilities related to cash. Otherwise, the bank reconciler could steal cash and manipulate the reconciliation to conceal the theft.

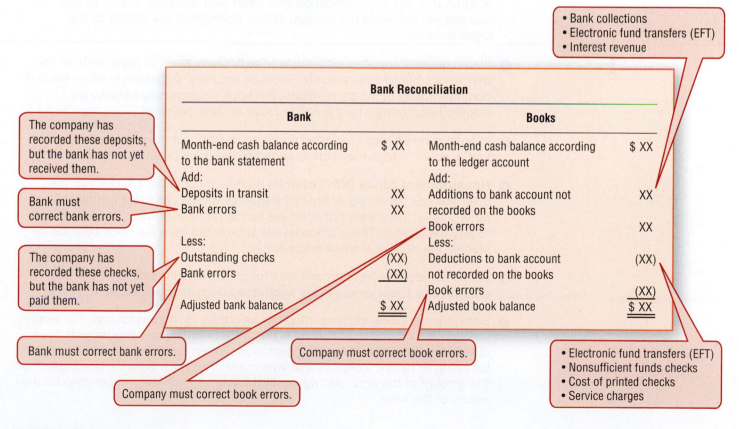

Bank Reconciliation				
Bank			**Books**	
Month-end cash balance according to the bank statement	$ XX		Month-end cash balance according to the ledger account	$ XX
Add:			Add:	
Deposits in transit	XX		Additions to bank account not	XX
Bank errors	XX		recorded on the books	
			Book errors	XX
Less:			Less:	
Outstanding checks	(XX)		Deductions to bank account	(XX)
Bank errors	(XX)		not recorded on the books	
			Book errors	(XX)
Adjusted bank balance	$ XX		Adjusted book balance	$ XX

Callouts:
- The company has recorded these deposits, but the bank has not yet received them.
- Bank must correct bank errors.
- The company has recorded these checks, but the bank has not yet paid them.
- Bank must correct bank errors.
- Company must correct book errors.
- Company must correct book errors.
- Bank collections
- Electronic fund transfers (EFT)
- Interest revenue
- Electronic fund transfers (EFT)
- Nonsufficient funds checks
- Cost of printed checks
- Service charges

Exhibit 7-3 ▲

Bank Side of the Reconciliation

When preparing a bank reconciliation, the following items are included on the bank side of the reconciliation:

❶ Deposits in transit are deposits that the business has recorded but the bank has not. Deposits in transit are added to the bank balance.

❷ Outstanding checks are checks that the business has recorded but the bank has not yet paid. Outstanding checks are subtracted from the bank balance.

❸ Bank errors include the bank recording a deposit or a check for the wrong amount. The bank may also record a deposit or check that belongs in another bank customer's account. The bank must correct the errors that it has made. Adjust the bank balance for the amount of the error, adding or subtracting as necessary depending on the nature of the error.

Book Side of the Reconciliation

When preparing a bank reconciliation, the following items are included on the book side of the reconciliation:

❶ Bank collections are cash collections made by the bank on behalf of the business. Many businesses have their customers pay their bank directly. One way customers make payment is through a **lock-box system** in which they send their payments to a business's post office box. The bank then collects payments from the box and deposits them in the business's account, thus reducing the chance of theft. Another example is a bank collection of a depositor's note receivable. Because the bank statement is often the first communication that cash was received, the business has not yet recorded the receipt. These collections are added to the book balance.

❷ Electronic fund transfers occur when the bank receives or pays cash on the depositor's behalf electronically. Because the bank statement is often the first communication of the transactions, the book balance may need to be adjusted accordingly for the cash receipt or cash payment.

❸ Interest revenue may be earned on an account depending on the balance in that account. Interest revenue is added to the book balance.

❹ Nonsufficient funds (NSF) checks represent customer checks that the business has previously deposited that have turned out to be worthless. In other words, there were not sufficient funds in the customers' bank accounts to pay the checks. These amounts are subtracted from the book balance to reverse the deposit amount made earlier.

❺ Service charges represent bank fees for processing transactions, printing checks, etc. These amounts are subtracted from the book balance.

❻ Book errors include mistakes made in recording cash transactions. For example, an error might involve recording a check in the accounting records for a different amount than what the check was written for. Another mistake might be failing to record a deposit that was made. The book balance is adjusted for the amount of the error, adding or subtracting as necessary depending on the nature of the error.

🌐 Accounting in Your World

I don't need a check register; I use online banking.

Chris got a job his senior year in high school and opened a bank account to put the money he earns in. Chris deposits his paychecks into the account and then uses a debit card to make purchases. Chris's dad encouraged him to keep track of his finances using a check register and to reconcile his account balance each month when his bank statement arrives. Instead, Chris decided to just check his account activity every few days online to see that the deductions from his account agree with what he remembers purchasing. A few days after going out for pizza with a couple of friends, Chris was looking at his account activity online. Chris happened to have his receipt from the pizza parlor in his wallet, which was unusual as he normally throws them away, and decided to check it against his account activity. The receipt from the pizza parlor showed that the cost of the pizza was $18.53 and that Chris had added a $2 tip bringing the total amount to $20.53. However, the amount deducted from Chris's account was $22.53. It appears that the amount of the tip was, accidentally or purposefully, added into the total amount charged twice. Chris feels lucky that he caught this mistake but wonders how many mistakes like this have occurred in the past that he didn't catch. Now, Chris understands why it is important to maintain a check register and to reconcile the account activity each month when he gets his bank statement.

Bank Reconciliation Illustrated

The January bank statement of Acrofab, Inc., is presented in **Exhibit 7-4** on the next page. The summary at the top shows the beginning balance, total deposits, total withdrawals, service charges, and the resulting ending balance. Details of the transactions for the month appear on the statement following this summary. The statement shows that the January 31 bank balance of Acrofab, Inc., is $5,875.

INWNB
INLAND NORTHWEST NATIONAL BANK.

Acrofab, Inc.
721 Front Street
Seattle, WA 98058

CHECKING ACCOUNT 136-213733

CHECKING ACCOUNT SUMMARY AS OF 1/31/2010

BEGINNING BALANCE	TOTAL DEPOSITS	TOTAL WITHDRAWALS	SERVICE CHARGES	ENDING BALANCE
6,500	4,362	4,972	15	5,875

DEPOSITS		DATE	AMOUNT
Deposits		4-Jan	1,000
Deposits		4-Jan	112
Deposits		8-Jan	200
EFT-Rent		17-Jan	905
Bank collection		26-Jan	2,115
Interest		31-Jan	30

CHARGES	DATE	AMOUNT
Service charges	31-Jan	15

CHECKS		DAILY BALANCE				
Number	Amount	Date	Balance		Date	Balance
956	100	31-Dec	6,500		20-Jan	4,845
732	3,000	4-Jan	7,560		26-Jan	6,960
733	160	6-Jan	7,360		31-Jan	5,875
734	100	8-Jan	7,560			
735	100	10-Jan	7,460			
736	1,100	17-Jan	5,205			

OTHER CHARGES		DATE	AMOUNT
NSF		4-Jan	52
EFT-Insurance		20-Jan	360

MONTHLY SUMMARY

Withdrawals: 8	Minimum Balance: 4,845	Average Balance: 6,085

Exhibit 7-4 ▲

Acrofab's Cash account has a balance of $3,147, as shown in **Exhibit 7-5**. Notice that the cash payments appear as one deduction, or credit, to the Cash account in the general ledger to make the process more efficient because businesses often write and record many checks at once.

General Ledger:

Cash Account No. 111

DATE	ITEM	POST REF.	DEBIT	CREDIT	BALANCE DEBIT	BALANCE CREDIT
2010						
Jan 1	Balance				6,500	
2		J. 30	1,112		7,612	
7		J. 30	200		7,812	
31		J. 32		6,265*	1,547	
31		J. 32	1,600		3,147	

Cash Payments: *Supporting Detail for Jan 31 Credit to Cash

CHECK NO.	AMOUNT	CHECK NO.	AMOUNT
732	$3,000	738	$ 320
733	610	739	85
734	100	740	205
735	100	741	460
736	1,100		
737	285	Total	$6,265

Exhibit 7-5 ▲

The bank reconciliation in **Exhibit 7-6** on the next page identifies and explains the differences between the balance according to the bank statement and the balance according to Acrofab's records, thus determining the correct Cash balance at the end of January. Exhibit 7-6, Panel A, lists the reconciling items, and Panel B shows the completed reconciliation.

PANEL A—Reconciling Items

a. Deposit in transit: $1,600

b. Bank error: The bank mistakenly deducted $100 for a check written by another company. Add $100 to bank balance because this balance will be $100 higher once the bank fixes its error.

c. Outstanding checks:

Check No.	Amount
737	$285
738	320
739	85
740	205
741	460

d. EFT receipt of rent revenue: $905

e. Bank collection of a note receivable: $2,115, which includes interest revenue of $115

f. Interest revenue earned on bank balance: $30

g. Book error: Check no. 733 for $160 paid to Brown Company on account was recorded as $610; add $450 to the book balance.

h. Bank service charge: $15

i. NSF check from L. Ross: $52

j. EFT payment of insurance expense: $360

PANEL B—Completed Reconciliation

Acrafab, Inc.
Bank Reconciliation
January 31, 2010

BANK		BOOKS	
Bal, Jan 31	$5,875	Bal, Jan 31	$3,147
Add:		Add:	
a. Deposit of January 31 in transit	1,600	d. EFT receipt of rent revenue	905
b. Correction of bank error	100	e. Bank collection of note receivable,	
	7,575	$2,000 plus interest revenue of $115	2,115
		f. Interest revenue earned on bank	
		balance	30
Less:		g. Correction of book error—overstated	
c. Outstanding checks		our check no. 733 ($610 – $160)	450
No. 737	(285)		6,647
No. 738	(320)	Less:	
No. 739	(85)	h. Service charge	(15)
No. 740	(205)	i. NSF check	(52)
No. 741	(460)	j. EFT payment of insurance expense	(360)
Adjusted bank balance	$6,220	Adjusted book balance	$6,220

These amounts must agree, or the reconciliation is not complete.

Here is a summary of how to treat the reconciling items encountered most often:

Bank Balance—Always:

- *Add* deposits in transit.
- *Subtract* outstanding checks.
- *Add* or *subtract* corrections of bank errors.

Book Balance—Always:

- *Add* bank collections, interest revenue, and EFT receipts.
- *Subtract* NSF checks, the cost of printed checks, service charges, and EFT payments.
- *Add* or *subtract* corrections of book errors.

Exhibit 7-6 ▲

Journalizing Transactions from the Reconciliation

Once the bank reconciliation has been prepared, the true balance of cash is known. However, the Cash account in the general ledger still reflects the original book balance. Journal entries must be made and posted to the general ledger so that it reflects the updated cash balance. *All items on the book side of the bank reconciliation require journal entries; whereas, none of the items on the bank side require journal entries.*

The journal entries listed here bring the Cash account up-to-date as a result of completing the reconciliation. The letters of the entries correspond to the letters of the reconciling items listed in Exhibit 7-6, Panel A. Entry (i), the entry for the NSF check, needs explanation. When L. Ross's check was first deposited, Inland Northwest National Bank added $52 to Acrofab's account. When L. Ross's check was returned to Inland Northwest National Bank due to insufficient funds, the bank deducted $52 from Acrofab's account. Because the funds are still receivable from Ross, Accounts Receivable—L. Ross is debited to reestablish the amount due from Ross.

DATE	ACCOUNTS	POST REF.	DR.	CR.
d.	Cash		905	
	Rent Revenue			905
	Record receipt of monthly rent.			
e.	Cash		2,115	
	Notes Receivable			2,000
	Interest Revenue			115
	Record note receivable and interest collected by bank.			
f.	Cash		30	
	Interest Revenue			30
	Record interest earned on bank balance.			
g.	Cash		450	
	Accounts Payable—Brown, Co.			450
	Correct recording of check no. 733			
h.	Miscellaneous Expense		15	
	Cash			15
	Record bank service charge.			
i.	Accounts Receivable—L. Ross		52	
	Cash			52
	Record NSF check returned by bank.			
j.	Insurance Expense		360	
	Cash			360
	Record payment of monthly insurance premium.			

Online Banking

Online banking allows businesses to pay bills and view account activity electronically. The company doesn't have to wait until the end of the month to get a bank statement. The account history is like a bank statement since it lists all transactions including deposits, checks, EFT receipts and payments, ATM withdrawals, and interest earned on the bank balance. Because of this, it can be used instead of a bank statement to reconcile the bank account at any time.

Decision Guidelines

Decision	Guideline	Analyze
Which cash balance is correct, the cash balance according to my books, or the cash balance according to the bank?	Neither, the correct cash balance can only be obtained by preparing a bank reconciliation.	The bank reconciliation identifies differences that arise from the following: • *Timing differences* resulting from items that have been recorded by the business but not yet by the bank or vice-versa • *Errors* that have been made by the business or by the bank Once the bank reconciliation has been completed, journal entries are made to adjust the business's cash account balance to the balance according to the bank reconciliation. This is the correct cash balance.

HOW IS CASH REPORTED ON THE BALANCE SHEET?

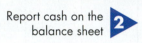

Report cash on the balance sheet

Remember from our discussion of the classified balance sheet in Chapter 4 that Cash is the first asset listed because it's the most liquid. Businesses often have several bank accounts but they customarily combine all cash amounts into a single total. On the balance sheet, this total may be called Cash, or it may be called **Cash and Cash Equivalents**.

Cash on the balance sheet includes coin, currency, checks on hand, **petty cash** (discussed in Appendix 7A), checking accounts, money orders, and traveler's checks. In short, cash consists of anything that a bank will take as a deposit.

Cash equivalents include very liquid, very safe short-term investments. They include time deposits, money market funds, certificates of deposit, and U.S. Treasury bills and Treasury notes. Although Treasury bills and Treasury notes and other cash equivalents can have maturity dates, they are considered cash equivalents if they mature within 90 days of the balance sheet date. These items are liquid because they can readily be converted into cash, and are safe because they have little risk of losing their value. Cash equivalents so closely resemble cash that they are included with cash on the balance sheet.

HOW DO YOU ACCOUNT FOR RECEIVABLES?

Types of Receivables

Identify the different types of receivables and discuss related internal controls for accounts receivable

As discussed earlier in the chapter, companies often make sales on account that create a receivable from the customer. The two major types of receivables are accounts receivable and notes receivable. Remember from Chapter 1 that a business's accounts receivable are current assets that reflect the amounts due from customers for credit sales of goods or services. Also recall from Chapter 2 that notes receivable are written promises by customers to pay an amount of cash to the business in the future. Notes receivable are more formal and usually longer in term than accounts receivable. Notes also usually include a charge for interest. A detailed discussion of Notes Receivable will follow later in the chapter.

A company may also have other receivables, such as loans to employees and interest receivable. These other receivables may be either current or long-term assets, depending on if they are due within one year or less.

Internal Control over Accounts Receivable

Most companies have a Credit Department to evaluate customers' credit applications. The extension of credit requires a balancing act. The company wants to avoid receivables that will never be collected while at the same time granting credit to as many customers as possible. Also, companies that sell on credit often receive the related payment by mail, so internal control over collections is important. Remember, a critical element of internal control is the separation of cash-handling and cash-accounting duties.

Good internal control over Accounts Receivable dictates that the granting of credit, the receipt of cash, and the recording of Accounts Receivable transactions is done by different individuals preferably from different departments. For example, if the employee who handles the daily cash receipts also records the Accounts Receivable transactions, the company would have no separation of duties. The employee could pocket money received from a customer. He or she could then label the customer's account as uncollectible, and the company would **write off** the account receivable, as discussed in the next section. The company would stop billing that customer, and the employee would have covered his or her theft. For this reason, separation of duties is important.

Accounting for Uncollectible Accounts Receivable

Unfortunately, when a business chooses to sell goods or services on account, there will likely be customers who fail to pay the amount owed. When this happens, the customer's account is referred to as an uncollectible account. Uncollectible accounts reflect a cost associated with selling goods and services on account. Companies who make sales on account expect that the benefit of granting credit to customers outweighs the cost.

- **The benefit:** Increased revenues and profits from making sales to a wider range of customers.
- **The cost:** Some customers don't pay, and that creates an expense called **uncollectible accounts expense**. Uncollectible accounts expense is also called **bad debts expense**. Both account names mean the same thing—a customer did not pay his or her account balance.

There are two methods of accounting for uncollectible receivables:

- The direct write-off method
- The allowance method

We will examine the direct write-off method first.

HOW DO YOU ACCOUNT FOR BAD DEBTS?

The Direct Write-Off Method

Use the direct write-off and allowance methods to account for uncollectible accounts

4

The simplest way to account for uncollectible accounts is to use the **direct write-off method**. Under the direct write-off method, at the time it is determined the business will not collect from a specific customer, the business writes off that customer's Account Receivable. The Account Receivable is written off by debiting Uncollectible Accounts Expense and crediting the customer's Account Receivable. For example, on

March 5, 2011, assume that Allied Enterprises determined that Bill Johnson's $400 Account Receivable was uncollectible. The entry to write off Bill Johnson's account under the direct write-off method would be as follows:

DATE	ACCOUNTS	POST REF.	DR.	CR.
Mar 5	Uncollectible Accounts Expense		400	
	Accounts Receivable—Bill Johnson			400
	Wrote off Bill Johnson's account.			

The direct write-off method is generally not allowed by GAAP because it does not always adhere to the matching principle that was discussed in Chapter 3. For example, let's assume Bill Johnson's $400 account, which was written off, originated from a credit sale that occurred in 2010. In this instance, Allied Enterprises would have recorded sales revenue in 2010. However, Allied Enterprises wrote off the bad debt by recording the Uncollectible Account Expense in 2011, a different year. As a result, Allied Enterprises fails to correctly match expenses with related revenues. The direct write-off method is typically used by small, non-public companies who are not required to follow GAAP. The materiality principle, discussed in Chapter 5, also allows companies who experience low amounts of uncollectible accounts expense to utilize the direct write-off method.

Direct Write-Off Method: Recovery of Accounts Previously Written Off

Occasionally after a company has written off a customer's account, the customer will unexpectedly pay part, or all, of the amount owed. There is a two-step process used to record the receipt of cash from the customer when this happens. First, the customer's Account Receivable is reinstated. This step is required as the customer's account no longer exists within the company's records. Next, the payment on the account is recorded. Let's assume that on August 10, 2011, Bill Johnson unexpectedly sent Allied Enterprises a check for $250 as payment on his account, which had previously been written off. Allied Enterprises would first reinstate the Account Receivable as follows:

DATE	ACCOUNTS	POST REF.	DR.	CR.
Aug 10	Accounts Receivable—Bill Johnson		250	
	Uncollectible Accounts Expense			250
	Reinstate Bill Johnson's account.			

Observe that only $250 of the account was reinstated. If Allied Enterprises believes Mr. Johnson will pay the remaining $150 owed on the account, the entire $400 could have been reinstated. Also notice that the accounts debited and credited in this entry are exactly opposite of those used in the entry to write off the account. Now that the account has been reinstated, Allied Enterprises records the receipt of cash as follows:

DATE	ACCOUNTS	POST REF.	DR.	CR.
Aug 10	Cash		250	
	Accounts Receivable—Bill Johnson			250
	Collected cash on account.			

Another method of accounting for uncollectible accounts that does adhere to the matching rule is the allowance method.

The Allowance Method

The **allowance method** is a method of accounting for bad debts in which uncollectible accounts expense is recorded in the same period as sales revenue. For this reason, the allowance method adheres to the matching principle and is, therefore, required by GAAP. Under the allowance method, a business will use an adjusting entry at the end of the period to record the uncollectible accounts expense for the period. Since the business does not know which customers will eventually not pay them, it must estimate the amount of uncollectible accounts expense based on past experience. The debit side of the adjusting entry will be to the Uncollectible Accounts Expense account. This is the same account that was debited when an account was written off using the direct write-off method. However, instead of crediting Accounts Receivable, a contra-account called **Allowance for Uncollectible Accounts** or **Allowance for Doubtful Accounts** will be credited. The Allowance for Uncollectible Accounts is "tied" to the Accounts Receivable account and serves to reduce the **net realizable value** of the Accounts Receivable. The adjusting entry will look like this:

DATE	ACCOUNTS	POST REF.	DR.	CR.
Dec 31	Uncollectible Accounts Expense		XXX	
	Allowance for Uncollectible Accounts			XXX
	To record estimated bad debts.			

The Allowance for Uncollectible Accounts is utilized because the specific customers who will ultimately not pay are unknown at the time the adjusting entry is made. Remember from Chapter 4 that in addition to the Accounts Receivable **control account** in the general ledger, each customer also has an account in the accounts receivable subsidiary ledger. In order to reduce Accounts Receivable, the specific customer would have to be known so that his or her Account Receivable could be reduced in the subsidiary ledger. As we will demonstrate later in the chapter, once it is known that a specific customer's account is uncollectible, his or her Account Receivable will be written off. The offset to this entry will be to reduce the Allowance for Uncollectible Accounts by an equal amount.

Estimating the Amount of Uncollectible Accounts

In order to estimate the amount of Uncollectible Accounts Expense, a company will use its past bad debt experience to make an educated guess of how much will be uncollectible. The state of the economy, the industry the business operates in, and other variables are also used in order to arrive at the best estimate possible. There are two basic ways to estimate the amount of uncollectible accounts:

- Percent of sales method
- Aging method

Percent of Sales Method The **percent of sales method** computes the estimated amount of uncollectible accounts as a percentage of **net credit sales**. To demonstrate, let's assume that Allied Enterprises has the following selected account balances as of December 31, 2010, prior to adjusting for bad debts:

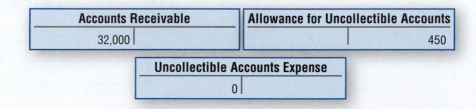

Accounts Receivable		Allowance for Uncollectible Accounts	
32,000			450

Uncollectible Accounts Expense	
0	

It is important to note that when using the allowance method, the Allowance for Uncollectible Accounts will almost always have a balance at the end of the period. The balance in the account may have a debit or a credit balance depending on the amount of the adjusting entry from the prior period and the amount of uncollectible accounts that have been written off during the current period. Also note that the Uncollectible Accounts Expense account will always have a zero balance. This is because, as an expense account, it was closed at the end of the prior period.

Now, let's assume that Allied Enterprises estimates Uncollectible Accounts Expense to be 1/2 of 1% of net credit sales, which totaled $300,000 during 2010. The estimated amount of uncollectible accounts is $1,500 ($300,000 × .005). Under the percent of sales method, once the estimated amount of uncollectible accounts has been determined, the adjusting entry is made for that amount. The required journal entry at December 31, 2010, would be as follows:

DATE	ACCOUNTS	POST REF.	DR.	CR.
Dec 31	Uncollectible Accounts Expense		1,500	
	Allowance for Uncollectible Accounts			1,500
	To record estimated bad debts.			

After posting the adjusting entry, Allied Enterprises' accounts would look like this:

Accounts Receivable		Allowance for Uncollectible Accounts	
32,000			450
			1,500
			1,950

Uncollectible Accounts Expense	
0	
1,500	
1,500	

The net realizable value of Allied Enterprises' Accounts Receivable is $30,050 at December 31, 2010 ($32,000 A/R less $1,950 Allowance for Uncollectible Accounts). Notice that Uncollectible Accounts Expense reflects the calculated amount of uncollectible accounts ($1,500), whereas Allowance for Uncollectible Accounts reflects a different amount ($1,950). This reflects why this method is also called the **income statement approach**. This method focuses more on the income statement than on the balance sheet. After the adjusting entry has been posted, the income statement account (Uncollectible Accounts Expense) reflects the calculated amount of uncollectible accounts rather than the balance sheet account (Allowance for Uncollectible Accounts).

Aging Method The other method for estimating uncollectible accounts is the **aging method**. Once again, let's assume Allied Enterprises had the following account balances at December 31, 2010, prior to adjusting for bad debts.

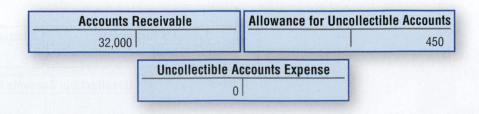

When using the aging method, a schedule is created that reflects all of the company's individual credit customers with their account balances broken down based on how long they've been outstanding. This is known as an Accounts Receivable aging report. **Exhibit 7-7** reflects the Accounts Receivable aging report for Allied Enterprises at December 31, 2010.

	Customer	Balance	Current	1–30	31–60	61–90	91–180	> 181
						Days Past Due		
1	B. Ashford	$ 450		150	300			
2	L. Clark	875	875					
32	M. Reynolds	575	575					
33	R. Turlock	225						225
34	K. Wilson	950				125	825	
	Total	$32,000	26,850	2,800	475	325	1,250	300

Exhibit 7-7 ▲

Once the aging has been prepared, an estimated percentage of uncollectible accounts is determined for each age category. This percentage is then multiplied by the balance for each age category to determine the estimated uncollectible amount for that category. These amounts are then added together to arrive at the total estimated amount of uncollectible accounts for the period. The calculation for Allied Enterprises would look like this:

Account Age	Balance	Estimated Percent Uncollectible	Estimated Uncollectible Amount
Current	$26,850	2%	$ 537
1–30	2,800	5%	140
31–60	475	20%	95
61–90	325	40%	130
91–180	1,250	50%	625
> 181	300	80%	240
Total	$32,000		$1,767

Now that we know the total estimated amount of uncollectible accounts, $1,767, we are ready to make the adjusting entry. Unlike we did when using the percent of sales method, we do not simply take the calculated amount of uncollectible accounts and use this as the amount of the journal entry (this is the biggest difference in the two methods). Instead, we must look at the existing balance in Allowance for Uncollectible Accounts and perform a calculation to determine the amount to use in the adjusting entry. When using the aging method, the goal is for Allowance for Uncollectible Accounts to reflect the calculated amount of uncollectible accounts *after* the adjusting entry has been recorded and posted. The easiest way to determine the correct amount of the required adjusting entry is to do a T-account analysis of Allowance for Uncollectible Accounts as follows:

Allowance for Uncollectible Accounts	
	450
	?
	1,767

The first step in the analysis is to enter the Allowance for Uncollectible Accounts balance that existed prior to making the adjusting entry. Next, skip a line and enter the desired ending balance in the T-account. This balance will be the calculated amount of the uncollectible accounts, $1,767. The question mark represents the adjusting entry amount that is required. This amount is determined by calculating the credit needed to bring the ending balance up to the desired amount. It is very important to pay attention to whether the Allowance for Uncollectible Accounts balance that existed prior to making the adjusting entry was a debit or a credit. Also, remember that the ending balance in the account will always be a credit balance. By looking at the T-account analysis, we can see that the required adjusting entry amount is $1,317 ($1,767 – $450). The required journal entry at December 31, 2010, would be as follows:

DATE	ACCOUNTS	POST REF.	DR.	CR.
Dec 31	Uncollectible Accounts Expense		1,317	
	Allowance for Uncollectible Accounts			1,317
	To record estimated bad debts.			

After posting the adjusting entry, Allied Enterprises' accounts would look like this:

Accounts Receivable	
32,000	

Allowance for Uncollectible Accounts	
	450
	1,317
	1,767

Uncollectible Accounts Expense	
0	
1,317	
1,317	

The net realizable value of Allied Enterprises' Accounts Receivable is $30,233 at December 31, 2010 ($32,000 A/R less $1,767 Allowance for Uncollectible Accounts). Notice that Allowance for Uncollectible Accounts reflects the calculated amount of uncollectible accounts ($1,767) whereas Uncollectible Accounts Expense reflects a different amount ($1,317). This reflects why this method is also called the **balance sheet approach**. This method focuses more on the balance sheet than on the income statement. After the adjusting entry has been posted, the balance sheet account (Allowance for Uncollectible Accounts) reflects the calculated amount of uncollectible accounts rather than the income statement account (Uncollectible Accounts Expense).

Writing Off Uncollectible Accounts Under the Allowance Method

The entry to write off a customer's account under the allowance method is similar to the entry used under the direct write-off method. At the time a company determines a customer's account in uncollectible, the Accounts Receivable will be credited to remove it from the company's books. However, the offsetting debit will not be made to Uncollectible Accounts Expense as it was under the direct write-off method. Instead, it will be made to Allowance for Uncollectible Accounts. Assume that on March 5, 2011, Allied Enterprises determined that Bill Johnson's $400 Account

Receivable was uncollectible. The entry to write off Bill Johnson's account under the allowance method would be as follows:

DATE	ACCOUNTS	POST REF.	DR.	CR.
Mar 5	Allowance for Uncollectible Accounts		400	
	Accounts Receivable—Bill Johnson			400
	Wrote off Bill Johnson's account.			

Remember that the expense related to writing off Bill Johnson's account was recognized in 2010 when Allied Enterprises made the adjusting entry to record the estimated bad debts.

☑ Concept Check...

Will writing off Bill Johnson's $400 account reduce the net realizable value of Allied Enterprises' Accounts Receivable?

Answer

No, the write off of uncollectible receivables has no impact on the net realizable value of Accounts Receivable. Remember that the net realizable value of Accounts Receivable equals the balance in the Accounts Receivable account less the balance in the related contra account, Allowance for Uncollectible Accounts. When Bill Johnson's account was written off, the asset account, Accounts Receivable, was reduced by $400. However, the Allowance for Uncollectible Accounts was also reduced by $400 so the total change in the net realizable value of the Accounts Receivable is zero.

Allowance Method: Recovery of Accounts Previously Written Off

The entries required to record the receipt of cash from a customer whose account was previously written off are similar under the allowance method to those used under the direct write-off method. First, the customer's Account Receivable is reinstated. Then, the payment on the account is recorded. Let's assume once again that on August 10, 2011, Bill Johnson unexpectedly sent Allied Enterprises a check for $250 as payment on his previously written off account. Allied Enterprises would first reinstate the Account Receivable as follows:

DATE	ACCOUNTS	POST REF.	DR.	CR.
Aug 10	Accounts Receivable—Bill Johnson		250	
	Allowance for Uncollectible Accounts			250
	Reinstated Bill Johnson's account.			

Notice again that the accounts debited and credited in this entry are exactly opposite of those used in the entry to write off the account. Allied Enterprises now records the receipt of cash in the same manner as was done under the direct write-off method as follows:

DATE	ACCOUNTS	POST REF.	DR.	CR.
Aug 10	Cash		250	
	Accounts Receivable—Bill Johnson			250
	Collected cash on account.			

Exhibit 7-8 summarizes the differences between the entries required when using the direct write-off method and those required when using the allowance method.

Event	Direct Write-off Method		Allowance Method	
Period-end adjusting entry	None required		Uncollectible Accounts Expense Allowance for uncollectible accounts	XXXX XXXX
Entry to write off customer account	Uncollectible Accounts Expense Accounts Receivable—customer name	XXXX XXXX	Allowance for Uncollectible Accounts Accounts Receivable—customer name	XXXX XXXX
Entries to record receipt of payment on an account previously written off	Accounts Receivable—customer name Uncollectible Accounts Expense Cash Accounts Receivable—customer name	XXXX XXXX XXXX XXXX	Accounts Receivable—customer name Allowance for Uncollectible Accounts Cash Accounts Receivable—customer name	XXXX XXXX XXXX XXXX

Exhibit 7-8 ▲

HOW ARE ACCOUNTS RECEIVABLE REPORTED ON THE BALANCE SHEET?

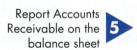

Report Accounts Receivable on the balance sheet **5**

Accounts receivable are reported at "net realizable value" in the current assets section of the balance sheet. There are two ways to show Accounts Receivable at net realizable value. For example, assume that at December 31, 2010, Allied Enterprises' Accounts Receivable balance is $32,000 and its Allowance for Uncollectible Accounts balance is $1,767. Allied Enterprises could report its accounts receivable in either of the two ways shown here:

Allied Enterprises Balance Sheet (partial): December 31, 2010	
Accounts Receivable	$32,000
Less: Allowance for Uncollectible Accounts	1,767
Accounts Receivable, Net	$30,233

Allied Enterprises Balance Sheet (partial): December 31, 2010	
Accounts Receivable, Net of Allowance for Uncollectible Accounts of $1,767	$30,233

Most companies use the second method, but either is acceptable. The key is to show Accounts Receivable at net realizable value.

Decision Guidelines

Decision		Guideline		Analyze
Should I use the direct write-off method or the allowance method to account for bad debts?		Generally Accepted Accounting Principles dictate the use of the allowance method.		Because the allowance method matches bad debt expense with the credit sales that resulted in the bad debts, it is generally viewed as the preferred method. The allowance method also reports accounts receivable at its net realizable value, which is a better indicator of the amount of cash that will ultimately be collected from the receivables.

HOW DO YOU ACCOUNT FOR NOTES RECEIVABLE?

Account for notes receivable **6**

Notes receivable are more formal than accounts receivable. The debtor signs a promissory note as evidence of the transaction. Before launching into the accounting, let's define the terms related to notes receivable.

- **Promissory note**: A written promise to pay a specified amount of money on a particular future date.
- **Maker of a note** (debtor): The entity that signs the note and promises to pay the required amount; the maker of the note is the **debtor**.
- **Payee of a note** (creditor): The entity to whom the maker promises future payment; the payee of the note is the **creditor**.
- **Principal:** The amount loaned out by the payee and borrowed by the maker of the note.
- **Interest:** The amount charged for loaning money. Interest is expense to the debtor and income to the creditor.
- **Interest rate:** The percentage rate of interest specified by the note. Interest rates are almost always stated for a period of one year. A 10% note means that the amount of interest for *one year* is 10% of the note's principal.
- **Maturity date:** This is the date when final payment of the note is due. Also called the **due date**.
- **Maturity value:** The sum of the principal plus interest due at maturity.
- **Note term:** The period of time during which interest is earned. It extends from the original date of the note to the maturity date.

Exhibit 7-9, on the next page, illustrates a promissory note. As you study the promissory note, look for the items mentioned previously.

Identifying Maturity Date

Some notes specify the maturity date. For example, March 31, 2011, is the maturity date of the note shown in Exhibit 7-9. Other notes state the period of the note in days or months. When the period is given in months, the note's maturity date falls on the same day of the month as the date the note was issued. For example, a three-month note dated March 1, 2010, would mature on June 1, 2010.

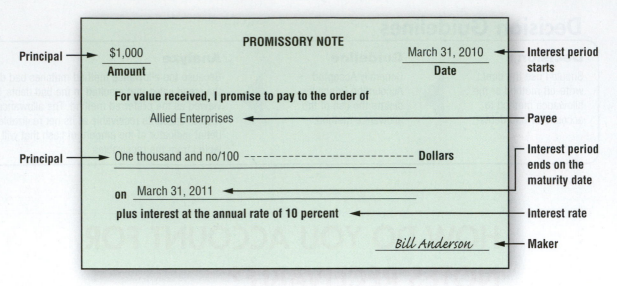

Exhibit 7-9 ▲

When the period is given in days, the maturity date is determined by counting the actual days from the date of issue. A 180-day note dated February 16, 2010, matures on August 15, 2010.

When counting the days for a note term remember to

- count the maturity date.
- omit the date the note was issued.

Origination of Notes Receivable

Notes receivable typically originate from a company doing one of the following:

- Lending money
- Providing goods or services in exchange for a promissory note
- Accepting a promissory note as payment on an account receivable

Assume that on August 1, 2010, Allied Enterprises lent $800 to Kim Simmons on a six-month, 8% promissory note. The journal entry to record the note would be as follows:

DATE	ACCOUNTS	POST REF.	DR.	CR.
Aug 1	Note Receivable—K. Simmons		800	
	Cash			800

Next, assume that on September 5, Allied Enterprises sells goods for $2,500 to Don Hammond. Hammond signs a nine-month promissory note at 10% annual interest. Allied Enterprises' entry to record the sale is as follows:

DATE	ACCOUNTS	POST REF.	DR.	CR.
Sep 5	Note Receivable—D. Hammond		2,500	
	Sales			2,500

A company may also accept a note receivable from a credit customer who is unable to pay his or her account receivable on time. The customer signs a promissory note and gives it to the creditor. Assume that on November 18, 2010, Sandra Fisher cannot pay her $1,200 account when it comes due and that Allied Enterprises accepts a 60-day, 12% note receivable in lieu of payment. Allied Enterprises would record this as follows:

DATE	ACCOUNTS	POST REF.	DR.	CR.
Nov 18	Note Receivable—S. Fisher		1,200	
	Accounts Receivable—S. Fisher			1,200

Computing Interest on a Note

The formula for computing the interest is as follows:

$$\text{Amount of interest} = \text{Principal} \times \text{Interest rate} \times \text{Time}$$

In the formula, multiplying by "Time" adjusts for the fact that the interest rate represents a year's worth of interest. The "Time," or time period, represents the portion of a year for which interest has accrued on the note. It may be expressed as a fraction of a year in months (x/12) or a fraction of a year in days (x/360 or x/365). When the interest period is stated in days, interest may be computed based on either a 360-day year or a 365-day year. Using the data in Exhibit 7-9, Allied Enterprises computes interest revenue for one year as follows:

$$\text{Amount of interest} = \text{Principal} \times \text{Interest rate} \times \text{Time}$$
$$\$100 = \$1,000 \times .10 \times 12/12$$

The maturity value of the note is $1,100 ($1,000 principal + $100 interest). The time element is 12/12 or 1 because the note's term is 1 year.

Interest on a $2,000 note at 6% for nine months is computed as follows:

$$\text{Amount of interest} = \text{Principal} \times \text{Interest rate} \times \text{Time}$$
$$\$90 = \$2,000 \times .06 \times 9/12$$

Interest on a $4,000 note at 8% for 90 days (assuming a 360 day year) is computed as follows:

$$\text{Amount of interest} = \text{Principal} \times \text{Interest rate} \times \text{Time}$$
$$\$80 = \$4,000 \times .08 \times 90/360$$

Accruing Interest Revenue

Notes receivable are often outstanding at the end of an accounting period. The interest revenue earned on the notes up to year-end should be recorded as part of that year's earnings. Recall that interest revenue is earned over time, not just when cash is received. Because of the matching principle, we want to record the earnings from notes in the year in which they were earned.

Let's continue with the Allied Enterprises note receivable from Exhibit 7-9. Allied Enterprises' accounting period ends December 31.

- How much of the total interest revenue does Allied Enterprises earn in 2010 (from March 31 through December 31, 2010)?

Amount of interest = Principal × Interest rate × Time

$75 = $1,000 × .10 × 9/12

Allied Enterprises makes the following adjusting entry at December 31, 2010:

DATE	ACCOUNTS	POST REF.	DR.	CR.
Dec 31	Interest Receivable		75	
	Interest Revenue			75
	Accrue interest revenue.			

- How much interest revenue does Allied Enterprises earn in 2011 (from January 1 through March 31, 2011)?

Amount of interest = Principal × Interest rate × Time

$25 = $1,000 × .10 × 3/12

On the note's maturity date, Allied Enterprises makes the following entry:

DATE	ACCOUNTS	POST REF.	DR.	CR.
Mar 31	Cash (Maturity Value)		1,100	
	Note Receivable—B. Anderson			1,000
	Interest Receivable			75
	Interest Revenue			25
	Record repayment of note at maturity.			

Earlier we determined that total interest on the note was $100 ($1,000 × .10 × 12/12). These entries assign the correct amount of interest to each year.

2010 = $ 75
2011 = $ 25
Total Interest = $100

FOCUS ON DECISION MAKING: RATIOS

Quick Ratio

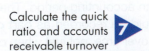

Calculate the quick ratio and accounts receivable turnover

In Chapter 4, we discussed the current ratio, which measures ability to pay current liabilities with current assets. A more stringent measure of a company's ability to pay current liabilities is the **quick ratio**. The quick ratio, also called the **acid-test ratio**, compares a company's **quick assets** to its current liabilities. The quick ratio reveals whether the entity could pay all of its current liabilities if they were to become due immediately. The formula for the quick ratio is as follows:

$$\text{Quick ratio} = \frac{\text{Cash} + \text{Net current receivables} + \text{Short-term investments}}{\text{Total current liabilities}}$$

Let's assume that Mackay Industries has the following current asset information for December 31, 2010: cash, $3,100; net current receivables, $2,500; inventory, $6,300; and short-term investments, $1,600. Current liabilities are $4,300. The quick ratio for Mackay Industries is calculated as follows:

$$\text{Quick ratio} = \frac{\$3,100 + \$2,500 + \$1,600}{\$4,300} = 1.67$$

Notice the $6,300 of inventory was not considered in the calculation of the quick ratio. This is because, although inventory is a current asset, it is not considered to be a "quick" asset.

The higher the quick ratio, the more able the business is to pay its current liabilities. Mackay Industries has a very strong quick ratio. Mackay Industries' quick ratio of 1.67 means that it has $1.67 of quick assets to pay each $1 of current liabilities.

What is an acceptable quick ratio? The answer depends on the industry. Wal-Mart operates smoothly with a quick ratio of less than 0.20. Several things make this low ratio possible: Wal-Mart collects cash rapidly and has almost no receivables. The quick ratios for most department stores cluster around 0.80, while travel agencies average 1.10. In general, a quick ratio of 1.00 is considered safe.

Decision Guidelines

Decision	Guideline	Analyze
Is there a way to determine if a business has an adequate amount of cash and receivables on hand?	Utilize the quick ratio.	The quick ratio provides an indicator of a business's ability to pay its obligations as they come due. Although the quick ratio takes into account a business's short-term investments, the primary components are cash and receivables. A quick ratio that is below 1.0 is generally an indicator that a business has an inadequate amount of cash and receivables on hand. If too many liabilities come due at once, the business is likely to encounter cash flow problems.

Accounts Receivable Turnover

Accounts receivable turnover measures the ability to collect cash from credit customers. The higher the ratio, the more successful the business is in collecting cash. However, an accounts receivable turnover that is too high may indicate that a company is not extending credit freely enough to make sales to all potentially good customers. Accounts receivable turnover is calculated as follows:

$$\text{Accounts receivable turnover} = \frac{\text{Net Credit Sales}}{\text{Average net Accounts Receivable}}$$

Assume that Mackay Industries has net credit sales for the year of $486,000, beginning net Accounts Receivable of $64,000, and ending net Accounts Receivable of $52,000. Mackay Industries would calculate the accounts receivable turnover for the year as follows:

$$\text{Accounts receivable turnover} = \frac{\$486,000}{\$58,000} = 8.38$$

The average net Accounts Receivable, $58,000, is figured by adding the beginning Accounts Receivable balance of $64,000 to the ending balance of $52,000 and dividing the result by two. The determination of whether a company's accounts receivable turnover rate is good or bad depends on the company's credit terms. If Mackay Industries grants 30-day credit terms, its 8.38 accounts receivable turnover rate would be viewed as poor. With 30-day credit terms, you would expect a ratio of closer to 12 (360 days divided by 30 days). If Mackay Industries grants 45-day credit terms, its 8.38 accounts receivable turnover rate would be viewed as good. With 45-day credit terms, you would expect a ratio of closer to 8 (360 days divided by 45 days).

Decision Guidelines

Decision	Guideline	Analyze
How can I evaluate a company's management of accounts receivable?	Utilize the accounts receivable turnover ratio.	A low accounts receivable turnover ratio is often an indicator that a business is not properly managing its credit accounts. A low ratio is usually the result of credit accounts becoming delinquent. This can adversely affect a company because it negatively impacts cash flows.

However, an accounts receivable turnover that is too high may also be an indicator that accounts receivable is being poorly managed. This often occurs when credit is not granted freely enough, resulting in lost sales. |

Demo Doc

Accounts Receivable

Learning Objective 4 ▶ Advantage Cycle accounts for its uncollectible accounts using the allowance method. Advantage Cycle had the following account balances as of September 1:

Accounts Receivable		Allowance for Uncollectible Accounts	
Bal 32,000			1,700 Bal

During the month of September, Advantage Cycle had the following transactions:

a. Made $57,000 of sales on account.

b. Collected $49,000 on account from credit customers.

c. Wrote off $2,300 of Accounts Receivable as uncollectible.

d. Unexpectedly collected $250 of Accounts Receivable that had previously been written off.

Requirements:

1 Journalize Transactions a–d (because information about individual customers has not been given, record all entries as summary entries to the Accounts Receivable control account). Post the entries to the Accounts Receivable and Allowance for Uncollectible Accounts T-accounts and calculate the account balances.

2 Assume that on September 30, based on an aging of its accounts receivable, Advantage Cycle estimates that $2,100 of Accounts Receivable will be uncollectible. Journalize the entry to record Uncollectible Accounts Expense for the month of September. What is the net realizable value of Accounts Receivable at September 30?

3 Ignoring Requirement 2, assume instead that Advantage Cycle estimates that Accounts Receivable equal to 3% of all credit sales will eventually be uncollectible. Journalize the entry to record Uncollectible Accounts Expense for the month of September. What is the net realizable value of Accounts Receivable at September 30?

Demo Doc Solutions

Requirement **1**

Journalize Transactions a–d.

Part 1	Part 2	Part 3	Demo Doc Complete

a. Made $57,000 of sales on account.

Because the sales were on account, Accounts Receivable is increased (debited) by $57,000. Sales is also increased (credited) by $57,000.

DATE	ACCOUNTS	POST REF.	DR.	CR.
	Accounts Receivable		57,000	
	Sales			57,000
	Sold merchandise on account.			

b. Collected $49,000 on account from credit customers.

When cash is collected from customers, Cash is increased (debited) by $49,000 and Accounts Receivable is decreased (credited) by $49,000.

DATE	ACCOUNTS	POST REF.	DR.	CR.
	Cash		49,000	
	Accounts Receivable			49,000
	Received cash on account.			

c. Wrote off $2,300 of Accounts Receivable as uncollectible.

When receivables are uncollectible, they no longer have value. Therefore, they are no longer considered to be valid assets so Accounts Receivable needs to be decreased (credited) by $2,300. Because Advantage Cycle uses the allowance method, the debit side of the entry is made to Allowance for Uncollectible Accounts. Remember that under the allowance method, the Allowance for Uncollectible Accounts is created when the period-end adjusting entry is made to record the estimated uncollectible accounts expense.

DATE	ACCOUNTS	POST REF.	DR.	CR.
	Allowance for Uncollectible Accounts		2,300	
	Accounts Receivable			2,300
	Wrote off uncollectible accounts.			

d. **Unexpectedly collected $250 of Accounts Receivable that had previously been written-off.**

When an account is written off, it is removed from the accounting records. If it is subsequently collected, it must first be put back into the accounting records. To reinstate the receivable, we must reverse the entry that removed the account. In other words, we must debit the accounts that were originally credited and credit the accounts that were originally debited. The entry to write off accounts receivable debits the allowance and credits the accounts receivable (as in Transaction c). To reverse this entry, we must do the opposite: Debit the accounts receivable and credit the allowance by $250.

DATE	ACCOUNTS	POST REF.	DR.	CR.
	Accounts Receivable		250	
	Allowance for Uncollectible Accounts			250
	Reinstated Accounts Receivable.			

Once this journal entry has been made, the cash collection is recorded as usual. Cash is increased (debited) by $250 and Accounts Receivable is decreased (credited) by $250.

DATE	ACCOUNTS	POST REF.	DR.	CR.
	Cash		250	
	Accounts Receivable			250
	Received cash on account.			

Post the entries to the Accounts Receivable and Allowance for Uncollectible Accounts T-accounts and calculate the account balances.

The entries are posted to the T-accounts and the ending balances are calculated as follows:

Accounts Receivable				Allowance for Uncollectible Accounts			
Bal	32,000	b.	49,000	c.	2,300	Bal	1,700
a.	57,000	c.	2,300			d.	250
d.	250	d.	250	Bal	350		
Bal	37,700						

Requirement ❷

Assume that on September 30, based on an aging of its accounts receivable, Advantage Cycle estimates that $2,100 of Accounts Receivable will be uncollectible. Journalize the entry to record Uncollectible Accounts Expense for the month of September. What is the net realizable value of Accounts Receivable at September 30?

Part 1	**Part 2**	Part 3	Demo Doc Complete

The phrase "based on an aging of its accounts receivable" tells us that Advantage Cycle is using the accounts receivable aging method to determine its allowance for uncollectible accounts. Under the aging method, the ending balance in the allowance account should equal the estimated amount of uncollectible accounts that was determined based on the aging of accounts receivable ($2,100).

What do we need to do to bring the allowance account to a balance of $2,100? By inserting the desired ending balance into the allowance account's T-account we can determine how much we must credit the account for in order to bring its balance to $2,100.

Allowance for Uncollectible Accounts			
c.	2,300	Bal	1,700
		d.	250
Bal	350		?
		Bal	2,100

The question mark represents the required credit to the account. Notice that the account has a debit balance prior to making the adjusting entry. This is because the amount of accounts written off during the period exceeds the balance that was in the allowance account at the beginning of the period. Remember, it is possible for the allowance account to have either a debit or a credit balance prior to making the period-end adjusting entry. It is very important to pay attention to whether the account has a debit or a credit balance as this has an impact on the calculation of the required adjusting entry.

In order to bring the account from a debit balance of $350 to a credit balance of $2,100 we must credit the account for a total of $2,450 ($350 + $2,100). This represents a credit of $350, which brings the account to a zero balance, plus an additional credit of $2,100, which brings the account to the desired $2,100 balance. The debit side of the entry is to Uncollectible Accounts Expense.

DATE	ACCOUNTS	POST REF.	DR.	CR.
Sep 30	Uncollectible Accounts Expense		2,450	
	Allowance for Uncollectible Accounts			2,450
	Record estimated uncollectible accounts.			

The net realizable value of Accounts Receivable is calculated by subtracting the ending Allowance for Uncollectible Accounts balance from the ending balance of Accounts Receivable calculated in Requirement 1.

Accounts Receivable	$37,700
− Allowance for Uncollectible Accounts	(2,100)
= Accounts Receivable, Net	$35,600

Requirement ❸

Ignoring Requirement 2, assume instead that Advantage Cycle estimates that Accounts Receivable equal to 3% of all credit sales will eventually be uncollectible. Journalize the entry to record Uncollectible Accounts Expense for the month of September. What is the net realizable value of Accounts Receivable at September 30?

Part 1	Part 2	**Part 3**	Demo Doc Complete

The phrase "that Accounts Receivable equal to 3% of all credit sales will eventually be uncollectible" tells us that Advantage Cycle is using the percent of sales method to determine its allowance for uncollectible accounts. From Requirement 1, Transaction a, we know that credit sales were $57,000 for the month. The amount of estimated uncollectible accounts is calculated as follows:

$$\text{Estimated uncollectible accounts} = 3\% \text{ of credit sales}$$
$$\$1,710 = 3\% \times \$57,000$$

Unlike with the aging method, it is not necessary to consider the Allowance for Uncollectible Accounts balance in order to determine the amount of the required period-end adjusting entry. Once the estimated amount of uncollectible accounts has been calculated, that amount is used as the debit to Uncollectible Accounts Expense and the credit to Allowance for Uncollectible Accounts as follows:

DATE	ACCOUNTS	POST REF.	DR.	CR.
Sep 30	Uncollectible Accounts Expense		1,710	
	Allowance for Uncollectible Accounts			1,710
	Record estimated uncollectible accounts.			

Before we can calculate the net realizable value of Accounts Receivable we need to post the adjusting entry to the allowance account and calculate the ending balance.

Allowance for Uncollectible Accounts

c.	2,300	Bal	1,700
		d.	250
Bal	350	Adj	1,710
		Bal	1,360

The net realizable value of Accounts Receivable can now be calculated as in Requirement 2.

Accounts Receivable	$37,700
− Allowance for Uncollectible Accounts	(1,360)
= Accounts Receivable, Net	$36,340

Demo Doc Complete

Part 1	Part 2	Part 3	**Demo Doc Complete**

Decision Guidelines

What decisions might you encounter while accounting for cash and receivables within your business?

Decision	Guideline	Analyze
How can my business maximize sales?	Consider granting credit to your customers or accepting alternate forms of payment other than cash.	Granting credit to your customers is an excellent way to increase a business's sales. On the other hand, if the credit accounts are not properly managed, the costs associated with bad debts can exceed the profits generated by the extra sales.
		Accepting debit and credit cards can also positively affect the amount of sales a business generates. However, because of the fees associated with accepting debit and credit cards, the profitability of those sales will be less than it is for cash sales.
Which cash balance is correct, the cash balance according to my books, or the cash balance according to the bank?	Neither, the correct cash balance can only be obtained by preparing a bank reconciliation.	The bank reconciliation identifies differences that arise from the following:
		• *Timing differences* resulting from items that have been recorded by the business but not yet by the bank or vice-versa
		• *Errors* that have been made by the business or by the bank
		Once the bank reconciliation has been completed, journal entries are made to adjust the business's cash account balance to the balance according to the bank reconciliation. This is the correct cash balance.
Should I use the direct write-off method or the allowance method to account for bad debts?	Generally Accepted Accounting Principles dictate the use of the allowance method.	Because the allowance method matches bad debt expense with the credit sales that resulted in the bad debts, it is generally viewed as the preferred method. The allowance method also reports accounts receivable at its net realizable value, which is a better indicator of the amount of cash that will ultimately be collected from the receivables.
Is there a way to determine if a business has an adequate amount of cash and receivables on hand?	Utilize the quick ratio.	The quick ratio provides an indicator of a business's ability to pay its obligations as they come due. Although the quick ratio takes into account a business's short-term investments, the primary components are cash and receivables. A quick ratio that is below 1.0 is generally an indicator that a business has an inadequate amount of cash and receivables on hand. If too many liabilities come due at once, the business is likely to encounter cash flow problems.
How can I evaluate a company's management of accounts receivable?	Utilize the accounts receivable turnover ratio.	A low accounts receivable turnover ratio is often an indicator that a business is not properly managing its credit accounts. A low ratio is usually the result of credit accounts becoming delinquent. This can adversely affect a company because it negatively impacts cash flows.
		However, an accounts receivable turnover that is too high may also be an indicator that accounts receivable is being poorly managed. This often occurs when credit is not granted freely enough, resulting in lost sales.

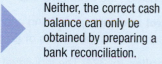

ACCOUNTING VOCABULARY

THE LANGUAGE OF BUSINESS

Accounts receivable turnover (p. 345) Net Credit Sales divided by net average Accounts Receivable; it measures a company's ability to collect cash from its credit customers.

Acid-test ratio (p. 344) Ratio that reveals how well the entity can pay its current liabilities. Also called the *quick ratio*.

Aging method (p. 336) The method of estimating uncollectible accounts that focuses on accounts receivable; the accountant calculates the end-of-period allowance balance based on an aging of the Accounts Receivable; also called the *balance sheet approach*.

Allowance for Doubtful Accounts (p. 335) A contra-asset account that holds the estimated amount of uncollectible accounts receivable; also called *Allowance for Uncollectible Accounts*.

Allowance for Uncollectible Accounts (p. 335) A contra-asset account that holds the estimated amount of uncollectible accounts receivable; also called *Allowance for Doubtful Accounts*.

Allowance method (p. 335) The method of accounting for uncollectible accounts that estimates these amounts and uses an allowance account so that the balance sheet shows the net amount of Accounts Receivable expected to be collected in the future.

Bad debt (p. 321) An account receivable that is unable to be collected; also called an *uncollectible account*.

Bad debts expense (p. 333) Selling expense caused by uncollectible accounts that reduce operating income; also called *uncollectible accounts expense*.

Balance sheet approach (p. 338) The method of estimating uncollectible accounts that focuses on accounts receivable. The accountant calculates the end-of-period allowance balance based on an aging of the Accounts Receivable; also called the *aging method*.

Bank balance (p. 325) The balance in the company's bank account according to the bank.

Bank collection (p. 326) Collection of money by the bank on behalf of a depositor.

Bank reconciliation (p. 325) A document that identifies and explains the differences between a depositor's record of a cash account and a bank's record of the same cash account.

Bank statement (p. 325) A document the bank prepares to report the changes in the depositor's cash account for a period of time. It shows the beginning bank account balance, lists the month's cash transactions, and shows the ending bank account balance.

Book balance (p. 325) The balance in a company's bank account according to the company's accounting records, or books.

Cash (p. 332) Coin, currency, checks, petty cash, checking accounts, payroll accounts, money orders, traveler's checks, and anything the bank will accept as a deposit.

Cash and cash equivalents (p. 332) The balance sheet item used to describe cash and items so closely resembling cash that they are presented as cash.

Cash equivalents (p. 332) Highly liquid, highly safe investments that so closely resemble cash that they may be shown with cash on the balance sheet.

Control account (p. 335) An account in the general ledger that summarizes the details of an account balance.

Controller (p. 324) The individual in an organization responsible for the accounting system and financial statements.

Creditor (p. 341) The entity to whom the debtor promises future payment; also called the *payee of a note*.

Debtor (p. 341) The entity that promises future payment; also called the *maker of a note*.

Deposits in transit (p. 326) Deposits that have been recorded by a company but not yet by its bank.

Direct write-off method (p. 333) The method of accounting for uncollectible accounts in which a customer's account is written off as uncollectible when the business determines that the customer will not pay.

Due date (p. 341) The date when final payment of the note is due; also called the *maturity date*.

Electronic data interchange (EDI) (p. 324) Direct electronic communication between suppliers and retailers.

Electronic funds transfer (EFT) (p. 324) System that transfers cash by electronic communication rather than by paper documents.

Income statement approach (p. 336) The method of estimating uncollectible accounts that focuses on net credit sales; also called the *percent of sales method*.

Interest (p. 341) The fee for using money; revenue to the creditor for loaning money; expense to the debtor for borrowing money.

Interest rate (p. 341) The percentage rate of interest specified by the note; almost always stated for a period of one year.

Lock-box system (p. 326) A system in which customers send payments to a post office box of a business. The bank collects payments from the box and deposits them into the business's account.

Maker of a note (p. 341) The entity that promises future payment; also called the *debtor*.

Maturity date (p. 341) The date when final payment of a note is due; also called the *due date*.

Maturity value (p. 341) The sum of the principal of a note plus interest due at maturity.

Net credit sales (p. 335) The total credit sales less sales discounts and sales returns and allowances related to the credit sales.

Net realizable value (p. 335) The net amount that the business expects to collect; the net realizable value of receivables is calculated by subtracting Allowance for Uncollectible Accounts from Accounts Receivable.

Note term (p. 341) The time span of the note during which interest is computed; it extends from the original date of the note to the maturity date.

Nonsufficient funds (NSF) check (p. 326) A check drawn against a bank account that has insufficient money to pay the check.

Outstanding checks (p. 326) Checks that have been issued by a company and recorded in its books but have not yet been paid by its bank.

Payee of a note (p. 341) The entity to whom the debtor promises future payment; also called the *creditor*.

Percent of sales method (p. 335) The method of estimating uncollectible accounts that focuses on net credit sales; also called the *income statement approach*.

Petty cash (p. 332) Fund containing a small amount of cash that is used to pay for minor expenditures.

Principal (p. 341) The amount loaned out by the payee and borrowed by the maker of the note.

Promissory note (p. 341) A written promise to pay a specified amount of money at a particular future date.

Purchase order (p. 323) A document showing details of merchandise being ordered from a supplier.

Purchasing agent (p. 324) The individual in an organization responsible for buying items for that organization.

Quick assets (p. 344) Highly liquid assets used to calculate the quick ratio, including cash and cash equivalents, short-term investments, and net accounts receivable.

Quick ratio (p. 344) Ratio that reveals how well the entity can pay its current liabilities; also called the *acid-test ratio*.

Receiving report (p. 323) A document evidencing the receipt of goods purchased.

Treasurer (p. 324) The individual in an organization responsible for the custody of assets, such as cash.

Uncollectible account (p. 321) An Account Receivable that is unable to be collected; also called a *bad debt*.

Uncollectible Accounts Expense (p. 333) Selling expense caused by uncollectible accounts that reduce operating income; also called *bad debts expense*.

Write off (p. 333) Removing a customer's receivable from the accounting records because it is considered uncollectible.

ACCOUNTING PRACTICE

DISCUSSION QUESTIONS

1. What duties should be segregated in the purchasing process? Why? That is, what could go wrong if two or more of those duties are not segregated?

2. After preparing a bank reconciliation, which reconciling items will require journal entries? Why?

3. What would be the surest way to eliminate the possibility of having any bad debts? Why don't companies operate this way if it could help them eliminate this costly expense?

4. Why does the allowance method of accounting for bad debts conform to GAAP while the direct write-off method does not?

5. How is Allowance for Doubtful Accounts reported on the financial statements? Why is it important for companies to report net realizable value of Accounts Receivable on the balance sheet?

6. Why is the percent of sales method called the "income statement approach" while the aging method is called the "balance sheet approach"?

7. Under which method, percent of sales or aging, would the balance in Allowance for Doubtful Accounts just before the adjusting entry affect the amount of the adjusting entry? Why?

8. How would the net realizable value of Accounts Receivable change when an account is written off under the allowance method?

9. If a company with a 12/31 year-end lends money in the form of a 6-month note on 11/1, which accounts will be credited when the note is paid off on 4/30?

10. In 2009 the United States was in a deep recession. What would be the expected effect of a recession on accounts receivable turnover ratios?

SELF CHECK

1. The document that identifies and explains all differences between the company's record of cash and the bank's record of that cash is the

  a. bank reconciliation.
  b. bank collection.
  c. bank statement.
  d. electronic fund transfer.

2. Which item(s) appears as a reconciling item(s) to the book balance in a bank reconciliation?

  a. Outstanding checks
  b. Deposits in transit
  c. Both a and b
  d. None of the above

3. Which item(s) appears as a reconciling item(s) to the bank balance in a bank reconciliation?

  a. Outstanding checks
  b. Deposits in transit
  c. Both a and b
  d. None of the above

4. On its books, Navarro Company's Cash account shows an ending balance of $770. The bank statement for the current period shows a $20 service charge and an NSF check for $100. A $250 deposit is in transit, and outstanding checks total $400. What is Navarro's adjusted book balance for Cash?

  a. $530   **b.** $650   **c.** $680   **d.** $1,050

5. After performing a bank reconciliation, journal entries are required for

  a. all items on the bank side of the reconciliation.
  b. all items on the book side of the reconciliation.
  c. all items on the reconciliation.
  d. no items from the reconciliation because the Cash account needs no adjustment.

6. Uncollectible accounts are the same as

  a. bad debts.
  b. notes receivable.
  c. both a and b.
  d. none of the above.

7. Which method of estimating uncollectible receivables focuses on net credit sales?

  a. Aging approach
  b. Percent-of-sales approach
  c. Net realizable value approach
  d. All of the above

8. Your business uses the allowance method to account for uncollectible receivables. At the beginning of the year, Allowance for Uncollectible Accounts had a credit balance of $1,100. During the year you wrote off bad receivables of $2,100 and recorded Uncollectible Accounts Expense of $2,000. What is your year-end balance in Allowance for Uncollectible Accounts?

  a. $1,000   **b.** $2,000   **c.** $3,100   **d.** $3,200

9. Which of the following is *true* regarding the direct write-off method of accounting for uncollectibles?

    a. The direct write-off method does not adhere to GAAP.
    b. The direct write-off method does not use an allowance for uncollectible accounts and, thus, overstates assets on the balance sheet.
    c. The direct write-off method does not match expenses against revenues very well.
    d. All of the above are true.

10. On December 31, you have a $10,000 note receivable from a customer. Interest of 8% has also accrued for six months on the note. What will your financial statements report for this situation?

    a. Nothing will be reported because you haven't received the cash yet.
    b. The balance sheet will report the note receivable of $10,000.
    c. The balance sheet will report the note receivable of $10,000 and interest receivable of $400.
    d. The income statement will report a note receivable of $10,000.

    Answers are given after Written Communication.

SHORT EXERCISES

S7-1. Bank reconciliation adjustments (*Learning Objective 1*) 5–10 min.

For each of the following, indicate whether the item is an adjustment to the bank balance or the book balance:

_____ 1. Bank service charge

_____ 2. Deposit in transit

_____ 3. Bank collection of amount due from customer

_____ 4. Interest revenue on bank balance

_____ 5. Outstanding check

S7-2. Bank reconciliation adjustments (*Learning Objective 1*) 10–15 min.

Classify each of the following items as one of the following:

Addition to the book balance (+ Book)

Subtraction from the book balance (– Book)

Addition to the bank balance (+ Bank)

Subtraction from the bank balance (– Bank)

_____ 1. Outstanding checks

_____ 2. Deposits in transit

_____ 3. NSF check

_____ 4. Bank collection of our note receivable

_____ 5. Interest earned on bank balance

_____ 6. Bank service charge

_____ 7. Book error: We credited Cash for $200. The correct amount of the check was $2,000.

_____ 8. Bank error: The bank decreased our account for a check written by another customer.

S7-3. Prepare a bank reconciliation (*Learning Objective 1*) 5–10 min.

The T-account for cash and the bank statement of Mee Auto Services for the month of March 2010 follows:

Cash			
Mar 1	3,200	Check #704	540
Mar 10 deposit	750	Check #705	210
Mar 31 deposit	200	Check #706	900
Pre-adjusted Bal @ Mar 31	2,500		

Bank Statement:			
Bal, Mar 1			$3,200
Deposits:			
Deposits		$750	
Bank collection		710	
Interest		10	1,470
Checks:	No.	Amount	
	704	540	
	705	210	(750)
Other Charges:			
Service charge		$ 20	(20)
Bal, Mar 31			$3,900

Prepare Mee Auto Services' bank reconciliation at March 31.

S7-4. Prepare bank reconciliation journal entries (*Learning Objective 1*) 5–10 min.

Make the necessary journal entries arising from Dee Zee Motor's bank reconciliation presented next. Date each entry March 31 and include an explanation with each entry.

Dee Zee Motors Bank Reconciliation March			
BANK		**BOOKS**	
Bal, Mar 31	$ 500	Bal, Mar 31	$ 740
Add:		Add:	
Deposit in transit	300	Interest revenue	10
	800		750
		Less:	
Less:		Service charge	(20)
Outstanding checks	(250)	NSF Checks	(180)
Adjusted bank balance	$ 550	Adjusted book balance	$ 550

S7-5. Balance sheet presentation of cash (*Learning Objective 2*) 5–10 min.

Prepare the current assets section of the balance sheet as of December 31, 2010, for Lipton, Inc., using the following information:

Accounts Receivable	$63,000
Petty Cash	500
Cash in Bank Accounts	22,000
Inventory	$55,500

S7-6. Receivable terms (*Learning Objectives 3 & 4*) 5–10 min.

Match the term with its definition by placing the corresponding letter in the space provided:

<u> c </u>   Example: Amounts owed to a business by another business or individual

_____ 1. A contra-account, related to accounts receivable, that holds the estimated amount of uncollectible receivables

_____ 2. A method of accounting for uncollectible receivables in which the company waits until a specific customer's account receivable is uncollectible before recording uncollectible accounts expense

_____ 3. A method of recording receivable losses on the basis of estimates instead of waiting to see which customers the company will not collect from

_____ 4. The party to a credit transaction who sells goods or a service and obtains a receivable

_____ 5. A way to estimate uncollectible accounts by analyzing individual accounts receivable according to the length of time they have been receivable

_____ 6. The party to a credit transaction who makes a purchase and has a payable

_____ 7. Cost to the seller of credit sales; arises from the failure to collect from credit customers

_____ 8. A method of estimating uncollectible receivables that calculates uncollectible accounts expense based on net credit sales

a. Creditor

b. Debtor

c. Receivables

d. Uncollectible Accounts Expense

e. Allowance method

f. Allowance for Uncollectible Accounts

g. Percent of sales method

h. Aging method

i. Direct write-off method

S7-7. Direct write-off method (*Learning Objective 4*) 5–10 min.

Antonio Galvan, an attorney, uses the direct write-off method to account for uncollectible receivables. On August 31, Galvan's accounts receivable were $8,000. During September, he earned service revenue of $20,000 on account and collected $22,000 from clients on account. He also wrote off uncollectible receivables of $2,000. What is Galvan's balance of Accounts Receivable on September 30? Does he expect to collect this entire amount? Why or why not?

S7-8. Percent of sales allowance method (*Learning Objective 4 & 5*) 5–10 min.

During its first year of operations, Atlas Travel earned revenue of $400,000 on account. Industry experience suggests that Atlas Travel's uncollectible accounts will amount to 2% of revenues. On December 31, 2010, accounts receivable total $90,000. The company uses the allowance method to account for uncollectibles.

Journalize Atlas Travel's Uncollectible Accounts Expense using the percent-of-sales method. Show how Atlas should report Accounts Receivable on its balance sheet on December 31, 2010.

S7-9. Percent of sales allowance method (*Learning Objectives 4*) 5–10 min.

Atlas Travel ended 2009 with Accounts Receivable of $90,000 and an Allowance for Uncollectible Accounts balance of $8,000. During 2010, Atlas Travel had the following activity:

a. Service revenue earned on account, $600,000.

b. Collections on account, $580,000.

c. Write-offs of uncollectibles, $15,000.

d. Uncollectible accounts expense, estimated as 2% of service revenue.

Journalize Atlas Travel's activity for 2010.

S7-10. Aging of accounts receivable allowance method (*Learning Objectives 4*) 5–10 min.

Gorav Dental Group started 2010 with Accounts Receivable of $120,000 and an Allowance for Uncollectible Accounts balance of $6,000. The following information relates to Gorav Dental's 2010 operations:

a. Credit sales, $400,000.

b. Collections on account, $320,000.

c. Write-offs of uncollectibles, $15,000.

d. At December 31, the aging of accounts receivable showed that Gorav will probably *not* collect $5,000 of its accounts receivable.

Journalize Gorav's 2010 transactions based on the information provided. Prepare a T-account for the Allowance for Uncollectible Accounts to show your computation of Uncollectible Accounts Expense for the year.

S7-11. Aging of accounts receivable allowance method (*Learning Objective 4*) 5–10 min.

Limo.com had the following balances on December 31, 2010, before the year-end adjustments:

Accounts Receivable	Allowance for Uncollectible Accounts
104,000	1,300

The aging of receivables yields these data:

	Age of Accounts				
	1–30 Days	31–60 Days	61–90 Days	Over 90 Days	Total Receivables
Accounts Receivable	$70,000	$20,000	$10,000	$4,000	$104,000
Estimate Percentage Uncollectible	× 1%	× 2%	× 5%	× 50%	

Journalize Limo's entry to adjust the allowance account to its correct balance on December 31, 2010.

S7-12. Internal controls—credit sales (*Learning Objective 3*) 10–15 min.

Claire Billiot, the office manager of a local office supply company, is designing its internal control system. Billiot proposes the following procedures for credit checks on new customers, sales on account, cash collections, and write-offs of uncollectible receivables:

a. The Credit Department runs a credit check on all customers who apply for credit. When an account proves uncollectible, the Credit Department authorizes the write-off of the account receivable.

b. Cash receipts come into the Credit Department, which separates the cash received from the customer remittance slips. The Credit Department lists all cash receipts by customer name and amount of cash received.

c. The cash goes to the treasurer for deposit in the bank. The remittance slips go to the Accounting Department for recording of the collections.

d. The controller compares the daily deposit slip to the total amount of the collections recorded. Both amounts must agree.

For each of the four procedures, indicate whether the procedure includes an internal control weakness. Explain how employee fraud could occur because of the weakness. What can Claire do to strengthen the internal control system?

S7-13. Notes receivable terms (*Learning Objective 6*) 10–15 min.

Match the term with its definition by placing the corresponding letter in the space provided:

_____ 1. A written promise to pay a specified amount of money at a particular future date

_____ 2. The date when final payment of the note is due; also called the due date

_____ 3. The percentage rate of interest specified by the note for one year

_____ 4. The entity to whom the maker promises future payment

_____ 5. The period of time during which interest is earned

_____ 6. The amount loaned out by the payee and borrowed by the maker of the note

_____ 7. The sum of the principal plus interest due at maturity

_____ 8. The entity that signs the note and promises to pay the required amount

_____ 9. The revenue to the payee for loaning money; the expense to the debtor

a. Interest

b. Note term

c. Interest rate

d. Maker of the note

e. Maturity date

f. Maturity value

g. Payee of the note

h. Principal

i. Promissory note

S7-14. Accounting for notes receivable (*Learning Objective 6*) 10–15 min.

For each of the following notes receivable, compute the amount of interest revenue earned during 2010. Use a 360-day year, and round to the nearest dollar.

	Principal	Interest Rate	Interest Period During 2010
Note 1	$100,000	8%	6 months
Note 2	30,000	12%	75 days
Note 3	20,000	9%	60 days
Note 4	50,000	10%	3 months

S7-15. Accounting for notes receivable (*Learning Objective 6*) 10–15 min.

Bank of America lent $100,000 to Christine Kleuters on a 90-day, 8% note. Record the following transactions for Bank of America (explanations are not required):

1. Lending the money on June 12.

2. Collecting the principal and interest at maturity. Specify the date. For the computation of interest, use a 360-day year.

S7-16. Quick ratio (*Learning Objective 7*) 5–10 min.

Calculate the quick assets and the quick ratio for each of the following companies:

	Jaxon	Kilborn
Cash	$10,000	$ 25,000
Short-term Investments	5,000	15,000
Net Receivables	45,000	52,000
Current Liabilities	45,000	100,000

S7-17. Accounts receivable turnover (*Learning Objective 7*) 5–10 min.

Calculate accounts receivable turnover for the following two companies.

	Moore	Noel
Net Credit Sales	$73,000	$45,625
Net Accounts Receivable, Beginning	12,000	23,000
Net Accounts Receivable, Ending	13,000	21,000

EXERCISES (GROUP A)

E7-18A. Bank reconciliation adjustments (*Learning Objective 1*) 10–15 min.

Calculate the answers for the missing data:

BANK		BOOKS	
Bal, Jan 31	$1,000	Bal, Jan 31	(c)
Add:		Add:	
Deposit in transit	600	Bank collection	425
	(a)	Interest revenue	15
			(d)
Less:		Less:	
Outstanding checks	(b)	Service charge	(30)
Adjusted bank balance	$1,200	Adjusted book balance	$1,200

E7-19A. Prepare a bank reconciliation and journal entries (*Learning Objective 1*) 20–25 min.

Dirk Cole's checkbook lists the following:

Date	Check No.	Item	Check	Deposit	Balance
9/ 1					$1,425
5	922	Mesilla Kitchen	$ 22		1,403
10		Dividends received		$ 115	1,518
14	923	Best Products	25		1,493
15	924	Fina (payment on account)	60		1,433
19	925	Cash	200		1,233
27	926	Staples	175		1,058
29	927	Hobart Properties	1,000		58
30		Paycheck		4,095	4,153

Dirk Cole's September bank statement shows the following:

Bal, Sep 1				$1,425
Deposits:				115
Checks:	No.	Amount		
	922	$ 22		
	923	25		
	924	70*		
	925	200		(317)
Other Charges:				
Printed checks			$20	
Service charge			15	(35)
Bal, Sep 30				$1,188

*This amount is correct for check no. 924.

Requirements

1. Prepare Dirk Cole's bank reconciliation on September 30, 2010. How much cash does Dirk Cole actually have on September 30?

2. Prepare all necessary journal entries for Dirk Cole to update the Cash account as a result of the bank reconciliation.

E7-20A. Prepare a bank reconciliation (*Learning Objective 1*) 20–25 min.

Information from Goddard Picture Frames' cash account as well as the January bank statement is presented next.

Cash				
Jan 1	1,400	Check #210	30	
Jan 30	2,700	Check #211	400	
		Check #212	110	
		Check #213	325	
		Check #214	200	
Pre-adjusted				
Bal @ Jan 31	3,035			

Bank Statement:				
Bal, Jan 1				$1,400
Deposits:				
EFT—rent				500
Checks:	No.	Amount		
	210	300		
	211	400		
	212	110		(810)
Other Charges:				
Service charge			$ 15	
Check printing			10	
NSF check #201			65	(90)
Bal, Jan 31				$1,000

Check #210 was written for $300 to pay salaries.

Quick solution: *1. Adjusted cash balance = $3,175*

Requirements

1. Prepare the bank reconciliation on January 31.

2. Prepare all necessary journal entries for Goddard Picture Frames to update the Cash account as a result of the bank reconciliation.

E7-21A. Direct write-off method (*Learning Objective 4*) 5–10 min.

Allied Industries uses the direct write-off method to account for bad debts. Record the following transactions that occurred during the year:

Feb	3	Provided $600 of services to Bill Hanson on account.
Aug	8	Wrote off Bill Hanson's $600 account as uncollectible.
Nov	10	Unexpectedly collected $400 from Bill Hanson on the account that had been written off. Allied Industries does not expect to collect the remaining balance.

E7-22A. Percent of sales allowance method (*Learning Objectives 4*) 10–15 min.

Rice Automotive ended December 2009 with Accounts Receivable of $30,000 and Allowance for Uncollectible Accounts of $1,500. During January 2010, Rice Automotive completed the following transactions:

- Sales of $180,000, which included $120,000 in credit sales and $60,000 of cash sales.
- Cash collections on account, $90,000.
- Write-offs of uncollectible receivables, $1,200.
- Uncollectible accounts expense, estimated as 2% of credit sales.

Requirements

1. Prepare journal entries to record sales, collections, write offs of uncollectibles, and uncollectible accounts expense by the percent-of-sales method.

2. Calculate the ending balances in Accounts Receivable, Allowance for Uncollectible Accounts, and net Accounts Receivable at January 31. How much does Rice Automotive expect to collect?

E7-23A. Aging of accounts receivable allowance method (*Learning Objective 4*) 15–20 min.

On December 31, 2010, the Accounts Receivable balance of Alterations Express is $300,000. The Allowance for Uncollectible Accounts has a $3,900 credit balance. Alterations prepares the following aging schedule for its accounts receivable:

	Age of Accounts			
	1–30 Days	31–60 Days	61–90 Days	Over 90 Days
Accounts Receivable.............................	$140,000	$80,000	$70,000	$10,000
Estimated Percentage Uncollectible	0.5%	1.0%	6.0%	50%

Requirements

1. Journalize the year-end adjusting entry for uncollectible accounts on the basis of the aging schedule. Calculate the resulting ending balance of the Allowance account based on the account aging. Show the T-account for the Allowance on December 31, 2010.

2. Assume that instead of a $3,900 credit balance, there is a $1,300 debit balance in the Allowance account prior to adjustment. Journalize the

year-end adjusting entry for uncollectible accounts on the basis of the aging schedule. Calculate the resulting ending balance of the Allowance account based on the account aging. Show the T-account for the Allowance on December 31, 2010.

E7-24A. Percent of sales and aging of accounts receivable allowance methods (*Learning Objective 4*) 15–20 min.

Inland Equipment uses the allowance method to account for uncollectible accounts. On December 31, 2010, Allowance for Uncollectible Accounts has a $600 credit balance. Journalize the year-end adjusting entry for uncollectible accounts assuming the following *independent* scenarios:

1. Inland Equipment estimates uncollectible accounts as ½ of 1% of net credit sales. Net credit sales for the year equal $550,000.

2. Based on an aging of Accounts Receivable, Inland Equipment estimates that uncollectible accounts will equal $2,575.

E7-25A. Accounting for notes receivable (*Learning Objective 6*) 15–20 min.

On April 30, 2010, Citibank loaned $100,000 to Grant Hughes on a one-year, 6% note.

Requirements

1. Compute the interest for the years ended December 31, 2010 and 2011, on the Hughes note.

2. Which party has
   a. a note receivable?
   b. a note payable?
   c. interest revenue?
   d. interest expense?

3. How much in total would Hughes pay the bank if he pays off the note early—say, on November 30, 2010?

E7-26A. Accounting for notes receivable (*Learning Objective 6*) 15–20 min.

Journalize the following transactions of Cramer, Inc., which ends its accounting year on June 30:

Apr 1	Loaned $20,000 cash to R. Simpson on a one-year, 8% note.
Jun 6	Sold goods to Friday, Corp., receiving a 90-day, 10% note for $3,000.
30	Made a single compound entry to accrue interest revenue on both notes. Use a 360-day year for interest computations.

E7-27A. Accounting for notes receivable (*Learning Objective 6*) 15–20 min.

Gorman Enterprises sells on account. When a customer account becomes four months old, Gorman converts the account to a note receivable. During 2010, Gorman completed these transactions:

Jun 29	Sold goods on account to I. Happy, $10,000.
Nov 1	Received a $10,000, 60-day, 9% note from I. Happy in satisfaction of his past-due account receivable.
Dec 31	Collected the I. Happy note at maturity.

Requirement

1. Record the transactions in Gorman Enterprises' journal.

E7-28A. Quick ratio (*Learning Objective 7*) 15–20 min.

Consider the following data:

	A	B	C	D
Cash..	$ 92,000	$ 64,000	$23,000	$107,000
Short-term Investments................	70,000	28,000	15,000	53,000
Net Receivables...........................	125,000	110,000	52,000	140,000
Current Liabilities.........................	205,000	101,000	60,000	350,000

Requirements

1. Calculate the quick assets and the quick ratio for each company.
2. Which of the companies should be concerned about its liquidity?

E7-29A. Quick ratio and accounts receivable turnover (*Learning Objective 7*) 15–20 min.

Vision Equipment reported the following items on February 28, 2010 (amounts in thousands, with last year's amounts also given as needed):

Accounts Payable........................	$ 449	Accounts Receivable, Net:	
Cash...	215	February 28, 2010..................	$ 220
Inventory:		February 28, 2009..................	150
February 28, 2010..................	190	Cost of Goods Sold.....................	1,200
February 28, 2009..................	160	Short-term Investments..............	165
Net Credit Sales..........................	1,930	Other Current Assets..................	90
Long-term Assets	410	Other Current Liabilities..............	145
Long-term Liabilities...................	10		

Requirements:

1. Compute Vision Equipment's (a) quick ratio and (b) accounts receivable turnover for 2010.
2. Evaluate each ratio value as strong or weak. Assume Vision Equipment sells on terms of net 30.

EXERCISES (GROUP B)

E7-30B. Bank reconciliation adjustments (*Learning Objective 1*) 10–15 min.

Calculate the answers for the missing data:

BANK		BOOKS	
Bal, Mar 31	$ 990	Bal, Mar 31	(c)
Add:		Add:	
Deposit in transit	680	Bank collection	420
	(a)	Interest revenue	100
			(d)
Less:		Less:	
Outstanding checks	(b)	Service charge	(40)
Adjusted bank balance	$1,240	Adjusted book balance	$1,240

**E7-31B. Prepare a bank reconciliation and journal entries (*Learning Objective 1*)
20–25 min.**

Dan Cryer's checkbook lists the following:

Date	Check No.	Item	Check	Deposit	Balance
10/ 1					$1,435
5	922	Rivertown Kitchen	$ 40		1,395
10		Dividends received		$ 125	1,520
14	923	Everyday Products	37		1,483
15	924	Fauna (payment on account)	63		1,420
19	925	Cash	200		1,220
27	926	Office Supply	117		1,103
28	927	North East Properties	984		119
31		Paycheck		5,285	5,404

Dan Cryer's October bank statement shows the following:

Bal, Oct 1					$1,435
Deposits:					125
Checks:	No.	Amount			
	922	$ 40			
	923	37			
	924	163*			
	925	200			(440)
Other Charges:					
Printed checks			$25		
Service charge			10		(35)
Bal, Oct 31					$1,085

*This amount is correct for check no. 924.

Requirements

1. Prepare Dan Cryer's bank reconciliation on October 31, 2010. How much cash does Dan Cryer actually have on October 31?

2. Prepare all necessary journal entries for Dan Cryer to update the Cash account as a result of the bank reconciliation.

E7-32B. Prepare a bank reconciliation (*Learning Objective 1*) 20–25 min.

Information from Sheppard Picture Frames' cash account as well as the November bank statement is presented next.

Cash			
Nov 1	2,100	Check #210	60
Nov 30	2,000	Check #211	400
		Check #212	137
		Check #213	310
		Check #214	180
Pre-adjusted			
Bal @ Nov 30	3,013		

Bank Statement:			
Bal, Nov 1			$ 2,100
Deposits:			
EFT—rent			750
Checks:	No.	Amount	
	210	600	
	211	400	
	212	137	(1,137)
Other Charges:			
Service charge		$ 30	
Check printing		16	
NSF check #201		80	(126)
Bal, Nov 30			$ 1,587

Check #210 was written for $600 to pay salaries.

Requirements

1. Prepare the bank reconciliation on November 30.

2. Prepare all necessary journal entries for Sheppard Picture Frames to update the Cash account as a result of the bank reconciliation.

E7-33B. Direct write-off method (*Learning Objective 4*) 5–10 min.

White Top Rafters uses the direct write-off method to account for bad debts. Record the following transactions that occurred during the year:

May 3	Provided $970 of services to Sam Martin on account.
Nov 8	Wrote off Sam Martin's $970 account as uncollectible.
Dec 10	Unexpectedly collected $200 from Sam Martin on the account that had been written off. White Top Rafters does not expect to collect the remaining balance.

E7-34B. Percent of sales allowance method (*Learning Objectives 4*) 10–15 min.

Ortiz Automotive ended December 2009 with Accounts Receivable of $20,000 and Allowance for Uncollectible Accounts of $5,900. During January 2010, Ortiz Automotive completed the following transactions:

- Sales of $260,000, which included $160,000 in credit sales and $100,000 of cash sales.
- Cash collections on account, $54,000.
- Write-offs of uncollectible receivables, $2,500.
- Uncollectible accounts expense, estimated as 4% of credit sales.

Requirements

1. Prepare journal entries to record sales, collections, write-offs of uncollectibles, and uncollectible accounts expense by the percent-of-sales method.

2. Calculate the ending balances in Accounts Receivable, Allowance for Uncollectible Accounts, and net Accounts Receivable at January 31. How much does Ortiz Automotive expect to collect?

E7-35B. Aging of accounts receivable allowance method (*Learning Objective 4*) 15–20 min.

On July 31, 2010, the Accounts Receivable balance of Questor Application, Inc., is $320,000. The Allowance for Uncollectible Accounts has a $6,400 credit balance. Questor prepares the following aging schedule for its accounts receivable:

	Age of Accounts			
	1–30 Days	31–60 Days	61–90 Days	Over 90 Days
Accounts Receivable.............................	$175,000	$70,000	$60,000	$15,000
Estimated Percentage Uncollectible	0.8%	3.0%	5.0%	60%

Requirements

1. Journalize the year-end adjusting entry for uncollectible accounts on the basis of the aging schedule. Calculate the resulting ending balance of the Allowance account based on the account aging. Show the T-account for the Allowance on July 31, 2010.

2. Assume that instead of a $6,400 credit balance, there is a $500 debit balance in the Allowance account prior to adjustment. Journalize the year-end adjusting entry for uncollectible accounts on the basis of the aging schedule. Calculate the resulting ending balance of the Allowance account based on the account aging. Show the T-account for the Allowance on July 31, 2010.

E7-36B. Percent of sales and aging of accounts receivable allowance methods (*Learning Objective 4*) 15–20 min.

Cotton, Corp., uses the allowance method to account for uncollectible accounts. On May 31, 2010, Allowance for Uncollectible Accounts has a $1,300 credit balance. Journalize the year-end adjusting entry for uncollectible accounts assuming the following *independent* scenarios:

1. Cotton, Corp., estimates uncollectible accounts as ¾ of 1% of net credit sales. Net credit sales for the year equal $750,000.

2. Based on an aging of Accounts Receivable, Cotton, Corp., estimates that uncollectible accounts will equal $3,120.

E7-37B. Accounting for notes receivable (*Learning Objective 6*) 15–20 min.

On June 30, 2010, Nature Bank loaned $2,000,000 to Gary Simon on a one-year, 7% note.

Requirements

1. Compute the interest for the years ended December 31, 2010 and 2011, on the Simon note.

2. Which party has

   a. a note receivable?

   b. a note payable?

   c. interest revenue?

   d. interest expense?

3. How much in total would Simon pay the bank if he pays off the note early— say, on January 31, 2011?

E7-38B. Accounting for notes receivable (*Learning Objective 6*) 15–20 min.

Journalize the following transactions of Coral, Inc., which ends its accounting year on April 30:

Feb	1	Loaned $15,000 cash to Carroll Fadal on a one-year, 10% note.
Apr	6	Sold goods to Lawn Pro, receiving a 90-day, 4% note for $6,000.
	30	Made a single compound entry to accrue interest revenue on both notes. Use a 360-day year for interest computations.

E7-39B. Accounting for notes receivable (*Learning Objective 6*) 15–20 min.

Professional Enterprises sells on account. When a customer account becomes four months old, Professional converts the account to a note receivable. During 2010, Professional completed these transactions:

Mar 29	Sold goods on account to Montclair, Inc., $21,000.
Aug 1	Received a $21,000, 60-day, 5% note from Montclair, Inc., in satisfaction of its past-due account receivable.
Sep 30	Collected the Montclair, Inc., note at maturity.

Requirement

1. Record the transactions in Professional Enterprises' journal.

E7-40B. Quick ratio (*Learning Objective 7*) 15–20 min.

Consider the following data:

	A	B	C	D
Cash	$ 93,000	$ 67,000	$23,000	$111,000
Short-term Investments	75,000	27,000	18,000	49,000
Net Receivables	126,000	110,000	54,000	144,000
Current Liabilities	335,000	280,000	35,000	220,000

Requirements

1. Calculate the quick assets and the quick ratio for each company.
2. Which of the companies should be concerned about its liquidity?

E7-41B. Quick ratio and accounts receivable turnover (*Learning Objective 7*) 15–20 min.

Algonquin Equipment reported the following items on November 30, 2010 (amounts in thousands, with last year's amounts also given as needed):

Accounts Payable	$ 434	Accounts Receivable, Net:	
Cash	210	November 30, 2010	200
Inventory:		November 30, 2009	110
November 30, 2010	170	Cost of Goods Sold	800
November 30, 2009	130	Short-term Investments	170
Net Credit Sales	2,450	Other Current Assets	30
Long-term Assets	410	Other Current Liabilities	170
Long-term Liabilities	60		

Requirements

1. Compute Algonquin Equipment's (a) quick ratio and (b) accounts receivable turnover for 2010.

2. Evaluate each ratio value as strong or weak. Assume Algonquin Equipment sells on terms of net 30.

EXERCISES (ALTERNATES 1, 2, AND 3)

These alternative exercise sets are available for your practice benefit at
www.myaccountinglab.com

PROBLEMS (GROUP A)

P7-42A. Prepare a bank reconciliation (*Learning Objective 1*) 20–25 min.

The May cash records of Nielson, Inc., follow:

Cash Receipts (CR)		Cash Payments (CP)	
Date	Cash Debit	Check No.	Cash Credit
May 4	$2,716	1416	$ 8
9	544	1417	775
14	896	1418	88
17	367	1419	126
31	2,037	1420	970
		1421	200
		1422	2,267

Nielson's Cash account shows the balance of $6,171 on May 31. On May 31, Nielson, Inc., received the following bank statement:

Bank Statement for May		
Beginning Balance		$ 4,045
Deposits and other additions		
May 1	$ 625 EFT	
5	2,716	
10	544	
15	896	
18	367	
31	1,000 BC	6,148
Checks and other deductions		
May 8	$ 441 NSF	
15 (Check no. 1416)	8	
19	340 EFT	
22 (Check no. 1417)	775	
29 (Check no. 1418)	88	
31 (Check no. 1419)	216	
31	25 SC	(1,893)
Ending Balance		$ 8,300

Explanations: BC—bank collection; EFT—electronic funds transfer; NSF—nonsufficient funds check; SC—service charge.

Additional data for the bank reconciliation:

a. The EFT deposit was a receipt of rent revenue. The EFT debit was payment of insurance expense.

b. The NSF check was received from a customer.

c. The $1,000 bank collection was for a note receivable.

d. The correct amount of check 1419 is $216. Nielson, Inc., mistakenly recorded the check for $126.

Requirement

1. Prepare Nielson's bank reconciliation at May 31.

P7-43A. Prepare a bank reconciliation (*Learning Objective 1*) 20–25 min.

The October 1, bank statement of Blake's Hamburger just arrived from First State Bank.

October Bank Statement:			
Bal, Oct 1			$12,769
Deposits:			
EFT—rent		$900	
EFT—deposit		200	
Interest		16	1,116
Checks:	No.	Amount	
	807	600	
	808	400	
	1668	410	(1,410)
Other Charges:			
Service charge		$ 7	
NSF check #998		67	
NSF check #201		192	(266)
Bal, Oct 31			$12,209

To prepare the bank reconciliation, you gather the following additional data:

a. The following checks are outstanding at October 31:

Check No.	Amount
800	$402
802	74
806	36
809	161
810	229
811	48

b. On October 31, Blake's Hamburger's treasurer deposited $381, but this deposit does not appear on the bank statement.

c. The bank statement includes a $410 deduction for check #1668 written by Danson Freight rather than Blake's Hamburger. Blake's Hamburger notified the bank of this bank error.

d. Blake's Hamburger's Cash account shows a balance of $11,200 on October 31.

Requirements

1. Prepare the bank reconciliation for October 31.

2. Record the entries called for by the reconciliation. Include an explanation for each entry.

P7-44A. Direct write-off method and percent of sales allowance method (*Learning Objectives 4 & 5*) 20–25 min.

On August 31, Pro Tennis Equipment had a $150,000 debit balance in Accounts Receivable. During September, Pro Tennis Equipment had the following transactions:

- Sales of $500,000, all on credit.
- Collections on account, $550,000.
- Write-offs of uncollectible receivables, $7,000.

Requirements

1. Assume that Pro Tennis Equipment uses the allowance method to account for uncollectible accounts and that there was a $9,000 credit balance in the allowance account on August 31. Prepare journal entries to record sales, collections on account, and write-offs of uncollectible accounts for the month of September. Next, assuming that uncollectible accounts expense is estimated at 2% of credit sales, prepare the adjusting journal entry to record bad debts expense. Enter the beginning balances and post all September activity in T-accounts for Accounts Receivable, Allowance for Uncollectible Accounts, and Uncollectible Accounts Expense.

2. Suppose that instead of the allowance method, Pro Tennis Equipment uses the direct write-off method to account for uncollectible receivables. Prepare journal entries to record sales, collections on account, and write-offs of uncollectible accounts for the month of September. Enter the beginning balances and post all September activity in T-accounts for Accounts Receivable and Uncollectible Accounts Expense.

3. What amount of uncollectible accounts expense would Pro Tennis Equipment report on its September income statement under each of the two methods? Which amount better matches expenses with revenue? Give your reason.

4. What amount of net accounts receivable would Pro Tennis Equipment report on its September 30 balance sheet under each of the two methods? Which amount is more realistic? Give your reason.

P7-45A. Aging of accounts receivable allowance method (*Learning Objectives 4 & 5*) 15–20 min.

Regents Supply completed the following selected transactions during the year:

Jan 17	Sold inventory to Abe Gomez, $600, on account. Ignore cost of goods sold.
Jun 29	Wrote off the Abe Gomez account as uncollectible after repeated efforts to collect from him.
Aug 6	Received $200 from Abe Gomez, along with a letter stating his intention to pay within 30 days. Reinstated his account in full.
Sep 4	Received the balance due from Abe Gomez.
Dec 31	Made a compound entry to write off the following accounts as uncollectible: Bernard Clark, $700; Marie Montrose, $300; and Terry Forman, $600.
Dec 31	Based on an aging of accounts receivable, estimated uncollectible accounts as $2,300.

Requirements

1. Open T-accounts for Allowance for Uncollectible Accounts and Uncollectible Accounts Expense. These accounts have beginning balances of $1,800 (cr.) and 0, respectively.

2. Record the transactions in the journal, and post to the two ledger accounts; remember to update the account balances but ignore posting references.

3. The December 31 balance of Accounts Receivable is $139,000. Show how Accounts Receivable would be reported on the balance sheet at that date.

Quick solution: 2. Adjusting journal entry amount to record bad debts expense = $2,100; Allowance for Uncollectible Accounts ending balance = $2,300; Uncollectible Accounts Expense ending balance = $2,100

P7-46A. Accounting for notes receivable (*Learning Objective 6*) 20–25 min.

The Bailey Insurance Agency received the following notes during 2010:

Note	Date	Principal Amount	Interest Rate	Term
(1)	Dec 23	$13,000	9%	1 year
(2)	Nov 30	12,000	12%	6 months
(3)	Dec 7	9,000	10%	30 days

Requirements

1. Identifying each note by number, compute interest using a 360-day year, and determine the due date and maturity value of each note.

2. Journalize a single adjusting entry on December 31, 2010, to record accrued interest revenue on all three notes. Explanations are not required.

3. For note (1), journalize the collection of principal and interest at maturity. Explanations are not required.

P7-47A. Accounting for notes receivable (*Learning Objective 6*) 20–25 min.

Record the following transactions in the journal of Bingham Phone Accessories. Explanations are not required.

2009	
Dec 19	Received a $3,000, 60-day, 12% note on account from Arnold Collins.
31	Made an adjusting entry to accrue interest on the Collins note.
31	Made a closing entry for interest revenue.
2010	
Feb 17	Collected the maturity value of the Collins note.
Jun 1	Loaned $10,000 cash to Electra Mann, receiving a six-month, 11% note.
Oct 31	Received a $1,500, 60-day, 12% note from Mark Phillips on his past-due account receivable.
Dec 1	Collected the maturity value of the Electra Mann note.

P7-48A. Quick ratio and accounts receivable turnover (*Learning Objective 7*) 20–25 min.

The comparative financial statements of Bien Taco Restaurants for 2010, 2009, and 2008 include the following selected data:

	(In Thousands)		
	2010	**2009**	**2008**
Balance Sheet			
Current Assets:			
Cash	$ 82	$ 80	$ 60
Short-term Investments	140	174	122
Receivables, Net of Allowance for			
Uncollectible Accounts of $6, $6,			
and $5 respectively	257	265	218
Inventory	429	341	302
Prepaid Expenses	21	27	46
Total Current Assets	929	887	748
Total Current Liabilities	$ 680	$ 700	$ 600
Income Statement			
Sales Revenue	$5,189	$4,995	$4,206
Cost of Goods Sold	2,734	2,636	2,418

Requirements

1. Compute these ratios for 2010 and 2009:

    a. Quick ratio.

    b. Accounts receivable turnover. Assume all sales are credit sales.

2. Write a memo explaining to the company owner which ratios improved from 2009 to 2010, which ratios deteriorated, and which items in the financial statements changed and caused changes in some ratios. Discuss whether this change conveys a favorable or an unfavorable impression about the company.

PROBLEMS (GROUP B)

P7-49B. Prepare a bank reconciliation (*Learning Objective 1*) 20–25 min.

The November cash records of Stenback, Inc., follow:

Cash Receipts (CR)		Cash Payments (CP)	
Date	Cash Debit	Check No.	Cash Credit
Nov 4	$2,725	1416	$ 9
9	530	1417	750
14	880	1418	93
17	353	1419	124
31	2,040	1420	960
		1421	210
		1422	2,250

Stenback's Cash account shows the balance of $6,172 on November 30. On November 30, Stenback received the following bank statement:

Bank Statement for November		
Beginning Balance		$ 4,040
Deposits and other additions:		
Nov 1	$ 635 EFT	
5	2,725	
10	530	
15	880	
18	353	
31	1,800 BC	6,923
Checks and other deductions:		
Nov 8	$ 452 NSF	
15 (Check no. 1416)	9	
19	350 EFT	
22 (Check no. 1417)	750	
29 (Check no. 1418)	93	
31 (Check no. 1419)	214	
31	45 SC	(1,913)
Ending Balance		$ 9,050

Explanations: BC—bank collection; EFT—electronic funds transfer; NSF—nonsufficient funds checks; SC—service charge.

Additional data for the bank reconciliation:

a. The EFT deposit was a receipt of rent revenue. The EFT debit was payment of insurance expense.

b. The NSF check was received from a customer.

c. The $1,800 bank collection was for a note receivable.

d. The correct amount of check number 1419 is $214. Stenback, Inc., mistakenly recorded the check for $124.

Requirement

1. Prepare Stenback's bank reconciliation on November 30.

P7-50B. Prepare a bank reconciliation (*Learning Objective 1*) 20–25 min.

The December 31, bank statement of Billy's Hamburger just arrived from Safety Bank.

Bank Statement for December			
Bal, Dec 1			$13,384
Deposits:			
EFT—rent		$700	
EFT—deposit		400	
Interest		12	1,112
Checks:	No.	Amount	
	807	$600	
	808	200	
	1668	410	(1,210)
Other Charges:			
Service charge		$ 19	
NSF check #998		60	
NSF check #201		205	(284)
Bal, Dec 31			$13,002

To prepare the bank reconciliation, you gather the following additional data:

a. The following checks are outstanding on December 31:

Check No.	Amount
800	$415
802	75
806	34
809	123
810	228
811	39

b. On December 31, Billy's Hamburger's treasurer deposited $330, but this deposit does not appear on the bank statement.

c. The bank statement includes a $410 deduction for a check written by Jenny's Jump Ropes rather than Billy's Hamburger. Billy's Hamburger notified the bank of this bank error.

d. Billy's Cash account shows a balance of $12,000 on December 31.

Requirements

1. Prepare the bank reconciliation for December 31.

2. Record the journal entries called for by the reconciliation. Include an explanation for each entry.

P7-51B. Direct write-off method and percent of sales allowance method (*Learning Objectives 4 & 5*) 20–25 min.

On March 31, Daisy Tennis Equipment had a $165,000 debit balance in Accounts Receivable. During April, Daisy Tennis Equipment had the following transactions:

- Sales of $490,000, all on credit.
- Collections on account, $425,000.
- Write-offs of uncollectible receivables, $6,000.

Requirements

1. Assume that Daisy Tennis Equipment uses the allowance method to account for uncollectible accounts and that there was a $8,000 credit balance in the allowance account on March 31. Prepare journal entries to record sales, collections on account, and write-offs of uncollectible accounts for the month of April. Next, assuming that uncollectible accounts expense is estimated at 2% of credit sales, prepare the adjusting journal entry to record bad debts expense. Enter the beginning balances and post all April activity in T-accounts for Accounts Receivable, Allowance for Uncollectible Accounts, and Uncollectible Accounts Expense.

2. Suppose that instead of the allowance method, Daisy Tennis Equipment uses the direct write-off method to account for uncollectible receivables. Prepare journal entries to record sales, collections on account, and write-offs of uncollectible accounts for the month of April. Enter the beginning balances and post all April activity in T-accounts for Accounts Receivable and Uncollectible Accounts Expense.

3. What amount of Uncollectible Accounts Expense would Daisy Tennis Equipment report on its April income statement under each of the two methods? Which amount better matches expense with revenue? Give your reasoning.

4. What amount of net accounts receivable would Daisy Tennis Equipment report on its April 30 balance sheet under each of the two methods? Which amount is more realistic? Give your reasoning.

P7-52B. Aging of accounts receivable allowance method (*Learning Objectives 4 & 5*) 15–20 min.

Beta Supply completed the following selected transactions during the year:

Jan 17	Sold inventory to Abe Gomez, $800 on account. Ignore cost of goods sold.
Jun 29	Wrote off Abe Gomez's account as uncollectible after repeated efforts to collect from him.
Aug 6	Received $250 from Abe Gomez, along with a letter stating his intention to pay within 30 days. Reinstated Gomez's account in full.
Sep 4	Received the balance due from Abe Gomez.
Dec 31	Made a compound entry to write off the following accounts as uncollectible: Brian Kemper, $1,000; Marie Montrose, $200; and Tanya Wayne, $900.
Dec 31	Based on an aging of accounts receivable, estimated uncollectible accounts as $2,600.

Requirements

1. Open T-accounts for Allowance for Uncollectible Accounts and Uncollectible Accounts Expense. These accounts have beginning balances of $1,500 (cr.) and 0, respectively.

2. Record the transactions in the journal, and post to the two ledger accounts that have been opened for you; remember to update account balances but ignore posting references.

3. The December 31 balance of Accounts Receivable is $133,000. Show how Accounts Receivable would be reported on the balance sheet at that date.

P7-53B. Accounting for notes receivable (*Learning Objective 6*) 20–25 min.

The Buffalo Insurance Agency received the following notes during 2010:

Note	Date	Principal	Interest Rate	Term
(1)	Oct 23	$13,000	8%	1 year
(2)	Sep 30	$ 8,000	11%	2 months
(3)	Oct 7	$10,000	12%	45 days

Requirements

1. Identifying each note by number, compute interest using a 360-day year, and determine the due date and maturity value of each note.

2. Journalize a single adjusting entry on October 31, 2010, to record accrued interest revenue on all three notes. Explanations are not required.

3. For note (1), journalize the collection of principal and interest at maturity. Explanations are not required.

P7-54B. Accounting for notes receivable (*Learning Objective 6*) 20–25 min.

Record the following transactions in the journal of Birds Eye Music. Explanations are not required.

2009	
Dec 19	Received a $6,000, 60-day, 12% note on account from AVC Company.
31	Made an adjusting entry to accrue interest on the AVC Company note.
31	Made a closing entry for interest revenue.
2010	
Feb 17	Collected the maturity value of the AVC Company note.
Jun 1	Loaned $12,000 cash to Lincoln Music, receiving a 6-month, 11% note.
Oct 31	Received a $5,500, 60-day, 13% note from Ying Yang Music on its past-due account receivable.
Dec 1	Collected the maturity value of the Lincoln Music note.

P7-55B. Quick ratio and accounts receivable turnover (*Learning Objective 7*) 20–25 min.

The comparative financial statements of Perfection Taco Restaurants for 2010, 2009, and 2008 include the following selected data:

	(In Thousands)		
	2010	**2009**	**2008**
Balance Sheet			
Current Assets:			
Cash	$ 82	$ 80	$ 55
Short-term Investments	130	178	125
Receivables, Net of Allowance for Uncollectible Accounts of $7, $6, and $4, respectively	290	305	256
Inventory	434	335	315
Prepaid Expenses	24	30	55
Total Current Assets	960	928	806
Total Current Liabilities	$ 780	$ 800	$ 625
Income Statement			
Sales Revenue	$5,223	$5,039	$4,250
Cost of Goods Sold	2,768	2,650	2,490

Requirements

1. Compute these ratios for 2010 and 2009:
   a. Quick ratio.
   b. Accounts receivable turnover. Assume all sales are credit sales.

2. Write a memo explaining to the company owner which ratios improved from 2009 to 2010, which ratios deteriorated, and which items in the financial statements changed and caused changes in some ratios. Discuss whether this change conveys a favorable or an unfavorable impression about the company.

PROBLEMS (ALTERNATES 1, 2, AND 3)

These alternative problem sets are available for your practice benefit at
www.myaccountinglab.com

CONTINUING EXERCISE

In this exercise, we continue our accounting for Graham's Yard Care, Inc. from Chapter 5. Refer to the continuing exercise from Chapter 5. On August 18, Graham's Yard Care, Inc., received $250 on account from Jim Henderson related to his July 15 purchase. On October 12, Jim notified Graham's Yard Care, Inc., that he was filing bankruptcy and that he would not be able to pay the remaining amount owed.

Requirement

1. Journalize the entry to record the payment from Jim and to record the write off of Jim's uncollectible account. Assume that Graham's Yard Care, Inc., uses the direct write-off method to account for uncollectible accounts.

CONTINUING PROBLEM

In this problem, we continue our accounting for Aqua Elite, Inc. from Chapter 5. Refer to the continuing problem in Chapters 4 and 5. Assume that all 13 of the spas Aqua Elite, Inc., sold in September were sold on account for $4,000 each. At September 30, Aqua Elite, Inc., estimates that 5% of the outstanding Account Receivable balance will not be collected.

Requirements

1. Calculate the ending balance in Accounts Receivable at September 30.

2. Journalize the entry to record Aqua Elite's uncollectible accounts expense for September.

3. How will Accounts Receivable be reflected on Aqua Elite's balance sheet at September 30?

APPLY YOUR KNOWLEDGE

ETHICS IN ACTION

Case 1. Ed Hanson is the controller of Casey's Collectibles. The business uses the accrual method of accounting and recognizes sales revenue in the period in which the sale is made. As a result, the Accounts Receivable balance at year-end was $92,480, which was net of the Allowance for Uncollectible Accounts of $1,260. Ed was completing the year-end financial statements for the business in order to apply for a much needed business loan when he saw a letter from a district court. The letter was to inform him as controller of Casey's Collectibles that Charlie Smith had declared bankruptcy. As it turned out, Charlie was Casey's Collectibles' largest customer and his account receivable balance was $24,295, which the bankruptcy notification letter stated was never going to be paid. When Ed looked over the account receivable aging schedule he saw that Charlie's account was more than 90 days past due, and even though Ed had been suspicious, he still hoped that Charlie would pay his account balance. Ed looked at his balance sheet and thought that if he wrote off Charlie's account, the bank would become concerned about all of the accounts receivable listed. He then thought that had he not been so quick to open the mail, he would have not known that Charlie was bankrupt, and the balance sheet he was about to present to the bank would be fine. Knowing how potentially damaging this new information could be, Ed decided to just ignore it for the moment and simply go ahead with the balance sheet he had originally planned to give to the bank.

Should Ed provide the bank with a new balance sheet that reflects this new information? Would Ed have been fine with the original balance sheet had he simply waited to open his mail? Are any ethical issues involved with updating financial statement information for subsequent events? Did Ed not properly use the allowance method as he only had a balance for doubtful accounts totaling $1,260? Would Ed need to inform the bank had the bankruptcy letter been from a customer with an account receivable balance of $120?

Case 2. Bob and Larry were finishing the financial statements for their business when they saw the net income for the year was not going to be as large as they had hoped. Concerned that the bank would question the lower reported net income, Bob suggested that they reduce the percentage used to estimate uncollectible accounts for the current year from 5% of credit sales to 1% of credit sales. Larry quickly pointed out that for the last seven years, the bad debts always approximated 5% of the total credit sales. Bob then said that the key was simply that an "estimate" was used to compute the bad debt expense, so why not simply change the percentage from the "5% estimate" to a "1% estimate"? Larry was concerned because the change was not due to new business information; rather it was due to pressure to increase the current year profit by reducing the amount of bad debt expense currently included in the income statement. He told Bob that the current year credit sales were $6,587,000 and the Uncollectible Accounts Expense should be 5% or $329,350, not 1% or $65,870, because they could expect that over the next fiscal year approximately $329,000 of Accounts Receivable would end up as uncollectible. Bob pointed out, however, that by only using a 1% estimate the current year net income would be much larger since the amount of Uncollectible Account Expense would only be $65,870 instead of the larger $329,350. He also noted that the allowance account would also be reduced so the net Accounts Receivable on the balance sheet would be larger as well. Besides, Bob told Larry that they could worry about it in the next fiscal year. Larry told Bob that the bank would find out what they had done, to which Bob said there would be no problem; they could just say they made a mistake in their estimate.

Would it be unethical to change the percentage used to compute the current year's Uncollectible Accounts Expense? Would it be acceptable to change the percentage amount if the change was disclosed? Would it be acceptable if they compromised and used 3%? If they had used a new screening method to determine the creditworthiness of customers and, as a result, they were certain that the bad debts would be drastically reduced, could they change the percentage amount used? What do you think would happen if they used the 1% of credit sales for the current year financial statements? What would you recommend?

KNOW YOUR BUSINESS

FINANCIAL ANALYSIS

Purpose: To help familiarize you with the financial reporting of a real company in order to further your understanding of the chapter material you are learning.

This case will address the accounts receivable reflected on Columbia Sportswear's Balance sheet. We will once again refer to the annual report for Columbia Sportswear located in Appendix A in order to answer some questions related to Columbia Sportswear's receivables.

Requirements

1. What was the Accounts Receivable balance as of December 31, 2008? What was the Accounts Receivable balance as of December 31, 2007? Did the amount of accounts receivable increase or decrease during the year?

2. Based on Columbia Sportswear's balance sheet, does it appear that the allowance method is used to account for uncollectible receivables? Why or why not?

3. Can you determine the total amount of Accounts Receivable Columbia Sportswear had as of December 31, 2008?

4. Did the amount of the allowance for doubtful accounts increase or decrease during 2008? What was the total amount of bad debts written off by Columbia Sportswear in 2008?

INDUSTRY ANALYSIS

Purpose: To help you understand and compare the performance of two companies in the same industry.

Find the Columbia Sportswear Company Annual Report located in Appendix A and go to the Financial Statements starting on page 681. Now access the 2008 Annual Report for Under Armour, Inc., from the Internet. Go to the company's Web page for Investor Relations at *http://investor.underarmour.com/investors.cfm* and under Downloads on the right-hand side, go to 2008 Annual Report. The company's Financial Statements start on page 49.

Requirement

1. Calculate the accounts receivable turnover for both companies for 2008. Who has the highest accounts receivable turnover? Is that good or bad? Is it better to have a high accounts receivable turnover or a low accounts receivable turnover? Explain your answer.

SMALL BUSINESS ANALYSIS

Purpose: To help you understand the importance of cash flows in the operation of a small business.

You're pretty excited about your cash balance at the end of the month because this was the month you were going to take the big bonus from the business and make a down payment on a new house. You were waiting on a big check to come in from a client who has owed you for several months. You had considered writing it off because you had heard through some business associates that the company had been experiencing some financial difficulties. However, after your telephone call to the company the first of the week, the check finally arrived. You rushed the check down to the bank and deposited it.

A couple days later, you access your account online at the bank to figure out how much of a bonus check you can afford to write yourself. After depositing the $30,000 from your client, you expect to have a balance of at least $40,000 and since you always like to keep a balance of at least $10,000 in your account as a buffer, you figure you can easily write a bonus check for $25,000 for your down payment. After reviewing your account, you're really concerned when you see that your bank balance is only $9,500! What happened? You scroll down through the screen for an explanation and you see the following:

- NSF check – Burns & Associates, Inc. – $30,000.00
- Return check charge $200.00
- Monthly service charge $300.00

Requirements

1. What happened? Explain why your bank balance is $30,500 lower than you had anticipated. When you prepare your bank reconciliation, what journal entries will you have to make as a result of these three items from your bank?

2. Assume you ultimately end up having to write off the amount owed by Burns & Associates, Inc. What would the journal entry be for that transaction assuming you use the allowance method to account for bad debts?

WRITTEN COMMUNICATION

Refer to the preceding Small Business Analysis case. Prepare an e-mail to the owner of Burns & Associates, Inc., explaining the situation with the returned check and the charge that the bank applied to your account for processing the returned check. Also request payment for this entire amount, as it is now several months overdue. However, keep in mind that the tone of the e-mail might have some bearing on whether or not Burns continues to utilize your services or not.

Self Check Answers
1. a 2. d 3. c 4. b 5. b 6. a 7. b 8. a 9. d 10. c

Appendix 7A

WHAT IS A PETTY CASH FUND?

(Appendix 7A) Account for the petty cash fund **8**

A business may choose to keep a petty cash fund, which is a fund containing a small amount of cash used to pay for minor expenditures, such as the purchase of postage stamps or a shipment of a small package. Cash is easy to steal and the thief is often able to do so without leaving evidence. For this reason, petty cash funds need controls such as the following:

- Designate a custodian for the petty cash fund. This assigns responsibility for the fund.
- Establish the fund by keeping a specific, fixed amount of cash on hand so that any missing amount can be easily identified.
- Keep the fund in a safe, locked location and only allow the custodian to have access to the fund.
- Support all payments from the fund with a written record documenting the purpose and amount of the payment.

Setting Up the Petty Cash Fund

Businesses establish a petty cash fund by writing a check for the designated amount, usually between $200 and $500, depending on the size and the needs of the business. They typically make the check payable to Petty Cash, cash the check, and place the money in the fund. Every business may have its own form for documenting petty cash payments, but the form is usually signed by the recipient of the petty cash and the custodian to verify the transaction. *The cash in the fund plus the total of the payment forms should always equal the fund balance at all times.*

Suppose that Inland Equipment established a petty cash fund of $200 on June 1. The journal entry to record the creation of the fund is as follows:

DATE	ACCOUNTS	POST REF.	DR.	CR.
Jun 1	Petty Cash		200	
	Cash			200
	Establish the petty cash fund.			

Now imagine that on June 21 Suzanne Kimmel, the fund custodian, approved a cash payment from the petty cash fund to Jim Dirks to reimburse Jim for $25 of envelopes he purchased for the business. Suzanne prepared a record of the disbursement, much like the petty cash ticket in **Exhibit 7A-1**, and both she and Jim signed it. Suzanne kept the form in the fund as a replacement for the cash taken.

```
              PETTY CASH TICKET

Date  Jun 21
Amount   $25
For   Envelopes
Debit  Office Supplies
Received by  Jim Dirks        Fund Custodian  SK
```

Exhibit 7A-1 ▲

Replenishing the Petty Cash Fund

Payments deplete the petty cash fund, so periodically it must be replenished. On July 31 the petty cash fund of Inland Equipment holds the following:

- $108 cash on hand
- $90 in petty cash tickets: office supplies, $53; delivery expense, $37

Notice that when the $108 of cash on hand is added to the $90 of petty cash tickets, the total comes to $198, which is $2 less than the fund balance of $200. The $2 difference signifies that $2 was misplaced from the fund. The petty cash fund can be reconciled as follows:

Cash on Hand.....................................	$108
+ Petty Cash Tickets	90
=	198
+ Cash Shortage	2
= Fund Balance	$200

To replenish the petty cash fund and make the cash on hand equal to $200 again, the company writes a check, payable to Petty Cash, for the $92 ($200 – $108) difference between the cash on hand and the fund balance. The fund custodian cashes this check and puts $92 back in the fund. Now the fund holds $200 cash as required. The following journal entry would be made to record the issuance of the check:

DATE	ACCOUNTS	POST REF.	DR.	CR.
Jul 31	Office Supplies Expense		53	
	Delivery Expense		37	
	Cash Short		2	
	Cash			92
	Replenish the petty cash fund.			

The accounts debited in the entry represent the expense accounts associated with what the petty cash funds were used to purchase. The cash shortage is debited to an expense account titled Cash Short. Notice that the journal entry included a credit to Cash, not Petty Cash. This is because the money to replenish the petty cash fund was taken from the Cash account. The Petty Cash account is only affected when

- the petty cash fund is established.
- the petty cash fund balance is increased or decreased.

Changing the Petty Cash Fund

Imagine that Inland Equipment wants to increase the size of its fund from $200 to $300 on August 1. The business writes a $100 check payable to Petty Cash, and the custodian cashes it and places the money in the fund. In this case, the journal entry to record this $100 increase will look like the following:

DATE	ACCOUNTS	POST REF.	DR.	CR.
Aug 1	Petty Cash		100	
	Cash			100
	Increase petty cash fund balance.			

ACCOUNTING PRACTICE

SHORT EXERCISES

S7A-1. Petty cash transactions (*Learning Objective 8*) 5–10 min.

Record the following petty cash transactions of Handy Dan in the journal; explanations are not required.

Nov	1	Established a petty cash fund with a $100 balance.
	30	The petty cash fund had $33 in cash and $67 in petty cash tickets that were issued to pay for postage. Replenished the fund with cash.

S7A-2. Petty cash transactions (*Learning Objective 8*) 5–10 min.

Record the following petty cash transactions of Xeno, Corp., in the journal; explanations are not required.

Jun	1	Established a petty cash fund with a $200 balance.
	30	The petty cash fund had $22 in cash and $174 in petty cash tickets that were issued to pay for office supplies ($104) and entertainment expense ($70). Replenished the fund.
	30	Increase the petty cash fund balance to $300.

EXERCISES (GROUP A)

E7A-3A. Petty cash transactions (*Learning Objective 8*) 10–15 min.

Jamie's Music School created a $200 petty cash fund on March 1. During the month, the fund custodian authorized and signed petty cash tickets as follows:

Petty Cash			
Ticket No.	Item	Account Debited	Amount
1	Delivery of programs to customers	Delivery Expense	$20
2	Mail package	Postage Expense	40
3	Newsletter	Supplies Expense	44
4	Key to closet	Miscellaneous Expense	16
5	Computer diskettes	Supplies Expense	30

Requirements

1. Record the journal entry to create the petty cash fund.
2. Assuming that the cash in the fund totals $45 on March 31, make the journal entry to replenish the petty cash fund.

E7A-4A. Petty cash transactions (*Learning Objective 8*) 10–15 min.

Hazelnut maintains a petty cash fund of $150. On November 30, the fund holds $7 cash, and petty cash tickets for office supplies, $90, and delivery expense, $50.

Requirements

1. Make the journal entry to replenish the petty cash fund.
2. Hazelnut decided to increase the petty cash fund by $100. Prepare the journal entry.

EXERCISES (GROUP B)

E7A-5B. Petty cash transactions (*Learning Objective 8*) 10–15 min.

Christine's Music School created a $220 petty cash fund on October 1. During the month, the fund custodian authorized and signed petty cash tickets as follows:

Petty Cash			
Ticket No.	Item	Account Debited	Amount
1	Delivery of programs to customers	Delivery Expense	$15
2	Mail package	Postage Expense	50
3	Newsletter	Supplies Expense	43
4	Key to closet	Miscellaneous Expense	19
5	Computer diskettes	Supplies Expense	10

Requirements

1. Record the journal entry to create the petty cash fund.
2. Assuming that the cash in the fund totals $55 on October 31, make the journal entry to replenish the petty cash fund.

E7A-6B. Petty cash transactions (*Learning Objective 8*) 10–15 min.

Maple maintains a petty cash fund of $250. On April 30, the fund holds $19 cash, petty cash tickets for office supplies, $185, and delivery expense, $40.

Requirements

1. Make the journal entry to replenish the petty cash fund.
2. Maple decided to increase the petty cash fund by $120. Prepare the journal entry.

EXERCISES (ALTERNATES 1, 2, AND 3)

These alternative exercise sets are available for your practice benefit at
www.myaccountinglab.com

PROBLEMS (GROUP A)

P7A-7A. Petty cash transactions (*Learning Objective 8*) 10–15 min.

On July 1, Chi Kong creates a petty cash fund with a balance of $300. During July, Elise Sautter, the fund custodian, signs the following petty cash tickets:

Petty Cash Ticket Number	Item	Amount
101	Office supplies	$86
102	Cab fare for executive	25
103	Delivery of package across town	17
104	Dinner money for president and a potential customer	90

On July 31, prior to replenishment, the fund contains these tickets plus cash of $62. The accounts affected by petty cash payments are Office Supplies Expense, Travel Expense, Delivery Expense, and Entertainment Expense.

Requirements

1. Record the journal entry to create the petty cash fund.

2. Record the journal entry to replenish the petty cash fund on July 31. Do you have any concerns regarding the Over/Short account?

3. Make the August 1 entry to increase the fund balance to $350. Include an explanation, and briefly describe what the custodian does when the balance is increased.

PROBLEMS (GROUP B)

P7A-8B. Petty cash transactions (*Learning Objectives 8*) 10–15 min.

On March 1, Fab Kong creates a petty cash fund with a balance of $300. During March, Elise Sautter, the fund custodian, signs the following petty cash tickets:

Petty Cash Ticket Number	Item	Amount
101	Office supplies	$86
102	Cab fare for executive	27
103	Delivery of package across town	10
104	Dinner money for president and a potential customer	110

On March 31, prior to replenishment, the fund contains these tickets plus cash of $37. The accounts affected by petty cash payments are Office Supplies Expense, Travel Expense, Delivery Expense, and Entertainment Expense.

Requirements

1. Record the journal entry to create the petty cash fund.

2. Record the journal entry to replenish the petty cash fund on March 31. Do you have any concerns over the Over/Short account?

3. Make the entry on April 1 to increase the fund balance to $375. Include an explanation, and briefly describe what the custodian does when the balance is increased.

PROBLEMS (ALTERNATES 1, 2, AND 3)

These alternative problem sets are available for your practice benefit at
www.myaccountinglab.com

Long-Term Assets

Regardless of whether you work for (or own) a service business, a merchandising business, or a manufacturing business, that business will likely own long-term assets. Many questions often arise with regard to long-term assets. What different types of long-term assets are there? How do you account for these assets? How do the different methods of accounting for these assets affect the financial statements? What happens when a long-term asset is sold? In this chapter, we will learn the answers to these and other questions as we study long-term assets.

Chapter Outline:

Learning Objectives

1. Describe the difference between plant assets, intangible assets, and natural resources
2. Calculate and record the acquisition of plant assets
3. Calculate and record the depreciation of plant assets
4. Account for repairs to plant assets
5. Account for the disposal of plant assets
6. Account for intangible assets
7. Account for natural resources
8. Account for other long-term assets
9. Report long-term assets on the balance sheet

WHAT ARE THE DIFFERENT TYPES OF LONG-TERM ASSETS?

Describe the difference between plant assets, intangible assets, and natural resources **1**

Most businesses will own at least one of the following types of long-term assets:

- **Plant assets. Plant assets**, also called **fixed assets**, are "physical assets"—meaning they can be seen, touched, or held. This includes assets such as land, buildings, vehicles, desks, and equipment. Plant assets are also sometimes referred to as **tangible assets**.

- **Intangible assets.** Patents, trademarks, and goodwill are examples of **intangible assets**. Unlike plant assets, intangible assets can not be seen, touched, or held. For example, even though there may a piece of paper that provides written evidence of a patent, the paper is not the patent. The patent (the intangible asset) is actually the specific rights that are conveyed to the owner of the patent.

- **Natural resources.** Assets that come from the earth and can ultimately be used up are called **natural resources**. Timber, oil, minerals, and coal are all examples of natural resources.

As we learned in Chapter 3, the cost of a long-term asset must be allocated to an expense as the asset is used up. Although the process of cost allocation is similar for the different types of assets, the terminology used to describe the process is different for each type of asset. **Exhibit 8-1** summarizes the different asset types and the cost allocation terminology used with each.

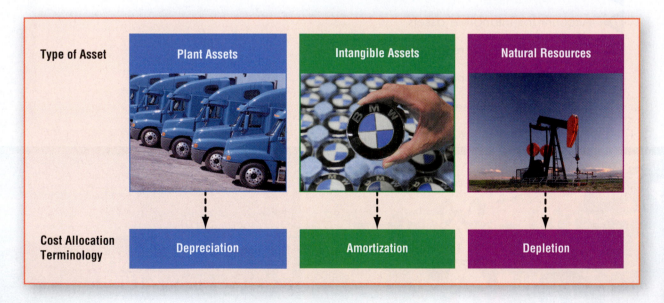

Exhibit 8-1 ▲

The cost allocation methods for each type of asset will be covered later in the chapter.

Companies may also own long-term assets that are classified as *other long-term assets*. Other long-term assets typically consist of long-term investments made by a business. These will be discussed near the end of the chapter.

HOW IS THE COST OF A PLANT ASSET CALCULATED?

Calculate and record the acquisition of plant assets **2**

Generally Accepted Accounting Principles require that the *cost principle,* which we learned about in Chapter 1, be applied when determining the cost of a plant asset. Therefore, the actual amount paid for an asset is to be used as the asset's cost. The amount paid for an asset should include all amounts paid to acquire the asset and to prepare it for its intended purpose. These costs vary depending on the type of plant asset being purchased, so let's discuss each asset type individually.

Land and Land Improvements

The cost of land includes, but is not limited to, the following amounts paid by the purchaser:

- Purchase price
- Realtor commissions
- Survey and legal fees
- Unpaid property taxes owed on the land
- Fees associated with transferring the ownership (title) on the land
- Cost of clearing the land and removing unwanted buildings

The cost of land does *not* include the following costs:

- Fencing
- Paving
- Sprinkler systems
- Lighting
- Signs

These costs are recorded as separate plant assets called **land improvements**.

Suppose that Apex Industries purchases land for $75,000 by signing a note payable for the same amount. Apex Industries also pays cash as follows: $2,500 in realtor commission, $1,200 in transfer fees, a $1,700 survey fee, $4,500 to remove an old building, $2,200 to have the land graded and leveled, $6,300 to have the land fenced, $1,300 for a sprinkler system, and $2,700 for outdoor lighting. What amount would Apex Industries record as the cost of the land? How much would Apex record as land improvements? Apex Industries would assign the costs to land and land improvements as follows:

Cost Incurred	Land	Land Improvements
Purchase price	$75,000	
Realtor commission	2,500	
Transfer fees	1,200	
Survey fee	1,700	
Building removal	4,500	
Grading	2,200	
Fencing		$ 6,300
Sprinkler system		1,300
Lighting		2,700
Total cost	$87,100	$10,300

The purchase of the land and the subsequent cash payments are recorded as follows:

DATE	ACCOUNTS	POST REF.	DR.	CR.
	Land		75,000	
	Note Payable			75,000
	Purchased land on a note payable.			
	Land		12,100	
	Land Improvements		10,300	
	Cash			22,400
	Paid cash for land and land improvements.			

We would say that Apex Industries *capitalized* the cost of the land at $87,100 ($75,000 + $12,100) and the land improvements at $10,300. **Capitalized** means that an asset account is debited (increased) for the cost of an asset. Notice that Land and Land Improvements are two entirely separate assets. Land is a special plant asset because it is never really used up. Therefore, land is not depreciated. However, the cost of land improvements *is* depreciated over the useful life of the improvements.

Buildings

The cost of a building depends on whether the building is constructed or whether an existing building is purchased. If a building is constructed the cost of the building includes the following:

- Architectural fees
- Building permit fees
- Contractor charges
- Payments for material, labor, and overhead

The time to complete a building can be months, even years. If a company constructs its own assets, the cost of a building may also include interest charged during the time of construction on any borrowed money.

If a company purchases an existing building, the cost of the building includes the following:

- Purchase price
- Realtor commissions
- Survey and legal fees
- Unpaid property taxes owed on the building
- Fees associated with transferring the ownership (title) on the building
- Costs of repairing and renovating the building for its intended use

Machinery and Equipment

The cost of machinery and equipment includes the following:

- Purchase price (less any discounts)
- Transportation (delivery) charges

- Insurance while in transit
- Sales and other taxes
- Purchase commission
- Installation costs
- Cost of testing the asset before it is used

After the asset is up and running, the company no longer debits insurance, taxes, and maintenance costs to the Equipment account. From that point on, insurance, taxes, repairs, and maintenance costs are recorded as expenses.

Furniture and Fixtures

Furniture and fixtures include desks, chairs, file cabinets, display racks, shelving, and so forth. The cost of furniture and fixtures includes the basic cost of each asset (less any discounts), plus all other costs to ready the asset for its intended use. For example, for a desk, this may include the costs to ship the desk to the business and the cost paid to a handyman to assemble the desk.

Exhibit 8-2 summarizes the costs associated with the different types of plant assets.

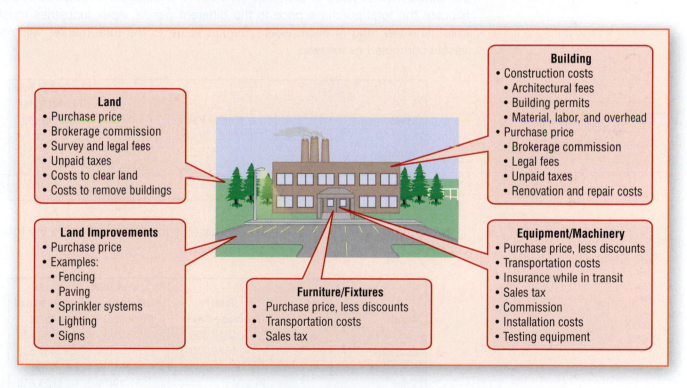

Land
- Purchase price
- Brokerage commission
- Survey and legal fees
- Unpaid taxes
- Costs to clear land
- Costs to remove buildings

Land Improvements
- Purchase price
- Examples:
  - Fencing
  - Paving
  - Sprinkler systems
  - Lighting
  - Signs

Building
- Construction costs
  - Architectural fees
  - Building permits
  - Material, labor, and overhead
- Purchase price
  - Brokerage commission
  - Legal fees
  - Unpaid taxes
  - Renovation and repair costs

Furniture/Fixtures
- Purchase price, less discounts
- Transportation costs
- Sales tax

Equipment/Machinery
- Purchase price, less discounts
- Transportation costs
- Insurance while in transit
- Sales tax
- Commission
- Installation costs
- Testing equipment

Exhibit 8-2 ▲

Lump-Sum (Basket) Purchase of Assets

When a company pays a single price for several assets as a group it is referred to as a **lump-sum purchase**, or **"basket" purchase**. For example, Apex Industries may pay one price ($625,000) for land, a building, and equipment. For accounting, the company must allocate a portion of the total cost to each individual asset, as shown in the following diagram:

The total cost is allocated to the different assets based on their relative market values. Let's assume that an appraisal revealed that the land's market value is $75,000, the building's market value is $480,000, and the equipment's market value is $130,000. Apex Industries got a good deal, paying only $625,000 for assets with a combined market value of $685,000 ($75,000 + $480,000 + $130,000). In order to allocate the total purchase price to the different assets, Apex Industries must first determine the ratio of each asset's market value to the total market value for all assets combined as follows:

Asset	Market Value		Percent of Total Market Value (Rounded)
Land	$ 75,000	÷ $685,000	11%
Building	480,000	÷ $685,000	70%
Equipment	130,000	÷ $685,000	19%
Total	**$685,000**		**100%**

Next, the cost that is allocated to each asset is found by multiplying the total purchase price by the ratios determined previously.

Asset	Total Purchase Price	×	Percent of Total Market Value (Rounded)	Cost Allocated to Asset
Land	$625,000	×	11%	$ 68,750
Building	$625,000	×	70%	437,500
Equipment	$625,000	×	19%	118,750
Total			**100%**	**$625,000**

If we assume that Apex Industries purchased the combined assets on a note payable, the purchase is recorded as follows:

DATE	ACCOUNTS	POST REF.	DR.	CR.
	Land		68,750	
	Building		437,500	
	Equipment		118,750	
	Note Payable			625,000
	Purchased land, building, and equipment on a note payable.			

Decision Guidelines

Decision	Guideline	Analyze
How do I determine the cost of an asset?	The matching principle dictates that all costs associated with acquiring an asset, and preparing it for its intended use, should be considered as part of the cost of the asset.	It is tempting to treat costs related to the purchase of an asset (delivery fees, taxes, set up costs, etc.) as current period expenses. However, if these costs are expensed in the current period, they are not properly matched against the future revenues that the asset will generate. This causes the current period's net income to be understated and future period's net income to be overstated.

HOW ARE PLANT ASSETS DEPRECIATED?

Calculate and record the depreciation of plant assets ▶ **3**

As we saw in Exhibit 8-1, the process of allocating a plant asset's cost to expense over its useful life is referred to as depreciation. Depreciation matches the asset's expense against the revenue generated from using the asset, thereby adhering to the matching principle. In accounting, the "using up" of a plant asset is also referred to as depreciation. For example, a delivery truck can only go so many miles before it is worn out, or used up. As the truck is driven, it depreciates, or is used up. Physical factors, like age and weather, will also contribute to the depreciation of assets. So, depreciation refers to the "using up" of a plant asset as well as to the process of allocating the asset's cost to expense over the asset's useful life.

Let's contrast this with what depreciation is **not**.

- **Depreciation is not a process of valuation.** Businesses do not record depreciation based on changes in the asset's market (sales) value.
- **Depreciation does not mean that the business sets aside cash to replace an asset when it is used up.** Depreciation has nothing to do with cash.

🌐 Accounting in Your World

Have you ever bought a new car, or know someone who has? If so, then you have probably heard people comment on how much the car "depreciated" the minute it was driven off the car lot. These people were referring to the fact that the resale value of the car was most likely less than what had been paid for it. In everyday life, the term depreciation is commonly used to describe a decrease in the market value of an asset, such as a car. However, from an accounting point of view, the car had not depreciated merely because it was driven off the lot. In accounting, depreciation refers to the allocation of the cost of an asset to expense during the life of the asset rather than to a decline in the market value of the asset.

Measuring Depreciation

Depreciation of a plant asset is based on three factors:

1 Cost

2 Estimated useful life

3 Estimated residual value

Cost is known and, as mentioned earlier in this chapter, includes all amounts incurred to prepare the asset for its intended purpose. The other two factors are estimates.

Estimated **useful life** represents the expected life of an asset during which it is anticipated to generate revenues. Useful life may be measured in years, or in units of output. For example, a building's life is usually stated in years, a truck's in the number of miles it can be driven, and a photocopier's in the number of copies it can make. For each asset, the goal is to define the estimated useful life that best matches the "using up" of the asset.

Some assets, such as computers and software, may become obsolete before they wear out. An asset is obsolete when a newer asset can perform the job more efficiently. As a result of obsolescence, an asset's useful life may be determined to be shorter than its physical life. In all cases, an asset's cost is depreciated over its useful life.

Estimated **residual value**—also called **salvage value**—is the asset's expected cash value at the end of its useful life. A delivery truck's useful life may be 150,000 miles. When the truck has driven that distance, the company will sell or scrap it. The expected cash value at the end of the truck's life is the truck's estimated residual value. Because the estimated residual value represents a portion of the asset's cost that will be recovered, it is *not* depreciated. The residual value is subtracted from the cost of the asset to arrive at the asset's **depreciable cost**.

> Cost
> − Residual Value
> = Depreciable cost

A business will use past experience as well as information obtained from other sources to make the best estimates it can of useful life and residual value.

Depreciation Methods

The most commonly used depreciation methods are as follows:

- Straight-line
- Units-of-production
- Declining-balance

These methods work differently in *how* the yearly depreciation amount is calculated, but they all result in the same total depreciation over the useful life of the asset. To demonstrate the different depreciation methods, let's assume that Apex Industries purchased and placed in service a new delivery truck on January 1. The data related to Apex Industries' new delivery truck is presented next:

Purchase price (cost)..	$43,000
Estimated residual (salvage) value..	$ 4,000
Estimated useful life..	5 years

Straight-Line Method The **straight-line (SL) depreciation method** allocates an equal amount of depreciation to each year. Apex Industries might want to use this method for the truck if it thinks time is the best indicator of the truck's depreciation. The equation to find yearly depreciation using straight-line depreciation is as follows:

$$\text{Straight-line depreciation} = \frac{\text{Cost} - \text{Residual value}}{\text{Estimated useful life in years}} = \text{Depreciation per year}$$

The yearly depreciation expense for Apex Industries' delivery truck is as follows:

$$\frac{\text{Cost} - \text{Residual value}}{\text{Estimated useful life}} = \frac{\$43,000 - \$4,000}{5} = \$7,800 \text{ per year}$$

Because Apex Industries purchased the delivery truck on January 1, an entire year's worth of depreciation will be recorded for the first year as follows on December 31:

DATE	ACCOUNTS	POST REF.	DR.	CR.
Dec 31	Depreciation Expense, Vehicles		7,800	
	Accumulated Depreciation, Vehicles			7,800
	Record yearly depreciation.			

Exhibit 8-3 demonstrates a straight-line depreciation schedule that has been prepared for Apex Industries' delivery truck.

Year	Asset Cost	Yearly Depreciation	Accumulated Depreciation	Book Value
0	$43,000			$43,000
1		$7,800	$ 7,800	35,200
2		7,800	15,600	27,400
3		7,800	23,400	19,600
4		7,800	31,200	11,800
5		7,800	39,000	4,000

Exhibit 8-3 ▲

The final column shows the asset's *book value*, which is its cost less accumulated depreciation.

Notice that as an asset is depreciated, its accumulated depreciation increases and its book value decreases. Observe the Accumulated Depreciation and Book

Value columns in Exhibit 8-3. At the end of its useful life, the asset is said to be **fully depreciated**. Once an asset has been fully depreciated its final book value should equal its residual value, $4,000 in this case.

Units-of-Production (UOP) Method The **units-of-production (UOP) depreciation method** allocates a fixed amount of depreciation to each unit of output as follows:

$$\text{Units-of-production depreciation} = \frac{\text{Cost} - \text{Residual value}}{\text{Estimated useful life in units}} = \text{Depreciation per unit}$$

Assume that instead of straight-line, Apex Industries depreciates its delivery truck using units-of-production depreciation. Apex Industries might want to use UOP depreciation for the truck if it thinks miles are the best measure of the truck's depreciation. The delivery truck is estimated to be driven 35,000 miles the first year, 30,000 the second, 30,000 the third, 20,000 the fourth, and 15,000 during the fifth (for a total of 130,000 miles). The UOP depreciation each period varies with the number of units (miles, in the case of the truck) the asset produces. The depreciation per unit for Apex Industries' delivery truck is calculated as follows:

$$\frac{\text{Cost} - \text{Residual value}}{\text{Estimated useful life in units}} = \frac{\$43,000 - \$4,000}{130,000 \text{ miles}} = \$0.30 \text{ per mile}$$

Apex Industries would record $10,500 (35,000 miles × $0.30) of depreciation at December 31, of the first year as follows:

DATE	ACCOUNTS	POST REF.	DR.	CR.
Dec 31	Depreciation Expense, Vehicles		10,500	
	Accumulated Depreciation, Vehicles			10,500
	Record yearly depreciation.			

A depreciation schedule similar to the one prepared for straight-line depreciation is presented in **Exhibit 8-4** for units-of-production depreciation.

Year	Asset Cost	Number of Units		Depreciation Per Unit		Depreciation Expense	Accumulated Depreciation	Book Value
0	$43,000							$43,000
1		35,000 miles	×	$0.30	=	$10,500	$10,500	32,500
2		30,000 miles	×	$0.30	=	9,000	19,500	23,500
3		30,000 miles	×	$0.30	=	9,000	28,500	14,500
4		20,000 miles	×	$0.30	=	6,000	34,500	8,500
5		15,000 miles	×	$0.30	=	4,500	39,000	4,000

Exhibit 8-4 ▲

Notice once again that the ending book value of the delivery truck, $4,000, equals its residual value as it did with straight-line depreciation.

Double-Declining-Balance Method The **double-declining-balance (DDB)** method is known as an **accelerated depreciation method**. An accelerated depreciation method writes off more depreciation near the start of an asset's life and less at the end. Although

DDB depreciation is generally used for income tax purposes, it can be used for "book" purposes. The use of DDB by Apex Industries would be appropriate if Apex anticipates the delivery truck will be significantly more productive in its early years. The DDB method multiplies the asset's decreasing book value by a constant rate that is twice the straight-line depreciation rate. DDB amounts can be computed using the following formula:

$$\text{Double-declining-balance depreciation} = \frac{1}{\text{Estimated useful life in years}} \times 2 \times \text{Book value} = \text{Depreciation per year}$$

Note that residual value is not included in the formula. Unlike with straight-line and units-of-production, with double-declining-balance depreciation, residual value is ignored until the end of an asset's life.

For the first year of the delivery truck, the calculation would be as shown here:

$$\frac{1}{5} \times 2 = 2/5 \times \$43{,}000 = \$17{,}200$$

Exhibit 8-5 reflects a depreciation schedule for the delivery truck using double-declining-balance depreciation.

Year	Asset Cost	DDB Rate*		Book Value		Depreciation Expense	Accumulated Depreciation	Book Value
				Yearly Depreciation				
0	$43,000							$43,000
1		2/5	×	$43,000	=	$17,200	$17,200	25,800
2		2/5	×	25,800	=	10,320	27,520	15,480
3		2/5	×	15,480	=	6,192	33,712	9,288
4		2/5	×	9,288	=	3,715**	37,427	5,573
5						1,573***	39,000	4,000

*1/5 × 2 = 2/5
**rounded
***5,573 − 4,000 = 1,573

Exhibit 8-5 ▲

Under double-declining-balance, the depreciation schedule is altered in the final years to prevent the asset from being depreciated below the residual value. In the case of Apex Industries' delivery truck, the residual value was given as $4,000. In the DDB schedule in Exhibit 8-5, notice that after year 4, the truck's book value is $5,573. Depreciation expense calculated using DDB would reduce the book value below the residual value. Therefore, in the final-year, the depreciation expense is reduced to $1,573, which is the book value of $5,573 less the $4,000 residual value. If the residual value is high enough, it is possible that the second to last year's depreciation expense could be reduced and there would be no depreciation in the final year.

Some companies change to the straight-line method during the last years of an asset's life to "level-off" the yearly depreciation expense in the final years. The yearly depreciation when switching to straight-line is calculated as follows:

$$\frac{\text{Remaining book value} - \text{Residual value}}{\text{Remaining useful life}} = \text{Depreciation per year}$$

Exhibit 8-6 reflects a depreciation schedule for the delivery truck using double-declining-balance depreciation with a switch to straight-line after year 3.

Year	Asset Cost	Yearly Depreciation			Depreciation Expense	Accumulated Depreciation	Book Value
		DDB Rate*		Book Value			
0	$43,000						$43,000
1		2/5	×	$43,000 =	$17,200	$17,200	25,800
2		2/5	×	25,800 =	10,320	27,520	15,480
3		2/5	×	15,480 =	6,192	33,712	9,288
4					2,644*	36,356	6,644
5					2,644*	39,000	4,000

*(9,288 − 4,000) ÷ 2 = 2,644

Exhibit 8-6 ▲

Comparing Depreciation Methods

Let's compare the depreciation methods. Annual amounts vary, but total accumulated depreciation equals $39,000 for all three methods.

	Depreciation per Year		
Year	Straight-Line	Units-of-Production	Double-Declining-Balance
1	$ 7,800	$10,500	$17,200
2	7,800	9,000	10,320
3	7,800	9,000	6,192
4	7,800	6,000	3,715
5	7,800	4,500	1,573
Total Depreciation	$39,000	$39,000	$39,000

Which method is best? That depends on the asset. A business should match an asset's expense against the revenue that the asset produces. Following are some guidelines:

- **Straight-Line.** For an asset that generates revenue evenly over time, the straight-line method follows the matching principle. Each period shows an equal amount of depreciation. For example, the straight-line method would be good for depreciating a building.

- **Units-of-Production.** The UOP method works best for an asset whose use varies from year to year. More use causes greater depreciation. For example, UOP might be good for depreciating copy machines, vehicles, and machinery.

- **Double-Declining-Balance.** The DDB method works best for assets that produce more revenue in their early years and less in their later years. Higher depreciation in the early years is matched against the greater revenue. For example, DDB would be good for depreciating computers. DDB is also often chosen for federal income tax purposes. The increased depreciation in the early years of an asset's life lowers the income in those years and, therefore, lowers the income tax paid.

Partial Year Depreciation

In the examples for Apex Industries' delivery truck, it was assumed that the truck was purchased on January 1 and used for an entire year. However, most assets are not purchased on the first day of the year and used for the entire year. When an asset is not used for an entire year, the depreciation expense for that year must be prorated for the number of months the asset was actually used during the year. If an asset is in service for more than one half of the month, it is considered to be in service for the entire month. The formula for prorating the depreciation expense is as follows:

$$\text{Depreciation expense for the entire year} \times \frac{\text{\# of months asset was used}}{12} = \text{Prorated yearly depreciation expense}$$

Let's return to our example using Apex Industries' delivery truck. Assume that instead of purchasing the delivery truck on January 1, Apex Industries purchased the delivery truck on May 1. **Exhibits 8-7** and **8-8** reflect new depreciation schedules for Apex Industries' delivery truck using straight-line and double-declining-balance depreciation respectively.

Year	Asset Cost	Yearly Depreciation	Accumulated Depreciation	Book Value
0	$43,000			$43,000
1		$7,800 × 8/12* = $5,200	$ 5,200	37,800
2		7,800	13,000	30,000
3		7,800	20,800	22,200
4		7,800	28,600	14,400
5		7,800	36,400	6,600
6		$7,800 × 4/12** = 2,600	39,000	4,000

*Prorated for May through December
**Prorated for January through April

Exhibit 8-7 ▲

Year	Asset Cost	DDB Rate	Book Value	Depreciation Expense*	Accumulated Depreciation	Book Value
				Yearly Depreciation		
0	$43,000					$43,000
1		2/5	× $43,000	= $17,200 × 8/12** = $11,467	$11,467	31,533
2		2/5	× 31,533	= 12,613	24,080	18,920
3		2/5	× 18,920	= 7,568	31,648	11,352
4		2/5	× 11,352	= 4,541	36,189	6,811
5		2/5	× 6,811	= 2,724	38,913	4,087
6				(4,087 − 4,000) = 87	39,000	4,000

*Rounded
**Prorated for May through December

Exhibit 8-8 ▲

Notice that both schedules now reflect six years even though the delivery truck has a five-year life. Because the truck was only depreciated for eight months in the first year instead of twelve, the sixth year is added to "pick up" the final four months of depreciation. With units-of-production depreciation, there is no need to prorate the depreciation for partial years. This is because UOP is based on the quantity of units produced by an asset, regardless of how many months the asset was in service during the year.

Changing the Useful Life of a Depreciable Asset

Estimating the useful life and residual value of a plant asset can be difficult. Sometimes, as the asset is used, a business may determine that it needs to revise the useful life and/or the residual value of the asset. For example, at the end of year 3, Apex Industries may find that its delivery truck is expected to last seven years instead of five. Accounting changes like this are not uncommon because the original estimates are not based on perfect foresight. The formula used to calculate the new yearly depreciation amount if the useful life or residual value is changed looks like this:

$$\frac{(\text{Remaining book value} - \text{New residual value})}{(\text{New estimated useful life} - \text{Number of years already depreciated})} = \text{Revised annual depreciation}$$

In effect, the asset's remaining depreciable book value is spread over the asset's remaining life.

Let's return to our Apex Industries' example. If we look back at Exhibit 8-3, we see that the remaining book value for Apex Industries' delivery truck after year 3 is $19,600. Now let's suppose that in addition to revising the estimated useful life from five to seven years, the residual value is also revised from $4,000 to $3,000. Apex Industries would calculate the new yearly depreciation as follows:

$$\frac{(\$19,600 - \$3,000)}{(7 \text{ years} - 3 \text{ years})} = \frac{\$16,600}{4} = \$4,150$$

A new straight-line depreciation schedule reflecting the changes in estimates appears in **Exhibit 8-9**.

Year	Yearly Depreciation	Accumulated Depreciation	Book Value
0			$43,000
1	$7,800	$ 7,800	35,200
2	7,800	15,600	27,400
3	7,800	23,400	19,600
4	4,150	27,550	15,450
5	4,150	31,700	11,300
6	4,150	35,850	7,150
7	4,150	40,000	3,000

Exhibit 8-9 ▲

Using Fully-Depreciated Assets

As explained earlier in the chapter, a fully-depreciated asset is one that has reached the end of its *estimated* useful life. No more depreciation is recorded for the asset. If the asset is no longer useful, it is disposed. If the asset is still useful, the company may continue using it. The asset account and its accumulated depreciation remain on the books, but no additional depreciation is recorded. In short, the asset never goes below residual value.

Decision Guidelines

Decision		Guideline		Analyze
Which depreciation method is the best for my assets?		The choice of depreciation method depends upon the specific asset being depreciated as well as what the intended use of that asset is. The best method is one that most closely matches the cost of an asset against the future revenues it helps generate.		Straight-line depreciation is best for assets that will be used evenly throughout their lives and that will incur repair and maintenance cost evenly.

Units-of-production depreciation is best for assets that will be utilized on an irregular basis throughout their lives.

Double-declining-balance depreciation is best for assets that will be utilized significantly more in the early years of their lives. It is also best for assets that will require significantly more repair and maintenance expenditures in the later years of the asset's life. |

HOW ARE COSTS OF REPAIRING PLANT ASSETS RECORDED?

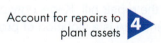

Account for repairs to plant assets

When a business has to repair an existing plant asset, the method of accounting for the expenditure is determined by the type of repair that occurred. Repairs are generally broken down into three types:

- Ordinary repairs
- Extraordinary repairs
- Betterments

Ordinary Repairs

Expenditures incurred to maintain an asset in proper working order are called **ordinary repairs**. For example, the cost of repairing the radiator, changing the oil and filter, or replacing the tires on a company vehicle would be considered to be ordinary repairs. Ordinary repairs do not extend the useful life of an asset beyond its original useful life nor do they increase the productivity of the asset. They simply keep the asset running. Ordinary repairs are recorded as an expense (usually by debiting Repairs and Maintenance Expense) in the period in which they are incurred. Ordinary repairs are also called **revenue expenditures** because the repair expense is matched against the revenues for the period.

Extraordinary Repairs

When an expenditure extends the useful life of an asset, it is called an **extraordinary repair**. Replacing the engine on a four-year-old company vehicle is an example of an extraordinary repair. This extraordinary repair would extend the vehicle's useful life past its original expected life. Extraordinary repairs are not expensed when they are incurred because they provide value beyond the current period. Instead, the expenditure is capitalized by debiting the cost of the repair to an asset account. The asset is then depreciated over its remaining useful life. For this reason, extraordinary repairs are also called **capital expenditures**.

Betterments

Expenditures that increase an asset's capacity or productivity are called **betterments**. An addition to an existing building is an example of a betterment. As with extraordinary repairs, betterments are capital expenditures that provide value that extends beyond the current period. The cost of a betterment is capitalized (debited to an asset account) and depreciated over the life of the betterment.

Treating a capital expenditure as an expense, or vice versa, creates an accounting error. Suppose Mackay Machine Works replaces the engine in a company vehicle. This would be an extraordinary repair because it increases the vehicle's life. If Mackay Machine Works expenses the cost by debiting Repair and Maintenance Expense, rather than capitalizing it (debiting an asset), Mackay Machine Works, makes an accounting error. This error would

- overstate Repair and Maintenance Expense.
- understate Net Income and therefore, Retained Earnings.
- understate Assets on the balance sheet.

Incorrectly capitalizing an expense creates the opposite error. Assume a minor repair, such as replacing the alternator on a vehicle, was incorrectly debited to an asset account. The error would result in expenses being understated and Net Income (and therefore Retained Earnings) being overstated. Furthermore, the balance sheet would overstate assets by the amount of the repair bill. Knowingly capitalizing an ordinary repair or expensing a capital expenditure is a violation of proper ethical behavior!

Decision Guidelines

Decision	Guideline	Analyze
Should I expense the cost of repairing my assets?	The matching principle dictates whether the cost of a repair should be expensed.	Ordinary repairs are repairs that simply maintain an asset in a state of operation. The cost of ordinary repairs is expensed in the period incurred because no future benefit is expected to arise from the repair.
		If a repair extends the useful life of an asset or makes it more efficient, it is known as an extraordinary repair. The cost of the repair should be capitalized and depreciated over the remaining life of the asset because it will provide future benefits.
		If an extraordinary repair is incorrectly expensed in the current period, the net income for that period will be understated and the net income for future periods will be overstated.

WHAT HAPPENS WHEN AN ASSET IS DISPOSED?

Account for the disposal of plant assets **5** ▶

In addition to acquiring and depreciating plant assets, businesses often dispose of plant assets. This may happen before, or after, the asset has reached the end of its useful life. The following are the most common ways that plant assets are disposed.

❶ The asset is discarded (thrown out).

❷ The asset is sold.

❸ The asset is exchanged for another asset. This occurs most often when an asset is used as a trade-in toward the purchase of another asset.

Regardless of the method of disposal, it is important to ensure that depreciation expense on the asset is up-to-date prior to recording the disposal. Therefore, for any asset that has not been fully depreciated, a business must record the current period's depreciation expense before recording the disposal of the asset. In many cases, the depreciation needs to be prorated because the asset is not in service for the entire year in which it is disposed. Prorating depreciation was covered earlier in the chapter in the discussion of partial-years depreciation.

Once depreciation is up-to-date, the disposal of an asset is recorded using the following steps.

Step 1 Record *"what you got."* In other words if you received any cash as part of the disposal transaction, then you would debit Cash for the amount of cash received. If you received a piece of equipment, then you would debit the Equipment account for the cost of the equipment you received.

Step 2 Record *"what you gave up."* You need to remove the asset that was disposed of from your books by debiting Accumulated Depreciation and crediting the Asset account (i.e., Office Equipment) for the respective amounts associated with the disposed of asset. Then, if you paid out any cash you would credit Cash. If you gave a note payable, you would credit Notes Payable.

Step 3 Record any gain or loss recognized on the transaction. You will recognize (debit) a loss if the value of "what you got" in the transaction is less than "what you gave up." You will recognize (credit) a gain if the value of "what you got" is more than the value of "what you gave up" in the transaction. In effect, the debit or credit needed in this part of the entry will equal the amount necessary to make the entire entry balance.

Prior to 2005, GAAP required that a business determine if an exchange of assets involved assets that were similar in their function, a **like-kind exchange**, or dissimilar in their function. Like-kind exchanges were accounted for differently than exchanges of dissimilar assets. Since 2005, the distinction of *similar versus dissimilar* has been abandoned by GAAP with regard to exchanges.[1] GAAP now requires that exchanges be evaluated to determine whether or not the exchange has "commercial substance." If an exchange lacks "commercial substance," then no gain or loss on the exchange is recognized. Due to the complex nature of how "commercial substance" is calculated, extended coverage of this topic will be deferred to more advanced accounting courses.

---

[1]For more information see FASB 153.

Let's demonstrate asset disposals by once again using the Apex Industries' delivery truck as an example. At the end of its useful life, the delivery truck is represented in the books as follows:

Truck		Accumulated Depreciation, Truck	
43,000			39,000

Consider these three situations in which Apex Industries disposes of the delivery truck. All disposals are assumed to take place after the delivery truck has been fully depreciated.

Situation A: The truck is completely worthless and is scrapped for $0.
Situation B: Apex Industries sells the truck for $5,000 cash.
Situation C: Apex Industries trades the delivery truck in on a new truck that costs $48,000. Apex is granted a trade-in allowance of $5,500 and pays for the difference in cash.

Situation A: The truck is completely worthless and is scrapped for $0. Let's apply the three steps for disposal outlined previously to demonstrate this:

Step 1 Record "what you got." In this case Apex Industries received nothing for the truck so there will be nothing to record.

Step 2 Record "what you gave up." In this case, Apex Industries gave up the old delivery truck and should remove it from the books. To remove the asset, we must zero out both the Asset and Accumulated Depreciation accounts. To do this we will need to debit the Accumulated Depreciation account for $39,000 and credit the Truck account for $43,000.

Step 3 Record any gain or loss on the transaction. This is a loss on disposal because Apex Industries received nothing for a truck that had a net book value (cost minus accumulated depreciation) of $4,000. Apex Industries will debit Loss on Disposal for $4,000.

Apex Industries will record the disposal as follows:

DATE	ACCOUNTS	POST REF.	DR.	CR.
	Accumulated Depreciation, Truck		39,000	
	Truck			43,000
	Loss on Disposal of Truck		4,000	
	Record discarding of truck.			

Notice that the debit to the loss account equals the amount needed to bring the entire entry into balance.

Situation B: Apex Industries sells the truck for $5,000 cash. The three steps for disposal outlined previously can be applied to this situation as follows:

Step 1 Record "what you got." In this case Apex Industries received $5,000 for the truck so Cash will be debited for $5,000.

Step 2 Record "what you gave up." Once again, Apex Industries gave up the old delivery truck and should remove it from the books. Accumulated

Depreciation is debited for $39,000 and the Truck account is credited for $43,000.

Step 3   Record any gain or loss on the transaction. This is a gain on sale because Apex Industries received $5,000 for a truck that had a net book value (cost-accumulated depreciation) of $4,000. Apex Industries will credit Gain on Sale for $1,000.

Apex Industries will record the disposal as follows:

DATE	ACCOUNTS	POST REF.	DR.	CR.
	Cash		5,000	
	Accumulated Depreciation, Truck		39,000	
	Truck			43,000
	Gain on Sale of Truck			1,000
	Record sale of truck.			

Observe that the credit to the gain account equals the amount needed to bring the entire entry into balance.

Situation C: Apex Industries trades the delivery truck in on a new truck that costs $48,000. Apex is granted a trade-in allowance of $5,500 and pays for the difference in cash. Here again we will apply the three-step process to record the disposal.

Step 1   Record "what you got." In this transaction, Apex Industries received a $48,000 new truck. So, Truck (new) will be debited for $48,000.

Step 2   Record "what you gave up." As in the previous situations, Apex Industries gave up the old delivery truck and should remove it from the books. Accumulated Depreciation is debited for $39,000 and the Truck (old) account is credited for $43,000. In addition to giving up the truck, Apex Industries paid cash in the amount of $42,500 so Cash is also credited for $42,500. With a trade-in, the amount of cash paid is determined by subtracting the trade-in allowance from the purchase price of the new asset. So, the $48,000 cost of the new truck less the $5,500 trade-in allowance equals the $42,500 cash paid. This same process is used to determine the amount of a note payable if a note is given instead of cash.

Step 3   Record any gain or loss on the transaction. A gain on the exchange occurs because Apex Industries received $48,000 of equipment for assets worth $46,500 (a truck that had a net book value of $4,000 plus cash of $42,500). Apex Industries will credit Gain on Exchange for $1,500.

Apex Industries will record the disposal as follows:

DATE	ACCOUNTS	POST REF.	DR.	CR.
	Truck (New)		48,000	
	Accumulated Depreciation, Truck		39,000	
	Truck (Old)			43,000
	Cash			42,500
	Gain on Exchange of Assets			1,500
	Record trade-in of old truck on a new truck.			

Once again, the gain equals the amount necessary to bring the entry into balance.

HOW DO YOU ACCOUNT FOR INTANGIBLE ASSETS?

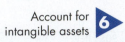

Account for intangible assets **6**

As we saw earlier, *intangible assets* have no physical form. Instead, in most cases, these assets convey special rights to their owner. Intangible assets include patents, copyrights, trademarks, and other creative works. The process of allocating the cost of an intangible asset to expense is called **amortization**. Amortization applies to intangible assets exactly as depreciation applies to plant assets and depletion to natural resources.

Amortization is computed over the intangible asset's estimated useful life—usually by the straight-line method. The residual value of most intangible assets is zero. Also, obsolescence can sometimes cause an intangible asset's useful life to be shortened from its original expected length. Amortization expense for an intangible asset is usually credited directly to the asset account instead of using an accumulated amortization account.

Specific Intangibles

Patents A **patent** is an intangible asset that is a federal government grant conveying an exclusive 20-year right to produce and sell an invention. The patent may cover a product, process, or technology. The useful life of a patent is often much less than 20 years because newer, better products and processes are invented, rendering the patent obsolete. From 1993 to 2007, IBM was granted over 38,000 US patents, more than any other US company. When an intangible asset is acquired, the acquisition cost is debited to an asset account.

Suppose Apex Industries pays $160,000 on January 1 to acquire a patent on a new manufacturing process. Apex Industries believes this patent's useful life is only five years, because it is likely a new, more efficient process will be developed within that time. Amortization expense is $32,000 per year ($160,000/5 years). The acquisition and year-end amortization entries for this patent are as follows:

DATE	ACCOUNTS	POST REF.	DR.	CR.
Jan 1	Patents		160,000	
	Cash			160,000
	Purchase patent.			
Dec 31	Amortization Expense		32,000	
	Patents			32,000
	Record yearly amortization.			

At the end of the first year, Apex Industries will report this patent at $128,000 ($160,000 minus first-year amortization of $32,000), the next year at $96,000, and so forth. Each year for five years the value of the patent will be reduced by $32,000 until the end of its five-year life, at which point its net book value will be $0.

Copyrights A **copyright** is the exclusive right to reproduce and sell a book, musical composition, film, or other work of art or intellectual property. Copyrights also protect computer software programs such as **Microsoft Vista™**. Copyrights are issued by the federal government and extend 70 years beyond the author's life, although the useful life of most copyrights is relatively short. A copyright is accounted for in the same manner as a patent.

Trademarks and Brand Names **Trademarks** and **brand names** (also known as **trade names**) convey the exclusive right to utilize a symbol, slogan, or name that represents a distinctive product or services such as **Sony's Blu-ray Disc**™ and **Intel's Centrino**®. One of the most widely recognized legally protected slogans is **Verizon Wireless**'s "Can you hear me now?" The cost of a trademark or trade name is amortized over its useful life.

Franchises and Licenses **Franchises** and **licenses** are privileges granted by a private business or a government to sell goods or services under specified conditions. The **Seattle Mariners** baseball team is a franchise granted by **Major League Baseball**. **Subway** restaurants and **Midas Muffler** centers are well-known business franchises. The acquisition cost of a franchise or license is amortized over its useful life.

Goodwill *Goodwill* in accounting has a different meaning from the everyday phrase "goodwill among men." In accounting, **goodwill** refers to the excess of the cost to purchase another company over the market value of its net assets (assets minus liabilities).

Suppose Apex Industries acquires Mackay Machine Works for $1,350,000. At the time of the purchase, the market value of Mackay Machine Works' assets is $1,750,000 and its liabilities total $500,000. In this case, Apex Industries pays $100,000 above the value of Mackay Machine Works' net assets of $1,250,000 ($1,750,000 − $500,000). The extra $100,000 is considered to be goodwill and is recorded as follows:

DATE	ACCOUNTS	POST REF.	DR.	CR.
	Assets (Cash, Accounts Receivable, Equipment, etc. recorded at market value)		1,750,000	
	Goodwill		100,000	
	Liabilities (Account Payable, Notes Payable, Accrued Liabilities, etc.)			500,000
	Cash			1,350,000
	To record purchase of Mackay Machine Works.			

Goodwill has some unique features unlike other intangible assets.

❶ Goodwill is recorded only by an acquiring company when it purchases another company. An outstanding reputation may create goodwill, but that company never records goodwill for its own business.

❷ According to Generally Accepted Accounting Principles (GAAP), goodwill is *not* amortized. Instead, the acquiring company measures the current value of its goodwill each year. If the goodwill has increased in value, there is nothing to record. But if goodwill's value has decreased, then the company records a loss and writes the goodwill down. For example, suppose Apex Industries' goodwill—which it acquired in the purchase of Mackay Machine Works—is worth only $80,000 a year after the purchase. In this case, Apex Industries would make the following entry:

DATE	ACCOUNTS	POST REF.	DR.	CR.
	Loss on Goodwill		20,000	
	Goodwill ($100,000 − $80,000)			20,000
	To record decrease in value of goodwill.			

Apex Industries would then report this goodwill at its reduced current value of $80,000.

▶ **Accounting for Research and Development Costs**

Research and development (R&D) costs are the lifeblood of companies such as **Sony**, **Johnson & Johnson**, **IBM**, and **Ford**. In general, companies don't report R&D costs as assets on their balance sheets because GAAP requires companies to expense R&D costs as they are incurred.

HOW ARE NATURAL RESOURCES ACCOUNTED FOR?

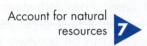

Account for natural resources **7**

Natural resources are assets that come from the earth. Examples include minerals, oil, natural gas, precious metals, coal, and timber. As stated earlier in the chapter, the process of allocating the cost of a natural resource to an expense is called **depletion**. Depletion expense is that portion of the cost of a natural resource that is used up in a particular period. Depletion expense is computed in a manner almost identical to units-of-production depreciation. The formula used to calculate the depletion per unit of nature resource is as follows:

$$\text{Depletion per unit of natural resource} = \frac{\text{Cost}}{\text{Estimated total units of natural resource}} = \text{Depletion expense per unit}$$

Notice that, unlike UOP depreciation, there is no residual value in the calculation of depletion expense. This is because when a natural resource is used up, there is nothing left to sell.

To illustrate, let's assume that Pegusus Gold owns gold reserves that cost $8,500,000. A geological study estimates that the reserves hold 20,000 ounces of gold. Pegusus Gold would calculate the depletion per ounce of gold as follows:

$$\frac{\$8,500,000}{20,000 \text{ ounces}} = \$425 \text{ per ounce}$$

If 600 ounces of gold are removed during the month, depletion is $255,000 (600 ounces × $425 per ounce) and would be recorded as follows:

DATE	ACCOUNTS	POST REF.	DR.	CR.
	Depletion Expense		255,000	
	Accumulated Depletion—Gold Reserves			255,000
	Record monthly depletion.			

Accumulated Depletion is a contra-account similar to Accumulated Depreciation. It is deducted from the cost of the natural resource to determine the net book value of the natural resource.

WHAT ARE THE OTHER TYPES OF LONG-TERM ASSETS?

Account for other long-term assets **8** ▶

Other long-term assets may consist of any assets a business owns that we have not already discussed. Two common long-term assets that a business might own are real estate (land or buildings) that are being held for resale rather than for use, and investments in marketable securities. Marketable securities are investments, such as stocks, also known as equity securities, and bonds, also called debt securities. Bonds will be discussed more in Chapter 9, but basically buying bonds is a way of loaning money to an entity. Marketable securities are classified as current assets if management intends to sell them, or they mature within a year. However, if they are often not intended to be sold, or they do not mature within a year, they are shown as other long-term assets.

A company investing in marketable securities earns income when it receives dividends on stock or interest on bonds that it holds. Also, changes in the value of a security can impact a company's income in two ways:

- Realized gains and losses occur when a security is sold for an amount different from its cost.

- Unrealized gains and losses occur when a security's market value changes while the company still owns it. These are considered "unreal" because the company won't actually gain or lose money until it sells the investment.

Accounting for marketable securities depends on the type of investment and on management's intention for the investment. Marketable securities are classified as trading securities, held-to-maturity securities, or available-for-sale securities.

- Trading securities include equity or debt securities that are actively managed in order to maximize profit as a result of short-term changes in price. These are shown as current assets on the balance sheet at their market value as of the balance sheet date. Any increase or decrease in price during the period is shown as an unrealized gain or loss on the income statement. Any interest or dividends earned during the period are also reported as income on the income statement.

- Held-to-maturity securities are debt securities that a company intends and is able to hold until they mature. These are valued at their cost on the balance sheet as either current or long-term assets based on their maturity date. Any interest income earned on these securities is reported on the income statement.

- Available-for-sale securities include equity or debt securities that cannot be classified as trading or held-to-maturity securities. These are valued at their current market value on the balance sheet date. Any interest or dividends earned during the period is included in net income on the income statement. However, increases or decreases in value during the period are not reported as part of net income on the income statement. Instead, they are shown as separate changes in stockholders' equity for the period.

HOW ARE LONG-TERM ASSETS REPORTED ON THE BALANCE SHEET?

In Chapter 4, we learned that current assets appear first on a classified balance sheet. Following the current assets, a business will report its long-term assets. Fixed assets are usually the first long-term asset reported and are often shown as "Property, Plant, and Equipment." Property, Plant, and Equipment includes the original cost, accumulated depreciation, and book value of assets such as land, buildings, and equipment. Natural resources are typically shown after the fixed assets and include the original cost, accumulated depletion, and book value of any natural resources the business owns. A business may choose to show only the net book value of fixed assets and natural resources on the balance sheet. In this case, the business will disclose the costs and accumulated depreciation or depletion for each asset group in the financial statement footnotes.

> Report long-term assets on the balance sheet **9**

When a business has intangible assets, the balance sheet will typically show the amount after the fixed assets and the natural resources. The footnotes to the financial statements will include a description of the intangible asset and its estimated useful life. Other long-term assets are typically shown last in the long-term assets section of a balance sheet. **Exhibit 8-10** illustrates a typical long-term assets section of a balance sheet:

Total Current Assets		$ 165,000
Property, Plant, and Equipment:		
Land	$ 175,000	
Buildings	680,000	
Equipment	240,000	
	1,095,000	
Less: Accumulated Depreciation	385,000	
Net Property, Plant, and Equipment		710,000
Gold Reserves, Net of Accumulated Depletion of $260,000		620,000
Patents		80,000
Other Long-Term Assets		145,000
Total Assets		$1,720,000

Exhibit 8-10 ▲

Demo Doc

Depreciation and Disposal of Depreciable Assets

Learning Objectives 3 & 5 ▶

Jensen, Inc., purchased a color laser printer for $100,000 on January 1, 2010. The printer was expected to last for six years and to print 180,000 pages during that time. The printer has a residual value of $10,000.

    Jensen, Inc., printed 50,000 pages in 2010, 20,000 in 2011, and 40,000 in 2012.

Requirements:

❶ Prepare a depreciation table showing depreciation calculations for the years 2010, 2011, and 2012 under the following depreciation methods: (a) straight-line, (b) units-of-production, and (c) double-declining-balance.

❷ On May 1, 2013, Jensen, Inc., sold the printer for $60,000 cash. Assume that Jensen, Inc., was using the straight-line method of depreciation. Journalize all transactions on this date.

Demo Doc Solutions
Requirement ❶

Prepare a depreciation table showing depreciation calculations for the years 2010, 2011, and 2012 under the following depreciation methods: (a) straight-line, (b) units-of-production, and (c) double-declining-balance.

Part 1	Part 2	Demo Doc Complete

Straight-Line

Refer to the straight-line depreciation table as shown in Exhibit 8-3. On the printer's purchase date (January 1, 2010), the printer's cost of $100,000 must be input. Because no depreciation has been taken yet, the book value is the same as the original cost.

Date	Asset Cost	Yearly Depreciation	Accumulated Depreciation	Book Value
Jan 1, 2010	$100,000			$100,000
Dec 31, 2010				
Dec 31, 2011				
Dec 31, 2012				

Remember that,

$$\text{Straight-line depreciation} = \frac{\text{Cost} - \text{Residual value}}{\text{Estimated useful life in years}} = \frac{\$100,000 - \$10,000}{6} = \$15,000 \text{ per year}$$

So for each year, the depreciation expense will be $15,000:

Date	Asset Cost	Yearly Depreciation	Accumulated Depreciation	Book Value
Jan 1, 2010	$100,000			$100,000
Dec 31, 2010		$15,000		
Dec 31, 2011		15,000		
Dec 31, 2012		15,000		

Accumulated depreciation is all of the depreciation expense that has *ever* been taken. So, to calculate accumulated depreciation, we take the previous year's accumulated depreciation and add on the current year's depreciation expense.

The first year of the printer's life is 2010 so in that year no prior depreciation has accumulated. Therefore, accumulated depreciation at December 31, 2010, is the same as the depreciation expense for 2010: $15,000.

For 2011, the accumulated depreciation is the December 31, 2010, accumulated depreciation plus the 2011 depreciation expense. So accumulated depreciation at December 31, 2011, is as follows:

$$\$15,000 + \$15,000 = \$30,000$$

For 2012, the accumulated depreciation is the December 31, 2011, accumulated depreciation plus the 2012 depreciation expense. So accumulated depreciation at December 31, 2012, is as follows:

$$\$30,000 + \$15,000 = \$45,000$$

Date	Asset Cost	Yearly Depreciation	Accumulated Depreciation	Book Value
Jan 1, 2010	$100,000			$100,000
Dec 31, 2010		$15,000	$15,000	
Dec 31, 2011		15,000	30,000	
Dec 31, 2012		15,000	45,000	

The book value of the printer is its cost minus its accumulated depreciation. So to calculate the book value for each year, subtract the accumulated depreciation from the total cost of $100,000.

Book Value at December 31, 2010 = $85,000 ($100,000 – $15,000)
Book Value at December 31, 2011 = $70,000 ($100,000 – $30,000)
Book Value at December 31, 2012 = $55,000 ($100,000 – $45,000)

Date	Asset Cost	Yearly Depreciation	Accumulated Depreciation	Book Value
Jan 1, 2010	$100,000			$100,000
Dec 31, 2010		$15,000	$15,000	85,000
Dec 31, 2011		15,000	30,000	70,000
Dec 31, 2012		15,000	45,000	55,000

Units-of-Production

Refer to the units-of-production depreciation table as shown in Exhibit 8-4. As with straight-line, the cost and starting book value of the printer are both $100,000.

Date	Asset Cost	Yearly Depreciation			Accumulated Depreciation	Book Value
		Number of Units	Depreciation Per Unit	Depreciation Expense		
Jan 1, 2010	$100,000					$100,000
Dec 31, 2010						
Dec 31, 2011						
Dec 31, 2012						

Remember that,

$$\text{Units of production depreciation per unit} = \frac{\text{Cost} - \text{Residual value}}{\text{Estimated useful life in units}} = \frac{\$100,000 - \$10,000}{180,000 \text{ pages}} = \$0.50 \text{ per page}$$

Each year, the depreciation expense is calculated as the depreciation cost per page multiplied by the number of pages printed.

2010 Depreciation Expense = $0.50 Depreciation expense per page × 50,000 Pages printed
= $25,000

2011 Depreciation Expense = $0.50 Depreciation expense per page × 20,000 Pages printed
= $10,000

2012 Depreciation Expense = $0.50 Depreciation expense per page × 40,000 Pages printed
= $20,000

Date	Asset Cost	Yearly Depreciation				Accumulated Depreciation	Book Value
		Number of Units		Depreciation Per Unit	Depreciation Expense		
Jan 1, 2010	$100,000						$100,000
Dec 31, 2010		50,000	×	$0.50	= $25,000		
Dec 31, 2011		20,000	×	$0.50	= $10,000		
Dec 31, 2012		40,000	×	$0.50	= $20,000		

Accumulated depreciation and book value are calculated in the same manner as was used for straight-line.

Accumulated Depreciation at December 31, 2010 = $0 + $25,000 = $25,000
Book Value at December 31, 2010 = $100,000 − $25,000 = $75,000

Accumulated Depreciation at December 31, 2011 = $25,000 + $10,000 = $35,000
Book Value at December 31, 2011 = $100,000 − $35,000 = $65,000

Accumulated Depreciation at December 31, 2012 = $35,000 + $20,000 = $55,000
Book Value at December 31, 2012 = $100,000 − $55,000 = $45,000

The completed table would look as follows:

Date	Asset Cost	Yearly Depreciation				Accumulated Depreciation	Book Value
		Number of Units		Depreciation Per Unit	Depreciation Expense		
Jan 1, 2010	$100,000						$100,000
Dec 31, 2010		50,000	×	$0.50	= $25,000	$25,000	75,000
Dec 31, 2011		20,000	×	$0.50	= $10,000	35,000	65,000
Dec 31, 2012		40,000	×	$0.50	= $20,000	55,000	45,000

Double-Declining-Balance

Refer to the double-declining-balance (DDB) depreciation table as shown in Exhibit 8-5. As with straight-line and units-of-production, the cost and starting book value of the printer are both $100,000.

Date	Asset Cost	Yearly Depreciation				Book Value
		DDB Rate*	Book Value	Depreciation Expense	Accumulated Depreciation	
Jan 1, 2010	$100,000					$100,000
Dec 31, 2010						
Dec 31, 2011						
Dec 31, 2012						

The DDB depreciation rate is calculated as follows:

$$\text{Double-declining-balance depreciation} = \frac{1}{\text{Estimated useful life in years}} \times 2 = 1/6 \times 2 = 2/6 \text{ or } 1/3$$

Each year, the depreciation rate is multiplied by the book value of the printer *at the beginning of the year*. So for 2010, the depreciation expense is as follows:

$$\$100,000 \times 1/3 = \$33,333$$

Accumulated depreciation and book value at the end of the year are calculated as under straight-line and units-of-production.

$$\text{Accumulated Depreciation at December 31, 2010} = \$0 + \$33,333 = \$33,333$$
$$\text{Book Value at December 31, 2010} = \$100,000 - \$33,333 = \$66,667$$

Date	Asset Cost	Yearly Depreciation				Book Value
		DDB Rate*	Book Value	Depreciation Expense*	Accumulated Depreciation	
Jan 1, 2010	$100,000					$100,000
Dec 31, 2010		1/3 ×	$100,000 =	$33,333	$33,333	66,667
Dec 31, 2011						
Dec 31, 2012						

*Rounded

Depreciation expense for 2011 is the book value of the printer *at the beginning* of 2011 multiplied by the depreciation rate. So for 2011, the depreciation expense is as follows:

$$\$66,667 \times 1/3 = \$22,222$$

$$\text{Accumulated Depreciation at December 31, 2011} = \$33,333 + \$22,222 = \$55,555$$
$$\text{Book Value at December 31, 2011} = \$100,000 - \$55,555 = \$44,445$$

Date	Asset Cost	Yearly Depreciation			Depreciation Expense*	Accumulated Depreciation	Book Value
		DDB Rate*		Book Value			
Jan 1, 2010	$100,000						$100,000
Dec 31, 2010		1/3	×	$100,000 =	$33,333	$33,333	66,667
Dec 31, 2011		1/3	×	66,667 =	22,222	$55,555	44,445
Dec 31, 2012							

*Rounded

Depreciation expense for 2012 is the book value of the printer *at the beginning* of 2012 multiplied by the depreciation rate. So for 2012, the depreciation expense is as follows:

$$\$44,445 \times 1/3 = \$14,815$$

$$\text{Accumulated Depreciation at December 31, 2012} = \$55,555 + \$14,815 = \$70,370$$
$$\text{Book Value at December 31, 2012} = \$100,000 - \$70,370 = \$29,630$$

The completed table would look like this:

Date	Asset Cost	Yearly Depreciation			Depreciation Expense*	Accumulated Depreciation	Book Value
		DDB Rate*		Book Value			
Jan 1, 2010	$100,000						$100,000
Dec 31, 2010		1/3	×	$100,000 =	$33,333	$33,333	66,667
Dec 31, 2011		1/3	×	66,667 =	22,222	$55,555	44,445
Dec 31, 2012		1/3	×	44,445 =	14,815	$70,370	29,630

*Rounded

Requirement ❷

On May 1, 2013, Jensen, Inc., sold the printer for $60,000 cash. Assume that Jensen, Inc., was using the straight-line method of depreciation. Journalize all transactions on this date.

Part 1	**Part 2**	Demo Doc Complete

Before Jensen, Inc., can record the disposal of the printer, it must update the depreciation on the printer. Depreciation represents use of an asset and because the asset was used for four months of 2013 (January, February, March, and April), four months of depreciation expense must be recorded.

From Requirement 1, we know that the annual depreciation expense on the printer under the straight-line method is $15,000 per year (12 months). To adjust for only four months we must multiply by the fraction of 4/12.

Depreciation Expense for 2013 is as follows:

$$\$15,000 \times 4/12 = \$5,000$$

This depreciation expense must now be recorded in a journal entry. Depreciation Expense is increased (debit) by $5,000, and Accumulated Depreciation is increased (credit) by $5,000.

DATE	ACCOUNTS	POST REF.	DR.	CR.
May 1	Depreciation Expense, Printer		5,000	
	Accumulated Depreciation, Printer			5,000
	To record four months' depreciation on printer.			

Now that this journal entry is made, we can calculate the balance in Accumulated Depreciation immediately before the disposal.

The transactions that have affected the Accumulated Depreciation account are the depreciation expense recorded in each year (2010, 2011, 2012, and 2013). We can add the 2013 depreciation expense to the Accumulated Depreciation balance from the prior year (2012).

Printer			Accumulated Depreciation, Printer		
Bal	100,000			Dec 31, 2012 Bal	45,000
				May 1, 2013	5,000
				May 1, 2013 Bal	50,000

Now we are ready to journalize the disposal of the printer.

Jensen, Inc., is receiving cash, so Cash increases (debit) by the $60,000 of cash received.

The printer is being sold, so the Printer asset will be decreased (credit) by its original cost of $100,000 (the amount in the printer T-account).

If the printer is sold, it no longer makes sense to have the accumulated depreciation on the printer. This account must be removed as well. Remember that Accumulated Depreciation is a contra-account, and so it goes wherever its associated asset goes. If we remove the printer from the accounting records, then the accumulated depreciation on that printer goes with it and is removed as well. We will, therefore, decrease Accumulated Depreciation (debit) by its balance of $50,000.

So far for the journal entry we have the following:

DATE	ACCOUNTS	POST REF.	DR.	CR.
May 1	Cash		60,000	
	Accumulated Depreciation, Printer		50,000	
	Printer			100,000

To complete the journal entry, we need to record the gain or loss on the sale of the printer. Remember that the amount of gain or loss can be calculated by comparing "what you got" to "what you gave up." In this case, Jensen got $60,000 for a printer with a book value of $50,000 ($100,000 − $50,000) so it had a $10,000 ($60,000 − $50,000) gain. The amount of the gain or loss can also equal the amount required to balance the journal entry. So far, the total debits in this entry are $110,000 ($60,000 + $50,000), and the total credits are $100,000. So a credit of $10,000 ($110,000 − $100,000) is needed to balance the entry.

Because the balancing amount is a credit, it is *similar* to revenue in that it will increase net income (be a positive number on the income statement). Therefore, it is a gain, so we will credit Gain on Sale of Printer for $10,000.

DATE	ACCOUNTS	POST REF.	DR.	CR.
May 1	Cash		60,000	
	Accumulated Depreciation, Printer		50,000	
	Printer			100,000
	Gain on Sale of Printer			10,000
	Record sale of printer.			

Demo Doc Complete

Part 1	Part 2	**Demo Doc Complete**

Decision Guidelines

Long-Term Assets

If your company has long-term assets, you will likely encounter one or more of the following decisions with regard to those assets:

Decision		Guideline		Analyze
How do I determine the cost of an asset?		The matching principle dictates that all costs associated with acquiring and asset, and preparing it for its intended use, should be considered as part of the cost of the asset.		It is tempting to treat costs related to the purchase of an asset (delivery fees, taxes, set up costs, etc.) as current period expenses. However, if these costs are expensed in the current period, they are not properly matched against the future revenues that the asset will generate. This causes the current period's net income to be understated and future period's net income to be overstated.
Which depreciation method is the best for my assets?		The choice of depreciation method depends upon the specific asset being depreciated as well as what the intended use of that asset is. The best method is one that most closely matches the cost of an asset against the future revenues it helps generate.		Straight-line depreciation is best for assets that will be used evenly throughout their lives and that will incur repair and maintenance cost evenly. Units-of-production depreciation is best for assets that will be utilized on an irregular basis throughout their lives. Double-declining-balance depreciation is best for assets that will be utilized significantly more in the early years of their lives. It is also best for assets that will require significantly more repair and maintenance expenditures in the later years of the asset's life.
Should I expense the cost of repairing my assets?		The matching principle dictates whether the cost of a repair should be expensed.		Ordinary repairs are repairs that simply maintain an asset in a state of operation. The cost of ordinary repairs is expensed in the period incurred because no future benefit is expected to arise from the repair. If a repair extends the useful life of an asset or makes it more efficient, it is known as an extraordinary repair. The cost of the repair should be capitalized and depreciated over the remaining life of the asset because it will provide future benefits. If an extraordinary repair is incorrectly expensed in the current period, the net income for that period will be understated and the net income for future periods will be overstated.

ACCOUNTING VOCABULARY

THE LANGUAGE OF BUSINESS

Accelerated depreciation method (p. 396) A depreciation method that writes off more of the asset's cost near the start of its useful life than the straight-line method does.

Amortization (p. 406) Systematic reduction of an intangibles asset's carrying value on the books. An expense that applies to intangibles in the same way depreciation applies to plant assets and depletion to natural resources.

Basket purchase (p. 391) Purchase of multiple assets for one price; also called a *lump-sum purchase*.

Betterment (p. 402) Expenditure that increases the capacity or efficiency of an asset.

Brand names (p. 407) Assets that represent distinctive identifications of a product or service; also called *trade names*.

Capital expenditure (p. 402) Expenditure that increases the capacity or efficiency of an asset or extends its useful life. Capital expenditures are debited to an asset account.

Capitalized (p. 390) The process of debiting (increasing) an asset account for the cost of an asset.

Copyright (p. 406) Exclusive right to reproduce and sell a book, musical composition, film, other work of art, or computer program. Issued by the federal government, copyrights extend 70 years beyond the author's life.

Depletion (p. 408) Systematic reduction of a natural resource's carrying value on the books. Expense that applies to natural resource in the same way depreciation applies to plant assets and amortization to intangible assets. It is computed in the same way as units-of-production depreciation.

Depreciable cost (p. 394) The cost of a plant asset minus its estimated residual value.

Double-declining-balance (DDB) method (p. 396) An accelerated depreciation method that computes annual depreciation by multiplying the asset's decreasing book value by a constant percent that is two times the straight-line rate.

Extraordinary repair (p. 402) Repair work that extends the life of an asset.

Fixed assets (p. 388) Tangible assets such as buildings and equipment; also called *plant assets*.

Franchises (p. 407) Privileges granted by a private business or a government to sell a product or service under specified conditions.

Fully-depreciated asset (p. 396) An asset that has reached the end of its estimated useful life. No more depreciation is recorded for the asset.

Goodwill (p. 407) Excess of the cost of an acquired company over the sum of the market values of its net assets (assets minus liabilities).

Intangible assets (p. 388) Assets with no physical form. They are valuable because of the special rights they carry. Examples included patents and copyrights.

Land improvements (p. 389) Depreciable improvements to land, such as fencing, sprinklers, paving, signs, and lighting.

Licenses (p. 407) Privileges granted by a private business or a government to sell a product or service under specified conditions.

Like-kind exchange (p. 403) Exchanging one asset for another asset that has similar functionality.

Lump-sum purchase (p. 391) Purchase of multiple assets for one price; also called a *basket purchase*.

Natural resources (p. 388) Assets that come from the earth. Examples include minerals, gas, oil, and timber.

Ordinary repair (p. 401) Repair work that is necessary to maintain an asset in normal operating condition.

Patent (p. 406) An intangible asset that is a federal government grant conveying an exclusive 20-year right to produce and sell a process or formula.

Plant assets (p. 388) Tangible assets such as buildings and equipment; also called *fixed assets*.

Residual value (p. 394) Expected cash value of an asset at the end of its useful life; also called *salvage value*.

Revenue expenditure (p. 401) Expenditure that is debited to an expense account.

Salvage value (p. 394) Expected cash value of an asset at the end of its useful life; also called *residual value*.

Straight-line (SL) depreciation method (p. 395) Depreciation method in which an equal amount of depreciation expense is assigned to each year of asset use.

Tangible assets (p. 388) Assets that are physical in form. They can be seen, touched, or held.

Trade names (p. 407) Assets that represent distinctive identifications of a product or service; also called *brand names*.

Trademarks (p. 407) Assets that represent distinctive identifications of a product or service.

Units-of-production (UOP) depreciation method (p. 396) Depreciation method by which a fixed amount of depreciation is assigned to each unit of output produced by an asset.

Useful life (p. 394) The expected life of an asset during which it is anticipated to generate revenues. May be expressed in years or units of output.

ACCOUNTING PRACTICE

DISCUSSION QUESTIONS

1. When a company makes an expenditure, it can either capitalize or expense the cost, depending on the nature of the expenditure. What does it mean to capitalize an expenditure? What determines whether an expenditure can be capitalized?

2. If a company were to purchase a piece of land with a building on it that it demolishes to make room for its new building, in which account would the cost of demolition be recorded (land, building, demolition expense, or something else)? Why?

3. What is a lump-sum purchase of assets? How does a company determine how much to allocate to each asset purchased in a lump-sum purchase?

4. What is depreciation and why is it used in accounting?

5. Are useful life and physical life the same thing relative to plant assets? Provide some examples that illustrate your answer.

6. Which depreciation method would be most appropriate for each of the following assets?

    a. This machine is used as a backup to the other machines in the production process. As a result there are some years where it sees a lot of action and others where it is seldom used. It is not a high-tech machine. It will not become obsolete in the foreseeable future.

    b. Typically this machine will work very effectively and with few repairs for the first three years, but will be down for maintenance quite a bit during its final four years of use.

    c. This machine is expected to run constantly over the entire period it is used. It requires regular maintenance over its lifetime in order to maintain its expected steady level of production.

7. What makes a repair "extraordinary" (as opposed to ordinary)? Give an example of an extraordinary and an ordinary repair. What is the financial statement effect of recording a repair as an extraordinary repair instead of an ordinary repair?

8. What is the book value of an asset? How is gain or loss on disposal of assets calculated?

9. If a machine that cost $10,000 was estimated to have a salvage value of zero after a useful life of 10 years and was sold for $4,500 after it had been owned for 6 complete years, what would be the amount of gain or loss recognized on the sale?

10. Complete the following analogies. What are some similarities and differences between the two concepts involved in each?

    a. Depreciation is to plant assets as _____ is to intangible assets.

    b. Depreciation is to plant assets as _____ is to natural resources.

SELF CHECK

1. Which cost is *not* recorded as part of the cost of a building?

    a. Construction materials, labor, and overhead
    b. Annual building maintenance
    c. Real estate commission paid to buy the building
    d. Earthmoving for the building's foundation

2. Orbit Airways bought two used Boeing 707 airplanes. Each plane was worth $35 million, but Orbit bought the combination for $60 million. How much is Orbit Airways' cost of each plane?

    a. $30 million
    c. $60 million

    b. $35 million
    d. $70 million

3. How should a capital expenditure be recorded?

    a. Debit capital
    c. Debit a liability

    b. Debit an expense
    d. Debit an asset

4. Which depreciation method usually produces the most depreciation in the first year?

 a. Straight-line
 b. Units-of-production
 c. Double-declining-balance
 d. All produce the same amount of depreciation for the first year.

5. A FedEx airplane costs $50 million and is expected to fly 500 million miles during its 10-year life. Residual value is expected to be zero because the plane was used when acquired. If the plane travels 20 million miles the first year, how much depreciation should FedEx record under the units-of-production method?

 a. $2 million
 b. $5 million
 c. $10 million
 d. Cannot be determined from the data given

6. Which depreciation method is generally preferable for income tax purposes? Why?

 a. Straight-line, because it is simplest
 b. Units-of-production, because it best tracks the asset's use
 c. Double-declining-balance, because it gives the most total depreciation over the asset's life
 d. Double-declining-balance, because it gives higher depreciation deductions in earlier years

7. A copy machine cost $40,000 when new and has accumulated depreciation of $37,000. Suppose Copies R Us junks this machine, receiving nothing in return. What is the result of the disposal transaction?

 a. Gain of $3,000
 b. Loss of $3,000
 c. Gain of $37,000
 d. Loss of $40,000

8. Using information from the preceding question, suppose Copies R Us sold the machine for $5,000. What is the result of this disposal transaction?

 a. Gain of $2,000
 b. Loss of $2,000
 c. Gain of $3,000
 d. Gain of $5,000

9. Depletion is calculated in a manner similar to which depreciation method?

 a. Accelerated method
 b. Straight-line method
 c. Units-of-production method
 d. Double-declining-balance method

10. Which intangible asset is recorded only as part of the acquisition of another company?

 a. Copyright
 b. Patent
 c. Franchise
 d. Goodwill

Answers are given after Written Communication.

SHORT EXERCISES

S8-1. Long-term asset terms (*Learning Objective 1*) 5–10 min.

Identify each of the following assets as a plant asset (P) or an intangible asset (I):

 ____ 1. Franchises
 ____ 2. Vehicles
 ____ 3. Buildings
 ____ 4. Furniture
 ____ 5. Patents
 ____ 6. Copyrights
 ____ 7. Trademarks
 ____ 8. Land improvements

S8-2. Long-term asset terms (*Learning Objective 1*) 5–10 min.

For each of the following long-term assets, identify the type of expense that will be incurred to allocate the asset's cost as depreciation expense (DR), depletion expense (DL), amortization expense (A), or none of these (NA).

_____ 1. Franchises

_____ 2. Land

_____ 3. Buildings

_____ 4. Furniture

_____ 5. Patents

_____ 6. Copyrights

_____ 7. Trademarks

_____ 8. Land improvements

_____ 9. Gold ore deposits

S8-3. Land or Land Improvements (*Learning Objective 2*) 5–10 min.

Identify each of the following as land (L) or land improvements (LI):

_____ 1. Survey fees

_____ 2. Fencing

_____ 3. Lighting

_____ 4. Clearing land

_____ 5. Parking lot

S8-4. Lump-sum purchase (*Learning Objective 2*) 5–10 min.

Johnson purchased land having a current market value of $80,000, a building with a market value of $64,000, and equipment with a market value of $16,000. Journalize the lump-sum purchase of the three assets purchased for a total cost of $120,000 in exchange for a note payable.

S8-5. Errors in accounting for long-term assets (*Learning Objective 2*) 5–10 min.

Orbit Airways repaired one of its Boeing 767 aircraft at a cost of $600,000, which Orbit Airways paid in cash. Orbit Airways erroneously capitalized this cost as part of the cost of the plane.

Journalize both the incorrect entry the accountant made to record this transaction and the correct entry that the accountant should have made. How will this accounting error affect Orbit Airways' net income? Ignore depreciation.

S8-6. Concept of depreciation (*Learning Objective 3*) 10–15 min.

Jessica Brooks just slept through the class in which Professor Dominguez explained the concept of depreciation. Because the next test is scheduled for Wednesday, Jessica Brooks telephones Hanna Svensen to get her notes from the lecture. Hanna Svensen's notes are concise: "Depreciation—Sounds like Greek to me." Jessica Brooks next tries Tim Lake, who says he thinks depreciation is what happens when an asset wears out. David Coe is confident that depreciation is the process of building up a cash fund to replace an asset at the end of its useful life. Explain the concept of depreciation for Jessica Brooks. Evaluate the explanations of Tim Lake and David Coe. Be specific.

S8-7. Depreciation methods (*Learning Objective 3*) 10–15 min.

At the beginning of the year, Orbit Airways purchased a used Boeing aircraft at a cost of $45 million. Orbit Airways expects the plane to remain useful for five years (3 million miles) and to have a residual value of $5 million. Orbit Airways expects the plane to be flown 750,000 miles the first year and 1.5 million miles the second year.

Compute Orbit Airways' first-year depreciation on the plane using the following methods:

a. Straight-line

b. Units-of-production

c. Double-declining-balance

Show the airplane's book value at the end of the first year under the straight-line method.

S8-8. Depreciation methods (Learning Objective 3) 10–15 min.

Refer to the data for S8-7. Compute second-year depreciation on the plane using the following methods:

a. Straight-line

b. Units-of-production

c. Double-declining-balance

S8-9. Straight-line depreciation method (Learning Objective 3) 5–10 min.

On March 31, 2010, Orbit Airways purchased a used Boeing aircraft at a cost of $45 million. Orbit Airways expects to fly the plane for five years and to have a residual value of $5 million. Compute Orbit Airways' depreciation on the plane for the year ended December 31, 2010, using the straight-line method.

S8-10. Straight-line depreciation method (Learning Objective 3) 5–10 min.

Big Boy's Hot Dogs purchased a hotdog stand for $40,000 with an estimated useful life of eight years, and no residual value. Suppose that after using the hotdog stand for four years, the company determines that the asset will remain useful for only two more years. Record Big Boy's Hot Dogs' depreciation on the hotdog stand for year 5 by the straight-line method.

S8-11. Capitalized versus expensed costs for long-term assets (Learning Objectives 2 & 4) 10–15 min.

Classify each of the following expenditures as a capital expenditure (CAP) or a revenue expenditure (REV):

a. Purchase price

b. Ordinary recurring repairs to keep the machinery in good working order

c. Lubrication of the machinery before it is placed in service

d. Periodic lubrication after the machinery is placed in service

e. Major overhaul to extend useful life by three years

f. Sales tax paid on the purchase price

g. Transportation and insurance while machinery is in transit from seller to buyer

h. Installation

i. Training of personnel for initial operation of the machinery

---

S8-12. Disposition of long-term assets (Learning Objective 5) 5–10 min.

Orbit Airways purchased a baggage-handling truck for $41,000. Suppose Orbit Airways sold the truck on December 31, 2010, for $28,000 cash, after using the truck for two full years and accumulating depreciation of $16,000. Make the journal entry to record Orbit Airways' sale of the truck.

S8-13. Goodwill (Learning Objective 6) 15–20 min.

When one media company buys another, goodwill is often the most costly asset acquired. World Media paid $700,000 to acquire the *Dandy Dime*, a weekly advertising paper. At the time of the acquisition, the *Dandy Dime's* balance sheet reported total assets of $1,200,000 and liabilities of $600,000. The fair market value of the *Dandy Dime's* assets was $800,000.

How much goodwill did World Media purchase as part of the acquisition of the *Dandy Dime?* Journalize World Media's acquisition of the *Dandy Dime*.

S8-14. Amortization *(Learning Objective 6)* 5–10 min.

On April 1, Keystone Applications paid $500,000 to acquire a patent on software. Keystone Application expects the patent to have a useful life of five years.

Journalize the entry to record the purchase of the patent on April 1. Journalize the entry to record amortization on December 31.

S8-15. Depletion *(Learning Objective 7)* 5–10 min.

Kent Oil, a small Texas oil company, holds huge reserves of oil and gas assets. Assume that at the end of 2010, Kent Oil's cost of mineral assets totaled approximately $18 million, representing 2.4 million barrels of oil and gas reserves in the ground.

Calculate Kent Oil's depletion expense per barrel of oil. Suppose Kent Oil removed 0.8 million barrels of oil during 2011 and sold all of these barrels during the year. Record Kent Oil's depletion expense for 2011.

S8-16. Other long-term assets *(Learning Objective 8)* 5–10 min.

Classify each of the following as:

Trading security (T)

Available-for-sale security (A)

Held-to-maturity security (H)

None of the above (N)

_____ 1. A bond that management plans on owning until it is repaid. Management does not believe it will need to sell the bond to generate cash before the bond's scheduled maturity date.

_____ 2. Land that management is holding as an investment.

_____ 3. Intel stock that company management plans on selling quickly, as soon as its price is 10% more than what the company paid at the time it purchased the stock.

_____ 4. Ford Motor Company stock. Management does not actively manage this stock and intends to sell it only if they need to generate cash.

_____ 5. A bond that management plans on owning until it is repaid. However, management believes it may have to sell the bond within the year in order to provide enough cash for operations.

_____ 6. Inventory that management intends to sell within the year.

S8-17. Other long-term assets *(Learning Objective 8)* 5–10 min.

Specify how each of the following items would be reported in the financial statements of Tanaka Enterprises for its current fiscal year. Also specify the amount that would appear on the statement. Some items may be reported on more than one financial statement. In these cases, specify the amount that would appear on each statement.

Income Statement (IS)

Balance Sheet (BS)

Change in Stockholders' Equity (SE)

1. Tanaka Enterprises received $55 of dividends during the year on stock it owned in Jasper, Inc.

2. At year-end, Tanaka Enterprises owned a $1,000 U.S. Treasury Bond.

3. Tanaka Enterprises sold stock for $110 cash that had been held as an available-for-sale security. The stock had been purchased for $90 and hadn't changed in value until the time of its sale.

4. Stock that Tanaka Enterprises purchased for $90 during the year as an available-for-sale security has a market value of $110 at the year-end balance sheet date.

5. Stock that Tanaka Enterprises purchased for $90 during the year as a trading security had a market value of $110 at the year-end balance sheet date.

6. $75 of interest earned on a bond that Tanaka Enterprises purchased from the State of Washington.

EXERCISES (GROUP A)

E8-18A. Capitalized costs for long-term assets *(Learning Objective 2)* 10–15 min.

Bozeman Systems purchased land, paying $80,000 cash as a down payment and signing a $120,000 note payable for the balance. In addition, Bozeman Systems paid delinquent property tax of $2,100, title insurance costing $2,500, and a $10,400 charge for leveling the land and removing an unwanted building. The company constructed an office building on the land at a cost of $800,000. It also paid $51,000 for a fence around the property, $15,000 for the company sign near the entrance, and $6,000 for special lighting of the grounds.

Quick solution:
Land = $215,000; Land Improvements = $72,000; Building = $800,000

Requirements

1. Determine the cost of the company's land, land improvements, and building.
2. Which of the assets will Bozeman depreciate?

E8-19A. Capitalized costs for long-term assets *(Learning Objective 2)* 10–15 min.

Lynch Brothers manufactures conveyor belts. Early in January 2011, Lynch Brothers constructed its own building at a materials, labor, and overhead cost of $900,000. Lynch Brothers also paid for architect fees and building permits of $72,000.

Requirements

1. How much should Lynch Brothers record as the cost of the building in 2011?
2. Record Lynch Brothers' transactions related to the construction of the building.

E8-20A. Capitalized costs for long-term assets *(Learning Objective 2)* 10–15 min.

Tonya's Tanning Salon bought three tanning beds in a $10,000 lump-sum purchase. An independent appraiser valued the tanning beds as follows:

Tanning Bed	Appraised Value
1	$3,000
2	5,000
3	4,000

Tonya's Tanning Salon paid $5,000 in cash and signed a note payable for $5,000. Record the purchase in the journal, identifying each tanning bed's cost by number in a separate Tanning Bed account. Round decimals to three places.

E8-21A. Errors in accounting for long-term assets *(Learning Objective 2)* 15–20 min.

Assume that early in year 1, Mariposa Company purchased equipment at a cost of $500,000. Management expects the equipment to remain in service for five years, with zero residual value. Mariposa Company uses the straight-line depreciation method. Through an accounting error, Mariposa Company accidentally expensed the entire cost of the equipment at the time of purchase.

Requirement

1. Prepare a schedule to show the overstatement or understatement in the following items at the end of each year over the five-year life of the equipment.
   a. Equipment, net
   b. Net income

E8-22A. Depreciation methods *(Learning Objective 3)* **15–20 min.**

Memorial Medical Center bought equipment on January 2, 2010, for $30,000. The equipment was expected to remain in service for four years and to perform 1,000 operations. At the end of the equipment's useful life, Memorial estimates that its residual value will be $6,000. The equipment performed 100 operations the first year, 300 the second year, 400 the third year, and 200 the fourth year.

Requirements

1. Prepare a schedule of depreciation expense per year for the equipment under the three depreciation methods. After two years under double-declining-balance depreciation, the company switched to the straight-line method. Show your computations.

2. Which method tracks the wear and tear on the equipment most closely?

3. Which method would Memorial prefer to use for income-tax purposes in the first years of the equipment's life? Explain in detail why a taxpayer prefers this method.

E8-23A. Straight-line depreciation *(Learning Objective 3)* **10–15 min.**

LHD Freight purchased a building for $700,000 and depreciated it on a straight-line basis over a 40-year period. The estimated residual value was $100,000. After using the building for 15 years, LHD realized that wear and tear on the building would force the company to replace it before 40 years. Starting with the sixteenth year, LHD began depreciating the building over a revised total life of 30 years and increased the estimated residual value to $175,000. Record depreciation expense on the building for years 15 and 16.

E8-24A. Straight-line depreciation and long-term asset disposal *(Learning Objectives 3 & 5)* **15–20 min.**

On January 2, 2010, Bright Lights purchased showroom fixtures for $10,000 cash, expecting the fixtures to remain in service for five years. Bright Lights has depreciated the fixtures on a straight-line basis, with zero residual value. On September 30, 2011, Bright Lights sold the fixtures for $5,000 cash. Record both the depreciation expense on the fixtures for 2011 and the sale of the fixtures on September 30, 2011.

E8-25A. Disposition of long-term assets *(Learning Objective 5)* **10–15 min.**

Assume that Henson Corporation's comparative balance sheet reported these amounts:

	December 31	
	2009	**2008**
Plant and Equipment	$ 600,000	$ 595,000
Less: Accumulated Depreciation	145,000	135,000
Net Plant and Equipment	$ 455,000	$ 460,000

Requirement

1. Assume that on January 2, 2010, Henson sold 1/10 of its plant and equipment for $75,500 in cash. Journalize this transaction for Henson.

E8-26A. Trade-in on purchase of new asset *(Learning Objectives 3 & 5)* **15–20 min.**

Mesilla Valley Transport is a large trucking company. Mesilla Valley Transport uses the units-of-production (UOP) method to depreciate its trucks. In 2009, Mesilla Valley Transport acquired a Mack truck costing $350,000 with a useful life of 10 years or 1 million miles. Estimated residual value was $100,000. The truck was driven 80,000 miles in 2009, 120,000 miles in 2010, and 160,000 miles in 2011. After 40,000 miles in 2012, Mesilla Valley Transport traded in the Mack truck for a new Freightliner that cost $480,000. Mesilla Valley Transport received a $275,000 trade-in allowance for the old truck and paid the difference in cash. Journalize the entry to record the purchase of the new truck.

E8-27A. Patents *(Learning Objective 6)* **10–15 min.**

Part 1. Millennium Printing manufactures high-speed printers. Millennium Printing recently paid $1 million for a patent on a new laser printer. Although it gives legal protection for 20 years, the patent is expected to provide a competitive advantage for only 8 years. Using the straight-line method of amortization, make journal entries to record (a) the purchase of the patent and (b) amortization for year 1.

Part 2. After using the patent for 4 years, Millennium Printing learns at an industry trade show that another company is designing a more efficient printer. On the basis of this new information, Millennium Printing decides, starting with year 5, to amortize the remaining cost of the patent over 2 remaining years, giving the patent a total useful life of 6 years. Record amortization for year 5.

E8-28A. Goodwill *(Learning Objective 6)* **10–15 min.**

Rutherford, Corp., aggressively acquired other companies. Assume that Rutherford, Corp., purchased Lancer, Inc., for $11 million cash. The market value of Lancer's assets is $15 million, and it has liabilities of $10 million.

Requirements

1. Compute the cost of goodwill purchased by Rutherford, Corp.
2. Record the purchase of Lancer, Inc., by Rutherford, Corp.

E8-29A. Depletion *(Learning Objective 7)* **10–15 min.**

Asarco Mining paid $398,500 for the right to extract mineral assets from a 200,000-ton mineral deposit. In addition to the purchase price, Asarco Mining also paid a $500 filing fee, a $1,000 license fee to the state of Colorado, and $60,000 for a geological survey of the property. Because the company purchased the rights to the minerals only, the company expected the asset to have zero residual value when fully depleted. During the first year, Asarco Mining removed 40,000 tons of minerals. Using the Mineral Assets account, make journal entries to record the following:

a. Purchase of the minerals
b. Payment of fees and other costs
c. Depletion for the first year (none of the minerals were sold during the year)

E8-30A. Balance sheet disclosure of long-term assets *(Learning Objective 9)* **10–15 min.**

At the end of 2010, Zeman, Corp., had total assets of $25 million and total liabilities of $13 million. Included in the assets were property, plant, and equipment with a cost of $9 million and accumulated depreciation of $3 million. During 2010, Zeman, Corp., earned total revenues of $20 million and had total expenses of $17 million. Show how Zeman, Corp., reported property, plant, and equipment on its balance sheet on December 31, 2010. What was the book value of property, plant, and equipment on that date?

EXERCISES (GROUP B)

E8-31B. Capitalized costs for long-term assets *(Learning Objective 2)* **10–15 min.**

Ogden Systems purchased land, paying $110,000 cash as a down payment and signing a $140,000 note payable for the balance. In addition, Ogden Systems paid delinquent property tax of $1,500, title insurance costing $3,500, and a $10,400 charge for leveling the land and removing an unwanted building. The company constructed an office building on the land at a cost of $600,000. It also paid $46,000 for a fence around the property, $7,000 for the company sign near the entrance, and $5,000 for special lighting of the grounds.

Requirements

1. Determine the cost of the company's land, land improvements, and building.
2. Which of the assets will Ogden depreciate?

E8-32B. Capitalized costs for long-term assets *(Learning Objective 2)* 10–15 min.

White Brothers manufactures conveyor belts. Early in May 2011, White Brothers constructed its own building at a materials, labor, and overhead cost of $970,000. White Brothers also paid for architect fees and building permits of $76,000.

Requirements

1. How much should White record as the cost of the building in 2011?
2. Record White Brothers' transactions related to the construction of the building.

E8-33B. Capitalized costs for long-term assets *(Learning Objective 2)* 10–15 min.

Amy's Tanning Salon bought three tanning beds in a $20,000 lump-sum purchase. An independent appraiser valued the tanning beds as follows:

Tanning Bed	Appraised Value
1	$ 7,000
2	8,000
3	11,000

Amy's Tanning Salon paid $10,000 in cash and signed a note payable for $10,000. Record the purchase in the journal, identifying each tanning bed's cost by number in a separate Tanning Bed account. Round decimals to three places.

E8-34B. Errors in accounting for long-term assets *(Learning Objective 2)* 15–20 min.

Assume that early in year 1, Marginal Company purchased equipment at a cost of $520,000. Management expects the equipment to remain in service for five years, with zero residual value. Marginal Company uses the straight-line depreciation method. Through an accounting error, Marginal Company accidentally expensed the entire cost of the equipment at the time of purchase.

Requirement

1. Prepare a schedule to show the overstatement or understatement in the following items at the end of each year over the five-year life of the equipment:
   a. Equipment, net
   b. Net income

E8-35B. Depreciation methods *(Learning Objective 3)* 15–20 min.

General Medical Center bought equipment on January 2, 2010, for $18,000. The equipment was expected to remain in service for four years and to perform 400 operations. At the end of the equipment's useful life, General estimates that its residual value will be $4,000. The equipment performed 40 operations the first year, 120 the second year, 160 the third year, and 80 the fourth year.

Requirements

1. Prepare a schedule of depreciation expense per year for the equipment under the three depreciation methods. After two years under double-declining-balance depreciation, the company switched to the straight-line method. Show your computations.
2. Which method tracks the wear and tear on the equipment most closely?
3. Which method would General prefer to use for income-tax purposes in the first years of the equipment's life? Explain in detail why a taxpayer prefers this method.

E8-36B. Straight-line depreciation *(Learning Objective 3)* 10–15 min.

Chapin Freight purchased a building for $800,000 and depreciated it on a straight-line basis over a 30-year period. The estimated residual value was $110,000. After using the building for 15 years, Chapin realized that wear and tear on the building would force the company to replace it before 30 years. Starting with the sixteenth year, Chapin began depreciating the building over a revised total life of 20 years and increased the estimated residual value to $170,000. Record depreciation expense on the building for years 15 and 16.

E8-37B. Straight-line depreciation and long-term asset disposal *(Learning Objectives 3 & 5)* **15–20 min.**

On January 2, 2010, Shine Lights purchased showroom fixtures for $18,000 cash, expecting the fixtures to remain in service for five years. Shine Lights has depreciated the fixtures on a straight-line basis, with zero residual value. On March 31, 2011, Shine Lights sold the fixtures for $5,000 cash. Record both the depreciation expense on the fixtures for 2011 and the sale of the fixtures on March 31, 2011.

E8-38B. Disposition of long-term assets *(Learning Objective 5)* **10–15 min.**

Assume that Hector Corporation's comparative balance sheet reported these amounts:

	December 31	
	2009	**2008**
Plant and Equipment	$ 610,000	$ 583,000
Less: Accumulated Depreciation	160,000	120,000
Net Plant and Equipment	$ 450,000	$ 463,000

Requirement

1. Assume that on January 2, 2010, Hector sold 1/2 of its plant and equipment for $237,000 in cash. Journalize this transaction for Hector.

E8-39B. Trade-in on purchase of new asset *(Learning Objectives 3 & 5)* **15–20 min.**

Regional Highway Transport is a large trucking company. Regional Highway Transport uses the units-of-production (UOP) method to depreciate its trucks. In 2009, Regional Highway Transport acquired a Mack truck costing $410,000 with a useful life of 10 years or 1,250,000 miles. Estimated residual value was $10,000. The truck was driven 85,000 miles in 2009, 110,000 miles in 2010, and 150,000 miles in 2011. After 10,000 miles in 2012, Regional Highway Transport traded in the Mack truck for a new Freightliner that costs $524,400. Regional Highway Transport received a $314,400 trade-in allowance for the old truck and paid the difference in cash. Journalize the entry to record the purchase of the new truck.

E8-40B. Patents *(Learning Objective 6)* **10–15 min.**

Part 1. Mayflower Printing manufactures high-speed printers. Mayflower Printing recently paid $9 million for a patent on a new laser printer. Although it gives legal protection for 20 years, the patent is expected to provide a competitive advantage for only 15 years. Using the straight-line method of amortization, make journal entries to record (a) the purchase of the patent and (b) amortization for year 1.

Part 2. After using the patent for 7 years, Mayflower Printing learns at an industry trade show that another company is designing a more efficient printer. On the basis of this new information, Mayflower Printing decides, starting with year 8, to amortize the remaining cost of the patent over 2 remaining years, giving the patent a total useful life of 9 years. Record amortization for year 8.

E8-41B. Goodwill *(Learning Objective 6)* **10–15 min.**

Richardson, Corp., aggressively acquired other companies. Assume that Richardson, Corp., purchased Lawrence, Inc., for $14 million cash. The market value of Lawrence's assets is $22 million, and it has liabilities of $14 million.

Requirements

1. Compute the cost of goodwill purchased by Richardson, Corp.
2. Record the purchase of Lawrence, Inc., by Richardson, Corp.

E8-42B. Depletion *(Learning Objective 7)* 10–15 min.

McKenzie Mining paid $831,600 for the right to extract mineral assets from a 600,000-ton mineral deposit. In addition to the purchase price, McKenzie Mining also paid a $600 filing fee, a $2,800 license fee to the state of Colorado, and $65,000 for a geological survey of the property. Because the company purchased the rights to the minerals only, the company expected the asset to have zero residual value when fully depleted. During the first year, McKenzie Mining removed 75,000 tons of minerals. Using the Mineral Assets account, make journal entries to record the following:

a. Purchase of the minerals

b. Payment of fees and other costs

c. Depletion for the first year (none of the minerals were sold during the year)

E8-43B. Balance sheet disclosure of long-term assets *(Learning Objective 9)* 10–15 min.

At the end of 2010, Zaney, Corp., had total assets of $26 million and total liabilities of $15 million. Included in the assets were property, plant, and equipment with a cost of $14 million and accumulated depreciation of $5 million. During 2010, Zaney, Corp., earned total revenues of $24 million and had total expenses of $15 million. Show how Zaney, Corp., reported property, plant, and equipment on its balance sheet on December 31, 2010. What was the book value of property, plant, and equipment on that date?

EXERCISES (ALTERNATES 1, 2, AND 3)

These alternative exercise sets are available for your practice benefit at
www.myaccountinglab.com

PROBLEMS (GROUP A)

P8-44A. Long-term asset costs and partial year depreciation *(Learning Objectives 2 & 3)* 20–25 min.

Gegax Manufacturing incurred the following costs in acquiring land, making land improvements, and constructing and furnishing a new building.

a.	Purchase price of four acres of land	$200,000
b.	Additional dirt and earthmoving	8,100
c.	Fence around the boundary of the property	17,600
d.	Attorney fee for title search on the land	1,000
e.	Unpaid property taxes on the land to be paid by Gegax	5,900
f.	Company signs at the front of the property	4,400
g.	Building permit for the building	500
h.	Architect's fee for the design of the building	22,500
i.	Labor to construct the building	709,000
j.	Materials used to construct the building	224,000
k.	Landscaping	6,400
l.	Parking lot and concrete walks	29,700
m.	Lights for the parking lot and walkways	10,300
n.	Salary of construction supervisor (85% to building; 15% to parking lot and concrete walks)	40,000
o.	Furniture for the building	107,100
p.	Transportation and installation of furniture	2,100

Gegax Manufacturing depreciates buildings over 40 years, land improvements over 20 years, and furniture over 8 years, all on a straight-line basis with zero residual value.

Requirements

1. Set up columns for Land, Land Improvements, Building, and Furniture. Show how to account for each cost by listing the cost under the correct account. Determine the total cost of each asset.

2. All construction was complete and assets were placed in service on May 1. Record partial-year depreciation for the year ended December 31. Round to the nearest dollar.

P8-45A. Journalize long-term asset transactions *(Learning Objectives 2, 3, & 5)* **20–25 min.**

Regal Freightway provides freight service. The company's balance sheet includes Land, Buildings, and Motor-Carrier Equipment. Regal Freightway uses a separate accumulated depreciation account for each depreciable asset. During 2010, Regal Freightway completed the following transactions:

Jan 1	Traded in motor-carrier equipment with accumulated depreciation of $90,000 (cost of $130,000) for new equipment with a cash cost of $176,000. Regal Freightway received a trade-in allowance of $70,000 on the old equipment and paid the remainder in cash.
Jul 1	Sold a building that cost $550,000 and had accumulated depreciation of $250,000 through December 31 of the preceding year. Depreciation is computed on a straight-line basis. The building has a 40-year useful life and a residual value of $50,000. Regal Freightway received $100,000 cash and a $600,000 note receivable.
Oct 31	Purchased land and a building for a cash payment of $300,000. An independent appraisal valued the land at $115,000 and the building at $230,000.
Dec 31	Recorded depreciation as follows: New motor-carrier equipment has an expected useful life of 1 million miles and an estimated residual value of $26,000. Depreciation method is the units-of-production method. During the year, Regal Freightway drove the truck 150,000 miles. Depreciation on buildings is straight-line. The new building has a 40-year useful life and a residual value equal to $20,000.

Requirement

1. Record the transactions in Regal Freightway's journal.

P8-46A. Capitalize long-term asset costs and several depreciation methods *(Learning Objectives 2, 3, & 9)* **20–25 min.**

On January 3, Jose Rojo, Inc., paid $224,000 for equipment used in manufacturing automotive supplies. In addition to the basic purchase price, the company paid $700 transportation charges, $100 insurance for the equipment while in transit, $12,100 sales tax, and $3,100 for a special platform on which to place the equipment in the plant. Jose Rojo, Inc., management estimates that the equipment will remain in service for five years and have a residual value of $20,000. The equipment will produce 50,000 units the first year, with annual production decreasing by 5,000 units during each of the next four years (i.e., 45,000 units in year 2; 40,000 units in year 3; and so on for a total of 200,000 units). In trying to decide which depreciation method to use, Jose Rojo, Inc., requested a depreciation schedule for each of the three depreciation methods (straight-line, units-of-production, and double-declining-balance).

Requirements

1. For each depreciation method, prepare a depreciation schedule showing asset cost, depreciation expense, accumulated depreciation, and asset book value. For the units-of-production method, round depreciation per unit to three decimal places.

2. Jose Rojo, Inc., prepares financial statements using the depreciation method that reports the highest income in the early years of asset use. For income tax purposes, the company uses the depreciation method that minimizes income taxes in the early years. Consider the first year Jose Rojo, Inc., uses the equipment. Identify the depreciation methods that meet Jose Rojo's objectives, assuming the income tax authorities permit the use of any method.

3. Show how Jose Rojo, Inc., would report equipment on the December 31, 2011, balance sheet of the first year.

P8-47A. Disposing of an Asset *(Learning Objective 5)* 15–20 min.

Atco Industries had a piece of equipment that cost $25,000 and had accumulated depreciation of $23,000.

Requirement

1. Record the disposition of the equipment assuming the following independent situations:

   a. Atco discarded the equipment, receiving $0.

   b. Atco sold the equipment for $3,000 cash.

   c. Atco traded the equipment in on a new piece of equipment costing $30,000. Atco was granted a $5,000 trade-in allowance for the old equipment and paid the difference in cash.

   d. Atco traded the equipment in on a new piece of equipment costing $20,000. Atco was granted a $1,000 trade-in allowance for the old equipment and signed a note payable for the difference.

Quick solution: a. $2,000 loss; b. $1,000 gain; c. $3,000 gain; d. $1,000 loss

P8-48A. Goodwill *(Learning Objective 6)* 15–20 min.

Benny's Restaurants acquired Hungry Boy Diners. The financial records of Hungry Boy Diners included the following:

Book Value of Assets	$2.4 million
Market Value of Assets	2.7 million
Liabilities	2.2 million

Requirements

1. Make the journal entry to record Benny's Restaurants' purchase of Hungry Boy Diners for $3 million cash, including any goodwill.

2. How should Benny's Restaurants account for this goodwill after acquiring Hungry Boy Diners? Explain in detail.

P8-49A. Depletion *(Learning Objective 7)* 20–25 min.

Wright Oil Company's balance sheet includes three assets: Natural Gas, Oil, and Coal. Suppose Wright Oil Company paid $2.8 million in cash for the right to work a mine with an estimated 100,000 tons of coal. Assume the company paid $60,000 to remove unwanted buildings from the land and $45,000 to prepare the surface for mining. Further, assume that Wright Oil Company signed a $30,000 note payable to a company that will return the land surface to its original condition after the mining ends. During the first year, Wright Oil Company removed 40,000 tons of coal, which it sold on account for $39 per ton. Operating expenses for the first year totaled $252,000, all paid in cash.

Requirements

1. Record all of Wright Oil Company's transactions, including depletion, for the year.

2. Prepare the company's income statement for its coal operations for the year.

PROBLEMS (GROUP B)

P8-50B. Long-term asset costs and partial year depreciation *(Learning Objectives 2 & 3)* 20–25 min.

Zed's Manufacturing incurred the following costs in acquiring land, making land improvements, and constructing and furnishing a new building.

a.	Purchase price of four acres of land	$192,000
b.	Additional dirt and earthmoving	8,800
c.	Fence around the boundary of the property	16,200
d.	Attorney fee for title search on the land	1,100
e.	Unpaid property taxes on the land to be paid by Zed's	6,300
f.	Company signs at the front of the property	5,000
g.	Building permit for the building	700
h.	Architect's fee for the design of the building	24,100
i.	Labor to construct the building	691,000
j.	Materials used to construct the building	217,000
k.	Landscaping	6,600
l.	Parking lot and concrete walks	28,700
m.	Lights for the parking lot and walkways	10,700
n.	Salary of construction supervisor (85% to building; 15% to parking lot and concrete walks)	80,000
o.	Furniture for the building	106,100
p.	Transportation and installation of furniture	2,300

Zed's Manufacturing depreciates buildings over 50 years, land improvements over 25 years, and furniture over 12 years, all on a straight-line basis with zero residual value.

Requirements

1. Set up columns for Land, Land Improvements, Building, and Furniture. Show how to account for each cost by listing the cost under the correct account. Determine the total cost of each asset.

2. All construction was complete and the assets were placed in service on November 1. Record partial-year depreciation for the year ended December 31. (Round to the nearest dollar.)

P8-51B. Journalize long-term asset transactions *(Learning Objectives 2, 3, & 5)* 20–25 min.

Russell Freightway provides freight service. The company's balance sheet includes Land, Buildings, and Motor-Carrier Equipment. Russell uses a separate accumulated depreciation account for each depreciable asset. During 2010, Russell Freightway completed the following transactions:

Jan 1 Traded in motor-carrier equipment with accumulated depreciation of $83,000 (cost of $136,000) for new equipment with a cash cost of $136,000. Russell received a trade-in allowance of $63,000 on the old equipment and paid the remainder in cash.

Jul 1 Sold a building that cost $565,000 and had accumulated depreciation of $265,000 through December 31 of the preceding year. Depreciation is computed on a straight-line basis. The building has a 40-year useful life and a residual value of $45,000. Russell received $90,000 cash and a $620,000 note receivable.

Oct 31 Purchased land and a building for a cash payment of $400,000. An independent appraisal valued the land at $140,000 and the building at $310,000.

Dec 31 Recorded depreciation as follows:
New motor-carrier equipment has an expected useful life of 1 million miles and an estimated residual value of $24,000. Depreciation method is the units-of-production method. During the year, Russell drove the truck 180,000 miles. Depreciation on buildings is straight-line. The new building has a 40-year useful life and a residual value equal to $20,000.

Requirement

1. Record the transactions in Russell Freightway's journal. (Round your depreciation expense to the nearest whole dollar.)

P8-52B. Capitalize long-term asset costs and several depreciation methods *(Learning Objectives 2, 3, & 9)* **20–25 min.**

On January 7, Red Tucker, Inc., paid $254,700 for equipment used in manufacturing automotive supplies. In addition to the basic purchase price, the company paid $500 transportation charges, $300 insurance for the equipment while in transit, $12,000 sales tax, and $2,500 for a special platform on which to place the equipment in the plant. Red Tucker, Inc., management estimates that the equipment will remain in service for five years and have a residual value of $30,000. The equipment will produce 60,000 units the first year, with annual production decreasing by 5,000 units during each of the next four years (i.e., 55,000 units in year 2, 50,000 units in year 3, and so on for a total of 250,000 units). In trying to decide which depreciation method to use, Red Tucker, Inc., requested a depreciation schedule for each of the three depreciation methods (straight-line, units-of-production, and double-declining-balance).

Requirements

1. For each depreciation method, prepare a depreciation schedule showing asset cost, depreciation expense, accumulated depreciation, and asset book value. For the units-of-production method, round depreciation per unit to three decimal places.

2. Red Tucker, Inc., prepares financial statements using the depreciation method that reports the highest income in the early years of asset use. For income tax purposes, the company uses the depreciation method that minimizes income taxes in the early years. Consider the first year Red Tucker, Inc., uses the equipment. Identify the depreciation methods that meet Red Tucker's objectives, assuming the income tax authorities permit the use of any method.

3. Prepare the balance sheet disclosure for Red Tucker's equipment at December 31 of the first year.

P8-53B. Disposing of an Asset *(Learning Objective 5)* **15–20 min.**

Mackay Industries had a piece of equipment that cost $32,000 and had accumulated depreciation of $28,000.

Requirement

1. Record the disposition of the equipment assuming the following independent situations:

   a. Mackay discarded the equipment receiving $0.

   b. Mackay sold the equipment for $6,000 cash.

   c. Mackay traded the equipment in on a new piece of equipment costing $35,000. Mackay was granted a $5,000 trade-in allowance for the old equipment and paid the difference in cash.

   d. Mackay traded the equipment in on a new piece of equipment costing $25,000. Mackay was granted a $3,000 trade-in allowance for the old equipment and signed a note payable for the difference.

P8-54B. Goodwill *(Learning Objective 6)* **15–20 min.**

Tico's Restaurants acquired Tin Bus Diners. The financial records of Tin Bus Diners included the following:

Book Value of Assets	$2,300,000
Market Value of Assets	2,750,000
Liabilities	2,250,000

Requirements

1. Make the journal entry to record Tico's Restaurants' purchase of Tin Bus Diners for $3,200,000 cash, including any goodwill.

2. How should Tico's Restaurants account for this goodwill after acquiring Tin Bus Diners? Explain in detail.

P8-55B. Depletion (*Learning Objective 7*) 20–25 min.

Airheart Oil Company's balance sheet includes three assets: Natural Gas, Oil, and Coal. Suppose Airheart Oil Company paid $1,900,000 cash for the right to work a mine with an estimated 200,000 tons of coal. Assume the company paid $68,000 to remove unwanted buildings from the land and $45,000 to prepare the surface for mining. Further, assume that Airheart Oil Company signed a $33,000 note payable to a company that will return the land surface to its original condition after the mining ends. During the first year, Airheart Oil Company removed 41,000 tons of coal, which it sold on account for $36 per ton. Operating expenses for the first year totaled $248,000, all paid in cash.

Requirements

1. Record all of Airheart Oil Company's transactions, including depletion, for the year.

2. Prepare the company's income statement for its coal operations for the year.

PROBLEMS (ALTERNATES 1, 2, AND 3)

These alternative problem sets are available for your practice benefit at *www.myaccountinglab.com*

CONTINUING EXERCISE

This exercise continues our accounting for Graham's Yard Care Inc., from previous chapters. In this exercise, we will account for the annual depreciation expense for Graham's Yard Care, Inc. In the Continuing Exercise in Chapter 2 we learned that Graham's Yard Care, Inc., had purchased a lawn mower and a weed whacker on June 3 and that they were expected to last four years.

Requirements

1. Calculate the annual depreciation expense amount for each asset assuming both assets are using straight-line depreciation.

2. Record the entry for the partial year's depreciation for 2010. Date it December 31, 2010. Assume that no depreciation has been recorded yet in 2010.

CONTINUING PROBLEM

This problem continues our accounting for Aqua Elite, Inc., from Chapter 7. During 2010, Aqua Elite made the following purchases:

- On May 3, Aqua Elite, Inc., purchased a copy machine for $4,700 cash. The copy machine has an estimated useful life of four years and no salvage value. Aqua Elite uses double-declining-balance depreciation for the copy machine.

- On May 18, Aqua Elite, Inc., purchased a $31,000 truck financed by a note payable bearing 8% annual interest. The truck has an estimated useful life of 200,000 miles and a residual value of $3,000. The truck was driven 28,000 miles in 2010 and is depreciated using the units-of-production method.

- On June 2, Aqua Elite, Inc., paid $15,000 for land.

- On June 22, $3,300 of furniture was purchased on account. The furniture has a five-year life and a residual value of $500. Furniture is depreciated using straight-line depreciation.

- On August 10, $1,200 of furniture was purchased. The furniture has a four-year life and no residual value, and is depreciated using straight-line depreciation.

- On September 1, Aqua Elite, Inc., purchased a building for $85,000 financed by a mortgage bearing 6% annual interest. The building has an estimated salvage value of $10,000 and is being depreciated over 25 years using the straight-line method.

Requirements

1. Calculate the depreciation expense as of December 31, 2010, for all assets purchased in 2010.

2. Assuming these are Aqua Elite's only assets, how will fixed assets be reflected on the balance sheet at December 31, 2010?

APPLY YOUR KNOWLEDGE

ETHICS IN ACTION

Case 1. Larry Johnson owns Larry's Limousine, which operates a fleet of limousines and shuttle buses. Upon reviewing the most recent financial statements, he became confused over the recent decline in net income. He called his accountant and asked for an explanation. The accountant told Larry that the numerous repairs and maintenance expenses, such as oil changes, cleaning, and minor engine repairs, had totaled up to a large amount. Further, because several drivers were involved in accidents, the fleet insurance premiums had also risen sharply. Larry told his accountant to simply capitalize all the expenses related to the vehicles rather than expensing them. These capitalized repair costs could then be depreciated over the next 10 or 20 years. By capitalizing those expenses, the net income would be higher, as would property and equipment assets; therefore, both the income statement and balance sheet would look better. His accountant, however, disagreed because the costs were clearly routine maintenance and because they did not extend the fleet's useful life. Larry then told his accountant that the estimated useful life of the vehicles needed to be changed from 5 years to 20 years to lower the amount of depreciation expense. His accountant responded that capitalizing costs that should be expensed and extending the estimated lives of assets just to increase the reported net income was unethical and wrong. Larry said that it was his business and, therefore, demanded that the financial statements be changed to show more net income. As a result, the accountant told Larry to pick up his files and find another accountant. What ethical concerns did the accountant have? If the total amount of repairs and maintenance were so large, couldn't a case be made that the amount should be capitalized? Is it unethical to change the estimated life of an asset? Was it unethical for the accountant to sever the business relationship? Do you have any suggestions?

Case 2. Table Corporation purchased Chairs Unlimited for $10 million. The fair market value of Chairs' net assets at the time was $8 million, so Table Corporation recorded $2 million of goodwill. Also included in the purchase was a patent valued at $1 million with an estimated remaining life of 10 years. To comply with GAAP, the goodwill was not amortized, but the patent was amortized over the remaining 10-year life. However, the Chairs Unlimited business was not as profitable as anticipated and as a result, the accountant for Table Corporation stated that the goodwill needed to be written off. Further, the accountant discovered that the remaining life of the patent was only 6 years and that it should be amortized over the remaining 6-year life rather than the 10-year life originally estimated. The CEO became concerned because these adjustments would cause net income to be extremely low for the year. As a result, he told the accountant to wait before writing off the goodwill because of the possibility that the purchase could be profitable in the future. Also, he argued, the life of the patent should be left alone because it was originally based upon what was thought to be a 10-year life. After much debate, the CEO then agreed with the accountant as long as the amount of goodwill was not completely written off in the current year. What ethical concerns are involved? Should the accountant change the amortizable life of an intangible asset? Should the accountant completely write off the goodwill account in the current year? Does the CEO's concern for higher net income create any ethical problems when the accountant agrees to not completely write off the goodwill? Do you have any other thoughts?

KNOW YOUR BUSINESS

FINANCIAL ANALYSIS

Purpose: to help familiarize you with the financial reporting of a real company in order to further your understanding of the chapter material you are learning.

This case addresses the long-term assets of Columbia Sportswear. The majority of these assets consist of property and equipment, and intangible assets. In the text, you learned how most long-term tangible assets used in business are capitalized and depreciated over their estimated useful lives. Further, you learned that certain intangible assets are amortized over time while others are not. In this case, you will not only see and understand the classification and presentation of these assets, but also explore the methods used by Columbia Sportswear to depreciate and amortize them. Refer to Columbia Sportswear's financial statements in Appendix A. Also, consider the information presented in footnote 2, under the headings Property, Plant, and Equipment, and Intangible Assets and in footnote 4 titled Property, Plant, and Equipment, net.

Requirements

1. What was the balance of net property, plant, and equipment on December 31, 2008? What was the balance of net property, plant, and equipment on December 31, 2007? Did the amount of ending net property, plant, and equipment increase or decrease? Assume Columbia Sportswear removed $357 (thousand) of fully depreciated assets from fixed assets in 2008. What effect did this have on the value of the net property, plant, and equipment balance? Explain your answer.

2. What methods of depreciation were used by Columbia Sportswear? What were the estimated useful lives? What kinds of intangible assets does Columbia Sportswear have? Which intangible assets are amortized by Columbia Sportswear and which are not? Why? In which year did Columbia Sportswear acquire most of its patents.

3. What was the percentage of net property, plant, and equipment compared to the total assets on December 31, 2008? What was the percentage of net property, plant, and equipment compared to the total assets on December 31, 2007? Did the percentage increase or decrease during the year?

4. Columbia Sportswear lists "Leasehold improvements" and "Construction in progress" as part of Property, Plant, and Equipment. Although these assets are not discussed in the textbook, can you describe what these assets represent?

INDUSTRY ANALYSIS

Purpose: To help you understand and compare the performance of two companies in the same industry.

Find the Columbia Sportswear Company Annual Report located in Appendix A and go to the Notes to the Consolidated Financial Statements starting on page 685. Now access the 2008 Annual Report for Under Armour, Inc., from the Internet. Go to the company Web page for Investor Relations at http://investor.underarmour.com/investors.cfm and under Downloads, on the right-hand side, go to 2008 Annual Report. The Notes to Unaudited Consolidated Financial Statements start on page 53.

Requirement

1. Find the section in the notes for each company where the company discusses its Property and Equipment, or its Property, Plant, and Equipment. Also find the section where the company discusses Intangible Assets. Compare the two and note any major differences.

SMALL BUSINESS ANALYSIS

Purpose: To help you understand the importance of cash flows in the operation of a small business.

You've made an appointment to take your year-end financial statements down to the bank. You know that your banker is usually concerned about two things, your net income and the amount of cash you have. You are a little concerned because you know that your current year net income was down a little bit from the prior year. You figure that a significant cause for the decline was due to a large equipment purchase you made early in the year, which resulted in a lot of depreciation expense. However, as you look at your balance sheet, it says that cash increased from last year to this year. That's a little puzzling, but you're hoping the banker can figure it out.

A couple of days later, you get a call from the banker. You're expecting him to tell you the bank won't be able to extend any more credit to you because your net income has declined. Imagine your surprise when he tells you how pleased he is with your financial performance this year, and that he doesn't anticipate any problems extending more credit to you. You want to know what he saw in your financial statements that you didn't see so you say to him, "Bob, thanks for the good news and the good report on my financial condition, even though our cash increased this year. I was afraid that the decline in our income might cause you some concern. How come it didn't?"

Requirement

1. What kind of response do you think that you might get from the banker regarding your net income as it relates to cash flow?

WRITTEN COMMUNICATION

A client of yours notified you that she just closed a deal to purchase an existing business. It's a pretty hefty purchase. As part of the purchase of the business, she received the land, the building, all the equipment, and the entire merchandise inventory of the company purchased. Your client e-mailed you a copy of the closing statement along with the breakdown of the purchase price shown below. In the e-mail, your client expressed concern about how the $1,500,000 paid for the Land and Building should be accounted for. She also wanted to know the proper way to account for the merchandise inventory and the goodwill that was purchased.

Asset List	
Description	**Amount**
Land and Building	$1,500,000
Equipment	675,000
Inventory	425,000
Goodwill	1,400,000
Total Purchase Price	$4,000,000

Requirement

1. Prepare an e-mail to your client explaining how the $1,500,000 should be allocated between the Land and Building as well as how the merchandise inventory and goodwill should be accounted for.

Self Check Answers
1. b 2. a 3. d 4. c 5. a 6. d 7. b 8. a 9. c 10. d

Current Liabilities and Long-Term Debt

In the past few chapters, we have examined the assets that most businesses have including Cash, Accounts Receivable, Inventory, and Long-Term Assets. We have seen how important it is to value assets properly, and to report them correctly in the financial statements. It is equally important, if not more important, for a business to properly value its liabilities and to report them correctly in the financial statements. When discussing liabilities, several questions may come to mind such as what different types of liabilities do most businesses have? Or, what happens if a company knows that a liability exists but doesn't know the amount of the liability? These, and other important questions, are answered here in Chapter 9 as we take a closer look at liabilities.

Chapter Outline:

WHAT IS THE DIFFERENCE BETWEEN KNOWN, ESTIMATED, AND CONTINGENT LIABILITIES? (p. 440)

HOW DO YOU ACCOUNT FOR CURRENT LIABILITIES OF A KNOWN AMOUNT? (p. 440)

HOW DO YOU ACCOUNT FOR CURRENT LIABILITIES OF AN UNCERTAIN AMOUNT? (p. 444)

HOW DO YOU ACCOUNT FOR A CONTINGENT LIABILITY? (p. 446)

HOW DO YOU ACCOUNT FOR LONG-TERM DEBT? (p. 447)

HOW ARE LIABILITIES REPORTED ON THE BALANCE SHEET? (p. 457)

FOCUS ON DECISION MAKING: RATIOS (p. 458)

Learning Objectives

1. Distinguish between known, estimated, and contingent liabilities

2. Account for current liabilities of a known amount

3. Account for liabilities of an uncertain amount

4. Account for contingent liabilities

5. Account for Long-Term Debt

6. Report liabilities on the balance sheet

7. Compute the debt ratio

8. (Appendix 9A) Account for payroll (Located at http://www.pearsonhighered.com/waybright)

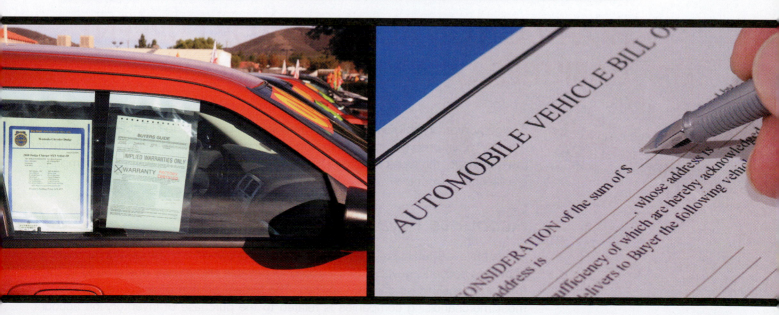

WHAT IS THE DIFFERENCE BETWEEN KNOWN, ESTIMATED, AND CONTINGENT LIABILITIES?

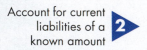

Distinguish between known, estimated, and contingent liabilities

Liabilities can generally be broken down into three categories as follows:

- **Known liabilities:** The majority of a company's liabilities fall into this category. Known liabilities can be defined as known obligations of known amounts. In other words, the business knows that it owes something and it knows how much it owes. Examples of known liabilities include accounts payable, notes payable, unearned revenues, and accrued liabilities such as interest or taxes payable.

- **Estimated liabilities:** An estimated liability is defined as a known obligation of an unknown amount. A business will sometimes encounter a situation where it knows that a liability exists but it does not know the exact amount of the liability. In these situations, the amount of the liability must be estimated. A typical example is estimated warranties payable, which is common for companies like **Ford** and **Apple**.

- **Contingent liabilities:** A **contingent liability** is a unique liability that differs from all other types of liabilities. A contingent liability arises because of a *past* event, but it is dependent upon the outcome of a *future* event. In other words, whether or not a company has an obligation depends upon the result of an event that has not yet occurred. In addition, the amount of a contingent liability may be either known or unknown. Current or pending litigation is an example of a contingent liability.

As we learned in Chapter 4, a liability is classified as a current liability if the related obligation will be settled within one year. All liabilities not classified as current liabilities are classified as long-term debt. It is possible for known, estimated, and contingent liabilities to be classified as either current or long term. We will begin our discussion of accounting for liabilities by looking at current liabilities of a known amount.

HOW DO YOU ACCOUNT FOR CURRENT LIABILITIES OF A KNOWN AMOUNT?

Account for current liabilities of a known amount

A large portion of liabilities for most companies will be made up of known liabilities that are due within one year. In the following paragraphs, we will learn how to account for the majority of the types of current liabilities of a known amount that most companies are likely to encounter.

Accounts Payable

As we have learned in previous chapters, amounts owed for purchases on account are known as accounts payable. Since accounts payable are typically due in 30 to 45 days, they are classified as current liabilities. The largest portion of accounts payable for most merchandising companies is related to the purchase of inventory on account.

Merchandising and service businesses also incur accounts payable when they purchase items such as supplies, electricity, or telephone service on account. Accounts payable transactions are recorded by debiting the related asset or expense account and crediting Accounts Payable. For example, assume that Mackay Industries receives a utility bill for $680. The bill represents prior electricity usage and is not due for 30 days. Mackay Industries would record the receipt of the bill as follows:

DATE	ACCOUNTS	POST REF.	DR.	CR.
	Utilities Expense		680	
	Accounts Payable			680
	Record utility bill due in 30 days.			

When Mackay Industries pays the utility bill, it will record the payment on account as follows:

DATE	ACCOUNTS	POST REF.	DR.	CR.
	Accounts Payable		680	
	Cash			680
	Record payment on account.			

Notes Payable

When a business borrows money, usually from a financial institution, the signing of a promissory note is generally required. Businesses also often finance purchases of long-term assets through the use of notes payable. Any note payable that must be paid within one year from the balance sheet date is classified as a current liability. All notes not classified as a current liability are classified as long-term debt (discussed later in the chapter).

In Chapter 7 we learned about promissory notes when we studied notes receivable. The terms and concepts we learned about then will also apply to notes payable. However, we are now learning about the promissory note transaction from the opposite perspective. To illustrate a note payable, assume that on September 1, 2010, Mackay Industries borrows $8,000 from First State Bank on a nine-month, 6% note payable. Mackay Industries would record the transaction as follows on September 1:

DATE	ACCOUNTS	POST REF.	DR.	CR.
Sep 1	Cash		8,000	
	Notes Payable			8,000
	Record 6%, nine-month note.			

At December 31, 2010, it is necessary for Mackay Industries to accrue interest expense for the four months from September to December (remember the matching principle). The accrued interest is recorded as follows:

DATE	ACCOUNTS	POST REF.	DR.	CR.
Dec 31	Interest Expense		160*	
	Interest Payable			160
	Accrue four months' interest expense.			

*$160 = ($8,000 × .06 × 4/12)

The interest accrual at December 31, 2010, allocated $160 of the interest on this note to 2010. The remaining $200 ($8,000 × .06 × 5/12) of interest expense on this note will be allocated to 2011 at the time the note is paid off as follows:

DATE	ACCOUNTS	POST REF.	DR.	CR.
Jun 1, 2011	Notes Payable		8,000	
	Interest Payable		160	
	Interest Expense		200	
	Cash			8,360
	Repay 6%, nine-month note.			

Notice that the $160 debit to Interest Payable zeros out the amount that was accrued in the liability account at December 31, 2010. The $8,000 debit to Notes Payable removes the note from Mackay Industries' books. The $200 debit to Interest Expense records the interest expense for 2011. In addition, the $8,360 credit to Cash reflects the payment of the entire maturity value of the note. If the term of the note had not spanned the end of the period, no adjusting entry to accrue interest would have been necessary. If this had been the case for Mackay Industries in the previous example, the final entry to repay the note would look like this:

DATE	ACCOUNTS	POST REF.	DR.	CR.
	Notes Payable		8,000	
	Interest Expense		360	
	Cash			8,360
	Repay 6%, nine-month note.			

Notice that Interest Expense is debited for the full amount of the interest on the note, $360. There is also no debit to Interest Payable because no interest had been accrued on the note.

Sales Tax Payable

Most states levy sales tax on retail sales. Retailers collect the sales tax from their customers in addition to the price of the item sold. The sales tax collected must then be remitted, or paid, to the state on a periodic basis, usually monthly or quarterly. Sales Tax Payable is a current liability because the retailer must pay the state in less than a year. Let's apply this to Mackay Industries.

Suppose December's taxable sales for Mackay Industries totaled $22,000. Assume that Mackay Industries is required to collect an additional 8% of sales tax, which would equal $1,760 ($22,000 × 0.08). Mackay Industries would record December sales as follows:

DATE	ACCOUNTS	POST REF.	DR.	CR.
	Accounts Receivable or Cash		23,760	
	Sales Revenue			22,000
	Sales Tax Payable			1,760
	Record December sales.			

The entry recorded when Mackay Industries remits the sales tax to the state looks like this:

DATE	ACCOUNTS	POST REF.	DR.	CR.
	Sales Tax Payable		1,760	
	Cash			1,760
	Remit sales tax.			

Accrued Expenses (Accrued Liabilities)

In Chapter 3, we learned that an accrued expense is any expense that has been incurred but has not yet been paid. That's why accrued expenses are also called accrued liabilities. Most businesses will often have accrued liabilities for one or more of the following:

- Interest
- Salaries and wages
- Payroll taxes
- Income taxes

Accrued liabilities are recorded by debiting the related expense account and crediting a liability account. For example, the entry to record $700 of accrued income tax would be as follows:

DATE	ACCOUNTS	POST REF.	DR.	CR.
	Income Tax Expense		700	
	Income Tax Payable			700
	Record accrued income tax expense.			

Unearned Revenues

As we saw in Chapter 3, unearned revenues, also called deferred revenues, arise when a business receives cash in advance of providing goods or services. As a result, the business has an obligation to provide goods or services to the customer in the future. Unearned revenues are typically classified as current liabilities because customers do not usually pay for more than one year's worth of goods or services in advance.

Current Portion of Long-Term Debt

Many long-term debt obligations (discussed later in the chapter) are paid in installments. The principal amount of these obligations, due within one year from the balance sheet date, is referred to as **current portion of long-term debt**. Because it is due within one year from the balance sheet date, current portion of long-term debt is classified as a current liability on the balance sheet. Let's assume that Mackay Industries signs a $30,000, 6% note payable on June 1, 2010. The note requires that annual installments of $6,000, plus interest, be paid on June 1 of each of the next five years. On Mackay Industries' December 31, 2010, balance sheet, what amount will be reflected as current portion of long-term debt? Because the $6,000 payment that is due on June 1, 2011, is due within one year from the balance sheet date, it will be classified as current portion of long-term debt. The remaining $24,000 ($30,000 – $6,000) will be classified as long term.

☑ Concept Check...

Jill and Alan both work in the Accounting Department of a large retail business that has a significant amount of long-term debt. Jill was commenting to Alan how important it is to ensure that the current portion of the company's long-term debt be properly classified as such on the balance sheet. Alan argued that it really doesn't matter how the debt was classified as long as the correct total amount of debt was included somewhere on the balance sheet. Is Alan's point of view correct?

Answer

No, Jill's point of view is correct. In Chapter 4 we learned that the current ratio is one of the most widely used tools investors, creditors, and suppliers use to evaluate a company's ability to pay its obligations as they come due. So, even though a company includes the correct amount of total liabilities on the balance sheet, if the liabilities are not properly classified as current versus long-term, the current ratio will not be correct. As a result, investors, creditors, and suppliers will be unable to correctly assess the ability of a business to pay its obligations as they come due. Therefore, it is very important for a business to analyze all of its long-term debt at the end of each accounting period to ensure that it is being properly classified as current versus long-term.

HOW DO YOU ACCOUNT FOR CURRENT LIABILITIES OF AN UNCERTAIN AMOUNT?

Account for liabilities of an uncertain amount **3**

A business may know that a liability exists but not know the exact amount of the liability. It cannot simply ignore the liability. The liability must be reported on the balance sheet. Although there are other types of estimated liabilities, the most common example occurs when a company guarantees its products or services against defects under a **warranty** agreement. Therefore, we will focus our attention on accounting for estimated warranties.

Estimated Warranty Liability

It is common for companies to provide either 90-day or 1 year warranties on the goods or services they provide. The matching principle requires that warranty expense be recorded in the same period the revenue related to the warranty is recorded. The expense, therefore, is incurred when sales are made, not when warranty claims are settled. At the time of sale, the company does not know how many warranty claims will be filed. Therefore, the amount of warranty expense for a period is unknown and must be estimated.

Assume that Mackay Industries makes sales of $75,000 during the month of August and that Mackay Industries extends its customers a 90-day warranty on all products sold. Mackay Industries estimates that 2% of its products will require warranty repairs. The company would record sales and warranty expense for the month of August as follows:

DATE	ACCOUNTS	POST REF.	DR.	CR.
	Accounts Receivable or Cash		75,000	
	Sales Revenue			75,000
	Record monthly sales.			
	Warranty Expense		1,500	
	Estimated Warranty Payable			1,500
	Record estimated warranty expense.			

Now assume that during September Mackay Industries paid $450 to settle warranty claims filed by customers. Mackay would make the following entry to record payment of the warranty claims:

DATE	ACCOUNTS	POST REF.	DR.	CR.
	Estimated Warranty Payable		450	
	Cash			450
	Settled warranty claims.			

If, instead of paying cash to settle the warranty claims, Mackay Industries had replaced the defective goods with new items, the entry would have been as follows:

DATE	ACCOUNTS	POST REF.	DR.	CR.
	Estimated Warranty Payable		450	
	Inventory			450
	Settled warranty claims.			

Estimated liabilities are generally current liabilities. However, if the estimated liability is expected to be settled more than one year from the balance sheet date, it would be classified as long-term.

Decision Guidelines

Decision		**Guideline**		**Analyze**
What should I do if I do not know the exact amount of a liability?		Utilize the conservatism principle and estimate the amount.		In order to properly reflect the true financial position and the results of operations of a company, it is important that all obligations of the business be recorded. When the exact amount of a liability is unknown, an estimate of the amount owed should be made. An effort should be made to err on the side of overestimating an obligation versus underestimating it. This will result in the net income of the business being understated rather than overstated. This helps prevent creditors and investors from making poor decisions because of relying on an overstated net income amount.

HOW DO YOU ACCOUNT FOR A CONTINGENT LIABILITY?

Account for
contingent liabilities **4**

IFRS

As stated earlier, although a contingent liability arises as the result of a *past* event, it is dependent upon the outcome of a *future* event. Therefore, a contingent liability represents a potential, rather than an actual obligation. The outcome of the future event will determine whether or not a company will incur an obligation. Examples of contingent liabilities are as follows:

■ Pending, or actual, legal action

■ Potential fines resulting from investigations conducted by regulatory agencies such as the Environmental Protection Agency (EPA) or the Occupational Safety and Health Administration (OSHA)

■ Loan guarantees that occur when one entity cosigns a note payable for another entity

Suppose Mackay Industries guarantees a note for Tucker Enterprises. If Tucker Enterprises fails to pay the note when it comes due, Mackay Industries would be obligated to pay the amount due. This represents a contingent liability to Mackay Industries. Although Mackay Industries cosigned the note (a past event) it will only incur an obligation if Tucker Enterprises fails to pay the note (the future event).

The accounting treatment of a contingent liability depends on the likelihood of an actual obligation occurring. **Exhibit 9-1** outlines the accounting treatment of contingent liabilities.

Likelihood of Obligation Occurring	Accounting Treatment
Remote (very unlikely)	No action is necessary.
Possible (it could occur)	Disclose the existence of the contingent liability in the financial statement footnotes. An explanation of the circumstances related to the contingent liability should be included in the footnote.
Probable (more likely than not)	If the amount of the potential obligation is known (or can be reasonably estimated) the contingent liability should be recorded. The circumstances related to the contingent liability should also be disclosed in the financial statement footnotes. If the amount of the obligation is not known and cannot be reasonably estimated, then only footnote disclosure is required.

Exhibit 9-1 ▲

Let's return to our example of the loan guarantee from earlier. As long as Tucker Enterprises is in sound financial condition, the likelihood of Mackay Industries being required to pay the loan is remote and, therefore, no action is required. If Mackay Industries becomes aware of the fact that Tucker Enterprises is experiencing financial difficulties, it is now possible that it will be obligated to repay the loan. In this case, Mackay Industries would be required to disclose the contingent liability in the notes to its financial statements. If Tucker Enterprises files for bankruptcy or defaults on the loan, it is probable that Mackay Industries will be obligated to repay the loan. Now, in addition to disclosing the contingent liability in the financial statement footnotes, Mackay Industries will have to record the contingent liability in the financial statements. The contingent liability would be recorded by debiting a loss account and crediting a liability account. Contingent liabilities are classified as current versus long-term based upon when the liability is expected to be paid.

HOW DO YOU ACCOUNT FOR LONG-TERM DEBT?

Account for Long-Term Debt **5**

The long-term debt of most companies is comprised of the following types of obligations:

- Notes payable
- Bonds payable
- Leases payable

There are many similarities in the accounting for these different obligations. However, there are also some unique differences. Therefore, we will examine each of the three separately.

Notes Payable

As discussed previously, a note payable is a debt obligation that is supported by a promissory note. Notes payable that are due to be repaid more than one year from the balance sheet date are classified as long-term debt. Most long-term notes payable represent loans taken out for the purchase of land, buildings, or both that are repaid over a long-term period. A note payable used to purchase land or buildings is a special type of note called a **mortgage**. A mortgage is an example of a secured note because it gives the lender the right to take specified assets, called **collateral**, if the borrower is unable to repay the loan.

🌐 Accounting in Your World

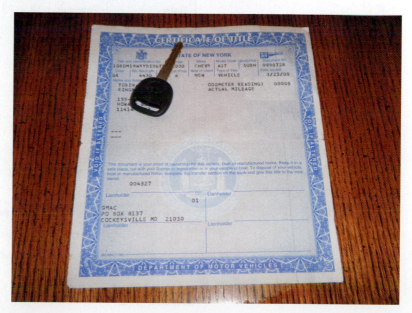

If you have ever borrowed money to purchase a car, then you probably know that you do not get the title to the car until the loan has been paid off. The vehicle title represents legal ownership of the vehicle. Lenders often secure car loans by using the car as collateral for the loan and placing a lien on the title. This means that the lender gets the title to the car (and has legal ownership of the car) until the loan is repaid. If the borrower fails to repay the loan, the lender has the right to repossess, or take back, the car to compensate it for the unpaid loan. Once the loan has been repaid, the lender will release the lien on the title by "signing it over" to the borrower. This transfers legal ownership of the car to the borrower. The title to a vehicle is often referred to as the "pink slip." So, if someone asks you if you have the pink slip to your car, he or she is asking if you owe any money on the car.

A mortgage is typically paid off through installment payments that include both principal and interest. The entries required to record mortgage note transactions are similar to those for note payable transactions. Let's assume that Mackay Industries issues a $155,000, 8%, 20-year mortgage note on January 1, 2010, to finance the purchase of a new building. Payments of $7,831 on the mortgage will be made semiannually on June 30 and December 31 of each year. The purchase of the building is recorded as follows:

DATE	ACCOUNTS	POST REF.	DR.	CR.
Jan 1	Buildings		155,000	
	Mortgage Payable			155,000
	Issued mortgage to purchase building.			

In order to keep track of the portion of each payment that is allocated to principal and to interest, an amortization schedule is usually prepared. **Exhibit 9-2** illustrates an amortization schedule for the first four years of Mackay Industries' mortgage:

	A	B	C	D
		Interest	**Principal**	**Loan Balance**
Date	**Payment**	**(D × .08 × 1/2)***	**(A – B)**	**(D – C)**
1/01/2010				$155,000
6/30/2010	$7,831	$6,200	$1,631	153,369
12/31/2010	7,831	6,135	1,696	151,673
6/30/2011	7,831	6,067	1,764	149,909
12/31/2011	7,831	5,996	1,835	148,074
6/30/2012	7,831	5,923	1,908	146,166
12/31/2012	7,831	5,847	1,984	144,182
6/30/2013	7,831	5,767	2,064	142,118
12/31/2013	7,831	5,685	2,146	139,972

*Rounded

Column B is calculated by multiplying the loan balance from the prior period (column D) by the interest rate (8%) and then multiplying by 1/2 to account for the fact that the payment is made semiannually.

Column C is calculated by subtracting the interest (column B) from the payment (column A).

Column D is calculated by subtracting the principal portion of the payment (column C) from the loan balance from the prior period (column D).

Exhibit 9-2 ▲

Based on information found in Exhibit 9-2, Mackay Industries will record the June 30, 2010, loan payment as follows:

DATE	ACCOUNTS	POST REF.	DR.	CR.
Jun 30	Interest Expense		6,200	
	Mortgage Payable		1,631	
	Cash			7,831
	Record semiannual loan payment.			

As discussed previously in the chapter, the principal portion of any mortgage payments due within one year from the balance sheet date will be classified under current portion of long-term debt on the balance sheet.

Bonds Payable

In addition to using notes payable to aquire needed cash, a business may obtain money by issuing **bonds payable**. Bonds payable are long-term, interest bearing notes that are issued to multiple lenders, called bondholders. By issuing bonds, it is often possible for a business to borrow hundreds of thousands (or even millions) of dollars. Instead of depending on one large loan from a single bank or lender, with bonds, a large number of smaller amounts are borrowed from different investors. For example, Mackay Industries could raise $1,000,000 by borrowing $1,000 each from 1,000 different investors.

Before we move on, let's explore some of the terminology associated with bonds.

- **Term bonds** all mature at the same specified time. For example, $500,000 of term bonds may all mature 10 years from today. With term bonds, the company issuing the bonds will have to repay all $500,000 at the same time.

- **Serial bonds** are bonds from the same bond issuance that mature at different times. For example, a $1,500,000 serial bond issuance may specify that one-third of the bonds mature in 10 years, one-third mature in 15 years, and one-third mature in 20 years.

- **Secured bonds** are bonds that are backed with some form of collateral. Secured bonds give the bondholders the right to take specified assets of the issuer if the issuer fails to pay principal or interest.

- **Unsecured bonds** are bonds that are not backed by any assets. They are backed only by the general credit of the company issuing the bond. Unsecured bonds are also called **debentures**.

- **Convertible bonds** are bonds that give the bondholder the option of exchanging the bond for common stock in the company.

- **Callable bonds** are bonds that may be bought back and retired (called) by the bond issuer at a pre-arranged price.

- **Principal amount** is the amount the borrower must pay back to the bond-holders on the maturity date. The pricipal amount is also called **maturity value**, or **par value**.

- **Maturity date** is the date on which the borrower must repay the principal amount to the bondholders.

- **Stated interest rate** determines the amount of cash interest the bond issuer pays each year. The stated interest rate is printed on the bond and *does not change* from year to year. For example, if a $1,000 bond has a stated interest rate of 9%, the bond issuer pays $90 of interest annually on the bond.
- **Market interest rate** is the rate of interest investors are willing to pay for similar bonds of equal risk at the current time. Bonds are often issued with a stated interest rate that differs from the market interest rate. This is due to the time gap between when the stated rate is determined and when the bonds are actually issued.

Bond Prices

A bond can be issued (sold) at a price that is equal to the par value of the bond, below the par value of the bond, or above the par value of the bond. Whether a bond sells at par, below par, or above par depends on the relationship between the stated interest rate on the bond and the current market rate of interest at the time the bond is sold. Bonds sold at a price equal to par value are said to be sold "at par." Bonds sold at a price below par are said to be sold "at a **discount**," and bonds sold at a price above par are said to be sold "at a **premium**."

To illustrate, let's assume that Mackay Industries issues 6% bonds when the market rate for similar bonds of equal risk is higher, say 6.5% or 7%. Mackay Industries will have a hard time attracting investors to buy its bonds when investors can earn higher returns on bonds of other companies. Therefore, to attract investors, Mackay Industries will offer to sell its bonds at a price less than maturity value, or at a discount. So, for example, Mackay Industries may offer to sell its $1,000, 6% bonds for only $920 each. Mackay Industries will pay the investors yearly interest payments equal to $60 ($1,000 par value × 6% stated interest) on each bond. However, because the investors only paid $920 for each bond, the $60 interest payment represents a return of approximately 6.5% ($60 interest/$920 invested).

On the other hand, if the market interest rate is 5% or 5.5%, Mackay Industries's 6% bonds will be so attractive that investors will pay more than maturity value, or a premium, for them. So, for example, Mackay Industries may offer to sell its $1,000, 6% bonds for $1,085 each. Mackay Industries will still pay the investors yearly interest payments equal to $60 ($1,000 par value × 6% interest) on each bond. However, because the investors paid $1,085 for each bond, the $60 interest payment represents a return of approximately 5.5% ($60 interest/$1,085 invested). The actual price of a bond represents a price that makes the return on the bond effectively the same as the market rate of interest at the time the bond is sold. **Exhibit 9-3** illustrates the relationship

Relationship of Stated Interest Rate to Current Market Interest Rate	Bond Is Sold At	Why?
Stated rate = Market rate	Par	Investors are willing to pay the full maturity value for the bond because it offers the same interest rate as similar bonds with equal risk.
Stated rate < Market rate	Discount	Investors demand a lower price for the bond because they will receive a lower return from this bond than from similar bonds with equal risk.
Stated rate > Market rate	Premium	Investors are willing to pay a higher price for the bond because they will receive a higher return from this bond than from similar bonds with equal risk.

Exhibit 9-3 ▲

between the stated interest rate and the market interest rate and how it effects the sales price of a bond.

The issue price of a bond determines the amount of cash the company receives when it issues the bond. However, the issue price of a bond does not affect the required payment at maturity. A company must always pay the maturity value (par value) of the bonds when they mature.

After bonds have been issued, investors may buy and sell them on the bond market just as they buy and sell stocks on the stock market. The most famous bond market is the New York Exchange, which lists several thousand bonds.

Bond prices are quoted as a percentage of maturity value. For example,

- a $1,000 bond quoted at 100 is bought or sold for 100% of maturity value, ($1,000. × 1.00).
- a $1,000 bond quoted at 96.4 has a price of $964 ($1,000 × .964).
- a $1,000 bond quoted at 102.8 has a price of $1,028 ($1,000 × 1.028).

Issuing Bonds Payable at Par

The journal entry to record the issuance of bonds payable depends on whether the bond is issued at par, at a discount, or at a premium. Let's assume that on April 1, 2010, Mackay Industries issues $500,000 of 8% bonds payable that mature in 10 years. The bonds will pay interest semiannually on March 31 and September 30 of each year. First, let's assume that the market rate of interest on April 1, 2010, is 8%. Because the stated interest rate equals the market interest rate, Mackay Industries will issue these bonds at maturity (par) value. The journal entry to record the receipt of cash and issuance of bonds payable is as follows:

DATE	ACCOUNTS	POST REF.	DR.	CR.
Apr 1	Cash		500,000	
	Bonds Payable			500,000
	Issued bonds at par.			

Interest payments occur March 31 and September 30 each year. Mackay Industries' first semiannual interest payment on September 30, 2010, is journalized as follows:

DATE	ACCOUNTS	POST REF.	DR.	CR.
Sep 30	Interest Expense		20,000*	
	Cash			20,000
	Paid semiannual interest.			

*$500,000 × .08 × 1/2

At maturity on March 31, 2020, after making the journal entry to record the final interest payment, Mackay Industries will record the repayment of the bonds as follows:

DATE	ACCOUNTS	POST REF.	DR.	CR.
2020				
Mar 31	Bonds Payable		500,000	
	Cash			500,000
	Repaid bonds at maturity.			

Now let's look at how bonds issued at a discount are accounted for.

Issuing Bonds Payable at a Discount

Suppose the market rate of interest is higher than 8% on April 1, 2010, when Mackay Industries issues the $500,000 of bonds. Remember from our previous discussion, if the market rate of interest is higher than the stated rate of interest, bonds will sell at a discount. The calculation of the actual sales price of bonds that are not sold at par will be left to more advanced accounting courses. Therefore, for this example we will assume that the Mackay Industries' bonds sold for $478,000. This equals the par value of the bonds, $500,000, less a $22,000 discount. Mackay Industries makes the following journal entry to record the issuance of the bonds at a discount:

DATE	ACCOUNTS	POST REF.	DR.	CR.
Apr 1	Cash		478,000	
	Discount on Bonds Payable		22,000	
	Bonds Payable			500,000
	Issued bonds at discount.			

After posting, the bond accounts have the following balances:

Bonds Payable		Discount on Bonds Payable	
	500,000	22,000	

Discount on Bonds Payable is a contra account to Bonds Payable and, therefore, has a debit balance. Bonds payable *minus* the discount gives the **carrying amount** of the bonds. The carrying amount of the bonds represents the "net" bond liability that is carried on the company's books. The carrying value of Mackay Industries' bonds immediately after issue would be as follows:

Bonds Payable	$500,000
Less, Discount on Bonds Payable	22,000
Carrying Value of Bonds Payable	$478,000

Interest Expense on Bonds Payable with a Discount

When Mackay Industries issued the bonds, it received $478,000 but it still must repay $500,000 when the bonds mature. The $22,000 difference between what it received and what it must pay back (the discount) ultimately represents additional interest expense to Mackay Industries. This additional interest effectively raises Mackay Industries' true interest rate on the bonds to the market interest rate, which was higher than the stated interest rate of 8%. The discount is allocated to interest expense through the process of amortization.

The simplest way of amortizing a bond discount is by using straight-line amortization. This is very similar to the straight-line method of amortizing intangible assets, like patents, which we learned about in Chapter 8. Under straight-line amortization, an equal amount of the discount is allocated to interest expense at the time of each semiannual interest payment. In our example, the initial discount is $22,000, and there are 20 semiannual interest periods during the bonds' 10-year life. Therefore, 1/20 of the $22,000 bond discount ($1,100) is amortized each interest period. Mackay Industries' first semiannual interest payment is recorded as follows:

DATE	ACCOUNTS	POST REF.	DR.	CR.
Sep 30	Interest Expense		21,100	
	Discount on Bonds Payable			1,100
	Cash			20,000
	Paid semiannual interest.			

The interest expense of $21,100 is the sum of

- the $20,000 of stated interest, which is paid to the bondholders in cash,
- plus the $1,100 amortization of the discount.

Discount on Bonds Payable has a debit balance. Therefore, when the bond discount is amortized, the Discount on Bonds Payable is credited to reduce its balance. As the balance in the discount account is reduced, the carrying value of the bonds increases. After 20 amortization entries, the discount will be reduced to zero and the carrying amount of the bonds payable will be $500,000.

Bonds Payable	$500,000
Less, Discount on Bonds Payable	-0-
Carrying Value of Bonds Payable	$500,000

At maturity, after making the journal entry to record the final interest payment, Mackay Industries will record the repayment of the bonds as follows:

DATE	ACCOUNTS	POST REF.	DR.	CR.
2020				
Mar 31	Bonds Payable		500,000	
	Cash			500,000
	Repaid bonds at maturity.			

Notice that the entry to record the repayment of the bonds is the same as it was for bonds that were issued at par. This is because, at maturity, the carrying value of the bonds is equal to the par value of the bonds.

Issuing Bonds Payable at a Premium

To illustrate a bond premium, let's change the Mackay Industries example. Assume that the market interest rate is less than the stated rate of 8% when Mackay Industries issues its 10-year bonds. Mackay Industries' 8% bonds are attractive when the market interest rate is less than 8% so investors will pay a premium to acquire them. Assume the bonds are priced at 103 (103% of maturity value). In this case, Mackay

Industries receives $515,000 cash upon issuance. Mackay Industries' entry to borrow money and issue these bonds is as follows:

DATE	ACCOUNTS	POST REF.	DR.	CR.
Apr 1	Cash		515,000	
	Premium on Bonds Payable			15,000
	Bonds Payable			500,000
	Issued bonds at premium.			

After posting, the bond accounts have the following balances:

Bonds Payable		Premium on Bonds Payable	
	500,000		15,000

Notice that Bonds Payable and Premium on Bonds Payable each have a credit balance. The Premium on Bonds Payable account is known as an **adjunct account**. Like a contra account, an adjunct account is a companion account to another account. However, unlike a contra account, an adjunct account serves to "add to" instead of "take away from" its companion account. Therefore, we add the Premium on Bonds Payable to Bonds Payable to determine the bond carrying value. The carrying value of the Mackay Industries' bonds immediately after issuance is as follows:

Bonds Payable	$500,000
Plus, Premium on Bonds Payable	15,000
Carrying Value of Bonds Payable	$515,000

Interest Expense on Bonds Payable with a Premium

When Mackay Industries issued the bonds it received $515,000 but it must pay back only $500,000 at maturity. The $15,000 difference between what it received and what it must pay back (the premium) ultimately represents a reduction of interest expense to Mackay Industries. This reduced interest effectively lowers Mackay Industries' true interest rate on the bonds to the market interest rate that was lower than the stated interest rate of 8%. As with a discount, a premium is allocated to interest expense through the process of amortization. Only, in the case of a premium, the amortization decreases interest expense over the life of the bonds.

In our example, the beginning premium is $15,000, and there are 20 semiannual interest periods during the bonds' 10-year life. Therefore, 1/20 of the $15,000 ($750) of bond premium is amortized each interest period. Mackay Industries' first semiannual interest entry is as follows:

DATE	ACCOUNTS	POST REF.	DR.	CR.
Sep 30	Interest Expense		19,250	
	Premium on Bonds Payable		750	
	Cash			20,000
	Paid semiannual interest.			

The interest expense of $19,250 is

- the $20,000 of stated interest which is paid to the bondholders in cash,
- minus the $750 amortization of the premium.

As the balance in the premium account is reduced, the carrying value of the bonds decreases. At maturity on March 31, 2020, the bond premium will have been fully amortized (it will have a zero balance), and the bond's carrying amount will be $500,000 (the amount in the Bonds Payable account). Therefore, the entry to record the repayment of the bonds will be the same as it was when the bonds were issued at par or at a discount.

Adjusting Entries for Bonds Payable

Interest payments on bonds seldom occur on December 31, so interest expense must be accrued at year end. The accrual entry should also amortize any related bond discount or premium. Let's return to our Mackay Industries example where Mackay Industries sold $500,000 of bonds at a discount for $478,000 on April 1, 2010. Mackay Industries made an interest payment on September 30, 2010. On December 31, Mackay Industries accrues interest and amortizes bond discount for three months (October, November, and December) as follows:

DATE	ACCOUNTS	POST REF.	DR.	CR.
Dec 31	Interest Expense		10,550	
	Discount on Bonds Payable			550
	Interest Payable			10,000
	Acrrued bond interest.			

The interest expense of $10,550 is the sum of

- the $10,000 of stated interest for October, November, and December;
- plus the $550 amortization of the discount for October, November, and December.

Interest payable is credited for the three months of interest owed to the bondholders, $10,000. The next semiannual interest payment occurs on March 31, 2011, and Mackay Industries makes the following journal entry:

DATE	ACCOUNTS	POST REF.	DR.	CR.
Mar 31	Interest Expense		10,550	
	Interest Payable		10,000	
	Discount on Bonds Payable			550
	Cash			20,000
	Paid semiannual interest.			

The interest expense of $10,550 is the sum of

- the $10,000 of stated interest for January, February, and March;
- plus the $550 amortization of the discount for January, February, and March.

Interest payable is debited for $10,000 to reflect the fact that the amount accrued at December 31, 2010, is being paid. The $20,000 credit to cash represents the stated interest that is paid to the bondholders.

Decision Guidelines

Decision		Guideline		Analyze
What should I do if my business needs more cash than the bank will lend me?		Consider issuing bonds.		With notes payable, a business typically borrows a large sum of money from one lender, usually a bank. With bonds, a business borrows smaller amounts, often in $1,000 increments, from many different investors. By utilizing bonds payable, a business can often borrow very large sums of money because no single investor is exposed to a significant amount of risk.

Lease Liabilities

A lease is an agreement in which one party (the lessee) agrees to pay another party (the lessor) for the use of an asset. Many businesses enter into leases for

- equipment such as computers, phone systems, and manufacturing equipment.
- vehicles, such as automobiles and delivery trucks.
- real estate, such as offices or warehouses.

Leases may be divided into two categories: operating leases and capital leases. The accounting treatment is different for each type of lease.

Operating Leases

An **operating lease** is basically a rental agreement. An operating lease grants the use of an asset to the lessee for the duration of the lease in exchange for regular payments. At the end of the lease, the lessee must return the leased asset to the lessor. The title (ownership) of the asset remains with the lessor. The lease payments are treated as an expense by the lessee and as revenue by the lessor. For example, assume that Mackay Industries entered into a lease agreement for the use of a copy machine. The agreement was an operating lease that required monthly payments of $250 for a three-year period. Mackay Industries would make the following entry to record the monthly lease payments:

DATE	ACCOUNTS	POST REF.	DR.	CR.
	Lease (or Rent) Expense		250	
	Cash			250
	Record monthly lease payment.			

At the end of the lease, Mackay Industries will return the copy machine to the lessor.

Capital Leases

A **capital lease** is treated as a financed purchase. In other words, it is treated as if the lessee borrowed money to purchase the asset. If a lease meets any one of the following criteria, it is classified as a capital lease:

1. Title (ownership) of the leased asset is transferred to the lessee at the end of the lease term.

2. The lease contains a bargain purchase option. In other words, the lessee has the option to purchase the asset at a price significantly less than fair market value at the end of the lease term.

❸ The duration of the lease is 75% or more of the estimated useful life of the leased asset.

❹ The present value of the lease payments equals 90% or more of the market value of the leased asset. The concept of present value is discussed in Appendix B at the end of the book.

Because a capital lease is treated as a financed purchase, the lessee will record the lease by debiting an asset account and crediting Lease Payable at the time the lease is entered into. For example, assume that Mackay Industries leases a delivery truck for a five-year period. The lease calls for monthly payments of $825 and has a bargain purchase option. Assume also that the liability under this capital lease is determined to be $38,000. (The calculation of the amount due under a capital lease is left to more advanced accounting courses.) Mackay Industries would record the lease as follows:

DATE	ACCOUNTS	POST REF.	DR.	CR.
	Delivery Truck		38,000	
	Lease Payable			38,000
	Acquired truck under a capital lease.			

Lease payments made under a capital lease agreement are similar to repayments of mortgage notes payable. The lessee allocates the lease payment between interest and principal, as demonstrated earlier in our discussion of accounting for mortgage note payments. Depreciation expense is recorded on a leased asset as it is for any other asset, as described in Chapter 8. As with mortgages, the principal portion of capital lease payments due within one year from the balance sheet date will be classified under current portion of long-term debt on the balance sheet.

Decision Guidelines

Decision	Guidelines	Analyze
When leasing an asset, am I better off with an operating lease or a capital lease?	Evaluate the costs and benefits associated with both types of leases.	The total lease payments made under an operating lease often seem to be expensive, especially considering that the asset must be returned at the end of the lease. However, operating leases are often attractive because they can take away some of the risks associated with owning an asset. Under an operating lease, the cost of repairing and maintaining the asset is often borne by the lessor. This helps the lessee budget his or her cash outflows knowing that they will not incur any unexpected repair bills. Also, with an operating lease, the risk of obsolescence of the asset is borne by the lessor.

HOW ARE LIABILITIES REPORTED ON THE BALANCE SHEET?

Report liabilities on the balance sheet **6** In Chapter 4, we learned how to prepare a classified balance sheet. Throughout the chapter, we have seen how all of a company's liabilities are classified as either current liabilities or long-term liabilities. This classification determines where the liabilities are reported on the company's classified balance sheet. An example of what the liabilities section of Mackay Industries' balance sheet might look like is presented in **Exhibit 9-4** on the following page.

Mackay Industries Balance Sheet—Partial	
Current Liabilities:	
Accounts Payable	$ 2,200
Salaries Payable	8,700
Payroll Taxes Payable	2,610
Interest Payable	1,850
Sales Tax Payable	975
Estimated Warranty Payable	1,310
Unearned Revenue	1,400
Income Tax Payable	6,200
Current Portion of Long-Term Debt	11,700
Total Current Liabilities	36,945
Long-Term Debt	
Mortgage Payable	85,000
Bonds Payable, Net of $20,350 Discount	479,650
Lease Payable	36,650
Total Long-Term Debt	601,300
Total Liabilities	638,245

Exhibit 9-4 ▲

Proper accounting for liabilities can also pose an ethical challenge. Classifying current liabilities as long-term, or vice versa, can have a big impact on a company's current ratio. Owners and managers may also be tempted to overlook expenses and their related liabilities at the end of the accounting period in an effort to make a business look more profitable. For example, a company might neglect to accrue warranty expense and the related warranty liability. This will cause reported liabilities and total expenses to be understated. Net income will also be overstated.

Contingent liabilities also pose an ethical challenge. Because contingencies are based on the outcome of a future event, they are easier to overlook. However, a contingency can turn into a real liability and can significantly change the company's financial position. Successful people refuse to play games with their accounting. Falsifying financial statements can result, and has resulted, in a prison term.

FOCUS ON DECISION MAKING: RATIOS

Compute the debt ratio **7**

In Chapter 4 we learned how the current ratio is used to analyze a business's ability to pay its obligations as they come due. The **debt ratio** also uses liabilities to help examine a business; however, instead of focusing on current liabilities, the debt ratio focuses on the total liabilities of an organization. The debt ratio is found by dividing the total liabilities (debt) of an organization by the total assets:

$$\text{Debt ratio} = \frac{\text{Total liabilities}}{\text{Total assets}}$$

The debt ratio reveals what percentage of a company's assets would be required to pay off all of its liabilities. The debt ratio is an indicator of a company's solvency. It is also a good indicator of a company's ability to incur, or take on, more debt. Let's assume that Mackay Industries has assets totaling $685,000, total liabilities of $425,000, and total stockholder's equity of $260,000. Mackay Industries debt ratio is as follows:

$$\text{Debt ratio} = \frac{\text{Total liabilities}}{\text{Total assets}} = \frac{\$425,000}{\$685,000} = 62\% \text{ (rounded)}$$

Mackay Industries' debt ratio of 62% indicates that 62% of Mackay Industries' assets would be required to pay off all of its liabilitites. Another way of looking at it is that after paying off all liabilities, 38% of Mackay Industries' assets would be left for the stockholders. The average debt ratio for most companies ranges from 57% to 67%, with relatively little variation from company to company. Mackay Industries' debt ratio falls right in the middle of the range of industry averages.

Demo Doc

Known and Estimated Current Liabilities

Learning Objectives 1–3 ▶

Advantage Audio, Inc., began operations on January 1, 2010, selling personal music players. Each player comes with a one-year warranty included in the selling price. Advantage Audio, Inc., also sells digital songs that owners can download to their players. Customers prepay $100 for 100 songs and can download them whenever they wish.

During 2010, Advantage Audio, Inc., had the following information:

Sales revenue from sale of music players sold to customers	$100,000
Purchase cost of music players sold to customers	$ 40,000
Sales tax rate (sales tax charged on player sales only)	7 %
Music downloads purchased by customers	20,000 songs
Songs downloaded by customers	6,000 songs
Repairs made to players under warranty	$ 1,200

Advantage Audio, Inc., estimates that the repairs it will have to make to music players under the warranty provided will cost 2% of the selling price. Advantage Audio, Inc., has contracted with a local repair shop to service any players required for an upfront cash payment.

At December 31, 2010, Advantage Audio, Inc., estimated that of the remaining prepaid music downloads, 10,000 songs would be downloaded in 2011, with the rest downloaded in 2012.

Requirements:

❶ Journalize the following transactions:

  a. The sale of all music players in 2010 (assume cash sales)

  b. Payment of the year's sales taxes to the state government

  c. The sale of music downloads in 2010 (assume cash sales)

  d. Song downloads in 2010

  e. Repairs made under warranty in 2010

❷ Are the following liabilities current or long-term for Advantage Audio, Inc.?

  a. Sales Tax Payable

  b. Unearned Music Downloads Revenue

  c. Estimated Warranty Payable

Demo Doc Solutions

Requirement ❶

Journalize the following transactions:

Part 1	Part 2	Demo Doc Complete

a. The sale of all music players in 2010 (assume cash sales)

When the players are sold, a number of accounts are affected. First, Advantage Audio, Inc., must record the sales revenue and cash collected. We are told in the problem that $100,000 of music players were sold, so "Sales Revenue—Players" increases (credit) by $100,000.

Cash also increases, but is $100,000 the *only* amount the customers paid? No, in addition to the selling price, customers must also pay sales tax when they buy a player. The total cash paid by customers was $107,000 [$100,000 + ($100,000 × 7%)]. So, Cash is increased (debit) by $107,000.

The extra $7,000 ($100,000 × 7%) collected by Advantage Audio, Inc., *does not belong* to it. It belongs to the state government and must be paid to the state at a future date. A future payment (or *obligation*) is a liability. Therefore, Advantage Audio, Inc., must record (credit) a Sales Tax Payable of $7,000.

DATE	ACCOUNTS	POST REF.	DR.	CR.
	Cash ($100,000 × 1.07)		107,000	
	Sales Revenue—Players			100,000
	Sales Tax Payable ($100,000 × 7%)			7,000
	Record sales for cash.			

In addition to recording the sales revenue, Advantage Audio, Inc., must record the cost of the players sold. The players cost $40,000 to purchase, so we must record (debit) Cost of Goods Sold for $40,000. As the players are sold, Inventory is also decreased (credit) by $40,000.

DATE	ACCOUNTS	POST REF.	DR.	CR.
	Cost of Goods Sold		40,000	
	Inventory			40,000
	Record cost of sales.			

One other issue must be addressed when recording the sales of the players: the warranties included in the selling price. Warranty costs are recorded *at the time of sale* to have proper matching (the expense of the warranty is recorded *at the same time* as the sales revenue).

Advantage Audio, Inc., estimates that the warranty costs will be 2% of selling price, so Advantage Audio, Inc., must record (debit) Warranty Expense for $2,000 ($100,000 × 2%). Advantage Audio, Inc., is now *obligated* to pay for these repairs when customer players break down. In accounting, *a future obligation is a liability*. So, Advantage Audio, Inc., must record an Estimated Warranty Payable liability (credit) of $2,000.

DATE	ACCOUNTS	POST REF.	DR.	CR.
	Warranty Expense ($100,000 × 0.02)		2,000	
	Estimated Warranty Payable			2,000
	Record estimated warranty expense.			

b. Payment of the year's sales taxes to the state government

The sales taxes must be sent to the state government. When this payment is made, Sales Tax Payable is decreased (debit) by $7,000 and Cash is decreased (credit) by $7,000.

DATE	ACCOUNTS	POST REF.	DR.	CR.
	Sales Tax Payable		7,000	
	Cash			7,000
	Record payment of sales tax collected.			

Notice that this entry is nearly identical to the entry to record payment of general accounts payable.

c. The sale of music downloads in 2010 (assume cash sales)

The customer pays for the music downloads before he or she receives them. In other words, Advantage Audio, Inc., has received the cash but has not provided the songs yet. So, Advantage Audio, Inc., has an *obligation* (a liability) to provide these songs to the customer.

Advantage Audio, Inc., *has not yet earned* the download revenue because it has not yet provided the songs to customers. Revenue will be earned as customers download their songs.

With 20,000 songs prepaid for $1 per song, we must record Unearned Music Download Revenue (credit) of $20,000 (20,000 × $1). We must also record an increase in Cash (debit) of $20,000.

DATE	ACCOUNTS	POST REF.	DR.	CR.
	Cash		20,000	
	Unearned Music Download Revenue			20,000
	Record cash received for music downloads in advance			
	of providing songs.			

d. Song downloads in 2010

Once songs are downloaded, Advantage Audio, Inc., earns the revenue from the sale of the songs. Then, it records "Sales Revenue—Music Downloads" of $6,000 (6,000 × $1). Because Advantage Audio, Inc., is now meeting its obligation to its customers by providing songs, the Unearned Music Download Revenue account is decreased (debit) by $6,000.

DATE	ACCOUNTS	POST REF.	DR.	CR.
	Unearned Music Download Revenue		6,000	
	Sales Revenue—Music Downloads (6,000 × $1)			6,000
	Record downloads revenue earned.			

After this transaction is recorded, the Unearned Revenue and related Sales Revenue accounts are as follows:

Unearned Music Download Revenue				Sales Revenues—Music Downloads	
		(Downloads prepaid)	20,000		6,000
(Songs downloaded)	6,000				
		Dec 31 Bal	14,000		

e. Repairs made under warranty in 2010

When repairs are made under warranty, Advantage Audio's obligation to pay for these repairs is being met. This causes Estimated Warranty Payable to decrease (debit) by $1,200.

The repairs are being paid for in cash, so Cash is also decreased (credit) by $1,200.

DATE	ACCOUNTS	POST REF.	DR.	CR.
	Estimated Warranty Payable		1,200	
	Cash			1,200
	Record payment of warranty claims.			

Notice that warranty expense is *not* affected by this transaction! The expense was *already* recorded back when the players were sold (see Transaction a). To record warranty expense now would be double-counting the expense.

After this transaction is recorded, the warranty-related accounts are as follows:

Estimated Warranty Payable				Warranty Expense	
	(Players sold)	2,000		2,000	
(Repairs made) 1,200					
	Dec 31 Bal	800			

Requirement ❷

Are the following liabilities current or long-term for Advantage Audio, Inc.?

Part 1	**Part 2**	Demo Doc Complete

a. Sales Tax Payable

Governments usually do not want to wait long for their money. Most sales taxes are remitted to the government within one month (or sooner) of being collected. In this example, Advantage Audio, Inc., already remitted the 2010 sales taxes before the end of the year. A real company could send sales tax collections to the state government once a month. Because sales tax liabilities are paid well within one year, the Sales Tax Payable account is a current liability.

b. Unearned Music Downloads Revenue

The prepaid music downloads are unearned revenue. But when will that revenue be earned? In 2010, 6,000 songs were downloaded, and Advantage Audio, Inc., expects that another 10,000 will be downloaded in 2011, with the remaining 4,000 songs (20,000 – 6,000 – 10,000) being downloaded in 2012.

At December 31, 2010, Advantage Audio, Inc., has an Unearned Music Download Revenue liability of $14,000 for 14,000 songs (see Transaction d). Of this $14,000, $10,000 is a current liability (because it will be earned during the next year of 2011 as songs are downloaded) and $4,000 is a long-term liability (for songs downloaded after 2011).

c. Estimated Warranty Payable

Warranties can cover many years, so it is possible that an Estimated Warranty Payable liability could have both current and long-term portions (as Advantage Audio's Unearned Revenue does). However, the warranties Advantage Audio, Inc., provides are only one year long, so we know that all obligations under the warranty will be met within one year. Therefore, the entire Estimated Warranty Payable is a current liability.

Demo Doc Complete

Part 1	Part 2	**Demo Doc Complete**

Decision Guidelines

Accounting for Current Liabilities and Long-Term Debt

Within your business, you will likely encounter some, or all, of these decisions related to liabilities:

Decision	**Guideline**	**Analyze**
What should I do if I do not know the exact amount of a liability?	Utilize the conservatism principle and estimate the amount.	In order to properly reflect the true financial position and results of operations of a company, it is important that all obligations of the business be recorded. When the exact amount of a liability is unknown, an estimate of the amount owed should be made. An effort should be made to err on the side of overestimating an obligation versus underestimating it. This will result in the net income of the business being understated rather than overstated. This helps prevent creditors and investors from making poor decisions because of relying on an overstated net income amount.
What should I do if my business needs more cash than the bank will lend me?	Consider issuing bonds.	With notes payable, a business typically borrows a large sum of money from one lender, usually a bank. With bonds, a business borrows smaller amounts, often in $1,000 increments, from many different investors. By utilizing bonds payable, a business can often borrow very large sums of money because no single investor is exposed to a significant amount of risk.
When leasing an asset, am I better off with an operating lease or a capital lease?	Evaluate the costs and benefits associated with both types of leases.	The total lease payments made under an operating lease often seem to be expensive, especially considering that the asset must be returned at the end of the lease. However, operating leases are often attractive because they can take away some of the risks associated with owning an asset. Under an operating lease, the cost of repairing and maintaining the asset is often borne by the lessor. This helps the lessee budget his or her cash outflows knowing that they will not incur any unexpected repair bills. Also, with an operating lease, the risk of obsolescence of the asset is borne by the lessor.

ACCOUNTING VOCABULARY

THE LANGUAGE OF BUSINESS

Adjunct account (p. 454) An account that is linked to another account (a companion account). An adjunct account will have a normal balance that is the same as its companion account.

Bonds payable (p. 449) Long-term, interest bearing notes payable issued to multiple lenders called bondholders.

Callable bonds (p. 449) Bonds that the issuer may call or pay off at a specified price whenever the issuer wants.

Capital lease (p. 456) A lease agreement that is treated as a financed purchase.

Carrying amount (p. 452) Bonds payable *minus* the discount or *plus* the premium.

Collateral (p. 447) Assets pledged to secure repayment of a loan. In the case of nonpayment by the borrower, the lender has the right to take the collateral.

Contingent liability (p. 440) A potential liability that depends on the outcome of a future event.

Convertible bonds (p. 449) Bonds that may be converted into the common stock of the issuing company at the option of the investor.

Current portion of long-term debt (p. 443) The principal portion of a long-term liability that is payable within one year.

Debentures (p. 449) Unsecured bonds backed only by the good faith of the borrower; also called *unsecured bonds*.

Debt ratio (p. 458) The ratio of a company's total liabilities (debt) to its total assets.

Discount (p. 450) Excess of a bond's maturity value over its issue price; also called a *bond discount*.

Market interest rate (p. 450) Interest rate investors are willing to pay for similar bonds of equal risk at the current time.

Maturity date (p. 449) The date on which the bond issuer (the borrower) must repay the principal amount to the bondholders.

Maturity value (p. 449) The amount a borrower must pay back to the bondholders on the maturity date; also called *principal amount* or *par value*.

Mortgage (p. 447) A long-term note payable that is secured by real estate.

Operating lease (p. 456) A lease (rental) agreement that grants the use of an asset to the lessee for the duration of the lease in exchange for regular payments.

Par value (p. 449) The amount a borrower must pay back to the bondholders on the maturity date; also called *principal amount* or *maturity value*.

Premium (p. 450) Excess of a bond's issue price over its maturity value; also called *bond premium*.

Principal amount (p. 449) The amount a borrower must pay back to the bondholders on the maturity date; also called *par value* or *maturity value*.

Secured bonds (p. 449) Bonds that give bondholders the right to take specified assets of the issuer if the issuer fails to pay principal or interest.

Serial Bonds (p. 449) Bonds from the same bond issuance that mature at different times.

Stated interest rate (p. 450) Interest rate that determines the amount of cash interest the borrower pays and the investor receives each year.

Term Bonds (p. 449) Bonds that all mature at the same time.

Unsecured bonds (p. 449) Bonds that are backed only by the general credit of the company issuing the bond; also called *debentures*.

Warranty (p. 444) A guarantee that a product or service is free from defect.

ACCOUNTING PRACTICE

DISCUSSION QUESTIONS

1. Provide an example of a known liability, an estimated liability, and a contingent liability.

2. If a company with a 12/31 year-end were to borrow money in the form of a four-month note on 11/1, what accounts would be debited on 3/1 when it pays the note off?

3. What journal entry is made when unearned revenue is earned?

4. What is the difference between a current liability for an uncertain amount and a contingent liability? Give an example of each and demonstrate how they differ with respect to the difference that you identified in the first part of this question.

5. What is the distinguishing feature of each of the following types of bonds:

   a. Convertible   **b.** Callable   **c.** Secured
   d. Unsecured   **e.** Serial   **f.** Term

6. What do we know about the relationship between the market rate of interest and the stated interest rate for a particular bond when the bond is sold at

   a. par?   **b.** a premium?   **c.** a discount?

7. Will interest expense be greater than, less than, or equal to the interest payment made on bonds when the bonds are sold at

   a. par?   **b.** a premium?   **c.** a discount?

8. What happens to the difference between the carrying amount of bonds and the principal amount of the bonds over time?

9. What are the differences between an operating lease and a capital lease?

10. What are some ways that companies might use improper recording of liabilities to manipulate financial statements?

SELF CHECK

1. Known liabilities of uncertain amounts should be

   a. estimated and accrued when they occur.
   b. ignored; record them when they are paid.
   c. reported on the income statement.
   d. described in the notes to the financial statements.

2. On January 1, 2010, you borrowed $10,000 on a five-year, 8% note payable. At December 31, 2010, you should record a journal entry that includes which of the following?

   a. Note Payable of $10,000
   b. Nothing; the note has already been recorded
   c. Interest Payable of $800
   d. Cash receipt of $10,000

3. Your company sells $100,000 of goods and you collect sales tax of 3%. What current liability does the sale create?

   a. Accounts Payable of $3,000   **b.** Unearned Revenue of $3,000
   c. Sales Revenue of $103,000   **d.** Sales Tax Payable of $3,000

4. Sony owed Estimated Warranty Payable of $1,000 at the end of 2009. During 2010, Sony made sales of $100,000 and expects product warranties to cost the company 3% of the sales. During 2010, Sony paid $2,500 for warranties. What is Sony's Estimated Warranty Payable at the end of 2010?

   a. $1,500   **b.** $2,500   **c.** $3,000   **d.** $3,500

5. What is the term used to describe an unsecured bond?

   a. Debenture bond   **b.** Mortgage bond   **c.** Serial bond   **d.** Callable bond

6. Which interest rate on a bond determines the amount of the semiannual interest payment?

   a. Market rate   **b.** Effective rate   **c.** Stated rate   **d.** None of the above

7. Plavix Corporation's bonds payable carry a stated interest rate of 7%, and the market rate of interest at the time of issuance is 8%. Plavix Corporation's bonds will be sold at

   a. a premium.   **b.** a discount.   **c.** par value.   **d.** maturity value.

8. Bonds issued at a premium always have

   a. interest expense less than the interest payments.
   b. interest expense greater than the interest payments.
   c. interest expense equal to the interest payments.
   d. none of the above.

9. Milton's bonds pay interest semiannually on July 1 and January 1. If its fiscal year ends on September 30, which statement is *true* of Milton's year-end adjusting journal entry for bond interest?

   a. Milton must record three month's accrued interest expense and amortize three month's discount or premium.

   b. Milton will record nine month's accrued interest expense and amortize nine month's discount or premium.

   c. Milton must record three month's accrued interest expense only.

   d. Milton will record nine month's accrued interest expense and amortize three month's discount or premium.

10. A company recognizes a lease as a capital lease when

    a. the lease term is less than 75% of the estimated useful life of the leased asset.

    b. the lease has no option to purchase the asset at the end of the lease term.

    c. the lease transfers title of the leased asset to the lessee at the end of the lease term.

    d. the present value of the lease payments is less than 90% of the market value of the leased asset.

    Answers are given after Written Communication.

SHORT EXERCISES

S9-1. Accounting for notes payable (*Learning Objective 2*) 5–10 min.

On June 30, 2010, Harper, Co., purchased $9,000 of inventory for a one-year, 9% note payable. Journalize the following for the company:

1. Accrual of interest expense on December 31, 2010
2. Payment of the note plus interest on June 30, 2011

S9-2. Accounting for notes payable (*Learning Objective 2*) 5–10 min.

On September 30, 2010, Tucker, Co., borrowed $15,000 on a one-year, 7% note payable. What amounts would Tucker, Co., report for the note payable and the related interest payable on its balance sheet at December 31, 2010, and on its income statement for the year ended December 31, 2010?

S9-3. Warranties (*Learning Objective 3*) 5–10 min.

Lake Country Boats guarantees its boats for three years or 1,500 hours, whichever comes first. Past experience of other boat makers indicates that Lake Country can expect warranty costs will equal 6% of sales. Assume in its first year Lake Country Boats had sales totaling $600,000, receiving cash for 30% of sales and notes receivable for the remainder. Warranty payments totaled $22,000 during the year.

1. Record the sales, warranty expense, and warranty payments for Lake Country Boats.

2. Post relevant portions of the journal entries to the Estimated Warranty Payable T-account. At the end of the first year, how much in estimated warranty payable does Lake Country owe its customers?

3. What amount of warranty expense will Lake Country report during its first year of operations? Does the warranty expense for the year equal the year's cash payments for warranties? Which accounting principle addresses this situation?

S9-4. Commitments and contingencies (*Learning Objective 4*) 5–10 min.

Phatboy Motorcycles, Inc., a motorcycle manufacturer, included the following note in its annual report:

Notes to Consolidated Financial Statements

9: Commitments and Contingencies

The Company self-insures its product liability losses in the United States up to $2.5 million.

Catastrophic coverage is maintained for individual claims in excess of $2.5 million up to $25 million.

1. Why are product liability losses considered contingent liabilities?

2. How can a contingent liability become a real liability for Phatboy Motorcycles?

S9-5. Accounting for mortgages (*Learning Objective 5*) 10–15 min.

Ling Company issued a $200,000, 8%, 30-year mortgage on January 1, 2010, to purchase a building. Payments of $8,840 are made semiannually. Complete the following amortization schedule (partial) for Ling Company.

Date	Payment	Interest	Principal	Loan Balance
Jan 1, 2010				$200,000
Jun 30, 2010	$8,840			
Dec 31, 2010				
Jun 30, 2011				
Dec 31, 2011				

S9-6. Accounting for mortgages (*Learning Objective 5*) 5–10 min.

Apex, Co., issued a $225,000, 9% mortgage on January 1, 2010. Payments of $10,900 are made semiannually on June 30 and December 31 each year. Record the journal entries for (a) issuance of mortgage on January 1, 2010, and (b) the first semiannual payment on June 30, 2010.

S9-7. Bond terms (*Learning Objective 5*) 5–10 min.

Match the following terms with the correct definition.

_____ 1. Bonds that all mature at the same time.

_____ 2. Interest rate investors are willing to pay for similar bonds of equal risk.

_____ 3. Unsecured bonds backed only by the good faith of the borrower.

_____ 4. Amount of a bond's issue price over its maturity value.

_____ 5. Bonds that may be converted into the common stock of the issuing company at the option of the investor.

_____ 6. Amount of a bond's maturity value over its issue price.

_____ 7. Interest rate that determines the amount of cash interest the borrower pays and the investor receives.

_____ 8. Bonds in the same bond issuance that mature at different times.

_____ 9. Bonds that the issuer may call or pay off at a specified price whenever the issuer wants.

a. Convertible bonds

b. Premium on bond

c. Callable bonds

d. Debentures

e. Term bonds

f. Serial bonds

g. Discount on bond

h. Stated interest rate

i. Market interest rate

S9-8. Determining the issue price for bonds (*Learning Objective 5*) 5–10 min.

Determine whether the following bonds payable will be issued at par, at a premium, or at a discount:

a. The market interest rate is 7%. Owens, Corp., issues bonds payable with a stated rate of 8 1/2%.

b. Bakers, Inc., issued 7% bonds payable when the market rate was 7 1/2%.

    c. Saratoga Corporation issued 8% bonds when the market interest rate was 8%.

    d. Tacoma Company issued bonds payable that pay cash interest at the stated rate of 7%. At the date of issuance, the market interest rate was 8 1/4%.

S9-9. Analyzing bond terms (*Learning Objective 5*) 10–15 min.

All Star Amusements is planning to issue long-term bonds payable to borrow for a major expansion. For each of the following questions, identify whether the bond price involves a discount, a premium, or par value.

    a. The stated interest rate on the bonds is 7%, and the market interest rate is 8%. What type of price can All Star Amusements expect for the bonds?

    b. All Star Amusements could raise the stated interest rate on the bonds to 9% (market rate is 8%). In that case, what type of price can All Star Amusements expect for the bonds?

    c. At what type of bond price will All Star Amusements have total interest expense equal to the cash interest payments?

    d. At which type of price will All Star Amusements' total interest expense be less than the cash interest payments?

    e. At which type of price will All Star Amusements' total interest expense be greater than the cash interest payments?

S9-10. Accounting for bonds (*Learning Objective 5*) 15–20 min.

Delta, Corp., issued 6%, five-year bonds payable with a maturity value of $5,000 on January 1, 2010. Journalize the following transactions and include an explanation for each entry. The market rate of interest equaled the stated rate at the date of issuance.

    a. Issuance of the bond payable at par on January 1, 2010.

    b. Payment of semiannual interest on July 1, 2010.

    c. Payment of the bonds payable at maturity. (Give the date.)

S9-11. Accounting for bonds (*Learning Objective 5*) 15–20 min.

Hastings, Corp., issued 6%, five-year bonds payable with a maturity value of $5,000 at a price of $4,570 when the market rate was 8% on January 1, 2010. Journalize the following transactions for Hastings, Corp. Include an explanation for each entry.

    a. Issuance of the bond payable on January 1, 2010.

    b. Payment of semiannual interest and amortization of bond discount on July 1, 2010. (Use the straight-line method to amortize the discount.)

S9-12. Accounting for bonds (*Learning Objective 5*) 15–20 min.

Hastings, Corp., issued 6%, five-year bonds payable with a maturity value of $5,000 at a price of $5,460 when the market rate was 4% on January 1, 2010. Journalize the following transactions for Hastings, Corp. Include an explanation for each entry.

    a. Issuance of the bond payable on January 1, 2010.

    b. Payment of semiannual interest and amortization of bond premium on July 1, 2010. (Use the straight-line method to amortize the premium.)

S9-13. Accounting for bonds (*Learning Objective 5*) 15–20 min.

Hastings, Corp., issued 6%, five-year bonds payable with a maturity value of $5,000 at par on May 1, 2010. Assume that the fiscal year ends on December 31. Journalize the following transactions and include an explanation for each entry.

    a. Issuance of the bonds payable on May 1, 2010.

    b. Payment of the first semiannual interest amount on November 1, 2010.

    c. Accrual of semiannual interest expense on December 31, 2010.

S9-14. Classification of liability accounts as current or long-term. (*Learning Objective 6*) 5–10 min.

Identify the section of the balance sheet in which the following accounts would be located: Current Assets (CA), Long-Term Assets (LTA), Current Liabilities (CL), or Long-Term Liabilities (LTL).

_____ 1. Bonds Payable

_____ 2. Interest Payable

_____ 3. Leased Equipment

_____ 4. Discount on Bonds Payable

_____ 5. Accumulated Depreciation on Leased Equipment

_____ 6. Lease Payable (due in four years)

_____ 7. Mortgage Notes Payable

S9-15. Balance sheet disclosure of long-term liabilities (*Learning Objective 6*) 5–10 min.

FastTrack Magazine, Inc., includes the following selected accounts in its general ledger at December 31, 2010:

Mortgage Notes Payable........	$100,000	Accounts Payable.....................	$19,000
Lease Payable, Long-Term.....	20,000	Discount on Bonds Payable	6,000
Bonds Payable	350,000		
Interest Payable (due next year).................	7,000		

Prepare the liabilities section of FastTrack Magazine's balance sheet at December 31, 2010, to show how the company would report these items. Report a total for current liabilities.

EXERCISES (GROUP A)

E9-16A. Sales tax payable (*Learning Objective 2*) 5–10 min.

Make journal entries to record the following transactions. Explanations are not required.

Mar 31	Recorded cash sales of $200,000 for the month, plus sales tax of 4% collected for the state of Illinois.
Apr 6	Sent March sales tax to the state.

E9-17A. Accounting for notes payable (*Learning Objective 2*) 5–10 min.

Record the following note payable transactions of Lisbon, Corp., in the company's journal. Explanations are not required.

2010	
May 1	Purchased equipment costing $15,000 by issuing a one-year, 6% note payable.
Dec 31	Accrued interest on the note payable.
2011	
May 1	Paid the note payable at maturity.

E9-18A. Subscriptions (*Learning Objective 2*) 5–10 min.

Ozark Publishing Company completed the following transactions during 2010:

Nov 1	Sold a six-month subscription, collecting cash of $180, plus sales tax of 5%.
Dec 15	Remitted the sales tax to the state of Illinois.
31	Made the necessary adjustment at year-end to record the amount of subscription revenue earned during the year.

Requirements

1. Journalize these transactions. Explanations are not required.

2. What amounts would Ozark Publishing Company report on the balance sheet at December 31, 2010?

Quick solution: 2. December 31, 2010 balance in Estimated Warranty Payable = $6,000

E9-19A. Warranties (*Learning Objective 3*) 5–10 min.

The accounting records of Osgood Carpets showed a balance of $3,000 in Estimated Warranty Payable at December 31, 2009. In the past, Osgood's warranty expense has been 5% of sales. During 2010, Osgood made sales of $300,000 on account and paid $12,000 to satisfy warranty claims.

Requirements

1. Journalize Osgood's sales, warranty expense, and cash payments made to satisfy warranty claims during 2010. Explanations are not required.

2. What balance of Estimated Warranty Payable will Osgood report on its balance sheet at December 31, 2010?

E9-20A. Accounting for mortgages (*Learning Objective 5*) 10–15 min.

Orbit, Corp., issued a $400,000, 10%, 15-year mortgage on January 1, 2010, to purchase warehouses.

Date	Payment	Interest	Principal	Loan Balance
Jan 1, 2010				$400,000
Jun 30, 2010	$26,021			
Dec 31, 2010				
Jun 30, 2011				
Dec 31, 2011				
Jun 30, 2012				

Requirements

1. Complete the amortization schedule for Orbit, Corp., assuming payments are made semiannually.

2. Record the journal entries for (a) issuance of mortgage on January 1, 2010, and (b) the first semiannual payment on June 30, 2010.

E9-21A. Accounting for bonds (*Learning Objective 5*) 15–20 min.

Pluto Corporation issued 8%, 20-year bonds payable with a maturity value of $500,000 on March 31. The bonds were issued at par and pay interest on March 31 and September 30. Record (a) issuance of the bonds on March 31, (b) payment of interest on September 30, and (c) accrual of interest on December 31.

E9-22A. Accounting for bonds (*Learning Objective 5*) 15–20 min.

On January 1, Quizmo, Corp., issues 8%, 20-year bonds payable with a maturity value of $100,000. The bonds sell at 98 and pay interest on January 1 and July 1. Quizmo, Corp., amortizes any bond discount or premium by the straight-line method. Record (a) the issuance of the bonds on January 1, and (b) the semiannual interest payment and amortization of any bond discount or premium on July 1.

E9-23A. Accounting for bonds (*Learning Objective 5*) 15–20 min.

Datil, Inc., issued $100,000 of 10-year, 6% bonds payable on January 1. Datil, Inc., pays interest each January 1 and July 1 and amortizes any discount or premium by the straight-line method. Datil, Inc., can issue its bonds payable under various conditions:

a. Issuance at par value

b. Issuance at a price of $90,000 when the market rate was 7%

c. Issuance at a price of $105,000 when the market rate was 5.5%

Requirements

1. Journalize Datil's issuance of the bonds and first semiannual interest payment for each situation. Explanations are not required.

2. Which condition results in the most interest expense for Datil, Inc.? Explain in detail.

E9-24A. Classifying notes payable as current or long-term (*Learning Objective 5 & 6*) 10–15 min.

Carruthers Medical Group borrowed $300,000 on July 1, 2010, by issuing a 9% long-term note payable that must be paid in three equal annual installments plus interest each July 1 for the next three years.

Requirement

1. Insert the appropriate amounts to show how Carruthers would report its current and long-term liabilities.

	December 31		
	2010	**2011**	**2012**
Current Liabilities:			
Current Portion of Long-Term Note Payable	$	$	$
Interest Payable			
Long-Term Liabilities:			
Long-Term Note Payable			

E9-25A. Balance sheet disclosure of liabilities (*Learning Objective 6*) 15–20 min.

At December 31, Deming Drapes owes $50,000 on accounts payable, plus salary payable of $14,000 and income tax payable of $8,000. Deming Drapes also has $300,000 of bonds payable that require payment of a $30,000 installment next year and the remainder in later years. The bonds payable also require an interest payment of $7,000 at the end of each year. Report Deming Drapes' liabilities on its year-end classified balance sheet.

E9-26A. Debt ratio (*Learning Objective 7*) 5–10 min.

Appleway Company had the following balances as of December 31, 2010:

Total Current Assets	$ 87,000
Total Long-Term Assets	358,000
Total Current Liabilities	42,000
Total Long-Term Liabilities	217,000
Total Stockholders' Equity	186,000

Requirement

1. Calculate Appleway Company's debt ratio as of December 31, 2010. Does it appear that Appleway Company is in a position to take on more debt?

EXERCISES (GROUP B)

E9-27B. Sales tax payable (*Learning Objective 2*) 5–10 min.

Make journal entries to record the following transactions. Explanations are not required.

Aug 31	Recorded cash sales of $770,000 for the month, plus sales tax of 7% collected for the state of Mississippi.
Sep 6	Sent August sales tax to the state.

E9-28B. Accounting for notes payable (*Learning Objective 2*) 5–10 min.

Record the following note payable transactions of Concilio, Corp., in the company's journal. Explanations are not required.

2010	
Oct 1	Purchased equipment costing $8,000 by issuing a one-year, 8% note payable.
Dec 31	Accrued interest on the note payable.
2011	
Oct 1	Paid the note payable at maturity.

E9-29B. Subscriptions (*Learning Objective 2*) 5–10 min.

TransWorld Publishing Company completed the following transactions during 2010:

Aug 1	Sold a six-month subscription, collecting cash of $3,000, plus sales tax of 4%.
Dec 15	Remitted the sales tax to the state of New York.
31	Made the necessary adjustment at year-end to record the amount of subscription revenue earned during the year.

Requirements

1. Journalize these transactions. Explanations are not required.
2. What amounts would TransWorld Publishing Company report on the balance sheet at December 31, 2010?

E9-30B. Warranties (*Learning Objective 3*) 5–10 min.

The accounting records of Atkinson Books showed a balance of $2,000 in Estimated Warranty Payable at December 31, 2009. In the past, Atkinson's warranty expense has been 6% of sales. During 2010, Atkinson made sales of $329,000 on account and paid $6,000 to satisfy warranty claims.

Requirements

1. Journalize Atkinson's sales, warranty expense, and cash payments made to satisfy warranty claims during 2010. Explanations are not required.
2. What balance of Estimated Warranty Payable will Atkinson report on its balance sheet at December 31, 2010?

E9-31B. Accounting for mortgages (*Learning Objective 5*) 10–15 min.

Jupiter, Corp., issued a $500,000, 8%, 15-year mortgage on January 1, 2010, to purchase warehouses.

Date	Payment	Interest	Principal	Loan Balance
Jan 1, 2010				$500,000
Jun 30, 2010	$28,915			
Dec 31, 2010				
Jun 30, 2011				
Dec 31, 2011				
Jun 30, 2012				

Requirements

1. Complete the amortization schedule for Jupiter, Corp., assuming payments are made semiannually.
2. Record the journal entries for (a) issuance of mortgage on January 1, 2010, and (b) the first semiannual payment on June 30, 2010.

E9-32B. Accounting for bonds (*Learning Objective 5*) 15–20 min.

Daffy Corporation issued 4%, 20-year bonds payable with a maturity value of $330,000 on January 31. The bonds were issued at par and pay interest on January 31 and July 31. Record (a) issuance of the bonds on January 31, (b) payment of interest on July 31, and (c) accrual of interest on December 31.

E9-33B. Accounting for bonds (*Learning Objective 5*) 15–20 min.

On January 1, Danvers, Corp., issues 5%, four-year bonds payable with a maturity value of $110,000. The bonds sell at 94 and pay interest on January 1 and July 1. Danvers, Corp., amortizes any bond discount or premium by the straight-line method. Record (a) the issuance of the bonds on January 1, and (b) the semiannual interest payment and amortization of any bond discount or premium on July 1.

E9-34B. Accounting for bonds (*Learning Objective 5*) 15–20 min.

Jefferson, Inc., issued $200,000 of 10-year, 4% bonds payable on January 1. Jefferson, Inc., pays interest each January 1 and July 1 and amortizes any discount or premium by the straight-line method. Jefferson, Inc., can issue its bonds payable under various conditions:

a. Issuance at par value
b. Issuance at a price of $130,000 when the market rate was 6.2%
c. Issuance at a price of $250,000 when the market rate was 3.2%

Requirements

1. Journalize Jefferson's issuance of the bonds and first semiannual interest payment for each situation. Explanations are not required.
2. Which condition results in the most interest expense for Jefferson, Inc.? Explain in detail.

E9-35B. Classifying notes payable as current or long-term (*Learning Objective 5 & 6*) 10–15 min.

Bon Secour Medical Group borrowed $600,000 on July 1, 2010, by issuing a 14% long-term note payable that must be paid in three equal annual installments plus interest each July 1 for the next three years.

Requirement

1. Insert the appropriate amounts to show how Bon Secour would report its current and long-term liabilities.

	December 31		
	2010	**2011**	**2012**
Current Liabilities:			
Current Portion of Long-Term Note Payable	$	$	$
Interest Payable			
Long-Term Liabilities:			
Long-Term Note Payable			

E9-36B. Balance sheet disclosure of liabilities (*Learning Objective 6*) 15–20 min.

At December 31, Trumpette Drapes owes $59,000 on accounts payable, plus salary payable of $15,000 and income tax payable of $13,000. Trumpette Drapes also has $270,000 of bonds payable that require payment of a $25,000 installment next year and the remainder in later years. The bonds payable also require an interest payment of $5,500 at the end of each year. Report Trumpette Drapes' liabilities on its year-end classified balance sheet.

E9-37B. Debt ratio (*Learning Objective 7*) 5–10 min.

Pine City Company had the following balances as of December 31, 2010:

Total Current Assets	$154,000
Total Long-Term Assets	501,000
Total Current Liabilities	95,000
Total Long-Term Liabilities	195,000
Total Stockholders' Equity	365,000

Requirement

1. Calculate Pine City Company's debt ratio as of December 31, 2010. Does it appear that Pine City Company is in a position to take on more debt?

EXERCISES (ALTERNATES 1, 2, AND 3)

These alternative exercise sets are available for your practice benefit at
www.myaccountinglab.com

PROBLEMS (GROUP A)

P9-38A. Accounting for several current liabilities (*Learning Objectives 2 & 3*) 20–25 min.

The following transactions of My Dollar stores occurred during 2010 and 2011:

2010

Feb 3	Purchased equipment for $10,000, signing a six-month, 9% note payable.
28	Recorded the week's sales of $51,000, one-third for cash, and two-thirds on account. All sales amounts are subject to a 5% sales tax.
Mar 7	Sent last week's sales tax to the state.
Apr 30	Borrowed $100,000 on a four-year, 9% note payable that calls for annual payment of interest each April 30.
Aug 3	Paid the six-month, 9% note at maturity.
Nov 30	Purchased inventory at a cost of $7,200, signing a three-month, 8% note payable for that amount.
Dec 31	Accrued warranty expense, which is estimated at 3% of total sales of $260,000.
31	Accrued interest on all outstanding notes payable. Accrued interest for each note separately.

2011

Feb 28	Paid off the 8% inventory note, plus interest, at maturity.
Apr 30	Paid the interest for one year on the long-term note payable.

Requirement

1. Record the transactions in the company's journal. Explanations are not required.

P9-39A. Accounting for several current and long-term liabilities (*Learning Objectives 2, 3, & 5*) 20–25 min.

Following are pertinent facts about events during the current year at Greely Snowboards.

a. December sales totaled $404,000, and Greely collected sales tax of 5%. The sales tax will be sent to the state of Washington early in January.

b. Greely owes $75,000 on a long-term note payable. At December 31, 6% interest for the year plus $25,000 of principal are payable within one year.

c. On August 31, Greely signed a six-month, 6% note payable to purchase a machine costing $80,000. The note requires payment of principal and interest at maturity.

d. Sales of $909,000 were covered by the Greely product warranty. At January 1, estimated warranty payable was $11,300. During the year, Greely recorded warranty expense of $27,900 and paid warranty claims of $30,100.

e. On October 31, Greely received cash of $2,400 in advance for the rent on a building. This rent will be earned evenly over six months.

Requirement

1. For each item, indicate the account and the related amount to be reported as a current liability on Greely's December 31 balance sheet.

P9-40A. Accounting for mortgages (*Learning Objective 5*) 20–25 min.

Jordan, Corp., completed the following transactions in 2010:

Jan 1	Purchased a building costing $100,000 and signed a 10-year, 10% mortgage note payable for the same amount.
Jun 30	Made the first semiannual payment on the mortgage note payable.
Dec 1	Signed a five-year lease to rent a warehouse for $7,000 per month due at the end of each month. The lease is considered an operating lease.
31	Paid for one month's rent on the warehouse.
31	Purchased 10 copiers and signed a $40,000, four-year lease with the option to buy the copiers at the end of the fourth year at a bargain price.
31	Made the second semiannual payment on the mortgage note payable.

Requirements

1. Complete the following amortization schedule for the first four mortgage payments on the $100,000 mortgage note, assuming semiannual payments of $8,024.

Date	Payment	Interest	Principal	Loan Balance
Jan 1, 2010				$100,000
Jun 30, 2010	$8,024			
Dec 31, 2010				
Jun 30, 2011				
Dec 31, 2011				

2. Record the journal entries for the 2010 transactions.

3. Prepare the long-term liabilities section of the balance sheet on December 31, 2010.

P9-41A. Analyzing bond terms and accounting for bonds (*Learning Objective 5*) 20–25 min.

Assume that on April 1, 2010, Roland, Corp., issues 8%, 10-year bonds payable with a maturity value of $400,000. The bonds pay interest on March 31 and September 30, and Roland amortizes any premium or discount by the straight-line method. Roland's fiscal year-end is December 31.

Requirements

1. If the market interest rate is 7 1/2% when Roland, Corp., issues its bonds, will the bonds be priced at par, at a premium, or at a discount? Explain.

2. If the market interest rate is 9% when Roland, Corp., issues its bonds, will the bonds be priced at par, at a premium, or at a discount? Explain.

3. Assume that the issue price of the bonds is $404,000. Journalize the following bonds payable transactions:

   a. Issuance of the bonds on April 1, 2010.

   b. Payment of interest and amortization of premium on September 30, 2010.

   c. Accrual of interest and amortization of premium on December 31, 2010.

   d. Payment of interest and amortization of premium on March 31, 2011.

P9-42A. Analyzing bond terms and accounting for bonds (*Learning Objective 5*)
20–25 min.

On January 1, 2010, Cave Creek Golf Club issued $600,000 of 20-year, 9% bonds payable. The bonds were sold for $600,000. The bonds pay interest each June 30 and December 31 and any discount or premium is amortized using straight-line amortization.

Requirements

1. Fill in the blanks to complete these statements:
   a. Cave Creek Golf Club's bonds are priced at (express the price as a percentage) ____.
   b. When Cave Creek Golf Club issued its bonds, the market interest rate was (higher than, lower than, or equal to) ____ 9%.
   c. The amount of bond discount or premium is $ ____.

2. Record the following transactions:
   a. Issuance of the bonds payable on January 1, 2010.
   b. Payment of interest (and amortization of discount or premium if any) on June 30, 2010.
   c. Payment of interest (and amortization of discount or premium if any) on December 31, 2010. Explanations are not required.

3. At what amount will Cave Creek Golf Club report the bonds on its balance sheet at December 31, 2010?

Quick solution: Total current liabilities = $153,000; total long-term liabilities = $383,000

P9-43A. Balance sheet disclosure of long-term liabilities (*Learning Objective 6*) 15–20 min.

The accounting records of Stokes, Corp., include the following items at December 31, 2010:

Salary Payable	$32,000	Accounts Payable	$ 60,000
Bonds Payable,		Mortgage Note Payable,	
Current Portion	25,000	Long-Term	90,000
Discount on Bonds Payable	7,000	Interest Payable	20,000
Income Tax Payable	16,000	Bonds Payable	300,000

Requirement

1. Report these liabilities on Stokes' balance sheet at December 31, 2010, including headings.

P9-44A. Calculation of debt ratio (*Learning Objective 7*) 10–15 min.

The classified balance sheet for Tipke, Inc., as of December 31, 2010, is presented next.

<table>
<tr><td colspan="6" align="center">**Tipke, Inc.**
Balance Sheet
December 31, 2010</td></tr>
<tr><td>Current Assets:</td><td></td><td></td><td>Current Liabilities:</td><td></td></tr>
<tr><td>Cash</td><td></td><td>$ 17,500</td><td>Accounts Payable</td><td>$ 1,100</td></tr>
<tr><td>Accounts Receivable</td><td></td><td>5,400</td><td>Salary Payable</td><td>2,400</td></tr>
<tr><td>Supplies</td><td></td><td>400</td><td>Unearned Service Revenue</td><td>650</td></tr>
<tr><td>Prepaid Rent</td><td></td><td>3,600</td><td>Note Payable</td><td>10,000</td></tr>
<tr><td>Total Current Assets</td><td></td><td>26,900</td><td>Total Current Liabilities</td><td>14,150</td></tr>
<tr><td></td><td></td><td></td><td></td><td></td></tr>
<tr><td>Fixed Assets:</td><td></td><td></td><td>Long-Term Debt:</td><td></td></tr>
<tr><td>Land</td><td></td><td>55,000</td><td>Mortgage Note Payable</td><td>10,000</td></tr>
<tr><td>Equipment</td><td>38,000</td><td></td><td>Bonds Payable</td><td>140,000</td></tr>
<tr><td>Less Accumulated</td><td></td><td></td><td>Total Long-Term Debt</td><td>150,000</td></tr>
<tr><td> Depreciation, Equipment</td><td>8,000</td><td>30,000</td><td></td><td></td></tr>
<tr><td></td><td></td><td></td><td>Stockholders' Equity:</td><td></td></tr>
<tr><td>Building</td><td>225,000</td><td></td><td>Common Stock</td><td>20,000</td></tr>
<tr><td>Less Accumulated</td><td></td><td></td><td>Retained Earnings</td><td>122,750</td></tr>
<tr><td> Depreciation, Building</td><td>30,000</td><td>195,000</td><td>Total Stockholders' Equity</td><td>142,750</td></tr>
<tr><td>Total Fixed Assets</td><td></td><td>280,000</td><td>Total Liabilities and</td><td></td></tr>
<tr><td>Total Assets</td><td></td><td>$306,900</td><td> Stockholders' Equity</td><td>$306,900</td></tr>
</table>

Requirements

1. Calculate Tipke's debt ratio as of December 31, 2010.

2. What percentage of Tipke's assets belong to the stockholders?

3. Would you be willing to extend credit to Tipke, Inc.? Why or why not?

PROBLEMS (GROUP B)

P9-45B. Accounting for several current liabilities (*Learning Objectives 2 & 3*) 20–25 min.

The following transactions of Crazy Craft stores occurred during 2010 and 2011:

2010

Feb 3	Purchased equipment for $11,000, signing a six-month, 8% note payable.
28	Recorded the week's sales of $93,000, one-third for cash, and two-thirds on account. All sales amounts are subject to a 5% sales tax.
Mar 7	Sent last week's sales tax to the state.
Apr 30	Borrowed $110,000 on a four-year, 10% note payable that calls for annual payment of interest each April 30.
Aug 3	Paid the six-month, 8% note at maturity.
Nov 30	Purchased inventory at a cost of $6,000, signing a three-month, 5% note payable for that amount.
Dec 31	Accrued warranty expense, which is estimated at 4% of total sales of $250,000.
31	Accrued interest on all outstanding notes payable. Accrued interest for each note separately.

2011

Feb 28	Paid off the 5% note, plus interest, at maturity.
Apr 30	Paid the interest for one year on the long-term note payable.

Requirement

1. Record the transactions in the company's journal. Explanations are not required.

P9-46B. Accounting for several current and long-term liabilities (*Learning Objectives 2, 3, & 5*) 20–25 min.

Following are pertinent facts about events during the current year at Laughton Snowboards.

a. December sales totaled $405,000, and Laughton collected sales tax of 5%. The sales tax will be sent to the state of Washington early in January.

b. Laughton owes $70,000 on a long-term note payable. At December 31, 6% interest for the year plus $45,000 of principal are payable within one year.

c. On August 31, Laughton signed a six-month, 6% note payable to purchase a machine costing $78,000. The note requires payment of principal and interest at maturity.

d. Sales of $101,000 were covered by a Laughton product warranty. At January 1, estimated warranty payable was $11,100. During the year, Laughton recorded warranty expense of $27,800 and paid warranty claims of $30,050.

e. On October 31, Laughton received cash of $3,990 in advance for the rent on a building. This rent will be earned evenly over six months.

Requirement

1. For each item, indicate the account and the related amount to be reported as a current liability on Laughton's December 31 balance sheet.

P9-47B. Accounting for mortgages (*Learning Objective 5*) 20–25 min.

Franco, Corp., completed the following transactions in 2010:

Jan 1	Purchased a building costing $140,000 and signed a 10-year, 11% mortgage note payable for the same amount.
Jun 30	Made the first semiannual payment on the mortgage note payable.
Dec 1	Signed a five-year lease to rent a warehouse for $9,000 per month due at the end of each month. The lease is considered an operating lease.
31	Paid for one month's rent on the warehouse.
31	Purchased 10 copiers and signed a $32,000, four-year lease with the option to buy the copiers at the end of the fourth year at a bargain price.
31	Made the second semiannual payment on the mortgage note payable.

Requirements

1. Complete the following amortization schedule for the first four mortgage payments on the $140,000 mortgage note, assuming semiannual payments of $9,633.

Date	Payment	Interest	Principal	Loan Balance
Jan 1, 2010				$140,000
Jun 30, 2010	$9,633			
Dec 31, 2010				
Jun 30, 2011				
Dec 31, 2011				

2. Record the journal entries for the 2010 transactions.

3. Prepare the long-term liabilities section of the balance sheet on December 31, 2010.

P9-48B. Analyzing bond terms and accounting for bonds (*Learning Objective 5*)
20–25 min.

Assume that on February 1, 2010, Atlantic, Corp., issued 9%, 10-year bonds payable with maturity value of $800,000. The bonds pay interest on January 31 and July 31, and Atlantic amortizes any premium or discount by the straight-line method. Atlantic's fiscal year-end is October 31.

Requirements

1. If the market interest rate is 8.5% when Atlantic, Corp., issues its bonds, will the bonds be priced at par, at a premium, or at a discount? Explain.

2. If the market interest rate is 10% when Atlantic, Corp., issues its bonds, will the bonds be priced at par, at a premium, or at a discount? Explain.

3. Assume that the issue price of the bonds is $832,000. Journalize the following bonds payable transactions:

   a. Issuance of the bonds on February 1, 2010.

   b. Payment of interest and amortization of premium on July 31, 2010.

   c. Accrual of interest and amortization of premium on October 31, 2010.

   d. Payment of interest and amortization of premium on January 31, 2011.

P9-49B. Analyzing bond terms and accounting for bonds (*Learning Objective 5*)
20–25 min.

On January 1, 2010, De La Terre Bistro issued $700,000 of 15-year, 7% bonds payable. The bonds were sold for $725,000. The bonds pay interest each June 30 and December 31, and any discount or premium is amortized using straight-line amortization.

Requirements

1. Fill in the blanks to complete these statements:

   a. De La Terre Bistro's bonds are priced at (express the price as a percentage) _____.

   b. When De La Terre Bistro issued its bonds, the market interest rate was (higher than, lower than, or equal to) _____ 7%.

   c. The amount of bond discount or premium is $_____.

2. Record the following transactions:

   a. Issuance of the bonds payable on January 1, 2010. Explanations are not required.

   b. Payment of interest (and amortization of discount or premium if any) on June 30, 2010. Explanations are not required.

   c. Payment of interest (and amortization of discount or premium if any) on December 31, 2010. Explanations are not required.

3. At what amount will De La Terre Bistro report the bonds on its balance sheet at December 31, 2010?

P9-50B. Balance sheet disclosure of long-term liabilities (*Learning Objective 6*)
15–20 min.

The accounting records of Green, Corp., include the following items at December 31, 2010:

Salary Payable........................	$10,000	Accounts Payable..................	$ 52,000
Bonds Payable,		Mortgage Note Payable,	
Current Portion	17,000	Long-Term	120,000
Discount on Bonds Payable	13,000	Interest Payable	16,000
Income Tax Payable	8,000	Bonds Payable	220,000

Requirement

1. Report these liabilities on Green's balance sheet at December 31, 2010, including headings.

P9-51B. Calculation of debt ratio (*Learning Objective 7*) 10–15 min.

The classified balance sheet for Thorn, Inc., as of December 31, 2010, is presented next.

Thorn, Inc. Balance Sheet December 31, 2010					
ASSETS			**LIABILITIES**		
Current Assets:			Current Liabilities:		
Cash		$ 6,600	Accounts Payable		$ 10,200
Accounts Receivable		10,100	Salary Payable		1,900
Supplies		1,300	Unearned Service Revenue		17,700
Prepaid Rent		2,800	Note Payable		10,000
Total Current Assets		$ 20,800	Total Current Liabilities		39,800
Fixed Assets:			Long-Term Debt:		
Land		55,000	Mortgage Note Payable		30,000
Equipment	$ 40,000		Bonds Payable		110,000
Less: Accumulated			Total Long-Term Debt		140,000
Depreciation, Equipment	14,000	26,000			
Building	225,000		**STOCKHOLDERS' EQUITY**		
Less: Accumulated			Common Stock		8,000
Depreciation, Building	90,000	135,000	Retained Earnings		49,000
Total Fixed Assets		216,000	Total Stockholders' Equity		57,000
			Total Liabilities and		
Total Assets		$236,800	Stockholders' Equity		$236,800

Requirements

1. Calculate Thorn's debt ratio as of December 31, 2010.
2. What percentage of Thorn's assets belong to the stockholders?
3. Would you be willing to extend credit to Thorn, Inc? Why or why not?

PROBLEMS (ALTERNATES 1, 2, AND 3)

These alternative problem sets are available for your practice benefit at
www.myaccountinglab.com

CONTINUING EXERCISE

In this exercise we will continue the accounting for Graham's Yard Care, Inc. Assume that on September 1, 2010, Graham's Yard Care, Inc., borrowed $5,000 from First State Bank, signing a nine month, 10% note.

Requirement

1. Prepare the journal required on September 1, 2010, December 31, 2010, and May 31, 2011, to record the transactions related to the note.

CONTINUING PROBLEM

This continues the Aqua Elite, Inc., example from the continuing problem in Chapter 8. Aqua Elite, Inc., purchased some of its fixed assets during 2010 using long-term debt. The following table summarizes the nature of this long-term debt.

Date	Item	Annual Interest Rate	Amount	Payment Terms
May 18	Note payable	8%	$31,000	Five equal annual payments of principal plus accrued interest are due on May 18 of each year.
Sep 1	Mortgage payable	6%	$85,000	Semiannual payments of $3,677 due on March 1 and September 1 of each year.

Requirements
1. Calculate the interest expense that Aqua Elite, Inc., should accrue as of December 31, 2010.
2. Prepare the balance sheet presentation for all long-term debt indicating the portion that should be classified as current and the portion that should be classified as long-term.

APPLY YOUR KNOWLEDGE

ETHICS IN ACTION

Case 1. The Transmission Shop was the largest company in the state specializing in rebuilding automobile transmissions. Every transmission rebuilt by the business was covered by a six-month warranty. The owner, Ron Wood, was meeting with his accountant to go over the yearly financial statements. In reviewing the balance sheet, Ron became puzzled by the large amount of current liabilities being reported, so he asked his accountant to explain them. The accountant said that most of the current liabilities were the result of accruals, such as the estimated warranty payable, some additional wages payable, and interest accrued on the note owed to the bank. The employees were not actually paid until the first week of the new year, so some of their wages had to be recorded and properly matched against revenues in the current period. Also, several months of interest expense had to be accrued on a bank loan, but the largest amount of the accrued liabilities was due to the estimated warranty expense. Ron asked whether the wages payable and the interest payable could be removed because they would be paid off shortly after the year ended. The accountant stated that accrued liabilities had to be properly recognized in the current accounting period, and, thus, they could not be removed. Ron agreed but then asked about the large accrued liability based upon the estimated warranty amounts. Again, the accountant stated that in previous years actual warranty cost had been about 5% of the total sales and, therefore, in the current year the estimate was accrued at 5%. Ron then informed the accountant that a new conditioning lubricant had been added to each transmission rebuilt, which dramatically reduced the amount of rebuilt transmissions being returned under warranty. As a result, Ron strongly felt that the warranty estimate should be reduced to only 2% of total sales and, thereby, the accrued warranty liability and related expense would also be reduced. The accountant argued that the only reason Ron wanted to reduce the estimated percentage was to improve the financial statements, which would be unethical and inappropriate.

Requirements
1. What is the impact of accrued liabilities on the financial statements? Should the accrued liabilities for wages and interest payable be removed from the balance sheet?

2. Does Ron have a valid reason for wanting to reduce the estimated warranty liability? Are the concerns expressed by the accountant valid?

3. What ethical issues are involved?

Case 2. Sam Gray, the CEO of Steele Corporation, was meeting with the company controller to discuss a possible major lease of a new production facility. Steele Corporation had a large amount of debt, and Sam was concerned that adding more debt to acquire the production facility would worry the stockholders. Sam knew that if the production facility could be classified as an operating lease rather than a capital lease, the lease obligation would not have to be reported on the balance sheet. Thus, the company could have a new production facility without having to report any additional debt. The accountant told Sam that if the title to the production facility transferred automatically to Steele at the end of the lease term, then the lease would have to be classified as a capital lease. Also, if the lease had a bargain purchase option, such that Steele Corporation could simply purchase the facility at the end of the lease term for a small option amount, it would also be classified as a capital lease. Sam said not to worry because he would make sure that the lease contract would not contain any title transfer or bargain purchase option. The accountant then said that the facility had a 20-year life and the lease was for 16 years, which was more than 75% of the economic life of the asset, so it would have to be classified as a capital lease. Sam then said he would change the lease term to 14 years so the lease term would be less than the 75% of the economic life of the facility. The accountant then computed the present value of all the lease payments, and the total was more than 90% of the market value of the facility. Again, Sam said he would make any needed changes so that the total present value of the lease payments would be 89% of the current market value of the facility. At this point the accountant became frustrated and told Sam that the rules of accounting used to determine the proper classification of a lease were not meant to be used in order to misclassify a leased asset and, thereby, provide misleading information. Sam then said the rules simply served as a guide for structuring the lease and that he was merely using the rules to allow the lease to be classified as an operating lease and, thus, the lease obligation would not have to be recorded. The accountant said that intentionally avoiding the rules was unethical and wrong.

Requirements

1. Why does Sam want to have the lease classified as an operating lease rather than a capital lease?

2. Does the accountant have a legitimate argument? Does Sam have a legitimate argument?

3. What ethical issues are involved?

4. Do you have any other thoughts?

KNOW YOUR BUSINESS

FINANCIAL ANALYSIS

Purpose: To help familiarize you with the financial reporting of a real company in order to further your understanding of the chapter material you are learning.

This case focuses on the liabilities of Columbia Sportswear Company. Current liabilities are those obligations that will become due and payable within the next year or operating cycle (whichever is longer), while long-term liabilities are those that are due and payable more than one year from the balance sheet date. It is important to properly classify and report these liabilities because they affect liquidity. We will now consider the current and long-term liabilities of Columbia Sportswear Company. Refer to the Columbia Sportswear Company financial statements found in Appendix A. Also, consider notes 6, 7, 9, & 11 in the footnotes included in the annual report.

Requirements

1. What was the balance of total current liabilities at December 31, 2008? What was the balance of total current liabilities at December 31, 2007? Did the amount of ending total current liabilities increase or decrease? What caused the biggest change in total current liabilities?

2. Look at the balance of accrued liabilities at December 31, 2008 and December 31, 2007. Then look at the footnote that provides the breakdown of the total accrued liabilities. What makes up the accrued liabilities and why would they be included in the current liability section? Which liability made up the biggest portion of the accrued liabilities?

3. Look at the financing activities section of the Consolidated Statements of Cash Flows. Can you see the amount of additions to notes payable and long-term debt over the last three years? Can you see the amount of reductions of notes payable and long-term debt over the last three fiscal years? Does it appear that Columbia Sportswear Company is borrowing more than it repays or repaying more than it borrows?

4. Compare the total amount of current liabilities to the total amount of long-term liabilities. Is the amount of total current liabilities more than or less than the total long-term liabilities? What do these results mean? Is the amount of total stockholders' equity more than or less than the total of all the liabilities at December 31, 2008? What does this result mean?

5. Examine the long-term liabilities section of the balance sheet. Can you determine what deferred income taxes are? Why does income taxes payable appear in both the current liabilities and long-term liabilities sections of the balance sheet?

INDUSTRY ANALYSIS

Purpose: To help you understand and compare the performance of two companies in the same industry.

Find the Columbia Sportswear Company Annual Report located in Appendix A and go to the Financial Statements starting on page 681. Now access the 2008 Annual Report for Under Armour, Inc., from the Internet. Go to the company Web page for Investor Relations at *http://investor.underarmour.com/investors.cfm* and under Downloads on the right-hand side, go to 2008 Annual Report. The company's Financial Statements start on page 49.

Requirement

1. Calculate the debt ratio for both companies for 2008 and 2007. Generally speaking, what does a debt ratio tell you? Specifically, what does the difference between the debt ratios for these two companies for the two years tell you?

SMALL BUSINESS ANALYSIS

Purpose: To help you understand the importance of cash flows in the operation of a small business.

Your business has been doing pretty well since you first opened the doors five years ago. You've been thinking for the last six months or so about expanding the business. There is some property right next door that would work well into your expansion plans. It would take some renovations to the building, but in order to continue to grow, you know you're going to need more room. But here's the problem. How are you going to pay for the building and the renovations? Your cash account is in pretty good shape, but you remember the sage advice of the business consultant that helped you when you were just getting started. That advice was to always have enough available cash to cover three months' worth of expenses just in case of some unexpected business interruption. Your available cash and short term investments of $100,000 is right at that benchmark.

Some preliminary investigation into the property next door indicates that the existing owner would probably be willing to accept $200,000 for the property. You also have a discussion with a contractor associate who tells you that the renovations to your specifications would cost about $50,000. So your dilemma is how are you going to come up with $250,000? You figure the best place to start is with a visit to your banker.

At that meeting with the banker, he tells you something like this:

"Frank, we would be pleased to help you out with your expansion plans. We would require you to take out a mortgage on the building and we would need a 20% down payment of the total amount up front. So the balance that we would be lending you would be 80% of the total you need, or $200,000. Your down payment amount would be $50,000. At 8% for 20 years, your monthly payments would be $1,672.88."

You are somewhat pleased with the outcome of the meeting, but you tell the banker you will get back to him in a day or two. You know that this is big step and a long-term investment for the business.

Requirements

1. After thinking through the details of the plan the banker gave you, what are your thoughts? Since the down payment is going to use up about half of your available cash, how does that concern you? What about the long-term commitment of 20 years?

2. Assuming you go ahead with the mortgage and the purchase and renovation of the property, journalize the transactions to acquire the property and make the renovations. Where will the building and the renovations show up on your financial statements? Where will the mortgage show up on your financial statements? If the interest portion of your first payment is going to be $1,333.33, journalize the transaction to make your first mortgage payment.

WRITTEN COMMUNICATION

Your boss has just asked you to write a short note to one of his clients that had expressed some concerns about the difference between liabilities that are of an unknown amount versus contingent liabilities. The client is in the midst of a lawsuit with a governmental agency that its attorney thinks has about a 50-50 chance of winning. However, if the company loses, it could cost a substantial amount of money. The client is wondering if it needs to account for the lawsuit, and if so, how?

Requirement

1. Write a note to the client explaining the difference between a liability of an unknown amount and a contingent liability. Also, make a suggestion as to how this particular situation might need to be accounted for.

Self Check Answers
1. a 2. c 3. d 4. a 5. a 6. c 7. b 8. a 9. a 10. c

10 Corporations: Paid-In Capital and Retained Earnings

Throughout the book, we have focused on the corporate form of business organization. We have made journal entries to record investments by stockholders in a corporation. We have also learned how to record the payment of dividends to stockholders. Maybe you've wondered, "Is issuing stock and paying dividends as simple as we have learned so far?" or, "How does a business actually become a corporation anyway?" You might have heard of stock dividends or stock splits and wondered what they are. As we explore corporations in greater detail in this chapter we will uncover the answers to these questions.

Chapter Outline:

Learning Objectives

1. Review the characteristics of a corporation

2. Describe the two sources of stockholders' equity and the classes of stock

3. Journalize the issuance of stock

4. Account for cash dividends

5. Account for stock dividends and stock splits

6. Account for treasury stock

7. Report stockholders' equity on the balance sheet

8. Evaluate return on stockholders' equity and return on common stockholders' equity

HOW ARE CORPORATIONS ORGANIZED?

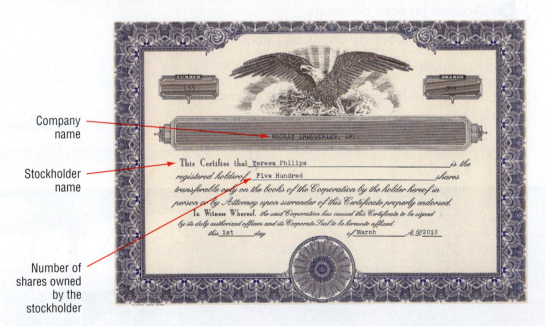

1 Review the characteristics of a corporation

As discussed in Chapter 1, a corporation is a separate legal entity from its owners. A corporation gets its legal standing from one of the 50 U.S. states. The process of becoming a corporation is known as incorporating. To incorporate, an organization's founders file **articles of incorporation** with the government of the state in which they wish to incorporate. The articles of incorporation, or **corporate charter**, describe the purpose, place of business, and other details of the corporation. Although a corporation may do business in multiple states, it is only incorporated in one state.

Once a state gives approval to an organization to become a corporation, the organization is authorized to sell individuals an ownership interest, or stock, in the corporation. Because the stock represents an individual's ownership of a corporation's capital it is also sometimes called **capital stock**. The basic unit of stock is a **share**. The number of shares of stock a company is authorized to sell is called **authorized stock**. Historically, a corporation would issue **stock certificates** to the stockholders when they buy stock. Today, many larger companies no longer issue physical stock certificates unless they are requested by the stockholders. Instead, records of stock ownership are maintained electronically. A corporation may issue a stock certificate for any number of shares. **Exhibit 10-1** shows a stock certificate for 500 shares of Mackay Industries, Inc., common stock owned by Teresa Philips. The certificate shows the following:

- Company name
- Stockholder name
- Number of shares owned by the stockholder

Company name

Stockholder name

Number of shares owned by the stockholder

Exhibit 10-1 ▲

Stock that is held by the stockholders is said to be **outstanding stock**. The outstanding stock of a corporation represents 100% of its ownership. The number of outstanding shares cannot exceed the number of authorized shares and is usually less than the number of authorized shares.

Corporations dominate business activity in the United States. Proprietorships and partnerships are more numerous, but corporations do much more business and are usually larger. Most well-known companies, such as **General Motors** and **Best Buy**, are corporations. Their full names include *Corporation* or *Incorporated* (abbreviated *Corp.* and *Inc.*) to show that they are corporations—for example, **General Motors Corporation** and **Best Buy, Inc.** The corporate form of organization is attractive for many reasons. **Exhibit 10-2** summarizes some of the advantages and disadvantages of the corporate form of business.

Advantages	Disadvantages
1. Stockholders have limited liability because the corporation is a separate legal entity.	1. Government regulation is cumbersome and expensive.
2. Corporations can raise more money than a proprietorship or partnership.	2. Double taxation.
3. A corporation has a continuous life.	
4. The transfer of corporate ownership is easy.	

Exhibit 10-2 ▲

WHAT MAKES UP THE STOCKHOLDERS' EQUITY OF A CORPORATION?

2 Describe the two sources of stockholders' equity and the classes of stock

Recall from Chapter 1 that the stockholders' equity of a corporation is divided into two categories:

- Paid-in capital (also called contributed capital) represents amounts received from the stockholders. Common stock, discussed in Chapter 1, is the main source of paid-in capital. This is *externally* generated capital and results from transactions with outsiders.

- Retained earnings is capital earned by profitable operations. This is *internally* generated capital and results from internal corporate decisions and earnings.

Stockholders' Rights

There are four basic rights a stockholder may have:

1. **Vote.** Stockholders participate in management by voting on corporate matters. This is the only way in which a stockholder can help to manage the corporation. Normally, each share of common stock carries one vote.

2. **Dividends.** Stockholders receive a proportionate part of any dividend. Each share of stock receives an equal dividend so, for example, a shareholder who owns 1% of the total shares in the company receives 1% of any dividend.

3. **Liquidation.** Stockholders receive their proportionate share of any assets remaining after the corporation pays its debts and liquidates (goes out of business).

4. Preemption. Stockholders can maintain their proportionate ownership in the corporation. Suppose you own 5% of a corporation's stock. If the corporation issues 100,000 new shares of stock, it must offer you the opportunity to buy 5% (5,000) of the new shares. Most states require that preemptive rights be specifically set forth in the corporate charter. For most companies, preemptive rights are the exception rather than the rule.

Classes of Stock

Every corporation must issue **common stock**, which represents the basic ownership of the corporation. The real "owners" of the corporation are the common stockholders. Some companies issue Class A common stock, which carries the right to vote, and Class B common stock, which is non-voting. There must be at least one voting "class" of stock. However, there is no limit to the number or types of classes of stock that a corporation may issue. Each class of stock has a separate account.

In addition to common stock a corporation may also issue **preferred stock**. Preferred stock gives its owners certain advantages over the owners of common stock. Most notably, preferred stockholders receive dividends before the common stockholders. They also receive assets before common stockholders if the corporation liquidates. Corporations pay a fixed dividend on preferred stock, which is printed on the face of the preferred stock certificate. Investors usually buy preferred stock to earn those fixed dividends. With these advantages, preferred stockholders take less investment risk than common stockholders.

Owners of preferred stock may also have the four basic stockholder rights, unless a right is withheld. The right to vote, however, is usually withheld from preferred stock. Companies may issue different series of preferred stock (Series A and Series B, for example). Each series is recorded in a separate account.

Par Value, Stated Value, and No-Par Stock

Stock may carry a par value, a stated value, or it may be no-par stock. **Par value** is an arbitrary amount assigned by a company to a share of its stock. The par value of **Johnson & Johnson**'s common stock is $1 per share. **Dell, Inc.**, has both common stock and preferred stock with a par value of $0.01 (1 cent) per share. Par value is arbitrary and is assigned when the organizers file the corporate charter with the state. There is no real "reason" for why par values vary. It is simply a choice made by the organizers of the corporation.

A company may also issue stock that has a **stated value**. Stated value is an arbitrary amount similar to par-value. Instead of being assigned when the corporate charter is filed, the stated value is assigned at a later date, such as when the company decides to issue stock. Most companies set par, or stated, value low to avoid legal difficulties that can occur if their stock is issued for a price below the par, or stated, value.

It is also possible for a company to issue stock that has no par (or stated) value, known as *no-par stock*. In addition to its $1 par common stock, **Johnson & Johnson** has preferred stock with no-par value.

✅ Concept Check...

John and Nancy are working on an assignment their accounting instructor gave them to do over the weekend. In the assignment, they are asked to record the issuance of 200,000 shares of $5 par value stock by a corporation for $30 per share. While working on the assignment, John commented to Nancy that he couldn't believe any investor would be dumb enough to pay a company $30 for a share of stock that is only worth $5. How should Nancy respond to John's comment?

Answer:

Nancy should explain to John that the $5 par value has nothing to do with the worth of each share of stock. Par value is an arbitrary amount assigned to each share of stock by the organizers of the corporation. Arbitrary means that the amount was determined by individual preference or convenience rather than by any underlying logic.

Let's review some stock issuance examples to illustrate accounting for par, stated, and no-par stock.

HOW IS THE ISSUANCE OF STOCK RECORDED?

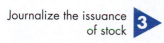
Journalize the issuance of stock 3

Corporations such as **IBM** and **Goodyear Tire** need huge quantities of money to operate. They cannot finance all their operations through borrowing, so they raise capital by issuing stock. A company can sell its stock directly to stockholders or it can use the services of an **underwriter**, such as the brokerage firm Morgan Stanley Smith Barney. An underwriter usually agrees to buy all the stock it cannot sell to its clients.

The price that the corporation receives from issuing stock is called the **issue price**. Usually, the issue price exceeds par value because par value is normally set quite low. In the following sections, we use Mackay Industries to show how to account for the issuance of stock.

Issuing Common Stock

Issuing Common Stock at Par

Suppose Mackay Industries' common stock carried a par value of $1 per share. The entry to record the issuance of 500,000 shares of stock at par value on January 1 would be as follows:

DATE	ACCOUNTS	POST REF.	DR.	CR.
Jan 1	Cash (500,000 × $1)		500,000	
	Common Stock			500,000
	Issued 500,000 shares of common stock for $1 per share.			

Issuing Common Stock above Par

As stated previously, most corporations set par value low and issue common stock for a price above par. Let's assume that the 500,000 shares of Mackay Industries' stock are issued for $15 a share on January 1. The $14 difference between the issue price ($15) and par value ($1) represents another type of paid-in capital account called **"Paid-in Capital in Excess of Par."** It is also called **Additional Paid-in Capital**.

Additional paid-in capital on the sale of common stock is not a gain, income, or profit for the corporation because the company is dealing with its own stock. This situation illustrates one of the fundamentals of accounting: A company can have no profit or loss when buying or selling its own stock.

With a par value of $1, Mackay Industries' entry to record the issuance of its stock at $15 per share on January 1 is as follows:

DATE	ACCOUNTS	POST REF.	DR.	CR.
Jan 1	Cash (500,000 × $15)		7,500,000	
	Common Stock (500,000 × $1 par)			500,000
	Paid-in Capital in Excess of Par—Common			
	[500,000 × ($15 − $1)]			7,000,000
	Issued 500,000 shares of common stock for $15 per share.			

The total paid-in capital should equal the amount of cash received. Altogether, it is the sum of the following:

$$\text{Total Paid-in Capital} = \text{Common Stock} + \text{Paid-in Capital in Excess of Par}$$
$$\$7{,}500{,}000 \quad = \quad \$500{,}000 \quad + \quad \$7{,}000{,}000$$

Issuing No-Par Stock

When a company issues no-par stock, there can be no paid-in capital in excess of par, because there isn't any par to be in excess of. Assume that, instead of $1 par value, Mackay Industries' common stock was no-par. How would that change the recording of the issuance of 500,000 shares for $15 on January 1? The entry to record the issuance of 500,000 shares of no-par stock for $15 per share would be as follows:

DATE	ACCOUNTS	POST REF.	DR.	CR.
Jan 1	Cash (500,000 × $15)		7,500,000	
	Common Stock			7,500,000
	Issued 500,000 shares of no-par common stock for			
	$15 per share.			

With no-par stock, Cash is debited and Common Stock is credited for the cash received regardless of the stock's price. Notice that the total paid-in capital of $7,500,000 remains the same as when there was a par value:

$$\text{Total Paid-in Capital} = \text{Common Stock} + \text{Paid-in Capital in Excess of Par}$$
$$\$7{,}500{,}000 \quad = \quad \$7{,}500{,}000 \quad + \quad \$0$$

Issuing No-Par Stock with a Stated Value

Accounting for stock with a stated value is almost identical to accounting for par-value stock. The only difference is that stock with a stated value uses an account titled Paid-in Capital in Excess of *Stated* Value to record amounts received above the stated value.

Issuing Stock for Assets Other Than Cash

A corporation may issue stock for assets other than cash. It records the assets received at their current market value and credits the stock accounts accordingly. The assets' prior book value is irrelevant. Now let's reconsider the January 1 entry for Mackay Industries. Assume that, instead of cash, Mackay Industries received a building worth $7,500,000 in exchange for the 500,000 shares of its $1 par common stock on January 1. How would the entry change?

DATE	ACCOUNTS	POST REF.	DR.	CR.
Jan 1	Building (fair market value)		7,500,000	
	Common Stock (500,000 × $1 par)			500,000
	Paid-in Capital in Excess of Par—Common			
	($7,500,000 – $500,000)			7,000,000
	Issued 500,000 shares of common stock in exchange for a building.			

As you can see, the only change is in the asset received; the Building account is debited instead of Cash.

Issuing Preferred Stock

Accounting for preferred stock is similar to the process illustrated for issuing common stock. Let's assume that Mackay Industries decides to issue 10,000 shares of its $20 par, 10% preferred stock on February 15 for $25 per share. The entry to record the issuance would be as follows:

DATE	ACCOUNTS	POST REF.	DR.	CR.
Feb 15	Cash (10,000 × $25)		250,000	
	Preferred Stock (10,000 × $20)			200,000
	Paid-in Capital in Excess of Par—Preferred			
	[10,000 × ($25 – $20)]			50,000
	Issued 10,000 shares of preferred stock for $25 per share.			

As with common stock, preferred stock can also be issued at par or it can be no-par stock.

HOW ARE CASH DIVIDENDS ACCOUNTED FOR?

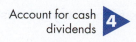

Account for cash dividends **4**

As discussed in Chapter 1, a profitable corporation may distribute cash to the stockholders in the form of *dividends*. Dividends cause a decrease in both Assets and Stockholders' Equity (Retained Earnings). Most states prohibit using paid-in capital for dividends. Accountants, therefore, use the term **legal capital** to refer to the portion of stockholders' equity that cannot be used for dividends. Corporations declare cash dividends from Retained Earnings and then pay them with cash.

Dividend Dates

A corporation declares a dividend before paying it. There are three dates associated with the declaration and payment of a cash dividend.

1. **Declaration date.** On the declaration date—say, March 5—the board of directors announces the intention to pay the dividend. The declaration of a cash dividend creates an obligation (liability) for the corporation.

2. **Date of record.** Those stockholders holding the stock at the end of business on the date of record—usually a week or two after declaration, say, March 19—will receive the dividend check.

3. **Payment date.** Payment of the dividend usually follows the record date by a week or two—say, March 31.

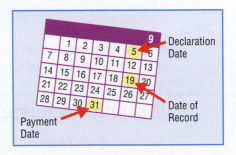

Declaring and Paying Dividends

The annual dividend rate on *preferred stock* is often expressed as a percentage of the preferred stock's par value, such as 10%. But sometimes annual cash dividends on preferred stock are expressed as a flat dollar amount per share, such as $2 per share. Therefore, preferred dividends are computed two ways, depending on how the preferred stock dividend rate is expressed. Let's look at the two ways to compute preferred dividends, using Mackay Industries' 10,000 outstanding shares of 10%, $20 par preferred stock. (Mackay Industries' flat rate instead of 10% could be stated as $2 per share.)

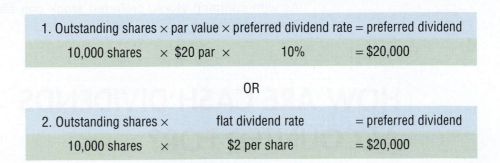

Cash dividends on *common stock* are computed the second way, because those cash dividends are not expressed as a percentage.

Remember from Chapter 3 that the Dividends account is closed to Retained Earnings at the end of the year. So, instead of using the Dividends account, companies often record the declaration of a dividend by debiting the Retained Earnings account instead of Dividends. In this case, there will be no entry required at year-end to close the Dividends account. To account for Mackay

Industries' declaration of a cash dividend we debit Retained Earnings and credit Dividends Payable on the date of declaration as follows:

DATE	ACCOUNTS	POST REF.	DR.	CR.
Mar 5	Retained Earnings		20,000	
	Dividends Payable			20,000
	Declared a cash dividend.			

On the date of record, no journal entry is required. On the payment date, Mackay Industries will record the payment of the dividend as follows:

DATE	ACCOUNTS	POST REF.	DR.	CR.
Mar 31	Dividends Payable		20,000	
	Cash			20,000
	Paid cash dividend.			

When a company has issued only common stock, the common stockholders will receive any dividend that is declared. However, if both preferred and common stock is issued, the preferred stockholders get their dividends first. The common stockholders receive dividends only if the total dividend declared is larger than the amount of the annual preferred dividend. In other words, the common stockholders get the leftovers. Let's see how dividends are divided between preferred and common stockholders.

Dividing Dividends Between Preferred and Common Shareholders

Assume that Mackay Industries has 500,000 shares of $1 par common stock outstanding and 10,000 shares of $20 par, 10% preferred stock outstanding. We calculated earlier that Mackay Industries' annual preferred dividend was $20,000. So, total declared dividends must exceed $20,000 for the common stockholders to get anything. **Exhibit 10-3** shows the division of dividends between preferred and common for two situations.

Situation A—Total Dividend of $15,000:		
Preferred dividend (the full $15,000 goes to the preferred stockholders because the annual preferred dividend is $20,000)		$15,000
Common dividend (none because the total dividend did not cover the preferred annual dividend)		0
Total dividend		$15,000
Situation B—Total Dividend of $30,000:		
Preferred dividend (10,000 shares × $20 par × 10%)		$20,000
Common dividend ($30,000 − $20,000)		10,000
Total dividend		$30,000

Exhibit 10-3 ▲

If Mackay Industries' dividend is large enough to cover the preferred dividend (Situation B), the preferred stockholders get their regular dividend ($20,000), and the common stockholders get the remainder ($10,000). But if the year's dividend falls below the annual preferred amount (Situation A), the preferred stockholders will receive the entire dividend, and the common stockholders get nothing that year.

Dividends on Cumulative and Noncumulative Preferred Stock

Preferred stock can be either

- cumulative or
- noncumulative.

Preferred stock is assumed to be cumulative unless it's specifically designated as noncumulative. Most preferred stock is cumulative. Let's see what effect the cumulative versus noncumulative designation has on the payment of dividends.

As we saw with Mackay Industries in Situation A in Exhibit 10-3, a corporation may fail to pay the entire annual preferred dividend. This may happen if, for example, the company does not have enough cash to fund the entire dividend. This is called *passing the dividend*, and the dividends are said to be in **arrears**. **Cumulative preferred stock** shareholders must receive all dividends in arrears before the common stockholders get any dividend.

The preferred stock of Mackay Industries is cumulative. How do we know this? Because it is not labeled as noncumulative.

Suppose Mackay Industries passed the entire 2010 preferred dividend of $20,000. Before paying any common dividend in 2011, Mackay Industries must first pay preferred dividends of $20,000 for 2010 and $20,000 for 2011, a total of $40,000. In 2011, Mackay Industries declares a $75,000 dividend. How much of this dividend goes to preferred? How much goes to common? The allocation of this $75,000 dividend is as follows:

Total dividend..		$75,000
Preferred stockholders get:		
2010 dividend (10,000 × $20 × 10%).................................	$20,000	
2011 dividend (10,000 × $20 × 10%).................................	20,000	
Total to preferred..		40,000
Common stockholders get the remainder...............................		$35,000

If Mackay Industries declared the $75,000 dividend on November 10, 2011, it would make the following entry:

DATE	ACCOUNTS	POST REF.	DR.	CR.
Nov 10	Retained Earnings		75,000	
	Dividends Payable—Preferred			40,000
	Dividends Payable—Common			35,000
	Declared a cash dividend.			

If the preferred stock is *noncumulative*, the corporation is not required to pay any dividends in arrears. Suppose Mackay Industries' preferred stock was noncumulative and the company passed the 2010 dividend. The preferred stockholders would lose the 2010 dividend of $20,000 forever. Then, before paying any common dividends in 2011, Mackay Industries would only have to pay the 2011 preferred dividend of $20,000, which would leave $55,000 for the common stockholders.

Dividends in arrears are *not* a liability. A liability for dividends arises only after the board of directors declares a dividend. It is possible that the board may never declare another dividend in the future. However, a corporation does report cumulative preferred dividends in arrears in the notes to the financial statements. This shows the common stockholders how big the declared dividend will need to be for them to get any dividends in the future.

Decision Guidelines

Decision	Guideline	Analyze
When is a cash dividend appropriate?	Consider the amount of available cash as well as the balance in Retained Earnings.	A cash dividend is a distribution of earnings to the company's stockholders. So, a company cannot declare and distribute dividends unless the balance in retained earnings (counting the current year's earnings) exceeds the amount of the desired dividend. In addition, the company must have the cash available to pay the dividend if it is declared. A business should carefully analyze its future cash needs so that it does not deplete its cash with a dividend and end up with cash flow issues in the future.

HOW ARE STOCK DIVIDENDS AND STOCK SPLITS ACCOUNTED FOR?

Stock Dividends

Account for stock dividends and stock splits **5**

A **stock dividend** is a distribution of a corporation's own stock to its shareholders. Unlike cash dividends, stock dividends do not give any assets to the shareholders. Stock dividends

- affect only stockholders' equity accounts (including Retained Earnings and Common Stock).
- have no effect on total stockholders' equity.
- have no effect on assets or liabilities.

A corporation distributes stock dividends to stockholders in proportion to the number of shares of stock they already own. Suppose you own 5,000 shares of Mackay Industries' common stock. If Mackay Industries distributes a 5% stock dividend, you would receive 250 (5,000 × .05) additional shares. You would now own 5,250 shares of the stock. All other Mackay Industries' stockholders also receive additional shares equal to 5% of the amount of stock they currently have. Because the amount of stock every stockholder has increases by 5%, the stockholders would all own the same percentage share of Mackay Industries' stock as they did before the stock dividend.

Companies issue stock dividends for several reasons including

❶ to continue a history of declaring dividends while conserving cash. A company may wish to continue dividends to keep stockholders happy but needs to keep its cash for operations. A stock dividend is a way to do so without using any cash.

❷ to reduce the market price of its stock. A stock dividend will usually cause the company's stock price to fall. This happens because after the stock dividend there will be more shares representing the same amount of value. Suppose that a share of Mackay Industries' stock was traded at $40 recently. Increasing the shares outstanding by issuing a 10% stock dividend would likely drop Mackay Industries' stock market price to around $36 per share. The objective behind a stock dividend is to make the stock less expensive and, therefore, more available and attractive to investors.

❸ to reward investors. Investors often feel like they've received something of value when they get a stock dividend.

Recording Stock Dividends

As with a cash dividend, there are three dates associated with a stock dividend:

- Declaration date
- Date of record
- Distribution date

The board of directors announces the stock dividend on the declaration date. The date of record determines who will receive the additional shares. The distribution date is the date the additional shares are distributed to the stockholders. Unlike with a cash dividend, the declaration of a stock dividend does *not* create a liability. This is because the corporation is not obligated to distribute any assets to the stockholders. (Recall that a liability is a claim on assets.) With a stock dividend, the corporation has simply declared its intention to distribute more of its stock. A stock dividend affects the following accounts:

- Retained Earnings is reduced (debited) by an amount equal to the number of shares being distributed times the current market price of the company's stock.
- Common Stock is increased (credited) by an amount equal to the number of shares being distributed times the par value of the company's stock.
- Paid-in Capital in Excess of Par is increased (credited) for the remainder.

The net effect of a stock dividend is to transfer an amount equal to the market value of the dividend from Retained Earnings into paid-in capital.

Assume that Mackay Industries has the following stockholders' equity on June 1, prior to declaring a stock dividend:

Mackay Industries, Inc.		
Stockholders' Equity		
June 1		
Paid-in Capital:		
Preferred Stock, 10%, $20 par, 500,000 shares authorized,		
10,000 shares issued and outstanding		$ 200,000
Paid-in Capital in Excess of Par—Preferred		50,000
Common Stock, $1 par, 2,000,000 shares authorized,		
500,000 shares issued and outstanding		500,000
Paid-in Capital in Excess of Par—Common		7,000,000
Total Paid-in Capital		7,750,000
Retained Earnings		2,000,000
Total Stockholders' Equity		$9,750,000

Now, assume Mackay Industries declares and distributes a 5% common stock dividend on June 15 when the market value of Mackay Industries' common stock is $40 per share. Although the declaration and distribution dates are normally different, we will assume they occurred on the same date for this example. Mackay would record the declaration and distribution of the stock dividend as follows:

DATE	ACCOUNTS	POST REF.	DR.	CR.
Jun 15	Retained Earnings (500,000 × .05 × $40 market value)		1,000,000	
	Common Stock (500,000 × .05 × $1 par)			25,000
	Paid-in Capital in Excess of Par—Common			975,000
	Declared and distributed stock dividend.			

As we did with cash dividends, we debited Retained Earnings directly instead of using a dividend account. Remember that a stock dividend does not affect assets, liabilities, or total stockholders' equity. A stock dividend merely rearranges the balances in the equity accounts, leaving total equity unchanged. Immediately after the stock dividend, Mackay Industries' stockholders' equity looks like this:

Mackay Industries, Inc. Stockholders' Equity June 30	
Paid-in Capital:	
Preferred Stock, 10%, $20 par, 500,000 shares authorized, 10,000 shares issued and outstanding	$ 200,000
Paid-in Capital in Excess of Par—Preferred	50,000
Common Stock, $1 par, 2,000,000 shares authorized, 525,000 shares issued and outstanding	525,000
Paid-in Capital in Excess of Par—Common	7,975,000
Total Paid-in Capital	8,750,000
Retained Earnings	1,000,000
Total Stockholders' Equity	$9,750,000

Note that the number of outstanding shares is now 525,000 [500,000 + (500,000 × .05)]. Note also that total stockholders' equity is still $9,750,000. The effect of the stock dividend was simply to transfer $1,000,000 from retained earnings to paid-in capital.

Stock Splits

Both a stock dividend and a **stock split** will increase the number of shares of stock outstanding. However, a stock split is fundamentally different from a stock dividend. A stock split increases not only the number of outstanding shares of stock, but also the number of authorized and issued shares. A stock split also decreases the par value per share, whereas stock dividends do not affect the par value or the number of authorized shares. For example, if Mackay Industries splits its common stock 2-for-1, the number of outstanding shares is doubled and par value per share is cut in half. A stock split also decreases the market price of the stock.

Assume the market price of a share of Mackay Industries common stock has been approximately $40. If Mackay Industries initiates a 2-for-1 split of its common stock on August 1, the market price per share will drop to around $20. A 2-for-1 stock split means that Mackay Industries will have twice as many shares of stock authorized and outstanding after the split as before. Each share's par value is also cut in half. **Exhibit 10-4** on the following page shows the before and after of how a 2-for-1 split affects Mackay Industries' stockholders' equity.

Study the exhibit and you'll see that a 2-for-1 stock split does the following:

- Cuts par value per share in half
- Doubles the shares of stock authorized and issued
- Leaves all account balances and total equity unchanged

Mackay Industries, Inc. Stockholders' Equity—Before Split August 1		
Paid-in Capital:		
Preferred Stock, 10%, $20 par, 500,000 shares authorized, 10,000 shares issued and outstanding		$ 200,000
Paid-in Capital in Excess of Par—Preferred		50,000
Common Stock, $1 par, 2,000,000 shares authorized, 525,000 shares issued and outstanding		525,000
Paid-in Capital in Excess of Par—Common		7,975,000
Total Paid-in Capital		8,750,000
Retained Earnings		1,000,000
Total Stockholders' Equity		$9,750,000

Mackay Industries, Inc. Stockholders' Equity—After Split August 1		
Paid-in Capital:		
Preferred Stock, 10%, $20 par, 500,000 shares authorized, 10,000 shares issued and outstanding		$ 200,000
Paid-in Capital in Excess of Par—Preferred		50,000
Common Stock, $.50 par, 4,000,000 shares authorized, 1,050,000 shares issued and outstanding		525,000
Paid-in Capital in Excess of Par—Common		7,975,000
Total Paid-in Capital		8,750,000
Retained Earnings		1,000,000
Total Stockholders' Equity		$9,750,000

Exhibit 10-4 ▲

🌐 Accounting in Your World

Robert invited three friends over to watch a football game and share a "take-and-bake" pizza he had purchased. On game day, Robert pulled the pizza out of the oven and was just about to slice it into eight pieces (two slices for each of them) when he began to wonder if there was enough pizza. Robert had an idea. He figured that if he cut the pizza into twelve slices instead of eight slices, each person would get three slices of pizza instead of two. Robert knew that each person would still receive the same amount of pizza but he figured that his friends would feel more satisfied if they received three slices instead of only two slices. It worked; no one complained that they did not get enough to eat.

The logic behind a stock split is similar to the logic behind Robert slicing the pizza into more pieces. When a company splits its stock, each shareholder still owns the same amount of the company (think the whole pizza). However, the shareholder's ownership is now represented by more shares of stock (think slices of pizza). For example, after a 3-for-2 stock split, each shareholder would own the same amount of the company. Each shareholder would just own three shares of stock now for every two shares he or she used to own.

Because the stock split does not affect any account balances, no formal journal entry is needed to record a stock split. Instead, the split is recorded in a **memorandum entry**, a journal entry that "notes" a significant event, but which has no debit or credit amount. Following is an example of a memorandum entry:

DATE	ACCOUNTS	POST REF.	DR.	CR.
Aug 1	Split the common stock 2-for-1.			
	OLD: 2,000,000 shares authorized; 525,000 shares			
	issued, $1 par			
	NEW: 4,000,000 shares authorized; 1,050,000 shares			
	issued, $.50 par			

Stock Dividends and Stock Splits Compared

Stock dividends and stock splits have some similarities and some differences. **Exhibit 10-5** summarizes the effects of each on stockholders' equity. Cash dividends have also been included in the exhibit for comparison purposes.

Event	Common Stock	Paid-In Capital in Excess of Par	Retained Earnings	Total Stockholders' Equity
Cash dividend	No effect	No effect	Decrease	Decrease
Stock dividend	Increase	Increase	Decrease	No effect
Stock split	No effect	No effect	No effect	No effect

Exhibit 10-5 ▲

Decision Guidelines

Decision		**Guideline**		**Analyze**
To decrease the market price of a company's stock is it better to use a stock dividend or a stock split?		The amount by which a company wishes to reduce the market price of the stock influences the decision to use a stock dividend or a stock split.		Because both a stock dividend and a stock split increase the number of outstanding shares (with no increase in the company's Stockholders' Equity), they both reduce the market value of a company's stock. A stock split usually increases the number of outstanding shares by a larger amount than a stock dividend. Therefore, it tends to have a bigger impact on the market price of the shares and should be used when a significant decrease in the market price is desired. For example, a 2-for-1 split will typically reduce the market price of a company's stock by 50%.

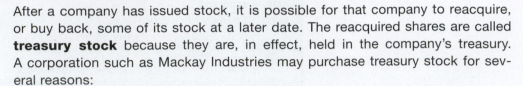

HOW IS TREASURY STOCK ACCOUNTED FOR?

Account for treasury stock **6** ▶

After a company has issued stock, it is possible for that company to reacquire, or buy back, some of its stock at a later date. The reacquired shares are called **treasury stock** because they are, in effect, held in the company's treasury. A corporation such as Mackay Industries may purchase treasury stock for several reasons:

❶ Management hopes to buy the stock when the price is low and sell it when the price goes higher.

❷ Management wants to support the company's stock price.

❸ Management wants to avoid a takeover by an outside party. If the company purchases the available shares, the shares are not available for others to purchase.

❹ Management wants to reward valued employees with stock. Treasury stock can be given to employees as a reward.

Treasury stock transactions are common among larger corporations.

Treasury Stock Basics

Before we see how treasury stock is accounted for, let's review some basic concepts related to treasury stock:

- The Treasury Stock account is a contra-equity account. Therefore, Treasury Stock has a debit balance, which is the opposite of the other equity accounts.
- Treasury Stock is recorded at cost (par value is ignored)
- The Treasury Stock account is reported beneath Retained Earnings on the balance sheet as a reduction to total stockholders' equity.

Although shares of treasury stock are still considered to be issued shares, they decrease the company's stock that is outstanding. This is because the shares are no longer held by outsiders (the stockholders). We compute outstanding stock as follows:

> Outstanding stock = Issued stock − Treasury stock

Outstanding shares are important because only outstanding shares have voting rights and receive cash dividends. Treasury stock doesn't have voting rights, and it gets no dividends. Now let's illustrate how to account for treasury stock, continuing with Mackay Industries.

Purchase of Treasury Stock

Mackay Industries' stockholders' equity, after the stock split discussed earlier in the chapter, appears in **Exhibit 10-6** on the following page.

Mackay Industries, Inc. Stockholders' Equity August 1		
Paid-in Capital:		
Preferred Stock, 10%, $20 par, 500,000 shares authorized,		
10,000 shares issued and outstanding		$ 200,000
Paid-in Capital in Excess of Par—Preferred		50,000
Common Stock, $.50 par, 4,000,000 shares authorized,		
1,050,000 shares issued and outstanding		525,000
Paid-in Capital in Excess of Par—Common		7,975,000
Total Paid-in Capital		8,750,000
Retained Earnings		1,000,000
Total Stockholders' Equity		$9,750,000

Exhibit 10-6 ▲

Assume that on August 10, Mackay Industries purchased 5,000 shares of treasury stock-common, paying $25 per share. To record the purchase, debit Treasury Stock and credit Cash as follows:

DATE	ACCOUNTS	POST REF.	DR.	CR.
Aug 10	Treasury Stock		125,000	
	Cash			125,000
	Purchased 5,000 shares of treasury stock.			

After posting the entry, the Treasury Stock account would look like this:

Treasury Stock	
8/10 125,000	

Sale of Treasury Stock

Companies buy their treasury stock hoping to sell it at a later date for more than they paid for it. However, companies may sell treasury stock at, above, or below what they paid for it.

Sale at Cost

If treasury stock is sold for cost, the same price the corporation paid for it, then there is no difference between cost and sale price to journalize. Let's assume Mackay Industries sells 500 of the treasury shares on September 5 for $25 each. The entry follows:

DATE	ACCOUNTS	POST REF.	DR.	CR.
Sep 5	Cash		12,500	
	Treasury Stock			12,500
	Sold 500 shares of treasury stock.			

After posting the entry, the Treasury Stock account would look like this:

Treasury Stock	
8/10 125,000 | 9/5 12,500	

Sale Above Cost

If treasury stock is sold for more than cost, the difference is credited to a new account, Paid-in Capital, Treasury Stock. This excess is additional paid-in capital because it came from the company's stockholders. It has no effect on net income. Suppose Mackay Industries resold 500 of its treasury shares for $28 per share on October 2. (Recall that cost was $25.) The entry to sell treasury stock for a price above cost is as follows:

DATE	ACCOUNTS	POST REF.	DR.	CR.
Oct 2	Cash (500 × $28)		14,000	
	Treasury Stock (500 × $25)			12,500
	Paid-in Capital, Treasury Stock (difference)			1,500
	Sold 500 shares of treasury stock.			

Paid-in Capital, Treasury Stock is reported with the other paid-in capital accounts on the balance sheet, beneath Common Stock and Paid-in Capital in Excess of Par. After posting the entry, the Treasury Stock and Paid-in Capital, Treasury Stock accounts would look like this:

Treasury Stock			
8/10	125,000	9/5	12,500
		10/2	12,500

Paid-in Capital, Treasury Stock	
10/2	1,500

Sale Below Cost

The resale price of treasury stock can be less than cost. The shortfall is debited first to Paid-in Capital, Treasury Stock. If this account's balance is too small, then Retained Earnings is debited for the remaining amount. To illustrate, let's assume Mackay Industries had two additional treasury stock sales. First, on October 28, Mackay Industries sold 1,000 treasury shares for $24 each. The entry to record the sale is as follows:

DATE	ACCOUNTS	POST REF.	DR.	CR.
Oct 28	Cash (1,000 × $24)		24,000	
	Paid-in Capital, Treasury Stock (difference)		1,000	
	Treasury Stock (1,000 × $25)			25,000
	Sold 1,000 shares of treasury stock.			

The total loss on the sale of the treasury shares is $1,000. Mackay Industries had previous gains of $1,500 from the October 2 sale of treasury stock, so there was enough Paid-in Capital from treasury stock transactions to cover the loss.

Now what happens if Mackay Industries sells an additional 1,500 treasury shares for $22 each on November 1?

DATE	ACCOUNTS	POST REF.	DR.	CR.
Nov 1	Cash (1,500 × $22)		33,000	
	Paid-in Capital, Treasury Stock (difference)		500	
	Retained Earnings		4,000	
	Treasury Stock (1,500 × $25)			37,500
	Sold 1,500 shares of treasury stock.			

The total loss on the sale is $4,500 [($25 cost per share minus $22 sales price per share) × 1,500 shares]. Only $500 remains in the Paid-in Capital, Treasury Stock account to absorb the loss. The remaining $4,000 ($4,500 – $500) in loss is debited to Retained Earnings.

So, what's left in stockholders' equity for Mackay Industries after the treasury stock transactions? First, let's post the treasury stock activity to the affected accounts:

Treasury Stock				Paid-in Capital, Treasury Stock				Retained Earnings			
8/10	125,000	9/5	12,500			10/2	1,500	11/1	4,000	8/1	1,000,000
		10/2	12,500	10/28	1,000					Bal	996,000
		10/28	25,000	11/1	500						
		11/1	37,500			Bal	-0-				
Bal	37,500										

Now, we can show the revised stockholders' equity for Mackay Industries in **Exhibit 10-7**:

Mackay Industries, Inc. Stockholders' Equity November 1	
Paid-in Capital:	
Preferred Stock, 10%, $20 par, 500,000 shares authorized,	
10,000 shares issued and outstanding	$ 200,000
Paid-in Capital in Excess of Par—Preferred	50,000
Common Stock, $.50 par, 4,000,000 shares authorized,	
1,050,000 shares issued, 1,048,500 shares outstanding	525,000
Paid-in Capital in Excess of Par—Common	7,975,000
Total Paid-in Capital	8,750,000
Retained Earnings	996,000
Less: Treasury Stock at cost (1,500 shares @ $25)	37,500
Total Stockholders' Equity	$9,708,500

Exhibit 10-7 ▲

HOW IS STOCKHOLDERS' EQUITY REPORTED ON THE BALANCE SHEET?

Report stockholders' equity on the balance sheet **7** ▶

Companies often report their stockholders' equity on the balance sheet in ways that differ from the examples we have shown in this chapter. In most cases the information is less detailed because it is assumed that investors understand the details. Two common differences are as follows:

❶ The heading Paid-in Capital does not usually appear. It is commonly understood that Preferred Stock, Common Stock, and Additional Paid-in Capital are elements of paid-in capital.

❷ All additional paid-in capital accounts are often combined and reported as a single amount labeled Additional Paid-in Capital. The Additional Paid-in Capital is most often reported following Common Stock.

Also, many companies often report a separate statement of stockholders' equity in addition to the regular financial statements. This statement is used to show investors the significant changes in all of the equity categories that occurred during the year. An example of a statement of stockholders' equity is presented in **Exhibit 10-8**.

		Common Stock	Additional Paid-in Capital	Retained Earnings	Treasury Stock	Total
	Balance, December 31, 2009	$80,000	$160,000	$130,000	$(25,000)	$345,000
	Issuance of Stock	20,000	60,000			80,000
	Net Income			69,000		69,000
	Cash Dividends			(20,000)		(20,000)
	Stock Dividends	8,000	26,000	(34,000)		0
	Purchase of Treasury Stock				(10,000)	(10,000)
	Sale of Treasury Stock		10,000		5,000	15,000
	Balance, December 31, 2010	$108,000	$256,000	$145,000	$(30,000)	$479,000

Example Company
Statement of Stockholders' Equity
Year Ended December 31, 2010

Exhibit 10-8 ▲

If a company has preferred stock, the statement would also include a column for Preferred Stock. Many companies will also have a column titled "Other Comprehensive Income," which reflects changes in stockholders' equity from things such as unrealized gains on available-for-sale securities which were discussed in Chapter 8.

FOCUS ON DECISION MAKING: RATIOS

 Evaluate return on stockholders' equity and return on common stockholders' equity

Investors are constantly evaluating companies' profits to determine performance. Two important ratios to use for comparison are return on stockholders' equity and return on common stockholders' equity.

Rate of Return on Stockholders' Equity

Rate of return on stockholders' equity, or **return on equity**, shows the relationship between net income and the average stockholders' equity. The numerator is net income and the denominator is average stockholders' equity. Let's assume Mackay Industries has the following data:

Net income for 2010	$136,000
Total stockholders' equity, 12/31/2010	$943,000
Total stockholders' equity, 12/31/2009	$825,000

Mackay Industries' rate of return on stockholders' equity for 2010 is computed as follows:

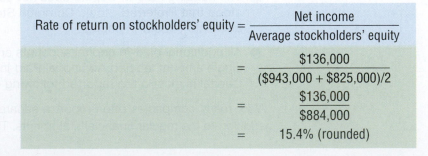

$$\text{Rate of return on stockholders' equity} = \frac{\text{Net income}}{\text{Average stockholders' equity}}$$

$$= \frac{\$136,000}{(\$943,000 + \$825,000)/2}$$

$$= \frac{\$136,000}{\$884,000}$$

$$= 15.4\% \text{ (rounded)}$$

Rate of Return on Common Stockholders' Equity

Rate of return on common stockholders' equity, or **return on common equity**, shows the relationship between the net income available to the common stockholders and their average stockholders' equity. The numerator is net income minus preferred dividends. The preferred dividends are subtracted because they represent part of the net income that is unavailable to the common stockholders. The denominator is average common stockholders' equity (total stockholders' equity minus preferred paid-in capital). Let's assume Mackay Industries has the following data:

Net income for 2010	$136,000
Preferred dividends for 2010	$ 18,000
Common stockholders' equity, 12/31/2010	$847,000
Common stockholders' equity, 12/31/2009	$723,000

Mackay Industries' rate of return on common stockholders' equity for 2010 is computed as follows:

$$\text{Rate of return on common stockholders' equity} = \frac{\text{Net income} - \text{preferred dividends}}{\text{Average common stockholders' equity}}$$

$$= \frac{\$136{,}000 - 18{,}000}{(\$847{,}000 + \$723{,}000)/2}$$

$$= \frac{\$118{,}000}{\$785{,}000}$$

$$= 15.0\% \text{ (rounded)}$$

Return on equity can be compared to returns that can be earned from other investments such as investments in other companies, or even investments in money market accounts or certificates of deposit. Returns on equity between 13% and 15% are generally considered to be good returns. Mackay Industries' return on equity of 15.4% and return on common equity of 15.0% are both strong.

Demo Doc

Equity Transactions

Learning Objectives 3–6 ▶

At January 1, 2010, Sara, Corp., had 2,000 common shares outstanding with a par value of $3 per share. During 2010, Sara had the following transactions:

Jan 31	Issued 500 common shares for $10 cash per share.
Mar 31	Declared cash dividends of $0.40 per common share.
May 31	Paid the cash dividends declared in March.
Jul 31	Purchased 300 shares of treasury stock for $11 cash per share.
Sep 30	Declared and distributed a 5% stock dividend when the market price was $12 per share.
Nov 30	Sold 200 shares of treasury stock for $12 cash per share.
Dec 31	Sold 100 shares of treasury stock for $9.50 per share.

Requirement:

❶ **Journalize all of Sara's equity transactions for 2010. After each transaction determine how many common shares are outstanding.**

Demo Doc Solutions

Requirement ❶

Journalize all of Sara's equity transactions for 2010. After each transaction determine how many common shares are outstanding.

Part 1	Demo Doc Complete

Jan 31   Issued 500 common shares for $10 cash per share.

Issuing common shares means that brand new share certificates were printed by Sara and sold to outside investors. It means an increase (credit) to Common Stock.

The Common Stock account *only* represents the par value of issued stock. Sara's common stock has a par value of $3 per share. So, Common Stock is increased by $1,500 (500 shares × $3 per share).

Sara receives $10 cash per share, so Cash is increased (debit) by $5,000 (500 shares × $10 per share).

The difference between the cash received and the par value of the stock is Paid-in Capital in Excess of Par. Paid-in capital is money the investors paid to the company. The investors are paying $10 per share to the company, all of which is paid-in capital. Of this amount, $1,500 relates to the par value and goes to the Common Stock account, and the remaining $3,500 ($5,000 – $1,500) is *excess*. So the $3,500 increases (credit) the Paid-in Capital in Excess of Par account.

DATE	ACCOUNTS	POST REF.	DR.	CR.
Jan 31	Cash (500 shares × $10)		5,000	
	Common Stock (500 shares × $3)			1,500
	Paid-in Capital in Excess of Par ($5,000 – $1,500)			3,500
	Issued stock at $10 per share.			

Selling common stock to outside investors increases the number of outstanding shares. So after this transaction, Sara has 2,500 (2,000 + 500) common shares outstanding.

Mar 31   Declared cash dividends of $0.40 per common share.

DATE	ACCOUNTS	POST REF.	DR.	CR.
Mar 31	Retained Earnings		1,000	
	Dividends Payable (2,500 shares × $0.40)			1,000
	Declared cash dividends.			

Declaring cash dividends decreases Retained Earnings (debit) and increases Dividends Payable (credit) by the amount to be paid. Sara declares $1,000 (2,500 shares outstanding × $0.40 per share) in cash dividends.

Declaring cash dividends does not change the number of outstanding shares, so 2,500 common shares remain outstanding after this transaction.

May 31 Paid the cash dividends declared in March.

When the dividends are paid, the Dividends Payable account is decreased (debit), in this case by $1,000, and Cash is also decreased (credit) by $1,000.

DATE	ACCOUNTS	POST REF.	DR.	CR.
May 31	Dividends Payable		1,000	
	Cash			1,000
	Paid cash dividends.			

Paying cash dividends does not change the number of outstanding shares, so 2,500 common shares remain outstanding after this transaction.

Jul 31 Purchased 300 shares of treasury stock for $11 cash per share.

When treasury stock is purchased, the Treasury Stock account is increased by the cost of the treasury stock. Treasury Stock is a *contra-equity* account, which means that it has a balance *opposite* to normal equity accounts. Most equity accounts have credit balances, so Treasury Stock has a debit balance. *Treasury stock decreases equity*. Cash is also decreased because Sara is *buying* (that is, paying for) the treasury shares.

In this case, the Treasury Stock account is increased (debit) by $3,300 (300 shares × $11 per share) and Cash is decreased (credit) by $3,300.

DATE	ACCOUNTS	POST REF.	DR.	CR.
Jul 31	Treasury Stock (300 shares × $11)		3,300	
	Cash			3,300
	Purchased treasury stock.			

Treasury shares are *no longer outstanding*. Because they are held by the company, they no longer have votes at shareholder meetings nor do they receive dividends. So the number of outstanding shares is now 2,200 (2,500 − 300).

Sep 30 Declared and distributed a 5% stock dividend when the market price was $12 per share.

Stock dividends are similar to cash dividends except that a stock dividend is distributed in stock instead of paid in cash. The stock dividend will issue brand new shares of common stock to investors who already own stock of the corporation.

Dividends (both stock and cash) only apply to *outstanding* shares. The treasury stock is considered inactive and *does not* receive dividends of any kind.

Just as with cash dividends, stock dividends decrease Retained Earnings. Retained Earnings is decreased by the *market value* of the new shares issued. Retained Earnings is decreased (debit) by $1,320 (2,200 shares × 5% × $12 per share).

The remainder of the entry is similar to the entry to issue common stock. The only difference between this transaction and the one on January 31 is that Retained Earnings is debited *instead of* Cash.

Common stock is increased by the *par value* of the new shares. So the Common Stock account is increased by $330 (2,200 shares × 5% × $3 per share).

The difference between the value of the dividend debited to Retained Earnings and the par value is Paid-in Capital in Excess of Par. This account is increased (credit) by the difference of $990 ($1,320 – $330).

DATE	ACCOUNTS	POST REF.	DR.	CR.
Sep 30	Retained Earnings (2,200 × 5% × $12)		1,320	
	Common Stock (2,200 × 5% × $3)			330
	Paid-in Capital in Excess of Par ($1,320 – $330)			990
	Declared and distributed a stock dividend.			

Because the stock dividend increases the number of common shares held by outside investors, it increases the number of outstanding common shares by 110 shares (2,200 shares × 5%). So after this transaction, Sara has 2,310 (2,200 + 110) common shares outstanding.

Nov 30   Sold 200 shares of treasury stock for $12 cash per share.

As seen in the July 31 transaction, purchasing treasury stock decreases equity. When treasury stock is sold, the opposite occurs and equity increases.

Treasury stock is decreased by the original cost of the treasury shares. These shares were purchased back on July 31 for $11 per share. The Treasury Stock account is decreased (credit) by $2,200 (200 shares × $11 per share).

When the treasury stock is sold, Sara receives the cash. Cash is increased (debit) by $2,400 (200 shares × $12 per share).

The difference between the cash received and the original cost of the treasury shares is an adjustment to Paid-in Capital, Treasury Stock. This adjustment represents additional cash (above cost) received by the company from the shareholders who purchased the stock. Paid-in Capital, Treasury Stock is increased by $200 ($2,400 – $2,200, or 200 shares times the difference of $12 – $11 = $1).

DATE	ACCOUNTS	POST REF.	DR.	CR.
Nov 30	Cash (200 shares × $12)		2,400	
	Treasury Stock (200 shares × $11 cost)			2,200
	Paid-in Capital, Treasury Stock ($2,400 – $2,200)			200
	Sold treasury stock.			

Purchasing treasury stock decreases the number of outstanding common shares. Selling the treasury shares makes them active again, thus increasing the number of outstanding shares. So after this transaction, 2,510 (2,310 + 200) common shares are outstanding.

Dec 31   Sold 100 shares of treasury stock for $9.50 per share.

As in the previous transaction, Treasury Stock is decreased by the original cost of the treasury shares. These shares were purchased back on July 31 for $11 per share, so Treasury Stock is decreased (credit) by $1,100 (100 shares × $11 per share). Cash is increased (debit) by $950 (100 shares × $9.50 per share).

As in the previous transaction, the difference between the cash received and the original cost of the treasury shares is an adjustment to Paid-in Capital, Treasury Stock. However, in this case, the cash received is *below* the original cost of the treasury stock, so the adjustment *decreases* paid-in capital. Paid-in Capital, Treasury Stock decreases by $150 ($1,100 – $950, or 100 shares times the difference of $11.00 – $9.50 = $1.50).

DATE	ACCOUNTS	POST REF.	DR.	CR.
Dec 31	Cash (100 shares × $9.50)		950	
	Paid-in Capital, Treasury Stock ($1,100 – $950)		150	
	Treasury Stock (100 shares × $11 cost)			1,100
	Sold treasury stock.			

Even though we are allowed to decrease Paid-in Capital, Treasury Stock, we *cannot* allow this account to become negative (have a debit balance). In this situation, we know the account holds $200 from the November 30 transaction, so we can decrease the account by $150 because a positive balance of $50 ($200 – $150) will remain.

If the Paid-in Capital, Treasury Stock account did not hold a sufficient balance, then we would have brought that account to zero and debited Retained Earnings for the rest.

Paid-in Capital, Treasury Stock			
Dec 31	150	Nov 30	200
		Bal	50

Selling the treasury shares increases the number of outstanding shares. After this transaction, 2,610 (2,510 + 100) common shares are outstanding.

Demo Doc Complete

Part 1	Demo Doc Complete

Decision Guidelines

Corporations: Paid-in Capital and Retained Earnings

The corporate form of business organization is very popular. You will possibly work for a corporation someday. Or, you may even have an opportunity to organize your own corporation. If you do, you will most likely encounter the following decisions.

Decision		Guideline		Analyze
When is a cash dividend appropriate?	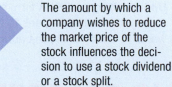	Consider the amount of available cash as well as the balance in Retained Earnings.	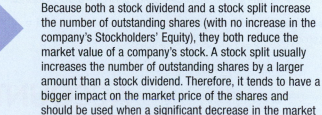	A cash dividend is a distribution of earnings to the company's stockholders. So a company cannot declare and distribute dividends unless the balance in retained earnings (counting the current year's earnings) exceeds the amount of the desired dividend. In addition, the company must have the cash available to pay the dividend if it is declared. A business should carefully analyze its future cash needs so that it does not deplete its cash with a dividend and end up with cash flow issues in the future.
To decrease the market price of a company's stock is it better to use a stock dividend or a stock split?		The amount by which a company wishes to reduce the market price of the stock influences the decision to use a stock dividend or a stock split.		Because both a stock dividend and a stock split increase the number of outstanding shares (with no increase in the company's Stockholders' Equity), they both reduce the market value of a company's stock. A stock split usually increases the number of outstanding shares by a larger amount than a stock dividend. Therefore, it tends to have a bigger impact on the market price of the shares and should be used when a significant decrease in the market price is desired. For example, a 2-for-1 split will typically reduce the market price of a company's stock by 50%.

ACCOUNTING VOCABULARY

THE LANGUAGE OF BUSINESS

Additional Paid-in Capital (p. 491) Paid-in capital that represents the amount by which the issue price of stock exceeds its par value; also called *Paid-in Capital in Excess of Par*.

Arrears (p. 496) A cumulative dividend on preferred stock that has not been paid for the year.

Articles of incorporation (p. 488) Describes the purpose, place, and other details of a corporation; also called *corporate charter*.

Authorized stock (p. 488) The number of shares of stock a corporation is authorized by a state to sell.

Capital stock (p. 488) Represents the individual's ownership of the corporation's capital.

Common stock (p. 490) The most typical kind of stock. It usually has voting rights, the rights to receive dividends, and the right to receive assets if the company liquidates.

Corporate charter (p. 488) Describes the purpose, place, and other details of a corporation; also called *articles of incorporation*.

Cumulative preferred stock (p. 496) Preferred stock whose owners must receive all dividends in arrears before the corporation pays dividends to the common stockholders.

Issue price (p. 491) The price the stock initially sells for the first time it is sold.

Legal capital (p. 493) The portion of stockholders' equity that cannot be used for dividends.

Memorandum entry (p. 501) A journal entry that "notes" a significant event, but which has no debit or credit amount.

Outstanding stock (p. 488) Stock in the hands of stockholders.

Paid-in Capital in Excess of Par (p. 491) Paid-in capital that represents the amount by which the issue price of stock exceeds its par value; also called *Additional Paid-in Capital*.

Par value (p. 490) Arbitrary amount assigned to a share of stock.

Preferred stock (p. 490) Stock that gives its owners certain advantages over common stockholders, such as the right to receive dividends before the common stockholders and the right to receive assets before the common stockholders if the corporation liquidates.

Rate of return on common stockholders' equity (p. 507) Net income minus preferred dividends, divided by average common stockholders' equity. It is a measure of profitability; also called *return on common equity*.

Rate of return on stockholders' equity (p. 506) Net income divided by average stockholders' equity. It is a measure of profitability; also called *return on equity*.

Return on common equity (p. 507) Net income minus preferred dividends, divided by average common stockholders' equity. It is measure of profitability; also called *rate of return on common stockholders' equity*.

Return on equity (p. 506) Net income divided by average stockholders' equity. It is a measure of profitability; also called *rate of return on stockholders' equity*.

Share (p. 488) The basic unit of stock.

Stated value (p. 490) An arbitrary amount that is similar to par value but is assigned after a corporation is organized.

Stock certificates (p. 488) Certificates that provide evidence of stock ownership.

Stock dividend (p. 497) A distribution by a corporation of its own stock to stockholders.

Stock split (p. 499) An increase in the number of outstanding shares of stock coupled with a proportionate reduction in the value of the stock.

Treasury stock (p. 502) A corporation's own stock that it has issued and later reacquired.

Underwriter (p. 491) A firm, such as Morgan Stanley Smith Barney, that usually agrees to buy all the stock a company wants to issue if the firm cannot sell the stock to its clients.

ACCOUNTING PRACTICE

DISCUSSION QUESTIONS

1. What are the four basic rights of stockholders?

2. Assume that you are a CFO of a company that is attempting to raise additional capital to finance an expansion of its production facility. You are considering either issuing bonds or additional stock. What are some of the differences in the two options?

3. What accounts are involved in the journal entry to record the issuance of stock at a price above the par value of the stock?

4. What accounts, if any, are involved in the journal entries to record the events associated with each of the following dates associated with cash dividends?

   a. Declaration date
   b. Date of record
   c. Payment date

5. With which type of stock would dividends in arrears be associated? Why?

6. What accounts are affected by the declaration and distribution of a stock dividend? What is the effect of a stock dividend on

   a. Total Stockholders' Equity?
   b. Total Assets?
   c. Total Liabilities?
   d. Cash?

7. What are some of the reasons for issuing a stock dividend?

8. What kind of account is treasury stock? What is its normal balance? Where would it be reported on the financial statements?

9. What could you reasonably conclude if a company reports more shares of stock issued than outstanding?

10. Why are preferred dividends subtracted from the numerator in calculating the return on common equity ratio?

SELF CHECK

1. Which characteristic of a corporation is considered to be an advantage?

   a. Ease of transferring ownership
   b. Indefinite life
   c. Limited stockholder liability
   d. All of the above

2. Which of the following is a disadvantage of organizing as a corporation?

   a. Separate legal entity
   b. Limited ability to raise capital
   c. Double taxation
   d. Limited stockholder liability

3. What are the two basic sources of corporate capital?

   a. Paid-in capital and retained earnings
   b. Stock and bonds
   c. Common stock and preferred stock
   d. Retained earnings and dividends

4. Suppose PETCO issued 100,000 shares of its $0.05 par common stock at $1 per share. Which journal entry correctly records the issuance of this stock?

DATE	ACCOUNTS	POST REF.	DR.	CR.
a.	Cash		100,000	
	Common Stock			100,000
b.	Common Stock		100,000	
	Cash			5,000
	Paid-in Capital in Excess of Par			95,000
c.	Cash		100,000	
	Common Stock			5,000
	Paid-in Capital in Excess of Par			95,000
d.	Common Stock		100,000	
	Cash			100,000

5. Chewning Corporation has 10,000 shares of 5%, $10 par, cumulative preferred stock and 50,000 shares of common stock outstanding. Chewning Corporation declared no dividends in 2010. In 2011, Chewning Corporation declares a total dividend of $25,000. How much of the dividends goes to the common stockholders?

   a. $ 5,000
   b. $10,000
   c. $15,000
   d. None; it all goes to preferred.

6. Techster Company has 10,000 shares of $1 par common stock outstanding, which Techster Company issued at $5 per share. Techster Company also has retained earnings of $80,000. How much is Techster Company's total stockholders' equity?

   a. $ 50,000
   b. $ 80,000
   c. $ 90,000
   d. $130,000

7. What is the term for a company's own stock that it has issued and repurchased?

   a. Issued stock
   b. Stock dividend
   c. Outstanding stock
   d. Treasury stock

8. What does a stock dividend do?

   a. Increases Common Stock
   b. Has no effect on total equity
   c. Decreases Retained Earnings
   d. All of the above

9. What happens with a stock split?

   a. Increases the number of shares of stock issued
   b. Decreases the par value of the stock
   c. Both a and b
   d. None of the above

10. Assume that Pier 1 Imports pays $10 per share to purchase 1,000 of its $1 par common stock as treasury stock. What is the effect of purchasing the treasury stock?

    a. Decreases total stockholders' equity by $1,000
    b. Decreases total stockholders' equity by $10,000
    c. Increases total stockholders' equity by $1,000
    d. Increases total stockholders' equity by $10,000

    Answers are given after Written Communication.

SHORT EXERCISES

S10-1. Stockholders' equity terminology (*Learning Objectives 1 & 2*) 10–15 min.

Match the following terms with the correct definition.

a. Common stock

b. Paid-in capital

c. Dividends

d. Legal capital

e. Outstanding stock

f. Par value

g. Preferred stock

h. Retained earnings

i. Treasury stock

j. Stockholders' equity

____ **1.** Paid-in capital plus Retained Earnings.

____ **2.** Capital from investments by the stockholders.

____ **3.** Capital earned through profitable operation of the business.

____ **4.** The basic form of capital stock.

____ **5.** Stock in the hands of stockholders.

____ **6.** Distributions by a corporation to its stockholders.

____ **7.** Stock that gives its owners certain advantages over common stockholders, such as the right to receive dividends before the common stockholders.

____ **8.** Arbitrary amount assigned to a share of stock at the time of incorporation.

____ **9.** The portion of stockholders' equity maintained for the protection of creditors.

____ **10.** A corporation's own stock that it reacquires.

S10-2. Stock issuance (*Learning Objective 3*) 5–10 min.

Tricor, Corp., issued stock above par on July 31. Answer the following questions about Tricor, Corp.

1. Tricor, Corp., received $30 million for the issuance of its stock. The par value of the Tricor, Corp., stock was only $30,000. Was the excess amount of $29,970,000 a profit to Tricor, Corp? Did the excess affect net income? If not, what was it?

2. Suppose the par value of the Tricor, Corp., stock had been $1 per share, $5 per share, or $10 per share. Would a change in the par value of the company's stock affect Tricor's total paid-in capital? When issuing stock, what does affect total paid-in capital?

S10-3. Issuance of stock for cash and noncash assets (*Learning Objective 3*) 10–15 min.

This exercise shows the similarity and the difference between two ways to acquire plant assets.

Case A—Issue stock and buy the assets in separate transactions:

Atar, Inc., issued 10,000 shares of its $10 par common stock for cash of $700,000. In a separate transaction, Atar, Inc., purchased a building for $500,000 and equipment for $200,000. Journalize the two transactions.

Case B—Issue stock to acquire the assets:

Atar, Inc., issued 10,000 shares of its $10 par common stock to acquire a building valued at $500,000 and equipment worth $200,000. Journalize this single transaction.

Compare the balances in all accounts after making both sets of entries. Are the account balances similar or different?

S10-4. Stock issuance (*Learning Objectives 2 & 3*) 5–10 min.

The Kingston Company reported the following on its balance sheet at December 31, 2010:

Common Stock, $0.25 par value, 500,000 shares authorized, 350,000 shares issued and outstanding	$ 87,500
Paid-in Capital in Excess of Par	385,500
Retained Earnings	2,500,000

1. Assume Kingston Company issued all of its stock during 2010. Journalize the company's issuance of the stock for cash.

2. Was Kingston Company's main source of stockholders' equity paid-in capital or profitable operations? How can you tell?

S10-5. Analyzing stockholders' equity (*Learning Objectives 2 & 3*) 5–10 min.

At December 31, 2010, Kingston Company reported the following on its comparative balance sheet, which included 2009 amounts for comparison (adapted, with all amounts in millions except par value per share):

	December 31	
	2010	**2009**
Common Stock, $0.25 par value, 500,000 shares authorized, 350,000 shares issued and outstanding in 2010; 349,000 shares in 2009	$ 87,500	$ 87,250
Paid-in Capital in Excess of Par	385,500	352,000
Retained Earnings	2,500,000	2,250,000

1. How much did Kingston Company's total paid-in capital increase during 2010? What caused total paid-in capital to increase? How can you tell?

2. Did Kingston Company have a profit or a loss for 2010? How can you tell?

S10-6. Stock issuance (*Learning Objectives 2 & 3*) 5–10 min.

Bruner Corporation has two classes of stock, $1 par common and $10 par preferred. Journalize Bruner's issuance of the following:

a. 1,000 shares of common stock for $50 per share

b. 1,000 shares of preferred stock for a total of $32,000

Explanations are not required.

S10-7. Accounting for cash dividends (*Learning Objective 4*) 10–15 min.

Midas Company earned net income of $85,000 during the year ended December 31, 2010. On December 15, 2010, Midas Company declared the annual cash dividend on its 6% preferred stock (total par value, $100,000) and a $0.50 per share cash dividend on its common stock (50,000 shares outstanding). Midas Company then paid the dividends on January 4, 2011.

Journalize for Midas Company

a. declaring the cash dividends on December 15, 2010.

b. paying the cash dividends on January 4, 2011.

S10-8. Accounting for cash dividends (*Learning Objective 4*) 10–15 min.

Holiday.com prepared the following stockholders' equity section as of December 31, 2010.

Stockholders' Equity	
Paid-in Capital:	
Preferred Stock, 5%, $100 par, 5,000 shares authorized,	
400 shares issued and outstanding	$ 40,000
Common Stock, $10 par, 20,000 shares authorized,	
5,000 shares issued and outstanding	50,000
Paid-in Capital in Excess of Par	70,000
Total Paid-in Capital	$160,000
Retained Earnings	90,000
Total Stockholders' Equity	$250,000

Answer the following questions about Holiday.com's dividends:

1. How much in dividends must Holiday.com declare each year before the common stockholders get any cash dividends for the year?

2. Suppose Holiday.com declares cash dividends of $20,000 for 2010. How much of the dividends goes to preferred? How much goes to common?

3. Is Holiday.com's preferred stock cumulative or noncumulative? How can you tell?

4. Suppose Holiday.com passed the preferred dividend in 2011 and 2012. In 2013, the company declares cash dividends of $9,000. How much of the dividends goes to preferred? How much goes to common?

S10-9. Accounting for stock dividends (*Learning Objective 5*) 10–15 min.

Transtech, Inc., has 200,000 shares of $2.50 par common stock outstanding. Transtech, Inc., declares and distributes a 5% stock dividend when the market value of its stock is $10 per share.

1. Journalize Transtech's declaration and distribution of the stock dividend on September 30. An explanation is not required.

2. What is the overall effect of the stock dividend on Transtech's total assets? On total stockholders' equity?

S10-10. Comparing cash and stock dividends (*Learning Objectives 4 & 5*) 10–15 min.

Compare and contrast the accounting for cash dividends and stock dividends. In the space provided, insert either "Cash dividends," "Stock dividends," or "Both" to complete each of the following statements:

1. _____ increase paid-in capital by the same amount that they decrease retained earnings.

2. _____ decrease both total assets and total stockholders' equity.

3. _____ decrease retained earnings.

4. _____ have no effect on a liability.

S10-11. Accounting for stock splits (*Learning Objective 5*) 5–10 min.

Suppose Pier 1 Imports has common stock, $1 par, 500,000 shares authorized, 100,000 shares issued and outstanding. The company decided to split its common stock 2-for-1 in order to decrease the market price of its stock. The company's stock was trading at $20 immediately before the split.

1. Show how the common stockholders' equity would appear in the stockholders' equity section of Pier 1 Imports' balance sheet after the stock split.

2. Which account balances changed after the stock split? Which account balances were unchanged?

S10-12. Accounting for treasury stock (*Learning Objective 6*) 10–15 min.

Classic Corporation began operations in 2010. After issuing its common stock to the public, Classic Corporation completed the following treasury stock transactions:

a. Purchased 2,000 shares of the company's $1 par common stock as treasury stock, paying cash of $5 per share.

b. Sold 1,000 shares of the treasury stock for cash of $8 per share.

Journalize these transactions. Explanations are not required. Show how Classic Corporation will report treasury stock on its December 31, 2010, balance sheet after completing the two transactions. In reporting the treasury stock, focus solely on the Treasury Stock account. You may ignore all other accounts.

S10-13. Balance sheet disclosure of stockholders' equity (*Learning Objective 7*) 5–10 min.

The financial statements of Nason Corporation reported the following accounts (in thousands except for par value):

Paid-in Capital in Excess of Par......	$170	Net Sales.....................................	$1,080
Cost of Goods Sold........................	588	Accounts Payable........................	60
Common Stock, $1 par, 400 shares		Retained Earnings.......................	166
issued and outstanding.............	400	Other Current Liabilities..............	52
Cash...	240	Operating Expenses....................	412
Long-Term Debt.............................	76	Total Assets...............................	?

Prepare the stockholders' equity section of Nason Corporation's balance sheet. Net income has already been closed to Retained Earnings.

S10-14. Analyzing stockholders' equity (*Learning Objective 7*) 10–15 min.

Use the statement of stockholders' equity in Exhibit 10-8, to answer the following questions:

1. Make journal entries to record the declaration and payment of cash dividends during 2010.

2. How much cash did the issuance of common stock bring in during 2010?

3. What was the cost of the treasury stock that was purchased during 2010?

What was the cost of the treasury stock that was sold during the year? For how much was the treasury stock sold during 2010?

EXERCISES (GROUP A)

E10-15A. Stock issuance (*Learning Objective 3*) 10–15 min.

Stanley Systems completed the following stock issuance transactions:

Apr 19	Issued 1,000 shares of $1 par common stock for cash of $10.50 per share.
May 3	Sold 300 shares of $4.50, no-par preferred stock for $15,000 cash.
11	Received inventory valued at $23,000 and equipment with a market value of $11,000. Issued 3,000 shares of the $1 par common stock in exchange.

Requirements

1. Journalize the transactions. Explanations are not required.
2. How much paid-in capital did these transactions generate for Stanley Systems?

E10-16A. Stock issuance (*Learning Objectives 3 & 7*) 10–15 min.

The charter for Zycor, Inc., authorizes the company to issue 100,000 shares of $3, no-par preferred stock and 500,000 shares of common stock with $1 par value. During its start-up phase, Zycor, Inc., completed the following transactions:

2010	
Aug 6	Issued 500 shares of common stock to the promoters who organized the corporation, receiving cash of $15,000.
12	Issued 300 shares of preferred stock for cash of $20,000.
14	Issued 1,000 shares of common stock in exchange for land valued at $26,000.

Requirements

1. Record the transactions in the journal.
2. Prepare the stockholders' equity section of Zycor's balance sheet at December 31, 2010. Assume that the company earned net income of $25,000 during this period.

E10-17A. Stock issuance (*Learning Objective 3*) 10–15 min.

Yates, Corp., issued 5,000 shares of no-par common stock for $10 per share.

Requirements

1. Record issuance of the stock if the stock
   a. is a no-par stock and
   b. actually has a stated value of $2 per share.
2. Which type of stock issuance results in more total paid-in capital?

E10-18A. Issuance of stock for cash and noncash assets (*Learning Objective 3*) 10–15 min.

Victor, Co., recently organized. The company issued common stock to an attorney in exchange for his patent with a market value of $40,000. In addition, Victor, Co., received cash for 2,000 shares of its $50 par preferred stock sold at par value and for 26,000 shares of its no-par common stock sold at $10 per share. Retained Earnings at the end of the first year was $70,000.

Requirement

1. Without making journal entries, determine the total paid-in capital created by these transactions.

Quick solution:

2010 dividends = $15,000 preferred, $0 common; 2011 dividends = $17,000 preferred, $33,000 common

E10-19A. Accounting for cash dividends (*Learning Objective 4*) 10–15 min.

Horizon Communications has the following stockholders' equity:

Horizon Communications Stockholders' Equity		
Paid-in Capital:		
Preferred Stock, 8%, $10 par, 100,000 shares authorized,		
20,000 shares issued and outstanding		$ 200,000
Common Stock, $0.50 par, 500,000 shares authorized,		
300,000 shares issued and outstanding		150,000
Paid-in Capital in Excess of Par		600,000
Total Paid-in Capital		$ 950,000
Retained Earnings		150,000
Total Stockholders' Equity		$1,100,000

Requirement

1. Assume the preferred stock is cumulative. Compute the amount of dividends to preferred and common shareholders for 2010 and 2011 if total dividends are $15,000 in 2010 and $50,000 in 2011.

E10-20A. Accounting for cash dividends (*Learning Objective 4*) 10–15 min.

The following elements of stockholders' equity are adapted from the balance sheet of Scribner Corporation.

Stockholders' Equity	$ Thousands
Preferred Stock, cumulative, $2 par (Note 7), 50,000 shares issued and outstanding	$100
Common Stock, $0.10 par, 9,000,000 shares issued and outstanding	900

Note 7. Preferred Stock: Designated annual cash dividend per share, $0.40.

Scribner Corporation paid no preferred dividends in 2010 but paid the designated amount of cash dividends per share to preferred shareholders in all prior years.

Requirement

1. Compute the dividends to preferred and common shareholders for 2011 if total dividends are $150,000.

E10-21A. Accounting for stock dividends (*Learning Objectives 5 & 7*) 10–15 min.

The stockholders' equity for Blade, Inc., on December 31, 2009, follows:

Stockholders' Equity	
Paid-in Capital:	
Common Stock, $1 par, 100,000 shares authorized,	
50,000 shares issued and outstanding	$ 50,000
Paid-in Capital in Excess of Par	400,000
Total Paid-in Capital	$450,000
Retained Earnings	120,000
Total Stockholders' Equity	$570,000

On April 30, 2010, the market price of Blade's common stock was $16 per share and the company distributed a 10% stock dividend.

Requirements

1. Journalize the declaration and distribution of the stock dividend.
2. Prepare the stockholders' equity section of the balance sheet after the stock dividend.

E10-22A. Accounting for cash and stock dividends (*Learning Objectives 4 & 5*) 10–15 min.

Rolly Racing Motors is authorized to issue 500,000 shares of $1 par common stock. The company issued 80,000 shares at $4 per share, and all 80,000 shares are outstanding. When the market price of common stock was $5 per share, Rolly Racing Motors declared and distributed a 10% stock dividend. Later, Rolly Racing Motors declared and paid a $0.50 per share cash dividend.

Requirements

1. Journalize the declaration and distribution of the stock dividend.
2. Journalize the declaration and the payment of the cash dividend.

E10-23A. Accounting for stock splits (*Learning Objectives 5 & 7*) 10–15 min.

Lipton Travel, Inc., had the following stockholders' equity at May 31:

Stockholders' Equity	
Paid-in Capital:	
Common Stock, $10 par, 200,000 shares authorized,	
50,000 shares issued and outstanding	$500,000
Paid-in Capital in Excess of Par	100,000
Total Paid-in Capital	$600,000
Retained Earnings	200,000
Total Stockholders' Equity	$800,000

On June 30, Lipton Travel, Inc., split its common stock 2-for-1.

Requirements

1. Make any necessary entry to record the stock split.
2. Prepare the stockholders' equity section of the balance sheet immediately after the split.

E10-24A. Accounting for stock issuance, splits, and treasury stock (*Learning Objectives 3, 5, & 6*) 20–25 min.

Consider each of the following transactions separately from every other transaction:

a. Issuance of 50,000 shares of $10 par common at $15.
b. Purchase of 1,000 shares of treasury stock (par value $0.50) at $5 per share.
c. Issuance of a 10% stock dividend. Before the dividend, 500,000 shares of $1 par common stock were outstanding; market value was $7 at the time of the dividend.
d. Sale of 600 shares of $1 par treasury stock for $5 per share. Cost of the treasury stock was $2 per share.
e. Split stock 3-for-1. Prior to the split, 60,000 shares of $4 par common were outstanding.

Requirement

1. Identify whether each transaction increased, decreased, or did not change total stockholders' equity.

E10-25A. Accounting for treasury stock (*Learning Objectives 3 & 6*) 20–25 min.

Journalize the following transactions of Goddard Sports, Inc., a chain of sports stores:

Feb 4	Issued 20,000 shares of no-par common stock at $15 per share.
Apr 22	Purchased 1,000 shares of treasury stock at $14 per share.
Aug 22	Sold 600 shares of treasury stock at $20 per share.

E10-26A. Accounting for treasury stock (*Learning Objectives 6 & 7*) 20–25 min.

Franklin, Inc., had the following stockholders' equity on November 30:

Stockholders' Equity	
Paid-in Capital:	
Common Stock, $5 par, 500,000 shares authorized,	
50,000 shares issued and outstanding	$250,000
Paid-in Capital in Excess of Par	150,000
Total Paid-in Capital	$400,000
Retained Earnings	520,000
Total Stockholders' Equity	$920,000

On December 30, Franklin, Inc., purchased 5,000 shares of treasury stock at $10 per share.

Requirements

1. Journalize the purchase of the treasury stock.
2. Prepare the stockholders' equity section of the balance sheet at December 31.

E10-27A. Balance sheet disclosure of stockholders' equity (*Learning Objective 7*) 10–15 min.

Casey Manufacturing, Co., has the following selected account balances at June 30, 2010.

Common Stock, no par with $1 stated value, 100,000 shares authorized, issued, and outstanding	$100,000	Inventory	$112,000
		Machinery and Equipment	109,000
		Preferred Stock, 5%, $20 par, 20,000 shares authorized, 5,000 shares issued and outstanding	100,000
Accumulated Depreciation, Machinery and Equipment	62,000		
Retained Earnings	110,000	Paid-in Capital in Excess of Stated Value	90,000
		Cost of Goods Sold	81,000

Requirement

1. Prepare the stockholders' equity section of the company's balance sheet.

E10-28A. Accounting for various stockholders' equity transactions (*Learning Objective 7*)
20–25 min.

At December 31, 2009, Eaton, Corp., reported the following stockholders' equity:

Paid-in Capital:	
Common Stock, $5 par, 200,000 authorized,	
120,000 shares issued	$ 600,000
Additional Paid-in Capital	100,000
Total Paid-in Capital	$ 700,000
Retained Earnings	700,000
Subtotal	$1,400,000
Less: Treasury Stock, 2,500 shares at cost	(80,000)
Total Stockholders' Equity	$1,320,000

During 2010, Eaton, Corp., completed these transactions and events in this order:

  a. Sold 1,000 shares of treasury stock for $35 per share; the cost of these shares was $30 per share.

  b. Issued 500 shares of common stock at $20 per share.

  c. Net income for the year was $200,000.

  d. Declared and paid cash dividends of $100,000.

Requirement

  1. Prepare Eaton's statement of stockholders' equity for 2010.

E10-29A. Accounting for various stockholders' equity transactions (*Learning Objectives 3, 5, & 7*) 20–25 min.

Olson Communications, Inc., began 2010 with 2.9 million shares of $1 par common stock issued and outstanding. Beginning paid-in capital in excess of par was $6 million, and retained earnings was $7 million. In February 2010, Olson Communications, Inc., issued 100,000 shares of stock at $11 per share. In September, when the stock's market price was $12 per share, the board of directors distributed a 10% stock dividend.

Requirements

  1. Make the journal entries for the issuance of stock for cash and for the declaration and distribution of the 10% stock dividend.

  2. Prepare the company's statement of stockholders' equity for the year ended December 31, 2010.

E10-30A. Calculating return on equity (*Learning Objective 8*) 10–15 min.

Assume that Apex, Inc., has the following data:

Net income for 2010	$ 127,000
Preferred dividends for 2010	$ 23,000
Total stockholder's equity, 12/31/2010	$1,627,000
Total stockholder's equity, 12/31/2009	$1,589,000
Common stockholder's equity, 12/31/2010	$1,484,000
Common stockholder's equity, 12/31/2009	$1,392,000

Requirements

  1. Calculate Apex's return on equity for 2010.

  2. Calculate Apex's return on common equity for 2010.

  3. Comment on Apex's performance during 2010.

EXERCISES (GROUP B)

E10-31B. Stock issuance (*Learning Objective 3*) 10–15 min.

Sierra Systems completed the following stock issuance transactions:

Sep 19	Issued 1,300 shares of $1 par common stock for cash of $10.00 per share.
Oct 3	Sold 500 shares of $4.00, no-par preferred stock for $25,000 cash.
11	Received inventory valued at $21,000 and equipment with a market value of $16,000. Issued 12,000 shares of the $1 par common stock in exchange.

Requirements

1. Journalize the transactions. Explanations are not required.
2. How much paid-in capital did these transactions generate for Sierra Systems?

E10-32B. Stock issuance (*Learning Objectives 3 & 7*) 10–15 min.

The charter for Zerron, Inc., authorizes the company to issue 500,000 shares of $4, no-par preferred stock and 700,000 shares of common stock with $1 par value. During its start-up phase, Zerron, Inc., completed the following transactions:

2010	
Jul 6	Issued 575 shares of common stock to the promoters who orginized the corporation, receiving cash of $17,250.
12	Issued 650 shares of preferred stock for cash of $23,000.
14	Issued 1,200 shares of common stock in exchange for land valued at $19,000.

Requirements

1. Record the transactions in the journal.
2. Prepare the stockholders' equity section of the Zerron's balance sheet at December 31, 2010. Assume that the company earned net income of $37,000 during this period.

E10-33B. Stock issuance (*Learning Objective 3*) 10–15 min.

Youken, Corp., issued 6,000 shares of no-par common stock for $15 per share.

Requirements

1. Record issuance of the stock if the stock
   a. is no-par stock and
   b. actually has a stated value of $4 per share.
2. Which type of stock issuance results in more total paid-in capital?

E10-34B. Issuance of stock for cash and noncash assets (*Learning Objective 3*) 10–15 min.

Arilla, Co., recently organized. The company issued common stock to an attorney in exchange for his patent with a market value of $52,000. In addition, Arilla, Co., received cash for 1,000 shares of its $60 par preferred stock sold at par value and for 30,000 shares of its no-par common stock sold at $15 per share. Retained Earnings at the end of the first year was $88,000.

Requirement

1. Without making journal entries, determine the total paid-in capital created by these transactions.

E10-35B. Accounting for cash dividends (*Learning Objective 4*) 10–15 min.

Eastern Communications has the following stockholders' equity:

Eastern Communications Stockholders' Equity		
Paid-in Capital:		
Preferred Stock, 15%, $10 par, 100,000 shares authorized		
28,000 shares issued and outstanding		$ 280,000
Common Stock, $0.50 par, 500,000 shares authorized		
320,000 shares issued and outstanding		160,000
Paid-in Capital in Excess of Par-Common		550,000
Total Paid-in Capital		990,000
Retained Earnings		160,000
Total Stockholders' Equity		$1,150,000

Requirement

1. Assume the preferred stock is cumulative. Compute the amount of dividends to preferred and common shareholders for 2010 and 2011 if total dividends are $36,000 in 2010 and $51,000 in 2011.

E10-36B. Accounting for cash dividends (*Learning Objective 4*) 10–15 min.

The following elements of stockholders' equity are adapted from the balance sheet of Sacchetti Corporation.

Stockholders' Equity	$ Thousands
Preferred Stock, cumulative, $2 par (Note 7), 45,000 shares issued and outstanding	$225
Common Stock, $0.10 par, 8,750,000 shares issued and outstanding	875

Note 7. Preferred Stock: Designated annual cash dividend per share, $0.75.

Sacchetti Corporation paid no preferred dividends in 2010 but paid the designated amount of cash dividends per share to preferred shareholders in all prior years.

Requirement

1. Compute the dividends to preferred and common shareholders for 2011 if total dividends are $185,000.

E10-37B. Accounting for stock dividends (*Learning Objectives 5 & 7*) 10–15 min.

The stockholders' equity for Pondwood, Inc., on December 31, 2009, follows:

Stockholders' Equity	
Paid-in Capital:	
Common Stock, $1 par, 350,000 shares authorized,	
40,000 issued and outstanding	$ 40,000
Paid-in Capital in Excess of Par	160,000
Total Paid-in Capital	200,000
Retained Earnings	360,000
Total Stockholders' Equity	$560,000

On September 30, 2010, the market price of Pondwood's common stock was $11 per share and the company distributed a 30% stock dividend.

Requirements

1. Journalize the declaration and distribution of the stock dividend.
2. Prepare the stockholders' equity section of the balance sheet after the stock dividend.

E10-38B. Accounting for cash and stock dividends (*Learning Objectives 4 & 5*) 10–15 min.

Artistic Expression is authorized to issue 1,000,000 shares of $1 par common stock. The company issued 71,000 shares at $4 per share, and all 71,000 shares are outstanding. When the market price of common stock was $12 per share, Artistic Expression declared and distributed a 20% stock dividend. Later, Artistic Expression declared and paid a $0.45 per share cash dividend.

Requirements

1. Journalize the declaration and distribution of the stock dividend.
2. Journalize the declaration and the payment of the cash dividend.

E10-39B. Accounting for stock splits (*Learning Objectives 5 & 7*) 10–15 min.

Clubhouse Landing, Inc., had the following stockholders' equity at May 31:

Stockholders' Equity	
Paid-in Capital:	
Common Stock, $1 par, 300,000 shares authorized,	
10,000 issued and outstanding	$ 10,000
Paid-in Capital in Excess of Par	20,000
Total Paid-in Capital	$ 30,000
Retained Earnings	700,000
Total Stockholders' Equity	$730,000

On June 30, Clubhouse Landing, Inc., split its common stock 5-for-1.

Requirements

1. Make any necessary entry to record the stock split.
2. Prepare the stockholders' equity section of the balance sheet immediately after the split.

E10-40B. Accounting for stock issuance, splits, and treasury stock (*Learning Objectives 3, 5, & 6*) 20–25 min.

Consider each of the following transactions separately from every other transaction:

a. Issuance of 57,000 shares of $1 par common at $13.
b. Purchase of 1,800 shares of treasury stock (par value at $0.50) at $8 per share.
c. Issuance of a 10% stock dividend. Before the dividend, 500,000 shares of $1 par common stock were outstanding; market value was $9 at the time of the dividend.
d. Sale of 200 shares of $1 par treasury stock for $10 per share. Cost of the treasury stock was $5 per share.
e. Split stocks 3-for-1. Prior to the split, 120,000 shares of $10 par common stock were outstanding.

Requirement

1. Identify whether each transaction increased, decreased, or did not change total stockholders' equity.

E10-41B. Accounting for treasury stock (*Learning Objectives 3 & 6*) 20–25 min.

Journalize the following transactions of Discount Sports, Inc., a chain of sports stores:

Feb 4	Issued 23,000 shares of no-par common stock at $14 per share.
Apr 22	Purchased 1,700 shares of treasury stock at $12 per share.
Aug 22	Sold 200 shares of treasury stock at $22 per share.

E10-42B. Accounting for treasury stock (*Learning Objectives 6 & 7*) 20–25 min.

Southern, Inc., had the following stockholders' equity on November 30:

Stockholders' Equity	
Paid-in Capital:	
Common Stock, $3 par, 500,000 shares authorized,	
40,000 shares issued and outstanding	$120,000
Paid-in Capital in Excess of Par	240,000
Total Paid-in Capital	360,000
Retained Earnings	510,000
Total Stockholders' Equity	$870,000

On December 10, Southern purchased 3,000 shares of treasury stock at $9 per share.

Requirements

1. Journalize the purchase of the treasury stock.
2. Prepare the stockholders' equity section of the balance sheet at December 31.

E10-43B. Balance sheet disclosure of stockholders' equity (*Learning Objective 7*) 10–15 min.

Bretton Manufacturing, Co., has the following selected account balances at April 30, 2010.

Common Stock, no par with		Inventory..................................	$ 55,000
$4 stated value,		Machinery and Equipment	77,000
140,000 shares authorized,		Preferred Stock, 5%, $17 par,	
issued, and outstanding	$560,000	20,000 shares authorized,	
Accumulated Depreciation,		6,000 shares issued and	
Machinery and Equipment...	14,000	outstanding	102,000
Retained Earnings	150,000	Paid-in Capital in Excess of	
		Stated Value	50,000
		Cost of Goods Sold................	76,000

Requirement

1. Prepare the stockholders' equity section of the company's balance sheet.

**E10-44B. Accounting for various stockholders' equity transactions (*Learning Objective 7*)
20–25 min.**

At December 31, 2009, Maloney, Corp., reported the following stockholders' equity.

Paid-in Capital:	
Common Stock, $2 par, 200,000 shares authorized,	
105,000 shares issued	$ 210,000
Additional Paid-in Capital	115,000
Total Paid-in Capital	325,000
Retained Earnings	690,000
Subtotal	1,015,000
Less: Treasury stock, 2,700 shares at cost	(86,400)
Total Stockholders' Equity	$ 928,600

During 2010 Maloney completed these transactions and events in this order:

a. Sold 1,000 shares of treasury stock for $42 per share; the cost of these shares was $32 per share.

b. Issued 1,400 shares of common stock at $15 per share.

c. Net income for the year was $215,000.

d. Declared and paid cash dividends of $115,000.

Requirement

1. Prepare Maloney's statement of stockholders' equity for 2010.

E10-45B. Accounting for various stockholders' equity transactions (*Learning Objectives 3, 5, & 7*) 20–25 min.

O'Grady Communications, Inc., began 2010 with 3.2 million shares of $1 par common stock issued and outstanding. Beginning paid-in capital in excess of par was $5.5 million, and retained earnings was $13.3 million. In May 2010, O'Grady Communications, Inc., issued 160,000 shares of stock at $17 per share. In October, when the stock's market price was $18 per share, the board of directors distributed a 20% stock dividend.

Requirements

1. Make the journal entries for the issuance of stock for cash and for the declaration and distribution of the 20% stock dividend.

2. Prepare the company's statement of stockholders' equity for the year ended December 31, 2010.

E10-46B. Calculating return on equity (*Learning Objective 8*) 10–15 min.

Assume that Skippito, Inc., has the following data:

Net income for 2010	$ 223,000
Preferred dividends for 2010	$ 23,000
Total stockholders' equity, 12/31/2010	$1,009,000
Total stockholders' equity, 12/31/2009	$1,384,000
Common stockholders' equity, 12/31/2010	$ 987,000
Common stockholders' equity, 12/31/2009	$1,207,000

Requirements

1. Calculate Skippito's return on equity for 2010.

2. Calculate Skippito's return on common equity for 2010.

3. Comment on Skippito's performance during 2010.

EXERCISES (ALTERNATES 1, 2, AND 3)

These alternative exercise sets are available for your practice benefit at
www.myaccountinglab.com

PROBLEMS (GROUP A)

P10-47A. Stock issuance (*Learning Objectives 3 & 7*) 10–15 min.

Partners Dempsey and Perry wish to avoid the unlimited personal liability of the
partnership form of business, so they are incorporating the company as D & P
Services, Inc. The charter from the state of Texas authorizes the corporation
to issue 10,000 shares of 6%, $100 par preferred stock and 250,000 shares of
no-par common stock. In its first month, D & P Services, Inc., completed the
following transactions:

Requirements

1. Record the transactions in the journal.
2. Prepare the stockholders' equity section of the D & P Services, Inc., balance
   sheet at December 31. The ending balance of Retained Earnings is $40,000.

Jan 3	Issued 6,300 shares of common stock to Dempsey and 3,800 shares to Perry, both for cash of $10 per share.
12	Issued 1,100 shares of preferred stock to acquire a patent with a market value of $110,000.
22	Issued 1,500 shares of common stock to other investors for $10 cash per share.

P10-48A. Analyzing stockholders' equity (*Learning Objectives 2, 3, 4, & 7*) 20–25 min.

Gamma Corporation was organized in 2009. At December 31, 2009, Gamma
Corporation's balance sheet reported the following stockholders' equity:

Stockholders' Equity	
Paid-in Capital:	
Preferred Stock, 5%, $10 par, 50,000 shares authorized,	
none issued	$ 0
Common Stock, $2 par, 100,000 shares authorized,	
10,000 shares issued and outstanding	20,000
Paid-in Capital in Excess of Par	30,000
Total Paid-in Capital	$50,000
Retained Earnings (deficit)	(5,000)
Total Stockholders' Equity	$45,000

Requirements

Answer the following questions and make journal entries as needed:

1. What does the 5% mean for the preferred stock? After Gamma Corporation
   issues preferred stock, how much in annual cash dividends would Gamma
   Corporation expect to pay on 1,000 shares?
2. At what price per share did Gamma Corporation issue the common stock
   during 2009?
3. Were first-year operations profitable? Give your reason.

4. During 2010, the company completed the following selected transactions. Journalize each transaction. Explanations are not required.

   a. Issued for cash 5,000 shares of preferred stock at par value.

   b. Issued for cash 1,000 shares of common stock at a price of $7 per share.

5. Prepare the stockholders' equity section of the Gamma Corporation balance sheet at December 31, 2010. Assume net income for the year is $50,000.

P10-49A. **Analyzing stockholders' equity (*Learning Objectives 2, 3, & 4*) 20–25 min.**

Radisson, Inc., included the following stockholders' equity on its year-end balance sheet at December 31, 2010, with all dollar amounts, except par value per share, adapted and in millions:

Stockholders' Equity	$ Millions
Paid-in Capital:	
Preferred Stock, 6% cumulative	$ 65
Common Stock, par value $1 per share; 650,000,000 shares authorized, 236,000,000 shares issued and outstanding	236
Paid-in Capital in Excess of Par	70
Total Paid-in Capital	$371
Retained Earnings	247
Total Stockholders' Equity	$618

Requirements

1. Identify the different issues of stock Radisson, Inc., has outstanding.

2. Give the two entries to record issuance of the Radisson, Inc., stock. Assume that all the stock was issued for cash. Explanations are not required.

3. Assume that preferred dividends are in arrears for 2009 and 2010. Record the declaration of a $50 million cash dividend on December 30, 2011. Use separate Dividends Payable accounts for preferred and common stock. Round to the nearest $1 million. An explanation is not required.

P10-50A. **Accounting for cash dividends (*Learning Objective 4*) 15–20 min.**

Klammer Consulting, Inc., has 10,000 shares of $4.50, no-par preferred stock and 50,000 shares of no-par common stock outstanding. Klammer Consulting, Inc., declared and paid the following dividends during a three-year period: 2008, $20,000; 2009, $100,000; and 2010, $200,000.

Requirements

1. Compute the total dividends to preferred stockholders and to common stockholders for each of the three years if

   a. preferred is noncumulative.

   b. preferred is cumulative.

2. For case 1(b), journalize the declaration of the 2010 dividends on December 28, 2010, and the payment of the dividends on January 17, 2011. Use separate Dividends Payable accounts for preferred and common stock.

P10-51A. Accounting for various stockholders' equity transactions (*Learning Objectives 4, 5, & 6*) 20–25 min.

Ralston Sports Corporation completed the following selected transactions during 2010:

Jan 6	Declared a cash dividend on the 10,000 shares of $2.25, no-par preferred stock outstanding. Declared a $0.20 per share dividend on the 10,000 shares of common stock outstanding. The date of record is January 17, and the payment date is January 20.
Jan 20	Paid the cash dividends.
Mar 21	Split common stock 2-for-1 by calling in the 10,000 shares of $10 par common and issuing new stock in its place.
Apr 18	Declared and distributed a 10% stock dividend on the common stock. The market value of the common stock was $27 per share.
Jun 18	Purchased 2,000 shares of treasury common stock at $25 per share.
Dec 22	Sold 1,000 shares of treasury common stock for $26 per share.

Requirement

1. Record the transactions in the journal.

P10-52A. Accounting for various stockholders' equity transactions (*Learning Objectives 5, 6, & 7*) 20–25 min.

The balance sheet of Quartz, Inc., at December 31, 2009, reported 500,000 shares of $1 par common stock authorized with 100,000 shares issued and outstanding. Paid-in Capital in Excess of Par had a balance of $300,000. Retained Earnings had a balance of $101,000. During 2010, the company completed the following selected transactions:

Feb 15	Purchased 5,000 shares of treasury stock at $4 per share.
Mar 8	Sold 2,000 shares of treasury stock for $7 per share.
Sep 28	Declared and distributed a 10% stock dividend on the 97,000 shares of *outstanding* common stock. The market value of Quartz's common stock was $5 per share.

Requirements

1. Record the transactions in the journal. Explanations are not required.

2. Prepare the stockholders' equity section of the balance sheet at December 31, 2010, assuming the company earned $73,000 of net income during the year.

P10-53A. Analyzing stockholders' equity (*Learning Objective 7*) 15–20 min.

Business Analysts, Inc., reported the following statement of stockholders' equity for the year ended September 30, 2010:

Business Analysts, Inc.
Statement of Stockholders' Equity
Year Ended September 30, 2010

(Dollar amounts in thousands)	COMMON STOCK	ADDITIONAL PAID-IN CAPITAL	RETAINED EARNINGS	TREASURY STOCK	TOTAL
Balance, September 30, 2009	$173	$2,118	$ 1,706	$(18)	$3,979
Net Income			520		520
Cash Dividends			(117)		(117)
Issuance of Stock (5,000 shares)	9	46			55
Stock Dividend	18	92	(110)		—
Sale of Treasury Stock		5		11	16
Balance, September 30, 2010	$200	$2,261	$(1,999)	$ (7)	$4,453

Requirements

1. What is the par value of the company's common stock?
2. At what price per share did the company issue its common stock during the year?
3. What was the cost of treasury stock sold during the year? What was the selling price of the treasury stock sold? What was the increase in total stockholders' equity from selling the treasury stock?
4. What overall effect did the stock dividend have on total stockholders' equity?

PROBLEMS (GROUP B)

P10-54B. Stock issuance (*Learning Objectives 3 & 7*) 10–15 min.

Partners Meeks and Olsen wish to avoid the unlimited personal liability of the partnership form of business, so they are incorporating the company as M & O Services, Inc. The charter from the state of Texas authorizes the corporation to issue 15,000 shares of 7%, $150 par preferred stock and 220,000 shares of no-par common stock. In its first month, M & O Services, Inc., completed the following transactions:

Jan	3	Issued 6,200 shares of common stock to Meeks and 3,700 shares to Olsen, both for cash of $12 per share.
	12	Issued 1,200 shares of preferred stock to acquire a patent with a market value of $180,000.
	22	Issued 1,700 shares of common stock to other investors for $12 cash per share.

Requirements

1. Record the transactions in the journal.
2. Prepare the stockholders' equity section of the M & O Services, Inc., balance sheet at December 31. The ending balance of Retained Earnings is $59,000.

P10-55B. Analyzing stockholders' equity (Learning Objectives 2, 3, 4, & 7) 20–25 min.

Robert Corporation was organized in 2009. At December 31, 2009, Robert Corporation's balance sheet reported the following stockholders' equity:

Stockholders' Equity	
Paid-in Capital:	
Preferred Stock, 6%, $10 par, 35,000 shares authorized,	
none issued	$ 0
Common Stock, $1 par, 120,000 shares authorized,	
11,000 shares issued and outstanding	11,000
Paid-in Capital in Excess of Par	33,000
Total Paid-in Capital	$44,000
Retained Earnings (deficit)	(5,000)
Total Stockholders' Equity	$39,000

Requirements

Answer the following questions and make journal entries as needed:

1. What does the 6% mean for the preferred stock? After Robert Corporation issues preferred stock, how much in annual cash dividends would Robert Corporation expect to pay on 1,000 shares?
2. At what price per share did Robert Corporation issue the common stock during 2009?
3. Were the first-year operations profitable? Give your reasons.
4. During 2010, the company completed the following selected transactions. Journalize each transaction. Explanations are not required.
   a. Issued for cash 2,000 shares of preferred stock at par value.
   b. Issued for cash 1,500 shares of common stock at a price of $5 per share.
5. Prepare the stockholders' equity section of the Robert Corporation balance sheet at December 31, 2010. Assume net income for the year was $65,000.

P10-56B. Analyzing stockholders' equity (*Learning Objectives 2, 3, & 4*) 20–25 min.

Madison Hotel, Inc., included the following stockholders' equity on its year-end balance sheet at December 31, 2010, with all dollar amounts, except par value per share, adapted and in millions:

Stockholders' Equity	$ Millions
Paid-in Capital:	
Preferred Stock, 6.5% cumulative	$ 45
Common Stock, par value $1 per share; 500,000,000 shares	
authorized, 176,000,000 shares issued and outstanding	176
Paid-in Capital in Excess of Par	52
Total Paid-in Capital	$273
Retained Earnings	142
Total Stockholders' Equity	$415

Requirements

1. Identify the different issues of stock Madison Hotel, Inc., has outstanding.

2. Give the two entries to record issuance of the Madison Hotel, Inc., stock. Assume all the stock was issued for cash. Explanations are not required.

3. Assume that preferred dividends are in arrears for 2009 and 2010. Record the declaration of a $37 million cash dividend on December 30, 2011. Use separate Dividends payable accounts for preferred and common stock. Round to the nearest $1 million. An explanation is not required.

P10-57B. Accounting for cash dividends (*Learning Objective 4*) 15–20 min.

Krystal Consulting, Inc., has 13,000 shares of $4.00 no-par preferred stock and 90,000 shares of no-par common stock outstanding. Krystal declared and paid the following dividends during a three-year period: 2008, $24,000; 2009, $115,000; and 2010, $230,000.

Requirements

1. Compute the total dividends to preferred stockholders and to common stockholders for each of the three years if

   a. preferred is noncumulative.

   b. preferred is cumulative.

2. For case 1(b), journalize the declaration of the 2010 dividends on December 28, 2010, and the payment of dividends on January 17, 2011. Use separate Dividends Payable accounts for preferred and common stock.

P10-58B. Accounting for various stockholders' equity transactions (*Learning Objectives 4, 5, & 6*) 20–25 min.

Triton Triathlete Corporation completed the following selected transactions during 2011:

Jan 6	Declared a cash dividend on the 7,000 shares of $3.00, no-par preferred stock outstanding. Declared a $0.10 per share dividend on the 15,000 shares of common stock outstanding. The date of record is January 17, and the payment date is January 20.
Jan 20	Paid the cash dividends.
Mar 21	Split common stock 2-for-1 by calling in the 15,000 shares of $6 par common and issuing new stock in its place.
Apr 18	Declared and distributed a 15% stock dividend on the common stock. The market value of the common stock was $34 per share.
Jun 18	Purchased 2,000 shares of treasury common stock at $31 per share.
Dec 22	Sold 1,000 shares of treasury common stock for $32 per share.

Requirement

1. Record the transactions in the journal.

P10-59B. Accounting for various stockholders' equity transactions (*Learning Objectives 5, 6, 7*) 20–25 min.

The balance sheet of Playtime, Inc., at December 31, 2009, reported 900,000 shares of $1 par common stock authorized with 90,000 shares issued and outstanding. Paid-in Capital in Excess of Par had a balance of $325,000. Retained Earnings had a balance of $102,000. During 2010, the company completed the following selected transactions:

Feb 15	Purchased 4,000 shares of treasury stock at $7 per share.
Mar 8	Sold 1,000 shares of treasury stock for $10 per share.
Sep 28	Declared and distributed a 5% stock dividend on the 87,000 shares of *outstanding* common stock. The market value of Playtime's common stock was $9 per share.

Requirements

1. Record the transactions in the general journal. Explanations are not required.
2. Prepare the stockholders' equity section of the balance sheet at December 31, 2010, assuming the company earned $77,000 of net income during the year.

P10-60B. Analyzing stockholders' equity (*Learning Objective 7*) 15–20 min.

Financial Analysts, Inc., reported the following statement of stockholders' equity for the year ended September 30, 2010.

	Financial Analysts, Inc. Statement of Stockholders' Equity Year Ended September 30, 2010				
(Dollar amounts in thousands)	COMMON STOCK	ADDITIONAL PAID-IN CAPITAL	RETAINED EARNINGS	TREASURY STOCK	TOTAL
Balance, September 30, 2009	$176	$2,114	$1,703	$(21)	$3,972
Net Income			523		523
Cash Dividends			(116)		(116)
Issuance of Stock (4,000 shares)	15	44			59
Stock Dividend	20	91	(111)		0
Sale of Treasury Stock		5		13	18
Balance, September 30, 2010	$211	$2,254	$1,999	$ 8	$4,456

Requirements

1. What is the par value of the company's common stock?
2. At what price per share did the company issue its common stock during the year?
3. What was the cost of treasury stock sold during the year? What was the selling price of the treasury stock sold? What was the increase in total stockholders' equity from selling the treasury stock?
4. What overall effect did the stock dividend have on total stockholders' equity?

PROBLEMS (ALTERNATES 1, 2, AND 3)

These alternative problem sets are available for your practice benefit at
www.myaccountinglab.com

CONTINUING EXERCISE

This exercise continues our accounting for Graham's Yard Care, Inc., from Chapter 9. In this exercise, we will account for the declaration and issuance of a cash dividend by Graham's Yard Care, Inc. On October 15, 2010, Graham's Yard Care, Inc., declared a $5,000 dividend. The dividend was payable to all common shareholders of record on October 31 and was paid on November 15, 2010.

Requirements

1. Journalize the entries related to the dividends.

2. What was the effect of the dividend on the following?

   ■ Cash

   ■ Retained Earnings

   ■ Total Stockholders' Equity

CONTINUING PROBLEM

This problem continues our accounting for Aqua Elite, Inc., from Chapter 9. Aqua Elite, Inc., has been authorized to sell 500,000 shares of $5 par value common stock and 100,000 shares of $10 par, 8% preferred stock. During the year, Aqua Elite had the following transactions related to stockholders' equity:

May 5	Issued 5,700 shares of common stock to Mike Hanson in exchange for $15,000 cash and a truck valued at $13,500.
Jun 13	Issued an additional 2,000 shares of stock to Mike Hanson for $10,000 cash.
Jul 18	Sold 4,000 shares of common stock to investors for $45,000.
Aug 6	Sold 1,500 shares of preferred stock to investors for $20,000.
Oct 22	Purchased 1,000 shares of common stock for $12 per share to hold in the company's treasury.
Nov 14	Declared a $5,000 dividend payable on December 15 to stockholders on record on December 1. Use separate payable accounts for preferred and common dividends.
Dec 15	Paid the dividend.
Dec 21	Sold 500 shares of treasury stock for $15 per share.

Requirements

1. Record the transactions in the journal. Explanations are not required.

2. Prepare the stockholders' equity section of the balance sheet at December 31, 2010, assuming Aqua Elite, Inc., earned $96,000 of net income during the year. In addition to the dividends paid on December 15, $3,400 of dividends were paid earlier in the year.

APPLY YOUR KNOWLEDGE

ETHICS IN ACTION

Case 1. Ted was a wealthy, 20% stockholder of TDS Corporation. He was looking over the financial statements of the corporation and saw that TDS Corporation was in need of a large loan. Furthermore, he knew that December sales were weaker than expected and that the yearly financial statements would show a lower net income than anticipated. He then decided to loan the company $3 million at 5% interest and also become a customer and purchase $250,000 of merchandise. By Ted becoming a customer, it would increase the business's December sales and net income, and give the company sufficient cash to meet expenses. When approached with the ideas, the CEO objected, stating that the "loan" would have to be recorded as additional capital because a stockholder could not loan money to a company. Ted stated that as long as the money was treated as a loan with interest and the expectation of repayment, it should be allowed. The CEO then stated that it would be unethical for the company to "borrow" money from a stockholder. Also, it would be unethical for the company to "sell" merchandise to a stockholder, because it would merely be done to improve the December sales. Ted stated that the loan agreement and 5% interest would make the arrangement reasonable. He stated that if the interest rate was 25%, then the CEO might have a valid ethical concern. Ted also argued that the sale of merchandise to him was completely ethical, because he was not going to return the merchandise. He further contended that it should not matter whether he was a stockholder because in these transactions he would be a lender and a customer, which would not involve any ethical issues.

Can a stockholder ethically lend money to the corporation? What potential ethical issues would be involved? Can a stockholder ethically become a customer in order to make purchases just to improve the sales and net income? Does the amount of the purchase matter? Why do you think the CEO was concerned?

Case 2. The board of directors for Atlantic Corporation met in January to address growing concerns about the declining stock price of the firm. Because the price per share was so low, the board decided that the company would buy back 10 million shares of outstanding stock. During the year, Atlantic Corporation repurchased the shares at a total cost of $62 million. With fewer shares in the hands of shareholders, the board of directors declared and paid a dividend on only those remaining shares outstanding. As a result of these activities, the price per share rose dramatically in only 10 months. The board of directors then felt it best to reissue the treasury stock at the highest per share price possible. Accordingly, Atlantic Corporation reissued the 10 million shares for $142 million. When the board of directors looked over the yearly financial statements, however, it could not find the $80 million "gain" from the treasury stock sale, equal to the reissue price of $142 million less the purchase cost of $62 million. The accountant had recorded the excess as "Additional Paid-in Capital" rather than as a gain on sale. The board of directors met with the accountant and demanded that a gain be recorded; the board wanted more revenue to be included on the income statement. It argued that stock had been sold at a price higher than it was purchased for, and, therefore, it really did not matter whether the stock was Atlantic Corporation stock or any other company's stock, because all stock sales result in either a gain or loss.

Why does the board of directors want to recognize the $80 million excess from the treasury stock transactions as a gain? Why does the accountant want to recognize the $80 million as an increase in total equity? Who is right and are any ethical issues involved? Does the board of directors have a strong argument that it does not matter whether the stock was Atlantic Corporation stock or any other company since all stock is the same? Do you have any additional thoughts?

KNOW YOUR BUSINESS

FINANCIAL ANALYSIS

Purpose: To help familiarize you with the financial reporting of a real company in order to further your understanding of the chapter material you are learning.

This case continues our examination of Columbia Sportswear. We will now study the stockholders' equity of Columbia Sportswear, which you will see titled as Shareholders' Equity. Refer to the Columbia Sportswear financial statements found in Appendix A. Look for the consolidated balance sheets as well as the consolidated statements of shareholders' equity.

Requirements

1. What was the balance of total stockholders' equity at December 31, 2008? What was the balance of total stockholders' equity at December 31, 2007? Did the amount of ending total stockholders' equity increase or decrease? What seems to be the main reason for the change in total stockholders' equity? What is the largest component of total stockholders' equity?

2. Does Columbia Sportswear have any preferred stock authorized? Can you determine the par value of the preferred stock? How many shares of preferred stock are issued and outstanding?

3. What is the par value of the common stock? Does Columbia Sportswear have any additional paid-in capital? Why or why not? How many shares of common stock are authorized? How many shares are issued and outstanding at the end of 2008? How many shares are issued and outstanding at the beginning of the year?

4. Look at the consolidated statements of shareholders' equity. Did Columbia Sportswear declare any dividends in 2008? If so, how much were the total dividends and what is the dividend per share? Has the amount of dividends per share increased or decreased from 2007 to 2008? Can you determine whether Columbia Sportswear has been repurchasing shares of its common stock? If so, has the amount of share repurchases been increasing or decreasing? What is the effect on total stockholders' equity?

INDUSTRY ANALYSIS

Purpose: To help you understand and compare the performance of two companies in the same industry.

Find the Columbia Sportswear Company Annual Report located in Appendix A and go to the Financial Statements starting on page 681. Now access the 2008 Annual Report for Under Armour, Inc., from the Internet. Go to the company Web page for Investor Relations at http://investor.underarmour.com/investors.cfm and under Downloads on the right-hand side, go to 2008 Annual Report. The company's Financial Statements start on page 49.

Requirement

1. On the Consolidated Balance Sheets for each company, look at the Stockholders' (Shareholders') Equity section. What type or class of stock has each company issued? How does the par value differ for each company? Do you see anything unusual with the Common Stock for Columbia Sportswear?

SMALL BUSINESS ANALYSIS

Purpose: To help you understand the importance of cash flows in the operation of a small business.

You are the chief operating officer (COO) of a small public corporation. The company just completed its fiscal year, and the annual meeting is just a few weeks away. Your company has had a pretty good year despite the rough economic climate your industry has been weathering. In spite of that, the stock price has maintained its high level. But here's the dilemma: The corporation has paid out a cash dividend every year since its inception, but this year you have some concerns about continuing that tradition. Cash flows during the latter part of the year have been slow because your customers are taking longer to pay than they normally do. There's also the concern about the lump sum payment on the mortgage that is due in a couple of months. You've got to have sufficient cash for that. You've already had some inquiries from stockholders about the amount of the dividend that the company will be paying out this year. You've answered all the inquiries with a very positive tone, but the whole while you're wondering if there will even **be** a dividend this year. You're certain that the important stockholders would understand if the corporation had to forego paying a dividend this year. Or would they? You decide to have a meeting with the controller to discuss the situation.

Requirement

1. What would be the most viable suggestion that your controller might make to you as an alternative to paying out a cash dividend this year? What are the implications of your recommendation?

WRITTEN COMMUNICATION

You just got off the telephone with one of your clients who is wanting to start a new business as a corporation. His question to you was concerning the different types of stock that can be issued to the potential stockholders of this new corporation. You had explained it to him during the telephone call, but you thought you should follow up your conversation with a letter.

Requirement

1. Prepare a letter to your client explaining the different types or classes of stock that can be issued, and the characteristics of each different type.

Self Check Answers
1. d 2. c 3. a 4. c 5. c 6. d 7. d 8. d 9. c 10. b

The Statement of Cash Flows

Throughout this book you have examined many different types of transactions businesses encounter each day. Did you notice how many of those transactions involved cash? Cash is a significant asset for most businesses and is important to their success. Because of this, business owners and managers, as well as investors and creditors, often have questions about a company's cash, such as "Where did the company get the cash it needed for the year?" and, "Where did all of the company's cash go?" The answers to these questions can be found in the statement of cash flows, which we will learn about in this chapter.

Chapter Outline:

Learning Objectives:

1. Identify the purposes of the statement of cash flows

2. Differentiate between cash flows from operating, investing, and financing activities

3. Prepare the statement of cash flows using the indirect method

4. Prepare the statement of cash flows using the direct method

5. Evaluate a company's performance with respect to cash

WHAT IS THE STATEMENT OF CASH FLOWS?

Identify the purposes of the statement of cash flows **1**

Cash is often considered to be the "life blood" of a business. As we have seen throughout the book, the balance sheet reports the amount of cash a business has at the end of the accounting period. Remember from Chapter 7, this cash balance typically includes cash as well as cash equivalents. When a comparative balance sheet is presented, the balance of cash the business has at the end of two consecutive periods is reported. The comparative balance sheet shows whether cash increased or decreased from one period to the next. However, the comparative balance sheet does not show *why* cash increased or decreased. Therefore, a **statement of cash flows**, or **cash flow statement**, is usually prepared to show why the cash amount changed during the year. The statement of cash flows reports

- all sources of cash during the period. In other words, it shows where a company got its cash during the year.
- all uses of cash during the period. In other words, it shows where a company spent its cash during the year.

🌐 Accounting in Your World

Have you ever taken a weekend "road trip" with some of your friends? If so, you probably went to the bank to get some cash before you took off. Then, at least once, you probably had to find an ATM in order to get a little more cash. When you got home, you probably looked in your wallet to see how much money you had left. Upon realizing that you had very little money left, you probably wondered "Where did all my money go?" At this point, you might have taken out a piece of paper and written down how much money you started with and how much additional cash you got along the way (your sources of cash). Then, you probably recorded all the things you spent money on, such as gas $120, food $73, movies $28, etc. (your uses of cash). Finally, you subtracted all of your uses of cash from your sources of cash and, sure enough, it equalled the amount of money left in your wallet. In essence, you prepared a statement of cash flows for the period of your "road trip."

The statement of cash flows helps investors and creditors do the following:

1. **Predict future cash flows.**   Past cash receipts and payments help predict future cash flows.

2. **Evaluate management decisions.**   Wise investment decisions help the business prosper. Unwise decisions cause problems. Investors and creditors use cash-flow information to evaluate managers' decisions.

3. **Predict ability to pay debts and dividends.**   Lenders want to know whether they'll collect on their loans. Stockholders want dividends on their investments. The statement of cash flows helps make these predictions.

The statement of cash flows also helps financial statement users understand why net income as reported on the income statement does not equal the change in cash according to the balance sheet. This is especially helpful for small business owners as they often do not trust the Net Income figure on the income statement. This is because Net Income often shows that the business made money at a time when there is little cash to show for it. Or the opposite may occur. Net Income may reflect that the business made little or no money at a time when the business has a lot of cash. In essence, the cash flow statement is the communicating link between the accrual based income statement and the cash reported on the balance sheet. **Exhibit 11–1** illustrates the relationships among the balance sheet, the income statement, and the statement of cash flows.

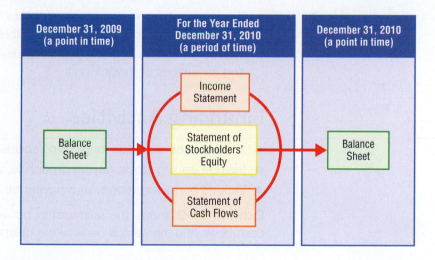

Exhibit 11-1 ▲

In order to provide more useful information, the statement of cash flows reports the sources and uses of cash for three different types of business activities:

- Operating activities
- Investing activities
- Financing activities

WHAT IS THE DIFFERENCE BETWEEN OPERATING, INVESTING, AND FINANCING ACTIVITIES?

Differentiate between cash flows from operating, investing, and financing activities

2

The cash flow statement is broken down into different sections based on three types of business activities; **operating activities**, **investing activities**, and **financing activities**. Let's explore each of the three types of activities.

Operating Activities

- Reflect the day-to-day operations of an organization.
- Create revenues, expenses, gains, and losses.
- Affect net income on the income statement.
- Affect current assets and current liabilities on the balance sheet.

Investing Activities

- Increase and decrease long-term assets, such as fixed assets (equipment, land, buildings, etc.) and notes receivable.
- Include purchases and sales of fixed assets, plus loans receivable from others and collections of those loans.

Financing Activities

- Increase and decrease long-term liabilities and equity.
- Include issuing stock, paying dividends, and buying and selling treasury stock.
- Include borrowing money and paying off loans.

Exhibit 11-2 shows the relationship between operating, investing, and financing cash flows and the various parts of the balance sheet they affect.

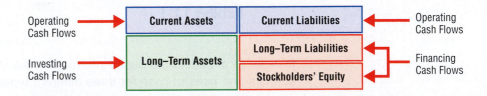

Exhibit 11-2 ▲

As you can see, operating cash flows affect the current accounts. Investing cash flows affect the long-term assets. Financing cash flows affect long-term liabilities and equity.

Two Formats for Operating Activities

There are two ways to format operating activities on the statement of cash flows:

- The **direct method** shows all cash receipts and all cash payments from operating activities. The direct method restates each (accrual based) item on the income statement on a cash basis.
- The **indirect method** starts with net income and adjusts it to net cash provided by operating activities.

    The direct and indirect methods

- produce the same amount of cash flow from operations through the use of different computations.
- have no effect on investing activities or financing activities.

Decision Guidelines

Decision		**Guideline**		**Analyze**
How do I determine how cash is being managed by a business?		Review the statement of cash flows.		The statement of cash flows shows all of the sources and all of the uses of cash for the period. The sources and uses of cash are reported separately for the operating activities, the investing activities, and the financing activities of the business. If a business is to remain successful, operating activities must be the main source of its cash over the long run.

HOW IS THE STATEMENT OF CASH FLOWS PREPARED USING THE INDIRECT METHOD?

Prepare the statement of cash flows using the indirect method **3**

Most businesses prefer to use the indirect method because its format makes it easier to reconcile net income to the change in cash for the period. In order to prepare the statement of cash flows you will need to have the other financial statements as well as some supplemental information about the company's operations. The format for the indirect method statement of cash flows for Mackay Industries is presented in **Exhibit 11-3** on the following page.

Mackay Industries' financial statements are presented in **Exhibit 11-4**, also on the following two pages.

Mackay Industries, Inc.
Statement of Cash Flows
Year Ended December 31, 2010

Cash flows from operating activities:			
Net Income			
Adjustments to reconcile net income to net cash			
provided by operating activities:			
+ Depreciation / amortization expense			
+ Loss on sale of long-term assets			
– Gain on sale of long-term assets			
– Increases in current assets other than cash			
+ Decreases in current assets other than cash			
+ Increases in current liabilities			
– Decreases in current liabilities			
Net cash provided by operating activities			
± **Cash flows from investing activities:**			
+ Cash receipts from sales of long-term assets			
(investments, land, building, equipment, and so on)			
– Purchases of long-term assets			
Net cash provided by (used for) investing activities			
± **Cash flows from financing activities:**			
+ Cash receipts from issuance of stock			
+ Sale of treasury stock			
– Purchase of treasury stock			
+ Cash receipts from issuance of notes or bonds			
payable (borrowing)			
– Payment of notes or bonds payable			
– Payment of dividends			
Net cash provided by (used for) financing activities			
= **Net increase (decrease) in cash during the year**			
+ Cash at December 31, 2009			
= Cash at December 31, 2010			

Exhibit 11-3 ▲

Mackay Industries, Inc.
Income Statement
Year Ended December 31, 2010

		Revenue:		
		Sales Revenue	$268,000	
		Interest Revenue	13,000	
		Dividend Revenue	5,000	
		Total Revenues		$286,000
		Expenses:		
		Cost of Goods Sold	$137,000	
		Salaries Expense	48,000	
	B	Depreciation Expense	18,000	
		Other Operating Expense	12,000	
		Interest Expense	11,000	
		Income Tax Expense	9,000	
	C	Loss on Sale of Plant Assets	3,000	
		Total Expenses		238,000
	A	Net Income		$ 48,000

Exhibit 11-4 ▲

Mackay Industries, Inc.
Statement of Retained Earnings
Year Ended December 31, 2010

	Retained Earnings, December 31, 2009	$121,000
	Add: Net Income for the Year	48,000
	Subtotal	169,000
M	Less: Dividends	23,000
	Retained Earnings, December 31, 2010	$146,000

Mackay Industries, Inc.
Balance Sheet
December 31, 2009 and 2010

		2010	2009	INCREASE (DECREASE)
	ASSETS			
	Current:			
	Cash	$ 18,000	$ 11,000	$ 7,000
D	Accounts Receivable	76,000	93,000	(17,000)
E	Inventory	132,000	124,000	8,000
	Total Current Assets	226,000	228,000	(2,000)
H/I	Plant Assets, Net	385,000	315,000	70,000
	Total Assets	$611,000	$543,000	$ 68,000
	LIABILITIES			
	Current:			
F	Accounts Payable	$ 84,000	$ 96,000	$(12,000)
G	Accrued Liabilities	12,000	8,000	4,000
	Total Current Liabilities	96,000	104,000	(8,000)
J/K	Long-Term Notes Payable	147,000	98,000	49,000
	Total Liabilities	243,000	202,000	41,000
	STOCKHOLDERS' EQUITY			
L	Common Stock	240,000	220,000	20,000
A/M	Retained Earnings	146,000	121,000	25,000
N	Less Treasury Stock	(18,000)	(0)	(18,000)
	Total Stockholders' Equity	368,000	341,000	27,000
	Total Liabilities and Stockholders' Equity	$611,000	$543,000	$ 68,000

Exhibit 11-4 ▲ *(continued)*

Now, let's prepare Mackay Industries' statement of cash flows one section at a time. To make things easier to follow, each item on the statement of cash flows has been cross referenced to the financial statements by a letter.

Cash Flows from Operating Activities

The operating activities section of Mackay Industries' statement of cash flows would look like this:

		Cash flows from operating activities:		
A		Net Income		$48,000
		Adjustments to reconcile net income to net cash		
		provided by operating activities:		
B		Depreciation Expense	$ 18,000	
C		Loss on sale of plant assets	3,000	
D		Decrease in Accounts Receivable	17,000	
E		Increase in Inventory	(8,000)	
F		Decrease in Accounts Payable	(12,000)	
G		Increase in Accrued Liabilities	4,000	22,000
		Net cash provided by operating activities		70,000

Operating cash flows begin with net income, taken from the income statement.

A Net Income

The statement of cash flows—indirect method—begins with net income because revenues and expenses, which affect net income, produce cash receipts and cash payments. Revenues bring in cash receipts and expenses must be paid. But net income is accrual based and the accrual basis of revenues and expenses don't always equal the cash flows (cash basis net income). For example, sales *on account* are revenues that increase net income, but the company hasn't yet collected cash from those sales. Accrued expenses decrease your net income, but you haven't paid cash *if the expenses are accrued*.

To go from net income to cash flow from operations, we must make some adjustments to net income on the statement of cash flows. These additions and subtractions follow net income and are labeled "Adjustments to reconcile net income to net cash provided by operating activities."

B Depreciation, Depletion, and Amortization Expenses

These expenses are added back to net income to reconcile it to cash flows from operations. Let's see why. Depreciation is recorded as follows:

DATE	ACCOUNTS	POST REF.	DR.	CR.
	Depreciation Expense		18,000	
	Accumulated Depreciation			18,000

You can see that depreciation does not affect cash because there's no Cash account in the journal entry. However, depreciation, like all the other expenses, decreases net income. Therefore, to go from net income to cash flows, we must add the depreciation back to net income.

Example: Suppose you had only two transactions during the period:

- $50,000 cash sale
- Depreciation expense of $20,000

Accrual basis net income is $30,000 ($50,000 – $20,000). But cash flow from operations is $50,000. To reconcile the net income of $30,000 to the cash flow from operations of $50,000, add back the $20,000 of depreciation expense. You would also add back depletion and amortization expenses because they are noncash expenses similar to depreciation.

C Gains and Losses on the Sale of Assets

Sales of long-term assets such as land and buildings are investing activities. The total cash proceeds from these sales are included in the investing section of the statement of cash flows. However, these sales usually result in a gain or a loss, which is included in net income. Gains and losses do not represent cash flows. They are simply a function of the difference between the cash proceeds and the book value of the asset. Therefore, gains and losses must be removed from net income on the statement of cash flows.

Mackay Industries' income statement includes a loss on the sale of plant assets. During 2010, Mackay Industries sold equipment resulting in a loss of $3,000 on the sale. Because the loss reduces net income, it is added back to net income to arrive at cash flows from operating activities. On the other hand, a gain on the sale of plant assets would increase net income. So, it would be subtracted from net income to arrive at cash flows from operating activities.

D, **E**, **F** & **G** Changes in the Current Assets and the Current Liabilities

Most current assets and current liabilities result from operating activities. For example,

- accounts receivable result from sales,
- inventory and accounts payable relate to cost of goods sold,
- prepaid assets and accrued liabilities relate to operating expenses, and so on.

Changes in the current asset and current liability accounts create adjustments to net income on the cash flow statement, as follows:

1. **A decrease in a current asset other than cash causes an increase in cash.** Mackay Industries' Accounts Receivable decreased by $17,000 **D**. What caused the decrease? During the year, Mackay Industries must have collected more cash from credit customers than the current year's credit sales. This means that $17,000 more was collected from customers than what is represented by the Revenues on the income statement. Therefore, the $17,000 decrease in Accounts Receivable is added to net income to arrive at cash flows from operating activities. A decrease in any current asset other than cash will be added to net income to arrive at cash flows from operating activities.

2. **An increase in a current asset other than cash causes a decrease in cash.** It takes cash to acquire assets. If Accounts Receivable, Inventory, or Prepaid Expenses increase, then Cash decreases. Therefore, subtract the increase in the current asset from net income to get cash flow from operations. For example, Mackay Industries' Inventory went up by $8,000 **E**. The $8,000 increase in inventory is not reflected in Cost of Goods Sold on the Income Statement. However, this increase required the payment of cash so it is deducted from net income to arrive at cash flows from operating activities. An increase in any current asset other than cash will be subtracted from net income to arrive at cash flows from operating activities.

3. **A decrease in a current liability causes a decrease in cash.** Mackay Industries' Accounts Payable went down $12,000 **F**. This means that Mackay Industries paid $12,000 more on its payables than it charged during the current year.

However, the amount that Mackay Industries charged on its payables is what is reflected in Cost of Goods Sold and Operating Expenses on the income statement. So, the $12,000 decrease in Accounts Payable is subtracted from net income to arrive at cash flows from operating activities. A decrease in any current liability will be subtracted from net income to arrive at cash flows from operating activities.

4. **An increase in a current liability causes an increase in cash.** Mackay Industries' Accrued Liabilities increased by $4,000 **G** . This means that $4,000 of the operating expenses on the income statement have not yet been paid for. Accordingly, even though net income was reduced by the $4,000, cash was not reduced. Therefore, the $4,000 increase in current liabilities is added to net income to arrive at cash flows from operations. An increase in any current liability will be added to net income to arrive at cash flows from operating activities.

During 2010, Mackay Industries' operations provided net cash flow of $70,000. This amount exceeds net income (due to the various adjustments discussed previously). However, to fully evaluate a company's cash flows, we must also examine its investing and financing activities.

Cash Flows from Investing Activities

As shown in Exhibit 11-2, investing activities affect long-term assets, such as Plant Assets and Investments. The investing section of Mackay Industries' statement of cash flows is presented next:

	Cash flows from investing activities:		
H	Acquisition of plant assets	$(195,000)	
I	Proceeds from sale of plant assets	104,000	
	Net cash used in investing activities		(91,000)

Computing Acquisitions and Sales of Plant Assets

Companies usually keep a separate account for each type of plant asset. However, for computing investing cash flows, it is helpful to combine all the plant assets into a single Plant Assets account. We subtract Accumulated Depreciation from the assets' cost in order to work with a single net figure for plant assets, such as Plant Assets, Net . . . $385,000. This simplifies the computations.

To illustrate, observe that Mackay Industries' financial statements presented in Exhibit 11-4 show the following:

- The balance sheet reports plant assets, net of depreciation, of $385,000 at the end of 2010 and $315,000 at the end of 2009.

- The income statement shows depreciation expense of $18,000 and a $3,000 loss on sale of plant assets.

The increase in the net amount of plant assets tells us that Mackay Industries acquired plant assets during 2010. Let's assume that Mackay Industries' acquisitions of plant assets during 2010 consisted of $195,000 of cash purchases. The $195,000 of cash used to purchase the plant assets will be reported as a cash outflow (item **H**) in the investing section of the statement of cash flows. If any portion of the purchase of plant assets is financed with notes payable, the amount financed is not included in the cash outflow.

The loss on sale of assets reported on the income statement indicates that Mackay Industries sold some older plant assets. This gives us an incomplete T-account as follows:

Plant Assets, Net			
12/31/09 Bal	315,000	2010 Depr exp	18,000
Acquisitions	195,000	Sales	?
12/31/10 Bal	385,000		

We can now solve for the net book value of the assets that were sold as follows:

12/31/2009 Balance + Acquisitions − Depreciation Expense − Sales? = 12/31/2010 Balance

$315,000	+ $195,000	−	$ 18,000	− Sales? =	$385,000
			$492,000	− Sales? =	$385,000
				Sales =	$107,000

Our completed T-account now looks like this:

Plant Assets, Net			
12/31/09 Bal	315,000	2010 Depr exp	18,000
Acquisitions	195,000	Sales	107,000
12/31/10 Bal	385,000		

Once we know the book value of the assets sold, we can calculate the amount of cash received from selling plant assets by using the journal entry approach:

DATE	ACCOUNTS	POST REF.	DR.	CR.
	Cash		??????	
	Loss of Sale of Plant Assets		3,000	
	Plant Assets, Net			107,000

So, we compute the cash receipt from the sale as follows:

Cash = Plant assets, net − loss
Cash = $107,000 − $3,000
Cash = $104,000

The cash receipt from the sale of plant assets of $104,000 is shown as item **1** in the investing activities section of the statement of cash flows. **Exhibit 11-5** on the following page summarizes the computation of the investing cash flows from the acquisition and sale of plant assets. Items to be computed are shown in blue.

The investing section of the statement of cash flows will also include cash outflows for the purchase of investments and for any amounts lent to others under long-term notes receivable. Cash inflows reported in the investing section of the statement of cash flows will include proceeds from the sale of investments and any payments received on long-term notes receivable.

Cash Receipts

| From sale of plant assets | Beginning plant assets (net) | + | Acquisition* | − | Depreciation Expense | − | Book value of assets sold | = | Ending plant assets (net) |

$$\text{Cash receipt} = \text{Book value of assets sold} \begin{cases} + & \text{Gain on sale} \\ \text{or} \\ − & \text{Loss on sale} \end{cases}$$

Cash Payments

| For acquisition of plant assets | Beginning plant assets (net) | + | Acquisition* | − | Depreciation Expense | − | Book value of assets sold | = | Ending plant assets (net) |

*Any portion of the acquisition that is financed by a note payable must be deducted from the amount of cash paid.

Exhibit 11-5 ▲

As we can see, Mackay Industries used $91,000 in investing activities. Now let's examine the financing section of the statement of cash flows.

Cash Flows from Financing Activities

As shown in Exhibit 11-2, financing activities affect the liability and stockholders' equity accounts, such as Long-Term Notes Payable, Bonds Payable, Common Stock, and Retained Earnings. The financing section of Mackay Industries' statement of cash flows is presented next:

	Cash flows from financing activities:		
J	Proceeds from issuance of notes payable	$ 75,000	
L	Proceeds from issuance of common stock	20,000	
K	Payment of notes payable	(26,000)	
M	Payment of dividends	(23,000)	
N	Purchase of treasury stock	(18,000)	
	Net cash provided by financing activities		28,000

Computing Issuances and Payments of Long-Term Notes Payable

The beginning and ending balances of Notes Payable or Bonds Payable are found on the balance sheet. If either the amount of new issuances or payments is known, the other amount can be computed. For Mackay Industries, Inc., let's assume that during 2010, $75,000 was borrowed on a long-term note payable. We can use the amount of the note proceeds and the beginning and ending balances of Notes Payable from Mackay Industries' balance sheet in Exhibit 11-4 to create the following incomplete T-account:

Notes Payable			
		12/31/09 Bal	98,000
Note payments	?	New notes	75,000
		12/31/10 Bal	147,000

Then, solve for the missing payments value:

$$12/31/09 \text{ Bal} + \text{New notes issued} - \text{Note payments?} = 12/31/10 \text{ Bal}$$

$98,000	+	$ 75,000	– Note payments? =	$147,000
		$173,000	– Note payments? =	$147,000
			Note payments =	$ 26,000

The completed T-account looks like this:

Notes Payable			
		12/31/09 Bal	98,000
Note payments	26,000	New notes	75,000
		12/31/10 Bal	147,000

The $75,000 cash received is reflected as a cash inflow (item **J**) in the financing section of the statement of cash flows. The payment of $26,000 is reflected as a cash outflow (item **K**) in the financing section of the statement of cash flows.

Computing Issuances of Stock

Cash flows for these financing activities can be determined by analyzing the stock accounts. We can see from looking at the data in Exhibit 11-4 that the balance in the Common Stock account increased by $20,000. Since we were not told about any stock retirements, we can assume there were none. Therefore, the $20,000 change in the Common Stock balance must be due to new stock issuances. We will assume the stock was issued in exchange for cash so the $20,000 will be reflected as a cash inflow (item **L**) in the financing section of the statement of cash flows.

Computing Dividend Payments

The amount of dividends that were declared during the year can be found on the statement of retained earnings. From the statement of retained earnings in Exhibit 11-4, we see that Mackay Industries declared $23,000 of dividends during 2010. Remember, a stock dividend has *no* effect on Cash and is, therefore, *not* reported on the statement of cash flows. We will assume that all of Mackay Industries dividends were cash dividends. Because there were no beginning or ending balances in Dividends Payable on the balance sheet, we can conclude that the entire $23,000 (and no more than) was paid during 2010. Therefore, the $23,000 will be reflected as a cash outflow (Item **M**) in the financing section of the statement of cash flows.

If the statement of retained earnings is unavailable, the amount of dividends can be computed by analyzing the Retained Earnings account. Remember, Retained Earnings increases when companies earn net income. Retained Earnings also decreases when companies have a net loss and when they declare dividends. We can use the amount of the Net Income and the beginning and ending balances of Retained Earnings (from Mackay Industries' financial statements in Exhibit 11-4) to create the following incomplete T-account:

Retained Earnings			
		12/31/09 Bal	121,000
Dividends	?	Net income	48,000
		12/31/10 Bal	146,000

Then, solve for the missing amount of dividends declared:

$$12/31/09 \text{ Bal} + \text{Net income} - \text{Dividends?} = 12/31/10 \text{ Bal}$$

$$\$121,000 + \$48,000 - \text{Dividends?} = \$146,000$$
$$\$169,000 - \text{Dividends?} = \$146,000$$
$$\text{Dividends} = \$23,000$$

The completed T-account looks like this:

Retained Earnings			
		12/31/09 Bal	121,000
Dividends	23,000	Net income	48,000
		12/31/10 Bal	146,000

Purchases and Sales of Treasury Stock

The last item that changed on Mackay Industries' balance sheet was Treasury Stock. Since we were not told that any Treasury Stock was sold, we must assume that 100% of the account change represents new acquisitions of Treasury Stock. So, $18,000 is shown as a cash outflow in the financing section of the cash flow statement for purchase of treasury stock (item **N**).

Net Change in Cash and Cash Balances

The cash provided by or used in operating, investing, and financing activities is totaled to arrive at the net increase of $7,000 in cash. Next, the beginning cash of $11,000 from December 31, 2009 is listed. The net increase of $7,000 is added to the beginning cash of $11,000 to get the ending cash balance on December 31, 2010 of $18,000. The completed statement of cash flows for Mackay Industries, Inc. is presented in **Exhibit 11-6** on the following page.

You can see why the statement of cash flows is so valuable. It explains why the cash balance for Mackay Industries increased by only $7,000, even though the company reported net income for the year of $48,000.

Noncash Investing and Financing Activities

The operating, investing, and financing sections of the statement of cash flows only reflect activity that results from the exchange of cash. But, companies may make investments that do not require cash. They may also obtain financing for other reasons than to acquire cash. These types of transactions are called noncash investing and financing activities. Although these transactions do not affect cash, they still affect the long-term assets, long-term liabilities, and equity of a business. In order to provide financial statement users with complete information, all noncash investing and financing activities are reported. Noncash investing and financing activities can be reported in a separate schedule that accompanies the statement of cash flows or they can be disclosed in a financial statement footnote.

Mackay Industries
Statement of Cash Flows
Year Ended December 31, 2010

	Cash flows from operating activities:		
A	Net Income		$ 48,000
	Adjustments to reconcile net income to net cash provided by operating activities:		
B	Depreciation Expense	$ 18,000	
C	Loss on sale of plant assets	3,000	
D	Decrease in Accounts Receivable	17,000	
E	Increase in Inventory	(8,000)	
F	Decrease in Accounts Payable	(12,000)	
G	Increase in Accrued Liabilities	4,000	22,000
	Net cash provided by operating activities		70,000
	Cash flows from investing activities:		
H	Acquisition of plant assets	(195,000)	
I	Proceeds from sale of plant assets	104,000	
	Net cash used in investing activities		(91,000)
	Cash flows from financing activities:		
J	Proceeds from issuance of notes payable	75,000	
L	Proceeds from issuance of common stock	20,000	
K	Payment of notes payable	(26,000)	
M	Payment of dividends	(23,000)	
N	Purchase of treasury stock	(18,000)	
	Net cash provided by financing activities		28,000
	Net increase in cash:		7,000
	Cash balance, December 31, 2009		11,000
	Cash balance, December 31, 2010		$ 18,000

Exhibit 11-6 ▲

Our Mackay Industries example did not include noncash transactions because the company did not have any transactions of this type during the year. So, to illustrate the reporting of noncash transactions, let's consider the following three noncash transactions for Tucker Enterprises.

❶ Tucker Enterprises issues $450,000 of no-par common stock in exchange for a building. The journal entry to record the purchase would be as follows:

DATE	ACCOUNTS	POST REF.	DR.	CR.
	Building		450,000	
	Common Stock			450,000
	Exchanged stock for a building.			

The purchase of the building is an investing activity. The issuance of common stock is a financing activity. However, this transaction is not reported in the investing and financing sections of the statement of cash flows because no cash is exchanged. Instead, this transaction is reported as a *noncash investing and financing activity.*

❷ Tucker Enterprises acquired $120,000 of land by issuing a note. The journal entry to record the purchase would be as follows:

DATE	ACCOUNTS	POST REF.	DR.	CR.
	Land		120,000	
	Notes Payable			120,000
	Purchased land.			

The purchase of the land is an investing activity. The issuance of the note is a financing activity. Once again, this transaction is not reported in the investing and financing sections of the statement of cash flows because no cash is exchanged. Instead, this transaction is reported as a *noncash investing and financing activity*.

❸ Tucker Enterprises issued $100,000 of no-par common stock to pay off a debt. The journal entry to record the purchase would be as follows:

DATE	ACCOUNTS	POST REF.	DR.	CR.
	Notes Payable		100,000	
	Common Stock			100,000
	Paid note with stock.			

The payment on the note and the issuance of the common stock are both financing activities. But, because no cash is involved, this transaction will not be reported in the financing section of the statement of cash flows. It is reported as a *noncash investing and financing activity*.

Exhibit 11-7 illustrates how the noncash investing and financing activities for Tucker Enterprises would be presented.

Tucker Enterprises Statement of Cash Flows—Partial Year Ended December 31, 2010			
	Noncash investing and financing activities:		
	Issued 10,000 shares of common stock in		
	exchange for a building		$450,000
	Issued a note in exchange for land		120,000
	Issued 1,800 shares of common stock as		
	repayment of note		100,000

Exhibit 11-7 ▲

☑ Concept Check

Alpine Manufacturing purchased a new piece of equipment costing $45,000. Alpine paid $5,000 cash down and signed a note for the remainder. What types of activities (operating, financing, or investing) are represented by this transaction? How would this transaction be reported in Alpine Manufacturing's statement of cash flows?

Answer

Because this transaction involves both the purchase of new plant assets and the issuance of a note payable, it represents both an investing activity and a financing activity. However, on Alpine Manufacturing's statement of cash flows, only $5,000 will be reflected in the investing section as an outflow of cash for the purchase of plant assets. The remaining $40,000 will be reflected as a noncash investing and financing activity in a separate schedule.

HOW IS THE STATEMENT OF CASH FLOWS PREPARED USING THE DIRECT METHOD?

Prepare the statement of cash flows using the direct method **4** ▶

Although most companies utilize the indirect method of reporting cash flows from operating activities, the Financial Accounting Standards Board (FASB) prefers the direct method. The direct method provides clearer information about the sources and uses of cash than the indirect method. Investing and financing cash flows are presented exactly the same under both direct and indirect methods.

To illustrate how the operating section of the statement of cash flows differs for the direct method, we will be using the Mackay Industries, Inc., data we used with the indirect method. The format for the direct method statement of cash flows for Mackay Industries is presented in **Exhibit 11-8**.

	Mackay Industries, Inc. Statement of Cash Flows Year Ended December 31, 2010		
	Cash flows from operating activities:		
	Receipts:		
	Collections from customers		
	Interest received		
	Dividends received on investments		
	Total cash receipts		
	Payments:		
	To suppliers		
	To employees		
	For interest and income tax		
	Total cash payments		
	Net cash provided by operating activities		
	± **Cash flows from investing activities:**		
	+ Cash receipts from sales of long-term assets (investments, land, building, equipment, and so on)		
	− Purchases of long-term assets		
	Net cash provided by (used for) investing activities		
	± **Cash flows from financing activities:**		
	+ Cash receipts from issuance of stock		
	+ Sale of treasury stock		
	− Purchase of treasury stock		
	+ Cash receipts from issuance of notes or bonds payable (borrowing)		
	− Payment of notes or bonds payable		
	− Payment of dividends		
	Net cash provided by (used for) financing activities		
	= **Net increase (decrease) in cash during the year**		
	+ Cash at December 31, 2009		
	= Cash at December 31, 2010		

Exhibit 11-8 ▲

Mackay Industries' completed direct method statement of cash flows for 2010 is presented in **Exhibit 11-9**.

Mackay Industries
Statement of Cash Flows
Year Ended December 31, 2010

		Cash flows from operating activities:		
		Receipts:		
A		Collections from customers	$ 285,000	
B		Interest received	13,000	
C		Dividends received	5,000	
		Total cash receipts		$ 303,000
		Payments:		
D		To suppliers	(165,000)	
E		To employees	(48,000)	
F		For interest	(11,000)	
G		For taxes	(9,000)	
		Total cash payments		(233,000)
		Net cash provided by operating activities		70,000
		Cash flows from investing activities:		
		Acquisition of plant assets	(195,000)	
		Proceeds from sale of plant assets	104,000	
		Net cash used in investing activities		(91,000)
		Cash flows from financing activities:		
		Proceeds from issuance of notes payable	75,000	
		Proceeds from issuance of common stock	20,000	
		Payment of notes payable	(26,000)	
		Payment of dividends	(23,000)	
		Purchase of treasury stock	(18,000)	
		Net cash provided by financing activities		28,000
		Net increase in cash:		7,000
		Cash balance, December 31, 2009		11,000
		Cash balance, December 31, 2010		$ 18,000

Exhibit 11-9 ▲

Now, we'll explain how we calculated each number.

Cash Flows from Operating Activities

In the indirect method, we start with net income and then adjust it to "cash-basis" through a series of adjusting items. In the direct method, we convert each line item on the income statement from accrual to cash basis. So, in essence, the operating activities section of the direct method statement of cash flows is really just a cash-basis income statement.

Depreciation, Depletion, and Amortization Expense

Because these expenses do not require the payment of cash, they are **not** reported on the direct method statement of cash flows.

Gains and Losses on the Sale of Plant Assets

The last item on the income statement is a loss on sale of plant assets of $3,000. Remember that gains and losses do not represent cash flows. The cash flow related to the sale of a plant asset equals the proceeds from the sale of the asset. As with the indirect method, the proceeds from the sale of the asset is reported in the investing section, not the operating section.

A Cash Collections from Customers

The first item on the income statement is Sales Revenue of $268,000. Sales Revenue represents the total of all sales, whether for cash or on account. The balance sheet accounts related to Sales Revenue are Accounts Receivable and Unearned Revenues. Accounts receivable decreased $17,000 from $93,000 at 12/31/09 to $76,000 at 12/31/10. A decrease in Accounts Receivable means that Mackay Industries collected more cash than it made in sales during the current year. This means that the cash receipts during the year are $17,000 greater than Sales Revenues. The balance sheet shows no unearned revenues so no adjustment is needed for unearned revenues. We can calculate the cash received from customers as follows:

Sales Revenue...	$268,000
Plus decrease in Accounts Receivable	17,000
Cash receipts from customers	$285,000

B Cash Receipts of Interest

The second item on the income statement is Interest Revenue of $13,000. The balance sheet account related to Interest Revenue is Interest Receivable. Since there is no Interest Receivable account on the balance sheet, the Interest Revenue must have all been received in cash. So, the cash flow statement shows Interest Received of $13,000. Had there been Interest Receivable in either year, the accrual basis Interest Revenue would have been converted to cash basis in a manner similar to that used for Sales Revenue and Accounts Receivable.

C Cash Receipts of Dividends

Dividend Revenue is the third item reported on the income statement of $5,000. The balance sheet account related to Dividend Revenue is Dividends Receivable. As with the interest, there is no Dividends Receivable on the balance sheet. Therefore, the Dividend Revenue must have all been received in cash. So, the cash flow statement shows cash received from dividends of $5,000.

D Payments to Suppliers

Payments to suppliers include all payments for

- inventory and
- operating expenses except employee compensation, interest, and income taxes.

Suppliers are those entities that provide the business with its inventory and essential services. The accounts related to payments to suppliers for inventory are Cost of Goods Sold, Inventory, and Accounts Payable. Cost of Goods Sold on the income statement was $137,000. Inventory increased from $124,000 at 12/31/09 to $132,000 at 12/31/10. The $8,000 ($132,000 – $124,000) increase in Inventory means that

Mackay Industries purchased more inventory than it sold during the year. This means that the total amount of inventory purchased during the year would be $145,000.

Cost of Goods Sold	$137,000
Plus increase in Inventory	8,000
Total inventory purchased	$145,000

Next we need to consider the change in Accounts Payable to determine the total cash payments for inventory purchased during the year. Accounts Payable decreased from $96,000 at 12/31/09 to $84,000 at 12/31/10. The $12,000 decrease ($96,000 − $84,000) in Accounts Payable means that Mackay Industries paid $12,000 more during the year than the amount of inventory purchased. So, the cash payments for inventory purchased during the year can be calculated as follows:

Total inventory purchased	$145,000
Plus decrease in Accounts Payable	12,000
Cash payments for inventory	$157,000

The accounts related to payments to suppliers for operating expenses are Operating Expenses, Prepaid Expenses, and Accrued Liabilities. Operating Expenses on the income statement were $12,000. There are no Prepaid Expenses on the balance sheet so no adjustment is needed for changes in prepaid expenses. Accrued Liabilities increased from $8,000 at 12/31/09 to $12,000 at 12/31/10. This means that Mackay Industries incurred more operating expenses than it paid for during the year. By subtracting the $4,000 ($12,000 − $8000) from the operating expenses we get the amount of cash payments made to suppliers for operating expense:

Operating Expenses	$12,000
Less increase in Accrued Liabilities	4,000
Cash payments for operating expenses	$ 8,000

Finally, by adding the cash paid to suppliers for inventory to the cash paid to suppliers for operating expenses we get the total cash paid to suppliers of $165,000.

Cash payments for inventory	$157,000
Cash payments for operating expenses	8,000
Total cash payments to suppliers	$165,000

E Payments to Employees

This category includes payments for salaries, wages, and other forms of employee compensation. The accounts related to employee payments are Salaries Expense from the income statement and Salaries Payable from the balance sheet. Since there aren't any Salaries Payable on the balance sheet, the Salaries Expense account must represent all amounts paid in cash to employees. So, the cash flow statement shows cash payments to employees of $48,000. Had there been any Salaries Payable, the Salaries Expense account would have been adjusted to arrive at the cash paid to employees in a manner similar to how operating expenses were adjusted for accrued liabilities above.

F Payments for Interest Expense

These cash payments are reported separately from the other expenses. The accounts related to interest payments are Interest Expense from the income statement and Interest Payable from the balance sheet. Since there is no Interest Payable on the balance sheet, the Interest Expense from the income statement must represent all amounts paid in cash for interest. So, the cash flow statement shows cash payments for interest of $11,000.

G Payments for Income Tax Expense

Like interest expense, these cash payments are reported separately from the other expenses. The accounts related to income tax payments are Income Tax Expense from the income statement and Income Tax Payable from the balance sheet. Again, since there is no Income Tax Payable on the balance sheet, the Income Tax Expense from the income statement must represent all amounts paid in cash for income tax. Therefore, the cash flow statement shows cash payments for income tax of $9,000.

Net Cash Provided by Operating Activities

To calculate net cash provided by operating activities using the direct method, we add all the cash receipts and cash payments described previously and find the difference. For Mackay Industries, Inc., total Cash receipts were $303,000. Total Cash payments were $233,000. So, net cash provided by operating activities is $70,000. If you refer back to the indirect method cash flow statement shown in Exhibit 11-6, you will find that it showed the same $70,000 for net cash provided by operating activities—only the method by which it was calculated was different.

The remainder of Mackay Industries' cash flow statement is exactly the same as what we calculated using the indirect method (see Exhibit 11-6).

Decision Guidelines

Decision		Guideline		Analyze
Should the direct or indirect method be used to prepare the cash flow statement?		Although, the direct method is preferred by GAAP, most financial statement users find the indirect method more useful.		Because the indirect method reconciles net income as reported on the income statement to net cash provided by operating activities, it is more useful to most financial statements users. It helps answer the questions "How can the company have so much income when it has so little cash?" or "How can the company have so much cash when it made so little income?"

FOCUS ON DECISION MAKING: FREE CASH FLOW AND THE CASH CONVERSION CYCLE

Free Cash Flow

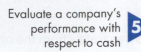

Evaluate a company's performance with respect to cash

The statement of cash flows is a useful tool for examining the sources and uses of cash during an accounting period. However, investors may want to know how much cash a company anticipates it can "free up" for new opportunities. **Free cash flow** is the amount of anticipated cash available from operations after paying for planned investments in long-term assets and paying dividends. Free cash flow can be computed as follows:

$$\text{Free cash flow} = \begin{array}{c}\text{Anticipated net}\\\text{cash provided by}\\\text{operating activities}\end{array} - \begin{array}{c}\text{Cash payments planned for}\\\text{investments in plant, equipment,}\\\text{and other long-term assets}\end{array} - \begin{array}{c}\text{Anticipated cash}\\\text{payments for dividends}\end{array}$$

Many companies use free cash flow to manage their operations. Suppose Tucker Enterprises expects net cash provided by operations of $160,000 during the next year. Tucker Enterprises also plans to spend $85,000 to purchase new equipment and anticipates paying another $15,000 in dividends. In this case, Tucker Enterprises' free cash flow would be $60,000 ($160,000 – $85,000 – $15,000). If a good investment opportunity comes along (or an anticipated need for cash), Tucker Enterprises should have $60,000 of free cash available.

Cash Conversion Cycle

The **cash conversion cycle** represents the time it takes a company to sell its inventory and collect its receivables less the time it takes the company to pay its payables. In other words, the cash conversion cycle represents the number of days a company's cash is "tied up" in the operations of the business. The cash conversion cycle is calculated as follows:

$$\text{Cash conversion cycle} = \text{Inventory turnover (in days)} + \begin{array}{c}\text{Accounts receivable}\\\text{turnover (in days)}\end{array} - \begin{array}{c}\text{Accounts payable}\\\text{turnover (in days)}\end{array}$$

The inventory turnover in days can be found by dividing 365 by the inventory turnover (discussed in Chapter 5). Alternatively, it can be found using the following formula:

$$\text{Inventory turnover in days} = \text{Average inventory} \div \text{Cost of goods sold} \times 365$$

The accounts receivable turnover in days can be found by dividing 365 by the accounts receivable turnover (discussed in Chapter 7). Alternatively, it can be found by using the following formula:

$$\text{Accounts receivable turnover in days} = \text{Average net accounts receivable} \div \text{Net credit sales} \times 365$$

The accounts payable turnover in days can is calculated as follows:

$$\text{Accounts payable turnover in days} = \text{Average accounts payable} \div \text{Cost of goods sold} \times 365$$

Let's assume that Tucker Enterprises has an inventory turnover of 52 days, an accounts receivable turnover of 34 days, and an accounts payable turnover of 39 days. Tucker Enterprises' cash conversion cycle would equal 47 days (52 + 34 − 39). This means that, on average, Tucker Enterprises' cash is tied up for 47 days. Generally, the lower the cash conversion cycle the healthier the company. This is because cash is the lifeblood of a business and the less amount of time it is "tied up" the better. Over time, if the cash conversion cycle for a business grows longer, it can be a sign that the business may be facing a pending cash flow "crunch."

Decision Guidelines

Decision	Guideline	Analyze
Does the company have sufficient cash available?	Calculate the company's free cash flow and its cash conversion cycle.	In order for a business to be able to take advantage of unforeseen opportunities, it is important that it has "free cash" available. A lack of "free cash" will probably not negatively impact a business's normal operations but it will most likely result in lost income due to foregone opportunities.
		The cash conversion cycle indicates how long a company's cash is being "tied up" in its operations. The longer cash is tied up, the more likely it is that the company will encounter cash flow problems in the future. A company with a long cash conversion cycle should consider obtaining a line of credit to provide some insurance against cash flow problems.

Demo Doc

Preparing the Statement of Cash Flows Using the Indirect Method

Learning Objective 3 ▶

Cassidy, Inc., has the following information for 2010:

Cassidy, Inc. Income Statement Year Ended December 31, 2010		
Sales Revenue		$550,000
Cost of Goods Sold		320,000
Gross Profit		230,000
Operating Expenses:		
Salary Expense	$165,000	
Depreciation Expense	21,000	
Insurance Expense	19,000	
Total Operating Expense		205,000
Income from Operations		25,000
Other items:		
Gain on Sale of Furniture		3,000
Net Income		$ 28,000

<table>
<tr><td colspan="7">Cassidy, Inc.
Balance Sheet
December 31, 2010 and 2009</td></tr>
<tr><td>ASSETS</td><td>2010</td><td>2009</td><td>LIABILITIES</td><td>2010</td><td>2009</td></tr>
<tr><td>Current:</td><td></td><td></td><td>Current:</td><td></td><td></td></tr>
<tr><td>Cash</td><td>$ 28,000</td><td>$ 33,000</td><td>Accounts Payable</td><td>$ 20,000</td><td>$ 23,000</td></tr>
<tr><td>Accounts Receivable</td><td>26,000</td><td>15,000</td><td>Salary Payable</td><td>10,000</td><td>8,000</td></tr>
<tr><td>Prepaid Insurance</td><td>30,000</td><td>42,000</td><td>Total Current</td><td></td><td></td></tr>
<tr><td>Total Current Assets</td><td>84,000</td><td>90,000</td><td>Liabilities</td><td>30,000</td><td>31,000</td></tr>
<tr><td>Furniture, net</td><td>90,000</td><td>74,500</td><td>Notes Payable</td><td>40,000</td><td>50,000</td></tr>
<tr><td></td><td></td><td></td><td>STOCKHOLDERS'
EQUITY</td><td></td><td></td></tr>
<tr><td></td><td></td><td></td><td>Common Stock (no par)</td><td>4,000</td><td>3,500</td></tr>
<tr><td></td><td></td><td></td><td>Retained Earnings</td><td>100,000</td><td>80,000</td></tr>
<tr><td></td><td></td><td></td><td>Total Liabilities and</td><td></td><td></td></tr>
<tr><td>Total Assets</td><td>$174,000</td><td>$164,500</td><td>Stockholders' Equity</td><td>$174,000</td><td>$164,500</td></tr>
</table>

During 2010 Cassidy

- sold furniture with a book value of $15,000 for cash. New furniture was purchased for cash.
- repaid notes payable with a principal value of $22,000. Issued new notes for cash.
- issued new common shares for cash.
- paid cash dividends.

Requirement:

1 Prepare Cassidy's statement of cash flows using the indirect method.

Demo Doc Solution

Requirement **1**

Prepare Cassidy's statement of cash flows using the indirect method.

Part 1	Demo Doc Complete

Operating Activities

As with income statements and balance sheets, every cash-flow statement needs a proper title. The first line of the title is the company name, next is the name of the statement (statement of cash flows), and last is the date (year ended December 31, 2010). Put all together, the title is as follows:

Cassidy, Inc.
Statement of Cash Flows
Year Ended December 31, 2010

The first section of the statement of cash flows is operating activities. This section begins with net income. We can find net income on the income statement. According to Cassidy's income statement, net income for the year is $28,000.

Items are added or subtracted on the statement of cash flows based on their impact to cash. In this case, net income increases cash, so it is added on the statement of cash flows.

Next, we must take a quick look through the income statement and look for any non-cash items. Noncash items are *not* part of cash flows, so any noncash items in net income must be removed.

The most frequent noncash item on the income statement is depreciation expense. Depreciation expense is subtracted to arrive at net income (if you look at the income statement, you will see a subtraction for depreciation expense), so to *remove* its impact, the *opposite* must be done: Depreciation expense of $21,000 must be added back to net income.

The other noncash item that you will see on many income statements is gains/losses on sale of assets. In this example, Cassidy has a gain on sale of furniture of $3,000. As you can see on the income statement, this gain was added to arrive at net income. To *remove* its effect, we do the *opposite*: subtract it. So the gain of $3,000 is subtracted.

Now that we have gotten all necessary information from the income statement, we can turn to the balance sheet.

Operating activities deal with everyday transactions of the business, the kind of things the company normally does to earn a profit. What kinds of accounts do businesses deal with on a daily basis? Some accounts are Accounts Receivable, Accounts Payable, Inventory, and so forth. In other words, they are the current assets and current liabilities of the company. Changes in the balances of these accounts impact income differently than they impact cash flows. So, adjustments must be made to reconcile net income to the cash flows for the period.

Other than Cash (which we are trying to analyze in preparing the statement of cash flows), what is the first current asset on the balance sheet? It is Accounts Receivable. What happened to Accounts Receivable during the year? It increased from $15,000 to $26,000. This means that $11,000 ($26,000 – $15,000) of the revenues on the income statement have not yet been collected in cash. So the $11,000 increase to Accounts Receivable is subtracted from net income on the statement of cash flows.

The other current asset is Prepaid Insurance. This account decreased from $42,000 to $30,000. A decrease to Prepaid Insurance indicates that part of the expenses for the period were not paid for with cash. Instead, we used something we had prepaid—that is something we had already paid for in an earlier period. So, the decrease of $12,000 ($42,000 – $30,000) will be added to net income on the statement of cash flows.

So far, operating activities show the following information:

Cash flows from operating activities:		
Net Income		$28,000
Adjustments to reconcile net income to net cash		
provided by operating activities:		
Depreciation Expense	$ 21,000	
Gain on sale of plant assets	(3,000)	
Increase in Accounts Receivable	(11,000)	
Decrease in Prepaid Insurance	12,000	

Now that we have looked at the current assets, we can look at the current liabilities. The first current liability is Accounts Payable. During the year, Accounts Payable decreased from $23,000 to $20,000. This means that $3,000 ($23,000 – $20,000) more was paid for during the current year than was charged on account. So, the $3,000 will be subtracted from net income on the statement of cash flows.

The other current liability is Salary Payable. During the year, Salary Payable increased from $8,000 to $10,000. The increase in this payable account means that part of the current year's salaries expense was not paid for with cash. So $2,000 ($10,000 – $8,000) will be added to net income on the statement of cash flows.

Now that we have looked at all of the current assets and liabilities, we can total the operating activities section:

Cash flows from operating activities:		
Net Income		$28,000
Adjustments to reconcile net income to net cash provided by operating activities:		
Depreciation Expense	$ 21,000	
Gain on sale of plant assets	(3,000)	
Increase in Accounts Receivable	(11,000)	
Decrease in Prepaid Insurance	12,000	
Decrease in Accounts Payable	(3,000)	
Increase in Salary Payable	2,000	18,000
Net cash provided by operating activities		46,000

Investing Activities

Investing activities deal with long-term assets. The only long-term asset is Furniture. Unfortunately, we cannot just say "increase in Furniture" or "decrease in Furniture" and look at the overall change because Furniture is a major account. We must look at each significant transaction affecting the account.

From the additional information we were given with the question, we know that Cassidy purchased furniture and sold furniture during the year. Each of these transactions will be a separate line in investing activities.

Cash flows from investing activities:		
Acquisition of furniture	???	
Proceeds from sale of furniture	???	
Net cash used for investing activities		???

We do not know these totals, but we can calculate them with the information we already have.

First, we should analyze the Furniture, Net T-account. From the balance sheet, we know that in 2010, Furniture, Net has a beginning balance of $74,500 and an ending balance of $90,000. During the year, Furniture, Net increased and decreased.

Furniture, Net			
Beginning balance	74,500		
Increases	???	Decreases	???
Ending balance	90,000		

Furniture, Net increases when new furniture is purchased (acquisitions). Furniture, Net decreases by the book value of furniture sold and when depreciation expense is recorded. Depreciation expense of $21,000 can be obtained from the income statement (or the operating activities section of the statement of cash flows). The book value of $15,000 for the assets sold was given in the problem. Putting these items into the T-account is shown next:

Furniture, Net			
Beginning balance	74,500	Depreciation	21,000
Acquisitions	X	Book value of assets sold	15,000
Ending balance	90,000		

We can use this information to calculate the cost of furniture purchased (acquisitions), X.

$$\$74{,}500 - \$21{,}000 - \$15{,}000 + X = \$90{,}000$$
$$X = \$90{,}000 - \$74{,}500 + \$21{,}000 + \$15{,}000$$
$$X = \$51{,}500$$

So acquisitions of furniture were $51,500. Purchasing furniture caused Cash to decrease, so the $51,500 will be subtracted on the statement of cash flows.

We still need to determine the cash received when furniture was sold (proceeds). We can use the gain/loss formula for this calculation:

Proceeds = Book value of assets sold + Gain, or − Loss

Proceeds = $15,000 Book value of assets sold + Gain of $3,000

Proceeds = $18,000

So the proceeds from sale of furniture were $18,000. Selling furniture caused Cash to increase, so the $18,000 will be added on the statement of cash flows. Filling this information into the investing activities, we have the following:

Cash flows from investing activities:		
Acquisition of furniture	$(51,500)	
Proceeds from sale of furniture	18,000	
Net cash used for investing activities		$(33,500)

Financing Activities

Financing activities deal with long-term liabilities (debt financing) and equity (equity financing).

Cassidy only has one long-term liability: Notes Payable. As with Furniture, we know that we must report the major transactions in this account separately.

From the additional information we were given with the question, we know that Cassidy paid off notes payable and issued new notes payable during the year. Each of these transactions will be a separate line in financing activities.

Cash flows from financing activities:		
Proceeds from issuance of long-term notes payable	???	
Payment of long-term notes payable	???	

We need to calculate the value of new notes issued. As we did with furniture, we can make this calculation by analyzing the T-account. In 2010, Notes Payable had a beginning balance of $50,000 and an ending balance of $40,000.

Notes Payable			
		Beginning balance	50,000
Decreases	???	Increases	???
		Ending balance	40,000

Notes Payable is increased when new notes are issued and is decreased when notes are paid off. From the additional information given in the problem, we know that $22,000 of notes were paid off. Putting this information into the T-account, we have the following:

Notes Payable			
		Beginning balance	50,000
Payments	22,000	Issuance of new notes payable	X
		Ending balance	40,000

We can use this information to calculate the value of new notes issued:

$$\$50,000 - \$22,000 + X = \$40,000$$
$$X = \$40,000 - \$50,000 + \$22,000$$
$$X = \$12,000$$

So, issuance of new notes payable was $12,000. Because issuing notes payable increased Cash, $12,000 will be added on the statement of cash flows.

Putting this information into the financing activities section, we have the following:

	Cash flows from financing activities:		
	Proceeds from issuance of long-term notes payable	$ 12,000	
	Payment of long-term notes payable	(22,000)	

Now that we have examined the long-term liabilities, we only have equity remaining. The first account in equity is Common Stock. From the additional information, we know that new common stock (no par) was issued during the year. Because this is the only transaction affecting Common Stock, we know that the change in the Common Stock account represents the issuance of these shares. Using the T-account we have the following:

Common Stock (no par)			
		Beginning balance	3,500
		Issuance of new stock	X
		Ending balance	4,000

We use this information to calculate the value of new common stock issued, X.

$$\$3,500 + X = \$4,000$$
$$X = \$4,000 - \$3,500$$
$$X = \$500$$

So issuance of common stock (proceeds) was $500. Because issuing common stock increases Cash, $500 will be added on the statement of cash flows.

The last account in equity is Retained Earnings. This account changed during 2010. Looking at the T-account we have the following:

Retained Earnings			
		Beginning balance	80,000
Decreases	???	Increases	???
		Ending balance	100,000

Retained Earnings is increased when the company earns net income and is decreased when the company declares dividends. If we put the net income from the income statement into the T-account, we have the following:

Retained Earnings			
		Beginning balance	80,000
Dividends	X	Net income	28,000
		Ending balance	100,000

We use this information to calculate the amount of cash dividends declared, X.

$$\$80,000 + \$28,000 - X = \$100,000$$
$$X = \$80,000 + \$28,000 - \$100,000$$
$$X = \$8,000$$

So, since there were no dividends payable, the cash dividends declared and paid were $8,000. Because the payment of dividends decreased Cash, $8,000 will be subtracted on the statement of cash flows.

Notice that we *do not record net income* in the financing activities (even though it affects Retained Earnings), because net income was already accounted for in the operating activities section.

Putting all of this information into the financing activities section, we have the following:

Cash flows from financing activities:			
Proceeds from issuance of long-term notes payable	$ 12,000		
Payment of long-term notes payable	(22,000)		
Proceeds from issuance of common stock	500		
Payment of dividends	(8,000)		
Net cash used for financing activities			$(17,500)

Finishing the Statement of Cash Flows

Now that we have completed the three main sections of the statement of cash flows, we can add the totals of the three sections together to determine cash flow (the net change in cash).

Net change in cash = Cash provided by operating activities – Cash used for investing activities – Cash used for financing activities

Net change in cash =	$46,000	–	$33,500	–	$17,500

Net change in cash = $(5,000)

Because the change in cash is negative, we know that it means a net *decrease* in cash. The statement began with net income (from the income statement). Now we tie it to the balance sheet to bring cash flows full circle. We add the decrease of $5,000 in cash to the cash balance at the beginning of the year of $33,000 (from Cassidy's balance sheet). This gives us the cash balance at the end of the year of $(5,000) + $33,000 = $28,000.

Putting this information in statement of cash flows format we have the following:

Net decrease in cash	$ (5,000)
Cash balance, December 31, 2009	33,000
Cash balance, December 31, 2010	$28,000

This section of the statement is also a nice check to ensure that our calculations are correct. The $28,000 calculated *is the number reported for cash* on the balance sheet at December 31, 2010.

To finish the statement of cash flows, we just put all of these pieces together:

Cassidy, Inc. Statement of Cash Flows Year Ended December 31, 2010		
Cash flows from operating activities:		
Net Income		$ 28,000
Adjustments to reconcile net income to net cash		
provided by operating activities:		
Depreciation Expense	$ 21,000	
Gain on sale of plant assets	(3,000)	
Increase in Accounts Receivable	(11,000)	
Decrease in Prepaid Insurance	12,000	
Decrease in Accounts Payable	(3,000)	
Increase in Salary Payable	2,000	18,000
Net cash provided by operating activities		$ 46,000
Cash flows from investing activities:		
Acquisition of furniture	(51,500)	
Proceeds from sale of furniture	18,000	
Net cash used for investing activities		(33,500)
Cash flows from financing activities:		
Proceeds from issuance of long-term notes payable	12,000	
Payment of long-term notes payable	(22,000)	
Proceeds from issuance of common stock	500	
Payment of dividends	(8,000)	
Net cash used for financing activities		(17,500)
Net decrease in cash		$ (5,000)
Cash balance, December 31, 2009		33,000
Cash balance, December 31, 2010		$ 28,000

Demo Doc Complete

Part 1	Demo Doc Complete

Decision Guidelines

The Statement of Cash Flows

As you examine the performance of a company (perhaps someday even your own) you may encounter some of the following decisions related to cash:

Decision	Guideline	Analyze
How do I determine how cash is being managed by a business?	Review the statement of cash flows.	The statement of cash flows shows all of the sources and all of the uses of cash for the period. The sources and uses of cash are reported separately for the operating activities, the investing activities, and the financing activities of the business. For a business to remain successful, operating activities must be the main source of its cash over the long run.
Should the direct or indirect method be used to prepare the cash flow statement?	Although, the direct method is preferred by GAAP, most financial statement users find the indirect method more useful.	Because the indirect method reconciles net income as reported on the income statement to net cash provided by operating activities, it is more useful to most financial statements users. It helps answer the questions "How can the company have so much income when it has so little cash?" or "How can the company have so much cash when it made so little income?"
Does the company have sufficient cash available?	Calculate the company's free cash flow and its cash conversion cycle.	In order for a business to be able to take advantage of unforeseen opportunities, it is important that it has "free cash" available. A lack of "free cash" will probably not negatively impact a business's normal operations but it will most likely result in lost income due to foregone opportunities.

The cash conversion cycle indicates how long a company's cash is being "tied up" in its operations. The longer cash is tied up, the more likely it is that the company will encounter cash flow problems in the future. A company with a long cash conversion cycle should consider obtaining a line of credit to provide some insurance against cash flow problems. |

ACCOUNTING VOCABULARY

THE LANGUAGE OF BUSINESS

Cash conversion cycle (p. 560) A measurement of the amount of time a company's cash is tied up in its operations.

Cash flow statement (p. 540) A financial statement that shows all of the sources and all of the uses of cash for an accounting period; also called the *statement of cash flows*.

Direct method (p. 543) Format of the operating activities section of the statement of cash flows; it lists the cash receipts and cash payments resulting from a company's day-to-day operations.

Financing activities (p. 542) Activities related to the issuance of, and repayment of, long-term debt or to the issuance of stock and the payment of dividends; it's a section of the statement of cash flows.

Free cash flow (p. 560) The anticipated amount of cash available from operations after paying for planned investments in long-term assets and paying dividends.

Indirect method (p. 543) Format of the operating activities section of the statement of cash flows; it starts with net income and reconciles to net cash provided by operating activities.

Investing activities (p. 542) Activities that increase or decrease long-term assets; it's a section of the statement of cash flows.

Operating activities (p. 542) Activities that create revenue or expense in the entity's major line of business; it's a section of the statement of cash flows. Operating activities affect the income statement.

Statement of cash flows (p. 540) A financial statement that shows all of the sources and all of the uses of cash for an accounting period; also called the *cash flow statement*.

ACCOUNTING PRACTICE

DISCUSSION QUESTIONS

1. What are some of the reasons why a statement of cash flows may be important to users of financial statements?

2. A company used cash to build a new factory and received cash when it sold off the machines in the old factory. In which section of the statement of cash flows would the cash flows from these activities be reported?

3. A company used cash to pay employees and received cash from performing services. In which section of the statement of cash flows would the cash flows from these activities be reported?

4. A company issued bonds during the year. Would this be reported as a source or use of cash on the statement of cash flows? In which section would it be reported?

5. Why is net income a good place to start when attempting to determine the cash flows from operating activities using the indirect method? Why is it not the same as the cash flows from operating activities?

6. When using the indirect method, why are gains on the sale of plant assets subtracted from net income in the operating activities section of the statement of cash flows? Why are losses on the sale of plant assets added to net income?

7. How does an increase in accounts receivable during the year affect the statement of cash flows (if at all)? Why?

8. Why would a decrease in accounts payable be shown as a decrease in cash when using the indirect method of calculating the cash flows from operating activities?

9. How would the sale of treasury stock that was acquired three years ago appear in the statement of cash flows (if at all)?

10. A company's cash conversion cycle increased from 55 days in Year 1 to 68 days in Year 3. What are the implications of this increase? What do you think happens to the cash conversion cycles of companies during a recession?

SELF CHECK

1. The three main categories of cash flows are
   a. direct, indirect, and hybrid.
   c. operating, investing, and financing.
   b. current, long-term, and fixed.
   d. short-term, long-term, and equity.

2. The purpose of the cash flow statement is to
   a. predict future cash flows.
   b. evaluate management decisions.
   c. predict ability to make payments to lenders.
   d. All of the above

3. Financing activities are most closely related to
   a. current assets and current liabilities.
   b. long-term assets.
   c. long-term liabilities and stockholder's equity.
   d. net income and dividends.

4. Which item does not appear on a statement of cash flows prepared by the indirect method?
   a. Collections from customers
   c. Depreciation
   b. Net income
   d. Gain on sale of land

5. Advanced Robotics earned net income of $60,000 after deducting depreciation of $4,000 and all other expenses. Current assets increased by $3,000 and current liabilities decreased by $5,000. Using the indirect method, how much was Advanced Robotics' cash flows from operating activities?
   a. $48,000
   c. $52,000
   b. $50,000
   d. $56,000

6. The Plant Assets account of Betterbuilt, Inc., shows the following:

Plant Assets, Net			
Beginning balance	100,000	Depreciation	30,000
Purchase	400,000	Sale	?
Ending balance	420,000		

Betterbuilt, Inc., sold plant assets at a $10,000 gain. How much should Betterbuilt, Inc., report for the sale?
   a. Cash flows from investing activities, $40,000
   b. Cash flows from investing activities, $50,000
   c. Cash flows from investing activities, $60,000
   d. Cash flows from investing activities, $10,000

7. Widget Corporation borrowed $15,000, issued common stock of $10,000, and paid dividends of $25,000. What was Widget Corporation's net cash provided or used by financing activities?
   a. $0
   c. $(25,000)
   b. $25,000
   d. $50,000

8. Which item appears on a statement of cash flows prepared by the indirect method?
   a. Net income
   c. Collections from customers
   b. Payment to suppliers
   d. Payment of income tax

9. Structural Systems, Inc., had accounts receivable of $20,000 at the beginning of the year and $50,000 at year-end. Revenue for the year totaled $100,000. How much cash did Structural Systems collect from customers?

   a. $170,000
   c. $120,000

   b. $150,000
   d. $70,000

10. Allied Enterprises had operating expenses of $40,000. At the beginning of the year, Allied Enterprises owed $5,000 on accrued liabilities. At year-end, accrued liabilities were $8,000. How much cash did Allied Enterprises pay for operating expenses?

   a. $35,000
   c. $43,000

   b. $37,000
   d. $45,000

Answers are given after Written Communication.

SHORT EXERCISES

S11-1. Purpose of the statement of cash flows *(Learning Objective 1)* 5–10 min.

Describe how the statement of cash flows helps investors and creditors perform each of the following functions:

1. Predict future cash flows
2. Evaluate management decisions
3. Predict the ability to make debt payments to lenders and pay dividends to stockholders

---

S11-2. Basics of statement of cash flows *(Learning Objectives 2 & 3)* 5–10 min.

Answer these questions about the statement of cash flows:

1. What is the "check figure" for the statement of cash flows? Where do you get this check figure?
2. List the categories of cash flows in order of importance.
3. What is the first dollar amount reported using the indirect method?

S11-3. Purpose of statement of cash flows *(Learning Objective 1)* 5–10 min.

Intermountain, Inc., experienced an unbroken string of 10 years of growth in net income. Nevertheless, the business is facing bankruptcy. Creditors are calling all of Intermountain's outstanding loans for immediate payment, and Intermountain, Inc., has no cash available to make these payments because managers placed undue emphasis on net income and gave too little attention to cash flows.

Write a brief memo in your own words to explain to the managers of Intermountain, Inc., the purposes of the statement of cash flows.

S11-4. Classification of items as operating, investing, or financing *(Learning Objective 3)* 10–15 min.

Identify each of the following transactions as one of the following:

- Operating activity (O)
- Investing activity (I)
- Financing activity (F)
- Noncash investing and financing activity (NIF)

For each item, indicate whether it represents an increase (+) or a decrease (–) in cash. The indirect method is used to report cash flows from operating activities.

____ a. Cash sale of land

____ b. Issuance of long-term note payable in exchange for cash

____ c. Depreciation of equipment

____ d. Purchase of treasury stock

____ e. Issuance of common stock for cash

____ f. Increase in Accounts Payable

____ g. Net income

____ h. Payment of cash dividend

____ i. Decrease in Accrued Liabilities

____ j. Loss on sale of land

____ k. Acquisition of building by issuance of notes payable

____ l. Payment of long-term debt

____ m. Acquisition of building by issuance of common stock

____ n. Decrease in Accounts Receivable

____ o. Decrease in Inventory

____ p. Increase in prepaid expenses

S11-5. Classification of items as operating, investing, or financing (Learning Objective 3) 10–15 min.

Indicate whether each of the following transactions would result in an operating activity, an investing activity, a financing activity, or a transaction that does affect cash for a statement of cash flows prepared by the indirect method.

DATE	ACCOUNTS	POST REF.	DR.	CR.
a.	Equipment		18,000	
	Cash			18,000
b.	Cash		7,200	
	Long-Term Investment			7,200
c.	Bonds Payable		45,000	
	Cash			45,000
d.	Building		164,000	
	Notes Payable, Long-Term			164,000
e.	Loss on Disposal of Equipment		1,400	
	Equipment			1,400
f.	Dividend Payable		16,500	
	Cash			16,500
g.	Cash		81,000	
	Common Stock			81,000
h.	Treasury Stock		13,000	
	Cash			13,000
i.	Cash		60,000	
	Sales Revenue			60,000
j.	Land		87,700	
	Cash			87,700
k.	Depreciation		9,000	
	Accumulated Depreciation			9,000

S11-6. Operating activities—indirect method (Learning Objective 3) 10–15 min.

C. Kirk Corporation reported the following data for 2010:

Income statement:	Net Income	$50,000
	Depreciation	8,000
Balance sheet:	Increase in Accounts Receivable	6,000
	Decrease in Accounts Payable	4,000

Compute C. Kirk Corporation's net cash provided by operating activities according to the indirect method.

S11-7. Operating activities—indirect method *(Learning Objective 3)* 10–15 min.

Inland Equipment's accountants assembled the following data for the year ended June 30, 2010.

Net Income	$60,000	Purchase of equipment	$40,000
Proceeds from issuance of		Decrease in	
common stock	20,000	current liabilities..................	5,000
Payment of dividends..............	6,000	Payment of note payable..........	30,000
Increase in current assets		Proceeds from	
other than cash	30,000	sale of land.........................	60,000
Purchase of treasury stock	5,000	Depreciation Expense...............	15,000

Prepare Inland Equipment's statement of cash flows for the year ended June 30, 2010 using the indirect method. The cash balance for Inland Equipment, Inc., at December 31, 2009 was $12,000.

S11-8. Operating activities—direct method *(Learning Objective 4)* 5–10 min.

Uhura Health Spas began 2010 with cash of $104,000. During the year, Uhura earned service revenue of $600,000 and collected $590,000 from customers. Expenses for the year totaled $420,000, of which Uhura paid $410,000 in cash to suppliers and employees. Uhura also paid $140,000 to purchase equipment and paid a cash dividend of $50,000 to its stockholders during 2010. Prepare the company's statement of cash flows for the year ended December 31, 2010. Format cash flows from operating activities by the direct method.

S11-9. Operating activities—direct method *(Learning Objective 4)* 5–10 min.

Inland Equipment, Inc., assembled the following data related to its cash transactions for the year ended June 30, 2010:

Payment of dividends..	$ 6,000
Proceeds from issuance of stock...	20,000
Collections from customers...	200,000
Proceeds from sale of land	60,000
Payments to suppliers	80,000
Purchase of equipment...	40,000
Payments to employees	70,000
Payment of note payable...	30,000

Prepare Inland Equipment's statement of cash flows for the year ended June 30, 2010 using the direct method. Inland Equipment's cash balance at December 31, 2009 was $12,000.

S11-10. Calculate certain operating information for direct method *(Learning Objective 4)* **5–10 min.**

McCoy Medical Company reported the following financial statements for 2010:

McCoy Medical Company
Income Statement
Year Ended December 31, 2010

Revenue:		
Sales Revenue		$710
Expenses:		
Cost of Goods Sold	$340	
Depreciation Expense	60	
Other Expenses	200	
Total Expense		600
Net Income		$110

McCoy Medical Company
Comparative Balance Sheet
December 31, 2010 and 2009

(in thousands) ASSETS	2010	2009	LIABILITIES	2010	2009
Current:			Current:		
Cash	$ 19	$ 16	Accounts Payable	$ 47	$ 42
Accounts Receivable	54	48	Salary Payable	23	21
Inventory	80	84	Accrued Liabilities	8	11
Prepaid Expenses	3	2	Long-Term Notes Payable	66	68
Long-Term Investments	75	90			
Plant Assets, Net	225	185	**STOCKHOLDERS' EQUITY**		
			Common Stock	40	37
			Retained Earnings	272	246
			Total Liabilities and		
Total Assets	$456	$425	Stockholders' Equity	$456	$425

Use the information in McCoy Medical Company's financial statements to compute the following:

1. Collections from customers
2. Payments for inventory

S11-11. Calculate certain investing and financing information from financial statements *(Learning Objective 3)* **10–15 min.**

Use the McCoy Medical Company data in S11-10 to compute the amount of plant assets acquired by McCoy Medical Company, assuming McCoy sold no plant assets in 2010.

S11-12. Calculate certain investing and financing information from financial statements *(Learning Objective 3)* 10–15 min.

Use the McCoy Medical Company data in S11-10 to compute the following amounts for 2010:

1. Borrowing or payment of long-term notes payable, assuming McCoy had only one long-term note payable transaction during the year

2. Issuance of common stock, assuming McCoy had only one common stock transaction during the year

3. Payment of cash dividends

EXERCISES (GROUP A)

E11-13A. Operating activities—indirect method *(Learning Objective 3)* 10–15 min.

The accounting records of Rising Star Talent Agency reveal the following:

Net Income	$22,000
Depreciation	12,000
Sales Revenue	9,000
Decrease in current liabilities	20,000
Loss on sale of land	5,000
Increase in current assets other than Cash	27,000
Acquisition of land	37,000

Requirements

1. Compute cash flows from operating activities by the indirect method. Use the format of the operating activities section shown in Exhibit 11-3.

2. Evaluate the operating cash flow of Rising Star Talent Agency. Give the reason for your evaluation.

E11-14A. Operating activities—indirect method *(Learning Objective 3)* 10–15 min.

The March accounting records of Jackson & Associates include these accounts:

Cash			
Mar 1	5,000	Payments	448,000
Receipts	447,000		
Mar 31	4,000		

Accounts Receivable			
Mar 1	18,000	Collections	447,000
Sales	443,000		
Mar 31	14,000		

Inventory			
Mar 1	19,000	Cost of goods sold	335,000
Purchases	337,000		
Mar 31	21,000		

Accounts Payable			
Payments	332,000	Mar 1	14,000
		Purchases	337,000
		Mar 31	19,000

Accumulated Depreciation			
		Mar 1	52,000
		Depreciation	3,000
		Mar 31	55,000

Retained Earnings			
Dividends	18,000	Mar 1	64,000
		Net income	69,000
		Mar 31	115,000

Requirement

1. Compute Jackson & Associates' net cash provided by operating activities during March. Use the indirect method.

E11-15A. Prepare statement of cash flows—indirect method *(Learning Objective 3)*
20–25 min.

The income statement and additional data of Specialized Services, Inc., follow:

Specialized Services, Inc. **Income Statement** Year Ended June 30, 2010		
Revenues:		
Sales Revenue	$229,000	
Dividend Revenue	8,000	
Total Revenues		$237,000
Expenses:		
Cost of Goods Sold	$103,000	
Salary Expense	45,000	
Depreciation Expense	28,000	
Advertising Expense	12,000	
Interest Expense	2,000	
Income Tax Expense	9,000	
Total Expenses		199,000
Net Income		$ 38,000

Additional data follows:

a. Acquisition of plant assets totaled $116,000. Of this amount, $101,000 was paid in cash and a $15,000 note payable was signed for the remainder.

b. Proceeds from sale of land totaled $24,000. No gain was recognized on the sale.

c. Proceeds from issuance of common stock totaled $30,000.

d. Payment of long-term note payable was $15,000.

e. Payment of dividends was $11,000.

f. Data from the comparative balance sheet follow:

June 30	2010	2009
Current Assets:		
Cash	$26,000	$20,000
Accounts Receivable	43,000	58,000
Inventory	92,000	85,000
Current Liabilities:		
Accounts Payable	$35,000	$22,000
Accrued Liabilities	13,000	21,000

Requirements

1. Prepare Specialized Services' statement of cash flows for the year ended June 30, 2010, using the indirect method.

2. Evaluate Specialized Services' cash flows for the year. In your evaluation, mention all three categories of cash flows and give the reason for your evaluation.

E11-16A. Calculate certain investing and financing information from financial statements *(Learning Objective 3)* **10–15 min.**

Compute the following items for the statement of cash flows:

1. The beginning and ending Retained Earnings balances are $45,000 and $73,000, respectively. Net income for the period is $62,000. How much are cash dividends?

2. The beginning and ending Plant Assets, Net, balances are $103,000 and $107,000, respectively. Depreciation for the period is $16,000, and acquisitions of new plant assets total $27,000. Plant assets were sold at a $1,000 loss. What were the cash proceeds of the sale?

E11-17A. Operating activities—direct method *(Learning Objective 4)* **10–15 min.**

The accounting records of The Fenceman, Inc., reveal the following:

Net Income	$ 22,000	Payment of	
Payment of income tax	13,000	salaries and wages	$34,000
Collection of		Depreciation	12,000
dividend revenue	7,000	Payment of interest	16,000
Payment to suppliers	54,000	Payment of	
Collections from customers	102,000	dividends	7,000

Requirements

1. Compute cash flows from operating activities by the direct method.

2. Evaluate the operating cash flow of The Fenceman, Inc. Give the reason for your evaluation.

E11-18A. Prepare statement of cash flows—direct method *(Learning Objective 4)* **20–25 min.**

The income statement and additional data of Specialized Services, Inc., follow:

Specialized Services, Inc. Income Statement Year Ended June 30, 2010		
Revenues:		
Sales Revenue	$229,000	
Dividend Revenue	8,000	
Total Revenues		$237,000
Expenses:		
Cost of Goods Sold	$103,000	
Salary Expense	45,000	
Depreciation Expense	28,000	
Advertising Expense	12,000	
Interest Expense	2,000	
Income Tax Expense	9,000	
Total Expenses		199,000
Net Income		$ 38,000

Additional data follows:

a. Collections from customers are $15,000 more than sales.

b. Payments to suppliers are the sum of cost of goods sold plus advertising expense.

c. Payments to employees are $2,000 more than salary expense.

d. Dividend revenue, interest expense, and income tax expense equal their cash amounts.

e. Acquisition of plant assets for cash is $101,000.

f. Proceeds from sale of land total $24,000.

g. Proceeds from issuance of common stock for cash total $30,000.

h. Payment of long-term note payable is $15,000.

i. Payment of dividends is $11,000.

j. Cash balance, June 30, 2009, was $20,000.

Requirement

1. Prepare Specialized Services' statement of cash flows for the year ended June 30, 2010. Use the direct method.

E11-19A. Calculate certain information for direct method *(Learning Objective 4)* **10–15 min.**

Compute the following items for the statement of cash flows:

1. The beginning and ending Accounts Receivable balances are $22,000 and $18,000, respectively. Credit sales for the period total $81,000. How much are cash collections?

2. Cost of Goods Sold is $90,000. Beginning Inventory balance is $25,000, and ending Inventory balance is $21,000. Beginning and ending Accounts Payable are $11,000 and $8,000, respectively. How much are cash payments for inventory?

E11-20A. Calculate certain information for direct method *(Learning Objective 4)* **20–25 min.**

Top Ten Corporation, a nationwide insurance chain, reported the following selected amounts in its financial statements for the year ended August 31, 2010 (adapted, in millions):

Income Statement

	2010	2009
Net Sales	$24,623	$21,207
Cost of Goods Sold	18,048	15,466
Depreciation Expense	269	230
Other Expenses	4,883	4,248
Income Tax Expense	537	486
Net Income	886	777

Balance Sheet

	2010	2009
Cash and Cash Equivalents	$ 17	$ 13
Accounts Receivable	798	615
Inventories	3,482	2,831
Property and Equipment, Net	4,345	3,428
Accounts Payable	1,547	1,364
Accrued Liabilities	938	848
Long-Term Liabilities	478	464
Common Stock	676	446
Retained Earnings	4,531	3,788

Requirement

1. Determine the following for Top Ten Corporation during 2010. (Enter all amounts in millions.)

   a. Collections from customers

   b. Payments for inventory

   c. Payments of operating expenses

   d. Acquisitions of property and equipment; no sales were made during 2010

   e. Long-term borrowing, assuming Top Ten made no payments on long-term liabilities

   f. Proceeds from issuance of common stock

   g. Payment of cash dividends

EXERCISES (GROUP B)

E11-21B. Operating activities—indirect method *(Learning Objective 3)* **10–15 min.**

The accounting records of Rodeo Talent Agency reveal the following:

Net Income	$30,000
Depreciation	6,000
Sales Revenue	10,000
Decrease in current liabilities	24,000
Loss on sale of land	6,000
Increase in current assets other than Cash	15,000
Acquisition of land	42,000

Requirements

1. Compute cash flows from operating activities by the indirect method. Use the format of the operating activities section shown in Exhibit 11-3.

2. Evaluate the operating cash flow of Rodeo Talent Agency. Give the reason for your evaluation.

E11-22B. Operating activities—indirect method *(Learning Objective 3)* **10–15 min.**

The October accounting records of Morrison & Associates include these accounts:

Cash			
Oct 1	12,000	Payments	400,000
Receipts	394,000		
Oct 31	6,000		

Accounts Receivable			
Oct 1	16,000	Collections	394,000
Sales	391,000		
Oct 31	13,000		

Inventory			
Oct 1	20,000	Cost of goods sold	309,000
Purchases	321,000		
Oct 31	32,000		

Accounts Payable			
Payments	319,000	Oct 1	19,000
		Purchases	321,000
		Oct 31	21,000

Accumulated Depreciation			
		Oct 1	49,000
		Depreciation	10,000
		Oct 31	59,000

Retained Earnings			
Dividends	24,000	Oct 1	67,000
		Net income	50,000
		Oct 31	93,000

Requirement

1. Compute Morrison & Associates' net cash provided by operating activities during October. Use the indirect method.

E11-23B. Prepare statement of cash flows—indirect method *(Learning Objective 3)*
20–25 min.

The income statement and additional data of Rayborn Services, Inc., follow:

Rayborn Services, Inc. Income Statement Year Ended April 30, 2010		
Revenues:		
Sales Revenue	$262,000	
Dividend Revenue	11,000	
Total Revenues		$273,000
Expenses:		
Cost of Goods Sold	$107,000	
Salary Expense	60,000	
Depreciation Expense	18,000	
Advertising Expense	14,000	
Interest Expense	9,000	
Income Tax Expense	8,000	
Total Expenses		216,000
Net Income		$ 57,000

Additional data follows:

a. Acquisition of plant assets totaled $116,000. Of this amount, $101,000 was paid in cash and a $15,000 note payable was signed for the remainder.

b. Proceeds from the sale of land totaled $22,000. No gain was recognized on the sale.

c. Proceeds from issuance of common stock total $34,000.

d. Payment of long-term note payable was $15,000.

e. Payment of dividends was $14,000.

f. Data from the comparative balance sheet follow:

June 30	2010	2009
Current Assets:		
Cash	$30,000	$21,000
Accounts Receivable	42,000	57,000
Inventory	89,000	83,000
Current Liabilities:		
Accounts Payable	$38,000	$31,000
Accrued Liabilities	12,000	20,000

Requirements

1. Prepare Rayborn Services' statement of cash flows for the year ended April 30, 2010, using the indirect method.

2. Evaluate Rayborn Services' cash flows for the year. In your evaluation, mention all three categories of cash flows and give the reason for your evaluation.

E11-24B. Calculate certain investing and financing information from financial statements *(Learning Objective 3)* **10–15 min.**

Compute the following items for the statement of cash flows:

1. The beginning and ending Retained Earnings balances are $47,000 and $71,000, respectively. Net income for the period is $93,000. How much are cash dividends?

2. The beginning and ending Plant Assets, Net, balances are $104,000 and $113,000, respectively. Depreciation for the period is $13,000, and acquisitions of new plant assets total $30,000. Plant assets were sold at a $6,000 loss. What were the cash proceeds of the sale?

E11-25B. **Operating activities—direct method** *(Learning Objective 4)* 10–15 min.

The accounting records of Fence Up, Inc., reveal the following:

Net Income	$ 64,000	Payment of	
Payment of income tax	20,000	salaries and wages	$30,000
Collection of		Depreciation	15,000
dividend revenue	7,000	Payment of interest	18,000
Payment to suppliers	36,000	Payment of	
Collections from customers	113,000	dividends	7,000

Requirements

1. Compute cash flows from operating activities by the *direct* method.

2. Evaluate the operating cash flow of Fence Up, Inc. Give the reason for your evaluation.

E11-26B. **Prepare statement of cash flows—direct method** *(Learning Objective 4)* 20–25 min.

The income statement and additional data of Rayborn Services, Inc., follow:

Rayborn Services, Inc.
Income Statement
Year Ended April 30, 2010

Revenues:		
Sales Revenue	$262,000	
Dividend Revenue	11,000	
Total Revenues		$273,000
Expenses:		
Cost of Goods Sold	$107,000	
Salary Expense	60,000	
Depreciation Expense	18,000	
Advertising Expense	14,000	
Interest Expense	9,000	
Income Tax Expense	8,000	
Total Expenses		216,000
Net Income		$ 57,000

Additional data follows:

a. Collections from customers are $15,000 more than sales.

b. Payments to suppliers are the sum of cost of goods sold plus advertising expense.

c. Payments to employees are $7,000 more than salary expense.

d. Dividend revenue, interest expense, and income tax expense equal their cash amounts.

e. Acquisition of plant assets for cash is $101,000.

f. Proceeds from sale of land total $22,000.

g. Proceeds from issuance of common stock for cash total $34,000.

h. Payment of long-term note payable is $15,000.

i. Payment of dividends is $14,000.

j. Cash balance, April 30, 2009, was $21,000.

Requirement

1. Prepare Rayborn Services' statement of cash flows for the year ended April 30, 2010. Use the direct method.

E11-27B. Calculate certain information for direct method *(Learning Objective 4)* **10–15 min.**

Compute the following items for the statement of cash flows:

1. The beginning and ending Accounts Receivable balances are $18,000 and $22,000, respectively. Credit sales for the period total $115,000. How much are cash collections?

2. Cost of Goods Sold is $76,000. Beginning Inventory balance is $26,000, and ending Inventory balance is $28,000. Beginning and ending Accounts Payable are $15,000 and $12,000, respectively. How much are cash payments for inventory?

E11-28B. Calculate certain information for direct method *(Learning Objective 4)* **20–25 min.**

A-One Corporation, a nationwide insurance chain, reported the following selected amounts in its financial statements for the year ended March 31, 2010 (adapted, in millions):

Income Statement		
	2010	**2009**
Net Sales	$24,859	$21,099
Cost of Goods Sold	18,026	15,497
Depreciation Expense	270	230
Other Expenses	4,801	4,460
Income Tax Expense	539	488
Net Income	1,223	424

Balance Sheet		
	2010	**2009**
Cash and Cash Equivalents	$ 30	$ 28
Accounts Receivable	804	626
Inventories	3,484	3,264
Property and Equipment, Net	4,225	3,825
Accounts Payable	1,543	1,373
Accrued Liabilities	939	848
Long-Term Liabilities	450	445
Common Stock	675	575
Retained Earnings	4,936	4,502

Requirement

1. Determine the following for A-One Corporation during 2010. (Enter all amounts in millions.)

    a. Collections from customers

    b. Payments for inventory

    c. Payments of operating expenses

    d. Acquisitions of property and equipment; no sales were made during 2010

    e. Long-term borrowing, assuming A-One made no payments on long-term liabilities

    f. Proceeds from issuance of common stock

    g. Payment of cash dividends

EXERCISES (ALTERNATES 1, 2, AND 3)

These alternative exercise sets are available for your practice benefit at
www.myaccountinglab.com

PROBLEMS (GROUP A)

P11-29A. **Prepare statement of cash flows—indirect method** *(Learning Objective 3)*
20–25 min.

O'Malley Corporation accountants assembled the following data for the year
ended December 31, 2010:

O'Malley Corporation		
December 31	**2010**	**2009**
Current Assets:		
Cash and Cash Equivalents	$85,000	$22,000
Accounts Receivable	69,200	64,200
Inventory	80,000	83,000
Current Liabilities:		
Accounts Payable	$57,800	$55,800
Income Tax Payable	14,700	16,700

Transaction Data for 2010:	
Net Income	$ 57,000
Purchase of treasury stock	14,000
Issuance of common stock for cash	41,000
Loss on sale of equipment	11,000
Payment of cash dividends	18,000
Depreciation Expense	21,000
Issuance of long-term note payable in exchange for cash	34,000
Purchase of building for cash	125,000
Retirement of bonds payable by issuing common stock	65,000
Sale of equipment for cash	58,000

Quick solution:

1. Cash provided by operating
activities = $87,000;
Cash used for investing
activities = ($67,000);
Cash provided by financing
activities = $43,000

Requirement

1. Prepare O'Malley Corporation's statement of cash flows using the indirect
   method to report operating activities. List noncash investing and financing
   activities on an accompanying schedule.

P11-30A. **Prepare statement of cash flows—indirect method** *(Learning Objective 3)*
20–25 min.

Data from the comparative balance sheet of Izzie Company at March 31, 2010, follow:

March 31	2010	2009
Current Assets:		
Cash and Cash Equivalents	$ 6,200	$ 4,000
Accounts Receivable	14,900	21,700
Inventory	63,200	60,600
Current Liabilities:		
Accounts Payable	$30,100	$27,600
Accrued Liabilities	10,700	11,100
Income Tax Payable	8,000	4,700

Izzie Company's transactions during the year ended March 31, 2010, included the following:

Payment of cash dividend........	$30,000	Depreciation Expense...............	$17,300
Purchase of equipment for cash	78,700	Purchase of building for cash	47,000
Issuance of long-term note payable in exchange for cash..............................	50,000	Net Income .... Issuance of common stock	70,000 11,000

Requirements

1. Prepare Izzie Company's statement of cash flows for the year ended March 31, 2010, using the indirect method to report cash flows from operating activities.

2. Evaluate Izzie's cash flows for the year. Mention all three categories of cash flows and give the reason for your evaluation.

P11-31A. Prepare statement of cash flows—indirect method *(Learning Objective 3)* **20–25 min.**

The 2010 comparative balance sheet and income statement of A. Karev Medical Supplies follow:

A. Karev Medical Supplies
Comparative Balance Sheet
December 31, 2010 and 2009

	2010	2009	INCREASE (DECREASE)
Current Assets:			
Cash and Cash Equivalents	$ 6,700	$ 5,300	$ 1,400
Accounts Receivable	25,300	26,900	(1,600)
Inventory	91,800	89,800	2,000
Plant Assets:			
Land	89,000	60,000	29,000
Equipment, Net	53,500	49,400	4,100
Total Assets	$266,300	$231,400	$ 34,900
Current Liabilities:			
Accounts Payable	$ 30,900	$ 35,400	$ (4,500)
Accrued Liabilities	30,600	28,600	2,000
Long-Term Liabilities:			
Notes Payable	75,000	100,000	(25,000)
Stockholders' Equity:			
Common Stock	88,300	64,700	23,600
Retained Earnings	41,500	2,700	38,800
Total Liabilities and Stockholders' Equity	$266,300	$231,400	$ 34,900

A. Karev Medical Supplies
Income Statement
Year Ended December 31, 2010

Revenues:		
Sales Revenue	$213,000	
Interest Revenue	8,600	
Total Revenues		$221,600
Expenses:		
Cost of Goods Sold	$ 70,600	
Salary Expense	27,800	
Depreciation Expense	4,000	
Other Operating Expenses	10,500	
Interest Expense	11,600	
Income Tax Expense	29,100	
Total Expenses		153,600
Net Income		**$ 68,000**

A. Karev Medical Supplies had no noncash investing and financing transactions during 2010. During the year, A. Karev Medical Supplies made no sales of land or equipment, no issuance of notes payable, no retirement of stock, and no treasury stock transactions.

Requirements

1. Prepare the 2010 statement of cash flows, formatting operating activities by the indirect method.

2. How will what you learned in this problem help you evaluate an investment in A. Karev Medical Supplies?

P11-32A. Prepare statement of cash flows—direct method (*Learning Objective 4*)
20–25 min.

The accounting records for R. Webber Associates, Inc., for the year ended April 30, 2010, contain the following information:

a. Purchase of plant assets for cash, $59,400
b. Proceeds from issuance of common stock, $8,000
c. Payment of dividends, $48,400
d. Collection of interest, $4,400
e. Payment of salaries, $93,600
f. Proceeds from sale of plant assets, $22,400
g. Collections from customers, $620,500
h. Cash receipt of dividend revenue, $4,100
i. Payments to suppliers, $368,500
j. Depreciation expense, $59,900
k. Proceeds from issuance of long-term notes, $19,600
l. Payments of long-term notes payable, $50,000
m. Interest expense and payments, $13,300
n. Income tax expense and payments, $37,900
o. Cash balances: April 30, 2009, $39,300; April 30, 2010, $47,200

Requirement

1. Prepare R. Webber Associates' statement of cash flows for the year ended April 30, 2010. Use the direct method for cash flows from operating activities.

P11-33A. Prepare statement of cash flows—direct method (*Learning Objective 4*)
20–25 min.

Use the A. Karev Medical Supplies data from P11-31A. The cash amounts for Interest Revenue, Salary Expense, Interest Expense, and Income Tax Expense are the same as the accrual amounts for these items.

Requirements

1. Prepare the 2010 statement of cash flows by the direct method.
2. How will what you learned in this problem help you evaluate an investment in A. Karev Medical Supplies?

P11-34A. Prepare statement of cash flows—direct method (*Learning Objective 4*)
20–25 min.

To prepare the statement of cash flows, accountants for C. Yang, Inc., summarized 2010 activity in the Cash account as follows:

Cash			
Beginning balance	53,600	Payment on accounts payable	399,100
Receipts of interest	17,100	Payment of dividends	27,200
Collections from customers	673,700	Payment of salaries and wages	143,800
Issuance of common stock	47,300	Payment of interest	26,900
		Payment for equipment	10,200
		Payment of operating expenses	34,300
		Payment of notes payable	67,700
		Payment of income tax	18,900
Ending balance	63,600		

Requirement

1. Prepare the statement of cash flows of C. Yang, Inc., for the year ended December 31, 2010, using the direct method for operating activities.

PROBLEMS (GROUP B)

P11-35B. Prepare statement of cash flows—indirect method (*Learning Objective 3*)
20–25 min.

Morgensen Corporation accountants assembled the following data for the year ended December 31, 2010:

Morgensen Corporation		
December 31	2010	2009
Current Assets:		
Cash and Cash Equivalents	$85,000	$23,000
Accounts Receivable	69,600	64,700
Inventory	80,900	83,500
Current Liabilities:		
Accounts Payable	$57,700	$55,600
Income Tax Payable	14,800	16,400

Transaction Data for 2010:	
Net Income	$ 57,800
Purchase of treasury stock	14,500
Issuance of common stock for cash	36,200
Loss on sale of equipment...	11,000
Payment of cash dividends	18,100
Depreciation Expense...	21,900
Issuance of long-term note payable in exchange for cash	34,500
Purchase of building for cash	122,000
Retirement of bonds payable by issuing common stock.....................	62,000
Sale of equipment for cash	57,000

Requirement

1. Prepare Morgensen Corporation's statement of cash flows using the indirect method to report operating activities. List noncash investing and financing activities on an accompanying schedule.

P11-36B. **Prepare statement of cash flows—indirect method** *(Learning Objective 3)* 20–25 min.

Data from the comparative balance sheet of Johnson Company, at March 31, 2010, follow:

March 31	2010	2009
Current Assets:		
Cash and Cash Equivalents	$13,400	$ 4,600
Accounts Receivable...	14,800	21,400
Inventory...	54,300	53,600
Current Liabilities:		
Accounts Payable..	$29,000	$28,400
Accrued Liabilities...	14,600	16,200
Income Tax Payable	8,300	4,800

Johnson Company's transactions during the year ended March 31, 2010, included the following:

Payment of cash dividend........	$33,500	Depreciation Expense...............	$17,500
Purchase of		Purchase of	
equipment for cash	78,300	building for cash	47,800
Issuance of long-term		Net Income	73,500
note payable in exchange		Issuance of	
for cash	56,000	common stock	13,000

Requirements

1. Prepare Johnson Company's statement of cash flows for the year ended March 31, 2010, using the indirect method to report cash flows from operating activities.

2. Evaluate Johnson Company's cash flows for the year. Mention all three categories of cash flows and give the reason for your evaluation.

P11-37B. Prepare statement of cash flows—indirect method *(Learning Objective 3)*
20–25 min.

The 2010 comparative balance sheet and income statement of Goldman Medical Supplies, follow:

Goldman Medical Supplies
Comparative Balance Sheet
December 31, 2010 and 2009

	2010	2009	INCREASE (DECREASE)
Current Assets:			
Cash and Cash Equivalents	$ 6,700	$ 5,400	$ 1,300
Accounts Receivable	25,200	26,800	(1,600)
Inventory	91,500	89,600	1,900
Plant Assets:			
Land	89,200	60,300	28,900
Equipment, Net	53,200	49,200	4,000
Total Assets	$265,800	$231,300	$ 34,500
Current Liabilities:			
Accounts Payable	$ 30,200	$ 35,400	$ (5,200)
Accrued Liabilities	30,400	28,100	2,300
Long-Term Liabilities:			
Notes Payable	72,000	100,000	(28,000)
Stockholders' Equity:			
Common Stock	88,900	64,700	24,200
Retained Earnings	44,300	3,100	41,200
Total Liabilities and Stockholders' Equity	$265,800	$231,300	$ 34,500

Goldman Medical Supplies
Income Statement
Year Ended December 31, 2010

Revenues:		
Sales Revenue	$217,000	
Interest Revenue	8,500	
Total Revenues		225,500
Expenses:		
Cost of Goods Sold	$ 70,700	
Salary Expense	27,400	
Depreciation Expense	4,400	
Other Operating Expenses	10,400	
Interest Expense	11,100	
Income Tax Expense	29,700	
Total Expenses		153,700
Net Income		$ 71,800

Goldman Medical Supplies had no noncash investing and financing transactions during 2010. During the year, Goldman Medical Supplies made no sales of land or equipment, no issuance of notes payable, no retirement of stock, and no treasury stock transactions.

Requirements

1. Prepare the 2010 statement of cash flows, formatting operating activities by the indirect method.

2. How will what you learned in this problem help you evaluate an investment in Goldman Medical Supplies?

P11-38B. Prepare statement of cash flows—direct method *(Learning Objective 4)*
20–25 min.

The accounting records for L. Lee Associates, Inc., for the year ended April 30, 2010, contain the following information:

a. Purchase of plant assets, $55,400

b. Proceeds from issuance of common stock, $45,000

c. Payment of dividends, $44,400

d. Collection of interest, $8,500

e. Payments of salaries, $93,600

f. Proceeds from sale of plant assets, $27,000

g. Collections from customers, $630,000

h. Cash receipt of dividend revenue, $4,600

i. Payments to suppliers, $374,800

j. Depreciation expense, $58,500

k. Proceeds from issuance of long-term notes, $46,100

l. Payments of long-term notes payable, $39,000

m. Interest expense and payments, $14,000

n. Income tax expense and payments, $45,000

o. Cash balance: April 30, 2009, $39,400; April 30, 2010, $134,400

Requirement

1. Prepare L. Lee Associates' statement of cash flows for the year ended April 30, 2010. Use the direct method for cash flows from operating activities.

P11-39B. Prepare statement of cash flows—direct method *(Learning Objective 4)*
20–25 min.

Use the Goldman Medical Supplies data from P11-37B. The cash amounts for Interest Revenue, Salary Expense, Interest Expense, and Income Tax Expense are the same as the accrual amounts for these items.

Requirements

1. Prepare the 2010 statement of cash flows by the direct method.

2. How will what you learned in this problem help you evaluate an investment in Goldman Medical Supplies?

P11-40B. Prepare statement of cash flows—direct method *(Learning Objective 4)*
20–25 min.

To prepare the statement of cash flows, accountants for H. Laurie, Inc., summarized 2010 activity in the Cash account as follows:

Cash			
Beginning balance	91,700	Payment on accounts payable	347,400
Receipts of interest	15,100	Payment of dividends	30,000
Collections from customers	492,300	Payment of salaries and wages	63,500
Issuance of common stock	90,000	Payment of interest	21,100
		Payment for equipment	11,000
		Payment of operating expenses	21,100
		Payment of notes payable	77,000
		Payment of income tax	18,900
Ending balance	99,100		

Requirement

1. Prepare the statement of cash flows of H. Laurie, Inc., for the year ended December 31, 2010, using the direct method for operating activities.

PROBLEMS (ALTERNATES 1, 2, AND 3)

These alternative problem sets are available for your practice benefit at
www.myaccountinglab.com

CONTINUING EXERCISE

This exercise continues the accounting for Graham's Yard Care, Inc., from the continuing exercise in Chapter 10. Assume that Graham's Yard Care, Inc., had the following comparative balance sheet at the end of 2011, its second year of operations.

Graham's Yard Care, Inc. Comparative Balance Sheet December 31, 2011 and 2010		2011	2010
ASSETS			
Cash		$1,500	$6,480
Accounts Receivable		2,200	150
Lawn Supplies		150	70
Equipment		4,900	1,400
(Less Accumulated Depreciation)		(495)	(146)
Total Assets		$8,255	$7,954
LIABILITIES			
Accounts Payable		$ 350	$1,400
Notes Payable			5,000
STOCKHOLDERS' EQUITY			
Common Stock		2,000	1,000
Retained Earnings		5,905	554
Total Liabilities and Stockholders' Equity		$8,255	$7,954

Requirement

1. Prepare the statement of cash flows for Graham's Yard Care, Inc., for 2011 using the indirect method. The following additional information applies to 2011:

   ■ Common stock was issued at par value.

   ■ No dividends were declared or paid during the year.

   ■ No equipment was sold during the year and all purchases of equipment were for cash.

CONTINUING PROBLEM

In this problem, we continue our accounting for Aqua Elite, Inc., from Chapter 10. We will assume that Aqua Elite, Inc., is now in its second year of operations.

Assume that the comparative balance sheet for Aqua Elite, Inc., at July 31, 2011, and the income statement for the month ended July 31, 2011, are as follows.

Aqua Elite, Inc.
Comparative Balance Sheets
July 31 and June 30, 2011

	July 31	June 30
ASSETS		
Cash	$ 5,333	$3,270
Accounts Receivable, net	2,280	1,000
Inventory	4,175	180
Supplies	105	125
Total Current Assets	11,893	4,575
Fixed Assets	67,250	2,250
Less: Accumulated Depreciation	(352)	(47)
Net Fixed Assets	66,898	2,203
Total Assets	$78,791	$6,778
LIABILITIES		
Accounts Payable	$ 1,805	$ 450
Unearned Revenue	5,800	2,000
Salary Payable	950	900
Interest Payable	375	17
Payroll Taxes Payable	188	—
Dividend Payable	500	—
Current Portion of Long-Term Debt	4,410	2,000
Total Current Liabilities	14,028	5,367
Notes Payable	20,000	—
Mortgage Payable	42,590	—
Total Liabilities	76,618	5,367
STOCKHOLDERS' EQUITY		
Common Stock	1,000	1,000
Retained Earnings	1,173	411
Total Stockholders' Equity	2,173	1,411
Total Liabilities & Stockholders' Equity	$78,791	$6,778

Aqua Elite, Inc.
Income Statement
Month Ended July 31, 2011

Revenue	$6,300
Expenses:	
Cost of Goods Sold	1,080
Depreciation Expense	305
Bad Debt Expense	220
Interest Expense	375
Insurance Expense	150
Supplies Expense	210
Salary Expense	2,400
Payroll Taxes Expense	268
Bank Service Fees	30
Net Income*	$1,262

*Income taxes ignored

Additional information follows:

Aqua Elite, Inc., purchased a $20,000 truck financed with a note payable; it purchased a $45,000 building site financed with a mortgage payable; and it did not sell any fixed assets during the month.

Requirement

1. Prepare the statement of cash flows using the indirect method for the month of July.

APPLY YOUR KNOWLEDGE

ETHICS IN ACTION

Case 1. Design Incorporated experienced a downturn in December sales. To make matters worse, many of the recent sales were on account and because many customers were not paying on their accounts, the ending balance of Accounts Receivable at December 31 was higher than the beginning balance. Because the business had a dramatic need for cash, a prime piece of land owned by the company was sold for cash in December at a substantial gain. Design had purchased the land 10 years earlier and properly classified it as a long-term investment. The CEO, Jim Shady, was looking over the financial statements and saw the company's weak operating cash flows. He approached the accountant to ask why the December cash flows provided from operations were so weak, given that the land had been sold. The accountant explained that because the indirect method was used in preparing the cash flow statement, certain adjustments to net income were required. To begin with, the increase in accounts receivable was a decreasing adjustment made in arriving at the net cash provided from operating activities. Next, the large gain recognized on the sale of land had to be adjusted by subtracting it from the net income in arriving at the cash provided by operating activities. These large negative adjustments drastically reduced the reported cash provided from that category of cash flows. The accountant then explained that all the cash proceeds from the land sale were included as cash inflows in the investing activities section.

Jim became worried because he remembered the bank telling him about the importance of strong operating cash flows, so he told the accountant to redo the statement but not to reduce the net income by the accounts receivable increase or the gain on the land sale. The accountant refused because these adjustments were necessary in order to properly arrive at the net cash provided from operating activities. If these adjustments were not made, then the net change in cash could not be reconciled. Jim finally agreed but then told the accountant to just include the cash proceeds from the sale of land in the operating activities rather than in the investing activities. The accountant said that would be wrong. Besides, everyone would know that proceeds from the sale of land should be an investing activity. Jim then suggested listing it as "other" in the operating section so no one would ever know that it wasn't an operating cash flow.

Why didn't Jim want the accountant to decrease the net income by the increase in accounts receivable and the gain on the land sale? Why do you think Jim finally agreed with the accountant? Could the operating cash flows be increased by including the cash proceeds from the sale but listing them as "other" rather than as land sale proceeds? What ethical concerns are involved? Do you have any other thoughts?

Case 2. Kevin Sailors, the CEO of Candle Corporation, was discussing the financial statements with the company accountant. Weak cash flows had resulted in the company borrowing a lot of money. Kevin wanted to know why the money borrowed was included as cash inflows in the financing section of the statement of cash flows but the interest paid on the amounts borrowed was not. The accountant replied that the interest paid on loans was an expense included in the calculation of net income, which was in the operating activities section. Kevin then asked why the dividends Candle Corporation paid to stockholders were included as an outflow of cash in the financing section. The accountant then explained that dividends paid, unlike interest paid, were a return to stockholders and not an expense; there-fore, it would not be included in net income, nor would it appear in the operating activities section. Kevin replied that he did not care, and instructed the accountant to include both the interest paid and the dividends paid in the financing section. The accountant said that such a move would not be proper. Kevin then said to not provide the statement of cash flows at all because too many people would see the weakening operating cash flows. He further stated that investors and creditors who really analyzed the income statements and balance sheets would be able to understand the company without the need for a statement of cash flows spelling out the net changes in cash flows.

Why would Kevin want the interest paid to be included in the financing activities section? Why would the accountant state that interest paid should not be included in the financing activities section? Can the statement of cash flows be omitted? What ethical issues are involved? Do you have any additional thoughts?

KNOW YOUR BUSINESS

FINANCIAL ANALYSIS

Purpose: To help familiarize you with the financial reporting of a real company in order to further your understanding of the chapter material you are learning.

This case focuses on the cash flows of Columbia Sportswear. Recall that inflows and outflows of cash are classified as operating activities, investing activities, or financing activities. The statement of cash flows presents cash flows from each of these three activities. It is, therefore, important to understand the information provided in this revealing financial statement. The statement of cash flows and additional related information for Columbia Sportswear are disclosed in its annual report found in Appendix A.

Requirements

1. Look at the operating activities section of the statements of cash flows. Compare the net cash provided by operating activities to the net income for each of the three years presented. Are the net income amounts reported on the cash flow statement the same as on the income statement? How does the total cash flows provided by operations compare to the net income? Why do they differ? Is this difference good or bad? Have the cash flows provided from operations been increasing or decreasing? On average, what is the largest adjustment item in the operating cash flows section? Why is this amount added back each year?

2. Look at the investing activities section of the statements of cash flows. What has created the largest inflows and outflows of cash related to investing activities? Can you determine whether Columbia Sportswear has been spending money to purchase more property and equipment? Did investing activities provide or use cash for the three years presented?

3. Look at the financing activities section of the statements of cash flows. Did financing activities provide or require cash for the three fiscal years presented? What is the significance of this information? What are the stock repurchase and dividend trends? What was the largest item in the financing section for the most recent year?

4. How do you feel about the overall sufficiency of cash flows? Does the cash provided from operations cover the cash required for investing activities? Does the cash provided from operations cover the cash required for financing activities?

5. What was the net change in cash and cash equivalents for the most recent fiscal year? Does the ending cash amount agree with the cash and cash equivalents reported on the balance sheet? Do you have any other observations about the statement of cash flows?

INDUSTRY ANALYSIS

Purpose: To help you understand and compare the performance of two companies in the same industry.

Find the Columbia Sportswear Company Annual Report located in Appendix A and go to the Consolidated Statements of Cash Flows on page 683. Now access the 2008 Annual Report for Under Armour, Inc., from the Internet. Go to their Web page for Investor Relations at *http://investor.underarmour.com/investors.cfm* and under Downloads on the right-hand side, go to 2008 Annual Report. The company's Consolidated Statements of Cash Flows is on page 52.

Requirement

1. Which method (direct or indirect) does each of these companies use to prepare their statement of cash flow? How can you tell? Which activities provided cash for each of the companies? Which activities used cash for each of these companies? What conclusions can you draw from these results?

SMALL BUSINESS ANALYSIS

Purpose: To help you understand the importance of cash flows in the operation of a small business.

You just received your year-end financial statements from your CPA. Although receiving the year-end financial package is important every year for your financing institutions and your investors, it is especially important this year because of the potential investment opportunity that just became available to you. Yesterday you got a telephone call from one of your competitors with whom you have been discussing the possibility of a merger. The gist of the conversation was that the board of directors wanted to sell outright to you instead of merging. You're pretty happy about that except for the fact that it could create some potential cash flow problems. The other company wants $1,000,000 cash and it wants to do it soon or the deal is off. You've got that amount of cash and cash equivalents available right now, but you know there are some cash commitments coming up soon for capital expenditures and dividend payments. You decide to call one of your financial investors. He or she suggests that you calculate free cash flow from the end of the year to determine if that amount of cash is available to complete the deal.

You look at your statement of cash flows from the financial statements and see that cash flows from operations was $1,725,000 and you expect that same amount for this year. From the capital budget, anticipated capital expenditures in the short term are $550,000. And from the board of director's minutes of the last meeting, the cash dividend approved for payout next month is $275,000.

Requirement

1. Define free cash flow and calculate it based on the information previously provided. With your understanding of free cash flow, is this new investment something that this company should pursue?

WRITTEN COMMUNICATION

You have been asked by your accounting professor to prepare a paper outlining the importance of the statement of cash flows, the details of what is included in each of the three sections of the statement, and how it provides a link between the income statement and the balance sheet.

12 Financial Statement Analysis

Throughout the book you have learned about the process of accounting. You have learned how to account for the transactions of a business and how to report the results of those transactions in the financial statements. However, have you ever wondered how the financial statements are utilized by managers, investors, and creditors to assess the performance of a business? In Chapter 12 you will learn several tools that can be applied to the financial statements to help assess a company's performance.

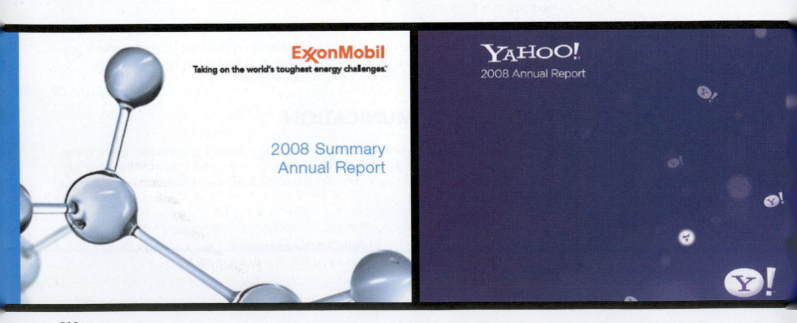

Chapter Outline:

Learning Objectives

1. Understand items on corporate income statements

2. Perform a horizontal analysis of financial statements

3. Perform a vertical analysis of financial statements

4. Compare one company to another using common-size financial statements and benchmarking

5. Compute various financial ratios

In Chapter 1, we learned that the study of accounting is important because it teaches us about the "language of business." In this chapter we will learn that another important reason to study accounting is that it teaches us how to use financial information to make better decisions. Managers, investors, and creditors can all benefit from being able to make better decisions regarding the performance of a company. As we begin our discussion of financial statement analysis, there are several important points that should be considered.

❶ Financial statement analysis usually does not indicate that a problem definitely exists within a company. Also, even if a problem does exist, financial statement analysis generally will not identify what the specific problem is. Instead, financial statement analysis indicates that a problem may exist and it gives clues as to what the problem might be.

❷ A company's performance is best evaluated by examining more than one year's data. This is why most financial statements cover at least two periods. In fact, most financial analysis covers trends of up to five years.

❸ A company's performance is best evaluated by comparing it against the following:

- Its own past performance
- The performance of competitors
- Industry averages for the industry the company is in

🌐 Accounting in Your World

So just how bad did you do on that test?

Have you ever received a test or an assignment back and, after looking at your score, you were sure you failed? Then you you found out your score wasn't so bad after all because there were only 80 points possible. Or perhaps you found out that your score, although low, was higher than the class average. Until you had a point of reference, your raw score did not tell the whole story about your performance. The results of financial statement analysis are similar. The results of financial statement analysis have minimal value without a point of reference. This is why, when conducting financial statement analysis, a company's performance is compared to past performance and industry averages.

There are three main ways to analyze financial statements:

- Horizontal analysis
- Vertical analysis
- Ratio analysis

Before we begin our discussion of financial statement analysis, let's take a closer look at the income statements of a corporation.

WHAT IS THE DIFFERENCE BETWEEN OPERATING INCOME AND NET INCOME ON THE INCOME STATEMENT?

Understand items on corporate income statements

In Chapter 4 we examined the multi-step income statement format. Recall that the multi-step format provides detailed information about the items comprising net income so that financial statement users can make more informed decisions about a company's results of operations. Corporate income statements often contain additional items that are reported in order to better inform users about a company's results of operations. The income items we will examine are as follows:

- Continuing operations
- Discontinued operations
- Extraordinary items
- Effects of changes in accounting principles

For illustration purposes, refer to the income statement for Best Way, Inc., presented in **Exhibit 12-1** on the following page.

Income from Continuing Operations

In Exhibit 12-1, the top most section reports income from continuing operations. Continuing operations consist of business activities that will most likely continue from period to period. Reporting income from continuing operations, therefore, helps investors make predictions about a company's future earnings. The continuing operations of Best Way, Inc., include two items that need explanation:

- *Other income (expense)* includes items that, although a normal part of business operations, fall outside of a company's core business activities. Therefore, these items are not included in sales, cost of goods sold, or operating expenses but are instead reported separately. Gains and losses on the sale of fixed assets as well as interest income and interest expense are examples of items reported as part of other income (expense). Best Way, Inc., reported interest expense of $32,000 and a loss on the sale of fixed assets of $14,000.
- *Income tax expense* reflects the income tax expense that is assessed on the company's operating income. Best Way, Inc., was assessed $72,000 of income tax on its operating income.

After continuing operations, an income statement may include the following items:

- Discontinued operations
- Extraordinary gains and losses

Best Way, Inc. Income Statement Year Ended December 31, 2010	
Net Sales Revenue	$1,877,000
Cost of Goods Sold	1,145,000
Gross Profit	732,000
Operating Expenses (detailed)	423,000
Operating Income	309,000
Other income (expense):	
Interest Expense	(32,000)
Loss on Sale of Fixed Assets	(14,000)
Income from continuing operations before income tax	263,000
Income tax expense	72,000
Income from continuing operations	191,000
Income from discontinued operations, net of income tax of $26,000	68,000
Income before extraordinary items	259,000
Extraordinary loss from hurricane, net of tax savings of $17,000	(42,000)
Net Income	$ 217,000
Earnings per share of common stock (100,000 shares outstanding):	
Income from continuing operations	$ 1.91
Income from discontinued operations	0.68
Extraordinary loss	(0.42)
Net Income	2.17

Exhibit 12-1 ▲

Discontinued Operations

Corporations often consist of many different business segments. A business segment is a distinguishable part of a business that is subject to a different set of risks and returns than other parts of the business. Information on any of the company's segments that have been sold (or otherwise discontinued) is reported separately from the results of continuing operations. This is because the discontinued segment will not be part of the company's operations in the future. The results of discontinued operations are generally reported net of income tax expense (or income tax savings in the case of a loss). Best Way, Inc., reported net income from discontinued operations of $68,000. This amount represents income of $94,000 less income tax expense of $26,000.

Extraordinary Gains and Losses

Extraordinary gains and losses, also called extraordinary items, are both unusual and infrequent in nature. Losses from natural disasters (floods, earthquakes, hurricanes, and tornadoes) and the taking of company assets by a foreign government (expropriation) are extraordinary items. Extraordinary items are generally reported net of their income tax effects and are reported separately from continuing operations because of their infrequent nature. Best Way, Inc., reported an extraordinary loss from a hurricane of $42,000 (net). This amount represents a loss of $59,000 net of tax savings of $17,000.

Effects of Changes in Accounting Principles

Occasionally, a company will change from the application of one accounting principle to another. For example, a business may change from LIFO to FIFO inventory valuation. Prior to 2006, the cumulative effect of a change in accounting principles was reported as a separate line item on the income statement. Beginning in 2006, GAAP requires retrospective application to account for the effects of most changes in accounting principles. Retrospective application means that a change in accounting principle is accounted for by restating comparative financial statements to reflect the new method as though it had been applied all along.

Earnings per Share

The final segment of a corporate income statement reports the company's earnings per share, abbreviated as EPS. Earnings per share reports the amount of net income for each share of the company's *outstanding common stock.* The computation of EPS is discussed later in the chapter. Corporations report a separate EPS figure for each element of income. Some corporations must report two sets of EPS figures, as follows:

- Basic EPS—EPS based on outstanding common shares.
- Diluted EPS—EPS based on outstanding common shares plus the additional shares of common stock that would arise if convertible preferred stock (or other dilutive items) were exchanged for common shares. Diluted EPS is always lower than basic EPS.

Best Way, Inc., had no convertible (dilutive) items and therefore reported only one set of EPS figures for each element of income.

Now let's examine financial statement analysis. As previously discussed, the three most popular forms of financial statement analysis are horizontal analysis, vertical analysis, and ratio analysis. We will begin our discussion with horizontal analysis.

WHAT IS HORIZONTAL ANALYSIS?

Perform a horizontal analysis of financial statements

The study of percentage changes in the line items on comparative financial statements is called **horizontal analysis**. Although it can be useful to know if individual financial statement amounts (such as sales, wages expense, or accounts receivable) have increased or decreased from the prior period, the *percentage change* is often more relevant and, therefore, more helpful to know. For example, sales may have increased by $80,000, but considered alone, this fact is not very helpful. For some companies, an $80,000 increase in sales would be significant while for others, it would be minor. It is better to know by what percentage sales have increased from the prior year. For instance, knowing that sales have increased by 15% is more meaningful than knowing sales increased by $80,000.

To compute the percentage change in the line items on comparative financial statements

❶ compute the dollar amount of the change from the earlier period to the later period.

❷ divide the dollar amount of change by the earlier period amount and multiply by 100. We call the earlier period the base period.

To illustrate horizontal analysis let's consider the comparative income statement and balance sheet for Tucker Enterprises presented in **Exhibits 12-2** and **12-3**.

Tucker Enterprises, Inc. Income Statement Years Ended December 31, 2010 and 2009		
(in thousands)	**2010**	**2009**
Net Sales	$824	$596
Cost of Goods Sold	375	277
Gross Profit	449	319
Operating Expenses:		
Selling, General, and Administrative	213	167
Other	48	34
Income Before Income Tax	188	118
Income Tax Expense	33	21
Net Income	$155	$ 97

Exhibit 12-2 ▲

Tucker Enterprises, Inc. Balance Sheet December 31, 2010 and 2009		
(in thousands)	**2010**	**2009**
Assets		
Current Assets:		
Cash and Cash Equivalents	$ 36	$ 47
Accounts Receivable, Net	61	52
Inventory	144	116
Total Current Assets	241	215
Property, Plant, and Equipment, Net	319	179
Total Assets	$560	$394
Liabilities		
Current Liabilities:		
Accounts Payable	$121	$ 74
Accrued Liabilities	24	33
Total Current Liabilities	145	107
Long-Term Liabilities	173	104
Total Liabilities	318	211
Stockholders' Equity		
Common Stock	35	30
Retained Earnings	207	153
Total Stockholders' Equity	242	183
Total Liabilities and Stockholders' Equity	$560	$394

Exhibit 12-3 ▲

The increase in sales is computed as follows:

Step 1 Compute the dollar amount of change in sales from 2009 to 2010:

$$\frac{\text{2010 amount}}{\$824} - \frac{\text{2009 amount}}{\$596} = \frac{\text{Dollar change}}{\$228}$$

Step 2 Compute the percentage change for the period by dividing the dollar amount of change by the base-period (2009) amount and multiplying the result by 100:

$$\text{Percentage change} = \frac{\text{Dollar change}}{\text{Base period amount}} \times 100 = \frac{\$228}{\$596} \times 100 = 38.3\% \text{ (rounded)}$$

The percentage changes in the remaining items are computed in the same manner. The completed horizontal analyses for Tucker Enterprises' financial statements are shown in **Exhibits 12-4** below and **12-5** on the next page.

Horizontal Analysis of the Income Statement

Tucker Enterprises' comparative income statement reveals strong growth during 2010. The 38.3% increase in Sales coupled with only a 35.4% increase in Cost of Goods Sold resulted in an increase in Gross Profit of 40.8%. The item on Tucker Enterprises' income statement with the lowest growth rate is Selling, General, and Administrative Expense, with an increase of only 27.5%. Even though Other Operating Expenses and Income Tax Expense increased by 41.2% and 57.1% respectively, they were the smallest dollar amounts on the income statement. So, on the bottom line, Net Income grew by a very respectable 59.8%.

Horizontal Analysis of the Balance Sheet

Tucker Enterprises' comparative balance sheet also shows significant growth with total assets increasing by 42.1%. Accounts Receivable and Inventory increased 17.3% and 24.1% respectively. These increases are likely related to the increase in Sales during the year. Cash actually decreased by 23.4%, which could be a concern for Tucker Enterprises' management. If a decrease in cash becomes a trend, the company could face cash flow problems in the future. Tucker Enterprises' Property, Plant, and Equipment also grew notably at a rate of 78.2%.

Tucker Enterprises, Inc.
Income Statement
Years Ended December 31, 2010 and 2009

(in thousands)	2010	2009	INCREASE (DECREASE) AMOUNT	PERCENTAGE
Net Sales	$824	$596	$228	38.3%
Cost of Goods Sold	375	277	98	35.4
Gross Profit	449	319	130	40.8
Operating Expenses:				
Selling, General, and Administrative	213	167	46	27.5
Other	48	34	14	41.2
Income Before Income Tax	188	118	70	59.3
Income Tax Expense	33	21	12	57.1
Net Income	$155	$ 97	58	59.8%

Exhibit 12-4 ▲

(in thousands)	2010	2009	INCREASE (DECREASE) AMOUNT	INCREASE (DECREASE) PERCENTAGE
Assets				
Current Assets:				
Cash and Cash Equivalents	$ 36	$ 47	$ (11)	(23.4)%
Accounts Receivable, Net	61	52	9	17.3
Inventory	144	116	28	24.1
Total Current Assets	241	215	26	12.1
Property, Plant, and Equipment, Net	319	179	140	78.2
Total Assets	$560	$394	$166	42.1 %
Liabilities				
Current Liabilities:				
Accounts Payable	$121	$ 74	$ 47	63.5
Accrued Liabilities	24	33	(9)	(27.3)
Total Current Liabilities	145	107	38	35.5
Long-Term Liabilities	173	104	69	66.3
Total Liabilities	318	211	107	50.7
Stockholders' Equity				
Common Stock	35	30	5	16.7
Retained Earnings	207	153	54	35.3
Total Stockholders' Equity	242	183	59	32.2
Total Liabilities and Stockholders' Equity	$560	$394	$166	42.1 %

Tucker Enterprises, Inc.
Balance Sheet
December 31, 2010 and 2009

Exhibit 12-5 ▲

Total liabilities increased by 50.7%. Accounts Payable increased notably at a rate of 63.5%, however, Accrued Liabilities actually decreased by 27.3%. The 66.3% increase in Long-Term Liabilities is probably not a concern for management as it is most likely related to the increase in Property, Plant, and Equipment. The strong growth in Net Income for the year helped Tucker Enterprises achieve a 32.2% increase in total stockholders' equity during 2010.

Trend Percentages

Trend percentages are a form of horizontal analysis. Trends indicate the direction a business is taking. How have sales changed over a five-year period? What trend does net income show? These questions can be answered by looking at trend percentages over a period of time, such as three to five years. To calculate trend percentages, a base-year must first be selected. The base-year amounts are then set equal to 100%. Next, the amounts for each subsequent year are expressed as a percentage of the base-year amount. To compute trend percentages, divide each item for the years following the base-year by the base-year amount and multiply the result by 100.

$$\text{Trend percentage} = \frac{\text{Any year \$}}{\text{Base year \$}} \times 100$$

Let's assume Tucker Enterprises' Net Sales were $387,000 in 2006 and rose to $824,000 in 2010. To illustrate trend analysis, let's review the trend of Net Sales during 2006–2010, with dollars in thousands. The base year is 2006, so that year's percentage is set equal to 100. We compute the trend percentages by dividing each year's net sales amount by the 2006 net sales amount and multiplying the result by 100.

(in thousands)	2010	2009	2008	2007	2006
Net Sales...	$ 824	$ 596	$ 467	$ 411	$387
Trend Percentage................................	212.9%	154.0%	120.7%	106.2%	100%

The trend analysis shows that Tucker Enterprises' Net Sales increased moderately from 2006 to 2008 and then more significantly in 2009 and substantially in 2010. You can perform a trend analysis on any one, or multiple items, you consider important. Trend analysis is widely used to predict future performance.

WHAT IS VERTICAL ANALYSIS?

Perform a vertical analysis
of financial statements **3**

In addition to a horizontal analysis, a **vertical analysis** can also be performed to help evaluate a company's performance. A vertical analysis of a financial statement reflects each item on the financial statement as a percentage of another item (the base amount) on the financial statement. The vertical analysis percentages are calculated as follows:

$$\text{Vertical analysis percentage} = \frac{\text{Financial statement item \$}}{\text{Base amount \$}} \times 100$$

On the income statement, net sales is used as the base amount and is shown as 100%. On the balance sheet, total assets is used as the base amount and is shown as 100%. The completed vertical analysis of Tucker Enterprises' 2009 and 2010 income statement and balance sheet is presented in **Exhibits 12-6** and **12-7**.

Tucker Enterprises, Inc.
Income Statement
Years Ended December 31, 2010 and 2009

(in thousands)	2010	PERCENT	2009	PERCENT
Net Sales	$824	100.0%	$596	100.0%
Cost of Goods Sold	375	45.5	277	46.5
Gross Profit	449	54.5	319	53.5
Operating Expenses:				
Selling, General, and Administrative	213	25.8	167	28.0
Other	48	5.8	34	5.7
Income Before Income Tax	188	22.8	118	19.8
Income Tax Expense	33	4.0	21	3.5
Net Income	$155	18.8%	$ 97	16.3%

Exhibit 12-6 ▲

(in thousands)	2010	PERCENT	2009	PERCENT
Tucker Enterprises, Inc.				
Balance Sheet				
December 31, 2010 and 2009				
Assets				
Current Assets:				
Cash and Cash Equivalents	$ 36	6.4%	$ 47	11.9%
Accounts Receivable, Net	61	10.9	52	13.2
Inventory	144	25.7	116	29.4
Total Current Assets	241	43.0	215	54.6
Property, Plant, and Equipment, Net	319	57.0	179	45.4
Total Assets	$560	100.0%	$394	100.0%
Liabilities				
Current Liabilities:				
Accounts Payable	$121	21.6%	$ 74	18.8%
Accrued Liabilities	24	4.3	33	8.4
Total Current Liabilities	145	25.9	107	27.2
Long-Term Liabilities	173	30.9	104	26.4
Total Liabilities	318	56.8	211	53.6
Stockholders' Equity				
Common Stock	35	6.3	30	7.6
Retained Earnings	207	37.0	153	38.8
Total Stockholders' Equity	242	43.2	183	46.4
Total Liabilities and Stockholders' Equity	$560	100.0%	$394	100.0%

Exhibit 12-7 ▲

A Note About Rounding

An interesting issue often arises when preparing vertical analyses of financial statements. This issue occurs when the calculated percentage amounts are added or subtracted from each other in the same manner that was used to prepare the financial statements (i.e. the Cost of Goods Sold percentage is subtracted from the Net Sales percentage to get the Gross Profit percentage, etc.). Some of the percentage amounts arrived at in this manner often differ slightly from the percentage amounts that were initially calculated when doing the vertical analysis. For example, in Exhibit 12-6 for 2010, if the calculated percentages for Operating Expenses are subtracted from the calculated percentage for Gross Profit, the result is 22.9 (54.5–25.8–5.8). This amount differs from the 22.8 which was calculated when preparing the vertical analysis of the Income statement. These differences are the result of the rounding that took place when calculating the percentages for the vertical analysis. These differences are insignificant and will be ignored for purposes of our discussion of vertical analysis. All of the amounts in the vertical analyses that are performed in this textbook will be based off of the calculated percentages.

Vertical Analysis of the Income Statement

The vertical analysis reveals that Tucker Enterprises' 2010 cost of goods sold is 45.5% of net sales compared to 46.5% in 2009. The fact that Tucker Enterprises was able to decrease the Cost of Goods Sold as a percent of Net Sales while increasing Net Sales by over $200,000 is a positive sign. The analysis also indicates that Tucker Enterprises was able to decrease Selling, General, and Administrative Expenses from 28.0% of Net Sales in 2009 to only 25.8% in 2010. This indicates that Tucker Enterprises' management appears to be doing a good job of controlling these expenses. We also see that Tucker Enterprises' 2010 Net Income is 18.8% of Net Sales. In other words, Tucker Enterprises earned $188 for every thousand dollars of net sales it had.

Vertical Analysis of the Balance Sheet

The vertical analysis of Tucker Enterprises' balance sheet reveals several things that warrant discussion. First, Cash and Cash Equivalents decreased from 11.9% of total assets to only 6.4% of total assets. This should concern management as it could indicate a potential cash flow problem in the future. In addition to Cash and Cash Equivalents, Accounts Receivable and Inventory also decrease as a percent of total assets. As a result, total current assets decreased from 54.6% of total assets to 43.0% of total assets. However, as we saw in the horizontal analysis, the current assets actually increased in total from 2009 to 2010. So, the decrease of current assets as a percentage of total assets was not due to a decrease in total current assets. It was actually the result of the significant increase in Property, Plant, and Equipment during the year. Also, total liabilities increased from 53.6% to 56.8% of total liabilities and stockholders' equity while total stockholders' equity decreased from 46.4 % to 43.2%. This indicates that creditors have claims to a higher percentage of Tucker Enterprises' assets in 2010 than they did in 2009.

HOW DO WE COMPARE ONE COMPANY WITH ANOTHER?

Compare one company to another using common-size financial statements and benchmarking

Horizontal and vertical analyses are useful tools to assess a company's performance. However, they only evaluate a company's performance against itself. In order to better asses a company's performance, it is often useful to compare the company against other companies. To compare Tucker Enterprises to another company we can use common-size statements. A **common-size statement** reports only percentages—the same percentages that appear in a vertical analysis. Common-size statements make it easier to compare companies of different sizes. By only reporting percentages, it removes **dollar value bias** when comparing the companies. Dollar value bias is the bias one sees from comparing numbers in absolute (dollars) rather than relative (percentages) terms. For example, it may appear that one company performed better than another because it had higher net income. However, the company with the lower net income might actually have been the better performer of the two companies in relative (percentage) terms.

To illustrate, let's assume that Tucker Enterprises, Inc., and Mackay Industries, Inc., compete in the same industry. Which company achieves a higher gross margin? Which company earns a higher percentage of revenues as profits for its shareholders? We can use a common-size income statement to compare the two companies and answer these questions. **Exhibit 12-8** on the next page gives both companies' common-size income statements for 2010 so that we may compare them on a relative, not absolute basis. The figures for Tucker Enterprises are taken from the vertical analysis in Exhibit 12-6 and the figures for Mackay Industries are assumed.

Exhibit 12-8 shows that in 2010, Tucker Enterprises was more profitable than Mackay Industries. Tucker Enterprises' gross profit percentage is 54.5%, compared to 52.8% for Mackay Industries. This means that Tucker Enterprises is getting more profit from every dollar of net sales than Mackay Industries. And, more importantly, Tucker Enterprises' percentage of net income to net sales is 18.8%.

Tucker Enterprises, Inc., Versus Mackay Industries, Inc.
Common-Size Income Statement
Year Ended December 31, 2010

(in thousands)	TUCKER ENTERPRISES	MACKAY INDUSTRIES
Net Sales	100.0%	100.0%
Cost of Goods Sold	45.5	47.2
Gross Profit	54.5	52.8
Operating Expenses:		
Selling, General, and Administrative	25.8	26.3
Other	5.8	4.9
Income Before Income Tax	22.8	21.6
Income Tax Expense	4.0	3.7
Net Income	18.8%	17.9%

Exhibit 12-8 ▲

That means that nearly one fifth of Tucker Enterprises' net sales end up as profits for the company's stockholders. On the other hand, although close, Mackay Industries' percentage of net income to net sales is 17.9%. Both percentages are good; however, the common-size statement highlights Tucker Enterprises' advantage over Mackay Industries.

A common-size balance sheet can also be prepared in order to compare the two companies' balance sheets. **Exhibit 12-9** on the next page gives both companies' common-size balance sheets for 2010 so that we may compare them. The figures for Tucker Enterprises are taken from the vertical analysis in Exhibit 12-7 and the figures for Mackay Industries are assumed.

As we can see from the figures in Exhibit 12-9, Tucker Enterprises' cash represents only 6.4% of its total assets compared to 11.1% for Mackay Industries. This might concern Tucker Enterprises' managers as it could indicate cash flow issues for Tucker Enterprises in the future. We can also see that Tucker Enterprises' total liabilities represents 56.8% of the total liabilities and stockholders' equity compared to 59.3% for Mackay Industries. This means that a higher percentage of assets are financed by creditors rather than stockholders for Mackay Industries.

Benchmarking

The practice of comparing a company with other leading companies is known as **benchmarking**. The common-size financial statements presented in Exhibits 12-8 and 12-9 represent benchmarking against a key competitor. Mackay Industries, Inc., is a good company to use to benchmark Tucker Enterprises' performance because the two companies compete in the same industry. As we saw in the common-size income statement, Tucker Enterprises is slightly more profitable than Mackay Industries.

It is also possible to utilize industry averages as a benchmark for evaluating a company. An industry comparison would show how Tucker Enterprises is performing alongside the average for the industry it operates in. A popular source for industry averages is *Annual Statement Studies* published by The Risk Management Association. You can even find industry averages online at BizStats.com. To compare Tucker Enterprises, Inc., to the industry average, simply insert the industry average common-size financial statements in place of Mackay Industries in Exhibits 12-8 and 12-9.

		TUCKER ENTERPRISES	MACKAY INDUSTRIES
Tucker Enterprises, Inc., Versus Mackay Industries, Inc. Common-Size Balance Sheet December 31, 2010			
(in thousands)			
Assets			
Current Assets:			
Cash and Cash Equivalents		6.4%	11.1%
Accounts Receivable, Net		10.9	9.3
Inventory		25.7	26.5
Total Current Assets		43.0	46.9
Property, Plant, and Equipment, Net		57.0	53.1
Total Assets		100.0%	100.0%
Liabilities			
Current Liabilities:			
Accounts Payable		21.6%	20.7%
Accrued Liabilities		4.3	6.4
Total Current Liabilities		25.9	27.1
Long-Term Liabilities		30.9	32.2
Total Liabilities		56.8	59.3
Stockholders' Equity			
Common Stock		6.3	5.2
Retained Earnings		37.0	35.5
Total Stockholders' Equity		43.2	40.7
Total Liabilities and Stockholders' Equity		100.0%	100.0%

Exhibit 12-9 ▲

Decision Guidelines

Decision	**Guideline**	**Analyze**
How is my business performing compared to others in the same industry?	Utilize common-size financial statements.	Common size financial statements can be utilized to compare two different companies even if they are of dissimilar sizes. This is because common-size financial statements report financial statement items as percentages instead of as dollar amounts. The percentages for the two companies can be compared to see which company has the highest gross profit percentage and the lowest expense percentages.

Common size financial statements can also be used to compare a company against the best companies in the industry. This is known as benchmarking. A business may not be able to achieve the same results as the industry leader, but benchmarking gives a company a goal to shoot for.

WHAT IS RATIO ANALYSIS?

Compute various financial ratios

Ratio analysis is a form of financial statement analysis in which items on the financial statements are expressed as ratios of one number to another. These ratios are then compared to ratios from prior years, ratios of other companies, or industry average ratios in order to evaluate a company's performance. Remember, however, that no single ratio tells the whole picture of any company's performance. Different ratios explain different aspects of a company. The ratios we discuss in this chapter may be classified as follows:

- *Liquidity ratios* measure a company's ability to meet short-term obligations with current assets.
- *Asset management ratios* measure how efficiently a company utilizes its operating assets.
- *Solvency ratios* measure a company's ability to meet its long-term obligations or take on more debt.
- *Profitability ratios* measure a company's ability to generate profits.
- *Market analysis ratios* are used to evaluate a company's stock market performance.

In earlier chapters, we introduced many of these ratios. In this chapter, we will review previously introduced ratios and examine new ratios. To illustrate ratio analysis, we will return to the comparative income statement and balance sheet for Tucker Enterprises, which were presented in Exhibits 12-2 and 12-3. Let's start by discussing liquidity ratios.

Liquidity Ratios

Working Capital

Working capital is defined as current assets less current liabilities. Working capital measures the amount of current assets that are left over after settling all current liabilities. Tucker Enterprises' working capital is $96,000 in 2010 and $108,000 in 2009 calculated as follows:

$$\text{Working capital} = \text{Current assets} - \text{Current liabilities} = \begin{array}{l} \textbf{2010} \ \$241,000 - 145,000 \ = \ \$\ 96,000 \\ \textbf{2009} \ \$215,000 - 107,000 \ = \ \$108,000 \end{array}$$

Current Ratio

The **current ratio** is the most widely used liquidity ratio. The current ratio is calculated by dividing current assets by current liabilities. Tucker Enterprises' current ratio for 2010 and 2009 is calculated as follows:

$$\text{Current ratio} = \frac{\text{Current assets}}{\text{Current liabilities}} = \begin{array}{cc} \textbf{2010} & \textbf{2009} \\ \dfrac{\$241,000}{\$145,000} = 1.66 & \dfrac{\$215,000}{\$107,000} = 2.01 \end{array}$$

A high current ratio indicates that the business has sufficient current assets to pay its current liabilities as they come due. But, what is an acceptable current ratio? The answer depends on the industry. For companies in most industries, a good current ratio is around 1.50, as reported by The Risk Management Association. Tucker Enterprises' current ratio of 1.66 in 2010 and 2.01 in 2009 are both strong. However, the decrease in the current ratio from 2009 to 2010 may be a cause of concern. Keep in mind that a current ratio that is too high would also be a cause for concern. This would indicate that the company is too liquid and, therefore, is not using its assets effectively.

Acid-Test Ratio

The **acid-test ratio** (or **quick ratio**) tells us whether the entity could pay all its current liabilities if they came due immediately. Inventory and prepaid expenses are *not* included in the acid-test ratio because they are not available to pay current liabilities. To compute the acid-test ratio, we add cash, short-term investments, and net current receivables (accounts and notes receivable, net of allowances) and divide this sum by current liabilities. Tucker Enterprises' acid-test ratios for 2010 and 2009 follow:

		2010	**2009**
Acid-test (Quick) ratio =	$\dfrac{\text{Cash} + \text{Short-term investments} + \text{Net current receivables}}{\text{Current liabilities}}$	$\dfrac{\$97,000}{\$145,000} = 0.67$	$\dfrac{\$99,000}{\$107,000} = 0.93$

The company's acid-test ratio declined from 0.93 in 2009 to 0.67 in 2010. An acid-test ratio of 0.90 to 1.00 is acceptable in most industries. Therefore, although it appears that Tucker Enterprises' acid-test ratio was acceptable in 2009, it is somewhat low in 2010.

Decision Guidelines

Decision	Guideline	Analyze
Will my business be able to meet its obligations as they come due?	Utilize liquidity ratios: • Working capital • Current ratio • Acid-test ratio	Monitoring a business's liquidity ratios can often provide an indicator that the business may experience cash flow problems. Action should be taken so that the business does not encounter difficulty meeting its obligations as they come due. For most businesses, a current ratio that drops below 1.50 or an acid-test ratio that drops below 0.90 may be cause for concern.

It is not only important for a company to have good liquidity ratios. It is also important that a company manage its operations effectively. There are three ratios we will look at that measure how well a company manages its inventory and accounts receivable.

Asset Management Ratios

Inventory Turnover

The **inventory turnover** measures the number of times a company sells its average level of inventory during a year. A high rate of turnover indicates ease in selling inventory; a low rate indicates difficulty. A value of 6 means that the company sold its average level of inventory six times, or once every two months, during the year. To compute inventory turnover, we divide cost of goods sold by the average inventory for the period. We use the cost of goods sold—not sales—because both cost of goods sold and inventory are stated *at cost*. Tucker Enterprises' inventory turnover for 2010 and 2009 is calculated as follows:

		2010
Inventory turnover ratio =	$\dfrac{\text{Cost of goods sold}}{\text{Average inventory}}$	$\dfrac{\$375,000}{(\$116,000 + \$144,000)/2} = 2.88$
		2009
		$\dfrac{\$277,000}{(\$68,000^* + \$116,000)/2} = 3.01$

*2008 inventory is $68,000.

Cost of goods sold comes directly from the income statement. Average inventory is figured by adding the beginning inventory to the ending inventory and dividing by two.

Inventory turnover varies widely with the nature of the business. For example, the inventory turnover ratio for a heavy equipment dealer will be significantly lower than that for a grocery store. Because of the high profit margin on heavy equipment, it is not necessary to turn the inventory over as many times and still be profitable. Let's assume the industry average inventory turnover ratio in Tucker Enterprises' industry is 2.5. In this case, Tucker Enterprises turnover ratio would be considered to be good in both 2009 and 2010. However, the decrease in the turnover from 2009 to 2010 should be investigated as it could be an indicator that Tucker Enterprises has some obsolete inventory.

Accounts Receivable Turnover

The **accounts receivable turnover** measures the ability to collect cash from credit customers. The higher the ratio, the faster the company collects cash. However, a receivable turnover ratio that is too high may indicate that credit is too tight, causing the loss of sales to good customers. To compute accounts receivable turnover, net credit sales is divided by average net accounts receivable. Average net accounts receivable is figured by adding the beginning and ending balances in net accounts receivable together and dividing the result by two. We will assume that all of Tucker Enterprises' sales were on account. Tucker Enterprises' accounts receivable turnover for 2010 and 2009 is computed as follows:

$$\text{Accounts receivable turnover ratio} = \frac{\text{Net credit sales}}{\text{Average net accounts receivable}}$$

2010

$$= \frac{\$824,000}{(\$52,000 + \$61,000)/2} = 14.58$$

2009

$$= \frac{\$596,000}{(\$43,000^* + \$52,000)/2} = 12.55$$

*2008 Accounts Receivable is $43,000.

Tucker Enterprises' receivable turnover of 14.58 in 2010 is an improvement over the 12.55 turnover in 2009. Considering Tucker Enterprises' credit terms are 2/10, n/30, it appears that Tucker Enterprises is doing a good job of collecting its receivables.

Days' Sales in Receivables

The **days' sales in receivables** also measures the ability to collect receivables. Days' sales in receivables tell us how many days' sales remain in Accounts Receivable. To compute, we divide 365 by the preceding accounts receivable turnover. Tucker Enterprises' days' sales in receivables for 2010 and 2009 is calculated as follows:

$$\text{Days' sales in receivables} = \frac{365}{\text{Accounts receivable turnover}}$$

2010

$$= \frac{365}{14.58} = 25 \text{ days}$$

2009

$$= \frac{365}{12.55} = 29 \text{ days}$$

An alternate method of calculating the days' sales in receivables is to do the following:

❶ Divide net sales by 365 days to figure average sales for one day.

❷ Divide this average day's sales amount into the average net accounts receivable.

Tucker Enterprises' ratio tells us that on average, 25 days' sales remain in Accounts Receivable in 2010 compared to 29 days in 2009. As with the accounts receivable turnover, this is an indicator that Tucker Enterprises has improved its ability to collect its accounts.

Decision Guidelines

Decision	Guideline	Analyze
Are Inventory and Accounts Receivable being managed effectively?	Utilize assets management ratios: • Inventory turnover • Accounts receivable turnover • Days' sales in receivables	Monitoring the asset management ratios can provide an indicator that a business is not managing its inventory and accounts receivables effectively. A decrease in the inventory turnover may indicate that a business has obsolete inventory or that it is purchasing too much inventory. Carrying high levels of inventory results in decreased profits due to the increased costs associated with maintaining the increased inventory levels. A decrease in the Accounts Receivable turnover may be due to poor collection practices related to past due accounts. This can result in decreased profits for the business due to increased bad debts expense. The longer a receivable is past due, the less likely it is to be collected.

Solvency Ratios

The ratios discussed so far yield insight into a company's ability to pay current liabilities and manage its assets. Most businesses also have long-term debt. Two key indicators of a business's ability to pay long-term liabilities are the *debt ratio* and the *times-interest-earned ratio.*

Debt Ratio

The **debt ratio** shows the relationship between total liabilities and total assets. In other words, it shows the proportion of assets financed with debt. If the debt ratio is 1, then all the assets are financed with debt. A debt ratio of 0.50 means that half the assets are financed with debt and the other half are financed by the owners of the business. The higher the debt ratio, the higher the company's financial risk. The debt ratios for Tucker Enterprises at the end of 2010 and 2009 follow:

		2010	**2009**
Debt ratio =	$\dfrac{\text{Total liabilities}}{\text{Total assets}}$ =	$\dfrac{\$318,000}{\$560,000} = 0.57$	$\dfrac{\$211,000}{\$394,000} = 0.54$

Tucker Enterprises' debt ratio in 2010 of 0.57 is slightly higher than the 2009 debt ratio of 0.54. However, neither ratio is considered to be very high. The Risk Management Association reports that the average debt ratio for most companies ranges from 0.57 to 0.67, with relatively little variation from company to company. Tucker Enterprises appears to be very solvent and in a position to take on more debt should the need arise.

Times-Interest-Earned Ratio

The **times-interest-earned ratio**, also known as **interest-coverage ratio**, indicates a company's ability to continue to service its debt. It measures the number of times operating income can cover (pay) interest expense. A high ratio means that a company is able to meet its interest obligations because earnings are significantly greater than annual interest obligations. A low ratio indicates that a company may encounter difficulty meeting its obligations. To compute this ratio, we divide operating income by interest expense. Before we can calculate the times-interest-earned ratio for Tucker Enterprises, we must calculate its operating income. If Tucker Enterprises' interest expense was $28,000 and $17,000 in 2010 and 2009 respectively, we can calculate operating income for the two years as follows:

$$\text{Operating income} = \text{Income before income tax} + \text{Interest expense}$$
$$2010 = \$188,000 + \$28,000 = \$216,000$$
$$2009 = \$118,000 + \$17,000 = \$135,000$$

Next, we can calculate the times-interest-earned ratios as follows:

		2010		2009	
Times-interest-earned ratio $=$	$\dfrac{\text{Operating income}}{\text{Interest expense}} =$	$\dfrac{\$216,000}{\$28,000} =$	7.7 times	$\dfrac{\$135,000}{\$17,000} =$	7.9 times

Tucker Enterprises' times-interest-earned ratio has declined slightly from 7.9 in 2009 to 7.7 in 2010. However, the norm for U.S. business, as reported by The Risk Management Association, falls in the range of 2.0 to 3.0. So, it appears that Tucker Enterprises will have little difficulty servicing its debt in the future.

Decision Guidelines

Decision		Guideline		Analyze
Will my business be able to service (pay off) its long-term debt?		Utilize solvency ratios: • Debt ratio • Times-interest-earned		Monitoring a company's solvency ratios can provide an indicator that the company may have difficulty servicing its long-term debt. In addition to creditors, a company's stockholders should pay attention to the solvency ratios. If a company is unable to pay back its creditors, there will be no value left in the company for the stockholders.

Now let's look at how the profitability of a business can be evaluated. We will examine four profitability ratios.

Profitability Ratios

Rate of Return on Net Sales

The **rate of return on net sales**, or simply **return on sales** shows the portion of each dollar of net sales that a firm is able to turn into income. Tucker Enterprises' rate of return on sales is calculated as follows:

		2010	2009
Rate of return on sales $=$	$\dfrac{\text{Net income}}{\text{Net sales}} =$	$\dfrac{\$155,000}{\$824,000} = 18.8\%$	$\dfrac{\$97,000}{\$596,000} = 16.3\%$

Companies strive for a high rate of return on sales. The higher the rate of return, the more sales dollars end up as profit. The increase in Tucker Enterprises' return on sales from 16.3% in 2009 to 18.8% in 2010 is a good sign.

Rate of Return on Total Assets

The **rate of return on total assets**, or simply **return on assets**, measures a company's effectiveness in using assets to generate earnings. In other words, it gives investors an idea of how well the company is converting the money they have invested into income. The assets of a company are financed by both debt and equity. The creditors have loaned money to the company and they earn interest. The shareholders have invested in stock and their return is net income. Therefore, the sum of interest expense and net income is added together when calculating the return to the two groups. The sum of these amounts is then divided by the average total assets to determine the return on assets. Average total assets is calculated by adding the beginning and ending total assets for the year together and dividing by two. Tucker Enterprises' return on assets for 2010 and 2009 is calculated as follows:

$$\text{Rate of return on total assets} = \frac{\text{Net income} + \text{Interest expense}}{\text{Average total assets}}$$

2010
$$= \frac{\$155,000 + \$28,000}{(\$394,000 + \$560,000)/2} = 38.4\%$$

2009
$$= \frac{\$97,000 + \$17,000}{(\$318,000^* + \$394,000)/2} = 32.0\%$$

*2008 Total Assets is $318,000.

Remember from our discussion of the times-interest-earned ratio that Tucker Enterprises' interest expense was $28,000 and $17,000 in 2010 and 2009 respectively. Investors would like Tucker Enterprises' return on assets for both years as they generally look for a return on assets that is high and growing.

Rate of Return on Common Stockholders' Equity

The **rate of return on common stockholders' equity**, often shortened to **return on common equity**, is another popular measure of profitability. The return on common equity shows the amount of net income returned as a percentage of common shareholders' equity.

To compute this ratio, we first subtract preferred dividends from net income to get net income available to the common stockholders. Because Tucker Enterprises has no preferred stock issued, preferred dividends are zero. The net income available to common stockholders is then divided by average common equity during the year. Common equity is total stockholders' equity minus preferred stockholders' equity. Average equity is the average of the beginning and ending balances.

The 2009 and 2010 rate of return on common stockholders' equity for Tucker Enterprises follows:

$$\text{Rate of return on common stockholders' equity} = \frac{\text{Net income} - \text{Preferred dividends}}{\text{Average common stockholders' equity}}$$

2010
$$= \frac{\$155,000 - \$0}{(\$183,000 + \$242,000)/2} = 72.9\%$$

2009
$$= \frac{\$97,000 - \$0}{(\$165,000^* + \$183,000)/2} = 55.7\%$$

*2008 Total common stockholders' equity is $165,000.

As we can see the return on equity was higher than 50% for both years, which is exceptional. The significant increase from 2009 to 2010 is sure to make the stockholders happy.

Earnings per Share of Common Stock

Perhaps the most widely quoted of all financial statistics is **earnings per share of common stock**, or simply earnings per share (EPS). EPS is the only ratio that is required to be shown on the income statement. EPS is the amount of net income earned for each share of the company's outstanding common stock.

Earnings per share is computed by dividing net income available to common stockholders by the number of common shares outstanding during the year. As with return on equity, preferred dividends are subtracted from net income because the preferred stockholders have a prior claim to dividends. Tucker Enterprises has no preferred stock outstanding and, therefore, paid no preferred dividends. In order to calculate earnings per share, we must know the number of common shares outstanding. Tucker Enterprises had 15,000 shares of common stock outstanding in 2009 and 17,000 shares outstanding in 2010. Tucker Enterprises earnings per share is calculated as follows:

$$\text{Earnings per share of common stock} = \frac{\text{Net income} - \text{preferred dividends}}{\text{Number of shares of common stock outstanding}}$$

2010

$$= \frac{\$155,000 - \$0}{17,000} = \$9.12$$

2009

$$\frac{\$97,000 - \$0}{15,000} = \$6.47$$

Tucker Enterprises' EPS increased by $2.65 from 2009 to 2010. This represents a 41% increase in the EPS. This is a good sign for Tucker Enterprises' stockholders; however, they should not expect this much increase in EPS every year. Most companies strive to increase EPS by 10% to 15% annually, and leading companies do so. But even the most successful companies have an occasional bad year.

Decision Guidelines

Decision	Guideline	Analyze
Should I be concerned with the profitability of my business?	Utilize profitability ratios: • Return on sales • Return on assets • Return on common equity • Earnings per share	The profitability of a business over the long run is critical to the survival of the business. By monitoring the profitability ratios, potential problems can be detected early and steps can be taken to prevent business failure. Many companies that have failed have shown warning signs well in advance of the company's collapse.

Market Analysis Ratios

Investors purchase stock with the hope of earning a return on their investments. There are two ways that investors earn returns on their stocks. They have gains (or losses) from selling stocks at prices above or below what they paid for them. They also may receive distributions of cash in the form of dividends from the company. The following tools are used to help people evaluate stock investments.

Price/Earnings Ratio

The **price/earnings ratio** is the ratio of the market price of a share of common stock to the company's earnings per share. This ratio, abbreviated P/E, shows how much investors are willing to pay per dollar of earnings. The stock market prices for publically traded companies can be found in the *Wall Street Journal*, or online from sources such as *Yahoofinance.com*. The market price of Tucker Enterprises' common stock was $67 at the end of 2010 and $44 at the end of 2009. Tucker Enterprises' P/E ratio for 2010 and 2009 are calculated as follows.

		2010	2009
Price/earnings ratio $= \dfrac{\text{Market price per share}}{\text{Earnings per share}} =$		$\dfrac{\$67.00}{\$9.12} = 7.35$	$\dfrac{\$44.00}{\$6.47} = 6.80$

Tucker Enterprises' P/E ratio increased slightly from 2009 to 2010. This indicates that investors are willing to pay more for $1 of earnings in 2010 than in 2009.

Dividend Yield

The ratio of dividends per share to a stock's market price per share is called the **dividend yield**. This ratio measures the percentage of a stock's market value that is returned annually as dividends. Dividend yield may be calculated on common stock, preferred stock, or both, depending on what type of stock a company issues. Because *preferred* stockholders invest primarily to receive dividends, they pay special attention to dividend yield.

Tucker Enterprises paid annual cash dividends on common stock of $3.50 per share in 2010 and $2.25 in 2009. Remember, Tucker Enterprises has no preferred stock. As noted previously, market prices of the company's common stock were $67 in 2010 and $44 in 2009. Tucker's dividend yield on common stock for 2010 and 2009 is calculated next.

		2010	2009
Dividend yield $= \dfrac{\text{Dividend per share}}{\text{Market price per share}} =$		$\dfrac{\$3.50}{\$67.00} = 5.2\%$	$\dfrac{\$2.25}{\$44.00} = 5.1\%$

Based on the dividend yield, investors who buy Tucker Enterprises' common stock can expect to receive about 5% of their investment in the form of cash dividends.

Red Flags in Financial Statement Analysis

As stated earlier in the chapter, financial statement analysis usually will not indicate that a problem definitely exists with a company. Also, even if a problem does exist, financial statement analysis generally will not identify what the specific problem is. Instead, financial statement analysis generates *red flags* that may signal financial trouble. Recent accounting scandals highlight the importance of these red flags. The following conditions may be cause for concern.

- **Decreased Cash Flow.** Cash flow validates net income. Is cash flow from operations consistently lower than net income? If so, the company is in trouble. Are the sales of plant assets a major source of cash? If so, the company may face a cash shortage.
- **Inability to Collect Receivables.** Are days' sales in receivables growing faster than for competitors? A cash shortage may be looming.
- **Buildup of Inventories.** Is inventory turnover too slow? If so, the company may have obsolete inventory, or it may be overstating inventory.
- **Movement of Sales, Inventory, and Receivables.** Sales, receivables, and inventory generally move together. Increased sales lead to higher receivables and require more inventory to meet demand. Unexpected or inconsistent movements among sales, inventory, and receivables make the financial statements look suspect.
- **Earnings Problems.** Has net income decreased significantly for several years in a row? Has income turned into a loss? Most companies cannot survive consecutive losses year after year.

■ **Too Much Debt.**   How does the company's debt ratio compare to that of major competitors? If the debt ratio is too high, the company may be unable to pay its debts.

Based on our financial statement analysis of Tucker Enterprises, the company appears to be in a strong financial condition. The only area of concern could be the company's cash position. Tucker Enterprises should monitor its cash position to ensure that it does not encounter any cash flow problems in the future.

Exhibit 12-10 summarizes the ratios we have learned in this chapter.

Liquidity Ratios	
Working capital	Current assets − Current liabilities
Current ratio	$\dfrac{\text{Current assets}}{\text{Current liabilities}}$
Acid-test (quick) ratio	$\dfrac{\text{Cash} + \text{Short-term investments} + \text{Net current receivables}}{\text{Current liabilities}}$
Asset Management Ratios	
Inventory turnover	$\dfrac{\text{Cost of goods sold}}{\text{Average inventory}}$
Accounts receivable turnover	$\dfrac{\text{Net credit sales}}{\text{Average net accounts receivable}}$
Days' sales in receivables	$\dfrac{365}{\text{Accounts receivable turnover ratio}}$
Solvency Ratios	
Debt ratio	$\dfrac{\text{Total liabilities}}{\text{Total assets}}$
Times-interest-earned ratio	$\dfrac{\text{Operating income}}{\text{Interest expense}}$
Profitability Ratios	
Rate of return on net sales	$\dfrac{\text{Net income}}{\text{Net Sales}}$
Rate of return on total assets	$\dfrac{\text{Net income} + \text{Interest expense}}{\text{Average total assets}}$
Rate of return on common stockholders' equity	$\dfrac{\text{Net income} - \text{Preferred dividends}}{\text{Average common stockholders' equity}}$
Earnings per share of common stock	$\dfrac{\text{Net income} - \text{Preferred dividends}}{\text{Number of shares of common stock outstanding}}$
Market Analysis Ratios	
Price/earnings ratio	$\dfrac{\text{Market price per share}}{\text{Earnings per share}}$
Dividend yield	$\dfrac{\text{Dividend per share}}{\text{Market price per share}}$

Exhibit 12-10 ▲

Demo Doc

Horizontal and Vertical Analysis

Learning Objectives 1 & 2 ▶   Cassidy, Inc., has the following information for 2010 and 2009:

<table>
<tr><td colspan="4">Cassidy, Inc.
Income Statement
Years Ended December 31, 2010 and 2009</td></tr>
<tr><td></td><td></td><th>2010</th><th>2009</th></tr>
<tr><td colspan="2">Sales Revenue</td><td>$550,000</td><td>$600,000</td></tr>
<tr><td colspan="2">Cost of Goods Sold</td><td>320,000</td><td>350,000</td></tr>
<tr><td colspan="2">Gross Profit</td><td>230,000</td><td>250,000</td></tr>
<tr><td colspan="2">Salary Expense</td><td>165,000</td><td>158,000</td></tr>
<tr><td colspan="2">Depreciation Expense</td><td>21,000</td><td>16,000</td></tr>
<tr><td colspan="2">Insurance Expense</td><td>19,000</td><td>23,000</td></tr>
<tr><td colspan="2">Income from Operations</td><td>25,000</td><td>53,000</td></tr>
<tr><td colspan="2">Gain on Sale of Furniture</td><td>3,000</td><td>0</td></tr>
<tr><td colspan="2">Net Income</td><td>$ 28,000</td><td>$ 53,000</td></tr>
</table>

<table>
<tr><td colspan="7">Cassidy, Inc.
Balance Sheet
December 31, 2010 and 2009</td></tr>
<tr><th>ASSETS</th><th>2010</th><th>2009</th><th>LIABILITIES</th><th>2010</th><th>2009</th></tr>
<tr><td>Current:</td><td></td><td></td><td>Current:</td><td></td><td></td></tr>
<tr><td>Cash</td><td>$ 28,000</td><td>$ 33,000</td><td>Accounts Payable</td><td>$ 20,000</td><td>$ 23,000</td></tr>
<tr><td>Accounts Receivable</td><td>26,000</td><td>15,000</td><td>Salary Payable</td><td>10,000</td><td>8,000</td></tr>
<tr><td>Prepaid Insurance</td><td>30,000</td><td>42,000</td><td>Total Current Liabilities</td><td>30,000</td><td>31,000</td></tr>
<tr><td>Total Current Assets</td><td>84,000</td><td>90,000</td><td>Notes Payable</td><td>40,000</td><td>50,000</td></tr>
<tr><td>Furniture, Net</td><td>90,000</td><td>74,500</td><td></td><td></td><td></td></tr>
<tr><td></td><td></td><td></td><td>STOCKHOLDERS' EQUITY</td><td></td><td></td></tr>
<tr><td></td><td></td><td></td><td>Common Stock (no par)</td><td>4,000</td><td>3,500</td></tr>
<tr><td></td><td></td><td></td><td>Retained Earnings</td><td>100,000</td><td>80,000</td></tr>
<tr><td></td><td></td><td></td><td>Total Liabilities and</td><td></td><td></td></tr>
<tr><td>Total Assets</td><td>$174,000</td><td>$164,500</td><td>Stockholders' Equity</td><td>$174,000</td><td>$164,500</td></tr>
</table>

Requirements:

❶ Prepare a horizontal analysis of Cassidy's income statement and balance sheet for 2010.
❷ Prepare a vertical analysis of Cassidy's income statement and balance sheet for 2010.

Demo Doc Solutions

Requirement ❶

Prepare a horizontal analysis of Cassidy's income statement and balance sheet for 2010.

Part 1	Part 2	Demo Doc Complete

Horizontal analysis goes across the rows of each financial statement, looking at one account and how it has changed from the prior year.

To prepare a horizontal analysis, we need to calculate the dollar amount of change and the percentage change for every number on the income statement and balance sheet.

> Dollar amount of change = This year's amount (balance) − Last year's amount (balance)

For example, the dollar amount of change for Sales Revenue and Accounts Receivable would be as follows:

> Sales Revenue = $550,000 − $600,000 = $(50,000) Change
> Accounts Receivable = $26,000 − $15,000 = $11,000 Change

Notice that the parentheses around the change in Sales Revenue indicates that it decreased, whereas the positive value of the change in the amount of Accounts Receivable indicates that it increased.

Expenses are assumed to be negative numbers on the income statement, in that they are subtracted to calculate net income. However, we use the absolute value of the expenses (ignoring the fact that they are already negative numbers) to calculate the dollar amount of change. So the dollar amount of change of Depreciation Expense and Insurance Expense would be as follows:

> Depreciation Expense = $21,000 − $16,000 = $5,000 Change
> Insurance Expense = $19,000 − $23,000 = $(4,000) Change

The positive amount of change indicates that Depreciation Expense increased and the negative amount of change indicates that Insurance Expense decreased.

$$\text{Percentage change} = \frac{\text{Dollar amount of change}}{\text{Base-year amount}}$$

The base-year amount is last year's amount (balance).

Using this formula, the percentage changes in Sales Revenue and Accounts Receivable would be as follows:

$$\text{Percentage Change in Sales Revenue} = \frac{\$(50,000)}{\$600,000}$$
$$= (8.3)\% \text{ Change}$$

$$\text{Percentage Change in Accounts Receivable} = \frac{\$11,000}{\$15,000}$$
$$= 73.3\% \text{ Change}$$

Notice that the percentage change numbers are negative for Sales Revenue (which had a dollar amount decrease for 2010) and positive for Accounts Receivable (which had a dollar amount increase for 2010).

The percentage changes of Depreciation Expense and Insurance Expense would be as follows:

$$\text{Percentage Change in Depreciation Expense} = \frac{\$5,000}{\$16,000}$$
$$= 31.3\% \text{ Change}$$

$$\text{Percentage Change in Insurance Expense} = \frac{\$(4,000)}{\$23,000}$$
$$= (17.4)\% \text{ Change}$$

If an account did not exist in the prior year (such as the Gain on Sale of Furniture in this example), then horizontal analysis is irrelevant and a percentage change cannot be calculated. Extending these calculations to all of the accounts on the income statement and balance sheet appear as follows:

Cassidy, Inc.
Income Statement
Years Ended December 31, 2010 and 2009

			2010	2009	INCREASE (DECREASE) AMOUNT	PERCENTAGE
		Sales Revenue	$550,000	$600,000	$(50,000)	(8.3)%
		Cost of Goods Sold	320,000	350,000	(30,000)	(8.6)%
		Gross Profit	230,000	250,000	(20,000)	(8.0)%
		Salary Expense	165,000	158,000	7,000	4.4 %
		Depreciation Expense	21,000	16,000	5,000	31.3 %
		Insurance Expense	19,000	23,000	(4,000)	(17.4)%
		Income from Operations	25,000	53,000	(28,000)	(52.8)%
		Gain on Sale of Furniture	3,000	0	3,000	—
		Net Income	$ 28,000	$ 53,000	$(25,000)	(47.2)%

Cassidy, Inc.
Balance Sheet
December 31, 2010 and 2009

			2010	2009	INCREASE (DECREASE) AMOUNT	PERCENTAGE
		ASSETS				
	Current:					
		Cash	$ 28,000	$ 33,000	$ (5,000)	(15.2)%
		Accounts Receivable	26,000	15,000	11,000	73.3 %
		Prepaid Insurance	30,000	42,000	(12,000)	(28.6)%
		Total Current Assets	84,000	90,000	(6,000)	(6.7)%
	Furniture, Net		90,000	74,500	15,500	20.8 %
	Total Assets		$174,000	$164,500	9,500	5.8 %
		LIABILITIES				
	Current:					
		Accounts Payable	$ 20,000	$ 23,000	$ (3,000)	(13.0)%
		Salary Payable	10,000	8,000	2,000	25.0 %
		Total Current Liabilities	30,000	31,000	(1,000)	(3.2)%
	Notes Payable		40,000	50,000	(10,000)	(20.0)%
	Total Liabilities		70,000	81,000	(11,000)	(13.6)%
		STOCKHOLDERS' EQUITY				
	Common Stock (no par)		4,000	3,500	500	14.3 %
	Retained Earnings		100,000	80,000	20,000	25.0 %
	Total Stockholders' Equity		104,000	83,500	20,500	24.6 %
	Total Liabilities and					
	Stockholders' Equity		$174,000	$164,500	$ 9,500	5.8 %

Requirement ❷

Prepare a vertical analysis of Cassidy's balance sheet and income statement for 2010.

Part 1	**Part 2**	Demo Doc Complete

Vertical analysis compares every number on a financial statement to all others in the same year (that is, down the columns of the financial statements).

To prepare a vertical analysis, we need to calculate the vertical analysis percentage for each account.

Income Statement

On the income statement, each number is calculated as a percentage of net sales revenues.

$$\text{Vertical analysis \% (Income statement)} = \frac{\text{Income statement account}}{\text{Net sales revenue}}$$

So in the case of Gross Profit it is as follows:

$$\text{Vertical analysis \% (2010 Gross Profit)} = \frac{\$230,000}{\$550,000}$$
$$= 41.8\%$$

This figure means that $0.418 of gross profit resulted from every dollar of sales revenue.

The calculation is the same for expenses. The vertical analysis percentages for Depreciation Expense and Insurance Expense would be as follows:

$$\text{Vertical analysis \% (2010 Depreciation Expense)} = \frac{\$21,000}{\$550,000}$$
$$= 3.8\%$$
$$\text{Vertical analysis \% (2010 Insurance Expense)} = \frac{\$19,000}{\$550,000}$$
$$= 3.5\%$$

Balance Sheet

On the balance sheet, each number, whether it be for an asset, a liability, or an equity account, is calculated as a percentage of total assets.

$$\text{Vertical analysis \% (Balance Sheet)} = \frac{\text{Balance Sheet Account}}{\text{Total Assets}}$$

So in the case of Accounts Receivable we have the following:

$$\text{Vertical analysis \% (2010 Accounts Receivable)} = \frac{\$26,000}{\$174,000}$$
$$= 14.9\%$$

In other words, approximately 15% of all the assets are Accounts Receivable.

Extending these calculations to all of the accounts on the balance sheet and income statement gives us the following:

Cassidy, Inc.
Income Statement
Years Ended December 31, 2010 and 2009

			2010		2009	
			AMOUNT	PERCENTAGE	AMOUNT	PERCENTAGE
		Sales Revenue	$550,000	100.0%	$600,000	100.0%
		Cost of Goods Sold	320,000	58.2%	350,000	58.3%
		Gross Profit	230,000	41.8%	250,000	41.7%
		Salary Expense	165,000	30.0%	158,000	26.3%
		Depreciation Expense	21,000	3.8%	16,000	2.7%
		Insurance Expense	19,000	3.5%	23,000	3.8%
		Income from operations	25,000	4.5%	53,000	8.8%
		Gain on sale of furniture	3,000	0.5%	0	0.0%
		Net Income	$ 28,000	5.1%	$ 53,000	8.8%

Cassidy, Inc.
Balance Sheet
December 31, 2010 and 2009

			2010		2009	
			AMOUNT	PERCENTAGE	AMOUNT	PERCENTAGE
		Assets				
		Current:				
		Cash	$ 28,000	16.1%	$ 33,000	20.1%
		Accounts Receivable	26,000	14.9%	15,000	9.1%
		Prepaid Insurance	30,000	17.2%	42,000	25.5%
		Total Current Assets	84,000	48.3%	90,000	54.7%
		Furniture, Net	90,000	51.7%	74,500	45.3%
		Total Assets	$174,000	100.0%	$164,500	100.0%
		Liabilities				
		Current:				
		Accounts Payable	$ 20,000	11.5%	$ 23,000	14.0%
		Salary Payable	10,000	5.7%	8,000	4.9%
		Total Current Liabilities	30,000	17.2%	31,000	18.8%
		Notes Payable	40,000	23.0%	50,000	30.4%
		Total Liabilities	70,000	40.2%	81,000	49.2%
		Stockholders' Equity				
		Common Stock (no par)	4,000	2.3%	3,500	2.1%
		Retained Earnings	100,000	57.5%	80,000	48.6%
		Total Stockholders' Equity	104,000	59.8%	83,500	50.8%
		Total Liabilities and Stockholders' Equity	$174,000	100.0%	$164,500	100.0%

Demo Doc Complete

Part 1	Part 2	**Demo Doc Complete**

Decision Guidelines

Financial Statement Analysis

The following guidelines can help you determine how best to analyze the financial statements of different companies.

Decision	Guideline	Analyze
How is my business performing compared to others in the same industry?	Utilize common-size financial statements.	Common size financial statements can be utilized to compare two different companies even if they are of dissimilar sizes. This is because common-size financial statements report financial statement items as percentages instead of as dollar amounts. The percentages for the two companies can be compared to see which company has the highest gross profit percentage and the lowest expense percentages. Common size financial statements can also be used to compare a company against the best companies in the industry. This is known as benchmarking. A business may not be able to achieve the same results as the industry leader, but benchmarking gives a company a goal to shoot for.
Will my business be able to meet its obligations as they come due?	Utilize liquidity ratios: • Working capital • Current ratio • Quick ratio	Monitoring a business's liquidity ratios can often provide an indicator that the business may experience cash flow problems. Action should be taken so that the business does not encounter difficulty meeting its obligations as they come due. For most businesses, a current ratio that drops below 1.50 or a quick ratio that drops below 0.90 may be cause for concern.
Are Inventory and Accounts Receivable being managed effectively?	Utilize assets management ratios: • Inventory turnover • Accounts receivable turnover • Days' sales in receivables	Monitoring the asset management ratios can provide an indicator that a business is not managing its inventory and accounts receivables effectively. An decrease in the inventory turnover may indicate that a business has obsolete inventory or that it is purchasing too much inventory. Carrying high levels of inventory results in decreased profits due to the increased costs associated with maintaining the increased inventory levels. A decrease in the Accounts Receivable turnover may be due to poor collection practices related to past due accounts. This can result in decreased profits for the business due to increased bad debts expense. The longer a receivable is past due, the less likely it is to be collected.
Will my business be able to service (pay off) its long-term debt?	Utilize solvency ratios: • Debt ratio • Times-interest-earned	Monitoring a company's solvency ratios can provide an indicator that the company may have difficulty servicing its long-term debt. In addition to creditors, a company's stockholders should pay attention to the solvency ratios. If a company is unable to pay back its creditors, there will be no value left in the company for the stockholders.
Should I be concerned with the profitability of my business?	Utilize profitability ratios: • Return on sales • Return on assets • Return on common equity • Earnings per share	The profitability of a business over the long run is critical to the survival of the business. By monitoring the profitability ratios, potential problems can be detected early and steps can be taken to prevent business failure. Many companies that have failed have shown warning signs well in advance of the company's collapse.

ACCOUNTING VOCABULARY

THE LANGUAGE OF BUSINESS

Accounts receivable turnover (p. 612) Measures a company's ability to collect cash from credit customers. To compute accounts receivable turnover, divide net credit sales by average net accounts receivable.

Acid-test ratio (p. 610) Quick assets (cash, short-term investments, and net current receivables) divided by current liabilities. It measures a company's ability to pay its current liabilities if they came due immediately; also called the *quick ratio*.

Benchmarking (p. 608) The practice of comparing a company with other companies that are leaders.

Common-size statement (p. 607) A financial statement that reports only percentages (no dollar amounts).

Current ratio (p. 610) Current assets divided by current liabilities. Measures a business's ability to meet its short-term obligations with its current assets.

Days' sales in receivables (p. 612) Measures a company's ability to collect receivables. To compute the ratio, divide 365 by the accounts receivable turnover.

Debt Ratio (p. 613) Total liabilities divided by total assets. It measures a business's ability to pay long-term liabilities.

Dividend yield (p. 617) Ratio of dividends per share of stock to the stock's market price per share. Tells the percentage of a stock's market value that the company returns to stockholders annually as dividends.

Dollar value bias (p. 607) The bias one sees from comparing numbers in absolute (dollars) rather than relative (percentages) terms.

Earnings per share of common stock (p. 616) Reflects the net income earned for each share of the company's outstanding common stock.

Horizontal analysis (p. 601) Study of dollar amount and percentage changes in comparative financial statements.

Interest-coverage ratio (p. 613) Ratio of income from operations to interest expense. It measures the number of times that operating income can cover interest expense; also called the *times-interest-earned ratio*.

Inventory turnover (p. 611) Measures the number of times a company sells its average level of inventory during a year.

Price/earnings ratio (p. 616) Ratio of the market price of a share of common stock to the company's earnings per share. It measures the value that the stock market places on $1 of a company's earnings.

Quick ratio (p. 610) Quick assets (cash, short-term investments, and net current receivables) divided by current liabilities. It measures a company's ability to pay its current liabilities if they came due immediately; also called the *acid-test ratio*.

Rate of return on common stockholders' equity (p. 615) Ratio of net income minus preferred dividends to common stockholders' equity. It is a measure of profitability; also called *return on common equity*.

Rate of return on net sales (p. 614) Ratio of net income to net sales. It is a measure of profitability; also called *return on sales*.

Rate of return on total assets (p. 615) Ratio of net income plus interest expense to total assets. It measures a company's effectiveness in using assets to generate earnings; also called *return on assets*.

Ratio analysis (p. 609) A form of financial statement analysis in which items on the financial statements are expressed as ratios of one number to another.

Return on assets (p. 615) Ratio of net income plus interest expense to total assets. It measures a company's effectiveness in using assets to generate earnings; also called *rate of return on total assets*.

Return on common equity (p. 615) Ratio of net income minus preferred dividends to common stockholders' equity. It is a measure of profitability; also called *rate of return on common stockholders' equity*.

Return on sales (p. 614) Ratio of net income to net sales. It is a measure of profitability; also called *rate of return on net sales*.

Times-interest-earned ratio (p. 613) Ratio of income from operations to interest expense. It measures the number of times that operating income can cover interest expense; also called the *interest-coverage ratio*.

Trend percentages (p. 604) A form of horizontal analysis in which percentages are computed by selecting a base year and then expressing amounts for following years as a percentage of the base year amounts.

Vertical analysis (p. 605) Analysis of a financial statement that reveals the relationship of each statement item to a specified base amount, which is the 100% figure.

Working capital (p. 610) Current assets minus current liabilities. It measures a business's ability to meet its short-term obligations with its current assets.

ACCOUNTING PRACTICE

DISCUSSION QUESTIONS

1. How is percentage change calculated?

2. Which amount is the base amount for vertical analysis on the income statement?

3. Which amount is the base amount for vertical analysis on the balance sheet?

4. What is the purpose for common-size financial statements?

5. The Financial Accounting Standards Board and the International Accounting Standards Board have identified the goal of comparability of financial statements as one toward which all companies should strive and consistency as the means toward achieving that goal. How are these characteristics important to horizontal and vertical analysis?

6. What is benchmarking? What should a company that wishes to use benchmarking look for in establishing benchmarks?

7. What are the major goals of each of the following types of ratios:

   a. Liquidity ratios
   b. Asset management ratios
   c. Solvency ratios
   d. Profitability ratios
   e. Market analysis ratios

8. How would you expect a recession to affect asset management ratios?

9. What is a "red flag" with respect to financial statement analysis?

10. A company has experienced increases in accounts receivable and inventory turnover ratios and has cash flows from operations that exceeds net income. All other things constant, what could you conclude about the company's performance this year relative to last year?

SELF CHECK

1. Net income was $245,000 in 2008, $240,000 in 2009, and $276,000 in 2010. The change from 2009 to 2010 is a (an)

   a. increase of 5%.
   b. increase of 10%.
   c. increase of 15%.
   d. increase of 20%.

2. Horizontal analysis of a financial statement shows

   a. the relationship of each statement item to a specified base.
   b. percentage changes in comparative balance sheets.
   c. percentage changes in comparative income statements.
   d. both b and c.

3. A statement that reports only percentages is called

   a. a comparative statement.
   b. a common-size statement.
   c. a condensed statement.
   d. a cumulative statement.

4. Working capital is

   a. a measure of the ability to meet short-term obligations with current assets.
   b. defined as current assets minus current liabilities.
   c. defined as current assets divided by current liabilities.
   d. both a and b.

5. Cash is $15,000, net accounts receivable amount to $6,000, inventory is $10,000, prepaid expenses total $4,000, and current liabilities are $20,000. What is the quick ratio?

   a. 1.05
   b. 1.55
   c. 1.25
   d. 1.75

6. Days' sales in receivables is computed by

   a. dividing net sales by 365.
   b. dividing 365 by accounts receivable turnover.
   c. dividing sales by average net accounts receivable.
   d. dividing accounts receivable turnover ratio by 365.

7. Rubble Company is experiencing a severe cash shortage due to its inability to collect accounts receivable. Which of the following would most likely identify this problem?

   a. Current ratio
   b. Working capital
   c. Accounts receivable turnover
   d. Return on sales

8. Which of the following statements is *true* of financial statement analysis?

   a. Horizontal analysis expresses all items on a financial statement as percentages of a common base.
   b. Vertical analysis involves comparing amounts from one year's financial statements to another year's statements.
   c. Ratio analysis is more important than either horizontal or vertical analysis.
   d. None of the above

9. Which statement is most likely to be *true*?

   a. An increase in inventory turnover indicates that inventory is not selling as quickly as it was.
   b. A decrease in inventory turnover indicates that inventory is not selling as quickly as it was.
   c. A change in inventory turnover cannot be accurately assessed without considering the change in profit margin.
   d. None of the above

10. How are financial ratios used in decision making?

    a. They eliminate uncertainty regarding cash flows.
    b. They can be used as a substitute for consulting financial statements.
    c. They are only used in evaluating business liquidity.
    d. They help to identify reasons for business success and failure.

    Answers are given after Written Communication.

SHORT EXERCISES

S12-1. Corporate financial statements (*Learning Objective 1*) 5–10 min.

Identify whether each of the following items would be classified as:

- Income from continuing operations (C)
- Income from discontinued operations (D)
- An extraordinary item (E)
- A change in accounting principle (P)

_____ a. $5,000 insurance proceeds on a fully depreciated piece of equipment that was lost in a hurricane.

_____ b. $2,500 gain on the sale of office furniture.

_____ c. $18,000 increase in income as a result of changing from DDB depreciation to straight-line depreciation.

_____ d. Income tax expense

_____ e. $85,000 loss incurred as a result of closing the Coeur d'Alene, Idaho store location.

_____ f. $4,600 loss incurred as a result of a company vehicle being involved in an accident.

S12-2. Horizontal analysis (*Learning Objective 2*) 10–15 min.

Aztec, Inc., had net sales of $250,000 and cost of goods sold of $150,000 in 2008, net sales of $275,000 and cost of goods sold of $165,000 in 2009, and net sales of $300,000 and cost of goods sold of $177,000 in 2010.

1. Find the percentage of increase in net sales from 2008 to 2009 and from 2009 to 2010.

2. Find the percentage of increase in gross profit from 2008 to 2009 and from 2009 to 2010.

S12-3. Vertical analysis (*Learning Objective 3*) 10–15 min.

The 2010 accounting records of Star Records showed the following: Cash, $15,000; Net Accounts Receivable, $8,000; Inventory, $5,000; Prepaid Expenses, $4,000; Net Plant and Equipment, $18,000.

Construct a vertical analysis of the asset section of Star Records' balance sheet for 2010.

S12-4. Ratio definitions (*Learning Objective 5*) 10–15 min.

Match the following terms to their definitions:

_____ 1. Tells whether a company can pay all its current liabilities if they become due immediately

_____ 2. Measures a company's success in using assets to earn income

_____ 3. The practice of comparing a company with other companies that are leaders

_____ 4. Indicates how rapidly inventory is sold

_____ 5. Shows the proportion of a company's assets that is financed with debt

_____ 6. Tells the percentage of a stock's market value that the company returns to stockholders annually as dividends

_____ 7. A measure of profitability

_____ 8. Measures a company's ability to collect cash from credit customers

a. Inventory turnover

b. Return on sales

c. Quick ratio

d. Dividend yield

e. Return on assets

f. Accounts receivable turnover

g. Benchmarking

h. Debt ratio

S12-5. Purpose of select ratios (*Learning Objective 5*) 10–15 min.

Identify each of the following financial ratios as follows:

- Profitability ratio (P)
- Asset management ratio (A)
- Liquidity ratio (L)
- Solvency ratio (S)

_____ a. Inventory turnover

_____ b. Debt ratio

_____ c. Return on equity

_____ d. Days' sales in receivables

_____ e. Quick ratio

_____ f. Return on assets

_____ g. Return on sales

_____ h. Receivables turnover

_____ i. Current ratio

_____ j. Earnings per share

_____ k. Times-interest-earned ratio

S12-6. Accounts receivable turnover, days' sales in accounts receivable, and inventory turnover (*Learning Objective 5*) 10–15 min.

The 2009 and 2010 balance sheets for Jackson and Sons showed net accounts receivable of $10,000 and $14,000, respectively, and inventory of $8,000 and $6,000, respectively. The company's 2010 income statement showed net sales of $109,500 and cost of goods sold of $70,000. Compute the following ratios for 2010:

1. Accounts receivable turnover
2. Days' sales in receivables
3. Inventory turnover

S12-7. Current ratio and quick ratio (*Learning Objective 5*) 10–15 min.

In addition to the information from S12-6, assume that cash on the 2010 balance sheet was $20,000 and current liabilities totaled $24,000. Compute the following ratios for 2010:

1. Current ratio
2. Quick ratio

S12-8. Return on sales, return on assets, return on common equity, times-interest-earned ratio, and debt ratio (*Learning Objective 5*) 10–15 min.

The 2010 financial statements for Country Cousin Stores show total assets of $490,000, total liabilities of $290,000, net sales of $1,800,000, net income of $450,000, income from operations of $520,000, cost of goods sold of $1,080,000, preferred dividends of $225,000, and interest expense of $20,000. Total assets and total liabilities for 2009 were $430,000 and $270,000, respectively. Preferred equity for both years is $35,000. Compute the following ratios for 2010:

1. Return on sales
2. Return on assets
3. Return on common equity
4. Times-interest-earned ratio
5. Debt ratio

S12-9. EPS and price/earnings ratio (*Learning Objective 5*) 10–15 min.

Using the information from S12-8, a market price of $25 per share, and 100,000 shares of common stock outstanding, compute the following for 2010:

1. Earnings per share
2. Price/earnings ratio

S12-10. Dividend yield (*Learning Objective 5*) 10–15 min.

In 2010, common stockholders received $2 per share in annual dividends. The market price per share for common stock was $12. Compute the dividend yield for common stock.

EXERCISES (GROUP A)

E12-11A. Horizontal analysis (*Learning Objective 2*) 15–20 min.

What were the dollar and percentage changes in Axel's Pawn Shop's working capital during 2009 and 2010? Is this trend favorable or unfavorable?

	2010	2009	2008
Total Current Assets	$410,000	$380,000	$360,000
Total Current Liabilities	250,000	217,000	240,000

E12-12A. Horizontal analysis (*Learning Objective 2*) 15–20 min.

Prepare a horizontal analysis of the following comparative income statement of R. Hanson, Inc. Round percentage changes to the nearest tenth of a percent.

	2010	2009
R. Hanson, Inc. **Comparative Income Statement** Years Ended December 31, 2010 and 2009		
Revenue	$492,000	$447,600
Expenses:		
Cost of Goods Sold	242,000	226,000
Selling and General Expenses	117,600	111,600
Interest Expense	8,000	5,000
Income Tax Expense	50,500	44,600
Total Expenses	418,100	387,200
Net Income	$ 73,900	$ 60,400

Requirement

1. Why did net income increase by a higher percent than total revenues increased during 2010?

E12-13A. Horizontal analysis (*Learning Objective 2*) 15–20 min.

Compute trend percentages for net sales and net income for the following five-year period, using year 1 as the base year:

	Year 5	Year 4	Year 3	Year 2	Year 1
Net Sales..................	$2,405	$2,185	$2,125	$2,005	$2,045
Net Income	717	714	683	671	685

Requirement

1. Which grew faster during the period, net sales or net income?

E12-14A. Vertical analysis (*Learning Objective 3*) 15–20 min.

Lori's Boutique requested that you perform a vertical analysis of its balance sheet to determine the component percentages of its assets, liabilities, and stockholders' equity. Round to the nearest tenth of a percent.

Lori's Boutique
Balance Sheet
December 31, 2010

ASSETS		LIABILITIES	
Total Current Assets	$108,000	Total Current Liabilities	$ 87,000
Long-Term Investments	52,500	Long-Term Debit	177,000
Property, Plant, and		Total Liabilities	264,000
Equipment, Net	325,500		
		STOCKHOLDERS' EQUITY	
		Total Stockholders' Equity	222,000
		Total Liabilities and	
Total Assets	$486,000	Stockholders' Equity	$486,000

E12-15A. Common-size income statement (*Learning Objective 4*) 15–20 min.

Prepare a comparative common-size income statement for R. Hanson, Inc., using the 2010 and 2009 data of E12-12A. Round percentages to the nearest tenth of a percent.

E12-16A. Current ratio, quick ratio, inventory turnover, accounts receivable turnover, and days' sales in accounts receivable (*Learning Objective 5*) 15–20 min.

The financial statements of Hernandez & Sons, Inc., include the following items:

	Current Year	Previous Year
Balance Sheet		
Cash	$ 27,000	$ 33,000
Short-Term Investments	22,000	28,000
Accounts Receivable, Net	54,000	72,000
Inventory	65,000	42,000
Prepaid Expenses	7,000	9,000
Total Current Assets	175,000	184,000
Total Current Liabilities	87,500	92,000
Income Statement		
Net Credit Sales	554,800	
Cost of Goods Sold	331,700	

Requirement

1. Compute the following ratios for the current year: (a) current ratio, (b) quick ratio, (c) inventory turnover, (d) accounts receivable turnover, and (e) days' sales in accounts receivable.

E12-17A. Current ratio, quick ratio, debt ratio, times-interest-earned ratio (*Learning Objective 5*) 15–20 min.

Brandy Pitts Winery requested that you determine whether the company's ability to pay its current liabilities and long-term debts improved or deteriorated during 2010. To answer this question, compute the following ratios for 2010 and 2009: (a) current ratio, (b) quick ratio, (c) debt ratio, and (d) times-interest-earned ratio. Summarize the results of your analysis.

	2010	2009
Cash	$ 32,000	$ 45,000
Short-Term Investments	35,000	–
Accounts Receivable, Net	130,000	142,000
Inventory	340,000	360,000
Prepaid Expenses	15,000	12,000
Total Assets	580,000	560,000
Total Current Liabilities	220,800	245,600
Long-Term Liabilities	24,200	29,400
Income From Operations	185,000	179,000
Interest Expense	42,000	44,000

E12-18A. Financial statement analysis (*Learning Objective 5*) 15–20 min.

For 2009 and 2010, compute the four ratios that measure the ability to earn profits for Fabulous Fashions, Inc., whose comparative income statement follows:

Fabulous Fashions, Inc. Income Statement Years Ended December 31, 2010 and 2009		
	2010	**2009**
Net Sales	$261,000	$237,000
Cost of Goods Sold	140,000	132,000
Gross Profit	121,000	105,000
Selling and General Expenses	72,000	65,000
Income From Operations	49,000	40,000
Interest Expense	32,000	15,000
Income Before Income Tax	17,000	25,000
Income Tax Expense	5,000	8,000
Net Income	$ 12,000	$ 17,000

Additional data follow:

	2010	2009	2008
Total Assets	$320,000	$292,000	$282,000
Common Stockholders' Equity	148,000	140,000	132,000
Preferred Dividends	4,000	4,000	
Shares of Common Stock Outstanding	25,000	25,000	

Requirement

1. Did the company's operating performance improve or deteriorate during 2010?

E12-19A. Financial statement analysis (*Learning Objective 5*) 15–20 min.

Evaluate the common stock of TomCat Incorporated as an investment. Specifically, use the two market analysis ratios to determine whether the stock increased or decreased in attractiveness during the past year. Assume that TomCat Incorporated paid the full amount of preferred dividends.

Quick solution:

Price/earnings ratio = 22 in 2010 and 17.9 in 2009; Dividend yield = 2.0% in 2010 and 2.6% in 2009

	2010	2009
Net Income	$ 87,000	$ 83,000
Total Dividends	48,000	48,000
Common Stockholders' Equity at Year-End (100,000 shares)	780,000	750,000
Preferred Stockholders' Equity, 6%, $100 Par at Year-End	300,000	300,000
Market Price of Common Stock at Year-End	$ 15.18	$ 11.63

E12-20A. Complete financial statement given certain information (*Learning Objective 5*) 15–20 min.

The following data (dollar amounts in millions) are adapted from the financial statements of Valco, Inc.:

Total Current Assets	$12,201
Accumulated Depreciation	1,738
Total Liabilities	14,755
Preferred Stock	10
Debt Ratio	55.145%
Current Ratio	2.1

Requirement

1. Complete the following condensed balance sheet. Report amounts rounded to the nearest $1 million:

Current Assets		$?
Property, Plant, and Equipment	$?	
Less: Accumulated Depreciation	(?)	?
Total Assets		$?
Current Liabilities		$?
Long-Term Liabilities		?
Stockholders' Equity		?
Total Liabilities and Stockholders' Equity		$?

EXERCISES (GROUP B)

E12-21B. Horizontal analysis (*Learning Objective 2*) 15–20 min.

What were the dollar and percentage changes in Hillary's Hair Salon's working capital during 2009 and 2010? Is this trend favorable or unfavorable?

	2010	2009	2008
Total Current Assets...	$600,000	$320,000	$270,000
Total Current Liabilities	479,000	232,000	190,000

E12-22B. Horizontal analysis (*Learning Objective 2*) 15–20 min.

Prepare a horizontal analysis of the following comparative income statement of Zinkowski, Inc. Round percentage changes to the nearest tenth of a percent.

Zinkowski, Inc. Comparative Income Statement Years Ended December 31, 2010 and 2009		2010	2009
Revenue		$480,000	$411,100
Expenses:			
Cost of Goods Sold		$254,000	$226,000
Selling and General Expenses		110,000	105,500
Interest Expense		6,500	2,000
Income Tax Expense		46,600	45,000
Total Expenses		417,100	378,500
Net Income		$ 62,900	$ 32,600

Requirement

1. Why did net income increase by a higher percent than total revenues increased during 2010?

E12-23B. Horizontal analysis (*Learning Objective 2*) 15–20 min.

Compute trend percentages for net sales and net income for the following five-year period, using year 1 as the base year:

	Year 5	Year 4	Year 3	Year 2	Year 1
Net Sales.................	$2,332	$2,310	$2,266	$2,244	$2,200
Net Income	755	717	659	640	640

Requirement

1. Which grew faster during the period, net sales or net income?

E12-24B. Vertical analysis (*Learning Objective 3*) 15–20 min.

Mary's Gift Store requested that you perform a vertical analysis of its balance sheet to determine the component percentages of its assets, liabilities, and stockholders' equity. Round to the nearest tenth of a percent.

Mary's Gift Store Balance Sheet December 31, 2010			
ASSETS		**LIABILITIES**	
Total Current Assets	$192,000	Total Current Liabilities	$120,000
Long-Term Investments	38,500	Long-Term Debt	155,000
Property, Plant, and		Total Liabilities	275,000
Equipment, Net	330,500		
		STOCKHOLDERS' EQUITY	
		Total Stockholders' Equity	286,000
		Total Liabilities and	
Total Assets	$561,000	Stockholders' Equity	$561,000

E12-25B. Common-size income statement (*Learning Objective 4*) 15–20 min.

Prepare a comparative common-size income statement for Zinkowski, Inc., using the 2010 and 2009 data of E12-22B. Round percentages to the nearest tenth of a percent.

E12-26B. Current ratio, quick ratio, inventory turnover, accounts receivable turnover, and days' sales in accounts receivable (*Learning Objective 5*) 15–20 min.

The financial statements of Vacation, Inc., include the following items:

	Current Year	Previous Year
Balance Sheet		
Cash	$ 25,000	$ 37,000
Short-Term Investments	10,000	24,000
Accounts Receivable, Net	64,000	86,000
Inventory	80,000	47,000
Prepaid Expenses	4,000	16,000
Total Current Assets	183,000	210,000
Total Current Liabilities	95,000	90,000
Income Statement		
Net Credit Sales	475,000	
Cost of Goods Sold	325,500	

Requirement

1. Compute the following ratios for the current year: (a) current ratio, (b) quick ratio, (c) inventory turnover, (d) accounts receivable turnover, and (e) days' sales in accounts receivable.

E12-27B. Current ratio, quick ratio, debt ratio, times-interest-earned ratio (*Learning Objective 5*) 15–20 min.

Hudson Crowe Winery requested that you determine whether the company's ability to pay its current liabilities and long-term debts improved or deteriorated during 2010. To answer this question, compute the following ratios for 2010 and 2009: (a) current ratio, (b) quick ratio, (c) debt ratio, and (d) times-interest-earned ratio. Summarize the results of your analysis.

	2010	2009
Cash	$ 41,000	$ 49,000
Short-Term Investments	50,000	—
Accounts Receivable, Net	90,000	156,000
Inventory	320,000	395,000
Prepaid Expenses		
Total Assets	570,000	650,000
Total Current Liabilities	250,000	244,700
Long-Term Liabilities	30,200	32,000
Income From Operations	145,000	203,000
Interest Expense	46,000	40,000

E12-28B. Financial statement analysis (*Learning Objective 5*) 15–20 min.

For 2009 and 2010, compute the four ratios that measure the ability to earn profits for Waldorf Fashions, Inc., whose comparative income statement and additional data follow:

Waldorf Fashions, Inc.
Income Statement
Years Ended December 31, 2010 and 2009

	2010	2009
Net Sales	$320,000	$298,000
Cost of Goods Sold	134,000	139,000
Gross Profit	186,000	159,000
Selling and General Expenses	66,000	68,000
Income From Operations	120,000	91,000
Interest Expense	32,000	19,000
Income Before Income Tax	88,000	72,000
Income Tax Expense	10,000	7,000
Net Income	$ 78,000	$ 65,000

Additional data follow:

	2010	2009	2008
Total Assets	$330,000	$286,000	$290,000
Common Stockholders' Equity	150,000	142,000	134,000
Preferred Dividends	6,000	6,000	
Shares of Common Stock Outstanding	45,000	45,000	

Requirement

1. Did the company's operating performance improve or deteriorate during 2010?

E12-29B. Financial statement analysis (*Learning Objective 5*) 15–20 min.

Evaluate the common stock of Shamrock Incorporated as an investment. Specifically, use the two market analysis ratios to determine whether the stock increased or decreased in attractiveness during the past year. Assume that Shamrock Incorporated paid the full amount of preferred dividends.

	2010	2009
Net Income	$117,000	$113,000
Total Dividends	30,000	30,000
Common Stockholders' Equity at Year-End (130,000 shares)	887,000	800,000
Preferred Stockholders' Equity, 4%, $100 Par at Year-End	370,000	370,000
Market Price of Common Stock at Year-End	$ 9.40	$ 11.63

E12-30B. Complete financial statement given certain information (*Learning Objective 5*)
15–20 min.

The following data (dollar amounts in millions) are adapted from the financial statements of Drawler, Inc.

Total Current Assets...	$11,983
Accumulated Depreciation	1,429
Total Liabilities..	15,200
Preferred Stock..	8
Debt Ratio..	77.79%
Current Ratio..	1.4

Requirement

1. Complete the following condensed balance sheet. Report amounts rounded to the nearest $1 million:

Current Assets		$?
Property, Plant, and Equipment	$?	
Less: Accumulated Depreciation	(?)	?
Total Assets		$?
Current Liabilities...		$?
Long-Term Liabilities		?
Stockholders' Equity		?
Total Liabilities and Stockholders' Equity..................		$?

EXERCISES (ALTERNATES 1, 2, AND 3)

These alternative exercise sets are available for your practice benefit at
www.myaccountinglab.com

PROBLEMS (GROUP A)

P12-31A. Horizontal and vertical analysis (*Learning Objectives 2 & 3*) 20–25 min.

Net sales, net income, and total assets for Gene Blue Clothing Emporium for a four-year period follow:

(in thousands)	2010	2009	2008	2007
Net Sales...	$381	$357	$321	$331
Net Income	31	23	16	24
Ending Total Assets	193	177	165	148

Requirements

1. Compute trend percentages for each item for 2007–2010. Use 2007 as the base year.

2. Compute the rate of return on net sales for 2008–2010, rounding to three decimal places. In this industry, rates of 6% are average, rates above 8% are considered good, and rates above 10% are viewed as outstanding.

3. How does Gene Blue Clothing Emporium's return on net sales compare with the industry?

P12-32A. Common-size financial statements and profitability ratios (*Learning Objectives 4 & 5*) 20–25 min.

Love Bug Used Auto Sales asked for your help in comparing the company's profit performance and financial position with the average for the auto sales industry. The proprietor has given you the company's income statement and balance sheet as well as the industry average data for retailers of used autos.

Love Bug Used Auto Sales Income Statement Compared with Industry Average Year Ended December 31, 2010		
	LOVE BUG	INDUSTRY AVERAGE
Net Sales	$521,000	100.0%
Cost of Goods Sold	331,000	62.1%
Gross Profit	190,000	37.9%
Operating Expenses	110,000	27.8%
Operating Income	80,000	10.1%
Other Expenses	3,000	0.4%
Net Income	$ 77,000	9.7%

Love Bug Used Auto Sales Balance Sheet Compared with Industry Average December 31, 2010		
	LOVE BUG	INDUSTRY AVERAGE
Current Assets	$230,000	70.9%
Plant Assets, Net	49,000	23.6%
Intangible Assets, Net	3,000	0.8%
Other Assets	15,000	4.7%
Total Assets	$297,000	100.0%
Current Liabilities	$136,000	48.1%
Long-Term Liabilities	41,000	16.6%
Stockholders' Equity	120,000	35.3%
Total Liabilities and Stockholders' Equity	$297,000	100.0%

Requirements

1. Prepare a two-column, common-size income statement and a two-column, common-size balance sheet for Love Bug Used Auto Sales. The first column of each statement should present Love Bug Used Auto Sales' common-size statement and the second column should show the industry averages.

2. For the profitability analysis, examine Love Bug Used Auto Sales' (a) ratio of gross profit to net sales, (b) ratio of operating income to net sales, and (c) ratio of net income to net sales. Compare these figures with the industry averages. Is Love Bug's profit performance better or worse than the industry average?

3. For the analysis of financial position, examine Love Bug Used Auto Sales' (a) ratio of current assets to total assets, and (b) ratio of stockholders' equity to total assets. Compare these ratios with the industry averages. Is Love Bug Used Auto Sales' financial position better or worse than the industry average?

P12-33A. Current ratio, debt ratio, EPS (*Learning Objective 5*) 20–25 min.

Financial statement data of Barb Wired Fencing, Inc., include the following items:

Cash..	$ 17,000
Short-Term Investments..	22,000
Accounts Receivable, Net...	103,000
Inventory...	119,000
Prepaid Expenses..	10,000
Total Assets	660,000
Short-Term Notes Payable..	45,000
Accounts Payable..	105,000
Accrued Liabilities...	40,000
Long-Term Notes Payable..	158,000
Other Long-Term Liabilities	33,000
Net Income	75,000
Number of Common Shares Outstanding	35,000

Quick solution:

1. Current ratio = 1.43;
debt ratio = 0.58;
earnings per share = $2.14

Requirements

1. Compute Barb Wired Fencing's current ratio, debt ratio, and earnings per share. Assume that the company had no preferred stock outstanding. Round all ratios to two decimal places.

2. Compute each of the same three ratios after evaluating the effect of each transaction that follows.

   a. Purchased merchandise of $38,000 on account, debiting Inventory.

   b. Issued 2,000 shares of common stock, receiving cash of $80,000.

   c. Borrowed $80,000 on a long-term note payable.

   d. Received cash on account, $22,000.

P12-34A. Calculate various ratios for analysis (*Learning Objective 5*) 20–25 min.

Comparative financial statement data of Lounge Around Furniture Company follow:

Lounge Around Furniture Company **Income Statement** Years Ended December 31, 2010 and 2009		2010	2009
Net Sales		$482,000	$457,000
Cost of Goods Sold		238,000	229,000
Gross Profit		244,000	228,000
Operating Expenses		140,000	138,000
Income from Operations		104,000	90,000
Interest Expense		12,000	14,000
Income Before Income Tax		92,000	76,000
Income Tax Expense		28,000	23,000
Net Income		$ 64,000	$ 53,000

Lounge Around Furniture Company
Balance Sheet
December 31, 2010 and 2009
(Selected 2008 amounts given for computation of ratios)

		2010	2009	2008
Current Assets:				
	Cash	$ 98,000	$ 99,000	
	Accounts Receivable, Net	108,000	112,000	$104,000
	Inventory	164,000	154,000	185,000
	Prepaid Expenses	28,000	20,000	
	Total Current Assets	398,000	385,000	
Property, Plant, and Equipment, Net		191,000	180,000	
Total Assets		$589,000	$565,000	
Total Current Liabilities		$208,000	$228,000	
Long-Term Liabilities		121,000	117,000	
Total Liabilities		329,000	345,000	
Preferred Stockholders' Equity, 8%, $100 Par		100,000	100,000	
Common Stockholders' Equity, no Par		160,000	120,000	100,000
Total Liabilities and Stockholders' Equity		$589,000	$565,000	

Other information follows:

a. Market price of common stock was $48 at December 31, 2010, and $30.75 at December 31, 2009.

b. Common shares outstanding were 10,000 during 2010 and 9,000 during 2009.

c. All sales were made on credit.

d. The full amount of preferred dividends was paid.

Requirements

1. Compute the following ratios for 2010 and 2009:
   a. Current ratio
   b. Inventory turnover
   c. Accounts receivable turnover
   d. Times-interest-earned ratio
   e. Return on common stockholders' equity
   f. Earnings per share of common stock
   g. Price/earnings ratio

2. Decide (a) whether Lounge Around Furniture Company's financial position improved or deteriorated during 2010 and (b) whether the investment attractiveness of its common stock appears to have increased or decreased.

3. How will what you learned in this problem help you evaluate an investment?

P12-35A. Calculate various ratios for analysis (*Learning Objective 5*) 20–25 min.

Assume you are purchasing an investment and decide to invest in a company in the home remodeling business. You narrow the choice to Build It Right, Inc., or Structurally Sound, Corp. You assemble the following selected data:

Selected income statement data for the current year follow:

	Build It Right, Inc.	Structurally Sound, Corp.
Net Sales (all on credit).................................	$298,000	$223,000
Cost of Goods Sold.......................................	155,000	125,000
Income from Operations	83,000	47,000
Interest Expense	13,000	—
Net Income	43,000	29,000

Selected balance sheet and market price data at the end of the current year follow:

	Build It Right, Inc.	Structurally Sound, Corp.
Current Assets:		
Cash..	$ 12,000	$ 13,000
Short-Term Investments	11,000	12,000
Accounts Receivable, Net..........................	28,000	25,000
Inventory..	60,000	52,000
Prepaid Expenses.....................................	2,000	1,000
Total Current Assets................................	113,000	103,000
Total Assets	197,000	159,000
Total Current Liabilities	59,000	65,000
Total Liabilities..	79,000	65,000
Preferred Stock, 5%, $100 Par	20,000	
Common Stock, $1.00 Par, 6,000 Shares......		6,000
$2.50 Par, 3,000 Shares......	7,500	
Total Stockholders' Equity	118,000	94,000
Market price per share of common stock.......	$ 67	$ 31

Selected balance sheet data at the beginning of the current year follow:

	Build It Right, Inc.	Structurally Sound, Corp.
Accounts Receivable, Net	$ 29,000	$ 24,000
Inventory	53,000	56,000
Total Assets	162,000	155,000
Preferred Stock, 5%, $100 Par	20,000	
Common Stock, $1.00 Par, 6,000 Shares		6,000
$2.50 Par, 3,000 Shares	7,500	
Total Stockholders' Equity	76,000	71,000

Your investment strategy is to purchase the stock of the company that has a low price/earnings ratio but appears to be in good shape financially. Assume that you analyzed all other factors and your decision depends on the results of the ratio analysis to be performed.

Requirement

1. Compute the following ratios for both companies for the current year and decide which company's stock better fits your investment strategy.

   a. Quick ratio

   b. Inventory turnover

   c. Days' sales in receivables

   d. Debt ratio

   e. Earnings per share of common stock

   f. Price/earnings ratio

P12-36A. Financial statement ratio analysis (Learning Objective 5) 20–25 min.

You have been hired as an investment analyst at McNeice Securities, Inc. It is your job to recommend investments for your client. The only information you have are the following ratio values for two companies in the video game industry.

Ratio	Tomb Crater, Co.	Resident Upheaval, Inc.
Days to collect receivables	46	52
Inventory turnover	8	10
Gross profit percentage	67%	59%
Net income as a percent of sales	15%	21%
Times-interest-earned ratio	16	12
Return on equity	35%	26%
Return on assets	13%	18%

Requirement

1. Write a memo to your client recommending the company you believe to be a more attractive investment. Explain the reasons for your recommendation.

PROBLEMS (GROUP B)

P12-37B. Horizontal and vertical analysis (Learning Objectives 2 & 3) 20–25 min.

Net sales, net income, and total assets for Armanix Clothing Emporium for a four-year period follow:

(in thousands)	2010	2009	2008	2007
Net Sales	$386	$357	$324	$337
Net Income	31	26	12	22
Ending Total Assets	196	177	170	152

Requirements

1. Compute trend percentages for each item for 2007–2010. Use 2007 as the base year.

2. Compute the rate of return on net sales for 2008–2010, rounding to three decimal places. In this industry, rates of 6% are average, rates above 8% are considered good, and rates above 10% are viewed as outstanding.

3. How does Armanix Clothing Emporium's return on net sales compare with the industry?

P12-38B. Common-size financial statements and profitability ratios (*Learning Objectives 3 & 4*) 20–25 min.

Verifine Used Auto Sales asked for your help in comparing the company's profit performance and financial position with the average for the auto sales industry. The proprietor has given you the company's income statement and balance sheet as well as the industry average data for retailers of used autos.

Verifine Used Auto Sales Income Statement Compared with Industry Average Year Ended December 31, 2010		
	VERIFINE	**INDUSTRY AVERAGE**
Net Sales	$548,000	100.0%
Cost of Goods Sold	348,528	62.1%
Gross Profit	199,472	37.9%
Operating Expenses	122,752	27.8%
Operating Income	76,720	10.1%
Other Expenses	1,096	0.4%
Net Income	$ 75,624	9.7%

Verifine Used Auto Sales Balance Sheet Compared with Industry Average December 31, 2010		
	VERIFINE	**INDUSTRY AVERAGE**
Current Assets	$229,034	70.9%
Plant Assets, Net	50,830	23.6%
Intangible Assets, Net	8,970	0.8%
Other Assets	10,166	4.7%
Total Assets	$299,000	100.0%
Current Liabilities	$118,105	48.1%
Long-Term Liabilities	50,830	16.6%
Stockholders' Equity	130,065	35.3%
Total Liabilities and Stockholders' Equity	$299,000	100.0%

Requirements

1. Prepare a two-column, common-size income statement and a two-column, common-size balance sheet for Verifine Used Auto Sales. The first column of each statement should present Verifine Used Auto Sales' common-size statement and the second column should show the industry averages.

2. For the profitability analysis, examine Verifine Used Auto Sales' (a) ratio of gross profit to net sales, (b) ratio of operating income to net sales, and (c) ratio of net income to net sales. Compare these figures with the industry averages. Is Verifine Used Auto Sales' profit performance better or worse than the industry average?

3. For the analysis of financial position, examine Verifine Used Auto Sales' (a) ratio of current assets to total assets and (b) ratio of stockholders' equity to total assets. Compare these ratios with the industry averages. Is Verifine Used Auto Sales' financial position better or worse than the industry average?

P12-39B. Current ratio, debt ratio, EPS (*Learning Objective 5*) 20–25 min.

Financial statement data of ABC Fencing, Inc., include the following items:

Cash	$ 21,000
Short-Term Investments	25,000
Accounts Receivable, Net	102,000
Inventory	121,000
Prepaid Expenses	15,000
Total Assets	660,500
Short-Term Notes Payable	45,000
Accounts Payable	106,000
Accrued Liabilities	44,000
Long-Term Notes Payable	160,000
Other Long-Term Liabilities	37,000
Net Income	77,000
Number of Common Shares Outstanding	37,000

Requirements

1. Compute ABC Fencing's current ratio, debt ratio, and earnings per share. Assume that the company had no preferred stock outstanding. Round all ratios to two decimal places.

2. Compute each of the same three ratios after evaluating the effect of each transaction that follows:

   a. Purchased merchandise of $40,000 on account, debiting Inventory.

   b. Issued 2,000 shares of common stock, receiving cash of $78,000.

   c. Borrowed $78,000 on a long-term note payable.

   d. Received cash on account, $18,000.

P12-40B. Calculate various ratios for analysis (*Learning Objective 5*) 20–25 min.

Comparative financial statement data of Danfield Furniture Company follow:

Danfield Furniture Company Income Statement Years Ended December 31, 2010 and 2009		
	2010	**2009**
Net Sales	$483,000	$458,000
Cost of Goods Sold	244,000	234,000
Gross Profit	239,000	224,000
Operating Expenses	145,000	137,000
Income from Operations	94,000	87,000
Interest Expense	14,000	24,000
Income Before Income Tax	80,000	63,000
Income Tax Expense	28,000	24,000
Net Income	$ 52,000	$ 39,000

Danfield Furniture Company
Balance Sheet
December 31, 2010 and 2009
(Selected 2008 amounts given for computation of ratios)

	2010	2009	2008
Current Assets:			
Cash	$ 95,000	$ 98,000	
Accounts Receivable, Net	104,000	114,000	$107,000
Inventory	161,000	151,000	193,000
Prepaid Expenses	38,000	28,000	
Total Current Assets	398,000	391,000	
Property, Plant, and Equipment, Net	196,000	175,000	
Total Assets	$594,000	$566,000	
Total Current Liabilities	$212,000	$228,000	
Long-Term Liabilities	129,000	116,000	
Total Liabilities	341,000	344,000	
Preferred Stockholders' Equity, 8%, $100 Par	99,000	99,000	
Common Stockholders' Equity, No Par	154,000	123,000	97,000
Total Liabilities and Stockholders' Equity	$594,000	$566,000	

Other information follows:

1. Market price of common stock was $48.50 at December 31, 2010, and $31.75 at December 31, 2009.
2. Common shares outstanding were 17,000 during 2010 and 15,000 during 2009
3. All sales were made on credit
4. The full amount of preferred dividends was paid.

Requirements

1. Compute the following ratios for 2010 and 2009:
   a. Current ratio
   b. Inventory turnover
   c. Accounts receivable turnover
   d. Times-interest-earned ratio
   e. Return on common stockholders' equity
   f. Earnings per share of common stock
   g. Price/earnings ratio
2. Decide (a) whether Danfield Furniture Company's financial position improved or deteriorated during 2010 and (b) whether the investment attractiveness of its common stock appears to have increased or decreased.
3. How will what you learned in this problem help you evaluate an investment?

P12-41B. Calculate various ratios for analysis (*Learning Objective 5*) 20–25 min.

Assume you are purchasing an investment and decide to invest in a company in the home remodeling business. You narrow the choice to Bob's Home Repair, Inc., or Stellar Stability, Corp. You assemble the following selected data.

Selected income statement data for the current year follow:

	Bob's Home Repair, Inc.	Stellar Stability, Corp.
Net Sales (all on credit)	$282,000	$226,000
Cost of Goods Sold	158,000	129,000
Income from Operations	88,000	48,000
Interest Expense	15,000	—
Net Income	44,000	24,000

Selected balance sheet and market price data at the end of the current year follow:

	Bob's Home Repair, Inc.	Stellar Stability, Corp.
Current Assets:		
Cash	$ 13,000	$ 14,000
Short-Term Investments	12,000	15,000
Accounts Receivable, Net	30,000	25,000
Inventory	69,000	50,000
Prepaid Expenses	5,000	4,000
Total Current Assets	129,000	108,000
Total Assets	201,000	166,000
Total Current Liabilities	54,000	68,000
Total Liabilities	80,000	71,000
Preferred Stock, 5%, $100 Par	18,000	
Common Stock, $1.00 Par, 7,000 Shares		7,000
$2.50 Par, 4,000 Shares	10,000	
Total Stockholders' Equity	121,000	95,000
Market price per share of common stock	$ 43.12	$ 30.87

Selected balance sheet data at the beginning of the current year follow:

	Bob's Home Repair, Inc.	Stellar Stability, Corp.
Accounts Receivable, Net	$ 29,000	$ 26,000
Inventory	52,000	62,000
Total Assets	162,000	157,000
Preferred Stock, 5%, $100 Par	18,000	
Common Stock, $1.50 Par, 7,000 Shares		7,000
$2.50 Par, 4,000 Shares	10,000	
Total Stockholders' Equity	77,000	72,000

Your investment strategy is to purchase the stock of the company that has a low price/earnings ratio but appears to be in good shape financially. Assume that you analyzed all other factors and your decision depends on the results of the ratio analysis to be performed.

Requirement

1. Compute the following ratios for both companies for the current year and decide which company's stock better fits your investment strategy.

   a. Quick ratio

   b. Inventory turnover

   c. Days' sales in receivables

   d. Debt ratio

   e. Earnings per share of common stock

   f. Price/earnings ratio

P12-42B. Financial statement ratio analysis (*Learning Objective 5*) 20–25 min.

You have been hired as an investment analyst at Harriet Winston Company. It is your job to recommend investments for your client. The only information you have are the following ratio values for two companies in the video game industry.

Ratio	Mario and Luco, Co.	Witches and Warlocks, Inc.
Days to collect receivables	60	54
Inventory turnover	10	8
Gross profit percentage	69%	75%
Net income as a percent of sales	17%	11%
Times-interest-earned ratio	14	18
Return on equity	37%	45%
Return on assets	15%	13%

Requirement

1. Write a memo to your client recommending the company you believe to be a more attractive investment. Explain the reasons for your recommendation.

PROBLEMS (ALTERNATES 1, 2, AND 3)

These alternative problem sets are available for your practice benefit at
www.myaccountinglab.com

CONTINUING EXERCISE

This concludes the accounting for Graham's Yard Care, Inc., that we began in Chapter 1. For this exercise, refer to the comparative balance sheet that was presented in the continuing exercise in Chapter 11.

Requirements

1. Prepare a horizontal analysis of the balance sheet for Graham's Yard Care, Inc.

2. Prepare a vertical analysis of the balance sheet for Graham's Yard Care, Inc.

CONTINUING PROBLEM

In Chapter 11, we prepared a cash flow statement for Aqua Elite, Inc. Now, we will analyze Aqua Elite's financial statements using the tools we learned in this chapter.

Following are the balance sheets for the months ended July 31 and June 30, 2011 and the income statement for the month ended July 31, 2011, for Aqua Elite, Inc.

Aqua Elite, Inc.
Comparative Balance Sheets
July 31 and June 30, 2011

			JULY 31	JUNE 30
		Assets		
		Cash	$ 5,333	$3,270
		Accounts Receivable, Net	2,280	1,000
		Inventory	4,175	180
		Supplies	105	125
		Total Current Assets	11,893	4,575
		Fixed Assets	67,250	2,250
		Less: Accumulated Depreciation	(352)	(47)
		Net Fixed Assets	66,898	2,203
		Total Assets	$78,791	$6,778
		Liabilities		
		Accounts Payable	$ 1,805	$ 450
		Unearned Revenue	5,800	2,000
		Salary Payable	950	900
		Interest Payable	375	17
		Payroll Taxes Payable	188	—
		Dividend Payable	500	—
		Current Portion of Long-Term Debt	4,410	2,000
		Total Current Liabilities	14,028	5,367
		Notes Payable	20,000	—
		Mortgage Payable	42,590	—
		Total Liabilities	76,618	5,367
		Stockholders' Equity		
		Common Stock	1,000	1,000
		Retained Earnings	1,173	411
		Total Stockholders' Equity	2,173	1,411
		Total Liabilities & Stockholders' Equity	$78,791	$6,778

Aqua Elite, Inc.
Income Statement
Month Ended July 31, 2011

		Revenue	$6,300
		Expenses:	
		Cost of Goods Sold	1,080
		Depreciation Expense	305
		Bad Debt Expense	220
		Interest Expense	375
		Insurance Expense	150
		Supplies Expense	210
		Salary Expense	2,400
		Payroll Taxes Expense	268
		Bank Service Fees	30
		Net Income*	$1,262

*Income taxes ignored

Requirements

1. Prepare a vertical analysis of the income statement using a multi-step income statement.

2. Calculate the current ratio for Aqua Elite, Inc., at July 31, 2011.

3. Calculate the quick ratio for Aqua Elite, Inc., at July 31, 2011

4. Why do you think the current and quick ratios are unfavorable? Do you believe that this is a temporary problem or a long-term problem?

APPLY YOUR KNOWLEDGE

ETHICS IN ACTION

Case 1. Robin Peterson, the CEO of Teldar Incorporated, was reviewing the financial statements for the first three months of the year. He saw that sales and net income were lower than expected. Because the reported net income and the related earnings per share were below expectations, the price of the stock declined. Robin held a meeting with top management and expressed his concerns over the declining trend in sales and income. He stated that the reduced profitability meant that he needed to formulate a plan to somehow increase the earnings per share. The vice president of marketing suggested that more advertising might help sales increase. Robin stated that spending more money on advertising would not guarantee an increase in sales. Then he announced that the excess company cash would instead be used to buy back shares of outstanding common stock; this move would help increase the earnings per share because fewer shares would be outstanding. Robin reminded everyone that the yearly financial statements would be analyzed and the current year would be compared to previous years' results. He then stated that the treasury stock would lower the total stockholders' equity, which could then provide a stronger EPS so the current year would not look as bad. Finally, Robin reminded everyone that with fewer shares of stock outstanding, the dividend per share could be increased and that would help make Teldar stock more attractive. The CFO argued that buying back stock merely to increase performance measures such as EPS was manipulative and unethical and financial analysts would easily see what Teldar was trying to do.

Why did the CEO want to repurchase shares of Teldar common stock? Would the repurchase of common stock really have any impact on the financial ratios? Would an investor or financial analyst be able to see that financial performance measures were improved because of the stock repurchase? Are any ethical issues involved? Were the concerns expressed by the CFO valid? Do you have any other thoughts?

Case 2. Crane Corporation was in the process of completing the financial statements for the latest fiscal year. Susan Randal, Crane's CEO, was reviewing the comparative financial statements and expressed some concerns. In comparing the current year income statement against those of the prior years, she noticed that total sales had decreased slightly. Further, the salary expense had increased while the advertising and research and development expenses had decreased. Although the total operating expenses were essentially the same, Susan was concerned that the increased salary expense would be questioned by the investors and financial analysts in light of the decreases in advertising and research and development. She knew that the lower sales would be blamed on reduced advertising and less spending on research and development. As a result, Susan ordered the accountants to issue a condensed income statement that would present all operating expenses as a single amount. Also, during the year Crane Corporation had purchased another company for a price higher than the total fair market value of the purchased business. Crane properly recorded the excess cost as goodwill, but the total amount of goodwill had increased substantially because of this purchase. Susan was concerned that this rather large increase in goodwill would be seen as an unnecessary purchase and investors and analysts would become upset. Thus, Susan ordered that the goodwill be lumped in with the other assets rather than listed separately on the balance sheet where it could easily be seen. The accountants argued that attempting to hide these items from investors and analysts would be unethical. They further argued that GAAP required full disclosure, and that if Susan insisted on providing condensed statements, details would need to be provided in the footnotes anyway. Susan reluctantly agreed to the disclosure, knowing that often footnotes are not read.

Why would Susan want all the operating expenses lumped together? Why would Susan want the goodwill included as other assets? Were the ethical concerns raised by the accountants valid? Are any ethical issues involved in providing condensed information with the details included in the footnotes? Do you have any additional thoughts?

KNOW YOUR BUSINESS

FINANCIAL ANALYSIS

Purpose: To help familiarize you with the financial reporting of a real company in order to further your understanding of the chapter material you are learning.

This case focuses on the financial statement analysis of Columbia Sportswear. Recall from the chapter that stakeholders use numerous ways to analyze and, thus, better understand the financial position and results of operations of a company. Tools such as vertical and horizontal analyses are available. In addition, financial ratios can be used to gain further insight into areas such as liquidity and profitability. Other measures include earnings per share and ratios that consider the share price of the company. Finally, nonfinancial information provides additional insights into the performance and financial position of the company. We will now apply some of the analytical tools contained in the chapter. Refer to the Columbia Sportswear annual report found in Appendix A.

Requirements

1. Perform a vertical analysis on the income statements (Consolidated Statements of Operations). Discuss your results. What benefit do you see in performing this analysis? Perform a horizontal analysis of the balance sheets (Consolidated Balance Sheets). Discuss your results. What benefit do you see in performing this analysis?

2. Look at the income statements (Consolidated Statements of Operations). Can you find the Basic EPS for each fiscal year presented? Has the Basic Earnings per Share increased or decreased each year? Why do you think the Basic EPS has been changing?

3. Determine the liquidity of Columbia Sportswear by computing the working capital, current ratio, and quick ratio at December 31, 2008 and December 31, 2007. Has Columbia Sportswear's liquidity improved or deteriorated? Compute the return on sales and the return on equity ratio for 2008 and 2007. Has Columbia Sportswear's profitability improved or deteriorated.

4. The market price for a share of Columbia Sportswear's common stock was $35.37 on December 31, 2008. Using this price, determine the price/earnings ratio and the dividend yield at December 31, 2008 (the dividends per share can be found on the Consolidated Statements of Stockholders' Equity). What do your results mean? Assume that the industry average P/E ratio was 12 times earnings and the dividend yield was 1.7% for the industry. Evaluate your results against the industry averages.

INDUSTRY ANALYSIS

Purpose: To help you understand and compare the performance of two companies in the same industry.

Find the Columbia Sportswear Company Annual Report located in Appendix A and go to the Selected Financial Data starting on page 663. Now access the 2008 Annual Report for Under Armour, Inc,. from the Internet. Go to the company's Web page for Investor Relations at *http://investor.underarmour.com/investors.cfm* and under Downloads on the right-hand side, go to 2008 Annual Report. The company's Selected Financial Data start on page 27.

The Selected Financial Data is the area of the Notes to the Financial Statements where the companies do their trend analysis. Each company has supplied the reader of the financial statements with five years of data to analyze. It is then up to the reader to determine the trend of the company.

Requirement

1. In your opinion and based on what you have learned from this chapter, what is the trend of each of these companies? And based on this data, which company would you invest in?

SMALL BUSINESS ANALYSIS

Purpose: To help you understand the importance of cash flows in the operation of a small business.

You just returned from a meeting with your bank loan officer and you were a little taken aback by his comments. You've been doing business with this bank for a number of years and he always seemed happy with your company's performance. This is why you can't understand the bank's hesitation to continue extending credit to your company. At this meeting, you had supplied him with the current year's financial information and even ran some of the financial ratios that you know the bank asks about. You thought the numbers looked decent for the current year, maybe not the best, but decent. Sure, sales had fallen a little bit since the previous year, but they were still pretty good. So when the discussion turned to a comparison of the last couple of year's financial information with this year's, you had to question what that has to do with anything. "Why shouldn't each and every year stand by itself?" you asked the banker. His comments to you were, "A company's performance is best evaluated by examining more than one year's data. This is why most financial statements cover at least two periods. In fact, most financial analysis covers trends of up to five years." He also said that a company's performance is best evaluated by comparing it against its own past performance, the performance of competitors, and the industry averages for the industry the company is in.

Requirement

1. Below are some selected financial data from the last four years. Calculate the trend percentages using 2007 as the base year and the return on sales for these four years and see if you can figure out what the concern is that the banker has for the financial health of your company.

	2010	2009	2008	2007
Total Sales	1,010,000	1,050,000	1,080,000	1,000,000
Total Expenses	896,000	888,000	880,000	800,000
Net Income	114,000	162,000	200,000	200,000

WRITTEN COMMUNICATION

Below are selected financial data for your client for the current year and corresponding data for the client's industry.

	Company	Industry
Return on Sales	12.5%	10.0%
Return on Assets	23.0%	20.0%
Current Ratio	1.6	1.5
Inventory Turnover	8.5	7.1
Accounts Receivable Turnover	8.5	11.0
Days Sales in Receivables	42.9	33.2
Debt Ratio	0.6	0.5

Requirement

1. Write a memo to your client comparing his or her business to the industry averages and explain to the client the value of common-size financial statements.

COMPREHENSIVE PROBLEM FOR CHAPTERS 11–12

ANALYZING A COMPANY FOR ITS INVESTMENT POTENTIAL

In its annual report, BALLI Supply includes the following five-year financial summary:

BALLI Supply, Inc. Five-Year Financial Summary (partial)					
(Dollar Amounts in Thousands Except per Share Data)	**2010**	**2009**	**2008**	**2007**	**2006**
Net Sales	$244,524	$217,799	$191,329	$165,013	$137,634
Net sales increase	12%	14%	16%	20%	17%
# of store increase	5%	6%	5%	8%	9%
Other Income, Net	2,001	1,873	1,787	1,615	1,391
Cost of Goods Sold	191,838	171,562	150,255	129,664	108,725
Selling, General, and					
Administrative Expenses	41,043	36,173	31,550	27,040	22,363
Interest Costs					
Interest Expense	1,063	1,357	1,383	1,045	803
Interest Income	(138)	(171)	(188)	(204)	(189)
Net Income	8,039	6,671	6,295	5,377	4,430
Per Share of Common Stock:					
Net Income	1.81	1.49	1.41	1.21	0.99
Dividends	0.30	0.28	0.24	0.20	0.16
Financial Position					
Current Assets	$ 30,483	$ 27,878	$ 26,555	$ 24,356	$ 21,132
Inventories at LIFO Cost	24,891	22,614	21,442	19,793	17,076
Net Property, Plant, and Equipment	51,904	45,750	40,934	35,969	25,973
Total Assets	94,685	83,527	78,130	70,349	49,996
Current Liabilities	32,617	27,282	28,949	25,803	16,762
Long-Term Debt	19,608	18,732	15,655	16,674	9,607
Shareholders' Equity	39,337	35,102	31,343	25,834	21,112
Financial Ratios					
Current ratio	0.9	1.0	0.9	0.9	1.3
Return on assets	9.2%	8.5%	8.7%	9.5%	9.6%
Return on shareholders' equity	21.6%	20.1%	22.0%	22.9%	22.4%

Requirement

1. Analyze the company's financial summary for the fiscal years 2006–2010 to decide whether to invest in the common stock of BALLI. Include the following sections in your analysis, and fully explain your final decision.

   a. Trend analysis for net sales and net income (use 2006 as the base year)

   b. Profitability analysis

   c. Measuring ability to sell inventory

   d. Measuring ability to pay debts

   e. Measuring dividends

Appendix A

2008 Annual Report to Shareholders

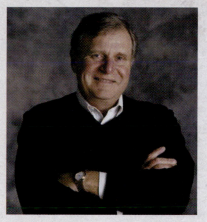

Dear Fellow Shareholders,

2008 was a year of unexpected challenges and deliberate investments for Columbia Sportswear.

Unexpected challenges came from the sudden crisis in U.S. and European credit markets followed by contraction of consumer spending at a pace unseen in more than a generation.

I'm not going to place blame for Columbia's 3 percent decline in net sales or 34 percent decline in net income in 2008 on the global credit crisis, the consumer, the economy, the burst housing bubble, or rising unemployment. Those are all external factors that we can't control.

We measure our success in terms of growth – growth in net sales, growth in operating margins, growth in net income, and growth in return on invested capital.

The sobering fact is that many of our key outdoor apparel and footwear competitors grew their revenues and earnings in 2008 in spite of those same macro-economic headwinds.

And we did not. In fact, we ended a string of annual net sales increases spanning the 10 years since we went public in 1998. (And, if you'll allow me to cite from memory, a record of sustained growth that stretched back into the 1970s.) While that's certainly a record to be proud of, we are disappointed to see it end and are committed to making it a brief pause before the beginning of our next growth phase.

As shareholders, it is important to remember that the strategic initiatives we adopted in 2007 have only recently become visible in the marketplace where consumers can begin to experience them. Those initiatives are to:

1. *Design authentic, innovative products that address activity-specific performance needs of active outdoor enthusiasts;*

2. *Expand our direct-to-consumer business by opening branded retail stores in key metro markets and outlet stores in leading outlet centers, and establishing an e-commerce platform;*

3. *Build stronger emotional connections with consumers by investing in enhanced brand advertising supported by clear seasonal product and technology messages;*

4. *Expand our global outdoor footwear business by developing a world-class footwear organization and creating innovative, performance-driven products; and*

5. *Complete the realignment of our European product assortments and marketing programs to leverage our global brand position and marketing communications.*

By using our fortress balance sheet and strong cash flow to invest in these strategic initiatives, we believe we are improving our competitive posture and positioning the company for renewed growth and increased profitability when the economy begins to recover.

Despite the difficult economic backdrop and our deliberate $35 million incremental investment in retail expansion and demand-creation, we were still able to return over $100 million in cash to shareholders in 2008 through a combination of share repurchases and dividends, ending the year with cash and short term investments totaling over $250 million, and zero long term debt.

With these incremental investments, we believe we are in a much better competitive position today:

*   *We have renewed our focus on innovation and enhanced design across all product categories. What we refer to as "The Science of the Greater Outdoors" is brought to life in Columbia's Omni-Shade and Omni-Tech apparel, as well as our Techlite footwear products and our expanded line of accessories and equipment. These products generated improved sell-throughs for many of our retail partners in 2008. In 2009, we will add Omni-Shield technology, providing advanced repellency against liquids and stains, to extend our performance foundation for future innovations.*

*   *Our Mountain Hardwear and Sorel brands achieved net sales growth of 15 percent and 5 percent, respectively. Both of these brands are founded on uncompromising commitments to performance and design, but both are still small and relatively unknown outside North America. We see great opportunities for each of these highly-regarded brands to contribute significant growth as we draw more attention to their performance features and broaden their design appeal to more consumers in more markets.*

- During 2008 we opened five new branded retail stores in the U.S., including Columbia stores in Minneapolis' Mall of America and in downtown Seattle, each featuring a broad assortment of Columbia and Sorel products. We opened Mountain Hardwear stores adjacent to the new Columbia store in downtown Seattle and adjacent to our remodeled Portland store, and a small Columbia store at the Portland International Airport. We also announced plans to open a Columbia store on Chicago's famed Michigan Avenue in spring 2010 that will feature our Columbia and Sorel brands.

- We opened 18 new outlet stores in 2008, including 15 in the U.S., one in the U.K, two in Japan and one in Korea. Globally, we operated a total of 50 outlet stores at December 31, 2008, providing us with a more profitable channel to liquidate end-of-season inventory without relying on brand-detracting discount channels.

- We began developing an e-commerce platform targeted to launch in the U.S. in summer 2009. In addition to enabling a more direct relationship with our consumers, we believe the site will also enhance our wholesale business by equipping consumers with important product information, knowledge of our innovative technologies and key brand messages in preparation for a visit to their nearest retailer.

- We developed and launched a new brand advertising campaign in October 2008. "The Pioneers of Columbia's Greater Outdoors" is a global brand platform that celebrates the accessibility of the outdoors. The primary message of this new campaign is that, while our best products are frequently used by elite athletes for summit assaults, our brands connect with everyone who shares a passion for the outdoors, regardless of skill level, income level or background.

- We continued to build a much stronger footwear team that is bringing meaningful innovation and increased confidence in this important category. We believe our Fall 2009 Columbia and Sorel footwear lines are strong and that 2010 holds even more promise for growth.

- We added key talent to our European management team and made great progress in realigning the European product assortment to better leverage our global brand messaging and seasonal product initiatives. These are important steps in regaining the trust and commitment of our European retail partners and reconnecting with European consumers.

- The Latin America/Asia Pacific region (LAAP) was our strongest region during 2008, contributing 13 percent revenue growth despite significant currency headwinds in Korea during the second half. This growth was fueled by an expanding base of retail stores in Japan and Korea and increased sales to our independent distributors across the region.

- Our worldwide marketing efforts benefited in 2008 from the success of the Team Columbia-Highroad professional cycling team, which debuted at the 2008 Tour de France and finished the year as the #1 professional cycling team in the world. We are looking forward to another very successful year in 2009 as the team's title co-sponsor.

I was pleased with our team's efforts in 2008 and their commitment to executing on our strategic initiatives, despite the weak macro-economic backdrop. Our strong financial position enables us to continue investing prudently in new growth platforms, even though we expect wholesale customers and consumers to remain very cautious throughout 2009.

During 2009 we plan to expand our retail store base with new Columbia branded stores in several key European markets, and add more outlet stores, primarily in the U.S. and Europe. At the same time, we have postponed plans to open branded retail stores in several key metro areas in the U.S., adjusted our 2009 marketing and advertising budgets, and are actively managing personnel and other overhead expenses across the entire organization to achieve targeted cost savings without compromising our commitment to innovation.

What really matters now is how quickly we are able to generate renewed top-line growth and achieve incremental profitability from our on-going investments.

In a world in which consumers have a renewed appreciation for performance and value, we think Columbia Sportswear is well positioned with a portfolio of brands and innovative products that offer outdoor enthusiasts plenty of both.

Sincerely,

Timothy P. Boyle
President and Chief Executive Officer

PART I

Item 1.   *BUSINESS*

General

Founded in 1938 in Portland, Oregon, as a small, family-owned, regional hat distributor and incorporated in 1961, Columbia Sportswear Company has grown to become a global leader in the design, sourcing, marketing and distribution of active outdoor apparel, footwear and related accessories and equipment. Unless the context indicates otherwise, the terms "we", "us", "our", "the Company" and "Columbia" refer to Columbia Sportswear Company and its consolidated subsidiaries.

As one of the largest outdoor apparel and footwear companies in the world, our products have earned an international reputation for innovation, quality, performance, durability, functionality, dependability and value. In addition to our flagship Columbia Sportswear® brand, we also design, develop, market and distribute active outdoor apparel, footwear and related accessories and equipment under the Mountain Hardwear®, Sorel®, Montrail® and Pacific Trail® brands. Our brands complement each other to address the diverse outdoor performance needs of a wide variety of outdoor consumer segments. We have sought to leverage our brand equity by expanding directly and through licensees into related outdoor and lifestyle merchandise categories, promoting a "head-to-toe" outfitting concept.

Each of our brands is distributed through a mix of wholesale distribution channels, independent distributors, our own retail stores and licensees. In 2008, we distributed our products to over 9,000 wholesale customers in over 100 countries. We employ creative marketing strategies designed to increase demand and reinforce consumer awareness of each of our brands. All of our products are manufactured by independent contractors in facilities located outside the United States.

As a consumer products company, the popularity of outdoor activities and changing design trends affect the desirability of our products. Therefore, we seek to influence, anticipate and respond to trends and shifts in consumer preferences by adjusting the mix of available product offerings, developing new products with innovative performance features and designs, and by creating persuasive and memorable marketing communications to drive consumer awareness and demand. Failure to respond to consumer needs and preferences in a timely and adequate manner could have a material adverse effect on our sales and profitability.

Our business is subject to many risks and uncertainties that may have a material adverse effect on our financial condition, results of operations or cash flows. Some of these risks and uncertainties are described below under Item 1A, Risk Factors.

Seasonality and Variability of Business

Our business is affected by the general seasonal trends common to the outdoor apparel industry and is heavily dependent upon discretionary consumer spending patterns. Our products are marketed on a seasonal basis and our product mix is weighted substantially toward the fall season, resulting in sales and profits being highest in the third calendar quarter. We expect the expansion of our owned retail operations to have a modest effect on the seasonality of our business, increasing the proportion of sales and profits that we generate in the fourth calendar quarter.

Results of operations in any period should not be considered indicative of the results to be expected for any future period, particularly in light of the current macro-economic environment. Sales of our products are subject to substantial cyclical fluctuation, the effects of unseasonable weather conditions, and the continued popularity of outdoor activities as part of an active lifestyle in key markets. Our net sales volumes have been affected by the volatility of the global economy, its impact on consumer purchasing patterns and placement of advanced orders, order cancellations and seasonal reorders by retailers. Sales tend to decline in periods of recession or uncertainty regarding future economic prospects that affect consumer spending, particularly on discretionary items. This cyclicality and any related fluctuation in consumer demand could have a material adverse effect on our financial position, results of operations or cash flows.

For further discussion regarding the effects of the current macro-economic environment on our business, see Part II, Item 7, Management's Discussion and Analysis of Financial Condition and Results of Operations.

Products

We provide high quality apparel, footwear, accessories and equipment for use in a wide range of outdoor activities by men, women and youth. A large percentage of our products are also worn for casual or leisure purposes. The durability, functionality and affordability of our products make them ideal for a wide range of outdoor activities. Our products serve consumers ranging from elite mountain climbers who use Columbia and Mountain Hardwear apparel and accessories, winter outdoor enthusiasts who wear Columbia and Sorel cold weather boots, hunting and fishing enthusiasts who wear our Columbia PFG® (Performance Fishing Gear) and PHG® (Performance Hunting Gear) apparel, top endurance trail runners who wear Montrail shoes, and outdoor-inspired consumers who wear Columbia sportswear and footwear for a variety of active outdoor pursuits. We also market apparel and accessories with licensed college team logos.

We categorize our merchandise in four principal categories: (1) sportswear, (2) outerwear, (3) footwear and (4) related accessories and equipment. Our product innovations and designs are inspired by the performance needs of consumers who participate in activities that we group into six end-user activity-based categories: (1) winter, (2) water, (3) trail, (4) travel, (5) fishing/hunting and (6) golf.

The following table presents the net sales and approximate percentages of net sales attributable to each of our principal product categories for each of the last three years ended December 31 (dollars in millions):

	2008		2007		2006	
	Net Sales	% of Sales	Net Sales	% of Sales	Net Sales	% of Sales
Sportswear	$ 540.9	41.0%	$ 565.6	41.7%	$ 509.1	39.5%
Outerwear	491.7	37.3	497.6	36.7	496.5	38.6
Footwear	217.2	16.5	227.4	16.8	219.7	17.1
Accessories and equipment	68.0	5.2	65.4	4.8	62.4	4.8
Total	$1,317.8	100.0%	$1,356.0	100.0%	$1,287.7	100.0%

Sportswear

We design, develop, market and distribute sportswear products for men and women under our Columbia and Mountain Hardwear brands and for youth under our Columbia brand. Our sportswear products incorporate various fabrication and construction technologies that protect consumers from the outdoor elements and enable consumers to enjoy the outdoors longer and in greater comfort year round. Our sportswear products are designed to be worn as a layering system with our outerwear and footwear products during fall and winter outdoor activities, or individually during milder weather commonly encountered in spring and summer outdoor activities such as hiking, trekking, fishing, golfing, adventure travel and water-sports. Mountain Hardwear-branded sportswear consists primarily of performance styles designed for backpacking, rock climbing and adventure sports. Our Columbia and Mountain Hardwear sportswear product assortments also include casual styles designed to appeal to a broader consumer base.

Outerwear

We design, develop, market and distribute outerwear products for men and women under our Columbia, Mountain Hardwear, Sorel and Pacific Trail brands and for youth under our Columbia and Pacific Trail brands.

Outerwear is our most established and iconic product category and incorporates the cumulative design, fabrication, fit and construction technologies that we have pioneered over several decades and that we continue to innovate. Our outerwear is designed to protect the wearer from the harsher inclement weather commonly encountered in fall and winter outdoor activities, such as skiing, snowboarding, hiking, hunting, fishing and adventure travel. Our Mountain Hardwear brand features technically advanced shells, down parkas and technical clothing designed for specialized outdoor activities such as mountaineering, backpacking and climbing. These products are used by elite mountaineering athletes and serious outdoor enthusiasts around the globe.

Footwear

We design, develop, market and distribute footwear products for men and women under our Columbia, Sorel and Montrail brands and for youth under our Columbia and Sorel brands. Our footwear products address the needs of outdoor consumers who participate in activities that typically involve challenging or unusual terrain that requires superior stability, cushioning and traction features. Our footwear products include durable, lightweight hiking and trekking boots, trail running shoes, rugged cold weather boots for activities on snow and ice, sandals for use in amphibious activities, and casual shoes for everyday use.

Accessories and Equipment

We design, develop, market and distribute a line of Columbia-branded accessories and equipment, including bags, packs, headwear, scarves and gloves. These products incorporate many of our performance technologies and complement our apparel and footwear collections to protect consumers during a multitude of outdoor activities in virtually any climate. We also design, develop, market and distribute a line of Mountain Hardwear accessories and equipment that includes technically-advanced tents, sleeping systems and backpacks. These equipment products are designed for mountaineering, ultralight backpacking and camping.

Licensed Products

We also license our Columbia, Pacific Trail and Sorel trademarks across a range of product categories that complement our current offerings. Licensing enables us to develop our "head-to-toe" outfitting concept by expanding the reach of our brands to appropriate and well-defined categories. In 2008, we licensed our brands in fifteen product categories, including, among others, socks, performance base layer, leather outerwear and accessories, camping gear, eyewear, home furnishings, watches and bicycles.

Product Design and Innovation

We believe our product innovation efforts are a key factor in our past and future success. We are committed to designing innovative and functional products that deliver relevant performance benefits to consumers who participate in a wide range of competitive and recreational outdoor activities, enabling them to enjoy their outdoor activities longer and more frequently. We also place significant value on product designs (the overall appearance and image of our products) that, along with technical performance features, distinguish our products in the marketplace.

Our research and development efforts involve working closely with independent fabric and component suppliers to develop products that address the unique performance problems encountered by consumers during outdoor activities. The most important performance features of our sportswear and outerwear products include water resistant or waterproof fabrics, insulation from cold ambient air temperatures and the chilling effects of wind, body warmth retention, skin protection from the damaging effects of UVA and UVB rays emitted by the sun, moisture wicking, breathability to minimize internal water vapor and moisture accumulation, protection from abrasion, liquid and stain repellency, light weight, and intelligent placement and operation of pockets and zippers for ample storage and easy access to important equipment and accessories. The most important performance features of our outdoor footwear products include cushioning, stability, superior traction in varying outdoor terrain and soil/moisture conditions, insulation from cold air or ground conditions such as snow and ice, water resistant or waterproof upper fabrics, water channeling and expulsion during aquatic activities, breathability of the upper fabrics, protection from bruising and abrasion, liquid and stain repellency, and fit.

Intellectual Property

We own many trademarks, including Columbia®, Columbia Sportswear Company®, Convert®, Bugaboo®, Bugabootoo®, OMNI-TECH®, OMNI-SHADE®, OMNI-SHIELD™, OMNI-DRY®, OMNI-GRIP®, TECHLITE®, GRT®, PFG®, PHG®, Columbia Interchange System®, Titanium®, Sorel®, Mountain Hard Wear®, Montrail®, Pacific Trail®, the Columbia diamond shaped logo and arrow-circle design, the Mountain Hardwear nut logo and the Sorel polar bear logo. Our trademarks, many of which are registered or subject to pending applications in the United States and other nations, are used on virtually all of our products. We believe that our trademarks are an important factor in creating a market for our products, in identifying the Company, and in differentiating our products from competitors' products. We vigorously protect these proprietary rights against counterfeit reproductions or other infringing activities.

Sales and Distribution

We sell our products through a mix of wholesale distribution channels, independent distributors, our own retail stores and licensees. Wholesale distribution channels include small, independently operated specialty stores, regional and national sporting goods chains, and large regional and national department store chains. We sell our products directly to consumers through a growing network of our own branded and outlet retail stores, and plan to begin selling our products to U.S. consumers on-line in the summer of 2009 through a new company-owned e-commerce website currently under development. In addition to our own retail operation, independent distributors, franchisees and licensees operate a total of over 400 Columbia and Mountain Hardwear-branded and outlet retail stores in various locations.

The following table presents net sales to unrelated entities and approximate percentages of net sales by geographic segment for each of the last three years (dollars in millions):

	2008 Net Sales	2008 % of Sales	2007 Net Sales	2007 % of Sales	2006 Net Sales	2006 % of Sales
United States	$ 727.7	55.2%	$ 767.2	56.6%	$ 752.0	58.4%
Europe, Middle East and Africa ("EMEA")	267.2	20.3	287.0	21.1	272.6	21.2
Latin America and Asia Pacific ("LAAP")	198.2	15.0	175.7	13.0	142.9	11.1
Canada	124.7	9.5	126.1	9.3	120.2	9.3
Total	$1,317.8	100.0%	$1,356.0	100.0%	$1,287.7	100.0%

See Note 15 of Notes to Consolidated Financial Statements for net sales to unrelated entities, income before income tax, interest income (expense), income tax expense, depreciation and amortization expense, goodwill and identifiable assets by geographic segment.

United States and Canada

We sell our products in the United States and Canada to wholesale customers, through our own retail stores, and through licensees. Approximately 49% of the wholesale customers that offer our products worldwide are located in the United States and Canada. As of December 31, 2008, we operated 29 outlet retail stores and 8 branded retail stores in various locations throughout North America. In 2008, we licensed our Columbia, Sorel and Pacific Trail trademarks through 18 licensees in the United States. Sales in these two countries accounted for 64.7% of our net sales for 2008.

We distribute the majority of our products sold to United States wholesale customers and our own retail stores from distribution centers in Portland, Oregon and Robards, Kentucky. We own and operate both of these facilities. We distribute the majority of our products in Canada through two distribution centers in Strathroy, Ontario. We lease one of these facilities and completed construction of our owned facility in June 2008. In some instances, we arrange to have products shipped directly from our independent manufacturers to customer-designated facilities in the United States and Canada.

EMEA

We sell our products in our EMEA segment to wholesale customers, independent distributors, and through our own retail stores. Approximately 48% of the wholesale customers that offer our products worldwide are located in Western Europe. Approximately 62% of independent distributors that offer our products worldwide are located in our EMEA segment. As of December 31, 2008, we operated three outlet retail stores in Europe: one each in France, Spain and the United Kingdom. Sales in our EMEA region accounted for 20.3% of our net sales for 2008.

We distribute our apparel and footwear products in direct markets in Europe through our distribution center in Cambrai, France, that we own and operate. Independent distributors in our EMEA region serve wholesale and retail customers in several locations throughout the EMEA region, including Russia, portions of Europe, the Middle East and Africa. The majority of sales to our EMEA distributors are factory-direct shipments.

LAAP

We sell our products in our LAAP segment to independent distributors, through our own retail stores, to franchisees, to licensees and to wholesale customers. Approximately 38% of independent distributors that offer our products worldwide are located in our LAAP segment. As of December 31, 2008, we operated 59 branded retail stores and 18 outlet retail stores in Japan and Korea within our LAAP region. Approximately 3% of the wholesale customers that offer our products worldwide are located in Japan and Korea. Sales in our LAAP region accounted for 15.0% of our net sales for 2008.

Independent distributors in our LAAP region serve wholesale and retail customers in several locations throughout the LAAP region, including Australia, New Zealand, Latin America, and Asia. The vast majority of sales to our LAAP distributors are factory-direct shipments. We distribute our products in Japan through an independent logistics company that owns and operates a warehouse located near Tokyo, Japan. We distribute our products in Korea from a leased warehouse near Seoul, Korea.

Advertising, Marketing, and Promotion

Advertising, marketing and promotional programs are integral parts of our global strategy to build brand equity, raise global brand awareness, infuse our brands with excitement and stimulate consumer demand for our products worldwide. Our advertising, marketing and promotional efforts consist of integrated marketing activities, including print, television, outdoor and Internet advertising; enhanced in-store displays and merchandising techniques executed in partnership with various wholesale customers; public relations and brand communications focused on our innovative apparel, footwear, accessories and equipment technologies, performance features and styling. Our key brand messages are reinforced consistently at our wholesale customers' stores using concept shops, focus areas and other visual merchandising displays dedicated exclusively to selling our merchandise on a year-round basis.

We also reinforce our marketing and product innovation messages through selected sponsorships of individual outdoor athletes, personalities and teams who serve as inspirational models of excellence to consumers. In 2008 we debuted a new 3-year sponsorship of the Team Columbia-Highroad professional cycling team at the 2008 Tour de France. Team Columbia-Highroad finished 2008 as the number one cycling team in the world with more stage victories over the course of the professional cycling season than any other team. The team's success has continued to generate substantial media attention and generate favorable visibility for the Columbia brand in key markets around the world, especially in Europe, Australia and Latin American markets where professional cycling is among the most popular spectator and participant sports.

Working Capital Utilization

We design, develop, market and distribute our products, but do not own or operate our own manufacturing facilities. As a result, most of our capital is invested in short-term working capital assets, including cash and cash equivalents, short term investments, accounts receivable from customers, and finished goods inventory. At December 31, 2008, working capital assets accounted for approximately 76% of total assets. As a result, the degree to which we efficiently utilize our working capital assets can have a significant impact on our profitability and return on invested capital. The overall goals of our working capital management efforts are to maintain the minimum level of inventory necessary to deliver goods on time to our customers to satisfy end consumer demand, and to minimize the cycle time from the purchase of inventory from our suppliers to the collection of accounts receivable balances from our customers.

Demand Planning and Inventory Management

As a branded consumer products company, inventory represents one of the largest and riskiest capital commitments in our business model. We design and develop our seasonal product lines twelve to eighteen months in advance of their availability to consumers in retail stores. As a result, our ability to estimate seasonal consumer demand and to purchase appropriate levels of finished goods from our suppliers can significantly affect our sales, gross margins and profitability. For this reason, we maintain and continue to make substantial investments in information systems, processes and personnel in support of our ongoing demand planning efforts. The goals of our demand planning efforts are to purchase an adequate amount of inventory to service a targeted percentage of total consumer demand while minimizing excess inventory to avoid the negative effect that liquidating excess, end-of-season goods at discounted prices has on our gross margins and profitability.

In order to manage inventory risk, we use incentive discounts to encourage our wholesale customers to place advance orders approximately four to six months in advance of scheduled delivery. We use those advance orders, together with forecasted demand from our own retail stores, market trends, historical data, customer and sales feedback and several other important factors, to determine the volumes of each product to purchase from our suppliers around the world. From the time of initial order through production, receipt and delivery, we attempt to manage our inventory to reduce risk.

Our inventory management efforts cannot entirely eliminate inventory risk due to the inherently unpredictable nature of consumer demand, the ability of customers to cancel their orders prior to shipment, and other variables that affect our customers' ability to take delivery of their orders when originally scheduled. In addition, we build calculated amounts of speculative inventory to support estimated at-once orders from customers and auto-replenishment orders on certain long-lived styles.

Credit and Collection

We extend credit to our customers based on an assessment of the customer's financial condition, generally without requiring collateral. To assist us in scheduling production with our suppliers and delivering seasonal products to our customers on time, we offer customers discounts for placing advance orders and extended payment terms for taking delivery before the peak shipping season. These extended payment terms increase our exposure to the risk of uncollectible receivables. In order to manage the inherent risks of customer receivables, we maintain and continue to invest in information systems, processes and personnel skilled in credit and collections. In some markets and with some customers we use credit insurance or standby letters of credit to minimize our risk of credit loss.

Sourcing and Manufacturing

Virtually all of our products are produced to our specifications by independent manufacturers located outside the United States. We believe that the use of independent manufacturers enables us to substantially limit our capital expenditures and avoid the costs and risks associated with owning and operating large production facilities and managing large labor forces. We also believe that the use of independent manufacturers greatly increases our production capacity, maximizes our flexibility and improves our product pricing. We generally do not maintain long-term manufacturing contracts; however, we believe that our historical long-term relationships with various manufacturers will help to ensure that adequate sources are available to produce a sufficient supply of goods in a timely manner and on satisfactory economic terms in the future. Our four largest factory groups accounted for approximately 11% of our total global apparel production in 2008 and a single vendor supplies substantially all of the zippers used in our products. These companies, however, have multiple factory locations, many of which are in different countries, thus reducing the risk that unfavorable conditions at a single factory or location will have a material adverse effect on our business.

Our apparel is manufactured in more than fifteen countries with Vietnam and China accounting for approximately 67% of our 2008 apparel production. Our footwear is manufactured in three countries with China and Vietnam accounting for approximately 99% of our 2008 footwear production.

We maintain thirteen manufacturing liaison offices in a total of seven Asian countries. Personnel in these manufacturing liaison offices are direct employees of Columbia, and are responsible for overseeing production at our independent manufacturers. We believe that having employees physically located in these regions enhances our ability to monitor factories for compliance with our policies, procedures and standards related to quality, delivery, pricing and labor practices. Our quality assurance process is designed to ensure that our products meet the highest quality standards. We believe that our quality assurance process is an important and effective means of maintaining the quality and reputation of our products.

Backlog

We typically receive the majority of our advance orders from our wholesale customers for the fall and spring seasons by March 31 and September 30, respectively, based upon customer ordering deadlines that we establish. As a result, our order backlog at March 31 and September 30 has historically been a meaningful indicator of anticipated sales for the corresponding future period. Accordingly, we disclose our backlog at March 31 and at September 30 in our Quarterly Reports on Form 10-Q for those respective periods, rather than at December 31. Generally, orders are subject to cancellation prior to the date of shipment.

Our owned retail stores do not participate in the advance order program, nor will our e-commerce business scheduled for launch in the summer of 2009. Accordingly, to the extent that order cancellations from wholesale customers remain at elevated levels and our retail and e-commerce sales grow to represent a larger proportion of our total sales, our advance order backlog may become less indicative of anticipated sales for the corresponding future periods.

Competition

The markets for sportswear, outerwear, footwear, and related accessories and equipment are highly competitive. In each of our geographic markets, we face significant competition from numerous and varying competitors. Some of our large wholesale customers also pose a significant competitive threat by marketing apparel, footwear and equipment under their own private labels. Our licensees operate in very competitive markets, such as those for watches, leather outerwear and socks. In addition, our retail expansion initiative is exposing us to a new set of competitors who operate retail stores in outlet malls and key metropolitan markets. We believe that the primary competitive factors in the market for active sportswear, outerwear, footwear and related accessories and equipment are brand strength, product innovation, product design and functionality, durability and price.

Government Regulation

Many of our imports are subject to existing or potential governmental tariff and non-tariff barriers to trade, such as import duties and potential safeguard measures that may limit the quantity of various types of goods that may be imported into the United States and other countries. These trade barriers often represent a material portion of the cost of the merchandise. Our products are also subject to domestic and foreign product safety and environmental standards, laws and other regulations, which are increasingly restrictive and complex. Although we diligently monitor these standards and restrictions, the United States or other countries may impose new or adjusted quotas, duties, safety requirements, material restrictions, or other restrictions or regulations, any of which may have a material adverse effect on our results of operations and financial condition.

Employees

At December 31, 2008 we had the equivalent of 3,163 full-time employees. Of these employees, 1,737 were based in the United States, 985 in Asia, 320 in Europe and 121 in Canada.

Available Information

We file with the Securities and Exchange Commission ("SEC") our annual report on Form 10-K, quarterly reports on Form 10-Q, current reports on Form 8-K and all amendments to those reports, proxy statements and registration statements. You may read and copy any material we file with the SEC at the SEC's Public Reference Room at 100 F Street, NE, Washington, D.C. 20549. You may also obtain information on the operation of the Public Reference Room by calling the SEC at 1-800-SEC-0330. In addition, the SEC maintains an internet site at http://www.sec.gov that contains reports, proxy and information statements, and other information regarding issuers, including us, that file electronically. We make available free of charge on or through our website at www.columbia.com our annual reports on Form 10-K, quarterly reports on Form 10-Q, current reports on Form 8-K and amendments to these reports filed or furnished pursuant to Section 13(a) or 15(d) of the Exchange Act as soon as reasonably practicable after we file these materials with the SEC.

Item 6. *SELECTED FINANCIAL DATA*

Selected Consolidated Financial Data

The selected consolidated financial data presented below for, and as of the end of, each of the years in the five-year period ended December 31, 2008 have been derived from our audited consolidated financial statements. The consolidated financial data should be read in conjunction with the Consolidated Financial Statements and Accompanying Notes that appear elsewhere in this annual report and Management's Discussion and Analysis of Financial Condition and Results of Operations set forth in Item 7.

	Year Ended December 31,				
	2008	**2007**	**2006 (1)**	**2005**	**2004**
	(In thousands, except per share amounts)				
Statement of Operations Data:					
Net sales	$1,317,835	$1,356,039	$1,287,672	$1,155,791	$1,095,307
Net income	95,047	144,452	123,018	130,736	138,624
Per Share of Common Stock Data:					
Earnings per share:					
Basic	$ 2.75	$ 4.00	$ 3.39	$ 3.39	$ 3.44
Diluted	2.74	3.96	3.36	3.36	3.40
Cash dividends per share	0.64	0.58	0.14	—	—
Weighted average shares outstanding:					
Basic	34,610	36,106	36,245	38,549	40,266
Diluted	34,711	36,434	36,644	38,943	40,812

	December 31,				
	2008	**2007**	**2006**	**2005**	**2004**
Balance Sheet Data:					
Total assets	$1,148,236	$1,166,481	$1,027,289	$ 967,640	$ 947,625
Long-term obligations, net of current maturities	15	61	136	7,414	12,636

(1) Effective January 1, 2006, we adopted the fair value recognition provisions of Statement of Financial Accounting Standards ("SFAS") No. 123R, *Share-Based Payment,* under which compensation expense is recognized in the Consolidated Statement of Operations for the fair value of employee stock-based compensation. Prior to the adoption of SFAS No. 123R, we accounted for stock-based compensation using the intrinsic value method prescribed in Accounting Principles Board ("APB") Opinion No. 25, *Accounting for Stock Issued to Employees*, and related interpretations. Accordingly, under APB Opinion No. 25, no compensation expense was recognized because the exercise price of our employee stock options was equal to the market price of the underlying stock on the date of grant. We applied the disclosure provisions of SFAS No. 123, *Accounting for Stock Based Compensation*, as amended by SFAS No. 148, *Accounting for Stock Based Compensation—Transition and Disclosure*, as if the fair value method had been applied in measuring compensation expense. See Note 12 of Notes to Consolidated Financial Statements for further discussion.

Item 7. *MANAGEMENT'S DISCUSSION AND ANALYSIS OF FINANCIAL CONDITION AND RESULTS OF OPERATIONS*

This Annual Report, including Item 1 of Part I and Items 7 and 7A of Part II, contains forward-looking statements. Forward-looking statements include any statements related to our expectations regarding future performance or market position, including any statements regarding anticipated sales across markets, distribution channels and product categories, access to raw materials and factory capacity, and financing and working capital requirements and resources.

These forward-looking statements, and others we make from time to time, are subject to a number of risks and uncertainties. Many factors may cause actual results to differ materially from those projected in forward-looking statements, including the risks described above in Item 1A, Risk Factors. We do not undertake any duty to either update forward-looking statements after the date they are made or conform them to actual results or to changes in circumstances or expectations.

Our Business

As one of the largest outdoor apparel and footwear companies in the world, we design, develop, market and distribute active outdoor apparel, footwear and related accessories and equipment under the Columbia, Mountain Hardwear, Sorel, Montrail, and Pacific Trail brands. Each of our brands is distributed through a mix of wholesale distribution channels, independent distributors, our own retail stores and licensees.

As a consumer products company, the popularity of outdoor activities and changing design trends affect the desirability of our products. Therefore, we seek to influence, anticipate and respond to trends and shifts in consumer preferences by adjusting the mix of available product offerings, developing new products with innovative performance features and designs, and by creating persuasive and memorable marketing communications to drive consumer awareness and demand. Failure to respond to consumer needs and preferences in a timely and adequate manner could have a material adverse effect on our sales and profitability.

Strategy and Outlook

Our business, like other branded consumer product companies, is heavily dependent upon discretionary consumer spending patterns. Our net sales volumes have been negatively affected by the volatility of the global economy and its impact on consumer purchasing behavior, and retailers' behavior related to advance orders, order cancellations and seasonal reorders. The current macro-economic environment has caused tightening of credit for some of our wholesale customers, independent distributors and consumers and a significant slowing of retail sales. This has resulted in, and could continue to cause, a more cautious approach by many of our wholesale customers and independent distributors when placing advance orders for seasonal products and reducing, delaying delivery of, or cancelling advance orders placed in earlier periods. In addition, the effects of foreign currency exchange rates may amplify potential net sales decline if the U.S. dollar continues to strengthen compared to foreign currencies in our direct markets. We expect our retail revenues to partially offset some of this anticipated wholesale revenue decline.

We believe that we have appropriately factored into our plans our historical experiences, incremental sales from our new retail stores, and the estimated effect of changes in foreign currency exchange rates. However, unfavorable and unprecedented macro-economic conditions have increased the uncertainty of our planning and forecasts. In this challenging economic environment, we are also mindful of our reliance on the overall financial health of our wholesale customers and their ability to continue to access credit markets to fund their purchases and day-to-day operations.

Strategic Growth Initiatives

Our goal is to achieve sustainable, profitable growth by creating innovative products, elevating consumer perception of our brands, increasing consumer and retailer awareness and demand for our products, creating compelling retail environments, and building stronger emotional brand connections with consumers over time. Specifically, our growth strategies include:

- designing authentic, innovative products that address activity-specific performance needs of active outdoor enthusiasts. Our goal is to help consumers of every ability enjoy their outdoor lifestyles and activities more comfortably for longer periods;

- expanding our direct-to-consumer business by building a network of branded retail stores in key metropolitan cities, expanding our network of outlet retail stores in the United States, Europe and Canada, and establishing an e-commerce platform. We expect our branded retail stores and e-commerce platform to increase brand awareness and demand for our products by creating compelling retail environments that communicate key marketing initiatives and product innovation, and offering a larger breadth of product assortments than are available in any of our wholesale customers' stores. In addition, the goal of opening additional outlet retail stores in outlet centers in the United States, Europe and Canada is to support our brands by allowing us to liquidate end-of-season products with less reliance on traditional wholesale and discount channels. We expect this strategy to require significant long-term lease obligations, capital investments in leasehold improvements, information systems, additional personnel and other operating expenses.

- creating and delivering targeted brand-enhancing advertising and marketing programs that communicate distinct, inspiring brand positions for each of our outdoor brands, differentiate our brands from other branded competitors as well as from the private label brands developed and marketed by many of our large retail customers, and result in increasing demand and strong emotional connections with consumers;

- expanding our global footwear business by building a footwear organization with proven skills in designing, developing and marketing innovative, performance-driven products and by expanding distribution into leading footwear retail channels in key markets;

- increasing demand in our European business by offering product assortments and marketing programs that are consistent with our global focus on innovative products, compelling retail presentation and brand-enhancing communications.

Overview

The following discussion of our results of operations and liquidity and capital resources, including known trends and uncertainties identified by management, should be read in conjunction with the Consolidated Financial Statements and accompanying Notes that appear elsewhere in this annual report.

In 2007, we reclassified our geographical net sales and segment reporting to reflect changes in our internal management and oversight structure as well as growth of the international distributor business. Net sales to international distributors, previously included as part of "Other International," were regrouped into either the Europe, Middle-East and Africa ("EMEA") or Latin America and Asia Pacific ("LAAP") region, in accordance with the markets in which each distributor operates. Previously reported geographical net sales information for fiscal year 2006 has been reclassified to reflect this change.

All references to years relate to the calendar year ended December 31. Highlights for the year ended December 31, 2008 include the following:

- Net sales decreased $38.2 million, or 3%, to $1,317.8 million in 2008 from $1,356.0 million in 2007. Changes in foreign currency exchange rates compared to 2007 contributed one percentage point of benefit to the consolidated net sales comparison. The decrease in net sales was primarily the result of decreased sales of Columbia-branded products in the United States, EMEA direct and Canada, partially offset by increased sales of Mountain Hardwear-branded products and increased sales in the LAAP region and to our EMEA distributors.

- Our backlog for the spring 2009 selling season, reported as of September 30, 2008, decreased $43.5 million, or 10.5%, to $370.9 million from $414.4 million as of September 30, 2007. Changes in foreign currency exchange rates compared to 2007 contributed less than one percentage point of benefit to the spring 2009 backlog comparison. The decrease in our spring backlog was the result of a decline in orders in the United States, EMEA and Canada driven primarily by a decline in orders of Columbia-branded sportswear. Although we cannot predict with certainty any future results, our reported backlog is one indicator of our anticipated net sales for the spring 2009 selling season. Many factors, however, could cause actual sales to differ materially from reported order backlog, including cancellation of orders by customers, changes in foreign currency exchange rates and continued deterioration of macroeconomic conditions. We expect that incremental sales through our expanded base of branded and outlet retail stores will partially offset some of the anticipated wholesale sales decline for the spring 2009 season. Moreover, our spring 2009 backlog should not be used in forecasting sales beyond the spring 2009 selling season.

- Gross profit increased 30 basis points to 43.1% in 2008 from 42.8% in 2007. Gross profit margins expanded as a result of a lower volume of close-out product sales and an increase in average selling prices, partially offset by the negative effects of an increased mix of sales to distributors, which carry lower margins than wholesale customers, and the effects of changes in foreign currency exchange rates.

- Selling, general and administrative expense increased $44.6 million, or 12%, to $430.4 million in 2008 from $385.8 million in 2007. This increase was primarily due to our planned investment in incremental marketing activities in 2008 to drive consumer demand for our brands, together with initial investment and incremental operating costs of our new retail stores.

- A non-cash pre-tax charge of $24.7 million, or $0.46 per diluted share after-tax, was incurred in the fourth quarter of 2008 for the write-down of acquired intangible assets related to our acquisitions of the Pacific Trail and Montrail brands in 2006. The impairment charge related primarily to goodwill and trademarks and resulted from our annual evaluation of intangible asset values.

- Net income decreased 34% to $95.0 million in 2008 from $144.5 million in 2007, and diluted earnings per share decreased to $2.74 in 2008, including a $0.46 per diluted share after-tax impairment charge, compared to $3.96 in 2007. 2008 net income was unfavorably affected by reduced revenues, increased selling, general and administrative expenses and the non-cash pre-tax impairment charge, partially offset by a lower effective tax rate in 2008 compared to 2007. Our effective tax rate was 24.7% in 2008 compared to 30.6% in 2007. The reduced 2008 tax rate resulted primarily from a higher proportion of our income being generated in foreign jurisdictions with lower overall tax rates, increased foreign tax credits and the favorable conclusion of a European tax examination.

- Since the inception of our stock repurchase plan in 2004 through December 31, 2008, our Board of Directors has authorized the repurchase of $500 million of our common stock. As of December 31, 2008, we have repurchased 8,694,657 shares under this program at an aggregate purchase price of approximately $400 million. Shares of our common stock may be purchased in the open market or through privately negotiated transactions, subject to market conditions. The repurchase program does not obligate us to acquire any specific number of shares or to acquire shares over any specified period of time.

26

	Year Ended December 31,		
	2008	**2007**	**% Change**
	(In millions, except for percentage changes)		
Geographical Net Sales to Unrelated Entities:			
United States	$ 727.7	$ 767.2	(5)%
EMEA	267.2	287.0	(7)%
LAAP	198.2	175.7	13%
Canada	124.7	126.1	(1)%
	$1,317.8	$1,356.0	(3)%
Categorical Net Sales to Unrelated Entities:			
Sportswear	$ 540.9	$ 565.6	(4)%
Outerwear	491.7	497.6	(1)%
Footwear	217.2	227.4	(4)%
Accessories and Equipment	68.0	65.4	4%
	$1,317.8	$1,356.0	(3)%
Brand Net Sales to Unrelated Entities:			
Columbia	$1,162.0	$1,211.2	(4)%
Mountain Hardwear	95.0	82.6	15%
Sorel	48.1	45.6	5%
Montrail	10.2	12.7	(20)%
Pacific Trail	2.5	3.9	(36)%
	$1,317.8	$1,356.0	(3)%

Although we cannot predict future results with certainty and despite current global economic conditions, we are committed to our demand creation and retail expansion strategies to stimulate increased consumer demand and improve inventory management with minimal disruption to our wholesale distribution channels. With our commitment to investment in these strategies, a well-developed sourcing and distribution infrastructure and a proven design and product development team, we believe that we are well positioned to establish sustainable platforms that will support long-term growth and profitability.

Results of Operations

Net income decreased $49.5 million, or 34%, to $95.0 million in 2008 from $144.5 million in 2007. Diluted earnings per share decreased to $2.74 in 2008, including a $0.46 per diluted share after-tax impairment charge, from $3.96 in 2007. Net income increased $21.5 million, or 17%, to $144.5 million in 2007 from $123.0 million in 2006. Diluted earnings per share increased to $3.96 in 2007 from $3.36 in 2006.

The following table sets forth, for the periods indicated, the percentage relationship to net sales of specified items in our Consolidated Statements of Operations:

	2008	2007	2006
Net sales	100.0%	100.0%	100.0%
Cost of sales	56.9	57.2	58.0
Gross profit	43.1	42.8	42.0
Selling, general and administrative expense	32.7	28.5	28.5
Impairment of acquired intangible assets	1.9	—	—
Net licensing income	0.5	0.4	0.5
Income from operations	9.0	14.7	14.0
Interest income, net	0.6	0.6	0.4
Income before income tax	9.6	15.3	14.4
Income tax expense	(2.4)	(4.6)	(4.8)
Net income	7.2%	10.7%	9.6%

Year Ended December 31, 2008 Compared to Year Ended December 31, 2007

Net Sales: Consolidated net sales decreased $38.2 million, or 3%, to $1,317.8 million in 2008 from $1,356.0 million in 2007. Changes in foreign currency exchange rates compared to 2007 contributed one percentage point of benefit to the consolidated net sales comparison. The decrease in net sales was led by the United States, followed by the EMEA region and Canada, partially offset by increased net sales in the LAAP region. By product category, the reduction in net sales was led by sportswear, followed by footwear and outerwear, partially offset by increased net sales of accessories and equipment.

Sales by Product Category

Net sales of sportswear decreased $24.7 million, or 4%, to $540.9 million in 2008 from $565.6 million in 2007. The decrease in sportswear net sales was predominantly the result of decreased net sales in the United States, followed by the EMEA region, offset by increased net sales in the LAAP region and Canada. The sportswear net sales decrease was led by the United States wholesale business for the Columbia brand, partially offset by incremental net sales through our expanded base of branded and outlet retail stores. We primarily attribute the decrease in wholesale net sales of sportswear to the lower initial order volumes and the weak U.S. retail environment resulting from difficult macro-economic conditions.

Net sales of outerwear decreased $5.9 million, or 1%, to $491.7 million in 2008 from $497.6 million in 2007. The decrease in outerwear net sales was led by the United States, followed by the EMEA region and Canada, partially offset by an increase in the LAAP region. The decrease in outerwear net sales was predominantly the result of decreased sales of the Columbia brand in the United States wholesale and EMEA direct businesses. The decrease in both regions was primarily the result of lower initial order volumes for the spring and fall 2008 seasons as well as the weak retail environment resulting from difficult macro-economic conditions. The decrease in sales of Columbia-branded outerwear was partially offset by increased sales of Mountain Hardwear-branded outerwear.

Net sales of footwear decreased $10.2 million, or 4%, to $217.2 million in 2008 from $227.4 million in 2007. The decrease in footwear net sales was led by the EMEA region, followed by Canada, partially offset by increased net sales of footwear in the LAAP region and the United States. The decrease in footwear net sales in the EMEA region was led by EMEA direct footwear net sales, followed by EMEA distributor net sales. The decrease in EMEA direct footwear net sales was primarily the result of lower initial order volumes due to continued product assortment and marketing challenges, coupled with economic uncertainty in that region. The decrease in EMEA distributor footwear net sales was primarily a result of earlier shipments of spring 2008 product that occurred in the fourth quarter of 2007.

Net sales of accessories and equipment increased $2.6 million, or 4%, to $68.0 million in 2008 from $65.4 million in 2007. Accessories and equipment sales growth was led by the LAAP region, followed by Canada, partially offset by a decrease in net sales in the United States, while net sales of accessories and equipment remained flat in the EMEA region.

Sales by Geographic Region

Net sales in the United States decreased $39.5 million, or 5%, to $727.7 million in 2008 from $767.2 million in 2007. The reduction in net sales in the United States was led by sportswear, followed by outerwear and accessories and equipment, while sales of footwear remained essentially flat. The net sales decrease was led by the wholesale business for the Columbia brand, partially offset by increased net sales through our expanded base of branded and outlet retail stores. During 2008 we opened 15 new outlet retail stores and 5 branded retail stores in the United States, ending the year with 28 outlet retail stores and 8 branded retail stores in the United States.

Net sales in the EMEA region decreased $19.8 million, or 7%, to $267.2 million in 2008 from $287.0 million in 2007. Changes in foreign currency exchange rates contributed five percentage points of benefit to

EMEA net sales compared to 2007. The decrease in net sales in the EMEA region was led by footwear, followed by outerwear and sportswear, while net sales of accessories and equipment remained essentially flat. The decrease in net sales in the EMEA region included a decrease in EMEA direct net sales, partially offset by an increase in net sales to EMEA distributors. The decrease in EMEA direct net sales was the result of lower initial order volumes for the spring and fall 2008 seasons due to continued product assortment and marketing challenges, coupled with economic uncertainty in the region. The increase in net sales to EMEA distributors primarily reflects increased Columbia-branded outerwear and sportswear net sales to our largest distributor in the region.

Net sales in the LAAP region increased $22.5 million, or 13%, to $198.2 million in 2008 from $175.7 million in 2007. Changes in foreign currency exchange rates contributed less than one percentage point of benefit to LAAP net sales compared to 2007. Sales growth in the LAAP region was led by our Japan business, which benefited from foreign currency exchange rates, followed by our LAAP distributor business, while net sales in Korea remained essentially flat, including a negative impact from foreign currency exchange rates. The increase in Japan net sales was primarily the result of growth in our retail business as well as continued expansion with key wholesale partners, particularly in the sports chain channel.

Net sales in Canada decreased $1.4 million, or 1%, to $124.7 million in 2008 from $126.1 million in 2007. Changes in foreign currency exchange rates contributed two percentage points of benefit to Canada net sales compared to 2007. The decrease in net sales in Canada was led by outerwear, followed by footwear, partially offset by increased net sales of sportswear and accessories and equipment. The decrease in outerwear was primarily attributable to lower initial order volumes of Columbia-branded products for the fall 2008 season, partially offset by incremental sales of Mountain Hardwear-branded products that were previously sold through third party distributors.

Gross Profit: Gross profit as a percentage of net sales increased to 43.1% in 2008 from 42.8% in 2007. Gross profit margins expanded in all of our product categories primarily due to a lower volume of close-out product sales and an increase in average selling prices, partially offset by the negative effects of an increased mix of sales to distributors, which carry lower margins than wholesale customers, and the effects of changes in foreign currency exchange rates.

A decrease in 2008 close-out product sales at slightly lower gross margins compared to 2007 had a favorable affect on our consolidated gross profits. We primarily attribute this decrease to earlier close-out sales of fall 2007 product in the fourth quarter of 2007.

Our gross profits may not be comparable to those of other companies in our industry because some include all of the costs related to their distribution network in cost of sales. We, like others, have chosen to include these expenses as a component of selling, general and administrative expense.

Selling, General and Administrative Expense: Selling, general and administrative expense ("SG&A") includes all costs associated with our design, merchandising, marketing, distribution and corporate functions including related depreciation and amortization.

SG&A expense increased $44.6 million, or 12%, to $430.4 million in 2008 from $385.8 million in 2007. Selling expenses increased $8.2 million, or 7%, while general and administrative expenses increased $36.4 million, or 13%. As a percentage of net sales, SG&A expense increased to 32.7% of net sales in 2008 from 28.5% of net sales in 2007.

Selling expenses, including commissions and advertising, increased to 9.2% of net sales in 2008 from 8.3% of net sales in 2007. We attribute the increase in selling expenses as a percentage of net sales to our increased marketing investments to drive consumer demand for our brands, which was amplified by a decrease in consolidated net sales in 2008 compared with the same period in 2007.

29

The increase in general and administrative expenses primarily resulted from the start-up and operational costs of our new retail stores. Depreciation and amortization included in SG&A expense totaled $30.1 million for 2008, compared to $29.3 million for the same period in 2007. We expect SG&A to continue to increase as we pursue our retail expansion strategies.

Impairment of Acquired Intangible Assets: We incurred a $24.7 million non-cash pre-tax charge, or approximately $0.46 per diluted share after tax, for the write-down of acquired intangible assets related to our acquisitions of the Pacific Trail and Montrail brands in 2006. The impairment charge related primarily to goodwill and trademarks and resulted from our annual evaluation of intangible asset values. These brands have not achieved our sales and profitability objectives and the deterioration in the macro-economic environment and resulting effect on consumer demand have decreased the probability of realizing these objectives in the near future. Going forward we remain committed to marketing and distributing Montrail-branded footwear through the outdoor specialty, running specialty and sporting goods channels. Beginning in 2009, Pacific Trail products will be sold solely through licensing arrangements.

Net Licensing Income: Net licensing income increased $0.8 million, or 15%, to $6.0 million in 2008 from $5.2 million in 2007. In 2008, licensing income was led by Columbia-branded leather accessories, followed by Columbia-branded socks, eyewear, insulated products including soft-sided coolers, and camping gear.

Interest Income, Net: Interest income was $7.6 million in 2008 compared to $9.0 million in 2007. The decrease in interest income was primarily due to lower average investment yields compared with the same period in 2007. Interest expense was nominal in 2008 and 2007.

Income Tax Expense: Our provision for income taxes decreased to $31.2 million in 2008 from $63.6 million in 2007. This decrease resulted from lower income before tax combined with a decrease in our effective income tax rate to 24.7% in 2008 compared to 30.6% in 2007. The decrease in our tax rate resulted primarily from generating a higher proportion of our income in foreign jurisdictions with lower overall tax rates, increased foreign tax credits and the favorable conclusion of a European tax examination.

Year Ended December 31, 2007 Compared to Year Ended December 31, 2006

Net Sales: Consolidated net sales increased $68.3 million, or 5%, to $1,356.0 million in 2007 from $1,287.7 million in 2006. Changes in foreign currency exchange rates compared with 2006 contributed two percentage points of consolidated net sales growth. Increased net sales were realized in each major geographic region in which we operate, led by LAAP, followed by the United States, EMEA and Canada. By product category, increased net sales were led by sportswear, followed by footwear, accessories and equipment, while sales of outerwear remained essentially flat. Sales growth was primarily the result of an increase in the quantity of units sold in each geographic region.

Sales by Product Category

Net sales of sportswear increased $56.5 million, or 11%, to $565.6 million in 2007 from $509.1 million in 2006. As a result of continued strength in our sportswear business, it remained our largest product category, representing 41.7% of total sales. We primarily attribute the increase in sportswear sales to higher sales in the United States, followed by EMEA, LAAP and Canada. The increase in sportswear sales was driven by a broader assortment of products, competitive pricing and related consumer demand, particularly for fleece sweaters, knitted and woven tops and pants.

Net sales of outerwear increased $1.1 million, or less than 1%, to $497.6 million in 2007 from $496.5 million in 2006. We primarily attribute the increase in outerwear sales to an increase in sales in LAAP, followed by Canada, while sales of outerwear decreased in EMEA and the United States. Outerwear sales growth was driven by increased sales of our Columbia and Mountain Hardwear brands across all regions, except EMEA direct. Growth in Columbia-branded outerwear sales in the United States was largely offset by a significant decrease in Pacific Trail outerwear sales. The decrease in outerwear sales in EMEA direct was primarily due to the extended periods of unseasonably warm weather conditions throughout Western Europe during the fall and winter seasons of 2006, which resulted in lower pre-season orders from retailers for the 2007 fall season.

Net sales of footwear increased $7.7 million, or 4%, to $227.4 million in 2007 from $219.7 million in 2006. Footwear sales growth was led by LAAP, followed by EMEA and Canada, while sales of footwear decreased in the United States. We primarily attribute the increase in international footwear sales to higher sales of men's and women's spring footwear to key international distributor markets in the LAAP and EMEA regions. The decrease in footwear sales in the United States was primarily due to higher than average volumes of fall 2006 Columbia and Sorel cold weather footwear product remaining in inventories at retailers resulting in lower orders from those retailers for fall 2007 products.

Net sales of accessories and equipment increased $3.0 million, or 5%, to $65.4 million in 2007 from $62.4 million in 2006. Accessories and equipment sales growth was led by LAAP, followed by the United States and EMEA, partially offset by a decrease in net sales in Canada. The increase in sales of accessories and equipment in our LAAP region was primarily related to expanded distribution and increased consumer demand.

Sales by Geographic Region

Net sales in the United States increased $15.2 million, or 2%, to $767.2 million in 2007 from $752.0 million in 2006. The increase in net sales in the United States was attributable to increased sales of sportswear, followed by accessories and equipment, while sales of footwear and outerwear decreased. Sportswear sales growth was primarily attributable to strong sales of fleece and sweaters. Growth in sales of Columbia-branded outerwear was largely offset by a significant decrease in Pacific Trail outerwear sales. The decrease in footwear sales was primarily due to higher than average volumes of fall 2006 Columbia and Sorel cold weather footwear product remaining in inventories at retailers resulting in lower orders from those retailers for fall 2007 products and to a lesser degree, a decrease in Montrail footwear sales.

Net sales in the EMEA region increased $14.4 million, or 5%, to $287.0 million in 2007 from $272.6 million in 2006. Changes in foreign currency exchange rates compared with 2006 contributed six percentage points of EMEA net sales growth. The increase in net sales in the EMEA region was led by sportswear, followed by footwear and accessories and equipment, partially offset by a decrease in outerwear sales. Our EMEA direct business was negatively affected by extended periods of unseasonably warm weather conditions throughout Western Europe during the fall and winter seasons of 2006, which resulted in lower pre-season orders from retailers buying less outerwear for the 2007 fall season. EMEA direct net sales decreased as the result of decreased sales in the United Kingdom, Italy and Spain. In response to business challenges in EMEA direct, we reorganized our European management team in the second half of 2007 and reestablished strong connections between our European and U.S. product teams to ensure more direction and interaction as we realign our European product assortments with consumers' expectations. Our EMEA distributor business growth was largely the result of increased sales of outerwear, sportswear and footwear by our distributor in Russia.

Net sales in the LAAP region increased $32.8 million, or 23%, to $175.7 million in 2007 from $142.9 million in 2006. Changes in foreign currency exchange rates compared with 2006 contributed one percentage point of LAAP net sales growth. Sales growth in the LAAP region was led by our LAAP distributor business, followed by our Korea and Japan businesses. Sales growth was led by footwear, followed by sportswear, outerwear and accessories and equipment. Sales growth by our LAAP distributors was largely the result of increased sales by our distributor in China, primarily due to increased sales of footwear. The increase in Korea sales resulted from the opening of new stores and continued growth of Columbia outerwear sales. Japan sales growth resulted from more favorable weather during the fourth quarter of 2007 as well as increased sales from our own retail channel.

Net sales in Canada increased $5.9 million, or 5%, to $126.1 million in 2007 from $120.2 million in 2006. Changes in foreign currency exchange rates compared with 2006 contributed five percentage points of Canada's net sales growth. Sales growth was led by sportswear, followed by outerwear and footwear, while sales of accessories and equipment decreased. Cold weather conditions during the fourth quarter of 2007 resulted in a higher volume of close-out product sales compared to the same period in 2006.

Gross Profit: Gross profit as a percentage of net sales increased to 42.8% in 2007 from 42.0% in 2006. We primarily attribute the increase in gross profit margin to modest increases in our average selling prices on spring 2007 products, lower freight costs and favorable hedged currency rates. The favorable gross profit effect of these items was partially offset by increased sales of spring and fall close-out product and higher international distributor shipments, both at lower gross margins.

Improvement in foreign currency hedge rates for our spring and fall 2007 selling seasons favorably affected our gross profit. Since our global supply of inventory is generally purchased with U.S. dollars, the gross profit of our direct international businesses is partially dependent on the valuation of the U.S. dollar. For our spring and fall 2007 selling seasons, the hedge rates for our European and Canadian direct businesses improved from our spring and fall 2006 selling seasons.

An increase in 2007 close-out product sales at lower gross margins compared to 2006 had a negative effect on our consolidated gross profits. We primarily attribute this increase to elevated close-out sales levels in 2007, due to unseasonably cool weather conditions in the early part of the spring season in the United States and earlier shipments of fall 2007 close-outs compared to 2006.

Selling, General and Administrative Expense: SG&A expense increased $19.0 million, or 5%, to $385.8 million in 2007 from $366.8 million in 2006. Selling expenses decreased $1.6 million, or 1%, while general and administrative expenses increased $20.6 million, or 8%. As a percentage of net sales, SG&A remained flat at 28.5% for 2007 and 2006.

Selling expenses, including commissions and advertising, decreased to 8.3% of net sales for 2007 from 8.9% of net sales for 2006. We largely attribute the decrease in selling expenses as a percentage of net sales to reduced commission rates in the United States and changes to our sales agency structures in Europe as well as lower advertising expenses, offset by increased promotional spending and sample costs.

The increase in general and administrative expenses primarily resulted from an increase in depreciation expense and personnel related costs. Depreciation and amortization included in general and administrative expenses totaled $29.3 million for 2007 compared to $22.5 million for 2006. The increase in depreciation expense is primarily related to the Portland, Oregon and Cambrai, France distribution center projects. The increase in personnel related costs was to support our growth initiatives.

Net Licensing Income: Net licensing income decreased $0.3 million, or 5%, to $5.2 million in 2007 from $5.5 million in 2006. Licensing income in 2007 was led by Columbia licensed socks, followed by licensed leather accessories, bicycles, camping gear, and eyewear.

Interest Income, Net: Interest income was $9.0 million in 2007 compared to $6.8 million in 2006. The increase in interest income was primarily due to a higher combined cash equivalents and short-term investments balance compared to the same period in 2006. Interest expense decreased to $0.1 million in 2007 from $1.2 million in 2006. We primarily attribute the decrease in interest expense to a reduction in notes payable.

Income Tax Expense: Our provision for income taxes increased to $63.6 million in 2007 from $62.3 million in 2006. This increase resulted from higher income before tax offset by a decrease in our effective income tax rate to 30.6% in 2007 compared to 33.6% in 2006. The lower rate in 2007 was primarily the result of the favorable conclusion of various United States and European tax examinations and the geographic mix of taxable income.

Liquidity and Capital Resources

Our primary ongoing funding requirements are for working capital, investing activities associated with the expansion of our global operations and general corporate needs. At December 31, 2008, we had total cash and cash equivalents of $230.6 million compared to $192.0 million at December 31, 2007. In addition, we had short-term investments of $22.4 million at December 31, 2008 compared to $81.6 million at December 31, 2007.

Net cash provided by operating activities was $144.9 million in 2008 compared to $124.3 million in 2007. The increase in cash provided by operating activities was primarily the result of a reduction in inventory in 2008 compared to a significant increase in inventory in 2007 partially offset by lower net income, excluding the non-cash pre-tax charge for the impairment of acquired intangible assets, in 2008 compared to 2007.

Net cash provided by investing activities was $11.7 million in 2008 compared to $41.8 million in 2007. In 2008, our investing activities primarily consisted of net liquidation of short-term investments of $59.2 million partially offset by capital expenditures of $54.3 million, of which $6.7 million was incurred but not yet paid. Capital expenditures in 2008 consisted of approximately $12.8 million in maintenance capital expenditures and $41.5 million for retail expansion and other capacity initiatives. In 2007, our investing activities primarily consisted of net liquidation of short-term investments of $73.7 million partially offset by capital expenditures of $34.3 million, of which $2.3 million was incurred but not yet paid. Capital expenditures in 2007 consisted of approximately $10 million in maintenance capital expenditures and $24 million for other capacity and growth initiatives.

Cash used in financing activities was $102.4 million in 2008 compared to $40.4 million in 2007. In 2008, net cash used in financing activities included the repurchase of common stock at an aggregate price of $83.9 million, dividend payments of $22.1 million, partially offset by proceeds from the issuance of common stock under employee stock plans of $3.5 million. In 2007, net cash used in financing activities included the repurchase of common stock at an aggregate price of $31.8 million, dividends payments of $20.9 million, the net repayments of notes payable of $3.6 million, partially offset by proceeds from the issuance of common stock under employee stock plans of $14.2 million.

To fund our domestic working capital requirements, we have available unsecured revolving lines of credit with aggregate seasonal limits ranging from $50 million to $125 million, of which $25 million to $100 million is committed. At December 31, 2008, no balance was outstanding under these lines of credit and we were in compliance with all associated covenants. Internationally, our subsidiaries have local currency operating lines in place guaranteed by us with a combined limit of approximately $115.5 million at December 31, 2008, of which $3.5 million is designated as a European customs guarantee. At December 31, 2008, no balance was outstanding under these lines of credit.

In 2009, we intend to open additional branded and outlet retail stores, primarily in the United States and Europe. We expect to fund our future capital expenditures with existing cash, operating cash flows and credit facilities. If the need arises for additional expenditures, we may need to seek additional funding. Our ability to obtain additional financing will depend on many factors, including prevailing market conditions, our financial condition, and our ability to negotiate favorable terms and conditions. Financing may not be available on terms that are acceptable or favorable to us, if at all.

Our operations are affected by seasonal trends typical in the outdoor apparel industry, and have historically resulted in higher sales and profits in the third calendar quarter. This pattern has resulted primarily from the timing of shipments to wholesale customers for the fall season. We believe that our liquidity requirements for at least the next 12 months will be adequately covered by existing cash, cash provided by operations and existing short-term borrowing arrangements.

The following table presents our estimated contractual commitments (in thousands):

	Year ending December 31,						
	2009	2010	2011	2012	2013	Thereafter	Total
Installment payments (1)	$ 63	$ 15	$ —	$ —	$ —	$ —	$ 78
Inventory purchase obligations (2) ...	157,774	—	—	—	—	—	157,774
Operating leases (3):							
Non-related parties	21,134	21,504	19,871	18,998	18,613	133,565	233,685
Related party	478	478	478	—	—	—	1,434

We have recorded liabilities for net unrecognized tax benefits related to income tax uncertainties in our Consolidated Balance Sheet at December 31, 2008 of approximately $22.4 million; however, they have not been included in the table above because we are uncertain about whether or when such amounts may be settled. See Note 9 of Notes to Consolidated Financial Statements.

(1) Installment payments consist of purchase obligations made in the ordinary course of business for non-product purchases. The amounts represent the minimum payments required, including any imputed interest, by contracts and agreements.

(2) Inventory purchase obligations consist of open production purchase orders for sourced apparel, footwear, accessories and equipment, and materials used to manufacture apparel. The reported amounts exclude product purchase liabilities included in accounts payable on the Consolidated Balance Sheet at December 31, 2008.

(3) Operating lease obligations include retail space operating leases, which often include real estate taxes, insurance, common area maintenance ("CAM"), and other costs in addition to base rent. Operating lease obligations listed above do not include real estate taxes, insurance, CAM, and other costs for which we are obligated. Total expense related to real estate taxes, insurance, CAM, and other costs related to these leases for the year ended December 31, 2008 was $3.8 million and is included in SG&A expense in the Consolidated Statement of Operations. These operating lease commitments are not reflected on the Consolidated Balance Sheet.

Off-Balance Sheet Arrangements

We maintain unsecured and uncommitted lines of credit with a combined limit of $150.0 million at December 31, 2008, available for issuing import letters of credit. At December 31, 2008, we had letters of credit outstanding of $8.3 million issued for purchase orders for inventory.

Quantitative and Qualitative Disclosures About Market Risk

In the normal course of business, our financial position and results of operations are routinely subject to a variety of risks, including market risk associated with interest rate movements on borrowings and investments and exchange rate movements on non-U.S. dollar currency denominated assets, liabilities, income and expenses. We regularly assess these risks and have established policies and business practices that should result in an appropriate level of protection against the adverse effect of these and other potential exposures. We do not engage in speculative trading in any financial market.

Our foreign currency risk management objective is to mitigate the uncertainty of anticipated cash flows attributable to changes in exchange rates. We focus on anticipated cash flows resulting from firmly and non-firmly committed inventory purchases and the related receivables and payables, including third party or intercompany transactions.

We manage this risk primarily by using currency exchange, option and swap contracts. Anticipated, but not yet firmly committed, transactions that we hedge carry a high level of certainty and are expected to be recognized

34

within one year. We use cross-currency swaps to hedge foreign currency denominated payments related to intercompany loan agreements. Hedged transactions are denominated primarily in European euros, Canadian dollars, and Japanese yen.

The fair value of our hedging contracts was favorable by approximately $1.8 million at December 31, 2008 and unfavorable by approximately $3.1 million at December 31, 2007. A 10% change in the euro, Canadian dollar and yen exchange rates would have resulted in the fair value fluctuating approximately $6.2 million at December 31, 2008 and $9.8 million at December 31, 2007. Changes in fair value, resulting from foreign exchange rate fluctuations, would be substantially offset by the change in value of the underlying hedged transactions.

Our exposure to market risk for changes in interest rates relates primarily to our debt obligations. We did not have any long-term debt obligations at December 31, 2008 or 2007. We have cash flow exposure on our committed and uncommitted bank lines of credit since the interest is indexed to various reference rates such as Prime and LIBOR. At December 31, 2008 and 2007, our bank lines of credit did not have a balance.

Critical Accounting Policies and Estimates

Management's discussion and analysis of our financial condition and results of operations are based on our consolidated financial statements, which have been prepared in accordance with GAAP. The preparation of these financial statements requires us to make various estimates and judgments that affect reported amounts of assets, liabilities, sales, cost of sales and expenses and related disclosure of contingent assets and liabilities. We believe that the estimates, assumptions and judgments involved in the accounting policies described below have the greatest potential impact on our financial statements, so we consider these to be our critical accounting policies and estimates. Because of the uncertainty inherent in these matters, actual results could differ from the estimates we use in applying the critical accounting policies. We base our ongoing estimates on historical experience and other various assumptions that we believe to be reasonable under the circumstances. Many of these critical accounting policies affect working capital account balances, including the policy for revenue recognition, the allowance for uncollectible accounts receivable, the provision for potential excess, close-out and slow moving inventory, product warranty, income taxes and stock-based compensation.

Management and our independent auditors regularly discuss with our audit committee each of our critical accounting estimates, the development and selection of these accounting estimates, and the disclosure about each estimate in Management's Discussion and Analysis of Financial Condition and Results of Operations. These discussions typically occur at our quarterly audit committee meetings and include the basis and methodology used in developing and selecting these estimates, the trends in and amounts of these estimates, specific matters affecting the amount of and changes in these estimates, and any other relevant matters related to these estimates, including significant issues concerning accounting principles and financial statement presentation.

Revenue Recognition

We record wholesale and licensed product revenues when title passes and the risks and rewards of ownership have passed to the customer, based on the terms of sale. Title generally passes upon shipment or upon receipt by the customer depending on the country of the sale and the agreement with the customer. Retail store revenues are recorded at the time of sale.

In some countries outside of the United States where title passes upon receipt by the customer, predominantly where we sell directly in Western Europe, precise information regarding the date of receipt by the customer is not readily available. In these cases, we estimate the date of receipt by the customer based on historical and expected delivery times by geographic location. We periodically test the accuracy of these estimates based on actual transactions. Delivery times vary by geographic location, generally from one to five days. To date, we have found these estimates to be materially accurate.

35

At the time of revenue recognition, we also provide for estimated sales returns and miscellaneous claims from customers as reductions to revenues. The estimates are based on historical rates of product returns and claims. However, actual returns and claims in any future period are inherently uncertain and thus may differ from the estimates. If actual or expected future returns and claims are significantly greater or lower than the reserves that we have established, we will record a reduction or increase to net revenues in the period in which we make such a determination. Over the three year period ended December 31, 2008, our actual annual sales returns and miscellaneous claims from customers were approximately two percent of net sales.

Allowance for Uncollectible Accounts Receivable

We make ongoing estimates of the uncollectibility of our accounts receivable and maintain an allowance for estimated losses resulting from the inability of our customers to make required payments. In determining the amount of the allowance, we consider our historical level of credit losses and we make judgments about the creditworthiness of customers based on ongoing credit evaluations. We analyze specific customer accounts, customer concentrations, credit insurance coverage, standby letters of credit, current economic trends, and changes in customer payment terms. Current credit and market conditions may slow our collection efforts as customers experience increased difficulty in accessing credit and paying their obligations, leading to higher than normal accounts receivable. Because we cannot predict future changes in the financial stability of our customers, actual future losses from uncollectible accounts may differ from our estimates and may have a material effect on our consolidated financial position, results of operations or cash flows. If the financial condition of our customers deteriorates and results in their inability to make payments, a larger allowance may be required. If we determine that a smaller or larger allowance is appropriate, we will record a credit or a charge to SG&A expense in the period in which we make such a determination.

Inventory Obsolescence and Product Warranty

We make ongoing estimates of potential future excess, close-out or slow moving inventory and product warranty costs. We evaluate our inventory on hand considering our purchase commitments, sales forecasts, and historical experience to identify excess, close-out or slow moving inventory and make provisions as necessary to properly reflect inventory value at the lower of cost or estimated market value. When we evaluate our reserve for warranty costs, we consider our historical claim rates by season, product mix, current economic trends, and the historical cost to repair, replace, or refund the original sale. If we determine that a smaller or larger reserve is appropriate, we will record a credit or a charge to cost of sales in the period we make such a determination.

Income Taxes

We use the asset and liability method of accounting for income taxes. Under this method, we recognize income tax expense for the amount of taxes payable or refundable for the current year and for the amount of deferred tax liabilities and assets for the future tax consequences of events that have been recognized in our financial statements or tax returns. We make assumptions, judgments and estimates to determine our current provision for income taxes, our deferred tax assets and liabilities, and our uncertain tax positions in accordance with Financial Accounting Standards Interpretation No. 48 ("FIN 48"), *Accounting for Uncertainty in Income Taxes—an interpretation of FASB Statement No. 109*. Our judgments, assumptions and estimates relative to the current provision for income tax take into account current tax laws, our interpretation of current tax laws and possible outcomes of current and future audits conducted by foreign and domestic tax authorities. Changes in tax law or our interpretation of tax laws and the resolution of current and future tax audits could significantly affect the amounts provided for income taxes in our consolidated financial statements. Our assumptions, judgments and estimates relative to the value of a deferred tax asset take into account predictions of the amount and category of future taxable income. Actual operating results and the underlying amount and category of income in future years could cause our current assumptions, judgments and estimates of recoverable net deferred taxes to be inaccurate. Changes in any of the assumptions, judgments and estimates mentioned above could cause our actual income tax obligations to differ from our estimates, which could materially affect our financial position and results of operations.

On a quarterly basis, we estimate what our effective tax rate will be for the full fiscal year and record an appropriate quarterly income tax provision, in accordance with the anticipated effective rate. As the calendar year progresses, we periodically refine our estimate based on actual events and earnings by jurisdiction during the year. This ongoing estimation process can result in changes to our expected effective tax rate for the full calendar year. When this occurs, we adjust the income tax provision during the quarter in which the change in estimate occurs so that our year-to-date provision equals our expected annual effective tax rate.

Stock-Based Compensation

We account for stock-based compensation in accordance with Statement of Financial Accounting Standards ("SFAS") No. 123(R), *Share-Based Payment*. Under the provisions of SFAS No. 123R, stock-based compensation cost is estimated at the grant date based on the award's fair value and is recognized as expense over the requisite service period using the straight-line attribution method. As allowed under SFAS No. 123R, we estimate stock-based compensation for stock options granted using the Black-Scholes option pricing model, which requires various highly subjective assumptions, including volatility and expected option life. Further, as required under SFAS No. 123R, we estimate forfeitures for stock-based awards granted, which are not expected to vest. If any of these inputs or assumptions changes significantly, stock-based compensation expense may differ materially in the future from that recorded in the current period.

Recent Accounting Pronouncements

In May 2008, the Financial Accounting Standards Board ("FASB") issued SFAS No. 162, *The Hierarchy of Generally Accepted Accounting Principles.* This statement identifies the sources of accounting principles and the framework for selecting the principles used in the preparation of financial statements of entities that are presented in conformity with generally accepted accounting principles (the GAAP hierarchy). SFAS No. 162 will become effective 60 days following the Securities and Exchange Commission's approval of the Public Company Accounting Oversight Board amendments to AU Section 411, *The Meaning of Present Fairly in Conformity With Generally Accepted Accounting Principles.* We do not expect the adoption of SFAS No. 162 to have a material effect on our consolidated financial position, results of operations or cash flows.

In March 2008, the FASB issued SFAS No. 161, *Disclosures about Derivative Instruments and Hedging Activities.* This statement is intended to improve financial reporting about derivative instruments and hedging activities by requiring enhanced disclosures to enable investors to better understand their effects on an entity's financial position, financial performance, and cash flows. The provisions of SFAS No. 161 are effective for the fiscal years and interim quarters beginning after November 15, 2008. We do not expect the adoption of this statement to have a material effect on our consolidated financial position, results of operations or cash flows.

In December 2007, the FASB issued SFAS No. 160, *Noncontrolling Interests in Consolidated Financial Statements.* This statement amends Accounting Research Bulletin No. 51, *Consolidated Financial Statements,* to establish accounting and reporting standards for the noncontrolling interest in a subsidiary and for the deconsolidation of a subsidiary. SFAS No. 160 is effective for fiscal years beginning after December 15, 2008. We do not expect the adoption of this statement to have a material effect on our consolidated financial position, results of operations or cash flows.

In December 2007, the FASB issued SFAS No. 141R, *Business Combinations.* This statement replaces SFAS No. 141 and requires the acquirer of a business to recognize and measure the identifiable assets acquired, the liabilities assumed, and any non-controlling interest in the acquiree at fair value. SFAS No. 141R also requires transaction costs related to the business combination to be expensed as incurred. SFAS No. 141R is effective for business combinations for which the acquisition date is on or after fiscal years beginning after December 15, 2008. We do not expect the adoption of this statement to have a material effect on our consolidated financial position, results of operations or cash flows.

In February 2007, the FASB issued SFAS No. 159, *The Fair Value Option for Financial Assets and Financial Liabilities—including an amendment of FASB Statement No. 115*. This statement permits us to measure many financial instruments and certain other assets and liabilities at fair value on an instrument-by-instrument basis. SFAS No. 159 is effective for fiscal years beginning after November 15, 2007. The adoption of this statement did not have a material effect on our consolidated financial position, results of operations or cash flows.

In September 2006, the FASB issued SFAS No. 157, *Fair Value Measurements*. SFAS No. 157 establishes a framework for measuring the fair value of assets and liabilities. This framework is intended to increase consistency in how fair value determinations are made under various existing accounting standards that permit, or in some cases require, estimates of fair market value. SFAS No. 157 also expands financial statement disclosure requirements about a company's use of fair value measurements, including the effect of such measures on earnings. SFAS No. 157 is effective for fiscal years beginning after November 15, 2007, and interim periods within those fiscal years. The adoption of this statement did not have a material effect on our consolidated financial position, results of operations or cash flows. See Note 17 of Notes to Condensed Consolidated Financial Statements.

Item 7A. *QUANTITATIVE AND QUALITATIVE DISCLOSURES ABOUT MARKET RISK*

The information required by this item is included in Management's Discussion and Analysis of Financial Condition and Results of Operations and is incorporated herein by this reference.

Item 8. *FINANCIAL STATEMENTS AND SUPPLEMENTARY DATA*

Our management is responsible for the information and representations contained in this report. The financial statements have been prepared in conformity with accounting principles generally accepted in the United States, which we consider appropriate in the circumstances and include some amounts based on our best estimates and judgments. Other financial information in this report is consistent with these financial statements.

Our accounting systems include controls designed to reasonably assure that assets are safeguarded from unauthorized use or disposition and which provide for the preparation of financial statements in conformity with accounting principles generally accepted in the United States of America. These systems are supplemented by the selection and training of qualified financial personnel and an organizational structure providing for appropriate segregation of duties.

The Audit Committee is responsible for recommending to the Board of Directors the appointment of the independent accountants and reviews with the independent accountants and management the scope and the results of the annual examination, the effectiveness of the accounting control system and other matters relating to our financial affairs as they deem appropriate.

REPORT OF INDEPENDENT REGISTERED PUBLIC ACCOUNTING FIRM

To the Board of Directors and Shareholders
Columbia Sportswear Company
Portland, Oregon

We have audited the accompanying consolidated balance sheets of Columbia Sportswear Company and subsidiaries (the "Company") as of December 31, 2008 and 2007, and the related consolidated statements of operations, shareholders' equity and cash flows for each of the three years in the period ended December 31, 2008. Our audits also included the consolidated financial statement schedule listed on the Index at Item 15. These financial statements and financial statement schedule are the responsibility of the Company's management. Our responsibility is to express an opinion on these financial statements and financial statement schedule based on our audits.

We conducted our audits in accordance with the standards of the Public Company Accounting Oversight Board (United States). Those standards require that we plan and perform the audit to obtain reasonable assurance about whether the financial statements are free of material misstatement. An audit includes examining, on a test basis, evidence supporting the amounts and disclosures in the financial statements. An audit also includes assessing the accounting principles used and significant estimates made by management, as well as evaluating the overall financial statement presentation. We believe that our audits provide a reasonable basis for our opinion.

In our opinion, such consolidated financial statements present fairly, in all material respects, the financial position of the Company as of December 31, 2008 and 2007, and the results of its operations and its cash flows for each of the three years in the period ended December 31, 2008, in conformity with accounting principles generally accepted in the United States of America. Also, in our opinion, such financial statement schedule, when considered in relation to the basic consolidated financial statements taken as a whole, presents fairly, in all material respects, the information set forth therein.

We have also audited, in accordance with the standards of the Public Company Accounting Oversight Board (United States), the Company's internal control over financial reporting as of December 31, 2008, based on the criteria established in *Internal Control—Integrated Framework* issued by the Committee of Sponsoring Organizations of the Treadway Commission and our report dated February 27, 2009, expressed an unqualified opinion on the Company's internal control over financial reporting.

DELOITTE & TOUCHE LLP
Portland, Oregon
February 27, 2009

COLUMBIA SPORTSWEAR COMPANY

CONSOLIDATED BALANCE SHEETS
(In thousands)

	December 31, 2008	2007
ASSETS		
Current Assets:		
Cash and cash equivalents	$ 230,617	$ 191,950
Short-term investments	22,433	81,598
Accounts receivable, net (Note 2)	299,585	300,506
Inventories, net (Note 3)	256,312	265,874
Deferred income taxes (Note 9)	33,867	31,169
Prepaid expenses and other current assets	29,705	14,567
Total current assets	872,519	885,664
Property, plant, and equipment, net (Note 4)	229,693	210,450
Intangibles and other non-current assets (Note 2)	33,365	53,094
Goodwill (Note 2)	12,659	17,273
Total assets	$1,148,236	$1,166,481
LIABILITIES AND SHAREHOLDERS' EQUITY		
Current Liabilities:		
Accounts payable	$ 104,354	$ 95,412
Accrued liabilities (Note 6)	58,085	62,549
Income taxes payable (Note 9)	8,718	7,436
Deferred income taxes (Note 9)	1,969	949
Other current liabilities (Note 7)	63	185
Total current liabilities	173,189	166,531
Income taxes payable (Note 9)	20,412	18,663
Deferred income taxes (Note 9)	—	8,968
Other long-term liabilities (Note 7)	10,545	2,198
Total liabilities	204,146	196,360
Commitments and contingencies (Note 11)		
Shareholders' Equity:		
Preferred stock; 10,000 shares authorized; none issued and outstanding	—	—
Common stock (no par value); 125,000 shares authorized; 33,865 and 35,824 issued and outstanding (Note 8)	1,481	17,004
Retained earnings (Note 8)	909,443	895,476
Accumulated other comprehensive income (Note 14)	33,166	57,641
Total shareholders' equity	944,090	970,121
Total liabilities and shareholders' equity	$1,148,236	$1,166,481

See accompanying notes to consolidated financial statements.

41

COLUMBIA SPORTSWEAR COMPANY

CONSOLIDATED STATEMENTS OF OPERATIONS

(In thousands, except per share amounts)

	Year Ended December 31,		
	2008	2007	2006
Net sales	$1,317,835	$1,356,039	$1,287,672
Cost of sales	750,024	776,288	746,617
Gross profit	567,811	579,751	541,055
Selling, general, and administrative expenses	430,350	385,769	366,768
Impairment of acquired intangible assets (Note 2)	24,742	—	—
Net licensing income	5,987	5,157	5,486
Income from operations	118,706	199,139	179,773
Interest income, net	7,537	8,888	5,562
Income before income tax	126,243	208,027	185,335
Income tax expense (Note 9)	(31,196)	(63,575)	(62,317)
Net income	$ 95,047	$ 144,452	$ 123,018
Earnings per share:			
Basic	$ 2.75	$ 4.00	$ 3.39
Diluted	2.74	3.96	3.36
Cash dividends per share:	$ 0.64	$ 0.58	$ 0.14
Weighted average shares outstanding (Note 13):			
Basic	34,610	36,106	36,245
Diluted	34,711	36,434	36,644

See accompanying notes to consolidated financial statements.

COLUMBIA SPORTSWEAR COMPANY

CONSOLIDATED STATEMENTS OF CASH FLOWS
(In thousands)

	Year Ended December 31,		
	2008	2007	2006
Cash flows from operating activities:			
Net income	$ 95,047	$ 144,452	$ 123,018
Adjustments to reconcile net income to net cash provided by operating activities:			
Depreciation and amortization	31,158	30,338	23,547
Loss on disposal of property, plant, and equipment	253	237	705
Deferred income tax (benefit) expense	(10,338)	278	(2,429)
Stock-based compensation	6,302	7,260	10,120
Excess tax benefit from employee stock plans	(72)	(1,811)	(2,148)
Impairment of acquired intangibles	24,742	—	—
Other	—	—	302
Changes in operating assets and liabilities:			
Accounts receivable	(9,689)	(3,093)	4,259
Inventories	4,507	(46,010)	(15,448)
Prepaid expenses and other current assets	(15,787)	(1,355)	(898)
Intangibles and other assets	101	592	(905)
Accounts payable	8,944	1,381	1,930
Accrued liabilities	(1,047)	(4,400)	3,323
Income taxes payable	2,567	(5,665)	8,292
Other liabilities	8,242	2,111	(559)
Net cash provided by operating activities	144,930	124,315	153,109
Cash flows from investing activities:			
Purchases of short-term investments	(72,337)	(305,769)	(346,615)
Sales of short-term investments	131,565	379,460	350,520
Capital expenditures	(47,580)	(31,971)	(47,465)
Acquisitions, net of cash acquired	—	—	(35,377)
Proceeds from sale of licenses	—	—	1,700
Proceeds from sale of property, plant, and equipment	52	32	106
Net cash provided by (used in) investing activities	11,700	41,752	(77,131)
Cash flows from financing activities:			
Proceeds from notes payable	33,727	30,651	43,585
Repayments on notes payable	(33,727)	(34,276)	(86,531)
Repayment on long-term debt and other long-term liabilities	(21)	(22)	(13,759)
Proceeds from issuance of common stock	3,488	14,162	21,712
Excess tax benefit from employee stock plans	72	1,811	2,148
Repurchase of common stock	(83,865)	(31,819)	(75,490)
Cash dividends paid	(22,098)	(20,915)	(5,026)
Net cash used in financing activities	(102,424)	(40,408)	(113,361)
Net effect of exchange rate changes on cash	(15,539)	1,411	1,172
Net increase (decrease) in cash and cash equivalents	38,667	127,070	(36,211)
Cash and cash equivalents, beginning of year	191,950	64,880	101,091
Cash and cash equivalents, end of year	$ 230,617	$ 191,950	$ 64,880
Supplemental disclosures of cash flow information:			
Cash paid during the year for interest, net of capitalized interest	$ 47	$ 148	$ 1,329
Cash paid during the year for income taxes	48,521	73,293	58,651
Supplemental disclosures of non-cash investing activities:			
Capital expenditures incurred but not yet paid	6,760	2,318	3,444
Supplemental disclosures of non-cash financing activities:			
Assumption of Montrail debt	—	—	5,833

See accompanying notes to consolidated financial statements.

COLUMBIA SPORTSWEAR COMPANY

CONSOLIDATED STATEMENTS OF SHAREHOLDERS' EQUITY
(In thousands)

	Common Stock		Retained Earnings	Accumulated Other Comprehensive Income	Comprehensive Income	Total
	Shares Outstanding	Amount				
BALANCE, JANUARY 1, 2006	36,863	$ 13,104	$704,724	$ 24,962		$742,790
Components of comprehensive income:						
Net income	—	—	123,018	—	$123,018	123,018
Cash dividends ($0.14 per share)	—	—	(5,026)	—	—	(5,026)
Foreign currency translation adjustment	—	—	—	11,167	11,167	11,167
Unrealized holding loss on derivative transactions, net	—	—	—	(1,735)	(1,735)	(1,735)
Comprehensive income	—	—	—	—	$132,450	—
Exercise of employee stock options	682	21,712	—	—		21,712
Tax benefit from stock plans	—	4,147	—	—		4,147
Stock-based compensation expense	—	10,120	—	—		10,120
Repurchase of common stock	(1,547)	(24,713)	(50,777)	—		(75,490)
BALANCE, DECEMBER 31, 2006	35,998	24,370	771,939	34,394		830,703
Components of comprehensive income:						
Net income	—	—	144,452	—	$144,452	144,452
Cash dividends ($0.58 per share)	—	—	(20,915)	—	—	(20,915)
Foreign currency translation adjustment	—	—	—	25,394	25,394	25,394
Unrealized holding loss on derivative transactions, net	—	—	—	(2,147)	(2,147)	(2,147)
Comprehensive income	—	—	—	—	$167,699	—
Issuance of common stock under employee stock plans, net	416	14,162	—	—		14,162
Tax benefit from stock plans	—	3,031	—	—		3,031
Stock-based compensation expense	—	7,260	—	—		7,260
Repurchase of common stock	(590)	(31,819)	—	—		(31,819)
BALANCE, DECEMBER 31, 2007	35,824	17,004	895,476	57,641		970,121
Components of comprehensive income:						
Net income	—	—	95,047	—	$ 95,047	95,047
Cash dividends ($0.64 per share)	—	—	(22,098)	—	—	(22,098)
Foreign currency translation adjustment	—	—	—	(30,511)	(30,511)	(30,511)
Unrealized holding gain on derivative transactions, net	—	—	—	6,036	6,036	6,036
Comprehensive income	—	—	—	—	$ 70,572	—
Issuance of common stock under employee stock plans, net	131	3,488	—	—		3,488
Tax adjustment from stock plans	—	(430)	—	—		(430)
Stock-based compensation expense	—	6,302	—	—		6,302
Repurchase of common stock	(2,090)	(24,883)	(58,982)	—		(83,865)
BALANCE, DECEMBER 31, 2008	33,865	$ 1,481	$909,443	$ 33,166		$944,090

See accompanying notes to consolidated financial statements.

44

COLUMBIA SPORTSWEAR COMPANY
NOTES TO CONSOLIDATED FINANCIAL STATEMENTS

NOTE 1—BASIS OF PRESENTATION AND ORGANIZATION

Nature of the business:

Columbia Sportswear Company is a global leader in the design, manufacture, marketing and distribution of active outdoor apparel, including sportswear, outerwear, footwear, and related accessories and equipment.

Principles of consolidation:

The consolidated financial statements include the accounts of Columbia Sportswear Company and its wholly-owned subsidiaries (the "Company"). All significant intercompany balances and transactions have been eliminated in consolidation.

Estimates and assumptions:

The preparation of financial statements in conformity with accounting principles generally accepted in the United States of America requires management to make estimates and assumptions that affect the reported amounts of assets and liabilities and disclosure of contingent assets and liabilities at the date of the consolidated financial statements and the reported amounts of revenues and expenses during the reporting period. Actual results may differ from these estimates and assumptions. Some of these more significant estimates relate to revenue recognition, allowance for doubtful accounts, inventory, product warranty, intangible assets and income taxes.

Reclassifications:

Certain immaterial reclassifications of amounts reported in the prior period financial statements have been made to conform to classifications used in the current period financial statements.

Dependence on key suppliers:

The Company's products are produced by independent manufacturers worldwide. For 2008, the Company sourced nearly all of its products outside the United States, principally in the Southeast Asia. The Company's four largest factory groups accounted for approximately 11% of the Company's total global production for 2008 and another company produced substantially all of the zippers used in the Company's products. From time to time, the Company has had difficulty satisfying its raw material and finished goods requirements. Although the Company believes that it can identify and qualify additional raw material suppliers and manufacturers to produce these products, the unavailability of some existing suppliers or manufacturers for supply of these products may have a material adverse effect on the Company.

Concentration of credit risk:

Trade Receivables

At December 31, 2008, the Company had one customer in its EMEA segment and one customer in its Canadian segment that accounted for approximately 13.5% and 10.2% of consolidated accounts receivable, respectively. At December 31, 2007 the Company had one customer in its Canadian segment that accounted for approximately 12.4% of consolidated accounts receivable. No single customer accounted for greater than or equal to 10% of consolidated revenues for the year ended December 31, 2008 or 2007.

Derivatives

The Company routinely uses derivative instruments to hedge the foreign currency risk of anticipated transactions denominated in non-U.S. dollar currencies. At December 31, 2008, no contract had a remaining

COLUMBIA SPORTSWEAR COMPANY

NOTES TO CONSOLIDATED FINANCIAL STATEMENTS—(Continued)

maturity longer than one year. All the counterparties to these transactions had a Standard & Poor's ("S&P") / Moody's Investor Services ("Moody's") short-term credit rating of A-2 / P-1 or better. The net exposure to any single counterparty, which is generally limited to the aggregate unrealized gain of all contracts with that counterparty, was immaterial at December 31, 2008.

Cash and Investments

At December 31, 2008, approximately 75% of the Company's cash and cash equivalents were concentrated in domestic and international money market mutual funds. Substantially all of the Company's money market mutual funds were assigned a triple A rating from S&P, Moody's or Fitch Ratings.

On September 29, 2008, the U.S. Treasury Department announced a temporary guarantee program for money market mutual funds regulated under Rule 2a-7 of the Investment Company Act of 1940. The temporary guarantee program limits coverage to the lesser of fund balances at September 19, 2008 or fund balances immediately prior to an institution reporting a net asset value below $1 per share. On September 19, 2008, the Company had a total of approximately $50,000,000 of investments with two institutions qualifying for this guarantee program. At December 31, 2008, the eligible $50,000,000 remained invested and both institutions were actively participating in the guarantee program. The guarantee program is set to expire on April 30, 2009, but the U.S. Treasury Department could extend the program through September 18, 2009.

All the Company's remaining cash and cash equivalents and short-term investments were deposited with various institutions in the Company's primary operating geographies. All institutions were rated investment grade by both S&P and Moody's and most were rated AA- / Aa1 or better.

NOTE 2—SUMMARY OF SIGNIFICANT ACCOUNTING POLICIES

Cash and cash equivalents:

Cash and cash equivalents are stated at cost, which approximates fair value, and include investments with maturities of three months or less from the date of acquisition. At December 31, 2008 and 2007, cash and cash equivalents were $230,617,000 and $191,950,000, respectively, primarily consisting of money market funds and certificates of deposit.

Short-term investments:

Short-term investments consist of debt security mutual fund shares available for use in current operations and certificates of deposit with maturities of six months or less at December 31, 2008. At December 31, 2007, short-term investments consisted of variable rate demand notes and obligations that generally mature up to 30 years from the purchase date. Investments with maturities beyond one year may be classified as short-term based on their highly liquid nature and because such marketable securities represent the investment of cash that is available for current operations. All short-term investments are classified as available-for-sale securities and are recorded at fair value with any unrealized gains and losses reported, net of tax, in other comprehensive income. Realized gains or losses are determined based on the specific identification method. The Company did not hold any auction-rate securities at December 31, 2008 or 2007 and had no investments considered to be trading or held-to-maturity securities.

Accounts receivable:

Accounts receivable have been reduced by an allowance for doubtful accounts. The Company makes ongoing estimates of the uncollectibility of accounts receivable and maintains an allowance for estimated losses resulting from the inability of the Company's customers to make required payments. The allowance for doubtful accounts was $9,542,000 and $7,369,000 at December 31, 2008 and 2007, respectively.

COLUMBIA SPORTSWEAR COMPANY

NOTES TO CONSOLIDATED FINANCIAL STATEMENTS—(Continued)

Inventories:

Inventories are carried at the lower of cost or market. Cost is determined using the first-in, first-out method. The Company periodically reviews its inventories for excess, close-out or slow moving items and makes provisions as necessary to properly reflect inventory value.

Property, plant, and equipment:

Property, plant and equipment are stated at cost, net of accumulated depreciation. Depreciation is provided using the straight-line method over the estimated useful lives of the assets. The principal estimated useful lives are: buildings and building improvements, 15-30 years; land improvements, 15 years; furniture and fixtures, 3-10 years; and machinery and equipment, 3-5 years. Leasehold improvements are depreciated over the lesser of the estimated useful life of the improvement, which is most commonly 7 years, or the remaining term of the underlying lease.

The interest-carrying costs of capital assets under construction are capitalized based on the Company's weighted average borrowing rates if there are any outstanding borrowings. There was no capitalized interest for the years ended December 31, 2008 and 2007 and capitalized interest was $642,000 for the year ended December 31, 2006.

Intangible assets:

Intangible assets with indefinite useful lives are not amortized and are periodically evaluated for impairment. Intangible assets that are determined to have finite lives are amortized using the straight-line method over their useful lives.

The following table summarizes the Company's identifiable intangible assets balance (in thousands):

	December 31, 2008		December 31, 2007	
	Carrying Amount	Accumulated Amortization	Carrying Amount	Accumulated Amortization
Intangible assets subject to amortization:				
Patents	$ 898	$(534)	$ 1,603	$(556)
Intangible assets not subject to amortization:				
Trademarks and trade names	$26,872		$46,771	
Goodwill	12,659		17,273	
	$39,531		$64,044	

Patents are subject to amortization over the lesser of 17 years from the date filed with the U.S. Patent and Trademark Office or the estimated useful life of the patent. Amortization expense for the years ended December 31, 2008, 2007, and 2006 was $205,000, $175,000 and $150,000, respectively. Amortization expense for intangible assets subject to amortization is estimated to be $109,000 per year in 2009 and 2010 and $73,000 per year in 2011 and 2012. These patents are anticipated to become fully amortized during 2012.

Other non-current assets totaled $6,129,000 and $5,276,000 at December 31, 2008 and 2007, respectively.

Impairment of long-lived and intangible assets:

Goodwill and intangible assets with indefinite useful lives are not amortized but instead are measured for impairment in accordance with Statement of Financial Accounting Standards ("SFAS") No. 142, *Goodwill and Other Intangible Assets*. The Company reviews and tests its goodwill and intangible assets with indefinite useful

COLUMBIA SPORTSWEAR COMPANY

NOTES TO CONSOLIDATED FINANCIAL STATEMENTS—(Continued)

lives for impairment in the fourth quarter of each year and when events or changes in circumstances indicate that the carrying amount of such assets may be impaired. The Company's intangible assets with indefinite lives consist of trademarks. Impairment testing for goodwill is performed at the reporting unit level. The two-step process first compares the estimated fair value of reporting unit goodwill with the carrying amount of that reporting unit. The Company estimates the fair value of its reporting units using a combination of discounted cash flow analysis, comparisons with the market values of similar publicly traded companies and other operating performance based valuation methods. If step one indicates impairment, step two compares the estimated fair value of the reporting unit to the estimated fair value of all reporting unit assets and liabilities except goodwill to determine the implied fair value of goodwill. The Company calculates impairment as the excess of carrying amount of goodwill over the implied fair value of goodwill. In the impairment test for trademarks, the Company compares the estimated fair value of the asset to the carrying amount. The fair value of trademarks is estimated using the relief from royalty approach, a standard form of discounted cash flow analysis used in the valuation of trademarks. If the carrying amount of trademarks exceeds the estimated fair value, the Company calculates impairment as the excess of carrying amount over the estimate of fair value. Impairment charges are classified as a separate component of operating expense. The fair value estimates are based on a number of factors, including assumptions and estimates for projected sales, income, cash flows, discount rates and other operating performance measures. Changes in estimates or the application of alternative assumptions could produce significantly different results. These assumptions and estimates may change in the future due to changes in economic conditions, changes in the Company's ability to meet sales and profitability objectives or changes in the Company's business operations or strategic direction.

The Company determined that its Pacific Trail brand and Montrail brand goodwill and trademarks were impaired at December 31, 2008. These brands have not achieved their sales and profitability objectives. The deterioration in the macroeconomic environment and the resulting effect on consumer demand has decreased the probability of realizing these objectives in the near future. These brands were acquired in 2006. The Company has recorded impairment charges, before income taxes, of $12,250,000 in trademarks and $3,900,000 in goodwill for the Pacific Trail brand. The Pacific Trail brand has $2,300,000 in trademarks and no goodwill after the impairment charge. The Pacific Trail brand is a reporting unit for goodwill impairment testing and Pacific Trail brand intangible assets are included in the United States segment. The Company has recorded impairment charges, before income taxes, of $7,400,000 in trademarks and $714,000 in goodwill for Montrail brand. The Montrail brand has $2,600,000 in trademarks and no goodwill after the impairment charge. The Montrail brand is a reporting unit for goodwill impairment testing and Montrail brand intangible assets are included in the United States segment.

Other than Montrail brand goodwill and trademarks and Pacific Trail brand goodwill and trademarks at December 31, 2008, the Company has determined that its goodwill and intangible assets with indefinite lives at December 31, 2008 and 2007 were not impaired.

Long-lived and intangible assets that are determined to have finite lives are amortized over their useful lives and are measured for impairment only when events or circumstances indicate the carrying value may be impaired. In these cases, the Company estimates the future undiscounted cash flows to be derived from the asset or asset group to determine whether a potential impairment exists. If the carrying value exceeds the estimate of future undiscounted cash flows, the Company then calculates the impairment as the excess of the carrying value of the asset over the estimate of its fair value. Impairment charges are classified as a separate component of operating expense.

The Company has determined that a Montrail brand patent was impaired at December 31, 2008. There is no anticipated future use of the patent beyond 2009, resulting in an impairment charge, before income taxes, of $478,000. The Montrail brand patent was included in the United States segment and was acquired in 2006.

48

COLUMBIA SPORTSWEAR COMPANY

NOTES TO CONSOLIDATED FINANCIAL STATEMENTS—(Continued)

Other than the Montrail brand patent, the Company has determined that its long-lived and intangible assets that are determined to have finite lives at December 31, 2008 and 2007 were not impaired.

Deferred income taxes:

Income tax expense is provided at the U.S. tax rate on financial statement earnings, adjusted for the difference between the U.S. tax rate and the rate of tax in effect for non-U.S. earnings deemed to be permanently reinvested in the Company's non-U.S. operations. Deferred income taxes have not been provided for the potential remittance of non-U.S. undistributed earnings to the extent those earnings are deemed to be permanently reinvested, or to the extent such recognition would result in a deferred tax asset. Deferred income taxes are provided for the expected tax consequences of temporary differences between the tax bases of assets and liabilities and their reported amounts. Valuation allowances are recorded to reduce deferred tax assets to the amount that will more likely than not be realized.

In July 2006, the Financial Accounting Standards Board ("FASB") issued Financial Accounting Standards Interpretation No. 48 ("FIN 48"), *Accounting for Uncertainty in Income Taxes—an interpretation of FASB Statement No. 109.* FIN 48 creates a single model to address accounting for uncertainty in tax positions and clarifies the accounting for income taxes, by prescribing a minimum recognition threshold a tax position is required to meet before being recognized in the financial statements. FIN 48 also provides guidance on derecognition, measurement, classification, interest and penalties, accounting in interim periods, disclosure, and transition. The Company adopted the provisions of FIN 48 on January 1, 2007 which did not result in the recognition of a material adjustment in the liability for unrecognized tax benefits.

Revenue Recognition:

The Company records wholesale and licensed product revenues when title passes and the risks and rewards of ownership have passed to the customer, based on the terms of sale. Title generally passes upon shipment or upon receipt by the customer depending on the country of the sale and the agreement with the customer. Retail store revenues are recorded at the time of sale.

In some countries outside of the United States where title passes upon receipt by the customer, predominantly where the Company sells direct in Western Europe, precise information regarding the date of receipt by the customer is not readily available. In these cases, the Company estimates the date of receipt by the customer based on historical and expected delivery times by geographic location. The Company periodically tests the accuracy of these estimates based on actual transactions. Delivery times vary by geographic location, generally from one to five days. The Company periodically tests the accuracy of these estimates based on actual transactions. To date, the Company has found these estimates to be materially accurate.

At the time of revenue recognition, the Company also provides for estimated sales returns and miscellaneous claims from customers as reductions to revenues. The estimates are based on historical rates of product returns and claims. However, actual returns and claims in any future period are inherently uncertain and thus may differ from the estimates. If actual or expected future returns and claims are significantly greater or lower than the reserves that had been established, the Company would record a reduction or increase to net revenues in the period in which it made such determination. Over the three year period ended December 31, 2008, the Company's actual annual sales returns and miscellaneous claims from customers were approximately two percent of net sales. The allowance for outstanding sales returns and miscellaneous claims from customers was approximately $10,583,000 and $9,196,000 as of December 31, 2008 and 2007, respectively.

COLUMBIA SPORTSWEAR COMPANY

NOTES TO CONSOLIDATED FINANCIAL STATEMENTS—(Continued)

Cost of sales:

The expenses that are included in cost of sales include all direct product and conversion-related costs, and costs related to shipping, duties and importation. Product warranty costs and specific provisions for excess, close-out or slow moving inventory are also included in cost of sales.

Selling, general and administrative expense:

Selling, general and administrative expense consists of commissions, advertising, other selling costs, personnel-related costs, planning, receiving finished goods, warehousing, depreciation and other general operating expenses.

Shipping and handling costs:

Shipping and handling fees billed to customers are recorded as revenue. The direct costs associated with shipping goods to customers are recorded as cost of sales. Inventory planning, receiving and handling costs are recorded as a component of selling, general, and administrative expenses and were $57,700,000, $64,420,000 and $50,213,000 for the years ended December 31, 2008, 2007 and 2006, respectively.

Foreign currency translation:

The assets and liabilities of the Company's foreign subsidiaries have been translated into U.S. dollars using the exchange rates in effect at period end, and the net sales and expenses have been translated into U.S. dollars using average exchange rates in effect during the period. The foreign currency translation adjustments are included as a separate component of accumulated other comprehensive income (loss) in shareholders' equity and are not currently adjusted for income taxes when they relate to indefinite net investments in non-U.S. operations.

Fair value of financial instruments:

Based on borrowing rates currently available to the Company for bank loans with similar terms and maturities, the fair value of the Company's other long-term liabilities approximates the carrying value. Furthermore, the carrying value of all other financial instruments potentially subject to valuation risk (principally consisting of cash and cash equivalents, short-term investments, accounts receivable and accounts payable) also approximate fair value because of their short-term maturities.

Derivatives:

The Company accounts for derivatives in accordance with SFAS No. 133, *Accounting for Derivative Instruments and Hedging Activities*, as amended.

Substantially all foreign currency derivatives entered into by the Company qualify for and are designated as foreign currency cash flow hedges, including those hedging foreign currency denominated firm commitments. Changes in fair values of outstanding cash flow hedges are recorded in other comprehensive income, until earnings are affected by the hedged transaction. In most cases amounts recorded in other comprehensive income will be released to earnings some time after maturity of the related derivative. The Consolidated Statement of Operations classification of effective hedge results is the same as that of the underlying exposure. Results of hedges of product costs are recorded in cost of sales when the underlying hedged transaction affects earnings. Unrealized derivative gains and losses, which are recorded in current assets and liabilities, respectively, are non-cash items and therefore are taken into account in the preparation of the Consolidated Statement of Cash Flows based on their respective balance sheet classifications.

50

COLUMBIA SPORTSWEAR COMPANY

NOTES TO CONSOLIDATED FINANCIAL STATEMENTS—(Continued)

Stock-based compensation:

The Company accounts for stock-based compensation in accordance with SFAS No. 123(R), *Share-Based Payment*. Under the provisions of SFAS No. 123R, stock-based compensation cost is estimated at the grant date based on the award's fair value and is recognized as expense over the requisite service period using the straight-line attribution method. As allowed under SFAS No. 123R, the Company estimates stock-based compensation at the stock option grant date using the Black-Scholes option pricing model, which requires various highly subjective assumptions, including volatility and expected option life. Further, as required under SFAS No. 123R, the Company estimates forfeitures for stock-based awards granted, which are not expected to vest. If any of these inputs or assumptions changes significantly, stock-based compensation expense may differ materially in the future from that recorded in the current period.

Advertising costs:

Advertising costs are expensed in the period incurred and are included in selling, general and administrative expenses. Total advertising expense, including cooperative advertising costs, was $72,237,000, $55,290,000 and $56,813,000 for the years ended December 31, 2008, 2007 and 2006, respectively.

Through cooperative advertising programs, the Company reimburses its wholesale customers for some of their costs of advertising the Company's products based on various criteria, including the value of purchases from the Company and various advertising specifications. Cooperative advertising costs are included in expenses because the Company receives an identifiable benefit in exchange for the cost, the advertising may be obtained from a party other than the customer, and the fair value of the advertising benefit can be reasonably estimated. Cooperative advertising costs were $16,351,000, $17,884,000 and $16,942,000 for the years ended December 31, 2008, 2007 and 2006, respectively.

Product warranty:

Some of the Company's products carry limited warranty provisions for defects in quality and workmanship. A warranty reserve is established at the time of sale to cover estimated costs based on the Company's history of warranty repairs and replacements and is recorded in cost of sales. The reserve for warranty claims at December 31, 2008 and 2007 was $9,746,000 and $10,862,000, respectively.

Recent Accounting Pronouncements:

In May 2008, the FASB issued SFAS No. 162, *The Hierarchy of Generally Accepted Accounting Principles*. This statement identifies the sources of accounting principles and the framework for selecting the principles used in the preparation of financial statements of entities that are presented in conformity with generally accepted accounting principles (the GAAP hierarchy). SFAS No. 162 will become effective 60 days following the Securities and Exchange Commission's approval of the Public Company Accounting Oversight Board amendments to AU Section 411, *The Meaning of Present Fairly in Conformity With Generally Accepted Accounting Principles*. The Company does not expect the adoption of SFAS No. 162 to have a material effect on its consolidated financial position, results of operations or cash flows.

In March 2008, the FASB issued SFAS No. 161, Disclosures About Derivative Instruments and Hedging Activities. This statement is intended to improve financial reporting about derivative instruments and hedging activities by requiring enhanced disclosures to enable investors to better understand their effects on an entity's financial position, financial performance and cash flows. The provisions of SFAS No. 161 are effective for the fiscal years and interim quarters beginning after November 15, 2008. The Company does not expect the adoption of this statement to have a material effect on its consolidated financial position, results of operations or cash flows.

51

COLUMBIA SPORTSWEAR COMPANY

NOTES TO CONSOLIDATED FINANCIAL STATEMENTS—(Continued)

In December 2007, the FASB issued SFAS No. 160, *Noncontrolling Interests in Consolidated Financial Statements*. This statement amends Accounting Research Bulletin No. 51, *Consolidated Financial Statements,* to establish accounting and reporting standards for the noncontrolling interest in a subsidiary and for the deconsolidation of a subsidiary. SFAS No. 160 is effective for fiscal years beginning after December 15, 2008. The Company does not expect the adoption of this statement to have a material effect on its consolidated financial position, results of operations or cash flows.

In December 2007, the FASB issued SFAS No. 141R, *Business Combinations*. This statement replaces SFAS No. 141 and requires the acquirer of a business to recognize and measure the identifiable assets acquired, the liabilities assumed, and any non-controlling interest in the acquiree at fair value. SFAS No. 141R also requires transaction costs related to the business combination to be expensed as incurred. SFAS No. 141R is effective for business combinations for which the acquisition date is on or after fiscal years beginning after December 15, 2008. The Company does not expect the adoption of this statement to have a material effect on its consolidated financial position, results of operations or cash flows.

In February 2007, the FASB issued SFAS No. 159, *The Fair Value Option for Financial Assets and Financial Liabilities—including an amendment of FASB Statement No. 115*. This statement permits an entity to measure many financial instruments and certain other assets and liabilities at fair value on an instrument-by-instrument basis. SFAS No. 159 is effective for fiscal years beginning after November 15, 2007. The adoption of this statement did not have a material effect on the Company's consolidated financial position, results of operations or cash flows.

In September 2006, the FASB issued SFAS No. 157, *Fair Value Measurements*. SFAS No. 157 establishes a framework for measuring the fair value of assets and liabilities. This framework is intended to increase consistency in how fair value determinations are made under various existing accounting standards that permit, or in some cases require, estimates of fair market value. SFAS No. 157 also expands financial statement disclosure requirements about a company's use of fair value measurements, including the effect of such measures on earnings. SFAS No. 157 is effective for fiscal years beginning after November 15, 2007, and interim periods within those fiscal years. The adoption of this statement did not have a material effect on the Company's consolidated financial position, results of operations or cash flows. See Note 17.

NOTE 3—INVENTORIES, NET

Inventories consist of the following (in thousands):

	December 31,	
	2008	**2007**
Raw materials	$ 621	$ 392
Work in process	1,065	3,979
Finished goods	254,626	261,503
	$256,312	$265,874

COLUMBIA SPORTSWEAR COMPANY

NOTES TO CONSOLIDATED FINANCIAL STATEMENTS—(Continued)

NOTE 4—PROPERTY, PLANT, AND EQUIPMENT, NET

Property, plant, and equipment consist of the following (in thousands):

	December 31,	
	2008	2007
Land and improvements	$ 16,465	$ 16,602
Building and improvements	143,997	140,602
Machinery and equipment	171,091	165,504
Furniture and fixtures	37,886	29,365
Leasehold improvements	45,231	20,632
Construction in progress	5,929	5,812
	420,599	378,517
Less accumulated depreciation	190,906	168,067
	$229,693	$210,450

NOTE 5—SHORT-TERM BORROWINGS AND CREDIT LINES

The Company has available an unsecured and committed revolving line of credit providing for borrowings in an aggregate amount not to exceed, at any time, $100,000,000 during the period of August 15 through November 14 and $25,000,000 at all other times. The maturity date of this agreement is July 1, 2010. Interest, payable monthly, is computed at the bank's prime rate minus 195 to 205 basis points per annum or the LIBOR rate plus 45 to 65 basis points. The unsecured revolving line of credit requires the Company to comply with certain covenants including a Capital Ratio, which limits indebtedness to tangible net worth. At December 31, 2008, the Company was in compliance with all of these covenants. If the Company defaults on its payments, it is prohibited, subject to certain exceptions, from making dividend payments or other distributions. The Company also has available an unsecured and uncommitted revolving line of credit providing for borrowing to a maximum of $25,000,000. The revolving line accrues interest on the LIBOR plus 65 basis points. There were no balances outstanding under either of these lines at December 31, 2008 and 2007.

The Company's Canadian subsidiary has available an unsecured and uncommitted line of credit guaranteed by the parent company providing for borrowing to a maximum of C$30,000,000 (US$24,614,000) at December 31, 2008. The revolving line accrues interest at the bank's Canadian prime rate. There was no balance outstanding under this line at December 31, 2008 and 2007.

The Company's European subsidiary has available two separate unsecured and uncommitted lines of credit guaranteed by the parent company providing for borrowing to a maximum of 30,000,000 and 20,000,000 euros respectively (combined US$69,850,000) at December 31, 2008, of which US$3,493,000 of the 20,000,000 euro line is designated as a European customs guarantee. These lines accrue interest based on the ECB refinancing rate plus 50 basis points and EURIBOR plus 50 basis points, respectively. There was no balance outstanding under either line at December 31, 2008 and 2007.

The Company's Japanese subsidiary has an unsecured and uncommitted line of credit guaranteed by the parent company providing for borrowing to a maximum of 1,000,000,000 JPY (US$11,033,000) at December 31, 2008. The revolving line accrues interest at the bank's Best Lending Rate or the LIBOR rate plus 110 basis points. There was no balance outstanding under this line at December 31, 2008 and 2007.

COLUMBIA SPORTSWEAR COMPANY

NOTES TO CONSOLIDATED FINANCIAL STATEMENTS—(Continued)

The Company's Korean subsidiary also has an unsecured and uncommitted line of credit guaranteed by the parent company providing for borrowing to a maximum of US$10,000,000 at December 31, 2008. The revolving line accrues interest at the three month certificate of deposit rate plus 1.3%. There was no balance outstanding under this line at December 31, 2008 and 2007.

Off-Balance Sheet Arrangements

The Company has arrangements in place to facilitate the import and purchase of inventory through the issuance of sight letters of credit. The Company has available an unsecured and uncommitted $50,000,000 import letter of credit line subject to annual renewal. At December 31, 2008, the Company had outstanding letters of credit of $8,338,000 for purchase orders for inventory under this arrangement. The Company also has available an unsecured and uncommitted $100,000,000 import letter of credit line subject to annual renewal. At December 31, 2008, the Company did not have any outstanding letters of credit for purchase orders for inventory under this arrangement.

NOTE 6—ACCRUED LIABILITIES

Accrued liabilities consist of the following (in thousands):

	December 31,	
	2008	2007
Accrued salaries, bonus, vacation and other benefits	$29,437	$34,952
Accrued product warranty	9,746	10,862
Accrued cooperative advertising	6,457	6,877
Other	12,445	9,858
	$58,085	$62,549

NOTE 7—OTHER LONG-TERM LIABILITIES

Other long-term liabilities consist of installment purchase obligations for non-inventory purchases made in the ordinary course of business, long-term severance liabilities, deferred rent obligations, the effect of straight-line rent under various operating leases, and rental asset retirement obligations. Deferred rent, straight-line rent, and rental asset retirement obligation liabilities were $10,126,000 and $2,137,000 at December 31, 2008 and 2007, respectively. The corresponding lease obligations for these deferred and straight-line rent liabilities are disclosed in Note 11. Principal payments due on installment purchase obligations are $63,000 in 2009 and $15,000 in 2010.

NOTE 8—SHAREHOLDERS' EQUITY

Since the inception of the Company's stock repurchase plan in 2004 through December 31, 2008, the Company's Board of Directors has authorized the repurchase of $500,000,000 of the Company's common stock. As of December 31, 2008, the Company has repurchased 8,694,657 shares under this program at an aggregate purchase price of approximately $400,000,000. During the year ended December 31, 2008, the Company repurchased an aggregate of $83,865,000 of the Company's common stock under the stock repurchase plan, of which $58,982,000 was recorded as a reduction to total retained earnings; otherwise, the aggregate purchase price would have resulted in a negative common stock carrying amount. Shares of the Company's common stock may be purchased in the open market or through privately negotiated transactions, subject to the market conditions. The repurchase program does not obligate the Company to acquire any specific number of shares or to acquire shares over any specified period of time.

COLUMBIA SPORTSWEAR COMPANY

NOTES TO CONSOLIDATED FINANCIAL STATEMENTS—(Continued)

NOTE 9—INCOME TAXES

The Company applies an asset and liability method of accounting for income taxes that requires the recognition of deferred tax assets and liabilities for the expected future tax consequences of events that have been recognized in the Company's financial statements or tax returns. In estimating future tax consequences, the Company generally considers all expected future events other than enactment of changes in the tax laws or rates. Deferred taxes are provided for temporary differences between assets and liabilities for financial reporting purposes and for income tax purposes. Valuation allowances are recorded against net deferred tax assets when it is more likely than not that the asset will not be realized.

The Company had undistributed earnings of foreign subsidiaries of approximately $135,918,000 at December 31, 2008 for which deferred taxes have not been provided. Such earnings are considered indefinitely invested outside of the United States. If these earnings were repatriated to the United States, the earnings would be subject to U.S. taxation. The amount of the unrecognized deferred tax liability associated with the undistributed earnings was approximately $32,237,000 at December 31, 2008. The unrecognized deferred tax liability approximates the excess of the United States tax liability over the creditable foreign taxes paid that would result from a full remittance of undistributed earnings.

The Company adopted the provisions of FIN 48 on January 1, 2007. The Company did not recognize a material adjustment in the liability for unrecognized tax benefits as a result of the implementation of FIN 48. A reconciliation of the beginning and ending amount of gross unrecognized tax benefits is as follows (in thousands):

	December 31,	
	2008	**2007**
Balance at January 1	$20,694	$19,705
Increases related to prior year tax positions	583	1,148
Decreases related to prior year tax positions	(2,496)	(4,272)
Increases related to current year tax positions	4,768	5,284
Settlements	—	(1,117)
Lapses of statute of limitations	(1,710)	(54)
Balance at December 31	$21,839	$20,694

$20,096,000 and $19,002,000 of the unrecognized tax benefits balance would affect the effective tax rate if recognized at December 31, 2008 and 2007, respectively. In 2007, approximately $853,000 of gross increases and decreases from current year tax positions and $2,056,000 of gross increases and decreases from prior year tax positions have been presented on a net basis in the tabular unrecognized tax benefits reconciliation. These unrecognized tax benefits were a result of changes in estimates during the year relating to a European tax examination which was effectively settled in the fourth quarter of 2007.

The Company conducts business globally, and as a result, the Company or one or more of its subsidiaries files income tax returns in the U.S. federal jurisdiction and various state and foreign jurisdictions. The Company is subject to examination by taxing authorities throughout the world, including such major jurisdictions as Canada, China, France, Germany, Hong Kong, Italy, Japan, South Korea, Switzerland, the United Kingdom and the United States. The Company has effectively settled U.S. tax examinations of all years through 2005. Internationally, the Company has effectively settled French tax examinations of all years through 2006 and Italian tax examinations of all years through 2007. The Company is currently under examination in Canada for the tax years 2002 through 2004. The Company does not anticipate that adjustments relative to this ongoing tax audit will result in a material change to its consolidated financial position, results of operations or cash flows.

COLUMBIA SPORTSWEAR COMPANY

NOTES TO CONSOLIDATED FINANCIAL STATEMENTS—(Continued)

Due to the potential for resolution of income tax audits currently in progress, and the expiration of various statutes of limitation, it is reasonably possible that the unrecognized tax benefits balance may change within the twelve months from December 31, 2008 by a range of zero to $8,645,000. At December 31, 2007, the comparable range was zero to $6,674,000. Open tax years, including those previously mentioned, contain matters that could be subject to differing interpretations of applicable tax laws and regulations as they relate to the amount, timing, or inclusion of revenue and expenses or the sustainability of income tax credits for a given examination cycle.

The Company recognizes interest expense and penalties related to income tax matters in income tax expense. The Company recognized interest and penalties related to uncertain tax positions during 2008 of $313,000 and the Company recognized a net reversal of accrued interest and penalties of $117,000 during 2007. The Company had $3,234,000 and $2,922,000 of accrued interest and penalties related to uncertain tax positions at December 31, 2008 and 2007, respectively.

Consolidated income from continuing operations before income taxes consists of the following (in thousands):

	Year Ended December 31,		
	2008	2007	2006
U.S. operations	$ 44,478	$122,588	$114,027
Foreign operations	81,765	85,439	71,308
Income before income tax	$126,243	$208,027	$185,335

The components of the provision (benefit) for income taxes consist of the following (in thousands):

	Year Ended December 31,		
	2008	2007	2006
Current:			
Federal	$ 22,576	$40,490	$48,181
State and local	2,459	3,685	3,316
Non-U.S.	18,568	22,493	16,494
	43,603	66,668	67,991
Deferred:			
Federal	(10,444)	(2,726)	(3,490)
State and local	(1,228)	(222)	(93)
Non-U.S.	(735)	(145)	(2,091)
	(12,407)	(3,093)	(5,674)
Income tax expense	$ 31,196	$63,575	$62,317

COLUMBIA SPORTSWEAR COMPANY

NOTES TO CONSOLIDATED FINANCIAL STATEMENTS—(Continued)

The following is a reconciliation of the normal expected statutory federal income tax rate to the effective rate reported in the financial statements:

	Year Ended December 31,		
	2008	2007	2006
	(percent of income)		
Provision for federal income taxes at the statutory rate	35.0%	35.0%	35.0%
State and local income taxes, net of federal benefit	0.8	1.1	1.2
Non-U.S. income taxed at different rates	(4.1)	(1.4)	(1.6)
Foreign tax credits	(3.2)	—	—
Reduction of accrued income taxes	(3.3)	(2.8)	—
Tax-exempt interest	(0.8)	(1.0)	(1.0)
Other	0.3	(0.3)	—
Actual provision for income taxes	24.7%	30.6%	33.6%

Significant components of the Company's deferred taxes are as follows (in thousands):

	December 31,	
	2008	2007
Deferred tax assets:		
Non-deductible accruals and allowances	$14,886	$ 12,630
Capitalized inventory costs	14,703	14,411
Stock compensation	4,857	3,835
Net operating loss carryforward	2,130	1,400
Depreciation and amortization	972	420
Other	1,747	1,130
	39,295	33,826
Valuation allowance	(2,512)	(889)
Net deferred tax assets	36,783	32,937
Deferred tax liabilities:		
Deductible accruals and allowance	(1,396)	(961)
Depreciation and amortization	—	(4,677)
Foreign currency gain (loss)	(2,022)	(4,810)
Other	(744)	(793)
	(4,162)	(11,241)
Total	$32,621	$ 21,696

The Company had net operating loss carryforwards at December 31, 2008 and December 31, 2007 in certain international tax jurisdictions of $27,191,000 and $19,000,000, respectively which will begin to expire in 2014. The net operating losses result in a deferred tax asset at December 31, 2008 of $2,130,000 which was subject to a $2,130,000 valuation allowance and a deferred tax asset at December 31, 2007 of $1,400,000 which was subject to a $460,000 valuation allowance. To the extent that the Company reverses a portion of the valuation allowance, the adjustment would be recorded as a reduction to income tax expense.

Non-current deferred tax assets of $723,000 and $444,000 are included as a component of other assets in the consolidated balance sheet at December 31, 2008 and 2007, respectively.

COLUMBIA SPORTSWEAR COMPANY

NOTES TO CONSOLIDATED FINANCIAL STATEMENTS—(Continued)

NOTE 10—PROFIT SHARING PLAN

The Company has a 401(k) profit-sharing plan, which covers substantially all U.S. employees. Participation begins the first of the quarter following completion of thirty days of service. The Company may elect to make discretionary matching and/or non-matching contributions. All Company contributions to the plan as determined by the Board of Directors totaled $3,118,000, $5,083,000 and $4,937,000 for the years ended December 31, 2008, 2007 and 2006, respectively.

NOTE 11—COMMITMENTS AND CONTINGENCIES

Operating Leases

The Company leases, among other things, retail space, office space, warehouse facilities, storage space, vehicles and equipment. Generally, the base lease terms are between 5 and 10 years. Certain lease agreements contain scheduled rent escalation clauses in their future minimum lease payments. Future minimum lease payments are recognized on a straight-line basis over the minimum lease term and the pro rata portion of scheduled rent escalations is included in other long-term liabilities in the Consolidated Balance Sheet. Certain retail space lease agreements provide for additional rents based on a percentage of annual sales in excess of stipulated minimums (percentage rent). Certain retail space lease agreements require the Company to pay real estate taxes, insurance, common area maintenance ("CAM"), and other costs, collectively referred to as operating costs, in addition to base rent. Percentage rent and operating costs are recognized as incurred in SG&A expense in the Consolidated Statement of Operations. Certain retail space lease agreements also contain lease incentives, such as tenant improvement allowances and rent holidays. The Company recognizes the benefits related to the lease incentives on a straight-line basis over the applicable lease term.

Rent expense, including percentage rent, but excluding operating costs, for which the Company is obligated, was $25,220,000, $13,938,000 and $12,994,000 for non-related party leases during the years ended December 31, 2008, 2007 and 2006, respectively. Of these amounts $23,687,000, $12,504,000 and $11,749,000 were included as part of selling, general and administrative expense for the years ended December 31, 2008, 2007 and 2006, respectively, and $1,533,000, $1,434,000 and $1,245,000 were included as part of cost of goods sold for the years ended December 31, 2008, 2007 and 2006, respectively.

The Company leases certain operating facilities from a related party of the Company. Total rent expense for these leases was included as part of selling, general and administrative expense and amounted to $543,000, $583,000 and $515,000 for the years ended December 31, 2008, 2007 and 2006, respectively.

Approximate future minimum payments, including rent escalation clauses and stores that are not yet open, on all lease obligations at December 31, 2008, are as follows (in thousands). Future minimum payments listed below do not include percentage rent or operating costs for which the Company is obligated.

	Non-related Parties	Related Party	Total
2009	$ 21,134	$ 478	$ 21,612
2010	21,504	478	21,982
2011	19,871	478	20,349
2012	18,998	—	18,998
2013	18,613	—	18,613
Thereafter	133,565	—	133,565
	$233,685	$1,434	$235,119

COLUMBIA SPORTSWEAR COMPANY

NOTES TO CONSOLIDATED FINANCIAL STATEMENTS—(Continued)

Litigation

The Company is a party to various legal claims, actions and complaints from time to time. Although the ultimate resolution of legal proceedings cannot be predicted with certainty, management believes that disposition of these matters will not have a material adverse effect on the Company's consolidated financial statements.

Off-Balance Sheet Arrangements

The Company has letters of credit outstanding for inventory purchase obligations. See *Off-Balance Sheet Arrangements* in Note 5.

Indemnities and Guarantees

During its normal course of business, the Company has made certain indemnities, commitments and guarantees under which it may be required to make payments in relation to certain transactions. These include (i) intellectual property indemnities to the Company's customers and licensees in connection with the use, sale and/or license of Company products, (ii) indemnities to various lessors in connection with facility leases for certain claims arising from such facility or lease, (iii) indemnities to vendors and service providers pertaining to claims based on the negligence or willful misconduct of the Company, (iv) executive severance arrangements and (v) indemnities involving the accuracy of representations and warranties in certain contracts. The duration of these indemnities, commitments and guarantees varies, and in certain cases, may be indefinite. The majority of these indemnities, commitments and guarantees do not provide for any limitation of the maximum potential for future payments the Company could be obligated to make. The Company has not recorded any liability for these indemnities, commitments and guarantees in the accompanying Consolidated Balance Sheets.

NOTE 12—STOCK-BASED COMPENSATION

The following table shows total stock-based compensation expense included in the Consolidated Statement of Operations for the years ended December 31, (in thousands):

	2008	2007	2006
Cost of sales	$ 302	$ 415	$ 967
Selling, general, and administrative expense	6,000	6,830	9,113
Licensing	—	15	40
Pre-tax stock-based compensation expense	6,302	7,260	10,120
Income tax benefits	(2,088)	(2,383)	(3,434)
Total stock-based compensation expense, net of tax	$ 4,214	$ 4,877	$ 6,686

No stock-based compensation costs were capitalized for the years ended December 31, 2008, 2007 and 2006.

The Company realized a tax benefit for the deduction from stock-based award transactions of $636,000, $4,213,000, and $4,984,000 for the years ended December 31, 2008, 2007 and 2006, respectively.

1997 Stock Incentive Plan

The Company's 1997 Stock Incentive Plan (the "Plan") provides for issuance of up to 7,400,000 shares of the Company's Common Stock, of which 813,511 shares were available for future grants under the Plan at December 31, 2008. The Plan allows for grants of incentive stock options, non-statutory stock options, restricted stock awards, restricted stock units and other stock-based awards. The Company uses original issuance shares to satisfy share-based payments.

COLUMBIA SPORTSWEAR COMPANY

NOTES TO CONSOLIDATED FINANCIAL STATEMENTS—(Continued)

Stock Options

Options to purchase the Company's common stock are granted at prices equal to or greater than the fair market value on the date of grant. Options granted prior to 2001 generally vest and become exercisable ratably over a period of five years from the date of grant and expire ten years from the date of grant. Options granted after 2000 generally vest and become exercisable over a period of four years (twenty-five percent on the first anniversary date following the date of grant and monthly thereafter) and expire ten years from the date of the grant, with the exception of most options granted in 2005. Most options granted in 2005 vested and became exercisable one year from the date of grant and expire ten years from the date of grant.

The Company estimates the fair value of stock options using the Black-Scholes model. Key input assumptions used to estimate the fair value of stock options include the exercise price of the award, the expected option term, the expected volatility of the Company's stock over the option's expected term, the risk-free interest rate over the option's expected term, and the Company's expected annual dividend yield. Assumptions are evaluated and revised as necessary to reflect changes in market conditions and the Company's experience. Estimates of fair value are not intended to predict actual future events or the value ultimately realized by people who receive equity awards.

The following table shows the weighted average assumptions for the year ended December 31:

	2008	2007	2006
Expected term	4.43 years	5.04 years	5.13 years
Expected stock price volatility	25.03%	28.97%	32.74%
Risk-free interest rate	2.54%	4.55%	4.80%
Expected dividend yield (1)	1.57%	1.01%	—
Weighted average grant date fair value	$ 8.60	$ 18.87	$ 18.29

(1) On November 30, 2006, the Company began paying a quarterly cash dividend.

The following table summarizes stock option activity under the Plan:

	Number of Shares	Weighted Average Exercise Price	Weighted Average Remaining Contractual Life	Aggregate Intrinsic Value (in thousands)
Options outstanding at January 1, 2006	2,310,093	$39.07	5.47	$23,583
Granted	189,636	48.57		
Cancelled	(239,332)	48.24		
Exercised	(681,247)	31.87		
Options outstanding at December 31, 2006	1,579,150	41.93	6.78	21,761
Granted	263,272	61.44		
Cancelled	(81,160)	53.11		
Exercised	(402,845)	36.37		
Options outstanding at December 31, 2007	1,358,417	46.70	6.54	4,497
Granted	640,008	40.98		
Cancelled	(228,300)	49.49		
Exercised	(116,486)	32.42		
Options outstanding at December 31, 2008	1,653,639	$45.10	6.73	$ 1,042
Options vested and expected to vest at December 31, 2008	1,568,300	$45.08	6.64	$ 1,042
Options exercisable at December 31, 2008	903,580	$45.56	5.16	$ 1,042

COLUMBIA SPORTSWEAR COMPANY

NOTES TO CONSOLIDATED FINANCIAL STATEMENTS—(Continued)

The aggregate intrinsic value in the table above represents pre-tax intrinsic value that would have been realized if all options had been exercised on the last business day of the period indicated, based on the Company's closing stock price on that day. Total stock option compensation expense for the years ended December 31, 2008, 2007 and 2006 was $3,329,000, $4,417,000 and $9,297,000, respectively. At December 31, 2008, 2007 and 2006, unrecognized costs related to stock options totaled approximately $6,473,000, $6,515,000 and $7,099,000, respectively, before any related tax benefit. The unrecognized costs related to stock options are being amortized over the related vesting period using the straight-line attribution method. Unrecognized costs related to stock options at December 31, 2008 are expected to be recognized over a weighted average period of 2.80 years. The aggregate intrinsic value of stock options exercised was $1,071,000, $10,953,000 and $14,694,000 for the years ended December 31, 2008, 2007 and 2006, respectively. The total cash received as a result of stock option exercises for the years ended December 31, 2008, 2007 and 2006 was $3,731,000, $14,604,000 and $21,712,000, respectively.

Restricted Stock Units

Service-based restricted stock units are granted at no cost to key employees and generally vest over three years from the date of grant. Performance-based restricted stock units are granted at no cost to certain members of the Company's senior executive team, excluding the Chairman and the President and Chief Executive Officer and generally vest over a performance period of between two and one-half and three years with an additional required service period of one year. Restricted stock units vest in accordance with the terms and conditions established by the Compensation Committee of the Board of Directors, and are based on continued service and, in some instances, on individual performance and /or Company performance.

The fair value of service-based and performance-based restricted stock units is discounted by the present value of the future stream of dividends over the vesting period using the Black-Scholes model. The relevant assumptions used in the Black-Scholes model to compute the discount are the vesting period, dividend yield and closing price of the Company's common stock on the date of grant. Prior to 2007, the fair value of service-based and performance-based restricted stock units was determined based on the number of units granted and the closing price of the Company's common stock on the date of grant. This change in valuation method is the result of the Company's initiation of a quarterly cash dividend in the fourth quarter of 2006.

The following table presents the weighted average assumptions for the years ended December 31:

	2008	2007
Vesting period	3.06 years	3.11 years
Expected dividend yield	1.56%	1.01%
Estimated average fair value per restricted stock unit granted	$ 39.27	$ 60.16

For the year ended December 31, 2006, no assumptions are listed above because no restricted stock units were granted following the initiation of a quarterly cash dividend in the fourth quarter of 2006.

COLUMBIA SPORTSWEAR COMPANY

NOTES TO CONSOLIDATED FINANCIAL STATEMENTS—(Continued)

The following table summarizes the restricted stock unit activity under the Plan:

	Number of Shares	Weighted Average Grant Date Fair Value Per Share
Restricted stock units outstanding at January 1, 2006	—	$ —
Granted	110,227	49.07
Vested	—	—
Forfeited	(10,539)	49.14
Restricted stock units outstanding at December 31, 2006	99,688	49.06
Granted	98,422	60.16
Vested	(21,622)	49.79
Forfeited	(16,618)	53.72
Restricted stock units outstanding at December 31, 2007	159,870	55.31
Granted	168,347	39.27
Vested	(20,625)	51.85
Forfeited	(47,083)	49.25
Restricted stock units outstanding at December 31, 2008	260,509	$46.32

Restricted stock unit compensation expense for the years ended December 31, 2008, 2007 and 2006 was $2,973,000, $2,843,000 and $823,000, respectively. At December 31, 2008, 2007 and 2006, unrecognized costs related to restricted stock units totaled approximately $5,499,000, $5,963,000 and $3,706,000, respectively, before any related tax benefit. The unrecognized costs related to restricted stock units are being amortized over the related vesting period using the straight-line attribution method. These unrecognized costs at December 31, 2008 are expected to be recognized over a weighted average period of 1.76 years. The total grant date fair value of restricted stock units vested during the year ended December 31, 2008 and 2007 was $1,069,000 and $1,077,000, respectively. No restricted stock units vested during the year ended December 31, 2006.

1999 Employee Stock Purchase Plan

In 1999, the Company's shareholders approved the 1999 Employee Stock Purchase Plan ("ESPP"). There are 750,000 shares of common stock authorized for issuance under the ESPP, which allows qualified employees of the Company to purchase shares on a quarterly basis up to fifteen percent of their respective compensation. The purchase price of the shares is equal to eighty five percent of the lesser of the closing price of the Company's common stock on the first or last trading day of the respective quarter. Effective July 1, 2005, the Company suspended offerings under the ESPP indefinitely. As of December 31, 2008, a total of 275,556 shares of common stock had been issued under the ESPP.

NOTE 13—EARNINGS PER SHARE

SFAS No. 128, *Earnings per Share* requires dual presentation of basic and diluted earnings per share ("EPS"). Basic EPS is based on the weighted average number of common shares outstanding. Diluted EPS reflects the potential dilution that could occur if securities or other contracts to issue common stock were exercised or converted into common stock. For the calculation of diluted EPS, the basic weighted average number of shares is increased by the dilutive effect of stock options and restricted stock units determined using the treasury stock method.

COLUMBIA SPORTSWEAR COMPANY

NOTES TO CONSOLIDATED FINANCIAL STATEMENTS—(Continued)

A reconciliation of the common shares used in the denominator for computing basic and diluted EPS is as follows (in thousands, except per share amounts):

	Year Ended December 31,		
	2008	2007	2006
Weighted average common shares outstanding, used in computing basic earnings per share	34,610	36,106	36,245
Effect of dilutive stock options and restricted stock units	101	328	399
Weighted-average common shares outstanding, used in computing diluted earnings per share	34,711	36,434	36,644
Earnings per share of common stock:			
Basic	$ 2.75	$ 4.00	$ 3.39
Diluted	2.74	3.96	3.36

Stock options and service-based restricted stock units representing 1,410,849, 354,342 and 612,603 shares of common stock were outstanding for the years ended December 31, 2008, 2007 and 2006, respectively, but these shares were excluded in the computation of diluted EPS because their effect would be anti-dilutive. In addition, performance-based restricted stock units representing 41,799, 24,318 and 5,221 shares for the years ended December 31, 2008, 2007 and 2006, respectively, were excluded from the computation of diluted EPS, as these shares were subject to performance conditions that had not been met.

Since the inception of the Company's stock repurchase plan in 2004 through December 31, 2008, the Company's Board of Directors has authorized the repurchase of $500,000,000 of the Company's common stock. As of December 31, 2008, the Company has repurchased 8,694,657 shares under this program at an aggregate purchase price of approximately $400,000,000. During the year ended December 31, 2008, the Company repurchased an aggregate of $83,865,000 of the Company's common stock under the stock repurchase plan, of which $58,982,000 was recorded as a reduction to total retained earnings; otherwise, the aggregate purchase price would have resulted in a negative common stock carrying amount. Shares of the Company's common stock may be purchased in the open market or through privately negotiated transactions, subject to market conditions. The repurchase program does not obligate the Company to acquire any specific number of shares or to acquire shares over any specified period of time.

NOTE 14—COMPREHENSIVE INCOME

Accumulated other comprehensive income, net of applicable taxes, reported on the Company's Consolidated Balance Sheets consists of foreign currency translation adjustments and the unrealized gains and losses on derivative transactions. A summary of comprehensive income, net of related tax effects, for the year ended December 31, is as follows (in thousands):

	2008	2007	2006
Net income	$ 95,047	$144,452	$123,018
Other comprehensive income (loss):			
Unrealized derivative holding gains (losses) arising during period (net of tax expense (benefit) of $361, ($796) and $63 in 2008, 2007 and 2006, respectively)	6,425	(844)	(2,599)
Reclassification to net income of previously deferred (gains) losses on derivative transactions (net of tax benefit of ($36), ($608) and ($576) in 2008, 2007 and 2006, respectively)	(389)	(1,303)	864
Foreign currency translation adjustments	(30,511)	25,394	11,167
Other comprehensive income (loss)	(24,475)	23,247	9,432
Comprehensive income	$ 70,572	$167,699	$132,450

COLUMBIA SPORTSWEAR COMPANY

NOTES TO CONSOLIDATED FINANCIAL STATEMENTS—(Continued)

NOTE 15—SEGMENT INFORMATION

The Company operates in four geographic segments: (1) United States, (2) Europe, Middle East and Africa ("EMEA"), (3) Latin America and Asia Pacific ("LAAP"), and (4) Canada, which are reflective of the Company's internal organization, management, and oversight structure. Each geographic segment operates predominantly in one industry: the design, production, marketing and selling of active outdoor apparel, including sportswear, outerwear, footwear, and related accessories and equipment.

In 2007, the Company reclassified its geographical net sales and segment reporting to reflect changes in its internal management and oversight structure as well as growth of the international distributor business. Net sales to international distributors, previously included as part of "Other International," have been regrouped into either the EMEA or LAAP region, in accordance with the markets in which each respective distributor operates. Previously reported geographical net sales information for fiscal year 2006 has been reclassified to reflect this change.

The geographic distribution of the Company's net sales, income before income tax, interest income (expense), income tax expense (benefit), depreciation and amortization expense, identifiable assets and goodwill are summarized in the following tables (in thousands) for, and for the years ended, December 31, 2008, 2007 and 2006. In addition to the geographic distribution of net sales, the Company's net sales by major product line are also summarized below. Inter-geographic net sales, which are recorded at a negotiated mark-up and eliminated in consolidation, are not material.

	2008	2007	2006
Net sales to unrelated entities:			
United States	$ 727,706	$ 767,198	$ 751,984
EMEA	267,152	286,968	272,605
LAAP	198,236	175,725	142,844
Canada	124,741	126,148	120,239
	$1,317,835	$1,356,039	$1,287,672
Income before income tax:			
United States	$ 38,674	$ 112,986	$ 106,172
EMEA	26,167	29,210	25,465
LAAP	32,857	29,585	24,437
Canada	21,008	27,195	23,394
Interest and other income and eliminations	7,537	9,051	5,867
	$ 126,243	$ 208,027	$ 185,335
Interest income (expense), net:			
United States	$ 5,804	$ 9,602	$ 7,855
EMEA	45	(1,856)	(2,486)
LAAP	1,023	482	276
Canada	665	660	(83)
	$ 7,537	$ 8,888	$ 5,562
Income tax expense:			
United States	$ (13,363)	$ (41,227)	$ (47,631)
EMEA	(2,692)	(5,185)	(236)
LAAP	(8,312)	(7,084)	(6,299)
Canada	(6,829)	(10,079)	(8,151)
	$ (31,196)	$ (63,575)	$ (62,317)

64

COLUMBIA SPORTSWEAR COMPANY

NOTES TO CONSOLIDATED FINANCIAL STATEMENTS—(Continued)

	2008	2007	2006
Depreciation and amortization expense:			
United States	$ 21,866	$ 18,643	$ 15,765
EMEA	6,978	9,910	6,397
LAAP	1,865	1,540	952
Canada	449	245	433
	$ 31,158	$ 30,338	$ 23,547
Assets:			
United States	$ 857,228	$ 872,027	$ 808,519
EMEA	246,072	239,007	195,826
LAAP	93,773	78,308	80,436
Canada	89,463	97,815	71,240
Total identifiable assets	1,286,536	1,287,157	1,156,021
Eliminations and reclassifications	(138,300)	(120,676)	(128,732)
Total assets	$1,148,236	$1,166,481	$1,027,289
Goodwill:			
United States	$ 12,157	$ 16,771	$ 16,996
EMEA	502	502	502
LAAP	—	—	—
Canada	—	—	—
	$ 12,659	$ 17,273	$ 17,498
Net sales to unrelated entities:			
Sportswear	$ 540,903	$ 565,591	$ 509,134
Outerwear	491,777	497,551	496,509
Footwear	217,237	227,434	219,640
Accessories and equipment	67,918	65,463	62,389
	$1,317,835	$1,356,039	$1,287,672

NOTE 16— FINANCIAL INSTRUMENTS AND RISK MANAGEMENT

As part of the Company's risk management programs, the Company uses a variety of financial instruments, including foreign currency option and forward contracts. The Company does not hold or issue derivative financial instruments for trading purposes.

The Company hedges against the foreign currency risk associated with anticipated transactions for approximately the next twelve months denominated in European euros, Canadian dollars and Japanese yen. The Company accounts for these instruments as cash flow hedges. In accordance with SFAS No. 133, *Accounting for Derivative Instruments and Hedging Activities*, as amended, these financial instruments are marked to market with the effective portion offset to accumulated other comprehensive income and any ineffective portion offset to current earnings. Amounts accumulated in other comprehensive income are subsequently amortized to cost of goods sold when the underlying transaction is included in earnings. Hedge effectiveness is determined by evaluating the ability of a hedging instrument's cumulative change in fair value to offset the cumulative change in the present value of expected cash flows on the underlying exposures. Hedge ineffectiveness was not material during the years ended December 31, 2008, 2007 and 2006.

COLUMBIA SPORTSWEAR COMPANY

NOTES TO CONSOLIDATED FINANCIAL STATEMENTS—(Continued)

In the normal course of business, the Company's financial position and results of operations are routinely subject to a variety of risks, including market risk associated with interest rate movements on borrowings and investments and currency rate movements on non-U.S. dollar currency denominated assets, liabilities and income. The Company regularly assesses these risks and has established policies and business practices that serve to mitigate these potential exposures. The Company does not enter into foreign currency or interest rate transactions for speculative purposes.

The Company's foreign currency risk management objective is to mitigate the uncertainty of anticipated cash flows attributable to changes in exchange rates. Particular focus is put on anticipated cash flows resulting from anticipated inventory purchases and the related receivables and payables, including third party or intercompany transactions.

The Company manages this risk primarily by using currency forward exchange contracts and options. Anticipated transactions that are hedged carry a high level of certainty and are expected to be recognized within one year. The Company uses cross-currency swaps to hedge foreign currency denominated payments related to intercompany loan agreements. Hedged transactions are denominated primarily in euros, Canadian dollars and yen. The Company attempts to mitigate foreign currency risk through hedging practices. However, if recent foreign currency exchange rate volatility continues, it is reasonably possible that the Company could experience a materially adverse effect on the cost of goods sold during the next twelve months.

At December 31, 2008 and 2007, the notional value of outstanding forward contracts was approximately $60,000,000 and $90,500,000, respectively. At December 31, 2008, $2,477,000 of deferred gains (net of tax) on both outstanding and matured derivatives accumulated in other comprehensive income are expected to be reclassified to net income during the next twelve months as a result of underlying hedged transactions also being recorded in net income. Actual amounts ultimately reclassified to net income are dependent on the exchange rates in effect when derivative contracts that are currently outstanding mature.

NOTE 17—FAIR VALUE MEASURES

The Company adopted the provisions of SFAS No. 157 effective January 1, 2008. SFAS No. 157 defines fair value, establishes a consistent framework for measuring fair value, and expands disclosures for each major asset and liability category measured at fair value on either a recurring or nonrecurring basis. SFAS No. 157 clarifies that fair value is an exit price, representing the amount that would be received to sell an asset or paid to transfer a liability in an orderly transaction between market participants. SFAS No. 157 establishes a three-tier fair value hierarchy which prioritizes the inputs used in measuring fair value as follows:

Level 1 –   observable inputs such as quoted prices in active markets;

Level 2 –   inputs, other than the quoted market prices in active markets, which are observable, either directly or indirectly; and

Level 3 –   unobservable inputs for which there is little or no market data available, which require the reporting entity to develop its own assumptions.

COLUMBIA SPORTSWEAR COMPANY

NOTES TO CONSOLIDATED FINANCIAL STATEMENTS—(Continued)

Assets and liabilities measured at fair value on a recurring basis as of December 31, 2008 are as follows (in thousands):

	Total	Level 1 (1)	Level 2 (2)	Level 3
Assets:				
Cash and cash equivalents	$230,617	$230,617	$ —	—
Short-term investments	22,433	22,433	—	—
Derivative financial instruments	2,603	—	2,603	—
Liabilities:				
Derivative financial instruments	494	—	494	—

(1) Level 1 assets include money market funds and certificates of deposit which cost approximates fair value.
(2) Level 2 assets and liabilities include derivative financial instruments which are valued based on significant observable inputs. See Note 14 and Note 16 for further discussion.

There were no assets and liabilities measured at fair value on a nonrecurring basis.

SUPPLEMENTARY DATA—QUARTERLY FINANCIAL DATA (Unaudited)

The following table summarizes the Company's quarterly financial data for the past two years ended December 31, 2008 (in thousands, except per share amounts):

2008	First Quarter	Second Quarter	Third Quarter	Fourth Quarter
Net sales	$297,363	$213,147	$452,415	$354,910
Gross profit	130,555	85,765	202,053	149,438
Net income (loss)	19,931	(1,770)	58,329	18,557
Earnings (loss) per share				
Basic	$ 0.56	$ (0.05)	$ 1.70	$ 0.55
Diluted	0.56	(0.05)	1.69	0.55

2007	First Quarter	Second Quarter	Third Quarter	Fourth Quarter
Net sales	$289,640	$218,560	$471,081	$376,758
Gross profit	126,698	90,575	203,531	158,947
Net income	26,086	10,037	62,609	45,720
Earnings per share				
Basic	$ 0.72	$ 0.28	$ 1.73	$ 1.27
Diluted	0.71	0.27	1.72	1.26

Item 9. *CHANGES IN AND DISAGREEMENTS WITH ACCOUNTANTS ON ACCOUNTING AND FINANCIAL DISCLOSURE*

None.

Item 9A. *CONTROLS AND PROCEDURES*

Evaluation of Disclosure Controls and Procedures

Our management has evaluated, under the supervision and with the participation of our chief executive officer and chief financial officer, the effectiveness of our disclosure controls and procedures as of the end of the period covered by this report pursuant to Rule 13a-15(b) under the Securities Exchange Act of 1934 (the "Exchange Act"). Based on that evaluation, our chief executive officer and chief financial officer have concluded that, as of the end of the period covered by this report, our disclosure controls and procedures are effective in ensuring that information required to be disclosed in our Exchange Act reports is (1) recorded, processed, summarized and reported in a timely manner, and (2) accumulated and communicated to our management, including our chief executive officer and chief financial officer, as appropriate to allow timely decisions regarding required disclosure.

Design and Evaluation of Internal Control Over Financial Reporting

Report of Management

Our management is responsible for establishing and maintaining adequate internal control over financial reporting. All internal control systems, no matter how well designed, have inherent limitations. Therefore, even those systems determined to be effective can provide only reasonable assurance with respect to financial statement preparation and presentation.

Under the supervision and with the participation of our management, we assessed the effectiveness of our internal control over financial reporting as of December 31, 2008. In making this assessment, we used the criteria set forth by the Committee of Sponsoring Organizations of the Treadway Commission in Internal Control—Integrated Framework. Based on our assessment we believe that, as of December 31, 2008, the Company's internal control over financial reporting is effective based on those criteria.

There has been no change in our internal control over financial reporting that occurred during our fiscal quarter ended December 31, 2008 that has materially affected, or is reasonably likely to materially affect, our internal control over financial reporting.

Our independent auditors have issued an audit report on the effectiveness of our internal control over financial reporting as of December 31, 2008, which is included herein.

Report of Independent Registered Public Accounting Firm

To the Board of Directors and Shareholders
Columbia Sportswear Company
Portland, Oregon

We have audited the internal control over financial reporting of Columbia Sportswear Company and subsidiaries (the "Company") as of December 31, 2008, based on criteria established in *Internal Control—Integrated Framework* issued by the Committee of Sponsoring Organizations of the Treadway Commission. The Company's management is responsible for maintaining effective internal control over financial reporting and for its assessment of the effectiveness of internal control over financial reporting, included in the accompanying "Report of Management". Our responsibility is to express an opinion on the Company's internal control over financial reporting based on our audit.

We conducted our audit in accordance with the standards of the Public Company Accounting Oversight Board (United States). Those standards require that we plan and perform the audit to obtain reasonable assurance about whether effective internal control over financial reporting was maintained in all material respects. Our audit included obtaining an understanding of internal control over financial reporting, assessing the risk that a material weakness exists, testing and evaluating the design and operating effectiveness of internal control based on the assessed risk, and performing such other procedures as we considered necessary in the circumstances. We believe that our audit provides a reasonable basis for our opinion.

A company's internal control over financial reporting is a process designed by, or under the supervision of, the company's principal executive and principal financial officers, or persons performing similar functions, and effected by the company's board of directors, management, and other personnel to provide reasonable assurance regarding the reliability of financial reporting and the preparation of financial statements for external purposes in accordance with generally accepted accounting principles. A company's internal control over financial reporting includes those policies and procedures that (1) pertain to the maintenance of records that, in reasonable detail, accurately and fairly reflect the transactions and dispositions of the assets of the company; (2) provide reasonable assurance that transactions are recorded as necessary to permit preparation of financial statements in accordance with generally accepted accounting principles, and that receipts and expenditures of the company are being made only in accordance with authorizations of management and directors of the company; and (3) provide reasonable assurance regarding prevention or timely detection of unauthorized acquisition, use, or disposition of the company's assets that could have a material effect on the financial statements.

Because of the inherent limitations of internal control over financial reporting, including the possibility of collusion or improper management override of controls, material misstatements due to error or fraud may not be prevented or detected on a timely basis. Also, projections of any evaluation of the effectiveness of the internal control over financial reporting to future periods are subject to the risk that the controls may become inadequate because of changes in conditions, or that the degree of compliance with the policies or procedures may deteriorate.

In our opinion, the Company maintained, in all material respects, effective internal control over financial reporting as of December 31, 2008, based on the criteria established in *Internal Control—Integrated Framework* issued by the Committee of Sponsoring Organizations of the Treadway Commission.

We have also audited, in accordance with the standards of the Public Company Accounting Oversight Board (United States), the consolidated financial statements and financial statement schedule as of and for the year ended December 31, 2008 of the Company and our report dated February 27, 2009 expressed an unqualified opinion on those financial statements and financial statement schedule.

DELOITTE & TOUCHE LLP
Portland, Oregon
February 27, 2009

Item 9B. *OTHER INFORMATION*

None.

Appendix B

TIME VALUE OF MONEY—FUTURE AND PRESENT VALUE CONCEPTS

Money earns income over time, a fact called the **time value of money**. The time value of money idea is based on the thought that $1 today is worth more than $1 in the future. This is because $1 today can be invested and earn interest and therefore become worth more than $1 at a later date.

FUTURE VALUE

Future value refers to the amount that a given sum of money will be "worth" at a specified time in the future assuming a certain interest rate. The main application of future value is calculating the future value of an amount invested today (a present value) that earns a constant rate of interest over time. For example, assume that you invest $4,545 and it earns 10% interest per year. After one year, the $4,545 invested grows to a future value of $5,000, as shown next.

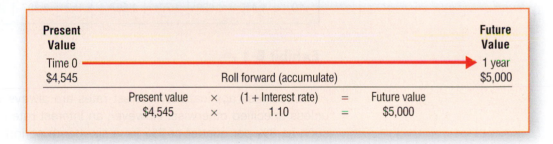

If the money was invested for five years, you would have to perform five such calculations. You would also have to consider the compound interest your investment is earning. **Compound interest** is the interest you earn not only on your principal amount, but also on the interest to date. Most business applications include compound interest. The following table shows the interest calculations for the first two years:

End of Year	Interest	Future Value
0	—	$4,545
1	$4,545 × 0.10 = $455	5,000
2	5,000 × 0.10 = 500	5,500

Earning 10%, a $4,545 investment grows to $5,000 at the end of one year, to $5,500 at the end of two years, and so on. (Throughout this discussion, we round dollar amounts to the nearest dollar.)

Future-Value Tables

Mathematical tables make computing a future value easy. Exhibit B-1 shows the table used to calculate the future value of $1 for various interest rates over various time periods. Future value depends on three factors:

❶ The amount of the investment

❷ The length of time the amount is invested

❸ The interest rate

The heading in **Exhibit B-1** states that the future value of $1 is being calculated. Future-value and present-value tables are based on $1 because $1 is so easy to work with. Look at the Period column and the interest rate columns from 4% to 16%.

					Future Value of $1					
Period	**4%**	**5%**	**6%**	**7%**	**8%**	**9%**	**10%**	**12%**	**14%**	**16%**
1	1.040	1.050	1.060	1.070	1.080	1.090	1.100	1.120	1.140	1.160
2	1.082	1.103	1.124	1.145	1.166	1.188	1.210	1.254	1.300	1.346
3	1.125	1.158	1.191	1.225	1.260	1.295	1.331	1.405	1.482	1.561
4	1.170	1.216	1.262	1.311	1.360	1.412	1.464	1.574	1.689	1.811
5	1.217	1.276	1.338	1.403	1.469	1.539	1.611	1.762	1.925	2.100
6	1.265	1.340	1.419	1.501	1.587	1.677	1.772	1.974	2.195	2.436
7	1.316	1.407	1.504	1.606	1.714	1.828	1.949	2.211	2.502	2.826
8	1.369	1.477	1.594	1.718	1.851	1.993	2.144	2.476	2.853	3.278
9	1.423	1.551	1.689	1.838	1.999	2.172	2.358	2.773	3.252	3.803
10	1.480	1.629	1.791	1.967	2.159	2.367	2.594	3.106	3.707	4.411

Exhibit B-1 ▲

In business applications, interest rates are always stated for a one-year period unless specified otherwise. However, an interest rate can be stated for any period, such as 3% per quarter or 5% for a six-month period. For example, an investment may offer a return of 3% per quarter for two years. In that case, you would be working with 3% interest for eight periods (two years multiplied by four quarters per year). It would be incorrect to use 3% for two years because the interest in this case is 3% compounded quarterly, and different future values would result. Take care when calculating future-value and present-value problems to select the proper interest rate and the appropriate number of periods.

Let's demonstrate using the tables in Exhibit B-1. The future value of $1.00 invested at 8% for one year is $1.08 ($1.00 × 1.080, which appears at the intersection of the 8% column and the Period 1 row). The future value factor 1.080 includes both the principal (1.000) and the compound interest for one period (0.080).

Suppose you deposit $5,000 in a savings account that pays annual interest of 8%. The account balance at the end of one year will be $5,400. To compute the future value of $5,000 at 8% for one year, multiply $5,000 by 1.080 to get $5,400.

Now suppose you invest $5,000 in a 10-year, 8% certificate of deposit (CD). What will be the future value of the CD at maturity? To compute the future value of $5,000 at 8% for 10 periods, multiply $5,000 by 2.159 (from Exhibit B-1) to get $10,795. This future value of $10,795 indicates that $5,000 earning 8% interest compounded annually grows to $10,795 at the end of 10 years. You can find any present amount's future value at a particular future date.

Future Value of an Annuity

In the preceding example, we made an investment of a single amount. Other investments, called **annuities**, include multiple investments of an equal periodic amount at fixed intervals over the length of the investment. Consider the Gomez family members investing for their child's education. Let's assume the Gomez family can invest $4,000 at the end of each year for three years to accumulate a college fund for 15-year-old Daniel. The investment can earn 7% annually until Daniel turns 18—a three-year investment. How much will be available for Daniel on the date of the last investment? The investment will have a future value of $12,860 as calculated next.

End of Year	Annual Investment +	Interest	=	Increase for the Year	Future Value of Annuity
0	—	—		—	0
1	$4,000	—		$4,000	$ 4,000
2	4,000	+ ($4,000 × 0.07 = $280) =		4,280	8,280
3	4,000	+ ($8,280 × 0.07 = $580) =		4,580	12,860

As with the Future Value of $1 table, mathematical tables make calculating the future value of annuities much easier. **Exhibit B-2**, Future Value of Annuity of $1 gives the future value of a series of investments, each of equal amount, made at regular intervals at the end of each period.

				Future Value of Annuity of $1						
Period	4%	5%	6%	7%	8%	9%	10%	12%	14%	16%
1	1.000	1.000	1.000	1.000	1.000	1.000	1.000	1.000	1.000	1.000
2	2.040	2.050	2.060	2.070	2.080	2.090	2.100	2.120	2.140	2.160
3	3.122	3.153	3.184	3.215	3.246	3.278	3.310	3.374	3.440	3.506
4	4.246	4.310	4.375	4.440	4.506	4.573	4.641	4.779	4.921	5.066
5	5.416	5.526	5.637	5.751	5.867	5.985	6.105	6.353	6.610	6.877
6	6.633	6.802	6.975	7.153	7.336	7.523	7.716	8.115	8.536	8.977
7	7.898	8.142	8.394	8.654	8.923	9.200	9.487	10.089	10.730	11.414
8	9.214	9.549	9.897	10.260	10.637	11.028	11.436	12.300	13.233	14.240
9	10.583	11.027	11.491	11.978	12.488	13.021	13.579	14.776	16.085	17.519
10	12.006	12.578	13.181	13.816	14.487	15.193	15.937	17.549	19.337	21.321

Exhibit B-2 ▲

What is the future value of an annuity of three investments of $1 each, made at the end of each year, that earn 7%? The answer is $3.215. The factor can be found in the 7% column and across from 3 in the Period column of Exhibit B-2. This factor can be used to compute the future value of the investment for Daniel's education, as follows:

Amount of Each Periodic Investment	×	Future Value of Annuity of $1(Exhibit B-2)	=	Future Value of Investment
$4,000	×	3.215	=	$12,860

You can compute the future value of any investment consisting of equal periodic amounts at regular intervals. Businesses make periodic investments to accumulate funds for plant expansion and other uses.

PRESENT VALUE

Often a person knows a future amount and needs to know the related **present value**. Present value is the value on a given date of a future amount, adjusted to reflect the time value of money. Suppose an investment promises to pay you $5,000 at the *end* of one year. How much would you pay *now* to acquire this investment? You would be willing to pay the present value of the $5,000 future amount.

Present value also depends on three factors:

❶ The amount of the future payment (or receipt)

❷ The time span between investment and future payment (or receipt)

❸ The interest rate

Computing a present value is called **discounting** because the present value is *always less* than the future value.

In our example, the future receipt is $5,000. The investment period is one year. Assume that you demand an annual interest rate of 10% on your investment. With all three factors specified, you can compute the present value of $5,000 at 10% for one year as follows:

$$\frac{\text{Future Value}}{(1 + \text{Interest Rate})} = \frac{\$5,000}{1.10} = \$4,545$$

By turning the data around into a future-value problem, we verify the present-value computation:

Amount Invested (present value)	$4,545
Expected Earnings ($4,545 × 0.10)	455
Amount to Be Received One Year from Now (future value)	$5,000

This example illustrates that present value and future value are based on the same equation:

$$\text{Present Value} \times (1 + \text{Interest Rate}) = \text{Future Value}$$

$$\frac{\text{Future Value}}{(1 + \text{Interest Rate})} = \text{Present Value}$$

If the $5,000 is to be received two years from now, you will pay only $4,132 for the investment, as shown next:

By turning the data around, we verify that $4,132 accumulates to $5,000 at 10% for two years:

Amount Invested (present value)	$4,132
Expected Earnings for First Year ($4,132 × 0.10)	413
Amount of Investment after One Year	4,545
Expected Earnings for Second Year ($4,545 × 0.10)	455
Amount to Be Received Two Years from Now (future value)	$5,000

You would pay $4,132, the present value of $5,000, to receive the $5,000 future amount at the end of two years at 10% per year. The $868 difference between the amount invested, $4,132, and the amount to be received, $5,000 is the return on the investment; it is the sum of the two interest receipts: $413 + $455 = $868.

Present-Value Tables

We have shown the simple formula for computing present value. However, figuring present value this way for investments spanning many years is tedious. Present-value tables ease our work. Let's reexamine our examples of present value by using **Exhibit B-3**, Present Value of $1.

Present Value of $1									
Period	4%	5%	6%	7%	8%	10%	12%	14%	16%
1	0.962	0.952	0.943	0.935	0.926	0.909	0.893	0.877	0.862
2	0.925	0.907	0.890	0.873	0.857	0.826	0.797	0.769	0.743
3	0.889	0.864	0.840	0.816	0.794	0.751	0.712	0.675	0.641
4	0.855	0.823	0.792	0.763	0.735	0.683	0.636	0.592	0.552
5	0.822	0.784	0.747	0.713	0.681	0.621	0.567	0.519	0.476
6	0.790	0.746	0.705	0.666	0.630	0.564	0.507	0.456	0.410
7	0.760	0.711	0.665	0.623	0.583	0.513	0.452	0.400	0.354
8	0.731	0.677	0.627	0.582	0.540	0.467	0.404	0.351	0.305
9	0.703	0.645	0.592	0.544	0.500	0.424	0.361	0.308	0.263
10	0.676	0.614	0.558	0.508	0.463	0.386	0.322	0.270	0.227

Exhibit B-3 ▲

For the 10% investment for one year, we find the intersection of the 10% column and the first row of the Period column. The factor 0.909 is computed as follows: 1/1.10 = 0.909. In preparing the table, this work has been done for us, so only the resulting present values are given in the table. The heading in Exhibit B-3 states that the present value of $1 is being determined. To figure present value for $5,000, we multiply $5,000 by 0.909. The result is $4,545, which matches the result we obtained previously by hand.

For the two-year investment, we read down the 10% column and across the Period 2 row. We multiply 0.826 by $5,000 and get $4,130, which confirms our preceding computation of $4,132; the difference is due to rounding in the present-value table. Using the table, we can compute the present value of any single future amount.

Present Value of an Annuity

Annuity investments provide multiple receipts of an equal amount at fixed intervals over the investment's length.

Consider an investment that promises *annual* cash receipts of $10,000 to be received at the end of each of three years. Assume that you demand a 12% return on your investment. What is the investment's present value? What would you pay today to acquire the investment? The investment spans three periods, and you would pay the sum of three present values. The computation follows:

Year	Annual Cash Receipt	×	Present Value of $1 at 12% (Exhibit B-3)	=	Present Value of Annual Cash Receipt
1	$10,000	×	0.893	=	$ 8,930
2	10,000	×	0.797	=	7,970
3	10,000	×	0.712	=	7,120
			Total Present Value of Investment =		$24,020

The present value of this annuity is $24,020. By paying this amount today, you will receive $10,000 at the end of each of the three years while earning 12% on your investment.

The example illustrates repetitive computations of the three future amounts. One way to ease the computational burden is to add the three present values of $1, 0.893 + 0.797 + 0.712, and multiply their sum of 2.402 by the annual cash receipt of $10,000 to obtain the present value of the annuity, $24,020 ($10,000 × 2.402).

An easier approach is to use a present value of an annuity table. **Exhibit B-4** shows the present value of $1 to be received at the end of each period for a given number of periods. The present value factor of a three-period annuity at 12% is 2.402, the junction of the Period 3 row and the 12% column. Thus, the present value of $10,000 received annually at the end of each of three years, discounted at 12%, is $24,020 ($10,000 × 2.402).

				Present Value of Annuity of $1					
Period	4%	5%	6%	7%	8%	10%	12%	14%	16%
1	0.962	0.952	0.943	0.935	0.926	0.909	0.893	0.877	0.862
2	1.886	1.859	1.833	1.808	1.783	1.736	1.690	1.647	1.605
3	2.775	2.723	2.673	2.624	2.577	2.487	2.402	2.322	2.246
4	3.630	3.546	3.465	3.387	3.312	3.170	3.037	2.914	2.798
5	4.452	4.329	4.212	4.100	3.993	3.791	3.605	3.433	3.274
6	5.242	5.076	4.917	4.767	4.623	4.355	4.111	3.889	3.685
7	6.002	5.786	5.582	5.389	5.206	4.868	4.564	4.288	4.039
8	6.733	6.463	6.210	5.971	5.747	5.335	4.968	4.639	4.344
9	7.435	7.108	6.802	6.515	6.247	5.759	5.328	4.946	4.607
10	8.111	7.722	7.360	7.024	6.710	6.145	5.650	5.216	4.833

Exhibit B-4 ▲

ACCOUNTING VOCABULARY

THE LANGUAGE OF BUSINESS

Annuities (p. 713) Multiple investments of an equal periodic amount at fixed intervals over the length of the investment.

Compound interest (p. 711) Interest earned not only on principal but also on the interest to date.

Discounting (p. 714) Computing a present value.

Future value (p. 711) The amount that a given sum of money will be "worth" at a specified time in the future assuming a certain interest rate.

Present value (p. 714) The value on a given date of a future amount, adjusted to reflect the time value of money.

Time value of money (p. 711) The concept that states that a dollar today is worth more than a dollar received in the future.

ACCOUNTING PRACTICE

EXERCISES

EB-1A. Calculate present and future values. 10–15 min.

Presented next are four independent situations related to future and present values.

Requirement

1. Using the tables in the appendix, calculate the future or present value of each item as needed.

    a. $5,000 is deposited in the bank today for a period of eight years. Calculate the value of the $5,000 at the end of eight years assuming it earns 5% interest.

    b. How much must you invest today in order to receive $1,500 at the end of each year for the next four years assuming you can earn 7% interest?

    c. $3,500 will be invested at the end of each year for a period of five years. Calculate the value of the investment at the end of five years assuming it earns 9% interest.

    d. The company you work for wants to purchase a new piece of equipment that is estimated to cost $18,000 ten years from now. How much must they invest today in order to have the $18,000 necessary to purchase the equipment if they can earn 8% interest?

EB-2A. Future value concepts. 15–20 min.

Allen Hamilton is considering two plans for building an education fund for his children.

Plan A—Invest $2,000 each year for six years. This investment will earn 10% annual interest.

Plan B—Invest $10,000 now, earning 8% annual interest for six years.

Requirement

1. Before making any calculations, which plan would you expect to provide the larger future amount? Using the tables provided in the appendix, calculate the future value of each plan. Which plan provides the larger amount at the end of six years?

EB-3A. Present value concepts. 15–20 min.

Aztec Electronics, Inc., needs new manufacturing equipment. Two companies can provide similar equipment but under different payment plans:

a. Fancher Manufacturing offers to let Aztec Electronics, Inc., pay $60,000 at the end of each year for five years. The payments include interest at 12% per year.

b. Phoenix, Corp., will let Aztec Electronics, Inc., make a single payment of $400,000 at the end of five years. This payment includes both principal and interest at 12%.

Requirements

1. Calculate the present value cost of each payment plan.

2. In addition to the present value cost of the equipment, what other factors should Aztec Electronics consider when deciding which company to purchase the equipment from?

Company Index

Glindex

A Combined Glossary and Subject Index

A

Accelerated depreciation method. A depreciation method that writes off more of the asset's cost near the start of its useful life than the straight-line method does, 396–398

Account form. A balance sheet format that lists assets on the left of the report and liabilities and stockholders' equity on the right, just as those accounts appear in the accounting equation, 193

Accountants, 6

Accounting. The information system that measures business activity, processes the results of activities into reports, and communicates the results to decision makers

  defined, 6

  principles, 9–10

  reasons to study, 4–6, 598

Accounting cycle. The sequence of steps used to record and report business transactions, 72

  completing, 123–124, 141

  defined, 110

Accounting equation

  closing accounts and, 124

  recording business transactions using, 10–17, 21–25

Accounting period. Generally, the time period reflected by a set of financial statements, 69, 110

Accounting standards

  cumulative effect of changes in, 601

  International Financial Reporting Standards, 302–304

Accounts. The basic summary device of accounting; the detailed record of all the changes in a specific asset, liability, or stockholders' equity item as a result of transactions

  adjunct, 454

  balancing, 67–68

  chart, 54

contra-accounts, 118

control, 335

defined, 54

net value of, 118

normal balance, 57–58

organizing, 54

permanent, 124

recovery of previously written off, 334, 339–340

T-accounts. *See* T-accounts

temporary, 123

uncollectible, 321, 333–340

Accounts payable. A liability backed by the general reputation and credit standing of the debtor, 13, 55

  accounting for, 440–441

  partial payment of, 16

Accounts receivable. An asset representing amounts due from customers to whom the business has sold goods or for whom the business has performed services, 15, 54, 332

  adjusting entries for, 113

  on balance sheet, 340

  demo doc, 346–350

  internal control over, 333

  uncollectible, 333

Accounts receivable turnover. Net Credit Sales divided by net average Accounts Receivable; it measures a company's ability to collect cash from its credit customers. To compute accounts receivable turnover, divide net credit sales by average net accounts receivable, 345–346, 612

Accrual accounting. Accounting method that records revenues when earned and expenses when incurred without regard to when cash is exchanged

  defined, 111

  updating accounts in. *See* Adjusting entries

Accruals. Revenues earned or expenses incurred before cash has been exchanged, 111, 113, 128

  See also Adjusting entries

Accrued expenses. Expenses that have been incurred prior to being paid for, 113–114, 443

Accrued liabilities, 55

Accumulated depreciation. A contra-asset account that reflects all of the depreciation recorded for an asset to date, 118–119

Acid-test ratio. Ratio that reveals how well the entity can pay its current liabilities. Also called the *quick ratio*, 344–345, 610–611

Additional Paid-in Capital. Paid-in capital that represents the amount by which the issue price of stock exceeds its par value; also called *Paid-in Capital in Excess of Par*, 491

Adjunct account. An account that is linked to another account (a companion account). An adjunct account will have a normal balance that is the same as its companion account, 454

Adjusted trial balance. A list of all the accounts of a business with their adjusted balances, 120–121

  preparation of, 137

Adjusting entries. Journal entries made at the end of the accounting period to measure the period's income accurately and bring the related asset and liability accounts to correct balances before the financial statements are prepared

  for accruals, 113–114

  for bonds payable, 455

  for deferrals, 114–119

  defined, 111

  for expenses, 113

  preparation of, 129–135

  role of, 111

  summary of process, 127–128

  types of, 112

defined, 543

preparing statement of cash flows using, 555–559

Direct write-off method. The method of accounting for uncollectible accounts in which a customer's account is written off as uncollectible when the business determines that the customer will not pay, 333–334, 340

Disbursement schemes. A form of employee embezzlement in which an employee tricks a company into giving up cash for an invalid reason. Examples include check tampering, cash register schemes, and expense schemes, 292

Disclaimer, 301

Discontinued operations, 600

Discount. Excess of a bond's maturity value over its issue price; also called a *bond discount,* 450

Discount period. Period in which the buyer can make early payment for a purchase and receive a discount on that purchase, 180

Discounting. Computing a present value, 714

Discounts

on bonds, 450

purchase, 178, 179–181

sales, 185

Dividend yield. Ratio of dividends per share of stock to the stock's market price per share. Tells the percentage of a stock's market value that the company returns to stockholders annually as dividends, 617

Dividends. Distribution of earnings by a corporation to its stockholders, 12, 55, 58

accounting for, 493–497

in arrears, 496

cash, 17, 493–497

cash receipts of, 557

computing payments of, 551–552

on cumulative and noncumulative preferred stock, 496

dates, 494

declaring and paying, 494–495

dividing between preferred and common shareholders, 495

stock, 497–501

to stockholders, 489

Documents, 297

Dollar value bias. The bias one sees from comparing numbers in absolute (dollars) rather than relative (percentages) terms, 607

Double-declining-balance (DDB). An accelerated depreciation method that computes annual depreciation by multiplying the asset's decreasing book value by a constant percent that is two times the straight-line rate, 396–398, 414–415

Double-entry accounting. The rule of accounting that specifies every transaction involves at least two accounts and is recorded with equal amounts of debits and credits, 56–57

Due date. The date when final payment of the note is due; also called the *maturity date,* 341

E

Earnings

retained, 12, 55, 58, 489

Earnings per share (EPS), 601, 616

Earnings per share of common stock. Reflects the net income earned for each share of the company's outstanding common stock, 616

Electronic data interchange (EDI). Direct electronic communication between suppliers and retailers, 324

Electronic funds transfer (EFT). System that transfers cash by electronic communication rather than by paper documents, 324, 326

Embezzlement, 292–293

Employee embezzlement. Fraud where employees steal from employers by taking assets, bribes, or kickbacks, or engaging in disbursement schemes to steal cash, 292–293

Employees

competent, 297

mandatory vacations for, 297

payments to, 558

Entity. An organization or a section of an organization that, for accounting purposes, stands apart as a separate economic unit, 9

eom. Credit term specifying that payment for a purchase is due by the end of the month; also referred to as *n/eom,* 179

Equipment, 55, 390–391

Equity securities, 409

Equity transactions, 507–511

Errors

bank, 326

book, 326

correcting, 70

inventory, 244–246

Estimated liabilities, 440, 444–445

Ethical dilemmas, 4–5, 458

Ethics. Principles of socially responsible behavior, 4

code of, 291

defined, 291

importance of, 291–292

Expense schemes. A fraud scheme in which an employee overcharges the company for travel and other business-related expenses, such as lunches, hotels, air travel, parking fees, and cab fares, 293

Expenses. Decreases to retained earnings caused by using resources to deliver goods or provide services to customers, 12, 55, 58

accrued, 113, 443

amortization, 546–547, 556, 559

bad debts, 333

deferred, 115–119

depreciation, 118

general and administrative, 191

income tax, 559, 599

interest, 452–455, 559

operating, 191

payment of, 16

prepaid, 13, 55, 112, 115–116

External audits. An audit of financial statements performed by Certified Public Accountants (CPAs), 300–301

of inventory on hand and the cost of the goods sold, 230

defined, 177

transaction analysis using, 196–200

Petty cash. Fund containing a small amount of cash that is used to pay for minor expenditures, 332

Petty cash funds

changing, 382

defined, 381

replenishing, 382

setting up, 381

Plant assets. The long-lived assets of a business including land, buildings, furniture, fixtures, and equipment; also called *fixed assets* and commonly shown on the balance sheet as property, plant, and equipment, 193

acquisitions and sales of, 548–550

calculating cost of, 389–393

changing useful life of, 400

costs of repairing, 401–402

defined, 388

depreciation of, 393–401

disposal of, 403–405

gains and losses from sale of, 557, 559

Post-closing trial balance. A list of the accounts and their balances at the end of the accounting period after closing entries have been journalized and posted

defined, 126–127

preparation of, 140–141

purpose of, 128

Posting. Copying information from the general journal to accounts in the general ledger, 58–59, 74–80

Posting reference. A notation in the journal and ledger that links these two accounting records together, 59

Preemption rights

of stockholders, 490

Preferred stock. Stock that gives its owners certain advantages over common stockholders, such as the right to receive dividends before the common stockholders and the right to receive assets before the common

stockholders if the corporation liquidates

cumulative, 496

defined, 490

dividend rate on, 494, 495

issuance of, 493

noncumulative, 496

Premium. Excess of a bond's issue price over its maturity value; also called *bond premium*, 450, 453–455

Prepaid expenses. Amounts that are assets of a business because they represent items that have been paid for but will be used later; also called *deferred expenses*, 13, 55, 112, 115–116

Prepaid rent, 115

Prepaid shipping costs, 187–188, 189–190

Present value. The value on a given date of a future amount, adjusted to reflect the time value of money

of an annuity, 715–716

computation of, 714–715

defined, 714

tables, 715

Price/earnings (P/E) ratio. Ratio of the market price of a share of common stock to the company's earnings per share. It measures the value that the stock market places on $1 of a company's earnings, 616–617

Principal. The amount loaned out by the payee and borrowed by the maker of the note, 341

Principal amount. The amount a borrower must pay back to the bondholders on the maturity date; also called *par value* or *maturity value*, 449

Profit. The difference between the revenues (the sales price of the goods or services sold by the business) and expenses (the cost of the resources used to provide these goods and services); also called *net income*

gross, 191

on income statement, 17

Profitability

determining, 19

Profitability ratios, 610, 614–616

Promissory notes. A written pledge to pay a fixed amount of money at a later date, 54, 341, 441

Property, plant, and equipment. A heading often seen on the balance sheet used to describe fixed, or plant, assets, 193

Purchase discounts. Discount received on purchases by paying early within a discount period, 178, 179–181

Purchase orders. A document showing details of merchandise being ordered from a supplier, 323

Purchase returns and allowances. A reduction in the amount owed for a purchase due to returning merchandise or accepting damaged goods, 178–179

Purchasing agents. The individual in an organization responsible for buying items for that organization, 324

Q

Qualified opinion, 301

Quick assets. Highly liquid assets used to calculate the quick ratio, including cash and cash equivalents, short-term investments, and net accounts receivable, 344

Quick ratio. Ratio that reveals how well the entity can pay its current liabilities; also called the *acid-test ratio*, 344–345, 610–611

R

Rate of return on common stockholders' equity. Net income minus preferred dividends, divided by average common stockholders' equity. It is a measure of profitability; also called *return on common equity*, 507, 615

Rate of return on net sales. Ratio of net income to net sales. It is a measure of profitability; also called *return on sales*, 614

Rate of return on stockholder's equity. Net income divided by average stockholders' equity. It is a measure of profitability; also called *return on equity*, 506

Sales revenue. The amount that a retailer earns from selling its inventory, 181

Sales tax payable, 442–443

Salvage value. The estimated value at the end of a long-term asset's useful life; also called *residual value*, 118, 394

Sarbanes-Oxley Act. A law passed in 2002 by the U.S. Congress in response to recent, large-scale fraud in publicly owned companies, 301–302

S-corporation. A corporation that does not pay income tax. Instead, its earnings are passed through to its owners, 8

Secured bonds. Bonds that give bondholders the right to take specified assets from the issuer if the issuer fails to pay principal or interest, 449

Security measures, 297

Selling expenses. Expenses related to advertising and selling products including sales salaries, sales commissions, advertising, depreciation on items used in sales, and delivery expense, 190

Separation of duties, 297, 323

Serial bonds. Bonds from the same bond issuance that mature at different times, 449

Service business. Businesses that provide services to customers, 7

Service charges, 326

Shareholders. A person who owns stock in a corporation; also called *stockholder*, 7

Shares. The basic unit of stock, 488

Shift in assets. Exchanging one asset for another; this generally has no effect on liabilities or stockholders' equity, 14

Shipping costs, 185–190

Single-step income statement. Income statement format that groups all revenues together and lists all expenses together, subtracting total expenses from total revenues and calculating net income or net loss without computing any subtotals, 190–191

Sole proprietorship. A business with a single owner, 7, 8

Solvency ratios, 610, 613–614

SOX. Acronym for the Sarbanes-Oxley Act, 301–302

Specific-identification method. Inventory costing method in which a business uses the specific cost of each unit of inventory; also called the *specific-unit cost* method, 230, 235

Specific-unit cost. Inventory costing method in which a business uses the specific cost of each unit of inventory; also called the *specific-identification* method, 235

Stated interest rate. Interest rate that determines the amount of cash interest the borrower pays and the investor receives each year, 450

Stated value. An arbitrary amount that is similar to par value but is assigned after a corporation is organized, 490

Statement of cash flows. Summary of the changes in a business's cash balance for a specific period. A financial statement that shows all of the sources and all of the uses of cash for an accounting period; also called the *cash flow statement*, 20
- business activities on, 542–543
- cash balances on, 552
- defined, 540–541
- direct method of preparing, 555–559
- financing activities on, 550–552
- indirect method of preparing, 543–554, 561–568
- investing activities on, 548–550
- net change in cash on, 552
- noncash investing and financing activities on, 552–554
- operating activities on, 546–548, 556–559
- uses of, 541

Statement of financial position. Summary of business's assets, liabilities, and stockholders' equity as of a specific date; also called the *balance sheet*, 20

See also Balance sheet

Statement of retained earnings. Summary of the changes in a business's retained earnings during a period, 19
- for merchandiser, 192, 194
- preparation of, 26, 138

Stock, 409
- authorized, 488
- capital, 488
- classes of, 490
- common, 12, 55, 58, 490–495
- earnings per share, 601, 616
- issuance of, 491–493, 551
- issue price, 491
- for non-cash assets, 493
- no-par, 490, 492
- outstanding, 488
- par value, 490, 491–492
- preferred, 490, 493, 494, 495
- stated value, 490
- treasury, 502–505

Stock certificates. Certificates that provide evidence of stock ownership, 488

Stock dividends. A distribution by a corporation of its own stock to stockholders
- accounting for, 497–501
- compared with stock splits, 501
- defined, 497
- reasons to issue, 497
- recording, 498–499

Stock preferred, 490

Stock splits. An increase in the number of outstanding shares of stock coupled with a proportionate reduction in the value of the stock
- compared with stock dividends, 501
- defined, 499–500
- recording, 501

Stockholders. A person who owns stock in a corporation; also called a *shareholder*, 11, 488
- rights of, 489–490

Unearned revenues. A liability created when a business collects cash from customers in advance of providing goods or services; also called *deferred revenue*, 112, 443

Units-of-production (UOP) depreciation. Depreciation method by which a fixed amount of depreciation is assigned to each unit of output produced by an asset, 396, 398, 412–413

Unqualified opinion, 301

Unsecured bonds. Bonds that are backed only by the general credit of the company issuing the bond; also called *debentures*, 449

Useful life. The expected life of an asset during which it is anticipated to generate revenues. May be expressed in years or units of output, 394

V

Vacations

mandatory, 297

Vertical analysis. Analysis of a financial statement that reveals the relationship of each statement item to a specified base amount, which is the 100% figure

of balance sheet, 607

defined, 605

demo doc, 619–623

of income statement, 606–607

rounding and, 606

Voting rights

of stockholders, 489

W

Warranty. A guarantee that a product or service is free from defect

defined, 444

estimated liability from, 444–445

Whistleblower. A person who reports unethical behavior, 292

Wholesalers. A businesses that purchases products from a manufacturer and sells them to a retail business, 7, 176

Work in process. Inventory of partially completed goods, 230

Working capital. Current assets minus current liabilities. It measures a business's ability to meet its short-term obligations with its current assets, 610

Write off. Removing a customer's receivable from the accounting records because it is considered uncollectible, 333

Credits

Text

Gear art © Pep | Dreamstime.com. Front Matter: xvi

The content/tabular material on the following pages are borrowed from POLLARD, MEG; MILLS, SHERRY T.; HARRISON, WALTER T., FINANCIAL AND MANAGERIAL ACCOUNTING, 1st, ©N/A. Electronically reproduced by permission of Pearson Education, Inc., Upper Saddle River, New Jersey. Chapter 4: 176, 178, 179, 180, 181, 182, 183, 184, 187, 188, 189, 190, 191, 194, 195, 196; Chapter 5: 236, 237, 238, 240, 242, 245, 247; Chapter 7: 323, 324, 325, 329, 330, 337, 365, 365, 369, 372, 383; Chapter 8: 391; Chapter 10: 494, 491, 492, 493, 495, 496, 498, 501, 503, 504, 508, 509, 510, 513, 515; Chapter 11: 546, 549, 553, 554, 573, 575, 577, 578, 585, 586; Chapter 12: 619, 621, 623, 630, 631, 637, 638, 639

The content/tabular material on the following pages are borrowed from HORNGREN, CHARLES T.; HARRISON, WALTER T.; OLIVER, M. SUZANNE, FINANCIAL AND MANAGERIAL ACCOUNTING, CHAPTERS 1-23, COMPLETE BOOK, 2nd, ©N/A. Electronically reproduced by permission of Pearson Education, Inc., Upper Saddle River, New Jersey. Chapter 10: 494, 503; Chapter 11: 542, 544, 553

Hybrid Approach SOURCE: Professor Clayton Hock, Miami University of Ohio, Accountancy. Chapters 2 and 3

Columbia Sportswear Inc. Annual Report. Chapter 2: 105, 106

Photo

Chapter 1, Page 2: Monkey Business Images Ltd\www.indexopen.com; Jupiter Unlimited; Page 3: photos.com\Jupiter Unlimited; Jupiter Unlimited; Page 5: Sergey Tumanov\iStockphoto.com

Chapter 2, Page 52: Brand X Pictures\Jupiter Unlimited; Comstock Images\Jupiter Unlimited; Page 53: Jupiter Unlimited; Jupiter Unlimited; Page 57: iStockphoto; Jupiter Unlimited; Steve Collender\Shutterstock; Jupiter Unlimited

Chapter 3, Page 108: Jupiter Unlimited; Jupiter Unlimited; Page 109: Bananna Stock Image \Jupiter Images - PictureArts Corporation/Brand X Pictures Royalty Free; Jupiter Unlimited; Page 116: Godfried Edelman\iStockphoto.com

Chapter 4, Page 174: Cathy Datwani; Cathy Datwani; Page 175: Cathy Datwani; Starbucks Coffee Company; Page 186: www.photos.com/Jupiter Images

Chapter 5, Page 228: Jupiter Unlimited; Jupiter Unlimited; Page 229: Photos to Go; Jupiter Unlimited; Page 231: www.photos.com/Jupiter Images

Chapter 6, Page 288: © Greg Smith / CORBIS All Rights Reserved; Shutterstock; Page 289: JOYCE NALTCHAYAN/Agence France Presse/Getty Images; Gerry Penn / Agence France Presse/Getty Images; Page 298: www.photos.com/Jupiter Images

Chapter 7, Page 318: Comstock Images\Jupiter Unlimited; Comstock Images\Jupiter Unlimited; Page 319: Comstock Images\Jupiter Unlimited; Jupiter Unlimited; Page 327: iStockphoto.com

Chapter 8, Page 386: Manfred Vollmer/Das Fotoarchiv\Peter Arnold, Inc.; MATTHIAS HIEKEL/DPA /Landov; Page 387: Jeff Greenberg\PhotoEdit Inc.; The Image Works; Page 388: Jupiter Unlimited; © Armin Weigel / CORBIS All Rights Reserved; Andrew Penner\iStockphoto.com; Page 392: haoliang\Shutterstock; www.photos.com/Jupiter Images; Southwest Airlines Co.; Page 393:Jupiter Unlimited

Chapter 9, Page 438: www.indexopen.com; Fogstock Llc\www.indexopen.com; Page 439: © Car Culture / CORBIS All Rights Reserved; Photos.com; Page 447: Kathy RIngrose\Kathy Ringrose

Chapter 10, Page 486: Steven Rubion\The Image Works; Photos to Go; Page 487: Photos to Go; Paul Sakuma\AP Wide World Photos; Page 500: Jupiter Unlimited

Chapter 11, Page 538: Cathy Datwani; Photos to Go; Page 539: Cathy Datwani; iStockphoto; Page 540: Radu Razvan\iStockphoto.com

Chapter 12, Page 596: Cathy Datwani\Pearson Business Publishing; Cathy Datwani\Pearson Business Publishing; Page 597: The Procter & Gamble Company; Teri Stratford\Pearson Education/PH College; Page 598: Jackie Burrele, About.com Guide to Parenting Young Adults, http://youngadults.about.com.

How to Use MyAccountingLab

If you have not yet had a chance to explore the benefits of the MyAccountingLab Web site, I would encourage you to log in now and see what a valuable tool it can be. MyAccountingLab is a terrific tool for helping you grasp the accounting concepts that you are learning. So what exactly is MyAccountingLab? MyAccountingLab is a homework management tool that allows you to complete homework online. ▼

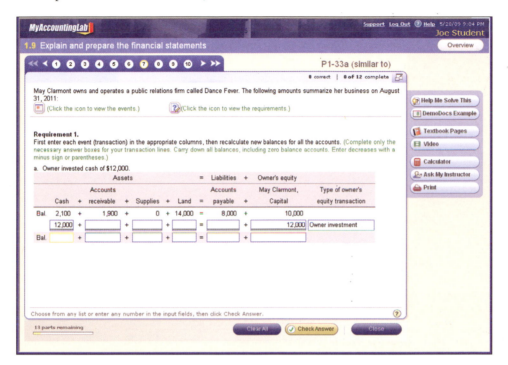

What is so great about completing the homework online, you might wonder?

Well, how about the ability to ask for and receive help *immediately* while you are working the problems? MyAccountingLab allows you to click on a **Help Me Solve This** button at anytime while you are working the problem, and a pop-up window appears with tips to help you solve the specific part of the problem that you are working on. It is similar to having someone standing over your shoulder to help you—right in the middle of the problem—so that you can get through it and understand how to solve it.

MyAccountingLab also has a button that you can click on that will open an ***online version of the textbook***—it even takes you right to the section of the textbook that explains the topic related to the problem that you are working on.

Another great feature of MyAccountingLab is the ***Ask My Instructor...*** button. If your instructor allows you to e-mail questions, you are able to send an e-mail to your instructor in which you can explain what you are having difficulties with. When your instructor receives the e-mail, there will be a link that will take the instructor right to the problem you were working on in MyAccountingLab.

You will also find two different types of problems in MyAccountingLab, ***bookmatch*** and ***algorithmic*** problems. The bookmatch problems are the exact problems right out of your textbook (your instructor must make these available in MyAccountingLab). The algorithmic problems are identical to the ones in the textbook, except they have several variables that change in the problem every time it is selected. The algorithmic problems allow you to have an unlimited number of problems you can work in order to master the material. This means that you can see how to do a problem similar to the one in the book.